The
DIMWIT'S
DICTIONARY

Other Books by Robert Hartwell Fiske

Robert Hartwell Fiske's Dictionary of Unendurable English
The Best Words
The Dictionary of Concise Writing
101 Elegant Paragraphs
Vocabula Bound 1: Outbursts, Insights, Explanations, and Oddities (editor)
Vocabula Bound 2: Our Wresting, Writhing Tongue (editor)

ROBERT HARTWELL FISKE'S

The
DIMWIT'S
DICTIONARY

Third Edition

Marion Street Press

Portland, Oregon

Published by Marion Street Press
4207 SE Woodstock Blvd # 168
Portland, OR 97206-6267
USA
http://www.marionstreetpress.com/

Orders and review copies: (800) 888-4741

Printed in the United States of America
ISBN 978-1-933338-98-9

Cover art direction by Nicky Ip
Back cover photo by Susan Hedman

Library of Congress Cataloging-in-Publication Data pending

Contents

The great enemy of clear language is insincerity. When there is a gap between one's real and one's declared aims, one turns as it were instinctively to long words and exhausted idioms, like a cuttlefish squirting out ink.

George Orwell, "Politics and the English Language"

Thoughts, that breathe, and words, that burn.

Thomas Gray, *The Progress of Poesy*

For I have neither wit, nor words, nor worth,
Action, nor utterance, nor the power of speech,
To stir men's blood

William Shakespeare, *Julius Caesar*, act 3, scene 2

Watch your thoughts; they become words.
Watch your words; they become actions.
Watch your actions; they become habits.
Watch your habits; they become character.
Watch your character; it becomes destiny.

Anonymous

How very convenient these cliché phrases are; how soothing to the pained mind, and how misleading, how concealing.

Iris Murdoch, *The Sea, The Sea*

Never do I ever want to hear another word. There isn't one I haven't heard.

Alan Jay Lerner and Frederick Loewe, *My Fair Lady*

The
DIMWIT'S
DICTIONARY

A Note on the Second Edition

Aside from new entries and commentary, throughout this second edition, you will find quotations from classic and contemporary authors of fiction. These quotations, however well written they or their surrounding words may be, are marred, adulterated by dimwitticisms:

> What you find out in your thirties is that clever children are a dime a dozen.—Christina Schwarz, *All Is Vanity*

a dime a dozen is a dimwitticism.

> But I can remember that from quite early on, for some reason, Isabel decided that Edith was rather a feather in her cap, someone that little bit special to be fed to her country neighbours in rationed morsels.—Julian Fellowes, *Snobs*

a feather in her cap is a dimwitticism.

> The two women were simply aiding and abetting each other to disband the Seraglio.—Penelope Fitzgerald, *Human Voices*

aiding and abetting is a dimwitticism.

> It has been a true labor of love, and something more—the only thing that has kept her calm during the long winter months of waiting for the hearing to begin.—Anita Shreve, *Fortune's Rocks*

a labor of love is a dimwitticism.

> For the time being he could see the line in the sand: on one side of it, all he had; on the other, all he'd lose.—Martin Amis, *Yellow Dog*

line in the sand is a dimwitticism.

> Poor Nelson. He has this bee in his bonnet—doing something for this girl nobody knows.—John Updike, *Rabbit Remembered*

bee in his bonnet is a dimwitticism.

> And now the dog was dead, and Morris was saying that, as the dog should have known, his was a losing battle, and that that not given in love would be redressed in blood.—David Mamet, *The Old Religion*

a losing battle is a dimwitticism.

> The do-gooder, the bleeding heart, the concerned citizen, the militant reformer: what a pain in the neck they are: always making us feel guilty about something.—Edward Abbey, *The Fool's Progress: An Honest Novel*

a pain in the neck is a dimwitticism.

> She gave me a rather disparaging look and took out a tin of Golden Virginia, which she opened to reveal a layer of tiny neat joints packed in like sardines.—Kate Atkinson, *Emotionally Weird*

packed in like sardines is a dimwitticism.

Each dimwitticism is a failure to write clearly and compellingly, an admission that the author could not manage an original thought or a better turn of phrase, or could not be bothered to think of one.

Dimwitticisms, as these examples make clear, yield only facile writing, only false sentiment.

A Note on the Third Edition

With the publication of this third edition, *The Dimwit's Dictionary* has been in print for more than fifteen years. Few books about words last so long. Almost all the word books that are written today are silly, indeed, insulting, narratives that talk down to people. Books of this sort rarely remain in print for long. You may disagree with the thesis of this book, but I offer a serious argument that has captured the interest of enough people to warrant the release of a third edition.

In this new edition, along with adding many more dimwitticisms, sentence examples, and commentary, I have identified the top-twenty dimwitticisms. Each of these entries is followed by the rubric A TOP-TWENTY DIMWITTICISM.

In 2006 and 2007, Factiva, a Dow Jones Company, provided *The Vocabula Review* with monthly graphs showing the top-twenty dimwitticisms used in U.S., U.K., Canadian, Australian, and Indian newspapers and magazines. I had supplied Factiva with a list of 200 dimwitticisms, and they searched for the terms among thousands of publications. Appendix A shows the graphs for April 2007.

To this third edition, I have also added more examples from works of fiction. The readability of a work of fiction is directly proportional to the number of dimwitticisms its author uses. The more dimwitticisms an author uses to help him tell his tale, the less readable the writing, the less compelling the story, the less able the author.

It is quite impossible to record every dimwitticism—there is simply no end to them—but those I have noted here are a good selection. Study them, and you will soon recognize all others. Substitute them, as I suggest, and you will soon no longer need to.

Foreword

When Robert Hartwell Fiske confronts Saint Peter, I hope he remembers to tell the man that he is the founding editor of *The Vocabula Review,* the online magazine devoted to contemporary language, its delights and its disasters. Saint Peter will immediately understand that Mr. Fiske has been on the side of the angels and therefore been doing the Lord's work. My worry is that, in reply, Saint Peter will commit one or another of the solecisms, illogicalities, or barbarisms that Mr. Fiske spends his days excoriating and that he will feel the need to correct him, causing him to lose his place on the other side of the gates. Meanwhile, on this side of the gates, to hew to this theological metaphor a bit longer, Robert Hartwell Fiske has been doing a hell of a job.

Mr. Fiske has signed on, evidently for life, for that best of all losing causes, the battle to keep language clear, fresh, free from the pollution of empty jargon, idiotic euphemism, self-serving imprecision, comic redundancy, nonsense generally. He has many famous comrades from among the dead in this battle: Jonathan Swift, H. L. Mencken, George Orwell, H. W. Fowler, Sir Ernest Gowers, and others. And, as I am sure he has discovered, many unknown, still living allies in unexpected places who get quite properly worked up over politicians, advertisers, social scientists, so-called educators, and others attempting to swindle the rest of us through nicely calculated verbal fog.

You are what you eat, the old food faddists used to say. As I read him, Robert Hartwell Fiske is saying that we are, or soon become, what we say and write. Use language slovenly, dully, dopily and we soon ourselves become sloppy, dull, dopey. In *The Dimwit's Dictionary,* he explains his reigning idea in the first paragraph of his first chapter, when he announces that "Dimwitticisms are worn-out words and phrases; they are expressions that dull our reason and dim our insight, formulas that we rely on when we are too lazy to express what we think or even to discover how we feel. The more we use them, the more we conform—in thought and feeling—to everyone else who uses them." We know soon enough what makes them "dim"; the witticism comes into play because most people who adopt such overworked words as "scenario" or such cumbersome academic locutions as "in terms of" think they are being clever, if not highly sophisticated.

Language mavens come in various intensities of aggression. Some come as a recent graduates of the Gestapo school of language correction; one has only to read them to feel the leather glove sting across one's cheeks, the word *schweinhund* ringing in one's ears. Some come on as school masters, simply unable to understand why anyone would wish to split an infinitive or end a sentence with a preposition. Some come on as pussycats passing along to us their amazement at the wild and wayward curiosities of language, but always attempting to avoid seeming either formidable or forbidding.

My own favorite among the great language mavens is H. W. Fowler, whose tone I should describe as superior commonsensical. Here, for example, is the great man on those damnable split infinitives: "The English-speaking world may be divided into (1) those who neither know nor care what a split infinitive is; (2) those who do not know but care very much; (3) those who know and condemn; (4) those who know and approve; and (5) those who know and distinguish." Such is Fowler's elevated superiority. Here is his commonsense: "We maintain, however, that a real split infinitive, though not desirable in itself, is preferable to either of two things, to real ambiguity and to patent artificiality." In other words, the Fowler line is, split away before writing anything stupid. But then he adds: "We will split infinitives sooner than be ambiguous or artificial; more than that, we will freely admit that sufficient recasting will get rid of any split infinitives without involving either of those faults, and yet reserve to ourselves the right of deciding in each case whether recasting is worthwhile." Superior, as I say, with a saving commonsense.

Robert Hartwell Fiske's desire—it informs his tone—is to bring us to our senses, to make us understand that "our knowledge of the world expands as our familiarity with words increases" and contracts when we fall back on the categories of ineptitude he has designated the Moribund Metaphor, the Overworked Word, the Plebeian Sentiment, all of which may be said—he, in fact, does say—"blunt our understanding and quash our creativity. They actually shield us from our thoughts and feelings, from any profound sense of ourselves." He is, *au fond,* a reformer who wants us to be the fully developed men and women we "were meant to be."

But Mr. Fiske's reforming impulse doesn't get in the way of his scorning clichés and trite sentiments. His lists of Overworked Words and of Torpid Terms—"off-putting," "operative," "prioritize," "pursuant to," qualify for the latter category—are there because they "keep us dumb and dispassionate. They elicit the least from us." He also suggests words that he thinks worthy of being revitalized—lovely words such as "bedizen," "bootless," "quondam"—while what he calls Withered Words ought, in the phrase of Paul Valery, the great French critic, to be turned over to the "numismaticians of language" to be put "away in their Cabinets, with many another verbal coin that has passed from circulation."

Robert Hartwell Fiske is a verbal trainer, the linguistic equivalent of the personal trainer one sees in gyms and health clubs. He wants us to trim the fat off our mental life; to knock off those Ineffectual Phrases, Inescapable Pairs, Infantile Phrases, and Wretched Redundancies.

He has the relentlessness but none of the dogmatism of the drill sergeant.

Reformer, verbal trainer, drill sergeant, in the end Robert Hartwell Fiske is a fisher of souls, a catcher in the wry, a man who, through looking carefully at language, understands its potency and loathes its power, when misused, for making life more dreary than it ought to be. After noting the spread of flat and predictable language in the contemporary world, he exclaims: "No wonder so many of us feel barren or inconsolable, there are few words that inspire us, few words that thrill or overwhelm us. Persuasion has lost much of its sway, conviction, much of its claim."

Mr. Fiske is, in short, a fanatic, an extremist who apparently believes that clear language is our only hope for clear thought, that dull language deadens the mind and dampens the imagination, that a felicitous phrase is good news, that a strong prose style is a gift to be cultivated and cherished, that nothing, no, nothing in the world exceeds language in its significance to the human enterprise. As it happens, I believe in all this, too, which makes it an honor to salute a fellow fanatic and wish him and his book the great good fortune both deserve.

—Joseph Epstein

Joseph Epstein is the author of *Snobbery: The American Version*, *Fabulous Small Jews: A Collection of Stories*, and *Envy*.

Apologia

The Dimwit's Dictionary will annoy some people and amuse others. People who feel as though I am referring to them in some of the commentary in this book may be annoyed by what I write; those who feel as though I am referring to others may be amused by it. This is an annoying, amusing book.

If the tone of my commentary is sometimes acerbic, it's because tempered persuasion is effete, and considered argument tiresome. Few of us are able to learn well by pedantic or rote methods. But if I disturb or annoy a person, is he not more likely to remember what bothered him; is he not more likely to retain what was said; is he not more likely to learn?

—Robert Hartwell Fiske
editor@vocabula.com

Part One

Expressions That Dull Our Reason and Dim Our Insight

Whereas a witticism is a clever remark or phrase—indeed, the height of expression—a "dimwitticism" is the converse; it is a commonplace remark or phrase. Dimwitticisms are worn-out words and phrases; they are expressions that dull our reason and dim our insight, formulas that we rely on when we are too lazy to express what we think or even to discover how we feel. The more we use them, the more we conform—in thought and feeling—to everyone else who uses them.

The Dimwit's Dictionary is a compilation of thousands of dimwitticisms (clichés, colloquialisms, idioms, slang, and the like) that people speak and write endlessly.*

The Dimwit's Dictionary categorizes dimwitticisms by the following types:†

- Foreign phrases
- Grammatical gimmicks
- Ineffectual phrases
- Inescapable pairs
- Infantile phrases
- Moribund metaphors
- Overworked words
- Plebeian sentiments
- Popular prescriptions
- Quack equations
- Suspect superlatives
- Torpid terms
- Withered words
- Wretched redundancies

---

* Many of the entries in this book are followed by synonyms that may be used in place of the worn-out word or phrase; others are followed by commentary; and still others by both. But even the mere inclusion of an entry—one unaccompanied by synonyms or commentary—damns it as a dimwitticism.

† Dimwitticisms, quite obviously, could be categorized by more than one of these fourteen types. Many wretched redundancies are also torpid terms, many moribund metaphors also infantile phrases, but I have sought to identify them by their principal type.

Foreign phrases

Expressions such as *ad infinitum, c'est la vie, crème de la crème, fait accompli, in loco parentis, je ne sais quoi, joie de vivre, mea culpa, mirabile dictu, modus vivendi, ne plus ultra, non compos mentis, par excellence, persona non grata, quid pro quo, raison d'être, sine qua non, très, verboten*, and *vive la différence,* though perfectly good foreign words and phrases, are, when used by English-speaking people, simply wearisome.

Grammatical gimmicks

Quite simply, *and everything* is a babbler's way of describing what he was unable to. This phrase and so many others like it—*and everything like that; and stuff (things); and (or) stuff (things) like that; and this and that; anyway; I mean; (and that) kind of stuff (thing); or something or other; or whatever; this, that, and the other (thing); you had to be there*— are grammatical gimmicks that we use to make up for the misfashioned words that precede them.

These are devices that we resort to whenever we are unable to adequately explain our thoughts or feelings. Grammatical gimmicks attest to just how dull and dimwitted we have become.

Ineffectual phrases

Ineffectual phrases are the expressions people use to delay or obstruct, to bewilder or make weary. The intent of those who use ineffectual phrases is to make it appear as though their sentences are more substantial than they actually are, but not one sentence is made more meaningful by their inclusion: *(please) be advised that; I'll tell you (something); it has come to (my) attention; it is important to realize (that); it is interesting to note (that); make no mistake (about it); (to) take this opportunity (to); the fact of the matter is; the fact remains; the thing about it is; what happened (is).*

How a person speaks often reveals how he thinks. And how he thinks determines how he behaves. A person who speaks ineffectually may think ineffectually, and a person who thinks ineffectually may behave ineffectually—perhaps badly.

Ineffectual phrases add only to our being ineffectual people.

Inescapable pairs

In an inescapable pair, the first word means much the same as the second, or so often accompanies the second that any distinction between them is, in effect, forfeited.

Only occasionally, that is, do we see the word *allied* without the word *closely; asset* without *valuable; baby* without *beautiful; balance* without *delicate; distinction* without *dubious; error* without *egregious; tied* without *inextricably; missed* without *sorely; poverty* without *abject; principle* without *basic.*

And only occasionally do we see the word *aid* without the word *abet; alive* without *well; effective* without *efficient; hope* without *pray; hue* without *cry; pure* without *simple.*

When two words are treated as though they were one—the plight of every inescapable pair—our keenness is compromised, our discernment endangered.

No longer does every word tell; the words themselves have become witless.

Infantile phrases

Any thought or feeling in which these expressions are found is likely to be made instantly laughable: *absolutely, positively; all of the above; because (that's why); because why?; (as) compared to what?; going on (19); I'll bet you any amount of money; in no way, shape, or form; intestinal fortitude; it takes one to know one; me, myself, and I; mission accomplished; mutual admiration society; never (not) in a million years; real, live; really and truly; (you) started it; (I) take it back; the feeling's mutual; the (L)-word; (my) whole, entire life; with a capital (A); (62) years young; (a) zillion(s) (of).*

Also included among these phrases that strike all but the dimwitted as derisory are notorious advertising slogans (*inquiring minds want to know; where's the beef*), song and film titles (*a funny thing happened to me on the way to; I can't get no satisfaction*), and alliterative or rhymed phrases (*a bevy of beauties; chrome dome*).

Other infantile phrases are more disturbing, for they reveal an adolescent, unformed reasoning. Explanations like *in the wrong place at the wrong time, it just happened, it's a free country,* and *everything's (it's all) relative* are as farcical as they are possibly fallacious.

Moribund metaphors*

Metaphors, like similes, should have the briefest of lives. Their vitality depends on their evanescence.

Yet must we ever endure the dimwitted *(it's) a jungle (out there), an emotional roller coaster, a stroll (walk) in the park, (like) being run over (getting hit) by a (Mack) truck, (as) cool as a cucumber, everything but the kitchen sink, (as) hungry as a horse, leak like a sieve, light at the end of the tunnel, out to lunch, over the hill, pass like ships in the night, (as) phony as a three-dollar bill, (a) piece of cake, rule the roost, window of opportunity, (every parent's) worst nightmare,* and countless other metaphors that characterize people as dull, everyday speakers and writers, indeed, as platitudinarians? Nothing new do they tell us. Nothing more do they show us.

Moreover, if it weren't for our plethora of metaphors, especially, sports images—*above par, a new ballgame, batting a thousand, do (make) an end run around, down for the count, hit a home run, move the ball forward, off base, pull no punches, stand on the sidelines, step up to*

---

* Rather than have a separate section on "insipid similes," I include them here. Since a metaphor can be thought of as a condensed simile (which often uses the word as or like) and a simile usually can be converted into a metaphor, this does not strike me as taking too much license.

the plate, took the ball and ran with it—and war images—*a call to arms, an uphill battle, battle lines are drawn, draw fire, earn his stripes, first line of defense, in the trenches, on the firing line, take by storm*—men and, even, women would be far less able to articulate their thoughts. We would speak and write more haltingly than we already do; our thoughts and feelings more misshapen than they already are.

Moribund metaphors interfere with our understanding not only when we use them singly but also, and especially, when we use them simultaneously, that is, when we use them together, metaphor on metaphor. Frequently incongruous, these metaphors disfigure any sentence in which they are found:

- Putting yourself under pressure to churn out work for the *cream of the crop* at the beginning of your writing career may *put the brakes on* your creativity.

- They want to get *all their ducks in a row* and make sure they're all *singing from the same hymn sheet.*

- And by last Christmas, for any defense contractor, the dwindling Soviet threat had evolved from *meal ticket* into *writing on the wall.*

- Our restaurant *cost* me and my wife *an arm and a leg,* but we didn't build it without planning and we certainly wouldn't let it *go down the drain.*

- Right now, USAir's problem is trying to determine whether this is *a soft landing* for the economy or a recession, and *the jury is still out.*

- For 20 years she was *a rising star* in the business, but by last year her success had *gone to the dogs.*

- In the face of mounting pressure to gut or eliminate the IRS, it continues to *shoot itself in the foot* by *biting the hands that feed them.*

- Looking at those things, *it didn't take a rocket scientist* to see there was *something rotten in Denmark.*

- Thanks to Clinton, Lewinsky, & Co., I'm *off the hook* and it's *on the table.*

- We expect them to *cast their net* as far and wide as possible because any *stone that's not unturned* will be questioned.

We rely on metaphors not because we feel they make our speech and writing more vivid and inviting but because we fail to learn how to express ourselves otherwise; we know not the words.

In truth, the more of these metaphors that we use, the less effective is our speech and writing. Neither interesting nor persuasive, their expression fatigues us where we thought it would inform us, annoys us where we believed it would amuse us, and benumbs us where we hoped it would inspire us.

Overworked words

The broader your knowledge of words, the greater your ability to express yourself precisely and persuasively. Many speakers and writers, however, rely on certain words—overworked words like *action, actively, amazing, appreciate, approach, attitude, awesome, basically, crisis, definitely, devastate, effect, excellence, great, impact, implement, incredible, interesting, lasting, major, meaningful, mindset, natural, nice, ongoing, parameter, pretty, really, scenario, significant, situation, strange, thing, unbelievable, very, weird.*

Words, when overworked, diminish the meaning of all that they are used to describe. Our thoughts and feelings both are enfeebled by these tired terms. Nothing that we express with these overworked words has the force or effectiveness of less habitually spoken, less repeatedly written words.

Moreover, since a person understands little more than what the words he is knowledgeable of conveying—a word means *only* so much—to rely on so few words reveals just how limited a person's understanding of himself, and those about him, is.

Our knowledge of the world increases as our familiarity with words does.

Plebeian sentiments

Plebeian sentiments reflect the views and values of the least thoughtful among us: *be nice; (I) gave (him) the best years of (my) life; (it) gives (me) something to do; (these things) happen to other people, not to (me); I (just) don't think about it; I just work here; I'm bored (he's boring); (it) keeps (me) busy; (it's) something to look forward to; there are no words to describe (express); you think too much; what can you do; why me?*

What's more, these expressions, base as they are, blunt our understanding and quash our creativity. They actually shield us from our thoughts and feelings, from any profound sense of ourselves.

People who use these expressions have not become who they were meant to be.

Popular prescriptions

Powerless to repeat an author's epigram, unfit to recite a poet's verse, more than many of us are utterly able to echo a society's slogans and clichés: *absence makes the heart grow fonder; actions speak louder than words; a picture is worth a thousand words; beauty is in the eye of the beholder; better late than never; do as I say, not as I do; forgive and forget; hope for the best but expect the worst; it takes two; keep (your) nose to the grindstone; live and learn; misery loves company; money isn't everything; neither a borrower nor a lender be; take it one day (step) at a time; the best things in life are free; the meek shall inherit the earth; the sooner the better; time flies when you're having fun; two wrongs don't make a right; what goes around, comes around; you can't be all things to all people; you can't have everything.*

Popular prescriptions are the platitudes and proverbs by which people live their lives. It is these dicta that determine who we are and how we act; they define our intellectual and moral makeup.

Dull-witted speakers and writers depend on prescriptions like these to guide them through life. For this poor populace, life is, we may surmise, laid out. From the popular or proper course, there is scant deviation. A stray thought is, for them, a gray thought. Popular prescriptions endure not for their sincerity but for their simplicity. We embrace them because they make all they profess to explain and all they profess to prescribe seem plain and uncomplicated.

Inexorably, we become as simple as they—we people, we platitudes.

Quack equations

a deal is a deal; a politician is a politician; a promise is a promise; a rule is a rule; bald is beautiful; bigger is better; enough is enough; ethics is ethics; fair is fair; God is love; it is what it is; less is more; more is better; perception is reality; (what's) right is right; seeing is believing; talk is cheap; the law is the law is the law; what happened happened; what's done is done. This is the sort of simplicity much favored by mountebanks and pretenders, by businesspeople and politicians. Quack equations too readily explain behavior that the undiscerning may otherwise find inexplicable and justify attitudes that they may otherwise find unjustifiable. No remedies for shoddy reasoning, no restoratives for suspect thinking, these palliatives soothe only our simple-mindedness.

Equally distressing is that there is no end to these quack equations: *alcohol is alcohol; he is who he is; math is math; money is money is money; people are people; plastic is plastic; prejudice is prejudice; their reasoning is their reasoning; the past is the past; wrong is wrong.* Forever being fabricated and continually being merchandized, shoddy thinking is far more easily dispensed than sound thinking.

Suspect superlatives

In dimwitted usage, superlatives are suspect. That which seems most laudable is often least; that which seems topmost, bottommost; that which seems best, worst: *an amazing person; (I'm) a perfectionist; area of expertise; celebrity; class; gentleman; great; personal friend; pursuit of excellence; the best and (the) brightest; the rich and famous.*

Torpid terms

Torpid terms are vapid words and phrases that we use in place of vital ones: *a majority of; a moving experience; a number of; a step (forward) in the right direction; cautiously optimistic; (take) corrective action; degree; effectuate; extent; (a) factor; incumbent upon; indicate; input; leaves a little (a lot; much; something) to be desired; move forward; negative feelings; off-putting; operative; prioritize; proactive; pursuant to; remedy the situation; represent(s); (the) same; send a message; shocked (surprised) and saddened (dismayed); significant other; subsequent to; utilize; weight in proportion (proportionate) to height.*

Formulas as flat as these keep us dumb and dispassionate. They elicit the least from us.

With these unsound formulas, little can be communicated and still less can be accomplished. Torpid terms interfere with our understanding and with our taking action; they thwart our thinking and frustrate our feeling.

Withered words

There are many rare and wonderful words that we would do well to become familiar with—words that would revitalize us for our revitalizing them—words like *bedizen; bootless; caliginous; compleat; cotquean; hebdomadal; helpmeet; logorrhea; quondam; wont*.

Withered words, however—words like *albeit; amidst; amongst; behoove; betwixt; ergo; forsooth; perchance; said; sans; save; thence; unbeknownst; verily; whence; wherein; whereon; wherewith; whilst*—are archaic and deserve only to be forgotten. People who use them say little that is memorable.

Wretched redundancies

Reckless writers and slipshod speakers use many words where few would do: *advance planning; at this time; consensus of opinion; dead body; due to the fact that; first and foremost; free gift; just recently; in advance of; in and of itself; in spite of the fact that; in terms of; make a determination; on a ... basis; on the part of; past experience; period of time; (the) reason (why) is because; refer back; the single best (most); until such time as*. Yet for all the words, their expression is but impoverished; more words do not necessarily signify more meaning.

Life is measured by its meaning, and a good deal of that meaning is inherent in the words we use. If so many of our words are superfluous—and thus do not signify—so much of our life is, ineluctably, meaningless.

In the end, we are no more superfluous than are the words we use.

* * *

In themselves, dimwitticisms are as innocuous as any other single word or phrase might be, but within sentences, among thoughts struggling to be expressed and ideas seeking to be understood, dimwitticisms ravage the writer's efforts as much as they do the reader's, the speaker's as much as the listener's.

Dimwitticisms give rise to ineloquence, and it is precisely this that marks so much of our speech and writing. Whatever the occasion, whether celebratory or funereal, quotidian or uncommon, people speak and write the same dimwitted words and phrases. No wonder so many of us feel barren or inconsolable: there are few words that inspire us, few words that move us, few words that thrill or overwhelm us. Persuasion has lost much of its sway, conviction, much of its claim.

Consider these further examples of dimwitted usage:

1. From a dialogue between a television correspondent and a school superintendent:
So you feel like you were *left holding the bag*?
Yes, it's fair to say we were *left out in the cold.*

Left holding the bag and *left out in the cold* are both moribund metaphors.

2. From the spoken words of a high school "genius":
It was *like her worst nightmare or something.*

Like is an infantile phrase, *her worst nightmare* is a moribund metaphor, and *or something* is a grammatical gimmick.

3. From the words of a computer scientist:
The encryption technology used today is the same as that used twenty years ago by military establishments *and that type of stuff.*

And that type of stuff is a grammatical gimmick.

4. From a business consultant's economic forecast:
Basically, it's a *pretty nice* forecast.

Basically, *pretty*, and *nice* are all overworked words.

5. From a political lobbyist's analysis:
If we could *level the playing field,* it would be better than having them *stick out like a sore thumb.*

Level the playing field and *stick out like a sore thumb* are both moribund metaphors.

6. From the author of a college textbook:
In the beginning, and certainly before democratic forms of government *arrived on the scene,* tribal chieftains used their armies to maintain order.

Arrive on the scene is an infantile phrase.

7. From a news program's report on the death of a woman:
The company released a statement saying she was an outstanding employee and her colleagues are *shocked and saddened* by her death.

Shocked and saddened is a torpid term.

8. From an article by a health-care professional:
It is interesting to note the impressive array of distinguished mental health professionals who have assumed a derogatory stance on prevention.

It is interesting to note is an ineffectual phrase.

9. From a meteorologist's weather forecast:
Averagewise, around November 10, we see the first snowflakes of the season fall.

Averagewise is a grammatical gimmick.

10. From a police report on the death of a vagrant:

This could have happened to anyone; he happened to be *in the wrong place at the wrong time.*

In the wrong place at the wrong time is an infantile phrase.

11. From a man speaking before a congressional committee:

There are no words to describe how *devastating* this experience has been.

There are no words to describe is a plebeian sentiment, and *devastating* is an overworked word.

12. From a questionnaire soliciting opinions about a business service:

Thank you in advance for your time and assistance; your answers can *make a difference.*

Thank you in advance is a plebeian sentiment, and *make a difference* is a suspect superlative.

13. From the CEO of a multimillion-dollar company:

A mensch is a man *with a capital M.*

With a capital M is an infantile phrase.

14. From an elementary school principal's letter to parents:

Please be advised that Mr. Kline will no longer be your child's fifth-grade teacher as of Monday, November 22.

Please be advised that is an ineffectual phrase.

15. From an interview with a local government official:

The fact of the matter is these are tolls that should have been removed long ago.

The fact of the matter is is an ineffectual phrase.

16. From a newspaper article:

But few couples even bother to discuss *the "F" word*—finances—before they *tie the knot.*

The "F" word is an infantile phrase, and *tie the knot* is a moribund metaphor.

17. From a U.S. government official:

We will *take corrective action to the extent that* we can; we're not going to be *caught asleep at the switch.*

Both *take corrective action* and *to the extent that* are torpid terms, and *caught asleep at the switch* is a moribund metaphor.

18. From a television news correspondent:

At the end of the day, the bottom line is, no matter how powerful Karl Rove is, defending their guy here does mean protecting the president, *period.*

At the end of the day and *the bottom line* are moribund metaphors, and *period* is an infantile phrase.

19. From a high school counselor's letter of recommendation:

If he continues to get support in college, with his *incredible* effort to overcome his difficulties, he can *definitely* succeed.

Both *incredible* and *definitely* are overworked words.

20. From a letter written by a lawyer:

The $325 is *an ounce of prevention* that will alleviate you having to *play* expensive *catch up later on down the road*.

An ounce of prevention is a moribund metaphor, *play catch up* is a moribund metaphor, and *later on down the road* is a wretched redundancy.

People who rely on dimwitticisms like these appear to express themselves more fluently and articulately than those few who do not. But this is a sham articulateness, for without the use of phrases like *left holding the bag, left out in the cold, her worst nightmare, and that type of stuff, basically, level the playing field, stick out like a sore thumb, arrive on the scene, shocked and saddened, it is interesting to note, in the wrong place at the wrong time, with a capital M, a breath of fresh air, incredible,* and *definitely,* most people would stammer helplessly.

As unsettling and dissatisfying as it can be to read a sentence in which a single dimwitticism occurs, more than one in a sentence heightens our perturbation. Moreover, to *mix* dimwitticisms, as in some of the preceding examples, compounds our distress. To mix metaphors, as in examples 5, 18, and 20 (and even example 1), has long been frowned upon by grammarians and careful users of the language. But equally disheartening is it to mix one of these categories with another. Joining a plebeian sentiment with an overworked word, as in example 11, or with a suspect superlative, as in example 12, makes a sentence, let us say, less convincing. Joining an infantile phrase with a moribund metaphor, as in examples 16 and 18, surely makes a sentence less clever. What's more, to join not two but three or more categories, as in example 2, makes a sentence altogether comical and inconsiderable. No less than mixed metaphors are these combinations worthy of our derision.

Dimwitticisms are ubiquitous, and we cannot easily escape them. Perhaps none of us can express a thought without them. We learn them unknowingly; insidiously do they become part of our wording unless we recognize what they are and withstand their onslaught. Genuine articulateness is writing and speech that scarcely makes use of dimwitticisms, and it is achieved only with effort.

Certainly, it is the least effective speakers and writers who use the most dimwitticisms. A person's ability to express himself well—compellingly, persuasively—is inversely proportional to the number of dimwitticisms he uses.

A person who expresses himself with genuineness instead of in jargon, with feeling instead of in formulas is capable as few have been, as few are, and as few will be; this is a person to heed.

Writing That Demands to Be Read Aloud, Speech That Calls to Be Captured in Print

The *Dimwit's Dictionary* would be incomplete without a brief discussion of what it means to express oneself well and *wittily*. Let us then consider the adoption of three categories of usage:

- Uneducated English
- Everyday English
- Elegant English

This scheme is largely an attempt to give recognition to speech and writing that is beyond standard, or everyday, English—to elegant English. Without such a listing, people may not understand that they *can* speak and write well, even elegantly. Certainly, as the superfluity of dimwitticisms makes plain, elegant English is English rarely heard, English seldom seen.

Here, first, are some examples of uneducated English.

Uneducated English
About uneducated English there is little to say—other than it is a lifeless, indeed, death-inducing, dialect that ought not to be said. Here, though, are a few examples:

- He knew they *was* out there for 10 to 15 minutes before he *done* anything.
- I *seen* things out there in the world that I never thought I would see.
- My mom is the one *that brung* me up.
- We were a close family; we *done* things together.
- Don't you have family members that you could *of went* to?
- Men have treated me *terrible*.
- I took everything *literate*.
- She wasn't being abused about *nothing*.
- We don't go to parties *no* more; we don't go *no* where.
- That *don't* matter, I'm still there with you, *ain't* I?
- I shot *me* a burglar.
- I shouldn't have *did* it.
- Let's start over here with the two of *yous*.
- I *gots* a lot of thinking to do.

Abuses of language abound, especially among those who speak and write uneducated English.

Whereas people who aspire to write and speak the language well still maintain standards of speech and observe distinctions between words, the uneducated, like some juggernaut, massacre and obliterate. They slay nearly all that they say:

alls. • *Alls* I can say is he was a good cop. Use *All.* • *Alls* you hear them talk about is their baby. Use *All.* • *Alls* I wanted to say is that I forgive him. Use *All.*

anyways. • *Anyways,* I have to go now. Use *Anyway* or Delete. • You shouldn't be sleeping around when you're married *anyways.* Use *anyway* or Delete.

being as how. • That's not so bad, *being as how* we didn't even know we would be on the ballot. Use *because, considering (that), in that,* or *since.*

better had. • You *better had* do as your father says. Use *had better, ought to,* or *should.*

complected. • I'm 5'2", 110 lbs., and very *light-complected.* Use *light-complexioned.*

could of. • I *could of* if I wanted to. Use *could have.*

drownded. • Two men *drownded* when their boat capsized. Use *drowned.*

drug. • He *drug* up the past and complained about the argument we had that time. Use *dragged.* • What I've done is *drug* all the chapters into one folder. Use *drag.*

heighth. • She's over 6 feet in *heighth.* Use *height.* • I am the same size as you in *heighth.* Use *height.*

irregardless (of). • Remember to treat all patients with respect and compassion *irregardless of* their health status. Use *despite, irrespective of, no matter what, regardless of,* or *whatever.* • This would have happened *irregardless of* the Chapter 11 decision. Use *despite, irrespective of, no matter what, regardless of,* or whatever.

leastways. • There's no sense of accomplishment, *leastways* not for me. Use *at least.*

most -(i)est. • We want to take this opportunity to humbly express to you our *most sincerest* appreciation for the many expressions of sympathy you have shown us. Use *most sincere* or *sincerest.* • The panel consisted of some of the town's *most lustiest* women. Use *most lusty* or *lustiest.*

not hardly. • Is she plump? *Not hardly.* Use *Hardly.* • I *couldn't hardly* breathe because he had broken my ribs. Use *could hardly.*

nowheres. • He was *nowheres* near their house. Use *nowhere.*

seeing as. • *Seeing as* you're a woman, does the audience respond to you differently? Use *Because, Considering (that), In that,* or *Since.*

theirself (theirselves). • Irish people I know don't think of *theirselves* as Irish. Use *themselves.*

thusly. • *Thusly,* I feel he was irresponsible and I feel I should tell him. Use *Thus.* • Because this was described as school shootings and *thusly* presented as gender neutral, the gendered nature of the killing and shooting was ignored. Use *thus.*

where at. • Nobody knows *where* the $100 is *at*. Delete *at*. • I know *where* she is *at*. Delete *at*. I know *where* he works *at*. Delete *at*.

with regards to. • Customers are looking for standard-based applications *with regards to* networking. Use *with regard to*. • *With regards to* the paper you gave out recently, I don't want to read about what you have against your opponent but what you are going to do for the city. Use *With regard to*.

Indeed, much uneducated English is everyday English. The language pullulates with people who hover between the uneducated and the everyday.

Everyday English

Everyday English is marked by an ignorance of both the structure of sentences (grammar) and the meanings of words (usage).Here are a few examples:

good. • He did *good* last night. Use *well*. • He helps me to do *good* in school. Use *well*.

graduated. • Even before *graduating* college, Hughes had published two books of poetry. Use *graduating from* or *he was graduated from*. • I *graduated* one of the finest medical schools in the country. Use *graduated from* or *was graduated from*.

like. • It's *like* déjà vu all over again. Delete *like*. • And she's *like*, "*Like*, he wasn't *like* anyone I've, *like*, ever met." Delete *like*. • And I'm *like* I just couldn't believe it. Delete *like*.

(my)self. • She told my sister and *myself* that she was pregnant by him. Use *me*. • Richard and *myself* are going to lunch. Use *I*. • Very large people like *yourselves* can eat tiny amounts of food and not lose an ounce. Use *you*. • Let's hope someone comes along, like *myself,* to take his place. Use *me*. • We feel Mr. Roedler's comments do an injustice to collectors like *ourselves* who currently pay $1,500 to $2,000 for radios of this type. Use *us*. • Neither the mayor nor *myself* desires to comment on the status of the matter. Use *I*.

where. • I saw on TV *where* he was awarded a prize. Use *that*. • I read *where* your neighbor was sentenced for soliciting sex. Use *that*. • It is wonderful, although I can see *where* they might have thought it went on too long. Use *that*.

who. • You all know exactly *who* I am talking about—which is odd considering that we don't have princes. Use *whom*. • This is a man *who* even Republican cohorts sometimes find disturbing, for the way he uses almost anything to his advantage. Use *whom*.

would have. • What I am sure of is if we *would have* never confronted them, these white kids would have never given in to us. Use *had*. • If I *would have* been Paula, I would not have started a sexual harassment lawsuit. Use *had*. • I wish none of this *would have* ever happened. Use *had*.

Everyday speakers and writers are also apt to confuse the meaning of one word for that of another. Half-conscious of the words they use and the meanings of them, these people speak and write words as if they scarcely mattered:

amount is confused with *number.* • Buy a qualifying *amount* of books and save 10% on all your subsequent purchases of non-discounted books. USE *number.* • All these methods will get you a minuscule *amount* of terrorists and a maximum *amount* of drug dealers instead. USE *number.*

breech is confused with *broach.* • I really respect that kind of honesty, and have *breeched* the subject at times to encourage fellow pioneers to bring some integrity to the table in such matters. USE *broached.* • When discussing changes in the current severance package, *breech* the topic within the context of changes of other benefit plans. USE *broach.* • Since we've *breeched* the subject, I have to say the Associated Press poll shows John Kerry doing better with women by 1 percentage point than Al Gore did with women. USE *broached.*

collaborate is confused with *corroborate.* • As our feedback reflects, we applaud some comments that *collaborate* our views on the proposals for further enhancement of relay services across the nation. USE *corroborate.* • At this point, we really only have Daniel's word and to back it up, it would be necessary to find Aerojet employees or White Sands people who could *collaborate* his statement. USE *corroborate.*

flaunt is confused with *flout.* • Why was Ted Kennedy a "pseudo-Catholic"—he claimed to be a Catholic but *flaunted* the rules of the church he belonged to. USE *flouted.* • Companies regularly *flaunt* the laws, collecting and disseminating personal information. USE *flout.* • North Korea continues to *flaunt* international law by speeding ahead with their nuclear program with no consequences whatsoever. USE *flout.*

irrelevant is confused with *irreverent.* • It was full of *irrelevant* fun almost to the point of Marx Brothers-style of antics, with a small dose of the horrors of war thrown in. USE *irreverent.* • His *irrelevant* style of humor is both witty and makes us think of how we see ourselves. USE *irreverent.*

meretricious is confused with *meritorious.* • I informed her that that was a *meretricious* plan except for the fact that it involves lying. USE *meritorious.* • They serve the public interest by reminding readers not to believe a message simply because it is widely distributed, and carries the *meretricious* authority of the published word. USE *meritorious.*

palatable is confused with *palpable.* • If only we could capture that *palatable* feeling in a bottle so that it can touch us on a more regular basis, it would do so much good. USE *palpable.* • About six months later I remember thinking that we were headed for a full-fledged recession, and there was an almost *palatable* uneasiness in the air. USE *palpable.*

proscribe is confused with *prescribe.* • We are on record to abide by the 1949 Geneva Conventions and their relevant sections that *proscribe* the rules of war. USE *prescribe.* • They often *proscribe* rules of behavior which we must follow to attain rewards or avoid punishment in this or the afterworld. USE *prescribe*.

respectively is confused with *respectfully*. • Graduates of St. Clare School will act *respectively* toward self and others. USE *respectfully*. • Behave *respectively* to adults and each other. USE *respectfully*.

straight-laced is confused with *strait-laced*. • He's as healthy and *straight-laced* a guy as you'll meet, and in today's society, that is amazing. USE *strait-laced*. • Anyone who's worked in advertising knows it's not exactly a *straight-laced* environment. USE *strait-laced*.

vociferous is confused with *voracious*. • No, he wasn't a *vociferous* reader or running a recycling business. USE *voracious*. • At the age of 18 she opened her own studio and began to teach; a *vociferous* reader, she read everything she could about dance and took master classes from all the recognized leaders. USE *voracious*.

Soon, it is clear, we will be a society unable to distinguish one word from another, sense from nonsense, truth from falsehood, good from evil. We will soon utter only mono- and disyllabic words, be entertained only by what pleases our peers, and adore whatever is easy or effortless. Unfamiliar wording and original phrasing will soon sound incoherent or cacophonic to us, while well-known inanities like *have a nice day, what goes around comes around,* and *hope for the best but expect the worst* will serve as our mantras, our maxims, our mottoes.

Elegant English

We all know far too well how to write everyday English, but few of us apparently know how to write elegant English—English that is expressed with music as well as meaning, style as well as substance. The point of this category is to show that the language can, indeed, be spoken or written with grace and polish—qualities that much contemporary English is bereft of and could benefit from.

So prevalent is everyday English that the person who speaks correctly and uses words deliberately is often thought less well of than the person who speaks solecistically and uses slang unreservedly. Today, fluency is in disfavor. Neither everyday nor even uneducated English seems to offend people quite as much as does elegant English. People neither fume nor flinch when they hear sentences like those illustrated earlier. But let them listen to someone who speaks, or read someone who writes, elegantly, and they may be instantly repelled. Doubtless, well-turned phrases and orotund tones suggest to them a soul unslain.

Even so, it is not classism but clarity, not snobbery but sensibility that users of elegant English prize and wish to promote. Nothing so patently accessible as usage could ever be justly called invidious. As long as we recognize the categories of usage available to us, we can decide whether to speak and write the language well or badly. And we might more readily decide that elegant English is indeed vital were it more widely spoken by our public figures and more often written in our better books. Countless occasions where elegant English might have been used—indeed, ought to have been used—by a president or politician, a luminary or other notable, have passed with uninspired, if not bumbling, speech or writing.

Further, elegant English needs to be reliably compiled in a new type of dictionary—one that does indeed pay more attention to the phrases and rhetorical figures we use or might use, one that can accommodate the category of elegant English. Such a dictionary would be as new as it is old, for it would also need to note and, more than that, endorse the distinctions between words. It would even prescribe distinctions between words where, perhaps, there have been none.

Although the first two categories of usage, uneducated and everyday English, comprise rudimentary structures—a single word misused, or two or three words misplaced—elegant English, a more rhetorical style, generally requires at least a few, and often many, words, as these examples illustrate:

1. I find it agreeable to sit here this morning, in a house of correct proportions, and hear across a century of time his flute, his frogs, and his seductive summons to the wildest revels of them all.—E. B. White, *A Slight Sound at Evening*

2. Take away but the pomps of death, the disguises and solemn bugbears, the tinsel, and the actings by candle-light, and proper and fantastic ceremonies, the ministrels and the noise-makers, the women and the weepers, the swoonings and the shriekings, the nurses and the physicians, the dark room and the ministers, the kindred and the watchers; and then to die is easy, ready, and quitted from its troublesome circumstances.—Jeremy Taylor, *The Rule and Exercises of Holy Dying*

3. Basil comfort those who sigh for the mother tongue. Plow under the fallow *aura, equation, creativity, imbalance, stance, normalcy, dichotomy, sociological, ambient, viable, escalate.* What a hailstone of torment, and a stroke of misery are *existential, confrontation, infiltrate, rationalize, sorted out,* and *activate.* Purge the unlearned mouth with a "combe of corn." Sing a benedictus praising *colewort, pillicock, jillflirt.* Our books are the dropping of starlings and the putrid blubber of seals lying on the wet shingle of Tierra del Fuego.—Edward Dahlberg, *Confessions of Edward Dahlberg*

4. Let me wither and wear out mine age in a discomfortable, in an unwholesome, in a penurious prison, and so pay my debts with my bones, and recompense the wastefulness of my youth, with the beggary of mine age; Let me wither in a spittle under sharp, and foul, and infamous diseases, and so recompense the wantonness of my youth, with that loathsomeness in mine age.—John Donne, *Let Me Wither*

5. A poor relation—is the most irrelevant thing in nature,—a piece of impertinent correspondency,— an odious approximation,—a haunting

conscience,—a preposterous shadow, lengthening in the noontide of your prosperity,—an unwelcome remembrancer,—a perpetually recurring mortification,—a drain on your purse,—a more intolerable dun upon your pride,—a drawback upon success,—a rebuke to your rising,—a stain in your blood,—a blot on your scutcheon,—a rent in your garment,—a death's head at your banquet,—Agathocles' pot,—a Mordecai in your gate,—a Lazarus at your door,—a lion in your path,—a frog in your chamber,—a fly in your ointment,—a mote in your eye,—a triumph to your enemy, an apology to your friends,—the one thing not needful,—the hail in harvest,—the ounce of sour in a pound of sweet.—Charles Lamb, *Poor Relations*

6. Perhaps her fading mind called up once more the shadows of the past to float before it, and retraced, for the last time, the vanished visions of that long history—passing back and back, through the cloud of years, to older and ever older memories—to the spring woods at Osborne, so full of primroses for Lord Beaconsfield—to Lord Palmerston's queer clothes and high demeanour, and Albert's face under the green lamp, and Albert's first stag at Balmoral, and Albert in his blue and silver uniform, and the Baron coming in through a doorway, and Lord M. dreaming at Windsor with the rooks cawing in the elm-trees, and the Archbishop of Canterbury on his knees in the dawn, and the old King's turkey-cock ejaculations, and Uncle Leopold's soft voice at Claremont, and Lehzen with the globes, and her mother's feathers sweeping down towards her, and a great old repeater-watch of her father's in its tortoise-shell case, and a yellow rug, and some friendly flounces of sprigged muslin, and the trees and the grass at Kensington.—Lytton Strachey, *Queen Victoria*

7. Listen! for if you are not totally callous, if your consciences are not seared, I will speak daggers to your souls, and awake you to all the horrors of guilty recollection. I will follow you with whips and stings through every maze of your unexampled turpitude, and plant thorns under the rose of ministerial approbation.—Edmund Burke, Speech

8. As to my old opinions, I am heartily sick of them. I have reason, for they have deceived me sadly. I was taught to think, and I was willing to believe, that genius was not a bawd, that virtue was not a mask, that liberty was not a name, that love had its seat in the human heart. Now I would care little if these words were struck out of the dictionary, or if I had never heard them. They are become to my ears a mockery and a dream. Instead of patriots and friends of freedom, I see nothing but the tyrant and the slave, the people linked with kings to rivet on the chains of despotism and superstition. I see folly join with knavery, and together make up public spirit and public opinions. I see the insolent Tory, the blind Reformer, the coward Whig! If mankind had wished for what is

right, they might have had it long ago.—William Hazlitt, *On the Pleasure of Hating*

9. Poor Cromwell,—great Cromwell! The inarticulate Prophet; Prophet who could not speak. Rude, confused, struggling to utter himself, with his savage depth, with his wild sincerity; and he looked so strange, among the elegant Euphemisms, dainty little Falklands, didactic Chillingworths, diplomatic Clarendons! Consider him. An outer hull of chaotic confusion, visions of the Devil, nervous dreams, almost semi-madness; and yet such a clear determinate man's-energy working in the heart of that. A kind of chaotic man. The ray as of pure starlight and fire, working in such an element of boundless hypochondria, unformed black of darkness! And yet withal this hypochondria, what was it but the very greatness of the man? The depth and tenderness of his wild affections: the quantity of sympathy he had with things,—the quantity of insight he would yet get into the heart of things, the mastery he would yet get over things: this was his hypochondria. The man's misery, as man's misery always does, came of his greatness. Samuel Johnson too is that kind of man. Sorrow-stricken, half-distracted; the wide element of mournful black enveloping him,—wide as the world. It is the character of a prophetic man; a man with his whole soul seeing, and struggling to see.—Thomas Carlyle, *Heroes and Hero Worship*

10. I confess I love littleness almost in all things. A little, convenient estate, a little cheerful house, a little company, and a very little feast; and, if I were to fall in love again (which is a great passion, and therefore, I hope, I have done with it), it would be, I think, with prettiness, rather than with majestical beauty.—Abraham Cowley, *Of Greatness*

No dimwitticisms clutter these examples of elegant English. They are full of wit and meaning and style and song; they are elegant. They do not have, nor do they need, the false allure, the empty zest of dim-witted words and phrases. Elegant English, as these examples show, is exhilarating; it stirs our thoughts and feelings as ably as dimwitted English blurs them.

* * *

The Dimwit's Dictionary will aid us in our quest for elegant, for *wittier,* speech and writing. The goal is to promote understanding and rouse people to action. The goal is to express ourselves as never before—in writing that demands to be read aloud, in speech that calls to be captured in print.

Part Two

The

DIMWIT'S
DICTIONARY

0-9

100 (110) percent ∎ An infantile phrase. 1. *altogether; categorically; completely; entirely; fully; perfectly; positively; quite; roundly; thoroughly; totally; unconditionally; unreservedly; utterly; wholly.* **2.** *all right; faultless; fine; fit; flawless; good; healthy; impeccable; okay; perfect; sound; thriving; unflawed; well.* • He said he is *100 percent* comfortable with the column. REPLACE WITH *altogether.* • I totally believe it, *110 percent.* DELETE *110 percent.* • My foot is *100 percent* now. REPLACE WITH *all right.*
  People uncomfortable with or unknowledgeable of words, and the precision they are capable of expressing, will use numbers—soaringly high, murmurously low numbers—where they can.

24/7 ∎ An infantile phrase. *always; ceaselessly; constantly; continually; continuously; day and night; endlessly; eternally; everlastingly; evermore; forever; forevermore; frequently; interminably; nonstop; permanently; perpetually; persistently; recurrently; regularly; repeatedly; unceasingly; unendingly; unremittingly.* • Back then, you did not have *24/7* email access. REPLACE WITH *constant.* • Our crews are cleaning Gulf beaches *24/7.* REPLACE WITH *ceaselessly.* Nothing recommends this silly phrase—especially when so many other words, true words, mean as much. *24/7* is favored by people who find words unwieldy and thought distasteful.

365/24/7 ∎ An infantile phrase. *always; ceaselessly; constantly; continually; continuously; endlessly; eternally; everlastingly; evermore; forever; forevermore; frequently; interminably; nonstop; permanently; perpetually; persistently; recurrently; regularly; repeatedly; unceasingly; unendingly; unremittingly.* • Today its fleet of 3,800 cabs are all GPS/ GPRS (general packet radio service) enabled and are available *365/24/7.* REPLACE WITH *always.*

Aa

(like) a bad penny (always turns up) ∎ A moribund metaphor. 1. *bastard; blackguard; cad; charlatan; cheat; cheater; fake; fraud; impostor; knave; mountebank; phony; pretender; quack; rascal; rogue; scoundrel; swindler; undesirable; villain; wretch.* 2. *adversity; calamity; hardship; misfortune; trouble.*

Dimwitticisms, as *a bad penny* nicely illustrates, are dull and uninspiring. Every one of the synonyms listed here is far more interesting than the expression *a bad penny.*

abandon all hope, ye who enter here ∎ An infantile phrase.

a barking dog never bites ∎ A popular prescription.

a barrage of ∎ A moribund metaphor. If our language seems languid, it's partly because our metaphors are moribund.

This, *a barrage of*, is one of a certain kind of moribund metaphor that is especially irksome to come upon: *a bastion of, a chorus of, a cloud of, a deluge of, a firestorm of, a flood of, a flurry of, a forest of, a hailstorm of, a mountain of, an army of, an avalanche of, an explosion of, an oasis of; an ocean of, an orgy of, a rising tide of, a sea of, a small army of, a spate of, a storm of, a symphony of, a torrent of, a whale of, a world of* are all shabby, unimaginative expressions.

These are the least evocative, the least metaphorical, of metaphors. • He says *a barrage of marketing* has made teens tougher to teach.

> After the name-calling and laughter, the rest was a blur, a barrage of hands and legs coming at him as he instinctively dropped to the ground and covered his head, rolling himself into what he imagined was a protective shell.—Gail Tsukiyama, *The Street of a Thousand Blossoms*

(like) a bat out of hell ∎ An insipid simile. *abruptly; apace; at once; briskly; directly; expeditiously; fast; forthwith; hastily; hurriedly; immediately; instantaneously; instantly; posthaste; promptly; quickly; rapidly; rashly; right away; speedily; straightaway; suddenly; swiftly; wingedly.*

> The word saved me, as words always have, and I could stir again, and stir I did, charging up the eastern loop of the trail back like a bat out of hell.—Jincy Willett, *Winner of the National Book Award: A Novel of Fame, Honor, and Really Bad Weather*

a beacon (ray) of hope ∎ A moribund metaphor. *anticipation; expectancy; expectation; hope; hopefulness; optimism; possibility; promise; prospect; sanguinity.*

(catch) a bear by the tail ∎ A moribund metaphor.

a beehive of activity ∎ A moribund metaphor. *active; astir; bustling; busy; buzzing; energetic; humming; hopping; hustling; lively; vigorous.*

a bee in (her) bonnet ∎ A moribund metaphor. 1. *caprice; crotchet; fancy; humor; impulse; maggot; notion; quirk; urge; vagary; whim.* 2. *craze; enthusiasm; fixation; infatuation; mania; obsession; passion; preoccupation.*

> Poor Nelson. He has this bee in his bonnet—doing something for this girl nobody knows.—John Updike, *Rabbit Remembered*

a bevy of beauties ∎ An infantile phrase.

(like) a big weight has been lifted from (my) shoulders ∎ An insipid simile. 1. *allay; alleviate; assuage; lighten; mitigate; relieve; soothe.* 2. *deliver; disburden; disencumber; disentangle; emancipate; extricate; free; liberate; manumit; release; relieve; save; set free; unburden; unchain; unencumber; unfetter; unshackle.*

a bird in the hand (is worth two in the bush) ∎ A popular prescription.

a bitter (tough) pill to swallow ∎ A moribund metaphor.

abject poverty ∎ An inescapable pair.

a blessing in disguise ∎ A moribund metaphor.

a blip on the (radar) screen ∎ A moribund metaphor. *frivolous; inappreciable; immaterial; inconsequential; inconsiderable; insignificant; meager; meaningless; minor; negligible; next to nothing; nugatory; paltry; petty; scant; scanty; scarcely anything; slight; trifling; trivial; unimportant; unsubstantial; worthless.* As laughable as it is moribund, *a blip on the (radar) screen* belies the writing ability of whoever uses it. • War and peace abroad was *barely a blip on the screen* compared with gun control at home. REPLACE WITH *inconsiderable.*

a bolt from (out of) the blue ∎ A moribund metaphor. *bombshell; shock; surprise; thunderbolt; thunderclap.*

abortive attempt (effort) ∎ An inescapable pair. *breakdown; failure; malfunction.*

above and beyond the call of duty ∎ A moribund metaphor.

above par ∎ A moribund metaphor. *excellent; exceptional; first-class; first-rate; outstanding; remarkable; superior; superlative.*

(like) a bowl of cherries ∎ An insipid simile. *agreeable; ambrosial; beguiling; celestial; charming; delectable; delicious; delightful; divine; enchanting; engaging; enjoyable; fun; heavenly; glorious; gratifying; inviting; joyful; joyous; luscious; pleasant; pleasing; pleasurable.*

> Maybe she was a complication he didn't want or need, but it wasn't like meeting him had made life a bowl of cherries for her, either.—Lara Adrian, *Kiss of Midnight*

a (welcome) breath of fresh air ∎ A moribund metaphor. *animating; arousing; bracing; enlivening; exciting; exhilarating; inspiring; inspiriting; invigorating; provoking; refreshing; rousing; stimulating; vivifying.*

Of what it purports to describe, *a (welcome) breath of fresh air* offers the opposite. If intelligent or heartfelt sentences are invigorating, this dimwitticism should make us gasp as though we've been throttled by foul-smelling thoughtlessness. • A toy industry analyst called the news *a breath of fresh air*. REPLACE WITH *exciting*. • Ordinarily, I find Friedman *a welcome breath of fresh air*—he has little patience for fools and plagiarists. REPLACE WITH *refreshing*.

> He was thumbing through his messages when his best friend and fellow attorney Charles Ryan bounced in. Charlie was a welcome breath of fresh air.—Renée Alexis, *Undying Love*

a breed apart (unto itself) ∎ A moribund metaphor. *aberrant; abnormal; anomalistic; anomalous; atypical; bizarre; curious; deviant; different; distinct; distinctive; eccentric; exceptional; extraordinary; fantastic; foreign; grotesque; idiosyncratic; independent; individual; individualistic; irregular; novel; odd; offbeat; original; peculiar; puzzling; quaint; queer; rare; remarkable; separate; singular; uncommon; unconventional; unexampled; unique; unnatural; unorthodox; unparalleled; unprecedented; unusual; weird.*

(it's) a breeze ∎ A moribund metaphor. *apparent; basic; clear; clear-cut; conspicuous; distinct; easily done; easy; effortless; elementary; evident; explicit; facile; limpid; lucid; manifest; obvious; patent; pellucid; plain; simple; simplicity itself; straightforward; translucent; transparent; unambiguous; uncomplex; uncomplicated;*

understandable; unequivocal; unmistakable.

absence makes the heart grow fonder ∎ A popular prescription.

absolutely ∎ An overworked word. *altogether; categorically; completely; entirely; fully; perfectly; positively; quite; roundly; thoroughly; totally; unconditionally; unreservedly; utterly; wholly.* SEE ALSO **100 (110) percent; definitely; most assuredly; most (very) definitely.**

absolutely, positively ∎ An infantile phrase. • A programmer must *absolutely, positively* keep a finger on the format's pulse. DELETE *absolutely, positively*. • On a wide range of topics, he is the go-to guy—when you *absolutely, positively* have to know what happened. DELETE *absolutely, positively*.

Here's a variation that the writer may have prided himself on: • But what you *positively, absolutely* do not want is to get hurt in a stupid exhibition game. DELETE *positively, absolutely*.

(like) a bull in a china closet (shop) ∎ An insipid simile. *awkward; blundering; bumbling; bungling; clumsy; gawky; gauche; ham-handed; heavy-handed; inapt; inept; lubberly; lumbering; maladroit; uncoordinated; uncouth; ungainly; ungraceful; unhandy; unskillful; unwieldy.*

> I took a moment to catch my breath. A bull in a china shop could not rival what had seemed like a herd of buffalos in a bookstore.—Joan Hess, *Damsels in Distress*

(like) a bump on a log ∎ An insipid simile. *dead; dormant; dull; immobile; immovable; inactive; inanimate; indolent; inert; inoperative; languid; latent; lethargic; lifeless; listless; motionless; phlegmatic; quiescent; quiet; sluggish; stagnant; static; stationary; still; stock-still; torpid; unresponsive.*

(open up) a can of worms ∎ A moribund metaphor. *complication; difficulty; dilemma; mess; muddle; ordeal; pickle; plight; predicament; problem; quandary; trial; trouble.*

(it's) a catch-22 ∎ A moribund metaphor. 1. *contradiction; dilemma; impasse; incongruity; paradox; plight; predicament; quandary; situation.* 2. *conundrum; enigma; puzzle; riddle.*

(like) a cat on a hot tin roof ∎ An insipid simile. *agitated; anxious; eager; edgy; excitable; excited; fidgety; frantic; jittery; jumpy; nervous; ill at ease; on edge; restive; restless; skittish; uncomfortable; uneasy.*

accentuate the positive ∎ An infantile phrase. *be confident; be encouraged; be heartened; be hopeful; be optimistic; be positive; be rosy; be sanguine.*

accidents will happen ∎ A popular prescription.

according to Hoyle ∎ An infantile phrase. *accurately; by the rules; conventionally; correctly; customarily; properly; regularly; rightly; traditionally.*

ace in the hole ∎ A moribund metaphor.

(running around) (like) a chicken with its head cut off ∎ An insipid simile. *agitated; chaotic; crazed; crazy; demented; deranged; distraught; frantic; frenetic; frenzied; harried; hysterical; insane; mad; raging; wild.*

> Next year, he would not be running around like a chicken with its head cut off, because next year, he would not have a parish.—Jan Karon, *Out to Canaan*

Achilles' heel (tendon) ∎ A moribund metaphor. *defect; deficiency; disadvantage; failing; fault; flaw; foible; fragility; frailness; frailty; handicap; imperfection; liability; limitation; shortcoming; susceptibility; susceptibleness; vulnerability; vulnerableness; weakness.* • If the Bruins had an *Achilles' heel* last season, it was that they were a tad oversized. REPLACE WITH *weakness.*

a chip off the old block ∎ A moribund metaphor. *carbon copy; clone; double; duplicate; mirror image; replica; twin.*

acid test ∎ A moribund metaphor. *assay; crucible; ordeal; proof; test; trial.*

a clear and present danger ∎ An infantile phrase. *danger; hazard; menace; peril; threat; troublemaker.* • He is *a clear and present danger.* REPLACE WITH *a menace.*

across the board ∎ A moribund metaphor. *(for) all; all over; (for) everyone; everyplace; everywhere; throughout (the land); universally.* • There is increased consumer confidence—not just here but *across the board.* REPLACE WITH *everywhere.*

> The war was over, things looked robust across the board, and Big Don was living the charmed life at the age of thirty-three.—Kevin Brennan, *Parts Unknown*

action plan ∎ A torpid term. *action; course; direction; intention; method; move; plan; policy; procedure; route; scheme; strategy.* • The UN is expected to produce a global *action plan* aimed at reducing demand and improving treatment, rehabilitation, and interdiction. REPLACE WITH *strategy.*

actions speak louder than words ∎ A popular prescription.

active ∎ An overworked word. Only thoughtless speakers and writers, apes and jackanapes, use the adjective *active* to modify a noun. In doing so, they emasculate the meaning of these words. So common is the adjectival *active*, we might easily wonder if anything is possible or achievable, serious or sincere that does not have this word preceding it.
 • Please believe me when I tell you that the only thing that stands between you and a better, more responsive government is your *active participation* in the process. DELETE *active.* • Nor did the president demonstrate *active interest* in the issue. DELETE *active.* • Some practitioners think that *active movement* might be the key to a cure. DELETE *active.* • An *active search* is on for the shooter. DELETE *active.* SEE ALSO **actively.**

actively ∎ An overworked word. The popular use of *actively* suggests that any verb not affixed to it is feckless.
 We cannot simply *consider* an idea lest we be accused of not thinking; we cannot simply *engage* in a pursuit lest we be accused of not trying; we cannot simply *participate* in a conversation lest we be accused of not speaking. • Another possibility is *actively being considered* by the administration: the use of force. DELETE *actively.* • The core group of ASC founders worried that the membership was restricted too narrowly to policing, so they *actively encouraged* others to participate. DELETE *actively.* • I have no intention of mailing a second letter to anyone who does not *actively show* an interest in becoming part of my collectors club. DELETE *actively.* • Police are *actively searching* for the killer, *actively looking* in all areas, and *actively examining* all the evidence. DELETE *actively.* • Not only do many people not enjoy speaking in public, they *actively dislike* and even fear it. DELETE *actively.* • Seek them out *actively.* DELETE *actively.* • Right now we're not *actively aware* of what her true motivation was. DELETE *actively.* • Reporters get mired in routine like everyone and need, from time to time, to *actively work* on expanding the number of places they go and the variety of people with whom they talk. DELETE *actively.*
 Here is an example of just how absurd our fixation on *actively* has become: • Among the new features of WSF2 R3.3 that he is *actively looking forward to* is the statistical information that can be provided through SMF records. DELETE *actively.* SEE ALSO **active.**

a cut above (the rest) ∎ A moribund metaphor. *abler; better; exceptional; greater; higher; more able (accomplished; adept; capable; competent; qualified; skilled; talented); outstanding; standout; superior; superlative.*

acutely aware ∎ An inescapable pair. • Fans have become *acutely aware* that player strikes and lockouts are battles over who gets the biggest piece of what the fan provides.

adamantly oppose ∎ An inescapable pair.

a dark day ∎ A moribund metaphor.

a day at the beach ∎ A moribund metaphor. 1. *easily done; easy; effortless; elementary; facile; simple; simplicity itself; straightforward; uncomplex; uncomplicated.* 2. *agreeable; beguiling; charming; delightful; enchanting; engaging; enjoyable; fun; glorious; gratifying; inviting; joyful; joyous; pleasant; pleasing; pleasurable.*

add fuel to the fire ∎ A moribund metaphor. *activate; aggravate; agitate; animate; arouse; awaken; encourage; enkindle; enliven; exacerbate; excite; feed; foment; heighten; ignite; impassion; incite; increase; inflame; intensify; invigorate; make worse; nourish; prod; provoke; rejuvenate; revitalize; revive; rouse; shake up; stimulate; stir up; vitalize; worsen.*

add insult to injury ∎ A moribund metaphor. *aggravate; arouse; enkindle; enliven; exacerbate; excite; feed; foment; heighten; ignite; impassion; incite; increase; inflame; intensify; invigorate; make worse; nourish; prod; provoke; rouse; shake up; stimulate; stir up; what's worse; worsen.*

a deal is a deal ∎ A quack equation.

a diamond in the rough ∎ A moribund metaphor. *bad-mannered; coarse; common; crass; crude; ill-bred; ill-mannered; impolite; rough; rude; uncivilized; uncouth; uncultured; unrefined; unsophisticated; vulgar.*

a dime a dozen ∎ A moribund metaphor. *average; basic; common; commonplace; customary; everyday; normal; omnipresent; ordinary; prevalent; quotidian; regular; standard; typical; ubiquitous; unexceptional; universal; unremarkable; usual; widespread.* • Sikhs in Kenya are *a dime a dozen.* REPLACE WITH *ubiquitous.*

> What you find out in your thirties is that clever children are a dime a dozen. It's what you do later that counts, and so far I had done nothing.—Christina Schwarz, *All Is Vanity*

ad infinitum ∎ A foreign phrase. *ceaselessly; endlessly; evermore; forever; forevermore; to infinity; without limit.*

a direct line to God ∎ An infantile phrase. • A pair of men spotted outside the Marshalls' house leads Dunning to the Preacher, a bookseller with questionable intentions and *a direct line to God.* • These nontraditionalist Christians frequently assert *a direct line to God*, purporting to know details about the consummation of the world.

> When she pictures *shefa*, she thinks of the red phone on the President's desk that is supposed to be a direct line to the Soviet Union. *Shefa* will be her red telephone, a direct line to God.—Myla Goldberg, *Bee Season*

a dirty word ∎ A moribund metaphor. *abhorrent; abominable; a curse; an abomination; anathema; antipathetic; detestable; execrable; hateful; loathsome; monstrous; offensive; repugnant.* • Some in the academic community may disagree, but to working families corporate takeovers are still *a dirty word.* REPLACE WITH *anathema.*

a dog-eat-dog world ∎ A moribund metaphor. *brutal; cruel; ferocious; fierce; vicious.*

a dog's age ∎ A moribund metaphor. *ages; a long time; a long while; an age; an eternity; decades; eons; forever; months; years.*

(lead) a dog's life ∎ A moribund metaphor. *misery; unhappiness; wretchedness.*

a done deal ∎ A infantile phrase. *absolute; completed; concluded; conclusive; consummated; definitive; final; finished.* • There seems to be a misconception that this is *a done deal.* REPLACE WITH *consummated.*

a dream (fairy tale) come true ∎ A plebeian sentiment.

a drop in the bucket (ocean) ∎ A moribund metaphor. *frivolous; inappreciable; immaterial; inconsequential; inconsiderable; insignificant; meager; meaningless; negligible; next to nothing; nugatory; paltry; petty; scant; scanty; scarcely anything; slight; trifling; trivial; unimportant; unsubstantial; worthless.* • Relative to need, it's *a drop in the bucket.* REPLACE WITH *next to nothing.* • When art is part of a larger construction budget, the money is usually *a drop in the bucket* compared with overall costs. REPLACE WITH *inconsiderable.*

a drowning man will clutch at a straw ∎ A popular prescription.

(like) a Dutch uncle ∎ An insipid simile.

advance planning ∎ A wretched redundancy. *planning.* • This project will require a lot of *advance planning.* DELETE *advance.*

advance warning ∎ A wretched redundancy. *warning.* • Although the bank's 17,000 employees have known for more than a month that the ax was about to fall, the *advance warning* did little to blunt the effect. DELETE *advance.* SEE ALSO **forewarn; warn in advance.**

advice is cheap ∎ A quack equation.

a dying breed ∎ A moribund metaphor. *declining; dying; moribund; waning.*

a feather in (his) cap ∎ A moribund metaphor. *accomplishment; achievement; feat; success; triumph; victory.*

> But I can remember that from quite early on, for some reason, Isabel decided that Edith was rather a feather in her cap, someone that little bit special to be fed to her country neighbours in rationed morsels.—Julian Fellowes, *Snobs*

(has) a few screws loose ∎ A moribund metaphor. *batty; cracked; crazy; daft; demented; deranged; fey; foolish; goofy; insane; lunatic; mad; maniacal; neurotic; nuts; nutty; psychotic; raving; silly; squirrelly; strange; touched; unbalanced; unhinged; unsound; wacky; zany.*

a fifth wheel ∎ A moribund metaphor. *excessive; extra; extraneous; immaterial; incidental; inconsequential; insignificant; irrelevant; needless; nonessential; superabundant; superfluous; unimportant; unnecessary.* • With his mother doing the cooking and other household chores, I would feel *like a fifth wheel*. REPLACE WITH *superfluous.*

a fine (pretty) kettle of fish ∎ A moribund metaphor. *complication; difficulty; dilemma; mess; muddle; ordeal; pickle; plight; predicament; problem; quandary; trial; trouble.*

(like) a fish out of water ∎ An insipid simile. *awkward; blundering; bumbling; bungling; clumsy; gawky; gauche; ham-handed; heavy-handed; inapt; inept; lubberly; lumbering; maladroit; uncoordinated; uncouth; ungainly; ungraceful; unhandy; unskillful; unwieldy.*

a fly on the wall ∎ A moribund metaphor.

> Some of you reading this may want to skip the next five pages, and discover what happened after I left the brothel, but others may want to stay with me now, and be a fly on the wall.—Alan Goodwin, *A Medic on the Mekong*

(bid) a fond farewell ∎ An infantile phrase.

a fool and his money are soon parted ∎ A popular prescription.

a force to be reckoned with ∎ An infantile phrase. *adversary; antagonist; challenger; competitor; contender; contestant; force; opponent; rival.* • The combination of Walsh, the broadcast of Celtics games this season, and hot Fox network programming will make WFXT *a force to be reckoned with.* REPLACE WITH *a contender.*

afraid (frightened; scared) of (his) own shadow ∎ A moribund metaphor. *afraid; alarmed; apprehensive; cowardly; craven; diffident; faint-hearted; fearful; frightened; pavid; pusillanimous; recreant; scared; terror-stricken; timid; timorous; tremulous.*

a friend in need (is a friend indeed) ∎ A popular prescription.

after (once; when) all is said and done ∎ A wretched redundancy. *all in all; all told; altogether; eventually; finally; in all; in the end; on the whole; overall; ultimately.* • *After all is said and done*, it truly was an exceptional decade. REPLACE WITH *On the whole.* • *When all is said and done*, we humans are a curious species. REPLACE WITH *All told.*

> Inside the sack was a spool of twine, a sugar cane knife to sever the umbilical cord, and a garden spade to bury the creature once all was said and done.—Kathy Hepinstall, *The House of Gentle Men*

after the fact ∎ A torpid term. *afterward; later.* • We don't have a choice, *after the fact.* REPLACE WITH *afterward.*

a funny thing happened to me on the way to ∎ An infantile phrase. • But *a funny thing happened on the way to* the Memorial Plaza.

age before beauty ∎ A popular prescription.

a glimmer of hope ∎ A moribund metaphor. *anticipation; expectancy; expectation; hope; hopefulness; optimism; possibility; promise; prospect; sanguinity.*

a goldmine of (information) ∎ A moribund metaphor. SEE ALSO **a barrage of.** • His diary is nonetheless *a goldmine of information* about earlier American gay social life.

a good man is hard to find ∎ A popular prescription.

a good read ∎ An infantile phrase. This is a hideous expression that only the very badly read—those, that is, who read merely to be entertained—could possibly verbalize. The people who use this phrase are the people who read *best-selling authors* (SEE). • This bookstore caters to those looking for *a good read in paperback.* REPLACE WITH *a readable paperback.* • While Foley's piece on football stadiums was *a good read*, it is entirely off the mark in terms of the proposed megaplex. REPLACE WITH *entertaining.* • It is hard to make air-conditioning repair *a good read.* REPLACE WITH *captivating.* SEE ALSO **a (must) read.**

> Then I come back, get the paper and settle down in the breakfast nook for a good read.—Anne George, *Murder on a Girls' Night Out*

(and) a good time was had by all ∎ An infantile phrase.

agree to disagree ∎ An infantile phrase.

a guilty conscience needs no accuser ∎ A popular prescription.

a hard (tough) act to follow ∎ A moribund metaphor.

a hard (tough) nut to crack ∎ A moribund metaphor. *conundrum; difficulty; dilemma; enigma; mystery; nut; plight; poser; predicament; problem; puzzle; quandary; question; riddle.*

ahead of the game ∎ A moribund metaphor. *advantageous; auspicious; blessed; charmed; enchanted; favored; felicitous; flourishing; fortuitous; fortunate; golden; happy; in luck; lucky; propitious; prosperous; successful; thriving.*

ahead of (his) time ∎ A moribund metaphor. *advanced; ground-breaking; innovative; inventive; new; original; pioneering; progressive; radical; revolutionary; unconventional.*

(has) a (good) head on (his) shoulders ∎ A moribund metaphor. *able; adroit; apt; astute; bright; brilliant; capable; clever; competent; discerning; effective; effectual; efficient; enlightened; insightful; intelligent; judicious; keen; knowledgeable; learned; logical; luminous; perceptive; perspicacious; quick; rational; reasonable; sagacious; sage; sapient; sensible; sharp; shrewd; smart; sound; understanding; wise.*

a heartbeat away ∎ A moribund metaphor.

(like) a herd of elephants ∎ An insipid simile.

a hop, skip, and a jump ∎ A moribund metaphor.

a house divided against itself cannot stand ∎ A popular prescription.

(like) a house of cards ∎ An insipid simile. *breakable; broken-down; crumbly; decrepit; dilapidated; flimsy; fragile; frangible; friable; precarious; ramshackle; rickety; shabby; shaky; tottering; unsound; unstable; unsteady; unsure; wobbly.* • He argued that the government's case against them is *a house of cards.* REPLACE WITH *rickety.*

aid and abet ∎ An inescapable pair. *abet; aid; assist; encourage; help; support.* • One of the best-known detectives comes from literature in the person of Sherlock Holmes, a private investigator *aided and abetted* by his friend Dr. Watson. REPLACE WITH *assisted.*

> The two women were simply aiding and abetting each other to disband the Seraglio.—Penelope Fitzgerald, *Human Voices*

airtight alibi ∎ An inescapable pair.

a (man) is known by the company (he) keeps ∎ A popular prescription.

a kick in the pants ∎ A moribund metaphor. 1. *encouragement; fillip; goad; impetus; impulse; incentive; incitation; incitement; inducement; jolt; motivation; motive; prod; provocation; push; shove; spur; stimulation; stimulus; thrust; urge.* 2. *animation; ebullience; elation; enthusiasm; excitement; exhilaration; exultation; jubilance; jubilation; liveliness; rapture; stimulation; vivacity.* 3. *admonishment; castigation; censure; chastisement; disapprobation; disapproval; rebuke; remonstrance; reprimand; reproof; scolding; upbraiding.*

a kick in the teeth ∎ A moribund metaphor. *abuse; affront; contempt; contumely; derision; disappointment; disdain; impertinence; indignity; insult; offense; outrage; rebuff; rebuke; rejection; scorn; slap; slight; slur; sneer; snub.* • We have received a judgment that has been *a kick in the teeth.* REPLACE WITH *an insult.*

(like) a kid in a candy shop (store) ∎ An insipid simile.

à la ∎ A foreign phrase. *according to; in the manner of; like.* • I don't want to put myself in a bad position and get beat *à la* this man. REPLACE WITH *like.* • The media may be engaged in a witch hunt *a la* the late U.S. Senator Joe McCarthy and perhaps should cut back on their coverage. REPLACE WITH *in the manner of.*

a labor of love ∎ A moribund metaphor.

> It has been a true labor of love, and something more—the only thing that has kept her calm during the long winter months of waiting for the hearing to begin.—Anita Shreve, *Fortune's Rocks*

alas ∎ A withered word. *regrettably; sadly; sorrowfully; unfortunately; unhappily.* • *Alas*, the program checks only the first two directory entries. REPLACE WITH *Unfortunately.*

alas and alack ∎ An infantile phrase. *regrettably; sadly; sorrowfully; unfortunately; unhappily.*

(for) a laugh ∎ A plebeian sentiment. This expression is spoken by people who tally their giggles and count their guffaws, people who value numbers and sums more than they do words and concepts, people who consider laughter a commodity and life a comedy. • I need *a laugh.* • Sue and I want to do these silly things to you *for a laugh.* • I'm always looking *for a laugh.* SEE ALSO **avid reader; on a scale of 1 to 10.**

albatross around (my) neck ∎ A moribund metaphor. *affliction; burden; charge; cross; difficulty; encumbrance; hardship; hindrance; impediment; load; obstacle; obstruction; onus; oppression; ordeal; problem; trial; trouble; weight.* • Then came that unspeakable song, "Begin the Beguine," which is still *an albatross around my neck.* REPLACE WITH *a burden.*

albeit ∎ A withered word. *although; even if; even though; though.* Like other withered words, *albeit* strikes some people as more exquisite sounding—and therefore, apparently, more intellectual sounding—than any of its synonyms. But this is perceived by only the deaf and the dimwitted. • *Albeit* somewhat dated, a study performed eight years ago is attracting attention once again. REPLACE WITH *Although*.

a legend in (his) own mind ∎ An infantile phrase.

(has) a leg up on ∎ A moribund metaphor. *advantage (over); predominance over; superiority to; supremacy over.* • This is expected to give auto makers *a natural leg up.* REPLACE WITH *a natural advantage.* • Even I have *a leg up on* him in that department. REPLACE WITH *an advantage over.*

a leopard cannot change his spots ∎ A popular prescription.

a level playing field ∎ A moribund metaphor. *egalitarianism; equality; equitableness; equity; fairness; impartiality; justice; justness.* • If you live in a democracy, there has to be *a level playing field.* REPLACE WITH *equality.* • Many people of goodwill sincerely, but mistakenly, believe that today we have achieved *a level playing field.* REPLACE WITH *fairness.*

a light went off (in my head) ∎ A moribund metaphor. *afflatus; brainwave; breakthrough; flash; idea; insight; inspiration; revelation.*

(draw) a (the) line in (the sand) ∎ A moribund metaphor. 1. *hold fast; persevere; stand firm.* 2. *assert; command; decree; dictate; insist; order; require.* 3. *deny; disallow; forbid; prohibit; refuse; reject.* • There is a time to *draw a line in the sand* and fight. REPLACE WITH *persevere.* So inexact an expression is *(draw) a (the) line in (the sand)* that it can mean other words as well: • Instead, they *draw a line in the sand* between good and bad, between timeless and fleeting. REPLACE WITH *distinguish.* • If you can't *draw a line in* the case law, you probably haven't analyzed the authorities enough. REPLACE WITH *distill information from.*

> If I didn't draw a line in the sand right now, the script would no longer be mine. It would be Allegra's.—Cady Kalian, *A Few Good Murders*

a little bird told me ∎ An infantile phrase.

a little (honesty) goes a long way ∎ A popular prescription.

a little knowledge is a dangerous thing ∎ A popular prescription.

alive and kicking ∎ A moribund metaphor. *alive; blooming; doing well; energetic; existent; existing; extant; flourishing; growing; hale; hardy; healthful; healthy; hearty; live; lively; living; prospering; robust; sound; still exists; strong; surviving; thriving; vigorous; vital; well; well-off.* One of the consequences of endlessly saying and hearing and writing and reading formulaic phrases is that, eventually, people *do* become weary of them.

But instead of expressing themselves differently—more eloquently or more inventively, perhaps—people will simply substitute one word in these selfsame formulas for another.

Thus, along with *alive and kicking,* there is, for instance, *alive and well* (SEE) and even *alive and thriving;* along with *a thing of the past,* there is *a phenomenon of the past;* along with *business as usual,* there is *politics as usual* (SEE) and *life as usual;* along with *mover and shaker,* there is *mover and shaper;* along with *neck of the woods,* there is the noisome *portion of the earth;* along with *needs and wants,* there is *needs and desires;* along with *in no way,* there is *in no way, shape, or form* and the preposterous *in no way, shape, form, or fashion;* along with *remedy the situation,* there is *rectify the situation;* along with *out the window,* there is *out the door;* and along with *nothing could be further from the truth,* there is, incomprehensibly, *nothing could be further from the actual facts.*

Would that it ended here, but there are also far too many people who begin with a hackneyed phrase and then transmogrify it into an ever-so-silly, garish one.

Thus, *between a rock and a hard place* (SEE) becomes: • In the past decade, newspaper publishers have feet squeezed *between the Net and a hard place.* • The Al Queda fighters are *between an anvil and a hammer.*

A needle in a haystack (SEE) becomes: • Her friend wrote back and said this was impossible, like looking for *a needle on the bottom of the ocean.*

From bad to worse (SEE) becomes: • Moscow now has about **90** days to try to keep a *bad situation from collapsing into something infinitely worse.*

Doesn't have a snowball's chance in hell (SEE) becomes: • There is nobody on Russia's political horizon who embraces Mr. Yeltsin's westernized brand of economic policy and *has a Siberian snowball's chance of winning a presidential election.*

An accident waiting to happen (SEE) becomes: • The holidays are *a cornucopia of awkward moments waiting to happen.* • Expectations are resentments *waiting to happen.*

Not with a bang but with a whimper (SEE) becomes: • This week *started out with a bang and ended with a whimper* for bank stocks. • Hurricane Bonnie hit New England *with a whimper, not a bang.* • After *beginning my career there with a bang, I cannot end with a whimper.* • It could *end with a whimper or a wallop.*

Walk softly and carry a big stick (SEE) becomes: • The guiding principle in foreign policy of this administration seems to be *speak loudly and carry a twig.*

Snatch victory from the jaws of defeat (SEE) becomes: • In the end, Republicans will simply *snatch defeat from the jaws of victory* if they successfully oust a president they loathe but lose their majorities in both houses of Congress as a result.

Light at the end of the tunnel (SEE) becomes: • Is it possible that we're actually seeing a *light at the end of* Star Trek's TV continuum?

Not worth the paper it's written (printed) on (SEE) becomes: • Consumers can put their trust in a few of these website seals, but in many cases they *aren't worth the pixels that they're painted with.*

Going to hell in a hand basket (SEE) becomes: • The good news, culturally speaking, is that if we're *going to Hell in a Saks shopping bag*, at least we are going there slowly.

People propagate these monstrosities. Equally distressing is that, in doing so, they think they *are* being clever and inventive. Among pedestrian people, this is what it means to be thoughtful, this is what it means to be creative.

Is it any wonder that speech is so often soporific, writing so often wearisome?

Calvin says there's an actual hog living in a swamp a few miles away and his favorite food is little girls eaten alive and kicking.—Joyce Carol Oates, *The Haunting*

alive and well ▌An infantile phrase. *alive; blooming; doing well; energetic; existent; existing; extant; fit; flourishing; growing; hale; hardy; healthful; healthy; hearty; live; lively; living; prospering; robust; sound; still exists; strong; surviving; thriving; vigorous; vital; well; well-off.* • Scholarship and readership are *alive and well* and will outlast the publishing binge of the commercial houses. REPLACE WITH *flourishing.* • The work ethic of American workers is unquestionably *alive and well.* REPLACE WITH *sound.*

a living hell ▌A moribund metaphor. *chthonian; chthonic; hellish; impossible; infernal; insufferable; insupportable; intolerable; painful; plutonic; sulfurous; unbearable; uncomfortable; unendurable; unpleasant; stygian; tartarean.* The force and colorfulness of this metaphor is no longer evident. An uncommonly used word—such as *chthonic, insupportable, plutonic, sulfurous, stygian,* or *tartarean*—is often more potent and captivating than a commonly used metaphor. SEE ALSO **hell on earth**.

a living legend ▌A suspect superlative.

all and sundry ▌A wretched redundancy. *all; everybody; everyone; everything.* SEE ALSO **various and sundry**.

From morning till night you saw her sitting on a low chair in the kitchen, surrounded by a Chinese cook and two or three native girls, giving her orders, chatting sociably with all and sundry, and tasting the savoury messes she devised.—W. Somerset Maugham, *The Moon and Sixpence*

all dressed up and no place to go ▌An infantile phrase.

all ears ▌A moribund metaphor. *attentive; heedful; listening; paying attention; paying heed.*

(as) all get-out ▌A moribund metaphor. *acutely; awfully; consumedly; exceedingly; extraordinarily; extremely; greatly; hugely; immensely; intensely; mightily; prodigiously; severely; terribly; very.* • He was *funny as all get-out.* REPLACE WITH *extremely funny.*

all hell broke loose ▌A moribund metaphor.

all mouth ▌A moribund metaphor. *boastful; vainglorious.*

all of the above ▌An infantile phrase. • Are you just looking for a companion or are you looking for a sexual partner? *All of the above.* SEE ALSO **none of the above**.

all over the lot (map) ▌A moribund metaphor. *diffuse; dispersed; disseminated; scattered; strewn; unfocused.*

all roads lead to Rome ▌A moribund metaphor.

all rolled into one ▌A moribund metaphor. *admixture; amalgam; blend; combination; mix; mixture.*

all's fair in love and war ▌A popular prescription.

all's well that ends well ▌A popular prescription.

all systems (are) go ▌A moribund metaphor.

all that glitters isn't gold ▌A popular prescription.

(and) all that jazz ▌A grammatical gimmick. • He tells me what to do *and all that jazz.* DELETE *and all that jazz.*

all the world's a stage ▌A moribund metaphor.

all things considered ▌A wretched redundancy. *all in all; all told; altogether; in all; on the whole; overall.*

all (good) things must end ▌A popular prescription.

all thumbs ▌A moribund metaphor. *ambisinister; awkward; blundering; bumbling; bungling; clumsy; gawky; gauche; ham-handed; heavy-handed; inapt; inept; lubberly; lumbering; maladroit; uncoordinated; uncouth; ungainly;*

ungraceful; unhandy; unskillful; unwieldy.

all-time record ▌ A wretched redundancy. *record.* • If anyone spent time skiing here this past winter, they'd be happy to find the boycott has resulted in an *all-time record* number of skiers. DELETE *all-time.* SEE ALSO **record-breaking; record-high.**

all to the good ▌ A moribund metaphor. *adequate; advantageous; beneficial; satisfactory; sufficient.*

(from) all walks of life ▌ A moribund metaphor.

all wet ▌ A moribund metaphor. *amiss; astray; deceived; deluded; erring; erroneous; fallacious; false; faulty; inaccurate; incorrect; in error; misguided; misinformed; mislead; mistaken; not correct; not right; wrong.* • Whoever told you that alcohol is less of a problem than drugs is *all wet.* REPLACE WITH *mistaken.*

all wool and a yard wide ▌ A moribund metaphor. *actual; authentic; earnest; genuine; heartfelt; honest; legitimate; pure; real; sincere; sterling; true; unadulterated; unalloyed; veritable.*

all work and no play makes Jack a dull boy ▌ A popular prescription.

along the lines of ▌ A wretched redundancy. *akin to; close to; like; resembling; similar to; such as.* • It's generally safe to ask people in the field if they've ever heard of anything *along the lines of* your idea. REPLACE WITH *similar to.*

> It turned out that Agent Samson was something along the lines of a circuit-court speech therapist.—David Sedaris, *Me Talk Pretty One Day*

a losing battle ▌ A moribund metaphor. *hopeless; impossible; incurable; irreclaimable; irredeemable; irremediable; irreparable; irretrievable; remediless.*

> And now the dog was dead, and Morris was saying that, as the dog should have known, his was a losing battle, and that that not given in love would be redressed in blood.— David Mamet, *The Old Religion*

a lot of times ▌ A wretched redundancy. *frequently; often.* • *A lot of times* people have a tendency to think that others are controlling their destiny. REPLACE WITH *Often.*

a lump in (her) throat ▌ A moribund metaphor.

a (the) ... majority (of) ▌ A torpid term. This phrase and others like it—*a large majority; an overwhelming majority; the vast majority*—are indispensable to those who luxuriate in circumlocutory language. They seldom mean more than an unpretentious *almost all, most,* or *nearly all.* • *The vast*

majority of those people don't receive death sentences. REPLACE WITH *Most.* • Within two years, *the overwhelming majority of* Americans will have health coverage. REPLACE WITH *nearly all.* • *A large majority of* the participatory lenders have now joined the major banks in supporting our plan. REPLACE WITH *Almost all.* SEE ALSO **a ... number (of).**

a man's home is his castle ▌ A popular prescription.

a marriage made in heaven ▌ A suspect superlative. *ideal; model; perfect; wonderful.*

(it's) a matter of life and death ▌ A moribund metaphor. *critical; crucial; essential; imperative; important; necessary; pressing; urgent; vital.*

amazing ▌ An overworked word. *astonishing; astounding; extraordinary; marvelous; outstanding; remarkable; spectacular; startling; stunning; wonderful; wondrous.*

(as) American as apple pie ▌ An insipid simile. *all-American; decent; good; honorable; moral; proper; pure; respectable; right; straight; upright; virtuous; wholesome.*

> And the truth was I wanted to fight just as much as every eighteen-year-old boy who'd up and enlisted the day after Pearl Harbor. Why not? I was as American as apple pie.— Susan Isaacs, *Shining Through*

amidst ▌ A withered word. *amid; among.* • *Amidst* all of life's distractions, what is it that keeps us going? REPLACE WITH *Amid.*

a mile a minute ▌ A moribund metaphor. *apace; briskly; expeditiously; fast; hastily; hurriedly; posthaste; quickly; rapidly; speedily; swiftly; wingedly.*

a mile wide and an inch deep ▌ A moribund metaphor. 1. *blowhard; boaster; braggadocio; braggart; know-it-all; showoff; swaggerer; trumpeter; windbag.* 2. *glib; silver-tongued; slick; smooth-tongued.*

a million miles away ▌ A moribund metaphor. *absent; absent-minded; absorbed; abstracted; bemused; captivated; daydreaming; detached; distracted; distrait; dreamy; engrossed; enraptured; faraway; fascinated; immersed; inattentive; lost; mesmerized; oblivious; preoccupied; rapt; spellbound.*

(has) a mind like a sieve ▌ An insipid simile. *forgetful; heedless; inattentive; lethean; neglectful; negligent; oblivious; remiss; thoughtless; unmindful; unthinking.*

(9:00) a.m. ... (in the) morning ▌ A wretched redundancy. *(9:00) a.m.; (in the) morning.* • Monday's events can be defined to occur from *8 a.m.* Monday *morning* to *8 a.m.* Tuesday *morning.* DELETE *morning.* • This *morning* at 9:35 *a.m.* a violent clash took place between prisoners. DELETE *a.m.*

31

a miss is as good as a mile A popular prescription.

amongst ∎ A withered word. *among.* • If there is a lack of confidence *amongst* those concerned, the strictly political element will be more obvious. REPLACE WITH *among.* • Someday, perhaps, you'll be able to find it *amongst* the software programs at the store, next to *SimCity:* the ultimate Language Architect simulator game. REPLACE WITH *among.* • I'm sorry to say that after passing this *amongst* some colleagues, we've agreed that it is not thorough enough to be a reference book. REPLACE WITH *among.*

a month of Sundays ∎ A moribund metaphor. *ages; a long time; a long while; an age; an eternity; decades; eons; forever; months; years.*

a (absolute) must ∎ An infantile phrase. *compulsory; critical; essential; imperative; important; indispensable; mandatory; necessary; needed; obligatory; required; requisite; vital.* • Prior experience writing user and technical documentation in the computer field is *a must.* REPLACE WITH *necessary.* • It is not *an absolute must* to read this part in order to use the second half of the book. REPLACE WITH *essential.* SEE ALSO **(a) must have; (a) must see; a (definite) plus.**

an accident waiting to happen ∎ A moribund metaphor. • Any network that does not have a standardized backup procedure in place is *an accident waiting to happen.* • The fire at the InterRoyal mill was a tragic *accident waiting to happen.*

An accident waiting to happen twists seriousness into silliness. The significance of what we say, the danger, perhaps, in what we do, the whole of who we are, we seldom see when we think with such frivolous phrases. Our understanding may be distorted, our responses dulled.

> She was an accident waiting to happen; an utterly naive, completely gullible woman with no life experience, no memories of pain or hurt or betrayal.—Kristin Hannah, *Waiting for the Moon*

analyze to death ∎ A moribund metaphor. *analyze; anatomize; dissect; examine; inspect; investigate; scrutinize; study.* SEE ALSO **to death.**

an amazing person ∎ A suspect superlative. *An amazing person* is so only in the eyes of another who, we can be confident, is not.

an apple a day keeps the doctor away ∎ A popular prescription.

(cost) an arm and a leg ∎ A moribund metaphor. 1. *a big (brobdingnagian; colossal; enormous; gargantuan; giant; gigantic; grand; great; huge; immense; large; massive; monstrous; prodigious; tremendous; vast)*

amount; a great deal; a lot. 2. *costly; dear; expensive; high-priced; precious; priceless; valuable.*

(as) ancient (old) as the hills ∎ An insipid simile. *aged; aging; ancient; antediluvian; antique; archaic; elderly; hoary; hoary-headed; old; patriarchal; prehistoric; seasoned; superannuated; venerable.*

(that's) ancient history ∎ A moribund metaphor. *aged; ancient; antediluvian; antique; archaic; elderly; history; hoary; old; past; prehistoric; seasoned; superannuated.*

> He knew that it had something to do with the scandal, but that was ancient history.—Frederick Buechner, *The Storm*

and all ∎ A grammatical gimmick. • We're going to look at all these nice buildings *and all.* DELETE *and all.* SEE ALSO **and all like that; and everything (else); and everything like that; and stuff (things); and (or) stuff (things) like that.**

and all like that ∎ A grammatical gimmick. • We went to different agencies for help *and all like that.* DELETE *and all like that.* • He caught me off guard by asking for my name and address *and all like that.* DELETE *and all like that.* SEE ALSO **and all; and everything (else); and everything like that; and stuff (things); and (or) stuff (things) like that.**

and etc. (et cetera) ∎ A wretched redundancy. *and so forth; and so on; and the like; etc.* • We bought the generic-brand products *and et cetera.* REPLACE WITH *and the like.*

and everything (else) ∎ A grammatical gimmick. • We're responsible for this baby *and everything else.* DELETE *and everything else.* • You guys fight *and everything,* but she really does love you. DELETE *and everything.* SEE ALSO **and all; and all like that; and everything like that; and stuff (things); and (or) stuff (things) like that.**

and everything like that ∎ A grammatical gimmick. • They adopted that way of speaking *and everything like that.* DELETE *and everything like that.* • Don't you feel cheap and used *and everything like that?* DELETE *and everything like that.* SEE ALSO **and all; and all like that; and everything (else); and stuff (things); and (or) stuff (things) like that.**

and/or ∎ A wretched redundancy. *and; or.* • Implant dentistry can be an effective alternative to dentures *and/or* missing teeth. REPLACE WITH *or.* • But computers may make both more attractive than the alternatives adopted by those who have abandoned wives *and/or* children by failing to meet their financial obligations. REPLACE WITH *and.*

and so on, and so forth ∎ A grammatical gimmick. *and so forth; and so on; and the like; etc.* • I'm more interested in films about human relationships *and so on, and so forth.* DELETE *and so on, and so forth.* SEE ALSO **blah, blah, blah; et cetera, et cetera**.

and stuff (things) ∎ A grammatical gimmick. • His legs had black bruises on them *and stuff.* DELETE *and stuff.* • The customers are really nice people; they're friends *and stuff.* DELETE *and stuff.* • They wanted him to go for a bike ride *and things.* DELETE *and things.* • We got invited to a lot of Hollywood parties *and things.* DELETE *and things.* SEE ALSO **and all; and all like that; and everything (else); and everything like that; and (or) stuff (things) like that**.

and (or) stuff (things) like that ∎ A grammatical gimmick. • I love women—the way they look *and stuff like that.* DELETE *and stuff like that.* • People shouldn't shoot others over money or things *or things like that.* DELETE *and things like that* • I was upset because my mother went through two divorces *and stuff like that.* DELETE *and stuff like that.* • As a big man, they look at you as big and healthy *and things like that.* DELETE *and things like that.* SEE ALSO **and all; and all like that; and everything (else); and everything like that; and stuff (things); and (or) stuff (things) like that**.

and that kind of stuff (thing) ∎ A grammatical gimmick. • He's a changed man; he's learned to read and write *and that kind of thing.* DELETE *and that kind of thing.* • I was working on getting the house settled *and that kind of stuff.* DELETE *and that kind of stuff.* SEE ALSO **(and that) sort of stuff (thing); (and that) type of stuff (thing)**.

and that sort of stuff (thing) ∎ A grammatical gimmick. • I enjoy walking in the park *and that sort of thing.* DELETE *and that sort of thing.* SEE ALSO **(and that) kind of stuff (thing); (and that) type of stuff (thing)**.

and that type of stuff (thing) ∎ A grammatical gimmick. • I like interesting conversation and interacting *and that type of thing.* DELETE *and that type of thing.* SEE ALSO **(and that) kind of stuff (thing); (and that) sort of stuff (thing)**.

and this and that ∎ A grammatical gimmick. • He told me how much he cared for me *and this and that.* DELETE *and this and that.* SEE ALSO **and this, that, and the other (thing)**.

and this, that, and the other (thing) ∎ A grammatical gimmick. • She would say to me, you've got the best of both worlds, you're special, you're loved, *and this, that, and the other thing.* DELETE *and this, that, and the other thing.* SEE ALSO **and this and that**.

an easy (simple) task ∎ A torpid term. *apparent; basic; clear; clear-cut; conspicuous; distinct; easily done; easy; effortless; elementary; evident; explicit; facile; limpid; lucid; manifest; obvious; patent; pellucid; plain; simple; simplicity itself; straightforward; translucent; transparent; unambiguous; uncomplex; uncomplicated; understandable; unequivocal; unmistakable.* • Identifying opinion leaders is not *a simple task* since they tend to be product specific and differ over time. REPLACE WITH *an easy.*

(like) (finding; looking for) a needle in a haystack ∎ A moribund metaphor.

an embarrassment of riches ∎ A moribund metaphor. • It's a city with *an embarrassment of riches.*

anent ∎ A withered word. *about; concerning.*

a (whole) new (different) ballgame ∎ A moribund metaphor. • Although the procedure is basically the same, recording a macro is slightly different in Word and PowerPoint than in Excel, and creating a macro in Access is *a whole different ballgame.* REPLACE WITH *wholly different.*

> Unfortunately, she didn't have extensive experience with mineral rights and royalties. Those were a whole new ballgame.—Maggie Sefton, *A Deadly Yarn*

a new lease on life ∎ A moribund metaphor. *animated; energized; enlivened; inspired; inspirited; invigorated; refreshed; reinvigorated; rejuvenated; revitalized; revived; roused; stimulated; stirred; vitalized.*

an eye for an eye (and a tooth for a tooth) ∎ A popular prescription.

angel of mercy ∎ A suspect superlative. *liberator; redeemer; rescuer; savior.*

an idea whose time has come ∎ An infantile phrase. • The good-news section is *an idea whose time has come.*

(it's) a nightmare ∎ A moribund metaphor. How impoverished our imaginations are. Nightmares ought to be terrifying, but this metaphor—so popular has it become—is hopelessly tame. *It was a nightmare* instills in us as little compassion as it does interest; it makes us yawn rather than yell. No longer is there terror to it.

Though an incident might well be *agonizing, alarming, appalling, awful, disgusting, disquieting, distressing, disturbing, dreadful, excruciating, frightening, frightful, ghastly, grisly, gruesome, harrowing, hideous, horrendous, horrible, horrid, horrific, horrifying, monstrous, nauseating, nightmarish, petrifying, repellent, repulsive, revolting, shocking, sickening, terrifying, tormenting, traumatic,* saying *it was a nightmare* makes it sound as though it were no more than an annoyance, no more than a mere inconvenience.

It was a nightmare, the metaphor, has hardly the force of a sweet dream. • It was *a nightmare*. REPLACE WITH *ghastly*. • If the birth mother shows up, it's *a nightmare* for the adopting mother. REPLACE WITH *disquieting*.

Altogether remarkable about this expression is that people use it to describe something that tormented or terrified them. They describe an extraordinary event with an ordinary phrase. How can we not doubt the sincerity of their words, the terror of their experience? Is this then what it is to be human, to be able to use language, expressing ourselves in platitudes to illustrate what affects us most deeply? Are so many of us still scribblers? SEE ALSO **(every person's) worst nightmare**.

an inspiration to us all ∎ A suspect superlative. How inspirational could anyone be when he is described with such an uninspired expression? • He's been *an inspiration to us all*.

an old hand ∎ A moribund metaphor. *able; adept; apt; capable; competent; deft; dexterous; experienced; expert; practiced; proficient; seasoned; skilled; skillful; veteran.*

anon ∎ A withered word. 1. *at another time; later.* 2. *shortly; soon.* 3. *at once; immediately.*

an open-and-shut case ∎ A moribund metaphor. *apparent; clear; evident; open; plain; straightforward; unambiguous; uncomplex; uncomplicated.*

an open book ∎ A moribund metaphor. 1. *apparent; clear; clear-cut; crystalline; evident; explicit; limpid; lucid; manifest; obvious; open; patent; pellucid; plain; translucent; transparent; unambiguous; uncomplex; uncomplicated; understandable; unequivocal; unmistakable.* 2. *aboveboard; artless; blunt; candid; direct; forthright; frank; genuine; guileless; honest; ingenuous; naive; sincere; straightforward; truthful; veracious; veridical.*

an (wide) open question ∎ A wretched redundancy. *a question; debatable; disputable; moot; open; questionable; uncertain; unclear; undecided; undetermined; unknown; unsettled; unsure.* • Whether it's still possible for us to complete the project by next season is *an open question* at this point. REPLACE WITH *questionable*.

another day, another dollar ∎ A popular prescription.

an ounce of prevention ∎ A moribund metaphor.

an ounce of prevention is worth a pound of cure ∎ A popular prescription.

ants in (his) pants ∎ A moribund metaphor. *aflame; agitated; animated; anxious; eager; ebullient; effervescent; enthusiastic; excitable; excited; fervent; fervid; fidgety; frantic; frenzied; impassioned; impatient; jittery; jumpy; lively; nervous; restive; restless; skittish; spirited.*

a ... number (of) ∎ A torpid term. • You can use the computer to discover students who are making *a large number of* mistakes. REPLACE WITH *many*. • *A good number of* troops have arrived in Moscow. REPLACE WITH *Hundreds*. • *An overwhelming number of* the participatory lenders have now joined the major banks in supporting our plan. REPLACE WITH *Almost all*. • They are dependent upon the teacher's pension, which is fully given at the age of 62 after *a large number of teaching years*. REPLACE WITH *years of teaching*. SEE ALSO **a (the) ... majority (of)**; **a sufficient number (of)**.

an uphill battle (fight) ∎ A moribund metaphor. 1. *an endeavor; an undertaking; a struggle; a task; drudgery; hard work; labor; moil; toil; travail; work.* • Alleging sexual harassment against a supervisor is *an uphill battle*. REPLACE WITH *a struggle*. 2. *arduous; difficult; hard; laborious; strenuous.* • Even though it's been *an uphill battle*, I've learned a lot. REPLACE WITH *difficult*. SEE ALSO **reach epidemic proportions**.

> The chances were good that the General would pass away before 1960, and even if he didn't, it would be an uphill battle for anybody in the Party to unseat me by then.—Robert Coover, *The Public Burning*

any and all ∎ A wretched redundancy. *all; any.* • *Any and all* accidental needle sticks must be reported to the physician at once. REPLACE WITH *All*. • We welcome *any and all* comments and suggestions regarding this project. REPLACE WITH *any*.

anyhow ∎ A grammatical gimmick. • *Anyhow*, we got the divorce in 1992. DELETE *Anyhow*. SEE ALSO **anyway**.

any port in a storm ∎ A moribund metaphor.

anything and everything ∎ A wretched redundancy. *anything; everything.* • A deadbeat is generally defined as a person dedicated to getting *anything and everything* possible for nothing. REPLACE WITH *anything* or *everything*.

anything (everything) is possible ∎ A popular prescription.

any (every) (reason) under the sun ∎ A moribund metaphor. *any; anything; every; everything.* • Americans sue each other for almost *every reason under the sun*. REPLACE WITH *every reason*. • Our catering staff has designed a menu and planned a party for almost *every reason under the sun*. REPLACE WITH *every reason*. • Capricorns have the ability to write about *any subject under the sun*.

> Maybe from the old habit of doing everything as one man; maybe when you have lived for four years in a world ordered completely by men's doings, even when it is danger and fighting, you don't want to quit that world: maybe the danger and the fighting are the reasons, because men have been pacifists for every reason under the sun except to avoid danger and fighting.—William Faulkner, *The Unvanquished*

anyway ▌ A grammatical gimmick. • But *anyway*, I'll talk to you later in the week. DELETE *anyway*. • So *anyway*, I just wanted to verify that with you. DELETE *anyway*. SEE ALSO **anyhow**.

a pain in the ass (butt; rear) ▌ A moribund metaphor. *affliction; annoyance; bane; bother; burden; curse; difficulty; inconvenience; irritant; irritation; load; nuisance; ordeal; pain; pest; plague; problem; torment; tribulation; trouble; vexation; weight; worry.*

a pain in the neck ▌ A moribund metaphor. *affliction; annoyance; bane; bother; burden; curse; difficulty; inconvenience; irritant; irritation; load; nuisance; ordeal; pain; pest; plague; problem; torment; tribulation; trouble; vexation; weight; worry.*

> The do-gooder, the bleeding heart, the concerned citizen, the militant reformer: what a pain in the neck they are: always making us feel guilty about something.—Edward Abbey, *The Fool's Progress: An Honest Novel*

a peach of ▌ A moribund metaphor. 1. *absolute; beautiful; consummate; excellent; exemplary; exquisite; faultless; flawless; ideal; impeccable; lovely; magnificent; matchless; nonpareil; model; peerless; perfect; pretty; pure; sublime; superb; supreme; transcendent; ultimate; unblemished; unequaled; unexcelled; unrivaled; unsurpassed; untarnished.* 2. *best; excellent; exceptional; fine; finest; first-class; first-rate; good; great; optimal; optimum; superior; superlative.*

a penny saved is a penny earned ▌ A popular prescription.

(I'm) a perfectionist ▌ A suspect superlative. Anyone who declares he is a perfectionist is most often someone who can barely manage his life, someone who trips over trying. SEE ALSO **I'm not perfect (you know); nobody's perfect**.

a picture is worth a thousand words ▌ A popular prescription.

> If one picture's worth a thousand words, that's the first two thousand right there, two thousand minus the hi howareya nicetameetcha.—Francine Prose, *A Changed Man*

(take) appropriate (corrective) action

a place for everything and everything in its place ▌ A popular prescription.

(he's) a poet but (he) doesn't know it ▌ An infantile phrase.

a point in time ▌ A wretched redundancy. *a time*. • There comes *a point in time* when we all pass into adulthood. REPLACE WITH *a time*.

(exact) a pound of flesh ▌ A moribund metaphor.

appearances can be deceiving ▌ A popular prescription.

(first) appear (arrive; come) on the horizon (scene) ▌ An infantile phrase. *appear; arise; become available; begin; be introduced; come forth; develop; emerge; occur; originate; present itself; rise; spring; start; surface; turn up.* • TTAPS first *appeared on the scene* in 1983 with a paper in *Science* on the global atmospheric consequences of nuclear war. REPLACE WITH *emerged*. • It is at the time of William the Conqueror and the Norman conquest of England that the office of shire reeve first *appears on the scene*. REPLACE WITH *appears*. • Clearly, oil used in the internal combustion engine presented such a change when it *came on the scene* in the early part of the twentieth century. REPLACE WITH *became available*. • The Component Object Model (COM) has caused more confusion since its inception than any other programming technology that has ever *appeared on the horizon*. REPLACE WITH *been introduced*.

apple polisher ▌ A moribund metaphor. *apparatchik; bootlicker; fawner; flatterer; flunky; follower; lackey; minion; stooge; sycophant; toady; yes-man.*

(like comparing) apples and oranges ▌ A moribund metaphor. *different; discordant; discrepant; dissimilar; dissonant; divergent; incommensurable; incommensurate; incomparable; incompatible; incongruent; incongruous; inconsistent; inconsonant; inharmonious; unlike.*

(I) appreciate (it) ▌ An overworked word. 1. *grateful for; thankful for; thank you.* 2. *admire; cherish; esteem; prize; relish; treasure; value; welcome.* • We *appreciate* your help. REPLACE WITH *are grateful for*. • We *appreciate* you being here. REPLACE WITH *thank you for*. • I *appreciate* every letter that I have received. REPLACE WITH *treasure*. SEE ALSO **common courtesy**.

(take) appropriate (corrective) action

▌ A torpid term. This ponderousness phrase will stem one person's drive while it saps another's desire. From such a phrase, only dull-minded deeds and uninspired acts may result, which is quite likely all that the user of it, bureaucrat he routinely is, either wishes for or can imagine. • If there's enough public pressure, they may rethink their defensiveness and begin to *take corrective action*. REPLACE WITH *behave differently*. • The bus driver was not exercising caution in this instance, and *corrective action has been taken*. REPLACE WITH *he was fired*. • By the time someone decides to *take corrective action*, the customer may be in too deep. REPLACE WITH *act*. • The district will *take appropriate action* to ensure such occurrences do not continue. REPLACE WITH *do what it must*.

a pretty picture ∎ A moribund metaphor.

April showers bring May flowers ∎ A popular prescription.

a prince among men ∎ A suspect superlative.

a promise is a promise ∎ A quack equation.

a race to the finish (line) ∎ A moribund metaphor.

a ray of light (sunshine) ∎ A moribund metaphor. *anticipation; expectancy; expectation; hope; hopefulness; optimism; possibility; promise; prospect; sanguinity.* • I don't see any *ray of sunshine* when we have all these interplaying forces in conflict. REPLACE WITH *hope*.

a (must) read ∎ An infantile phrase. Colloquial usage such as this leads only to everyday thoughts and commonplace actions; few insights, fewer epiphanies, can be had with mediocre language. In essence, *a (must) read* is an expression that secures the banality of what it describes. • Tom Wolfe's *Bonfire of the Vanities* is *an enormously entertaining read*. REPLACE WITH *enormously entertaining*. • This book is *a tough read* but one of the most important recent accounts of personal identity. REPLACE WITH *tough to understand*. • There are a few books on the list that I feel are clearly *easy reads*. REPLACE WITH *easy to read*. • There are thousands of great books out there, but how many are *must reads*? REPLACE WITH *compelling*. • It's a very challenging *read*. REPLACE WITH *book*. • Is it Tolstoy? is it Dostoyevsky? no, but it is a wonderfully satisfying *read*. REPLACE WITH *story*. • The manuscript is 312 pages long and *a pretty easy read*. REPLACE WITH *easily readable*. • But the problem with the "ho-hum" approach to a life story is that it makes for *a tiresome read*. REPLACE WITH *tiresome reading*. • I'm *having a quiet read*. REPLACE WITH *I'm reading quietly*. SEE ALSO **a good read; (a) must (miss); (a) must have; (a) must see**.

area of expertise ∎ A suspect superlative. *area; business; calling; craft; field; forte; job; line; métier; occupation; profession; specialty; strength; trade; vocation.*

(we) aren't going to take it anymore ∎ A popular prescription.

armed and dangerous ∎ An inescapable pair.

armed (themselves) to the teeth ∎ A moribund metaphor.

(like) a (an emotional) roller-coaster (ride) ∎ A moribund metaphor. Without relentless amusement, endless diversions, people might manage to speak tolerably well. As it is, the need to be entertained so overcomes us that we can speak in little but laughable images. The expression *(like) a (an emotional) roller-coaster (ride)*, one such image, results from and gives rise to only carnival-like conversation, sideshow prose. • But the next season, it's the same thing, a game filled with ups and downs; it really is *like a roller coaster ride*. • The stock market is *like a roller coaster ride*. • If you find that the everyday activities of your daily life are being interrupted by intense emotions or *a roller coaster of* emotions, call EAP Preferred to schedule a session. • When I started TTC again, I knew that this pregnancy would be a bit of *an emotional roller coaster,* but I had no idea just how terrified I would be.

> These past twenty-four hours have been like an emotional roller coaster for me. I don't know if I'm going to laugh or cry, from one moment to the next.—John Riedel, *Requiem in Red*

a rolling stone gathers no moss ∎ A popular prescription.

a roof over (their) heads ∎ A moribund metaphor. *asylum; cover; harbor; harborage; haven; home; housing; lodging; protection; refuge; retreat; safety; sanctuary; shelter.*

a rose by any other name (would smell as sweet) ∎ A popular prescription.

a rose is a rose (is a rose) ∎ A quack equation.

around about ∎ A wretched redundancy. *about; around.* • Let's meet *around about* noon. REPLACE WITH *about* or *around*.

a round peg in a square hole ∎ A moribund metaphor. *curiosity; deviant; eccentric; iconoclast; individual; individualist; maverick; misfit; nonconformist; oddball; oddity; renegade; undesirable.*

(work) around the clock ∎ A moribund metaphor. *always; ceaselessly; constantly; continually; continuously; endlessly; eternally; everlastingly; evermore; forever; forevermore; frequently; interminably; nonstop; permanently; perpetually; persistently; recurrently; regularly; repeatedly; unceasingly; unremittingly.*

(just; right) around the corner ∎ A moribund metaphor. *approaching; at hand; close; close by; coming; forthcoming; imminent; impending; near; nearby;*

nearing; pending; vicinal. • Deregulation of the utility industry was *just around the corner,* and several other companies were prepared to enter the market. REPLACE WITH *at hand.*

arrow in the heart ∎ A moribund metaphor. *injury; wound.*

(another) arrow in the quiver ∎ A moribund metaphor. *device; gambit; maneuver; means; plan; ploy; ruse; scheme; stratagem; strategy; tactic; tool; trick.*

art is long, and life is short ∎ A popular prescription.

a rule is a rule ∎ A quack equation.

a run for (his) money ∎ A moribund metaphor.

as a man sows so shall he reap ∎ A popular prescription.

as a matter of fact ∎ A wretched redundancy. *actually; indeed; in fact; in faith; in reality; in truth; truly.* • *As a matter of fact,* children get disappointed when they grow up to find the adult's prescription didn't match the real world. REPLACE WITH *In truth.*

as a result of ∎ A wretched redundancy. *after; because of; by; due to; following; for; from; in; out of; owing to; through; with.* • *As a result of* this letter, ten of us did not attend the wedding. REPLACE WITH *Because of.*

as defined in (the dictionary) ∎ An infantile phrase. This is a device that only abecedarian writers would ever use; even so, it should always be x'd. • *As defined in the dictionary,* "Health is the absence of disease." • Creationism, *as defined in Webster's New Universal Dictionary,* is the doctrine that matter and all things were created, substantially as they now exist, by an omnipotent creator, and not gradually evolved or developed. SEE ALSO **(the) dictionary defines**.

as far as ... (goes; is concerned) ∎ A wretched redundancy. *about; as for; as to; concerning; for; in; of; on; over; regarding; respecting; to; toward; with.* • *As far as* improvements *go,* you'd have a battle. REPLACE WITH *As for.* • *As far as* those bargains *are concerned,* attempts to place measures on the table would be regressive and an illegal act. REPLACE WITH *Concerning.* SEE ALSO **where ... is concerned**.

as far as the eye can see ∎ An insipid simile. *all around; all over; all through; broadly; everyplace; everywhere; extensively; panoramically; panoptically; throughout; ubiquitously; universally; widely.*

> The room was enormous, like something in a nightmare, one could hardly see from one end of it to the other, and as far as the eye could see was dotted with tables which were all full.—Barbara Pym, *Excellent Women*

(he's) a shadow of (his) former self ∎ A moribund metaphor. *apparition; specter; wraith.*

ashes to ashes (dust to dust) ∎ A moribund metaphor.

a shot across the bow ∎ A moribund metaphor. *admonition; caution; warning.*

a shot in the arm ∎ A moribund metaphor. *boost; encouragement; fillip; goad; impetus; impulse; incentive; incitation; incitement; inducement; jolt; motivation; motive; prod; provocation; push; shove; spur; stimulus; thrust; urge.* • Their success will give *a shot in the arm* to the rest of the economy. REPLACE WITH *a thrust.*

a shot in the dark ∎ A moribund metaphor. *appraisal; assessment; assumption; conjecture; estimate; estimation; guess; hypothesis; impression; opinion; presumption; speculation; supposition; surmise.*

(not) a shred of (evidence) ∎ A moribund metaphor. • There was not a *shred of evidence* to support his contentions.

(breathe; exhale; heave) a (collective) sigh of relief ∎ A torpid term. *be allayed; be alleviated; be assuaged; be calmed; be comforted; be mollified; be palliated; be relieved; be soothed; calm down; quiet down; relax; rest; unwind.* People who *breathe a collective sigh of relief* also *welcome a breath of fresh air* (SEE). They expire fetid words and inspire foolish thoughts.
• Investors *breathed a sigh of relief* there was nothing more in the report than they expected. REPLACE WITH *were relieved.*
• Emergency workers were *breathing a collective sigh of relief.* REPLACE WITH *relieved.* • Every morning when I come in and see them, I *breathe a sigh of relief.* REPLACE WITH *relax.* • After holding its breath for days, the city finally *exhaled a sigh of relief.* REPLACE WITH *relaxed.* • You are probably *breathing a sigh of relief knowing* that you won't have to mangle code any longer to render a display of a list within a list. REPLACE WITH *relieved to know.* SEE ALSO **reach epidemic proportions**.

a sight for sore eyes ∎ A moribund metaphor.

a significant part (portion; proportion) ∎ A wretched redundancy. *a good (great) deal; a good (great) many; almost all; many; most; much; nearly all.* • Many programmers spend *a significant portion* of their working day maintaining software. REPLACE WITH *a good deal.* SEE ALSO **a substantial part (portion; proportion)**.

as I live and breathe ▮ A moribund metaphor. *absolutely; certainly; definitely; positively; surely; undeniably; unquestionably.*

a sitting duck ▮ A moribund metaphor.

(like) asking for the moon ▮ An insipid simile.

ask me no questions and I'll tell you no lies ▮ A popular prescription.

a slap in the face ▮ A moribund metaphor. *abuse; affront; contempt; contumely; derision; disappointment; disdain; dishonor; impertinence; indignity; insult; offense; outrage; rebuff; rebuke; rejection; scorn; slap; slight; slur; sneer; snub.* • Megan's mother called the judge's decision *a slap in the face.* REPLACE WITH *an insult.* • The document is *a slap in the face* to the democratic principles that Americans expect their leaders to uphold. REPLACE WITH *an affront.*

> The fact that my father would spend even a nickel more than necessary was a slap in the face for all of the effort my mother put in trying to support us.—Brett Ellen Block, *The Grave of God's Daughter*

a slap on the wrist ▮ A moribund metaphor. *admonishment; admonition; animadversion; berating; castigation; censure; chastisement; chiding; condemnation; criticism; denouncement; denunciation; disapprobation; disapproval; disciplining; objurgation; punishment; rebuke; remonstrance; reprehension; reprimand; reproach; reprobation; reproof; revilement; scolding; upbraiding; vituperation; warning.* • Nearly as many seem willing to let him off with *a slap on the wrist* because they believe they see the changes involving mostly private matters. REPLACE WITH *a scolding.*

asleep at the switch (wheel) ▮ A moribund metaphor. 1. *forgetful; careless; heedless; inattentive; irresponsible; lethean; neglectful; negligent; oblivious; remiss; slack; thoughtless; unmindful; unthinking.* 2. *be oblivious to; disregard; ignore.* 3. *asleep; daydreaming.*

> Invitations of course came into the big house all the time, and that July, unless they perhaps touched his unfailing business sense, Mel usually ignored them. But Vicki was not asleep at the switch. She began to accept, all on her own.—Stephen Koch, *The Bachelor's Bride*

a slow boat to China (nowhere) ▮ A moribund metaphor.

(as) (wholesome) as mom and apple pie ▮ An insipid simile. *decent; ethical; exemplary; good; honest; honorable; just; moral; pure; righteous; straight; upright; virtuous; wholesome.*

(like) a soap opera ▮ An insipid simile. *exaggerated; excessive; histrionic; hyperbolic; maudlin; mawkish; melodramatic; overblown; overdone; overemotional; sensational; sentimental; soppy.*

a soft touch ▮ A moribund metaphor.

a sometime thing ▮ A torpid term. *erratic; fitful; haphazard; inconsistent; intermittent; irregular; occasional; random; sometime; spasmodic; sporadic; unpredictable.*

a square peg in a round hole ▮ A moribund metaphor. *curiosity; deviant; eccentric; iconoclast; individual; individualist; maverick; misfit; nonconformist; oddball; oddity; renegade; undesirable.*

as (you) sow, so shall (you) reap ▮ A popular prescription.

a step backward ▮ A torpid term. *backset; reversal; setback.*

a step forward ▮ A torpid term. *advancement; betterment; development; furtherance; growth; headway; improvement; progress.* • This is *a step forward* for us all. REPLACE WITH *betterment.* For some writers, *a step forward* isn't positive enough: • Although the IFS interface is *a positive step forward* for DOS, it remains in a sort of twilight zone. REPLACE WITH *an advancement.* SEE ALSO **a step (forward) in the right direction; go forward; move forward; move (forward) in the right direction; proceed forward.**

a step (forward) in the right direction ▮ A torpid term. *advancement; betterment; development; furtherance; growth; headway; improvement; progress.* Like many dimwitticisms, *a step forward in the right direction* is an ungainly creation. The English language is wonderfully expressive and infinitely flexible, but this phrase is stiff, wooden, awkward. • Incentives to attract and retain nurses would be *a step in the right direction.* REPLACE WITH *an improvement.* • Mr Singh described the arrests of Mr Saeed and other militants as *a step forward in the right direction* but said more action was necessary. REPLACE WITH *progress.* SEE ALSO **a step forward; go forward; move forward; move (forward) in the right direction; proceed forward.**

as the crow flies ▮ A moribund metaphor. *by air; directly; lineally; linearly; straight.*

(as) (vain) as the day is long ▮ An insipid simile. *acutely; awfully; consumedly; enormously; exceedingly; extraordinarily; extremely; greatly; hugely; immensely; intensely; mightily; prodigiously; severely; terribly; very.* • She's *as neurotic as the day is long.* REPLACE WITH *prodigiously neurotic.* • Celeste is *as bright as the day is long.* REPLACE WITH *enormously bright.*

as the saying goes (is) ∎ An infantile phrase. This phrase reminds us of our ordinariness. *As the saying goes (is)* announces our having spoken, and thought, words that countless others have spoken and thought. What thoughts are we missing, what images are unavailable to us because we use the same damn words and phrases again and again? Let us strive for better than banality.

a stitch in time saves nine ∎ A popular prescription.

a stone's throw (away) ∎ A moribund metaphor. *accessible (to); adjacent (to); bordering; at hand; close (to); close by; handy; near; nearby; neighboring; not far from; vicinal.*

> Of course, when I located the Park View hotel, not a stone's throw from the glorious Ansonia building, I had to take back my uncharitable thoughts.—Rhys Bowen, *In a Gilded Cage*

a stroll (walk) in the park ∎ A moribund metaphor 1. *casual; easily done; easy; effortless; elementary; facile; simple; simplicity itself; straightforward; uncomplex; uncomplicated.* 2. *agreeable; beguiling; charming; delightful; enchanting; engaging; enjoyable; fun; glorious; gratifying; inviting; joyful; joyous; pleasant; pleasing; pleasurable.* • Building high-rise buildings, dams, and bridges isn't exactly *a walk in the park.* REPLACE WITH *simple.* • Compared to NetWare 3.x, installing Windows NT Server is *a stroll in the park.* REPLACE WITH *effortless.*

a substantial part (portion; proportion) ∎ A wretched redundancy. *a good (great) deal; a good (great) many; almost all; many; most; much; nearly all.* • It is unconscionable that *a substantial proportion* of our population does not have adequate access to health care. REPLACE WITH *much.* • I assume that Boston will be eligible for *a substantial portion* of the distressed communities fund. REPLACE WITH *a good deal.* SEE ALSO **a significant part (portion; proportion).**

a sufficient number (of) ∎ A wretched redundancy. *enough.* • Effective groups contain *a sufficient number of* members to ensure good interaction. REPLACE WITH *enough.* SEE ALSO **a ... number (of).**

(even) as we speak ∎ An infantile phrase. *at present; currently; (just right) now; presently.* Whenever someone says *as we speak,* we should hear *as we misspeak,* for the person who uses this sad phrase instead of, say, *now* or even *at this moment,* speaks unhappily. • The team is having a pep rally on campus *as we speak.* REPLACE WITH *now.* • Are your forces, *even as we speak,* looking for him in a military way? REPLACE WITH *currently.* Most often, though, *as we speak,* as well as its synonyms, should be unspoken. • But

how can we not be afraid with weapons of mass destruction looming over our lives *even as we speak.* DELETE *even as we speak.* • The Reno police are holding a news conference right now *as we speak.* DELETE *as we speak.* • The hostage situation is still unfolding now *as we speak.* DELETE *as we speak.*

as you make your bed, so you must lie on it ∎ A popular prescription.

at a crossroad ∎ A moribund metaphor.

at a fast (good) clip ∎ A moribund metaphor. *apace; briskly; expeditiously; fast; hastily; hurriedly; posthaste; quickly; rapidly; speedily; swiftly; wingedly.*

a tale never loses in the telling ∎ A popular prescription.

at a loss ∎ A moribund metaphor. *baffled; befuddled; bewildered; confounded; confused; disconcerted; flummoxed; mixed up; muddled; nonplused; perplexed; puzzled.*

at a loss for what to say (words) ∎ A moribund metaphor. *dumb; mute; quiet; reserved; restrained; reticent; silent; speechless; still; taciturn; tongue-tied; uncommunicative; voiceless; withdrawn; wordless.*

> Gen, in his genius for languages, was often at a loss for what to say when left with only his own words.—Ann Patchett, *Bel Canto*

at a low ebb ∎ A moribund metaphor.

(hold) at arm's distance (length) ∎ A moribund metaphor.

> She had always felt that he wanted to keep her at arm's length, and she thought that by showing sympathy she might make him like her more.—Luanne Rice, *Stone Heart*

at a snail's pace ∎ A moribund metaphor. *deliberately; gradually; laggardly; languidly; lazily; leisurely; slothfully; slowly; sluggishly; snail-paced; unhurriedly.* • We have been working day after day with him, but he is improving *at a snail's pace.* REPLACE WITH *unhurriedly.*

at (my) beck and call ∎ A moribund metaphor. *accepting; accommodating; acquiescent; complacent; complaisant; compliant; cowed; deferential; docile; dutiful; obedient; passive; prostrate; resigned; submissive; subservient; tolerant; tractable; yielding.*

at death's door ∎ A moribund metaphor. *decaying; declining; deteriorating; disintegrating; dying; ebbing; expiring; fading; failing; near death; sinking; waning.*

at each other's throats ∎ A moribund metaphor. *arguing; battling; bickering; brawling; clashing; disagreeing; fighting; quarreling; squabbling; wrangling.*

at (my) fingertips ∎ A moribund metaphor. 1. *recall; recollect; remember; think of.* 2. *accessible; at hand; close; close by; handy; near; nearby; neighboring; vicinal.*

a (man) that (who) needs no introduction ∎ A torpid term.

a thing of beauty is a joy forever ∎ A popular prescription.

a thing of the past ∎ A torpid term. 1. *ceased; completed; concluded; dead; deceased; defunct; done; ended; exanimate; expired; extinct; extinguished; finished; gone; inanimate; lifeless; no more; over; perished; stopped; terminated.* 2. *antediluvian; antiquated; archaic; dead; obsolescent; obsolete; old; old-fashioned; outdated; outmoded; out of date; out of fashion; passé; superannuated.* • All agree that the days of students being able to work their way through college are *a thing of the past.* REPLACE WITH *over.* • The 8-hour day has become *a thing of the past.* REPLACE WITH *obsolete.* • Is the civil rights movement still alive in the United States or *a thing of the past?* REPLACE WITH *dead.*

> He was often on our campus, invited to address Municipal Government seminars on corruption. He told students that corruption was a thing of the past.—Saul Bellow, *More Die of Heartbreak*

a tip of the hat ∎ A moribund metaphor. *acknowledgment; greeting; nod; salutation.*

at loggerheads ∎ A moribund metaphor. *arguing; battling; bickering; brawling; clashing; disagreeing; disputing; fighting; quarreling; squabbling; wrangling.*

at loose ends ∎ A moribund metaphor. 1. *confused; disorganized; drifting; faltering; in between; irresolute; loose; shaky; swaying; tottering; uncertain; undecided; unfixed; unresolved; unsettled; unsteady; unsure; vacillating; wavering; wobbly.* 2. *bored; idle; inactive; unemployed; unoccupied.*

at (in) one fell swoop ∎ A moribund metaphor.

> "I was talking," he said through his teeth, and his arm flew in one fell swoop.—Kate Manning, *White Girl*

a trouble shared is a trouble halved ∎ A popular prescription.

(all) at sea ∎ A moribund metaphor. *baffled; befuddled; bewildered; confounded; confused; disconcerted; flummoxed; lost; mixed up; muddled; nonplused; perplexed; puzzled.*

at sixes and sevens ∎ A moribund metaphor. 1. *baffled; bewildered; confused; flummoxed; muddled; perplexed; uncertain.* 2. *disarranged; disorganized; entangled; jumbled; in disarray; in disorder; tangled.*

at that time ∎ A wretched redundancy. This phrase and several others like it, including *at that juncture in life, at that moment in our national life, at that point in time, at that stage in the history of my life, at that time in our history,* mean no more than *then.* • I wasn't happy with what I was doing *at that juncture in life.* REPLACE WITH *then.* • DFSMS did not include any cost input parameters *at that point in time.* REPLACE WITH *then.* SEE ALSO **at this time.**

at the back end (of) ∎ A torpid term. *at the end; finally; last; to conclude; to end; to finish; toward the close; toward the end.*

at the breaking point ∎ A moribund metaphor.

at the crack of dawn ∎ A moribund metaphor. *very early.*

(stand) at the crossroads of history ∎ A moribund metaphor.

at the drop of a hat ∎ A moribund metaphor. *at once; directly; fast; forthwith; hurriedly; immediately; instantly; momentarily; promptly; quickly; rapidly; right away; speedily; straightaway; summarily; swiftly; without delay.* • You can get additional information to reporters *at the drop of a hat* if you make up a press kit in advance. REPLACE WITH *speedily.*

> She also said there was a community of radicals who considered her a heroine and would help her at the drop of a hat.—Danzy Senna, *Caucasia*

at the eleventh hour ∎ A moribund metaphor. *belatedly; late.*

at the end of (my) rope (tether) ∎ A moribund metaphor. *dejected; despairing; desperate; despondent; disconsolate; distressed; forlorn; frantic; frenetic; frenzied; hopeless; in despair; woebegone; woeful; wretched.*

at the end of the day ∎ A TOP-TWENTY DIMWITTICISM. A moribund metaphor. 1. *eventually; finally; in the end; in time; ultimately.* 2. *all in all; all told; altogether; in all; on the whole; overall.*

The popular phrase was once the equally silly *in the final* (or *last*) *analysis.* More sensible phrases include *eventually, finally, in the end, in time, ultimately* (or, perhaps, *all in all, all told, overall*), but people, unsure of who they are, imitate one another; people today say *at the end of the day.* If we were less inclined to say what others say (and do what others do), the world might be a wholly different place. Reason might even prevail.

In most instances, *at the end of the day* is unnecessary and can, without forfeiting any meaning, be DELETEd from a sentence.

• We simply have to acknowledge the fact that the better side won *at the end of*

the day. DELETE *at the end of the day.* •
He wants each library, old or new, to be
a place people want to come to, think is
enjoyable, get a lot out of and have fun
at, because *at the end of the day,* it'll just
make their lives better. DELETE *at the end
of the day.* • Like every other relationship
you have personally or professionally you
don't always agree on things, but *at the
end of the day* he was the manager so even
if I didn't like something what could I do
about it? DELETE *at the end of the day.* •
That is a step in the right direction; I just
do hope that the alliance will work *at the
end of the day.* DELETE *at the end of the
day.*

at the front end (of) ▌ A torpid term. *at
first; at the start; beginning; first; initially;
to begin.* • Let me say a couple of things *at
the front end.* REPLACE WITH *first.* • The
recession produced a lot of casualties, and
now we're at the front end *of* the recovery.
REPLACE WITH *beginning.*

at the helm ▌ A moribund metaphor. *in
charge; in control.*

at the top of (his) game ▌ A moribund
metaphor.

at the top of (my) lungs ▌ A moribund
metaphor. *blaringly; boisterously; boomingly;
deafeningly; earsplittingly; loudly; noisily;
obstreperously; resoundingly; roaringly;
stentorianly; thunderingly; thunderously;
tumultuously; vociferously.*

at (behind) the wheel ▌ A moribund
metaphor. *in charge; in control.*

at this time ▌ A wretched redundancy. This
phrase and several others like it, including
*at the present time, at this juncture in life,
at this moment in our national life, at this
point in time, at this point in time right
now, at this stage in the history of my life,
at this time in our history,* mean no more
than *at present, now, today,* or *yet.* • We
don't see any significant breakthroughs
at this juncture. REPLACE WITH *now.* •
What can she do to help you *at this stage
of the game?* REPLACE WITH *now.* • *At
this point in time,* the conditions for an
agreement have not been met. REPLACE
WITH *The conditions for an agreement have
not yet been met.* SEE ALSO **at that time.**

attitude ▌ An overworked word. For example:
*attitude problem; holier-than-thou attitude;
patronizing attitude; superior attitude; wait-
and-see attitude.*

attributable to the fact that ▌ A wretched
redundancy. *because; considering; for; in that;
since.* • This is *attributable to the fact that*
people at Pan Am have done such a good
job. REPLACE WITH *because.* SEE ALSO
due to the fact that; owing to the fact that.

a tug of war ▌ A moribund metaphor. •
There's *a tug of war* between people who
like the economy and people who are
afraid.

a turn on ▌ A moribund metaphor. *animating;
arousing; bracing; enlivening; exciting;
exhilarating; inspiring; inspiriting;
invigorating; provoking; refreshing; rousing;
stimulating; vivifying.*

at (his) wit's end ▌ A moribund metaphor.
*baffled; befuddled; bewildered; confounded;
confused; disconcerted; flummoxed; mixed
up; muddled; nonplused; perplexed; puzzled.*

audible (inaudible) to the ear ▌ A
wretched redundancy. *audible (inaudible).* SEE
ALSO **visible (invisible) to the eye.**

au naturel ▌ A foreign phrase. *bare; disrobed;
naked; nude; stripped; unclothed; uncovered;
undressed.*

(your) average Joe ▌ A moribund
metaphor. *average; common; commonplace;
conventional; customary; everyday; familiar;
mediocre; middling; normal; ordinary;
quotidian; regular; standard; typical;
unexceptional; unremarkable; usual.*

avid reader ▌ A suspect superlative. An *avid
reader* suggests someone who reads little
more than mysteries, gothic novels, and
self-help books.
  These are people whose avidity is more
for how many books they read than it is
for any meaning in books—people, that
is, who prefer counting to reading. • I am
an *avid reader* and my advanced education
includes writing courses and an intensive
two-year writing course.

a vision of (loveliness) ▌ A moribund
metaphor.

> After talking for a couple of minutes, I asked
> Bruce who this vision of ebony beauty
> was.—E. Lynn Harris, *Invisible Life*

avoid (it) like the plague ▌ An insipid
simile. 1. *abhor; abominate; detest; hate;
loathe.* 2. *avoid; dodge; elude; eschew; evade;
recoil from; shirk; shrink from; shun; spurn.*
• Your clients will probably either love
Los Angeles or *avoid it like the plague.*
REPLACE WITH *loathe it.*

> The clientele were mostly businessmen in
> three-piece suits laughing boisterously and
> blowing cigarette smoke in each other's
> faces, or talking earnestly and confidently to
> well-dressed young women who were more
> probably their secretaries than their wives. In
> short, it was the kind of establishment that
> Robyn would normally have avoided like the
> plague.—David Lodge, *Nice Work*

a walking, talking ▌ An infantile phrase.

a watched pot never boils ▌ A popular
prescription.

awesome ▌ A TOP-TWENTY
DIMWITTICISM. An overworked word. Like
awful and *terrific,* the word *awesome* has
been made ridiculous by those who are bent
on using it solely in its most popular sense.

awful

Awesome means *awe-inspiring, majestic,* or *terrifying,* but of late, it most often merely means *fantastic* or *terrific* or *great,* worn words all. SEE ALSO **awful**; **terrific**.

awful ▮ An overworked word. *Awful* means *awe-inspiring* or *terrifying,* but of late, it means no more than *very bad* or *unpleasant.* SEE ALSO **awesome**; **terrific**.

a woman's place is in the home ▮ A popular prescription.

a woman's work is never done ▮ A popular prescription.

a work in progress ▮ A torpid term. *A work in progress* is often periphrastic for something or someone undone, unfinished, incomplete.
• Islamicizing liberal democracy is still *a work in progress.* • Georgia State is *a work in progress.* • She's *a work in progress* and a person to whom we can all relate.

a writhing mass of (human beings; (humanity) ▮ A moribund metaphor.

> The place was a hive, a termite's nest, a writhing mass of human beings, pressing against one another with every little movement of an arm or a leg.—Gregory David Roberts, *Shantaram*

ax (axe) to grind ▮ A moribund metaphor. *animosity; bitterness; enmity; grievance; grudge; hostility; indignation; ill will; offense; rancor; resentment; spite; umbrage.*

Bb

babe in the woods ∎ A moribund metaphor. *abecedarian; amateur; apprentice; beginner; greenhorn; neophyte; newcomer; novice; novitiate; tyro; young.* • He's a *babe in the woods* compared to Clinton and the Democrats. REPLACE WITH *neophyte.*

> In many ways, I'm still a babe in the woods, with an awful lot to learn.—Tony R. Woods, *The Road Rising*

back (up) against the wall ∎ A moribund metaphor. 1. *catch; corner; enmesh; ensnare; entangle; entrap; net; snare; trap.* 2. *at risk; endangered; imperiled; in danger; in jeopardy; threatened.* • People will do amazing things when *their backs are against the wall.* REPLACE WITH *they're endangered.*

(meanwhile) back at the ranch ∎ A moribund metaphor.

back in the saddle (again) ∎ A moribund metaphor.

> Maybe the convertible was not an attempt to get a concert pianist back in the saddle—back, as it were, on the horse that had thrown him—but an invitation to the mindless, happy, noisy, unambitious life that till then had been denied him.—Christopher Miller, *Sudden Noises from Inanimate Objects: A Novel in Liner Notes*

back into a corner ∎ A moribund metaphor. *catch; corner; enmesh; ensnare; entangle; entrap; net; snare; trap.*

(get) back on (his) feet ∎ A moribund metaphor. *ameliorate; amend; come round; convalesce; gain strength; get better; heal; improve; look up; meliorate; mend; rally; recover; recuperate; refresh; regain strength; renew; revive; strengthen.* • Even the construction industry is starting to *get back on its feet.* REPLACE WITH *recover.*

back on track ∎ A moribund metaphor.

back to basics ∎ A torpid term. • Banks and savings and loans are getting *back to basics* and concentrating on home mortgages.

back to square one ∎ A moribund metaphor.

(go) back to the drawing board ∎ A moribund metaphor. • Beware of protracted and angry discussions; they are usually a sign that there is not enough support for the idea, and you should go *back to the drawing board.*

back to the salt mines ∎ A moribund metaphor.

back to the wall ∎ A moribund metaphor. 1. *at risk; endangered; hard-pressed; imperiled; in a bind; in a fix; in a jam; in a predicament; in a quandary; in danger; in difficulty; in jeopardy; in peril; in trouble; jeopardized.* 2. *at bay; caught; cornered; enmeshed; ensnared; entangled; entrapped; netted; snared; trapped.*

bad apple ∎ A moribund metaphor. *brute; degenerate; fiend; knave; lout; rake; rascal; rogue; ruffian; scamp; scoundrel; villain.*

bad blood (between them) ∎ A moribund metaphor. *abhorrence; anger; animosity; antipathy; aversion; detestation; enmity; hate; hatred; hostility; ill will; loathing; malice; malignity; rancor; repugnance; revulsion; venom; virulence.*

bad egg ∎ A moribund metaphor. *brute; degenerate; fiend; knave; lout; rake; rascal; rogue; ruffian; scamp; scoundrel; villain.*

badge of courage (honor) ∎ A moribund metaphor.

bag and baggage ∎ An inescapable pair. 1. *accouterments; baggage; bags; belongings; cases; effects; encumbrances; equipment; gear; impedimenta; luggage; portmanteaus; possessions; property; sacks; satchels; stuff; suitcases; supplies; things.* 2. *altogether; completely; entirely; fully; roundly; thoroughly; totally; utterly; wholly.*

bag of bones ∎ A moribund metaphor. *asthenic; attenuated; bony; cachectic; emaciated; gaunt; lank; lanky; lean; narrow; rail-thin; scraggy; scrawny; skeletal; skinny; slender; slight; slim; spare; spindly; svelte; sylphid; thin; trim; wispy.*

bag (bagful) of tricks ∎ A moribund metaphor. *accouterment; equipage; equipment; gear; paraphernalia; resources; supplies; things; tools.*

baker's dozen ∎ A moribund metaphor. *thirteen.*

(as) bald as a baby's backside ∎ An insipid simile. *alopecic; bald; baldheaded; baldpated; glabrous; hairless; depilated; pilgarlic; smooth; tonsured.*

(as) bald as a billiard ball ∎ An insipid simile. *alopecic; bald; baldheaded; baldpated; glabrous; hairless; depilated; pilgarlic; smooth; tonsured.*

bald is beautiful ∎ A quack equation. .

ball of fire ∎ A moribund metaphor. *active; animated; ardent; dynamic; emotional; energetic; impassioned; intense; lively; passionate; spirited; sprightly; vigorous; vital; vivacious.*

ballpark figure ∎ A moribund metaphor. *appraisal; assessment; estimate; estimation; guess; idea; impression; opinion; sense.* • Can you give me a *ballpark figure* of how much you made last year? REPLACE WITH *idea.*

bang for (your) buck ∎ An infantile phrase. *quality; value; worth.*

banging (my) head against the wall ∎ A moribund metaphor.

baptism of fire ∎ A moribund metaphor.

bare-bones (budget) ∎ A moribund metaphor.

bare essentials (necessities) ∎ An inescapable pair.

barefaced (bold-faced) lie ∎ An inescapable pair.

bargaining chip ∎ A moribund metaphor.

bark at the moon ∎ A moribund metaphor.

(her) bark is worse than (her) bite ∎ A moribund metaphor.

bark up the wrong tree ∎ A moribund metaphor. *amiss; astray; deceived; deluded; erring; erroneous; fallacious; false; faulty; inaccurate; incorrect; in error; misguided; misinformed; mislead; mistaken; not correct; not right; wrong.*

> Ray had neither encouraged nor discouraged her over Minkie—he hadn't seemed at all interested in the party—although he said something about her barking up the wrong tree with John Lenier.—Tessa Hadley, *Everything Will Be All Right*

barrel of laughs ∎ A moribund metaphor. *hilarious; hysterical; side-splitting; uproarious.*

basically ∎ A TOP-TWENTY DIMWITTICISM. **An overworked word.** People often use *basically* thinking it lends an intellectual air to the meaning of their words. *Basically,* in truth, only steals the sense from whatever words accompany it, for it proclaims their uncertainty and inexactitude as loudly as it does the speaker's or writer's pomposity.

Of course, there are also people, with few pretensions, who use *basically* either because they do not know what they say or because they do not know what to say. • *Basically,* the program is designed to operate with the same skills used when doing the exercise with a pencil and paper. • If the man wants custody, he must prove the woman to be *basically* unfit. • The rest of the day will be *basically* partly cloudy.

• What *basically* began as an experiment to determine whether a family-type YMCA would survive quickly evolved into a challenge to serve a very enthusiastic community. • *Basically,* the next step is adding the molasses.

basic (and) fundamental ∎ A wretched redundancy. *basal; basic; elementary; essential; fundamental; primary; rudimentary.*

basic principle ∎ An inescapable pair. Seldom do we find *principle* without the word *basic* preceding it. A principle, however, is a basic truth or assumption. • Whether or not you are aware of it, there are *basic principles* of human interaction. DELETE *basic.* • The *basic principle* of laser protection is the same as for any direct fire weapon. DELETE *basic.*

basis in fact (reality) ∎ A wretched redundancy. *basis; fact; reality; truth; veracity.* • The June 2 editorial that describes the final, wheezy stages of the movement to eliminate cigarettes has no *basis in fact.* REPLACE WITH *basis.* • To see whether such beliefs have any *basis in fact,* five different brands of fruit cocktail were chosen. REPLACE WITH *veracity.*

bathed in tears ∎ A moribund metaphor.

(has) bats in (his) belfry ∎ A moribund metaphor. *batty; cracked; crazy; daft; demented; deranged; fey; foolish; goofy; insane; lunatic; mad; maniacal; neurotic; nuts; nutty; psychotic; raving; silly; squirrelly; touched; unbalanced; unhinged; unsound; wacky; zany.*

batten down the hatches ∎ A moribund metaphor.

batting a thousand ∎ A moribund metaphor.

> I was batting a thousand on predicting human behavior. Maybe *I* should become a psychologist.—Jane Mendle, *Kissing in Technicolor*

(good) batting average ∎ A moribund metaphor.

battle lines are drawn ∎ A moribund metaphor.

(please) be advised that ∎ An ineffectual phrase. This phrase is designed to make the reader pay attention to whatever follows it. The effect it has on anyone with sensibility, however, is quite the opposite: *(please) be advised that* stupefies the attentive reader thereby ensuring that whatever follows it is hardly attended to and, even, roundly ridiculed. • *Please be advised that* some of the ads in this category may require a fee for services or processing. DELETE *Please be advised that.* • *Please be advised that* the valuation below is proposed and not final. DELETE *Please be advised that.* • *Please be advised*

that this office has been retained by North American Mortgage Company to conduct real estate closing for the above-referenced property. DELETE *Please be advised that.*
• *Please be advised that* it takes seven to ten days to process any request for medical records information. DELETE *Please be advised that.* • *Please be advised that* the Norfolk County Mosquito Control Project is now accepting applications for the position of Assistant Superintendent. DELETE *Please be advised that.* • *Please be advised that* I will be on vacation from June 26 to July 10. DELETE *Please be advised that.* SEE ALSO **(please) be informed that: this is to inform you that.**

be-all and end-all ∎ A moribund metaphor. *acme; ideal; perfection; quintessence; ultimate.*

beard the lion (in his den) ∎ A moribund metaphor. *challenge; confront; defy.*

beat about (around) the bush ∎ A moribund metaphor. 1. *avoid; be equivocal; be evasive; dissemble; dodge; doubletalk; equivocate; evade; fence; hedge; palter; prevaricate; quibble; shuffle; sidestep; tergiversate; waffle.* 2. *defer; delay; dawdle; postpone; procrastinate; put off; stall.*

beat a path to (your door) ∎ A moribund metaphor. *dash; hasten; hurry; hustle; make haste; race; run; rush; scamper; scurry; sprint.*

beat a (hasty) retreat ∎ A moribund metaphor. *abscond; clear out; decamp; depart; desert; disappear; escape; exit; flee; fly; go; go away; leave; move on; part; pull out; quit; retire; retreat; run away; take flight; take off; vacate; vanish; withdraw.*

beat (his) brains out ∎ A moribund metaphor. 1. *assail; assault; attack; batter; beat; cudgel; flagellate; flog; hit; lambaste; lash; lick; mangle; pound; pummel; strike; thrash; trounce.* 2. *annihilate; assassinate; butcher; destroy; exterminate; kill; massacre; murder; slaughter; slay.* 3. *beat; conquer; crush; defeat; outdo; overcome; overpower; overwhelm; prevail; quell; rout; succeed; triumph; trounce; vanquish; win.* 4. *attempt; drudge; endeavor; essay; exert; grind; grub; labor; moil; slave; strain; strive; struggle; sweat; toil; travail; try; work.*

beat (them) hands down ∎ A moribund metaphor. *beat; conquer; crush; defeat; outdo; overcome; overpower; overwhelm; prevail; quell; rout; succeed; triumph; trounce; vanquish; win.*

(like) beating (flogging) a dead horse ∎ An insipid simile. *barren; bootless; effete; feckless; feeble; fruitless; futile; impotent; inadequate; inconsequential; inconsiderable; ineffective; ineffectual; infertile; insignificant; inutile; meaningless; meritless; nugatory; null; of no value; pointless; powerless; profitless; purposeless; redundant; sterile; superfluous; trifling; trivial;*

unavailing; unimportant; unnecessary; unproductive; unprofitable; unserviceable; unworthy; useless; vain; valueless; weak; worthless.

beat (smashed) into (to) a pulp ∎ A moribund metaphor. 1. *assail; assault; attack; batter; beat; cudgel; flagellate; flog; hit; lambaste; lash; lick; mangle; pound; pummel; strike; thrash; trounce.* 2. *beat; conquer; crush; defeat; outdo; overcome; overpower; overwhelm; prevail; quell; rout; succeed; triumph; trounce; vanquish; win.* 3. *crush; flatten; macerate; mash; pound; pulp; pulverize; squash.*

> He knew that the baby was going to hit first, and he would see it, would know it for a whole fraction of a second before he was smashed into a pulp himself.—Katherine Dunn, *Geek Love*

beat (it) into the ground ∎ A moribund metaphor. *debilitate; deplete; drain; empty; enervate; exhaust; fatigue; overdo; overwork; sap; tire; wear out; weary.*

beat the bushes ∎ A moribund metaphor. *hunt; look for; quest; ransack; rummage; scour; search; seek.*

beat the bejesus out of ∎ A moribund metaphor. 1. *assail; assault; attack; batter; beat; cudgel; flagellate; flog; hit; lambaste; lash; lick; mangle; pound; pummel; strike; thrash; trounce.* 2. *beat; conquer; crush; defeat; outdo; overcome; overpower; overwhelm; prevail; quell; rout; succeed; triumph; trounce; vanquish; win.* 3. *castigate; chastise; discipline; penalize; punish.*

beat the (living) daylights out of ∎ A moribund metaphor. 1. *assail; assault; attack; batter; beat; cudgel; flagellate; flog; hit; lambaste; lash; lick; mangle; pound; pummel; strike; thrash; trounce.* 2. *beat; conquer; crush; defeat; outdo; overcome; overpower; overwhelm; prevail; quell; rout; succeed; triumph; trounce; vanquish; win.* 3. *castigate; chastise; discipline; penalize; punish.*

beat the drum ∎ A moribund metaphor. *advertise; announce; broadcast; cry out; declaim; disseminate; exclaim; proclaim; promulgate; publicize; publish; shout; trumpet; yell.*

beat the stuffing out of ∎ A moribund metaphor. 1. *assail; assault; attack; batter; beat; cudgel; flagellate; flog; hit; lambaste; lash; lick; mangle; pound; pummel; strike; thrash; trounce.* 2. *beat; conquer; crush; defeat; outdo; overcome; overpower; overwhelm; prevail; quell; rout; succeed; triumph; trounce; vanquish; win.*

beat to death ∎ A moribund metaphor. 1. *annihilate; assassinate; butcher; destroy; exterminate; kill; massacre; murder; slaughter; slay.* 2. *debilitate; deplete; drain;*

beat (him) to the punch

empty; enervate; exhaust; fatigue; overdo; overwork; sap; tire; wear out; weary. SEE ALSO **to death**.

beat (him) to the punch ∎ A moribund metaphor.

beat up on (each other) ∎ A moribund metaphor. *assail; assault; attack; batter; beat; cudgel; flagellate; flog; hit; lambaste; lash; lick; mangle; pound; pummel; strike; thrash; trounce.*

beauteous ∎ A withered word. *beautiful.* • Saturday should be a *beauteous* day. REPLACE WITH *beautiful.*

beautiful baby ∎ An inescapable pair.

beauty and the beast ∎ A moribund metaphor.

beauty is in the eye of the beholder ∎ A popular prescription.

because (that's why) ∎ An infantile phrase. • Why did you hit him? *Because.* SEE ALSO **it just happened**.

because of the fact that ∎ A wretched redundancy. *because; considering; for; given; in that; since.* • I married him only *because of the fact that* his family has money. REPLACE WITH *because.* • Many people told me I had to break off my relationship with her *because of the fact that* I was being unfair to her. REPLACE WITH *because.* SEE ALSO **by virtue of the fact that; considering the fact that; given the fact that; in consideration of the fact that; in view of the fact that; on account of the fact that**.

because why? ∎ An infantile phrase. • They were afraid of him, too. *Because why?* DELETE *Because.*

(no) bed of roses ∎ A moribund metaphor. *agreeable; ambrosial; beguiling; celestial; charming; delectable; delicious; delightful; divine; enchanting; engaging; enjoyable; fun; heavenly; glorious; gratifying; inviting; joyful; joyous; luscious; pleasant; pleasing; pleasurable.*

(she's) been around the block (and back) ∎ A moribund metaphor. 1. *adult; aged; aging; elderly; full-grown; hoary; hoary-headed; mature; old; worn.* 2. *able; adept; apt; capable; competent; deft; dexterous; experienced; expert; practiced; proficient; seasoned; skilled; skillful; veteran.*

before (you) can say (Jack Robinson) ∎ A moribund metaphor. *abruptly; apace; at once; briskly; directly; expeditiously; fast; forthwith; hastily; hurriedly; immediately; instantaneously; instantly; posthaste; promptly; quickly; rapidly; rashly; right away; speedily; straightaway; suddenly; swiftly; unexpectedly; wingedly.*

beg, borrow, or steal ∎ A moribund metaphor.

beggars can't be choosers ∎ A popular prescription.

begin (start) a new chapter (in my life) ∎ A moribund metaphor.

behind closed doors ∎ A moribund metaphor. *clandestinely; confidentially; covertly; furtively; mysteriously; in private; in secret; privately; quietly; secludedly; secretly; slyly; stealthily; surreptitiously; undercover.*

behind every successful man stands a woman ∎ A popular prescription.

behind the eight ball ∎ A moribund metaphor. *at risk; endangered; hard-pressed; imperiled; in a bind; in a fix; in a jam; in a predicament; in a quandary; in danger; in difficulty; in jeopardy; in peril; in trouble; jeopardized.*

(work) behind the scenes ∎ A moribund metaphor. *clandestinely; confidentially; covertly; furtively; mysteriously; in private; in secret; privately; quietly; secludedly; secretly; slyly; stealthily; surreptitiously; undercover.*

behind the times ∎ A moribund metaphor. *antediluvian; antiquated; archaic; dead; obsolescent; obsolete; old; old-fashioned; outdated; outmoded; out of date; out of fashion; passé; superannuated.*

(I'll) be honest with you ∎ A plebeian sentiment.

behoove ∎ A withered word. 1. *be advantageous for; benefit; be worthwhile to.* 2. *be necessary for; be proper for.*

(please) be informed that ∎ An ineffectual phrase. • *Please be informed that* your wife has retained my office in the matter of her petition for a divorce. DELETE *Please be informed that.* • If you are running a version of Almanac earlier than 3.0, *please be informed that* the format of the desktop data files has been changed. DELETE *please be informed that.* SEE ALSO **(please) be advised that; this is to inform you that**.

(like) being run over (getting hit) by a (Mack) truck ∎ An insipid simile. *atomized; crushed; dashed; demolished; depleted; depressed; destroyed; devastated; distraught; distressed; exhausted; obliterated; overcome; overpowered; overwhelmed; prostrate; ravaged; ruined; shattered; undone; upset.* • I feel *like I've been run over by a Mac truck.*

bells and whistles ∎ A moribund metaphor. *adornments; attributes; characteristics; decorations; embellishments; features; flourishes; frills; highlights; innovations; novelties; ornaments; properties; qualities; specialties; traits.* • They sport few of the *bells and whistles* found in programs like Chrome and Firefox. REPLACE WITH *features.*

bell the cat ∎ A moribund metaphor.

> It was time to bell the cat, or at least inquire about its alibi.—Joan Hess, *The Murder at the Murder at the Mimosa Inn*

below par ∎ A moribund metaphor. *inferior; poor; second-class; second-rate; shoddy; subordinate; substandard.*

(hit) below the belt ∎ A moribund metaphor. *dishonorable; foul; inequitable; unconscientious; underhanded; unethical; unfair; unjust; unprincipled; unscrupulous; unsportsmanlike.*

below (under) the radar (of) (screen) ∎ A moribund metaphor. 1. *disregarded; hidden; ignored; imperceptible; indiscernible; invisible; overlooked; undetectable; undetected; unheard of; unknown; unnoticeable; unnoticed; unobserved; unperceived; unrevealed; unseen.* 2. *discreet; inconspicuous; self-effacing; unassuming; understated; unobtrusive.* • The underreported remain *below the radars of* most news organizations. REPLACE WITH *imperceptible to.* • We don't need to be *under the radar* anymore, we need to be out there. REPLACE WITH *unobtrusive.*

belt-tightening (measures) ∎ A moribund metaphor.

bend (my) ear ∎ A moribund metaphor.

bend over backward(s) ∎ A moribund metaphor. *aim; attempt; endeavor; essay; exert; labor; moil; strain; strive; struggle; toil; try hard; undertake; work at.* • If anything, he will have to *bend over backward* to not appear to be showing favoritism. REPLACE WITH *struggle.*

be nice ∎ A plebeian sentiment. "*Be nice,*" we often are admonished. There can be no complaint with being agreeable when agreeability is warranted, but to soporiferously accept niceness as a virtue, untarnished and true, is utterly benighted.

To be capable of expressing anger and indignation is thwarted by our society's placing a premium on politeness.

Let us not, of course, be rude gratuitously, nor seek to be singular for its own sake, nor foolish or fantastic for the quick cachet. Do, however, let us become more concerned with giving fuller expression to ourselves.

We do possibly irreparable harm to ourselves when we, to avoid unpleasantness, fail to show another how we truly feel. Unknown to ourselves and unknowable to others we homunculi are, for anonymity is won when anger is lost. SEE ALSO **if you can't say something nice, don't say anything; I'm sorry.**

bent out of shape ∎ A moribund metaphor. 1. *agitated; anxious; aroused; displeased; disquieted; excited; flustered; perturbed; troubled; upset; worried.* 2. *acerbated;*

angered; annoyed; bothered; disturbed; exasperated; galled; irked; irritated; miffed; nettled; provoked; rankled; riled; roiled; upset; vexed.

best of the bunch (lot) ∎ A suspect superlative. *best; brightest; choice; choicest; elite; excellent; finest; first-class; first-rate; foremost; greatest; highest; matchless; nonpareil; optimal; optimum; outstanding; paramount; peerless; preeminent; premium; prominent; select; superior; superlative; top; unequaled; unexcelled; unmatched; unrivaled; unsurpassed.*

best-selling author ∎ A suspect superlative. *Best-selling authors,* of course, are often responsible for the worst written books. SEE ALSO **a good read; a (must) read.**

bet (your) bottom dollar (life) ∎ A moribund metaphor. • I would have *bet my bottom dollar* that this would not have happened.

(my) better half ∎ An infantile phrase. *consort; helpmate; helpmeet; husband; mate; spouse; wife.*

better late than never ∎ A popular prescription.

better safe than sorry ∎ A popular prescription.

(it's) better than nothing ∎ A popular prescription.

bet the farm (ranch) (on) ∎ A moribund metaphor.

between a rock and a hard place ∎ A moribund metaphor. *at risk; endangered; hard-pressed; imperiled; in a bind; in a dilemma; in a fix; in a jam; in a predicament; in a quandary; in danger; in difficulty; in jeopardy; in peril; in trouble; jeopardized.* • When you need to regenerate a degraded stripe set with parity, you will be faced with a *rock and a hard place* dilemma. DELETE *rock and a hard place.*

> But now my father's advice and my sister's counsel war in my head. Between a rock and a hard place, I must find a middle ground.—Donna Hill, *An Ordinary Woman*

between Scylla and Charybdis ∎ A moribund metaphor. *at risk; endangered; hard-pressed; imperiled; in a bind; in a dilemma; in a fix; in a jam; in a predicament; in a quandary; in danger; in difficulty; in jeopardy; in peril; in trouble; jeopardized.*

between the devil and the deep blue sea ∎ A moribund metaphor. *at risk; endangered; hard-pressed; imperiled; in a bind; in a dilemma; in a fix; in a jam; in a predicament; in a quandary; in danger; in difficulty; in jeopardy; in peril; in trouble; jeopardized.*

between you and me (and the four walls) ∎ A moribund metaphor. *classified;*

confidential; personal; private; privy; restricted; secret.

betwixt ∎ A withered word. *between.*

betwixt and between ∎ An inescapable pair. *divided; drifting; faltering; in between; irresolute; loose; shaky; swaying; torn; tottering; uncertain; undecided; unfixed; unresolved; unsettled; unsteady; unsure; vacillating; wavering; wobbly.*

beware of Greeks bearing gifts ∎ A popular prescription.

beyond (without) a shadow of a doubt ∎ A moribund metaphor. *absolutely; conclusively; decidedly; definitely; incontrovertibly; indisputably; indubitably; irrefragably; irrefutably; positively; unconditionally; uncontestably; undeniably; undoubtedly; unequivocally; unmistakably; unquestionably.*

beyond the pale ∎ A moribund metaphor. *improper; inappropriate; unacceptable; unreasonable; unseemly; unsuitable; unthinkable.*

beyond (my) wildest dreams ∎ A moribund metaphor. *astonishing; astounding; beyond belief; beyond comprehension; breathtaking; extraordinary; fabulous; fantastic; implausible; imponderable; inconceivable; incredible; marvelous; miraculous; outlandish; overwhelming; prodigious; sensational; spectacular; unbelievable; unimaginable; unthinkable; wonderful.*

> He had succeeded beyond his wildest dreams, only too well, but in another sense, he had failed completely.—Jane Stevenson, *The Winter Queen*

(as) big as a house ∎ An insipid simile. *big; brobdingnagian; colossal; enormous; gargantuan; giant; gigantic; grand; great; huge; immense; large; massive; monstrous; prodigious; tremendous; vast.*

(as) big as life ∎ An insipid simile.

big cheese ∎ A moribund metaphor. 1. *administrator; boss; brass; chief; commander; director; executive; foreman; head; headman; leader; manager; master; (high) muckamuck; officer; official; overseer; president; principal; superintendent; supervisor.* 2. *aristocrat; dignitary; eminence; lord; luminary; magnate; mogul; notable; patrician; personage; ruler; sovereign; worthy.*

big deal ∎ An infantile phrase. *appreciable; central; climacteric; consequential; considerable; critical; crucial; essential; grave; major; material; important; meaningful; momentous; pivotal; pregnant; principal; serious; significant; substantial; vital; weighty.*

big fish in a small pond ∎ A moribund metaphor.

bigger is better ∎ A quack equation.

bigger isn't necessarily better ∎ A popular prescription.

big gun ∎ A moribund metaphor. 1. *administrator; boss; brass; chief; commander; director; executive; foreman; head; headman; leader; manager; master; (high) muckamuck; officer; official; overseer; president; principal; superintendent; supervisor.* 2. *aristocrat; dignitary; eminence; lord; luminary; magnate; mogul; notable; patrician; personage; ruler; sovereign; worthy.*

big shot ∎ A moribund metaphor. 1. *administrator; boss; brass; chief; commander; director; executive; foreman; head; headman; leader; manager; master; (high) muckamuck; officer; official; overseer; president; principal; superintendent; supervisor.* 2. *aristocrat; dignitary; eminence; lord; luminary; magnate; mogul; notable; patrician; personage; ruler; sovereign; worthy.*

big-ticket (item) ∎ A moribund metaphor. 1. *costly; expensive; high-priced.* 2. *all-important; central; chief; imperative; important; key; main; significant; vital.* • We can market these *big-ticket* items, which have a large profit margin. REPLACE WITH *expensive.*

> In the many months it had taken me to retrieve the box from the closet, I discovered that I had forgiven her for a number of things, although for none of the big-ticket items—like having existed at all, for instance, and then having lived so long.—Anne Lamott, *Plan B: Further Thoughts on Faith*

big wheel ∎ A moribund metaphor. 1. *administrator; boss; brass; chief; commander; director; executive; foreman; head; headman; leader; manager; master; (high) muckamuck; officer; official; overseer; president; principal; superintendent; supervisor.* 2. *aristocrat; dignitary; eminence; lord; luminary; magnate; mogul; notable; patrician; personage; ruler; sovereign; worthy.*

bird's-eye view ∎ A moribund metaphor. *outline; overview; profile; review; sketch; summary; survey.*

birds of a feather (flock together) ∎ A moribund metaphor. *akin; alike; commensurate; comparable; consonant; duplicate; equal; equivalent; identical; indistinguishable; interchangeable; like; same; similar; undifferentiated.* • Politically, they are *birds of a feather.* REPLACE WITH *indistinguishable.*

bite (his) head (nose) off ∎ A moribund metaphor. *admonish; animadvert; berate; castigate; censure; chasten; chastise; chide; condemn; criticize; denounce; denunciate; discipline; excoriate; fulminate against;*

imprecate; impugn; inveigh against; objurgate; punish; rebuke; remonstrate; reprehend; reprimand; reproach; reprobate; reprove; revile; scold; swear at; upbraid; vituperate.

bite off more than (he) can chew ∎ A moribund metaphor. 1. *overcommit; overpledge.* 2. *arrogant; brazen; cocksure; overconfident.* • Even in private circles, there is concern that the government has *bitten off more than it can chew.*

> The truth was that Joe was a talented but careless performer, liable to bite off more than he could chew.—Michael Chabon, *The Amazing Adventures of Kavalier & Clay*

bite the bullet ∎ A moribund metaphor. *bear; endure; put up with; stand; suffer; tolerate.*

bite the dust ∎ A moribund metaphor. 1. *be deceased; die; expire; extinguish; perish; terminate.* 2. *be beaten; be conquered; be crushed; be defeated; be outdone; be overcome; be overpowered; be overwhelmed; be quelled; be routed; be trounced; be vanquished.* 3. *cease; close; complete; conclude; derail; desist; discontinue; end; finish; halt; quit; settle; stop; terminate.* 4. *be unsuccessful; bomb; break down; collapse; fail; fall short; falter; fizzle; flop; fold; founder; mess up; miscarry; not succeed; stumble; topple.*

(they) bite the hand that feeds (them) ∎ A moribund metaphor. *unappreciative; ungrateful; unthankful.*

bite your tongue ∎ A moribund metaphor.

bits and pieces ∎ An inescapable pair. *bits; chunks; components; crumbs; elements; factors; fragments; ingredients; modicums; morsels; nuggets; parts; particles; pieces; scraps; segments; shreds; snips; snippets; specks.* • All the *bits and pieces* that make up the whole must be carefully and objectively examined. REPLACE WITH *elements.*

> The ancestors of the place hovered over the bits and pieces of their finished lives.—Annie Proulx, *That Old Ace in the Hole*

bitter acrimony ∎ An inescapable pair.

(as) black as coal ∎ An insipid simile. *black; blackish; caliginous; dark; ebony; ecchymotic; fuliginous; inky; jet; nigrescent; nigritudinous; raven; sable; swarthy; tenebrific; tenebrous.*

(as) black as night ∎ An insipid simile. *black; blackish; caliginous; dark; ebony; ecchymotic; fuliginous; inky; jet; nigrescent; nigritudinous; raven; sable; swarthy; tenebrific; tenebrous.*

> After that speech he glared at me in silence, then flung down the spear he had snatched up in his sudden rage and stalked out of the house and into the wood, but before long he was back again seated in his old place, brooding on my words with a face as black as night.—W. H. Hudson, *Green Mansions*

(as) black as pitch ∎ An insipid simile. *black; blackish; caliginous; dark; ebony; ecchymotic; fuliginous; inky; jet; nigrescent; nigritudinous; raven; sable; swarthy; tenebrific; tenebrous.*

(as) black as the ace of spades ∎ An insipid simile. *black; blackish; caliginous; dark; ebony; ecchymotic; fuliginous; inky; jet; nigrescent; nigritudinous; raven; sable; swarthy; tenebrific; tenebrous.*

black cloud ∎ A moribund metaphor. *anhedonia; cheerlessness; dejection; depression; despondency; disconsolateness; discouragement; dismay; dispiritedness; dolefulness; downheartedness; dreariness; forlornness; melancholia; misery; moroseness; mournfulness; negativity; pessimism; plaintiveness; sorrow; unhappiness; woe.*

black sheep (of the family) ∎ A moribund metaphor. *curiosity; deviant; eccentric; extremist; iconoclast; individual; individualist; maverick; misfit; nonconformist; oddball; oddity; renegade; undesirable.*

> Nate had been labeled the black sheep of the family years ago.—Robin Jones Gunn, *Gardenias for Breakfast*

blah, blah, blah ∎ A grammatical gimmick. • He told me, I want you to come out here; I miss you; *blah, blah, blah.* DELETE *blah, blah, blah.* SEE ALSO **and so on, and so forth; et cetera, et cetera.**

blast from the past ∎ An infantile phrase.

blatant lie ∎ An inescapable pair.

blessed event ∎ An infantile phrase. 1. *baby; infant; newborn.* 2. *birth; childbearing; childbirth; parturition.*

blessed with (has) the gift of gab ∎ An infantile phrase. *babbling; blathering; chatty; facile; fluent; garrulous; glib; jabbering; logorrheic; long-winded; loquacious; prolix; talkative; verbose; voluble; windy.*

(as) blind as a bat ∎ An insipid simile. 1. *blind; eyeless; purblind; sightless; unseeing; unsighted; visionless.* 2. *addleheaded; bovine; cretinous; decerebrate; dense; dull; dull-witted; fatuous; fat-witted; half-witted; harebrained; hebetudinous; idiotic; ignorant; imbecilic; incogitant; insensate; mindless; moronic; muddled; nescient; obtuse; phlegmatic; slow; slow-witted; sluggish; thick; torpid; undiscerning; unintelligent; vacuous; witless.*

blind faith ∎ An inescapable pair.

blondes have more fun ∎ An infantile phrase.

bloodcurdling scream (yell)

bloodcurdling scream (yell) ❚ An inescapable pair.

blood is thicker than water ❚ A popular prescription.

blood, sweat, and tears ❚ A moribund metaphor. *assiduity; diligence; discipline; drudgery; effort; endeavor; exertion; grind; hard work; industry; labor; moil; persistence; slavery; strain; struggle; sweat; toil; travail; work.* • However unautobiographical or fictional a book is, it still comes out by *blood, sweat, and tears.* REPLACE WITH *toil.*

blow a fuse ❚ A moribund metaphor. *bellow; bluster; clamor; explode; fulminate; fume; holler; howl; rage; rant; rave; roar; scream; shout; storm; thunder; vociferate; yell.*

blow a gasket ❚ A moribund metaphor. *bellow; bluster; clamor; explode; fulminate; fume; holler; howl; rage; rant; rave; roar; scream; shout; storm; thunder; vociferate; yell.*

blow away ❚ A moribund metaphor. 1. *annihilate; assassinate; butcher; destroy; exterminate; kill; massacre; murder; slaughter; slay.* 2. *amaze; astonish; astound; awe; dazzle; dumbfound; flabbergast; overpower; overwhelm; shock; startle; stun; stupefy; surprise.*

blow by blow ❚ A moribund metaphor.

blow (his) cover ❚ A moribund metaphor. *ascertain; discover; expose; find out; learn.*

blow (run) hot and cold ❚ A moribund metaphor. 1. *ambivalent; divided; indecisive; irresolute; torn; uncertain; uncommitted; undecided; unsure.* 2. *capricious; changeable; erratic; fickle; fitful; flighty; fluctuating; haphazard; inconsistent; inconstant; intermittent; irregular; mercurial; occasional; random; sometime; spasmodic; sporadic; unpredictable; unsettled; unstable; unsteady; vacillating; volatile; wavering; wayward.*

blow (my) mind ❚ A moribund metaphor. *amaze; astonish; astound; awe; dazzle; dumbfound; flabbergast; overpower; overwhelm; shock; startle; stun; stupefy; surprise.*

> And Elizabeth said one thing at the very end that really blew Rosie's mind, about how when she first got sober, she felt as if the mosaic she had been assembling out of life's little shards got dumped to the ground, and there was no way to put it back together.—Anne Lamott, *Crooked Little Heart*

blow off steam ❚ A moribund metaphor. 1. *bellow; bluster; clamor; complain; explode; fulminate; fume; holler; howl; object; protest; rage; rant; rave; roar; scream; shout; storm; thunder; vociferate; yell.* 2. *be merry; carouse; carry on; celebrate; debauch; disport; frolic; party; play; revel; riot; roister; rollick; romp; skylark.*

blow on the cue ball ❚ A moribund metaphor.

blow (things) out of proportion ❚ A moribund metaphor. *elaborate; embellish; embroider; enhance; enlarge; exaggerate; hyperbolize; inflate; magnify; overdo; overreact; overstress; overstate; strain; stretch.* • It was not the sort of event that has now been exaggerated and *blown out of proportion.* DELETE *and blown out of proportion.*

blow (them) out of the water ❚ A moribund metaphor. 1. *annihilate; assassinate; butcher; destroy; exterminate; kill; massacre; murder; slaughter; slay.* 2. *beat; conquer; crush; defeat; outdo; overcome; overpower; overwhelm; prevail; quell; rout; succeed; triumph; trounce; vanquish; win.* 3. *amaze; astonish; astound; awe; dazzle; dumbfound; flabbergast; overpower; overwhelm; shock; startle; stun; stupefy; surprise.*

blow (your) own horn ❚ A moribund metaphor. *acclaim; applaud; bluster; boast; brag; celebrate; cheer; commend; compliment; congratulate; crow; extol; flatter; gloat; hail; honor; laud; praise; puff; salute; self-congratulate; strut; swagger.*

blow smoke ❚ A moribund metaphor. *adumbrate; becloud; befog; camouflage; cloak; cloud; conceal; cover; disguise; dissemble; enshroud; harbor; hide; keep secret; mask; obfuscate; obscure; overshadow; screen; shroud; suppress; veil; withhold.*

blow (his) stack ❚ A moribund metaphor. *bellow; bluster; clamor; explode; fulminate; fume; holler; howl; rage; rant; rave; roar; scream; shout; storm; thunder; vociferate; yell.*

blow the whistle (on) ❚ A moribund metaphor. 1. *bare; betray; disclose; divulge; expose; give away; reveal; show; tell; uncover; unearth; unveil.* 2. *betray; deliver up; inform on; report; turn in.* • Fear of reprisals arises when people consider whether or not to *blow the whistle on* someone who violates ethical standards. REPLACE WITH *report.* • He *blew the whistle on* company corruption. REPLACE WITH *exposed.*

blow to bits ❚ A moribund metaphor. *annihilate; assassinate; butcher; demolish; destroy; devastate; eradicate; exterminate; kill; massacre; murder; obliterate; pulverize; rack; ravage; raze; ruin; shatter; slaughter; slay; smash; undo; wrack; wreck.*

blow (my) top ❚ A moribund metaphor. *bellow; bluster; clamor; explode; fulminate; fume; holler; howl; rage; rant; rave; roar; scream; shout; storm; thunder; vociferate; yell.*

blow to smithereens ❚ A moribund metaphor. *annihilate; assassinate; butcher; demolish; destroy; devastate; eradicate; exterminate; kill; massacre; murder; obliterate; pulverize; rack; ravage; raze; ruin;*

shatter; slaughter; slay; smash; undo; wrack; wreck.

(until) (I'm) blue in the face ∎ A moribund metaphor. 1. *angry; annoyed; enraged; exasperated; furious; incensed; infuriated; irate; irked; irritated; mad; raging; wrathful.* 2. *beat; bushed; debilitated; depleted; exhausted; fatigued; fed up; spent; tired; wearied; weary; worn out.*

blue-ribbon commission (committee; panel) ∎ A suspect superlative.

boggle (my) mind ∎ An infantile phrase. *baffle; befuddle; bemuse; bewilder; confound; confuse; disconcert; flummox; muddle; mystify; nonplus; perplex; puzzle.*

> They had been friends forever, sitting in this room for longer than Amy had been alive, although it boggled Amy's mind to think that—Elizabeth Strout, *Amy and Isabelle*

(as) bold as brass ∎ An insipid simile. *audacious; bold; brash; brass; brassy; brazen; cheeky; forward; impertinent; impudent; insolent; outrageous; saucy; shameless; unabashed.*

bone of contention ∎ A moribund metaphor.

bone to pick ∎ A moribund metaphor. *animosity; bitterness; enmity; grievance; grudge; hostility; indignation; ill will; offense; rancor; resentment; spite; umbrage.*

(cite) book, chapter, and verse ∎ A moribund metaphor. *explain; expound; lecture.* • She will *give me chapter and verse* about the merits of XYZ Chemical and why it should be a glorious investment. REPLACE WITH *lecture me.*

book of woes ∎ A moribund metaphor.

bore the pants off (me) ∎ A moribund metaphor. *annoy; bore; discourage; disgust; exasperate; exhaust; fatigue; irk; irritate; sicken; tire; wear out; weary.*

bore to death (extinction) ∎ A moribund metaphor. *annoy; bore; discourage; disgust; exasperate; exhaust; fatigue; irk; irritate; sicken; tire; wear out; weary.* SEE ALSO **to death**.

bore to tears ∎ A moribund metaphor. *annoy; bore; discourage; disgust; exasperate; exhaust; fatigue; irk; irritate; sicken; tire; wear out; weary.*

born to the purple ∎ A moribund metaphor.

born under a lucky star ∎ A moribund metaphor. *advantageous; auspicious; blessed; charmed; enchanted; favored; felicitous; flourishing; fortuitous; fortunate; golden; happy; in luck; lucky; propitious; prosperous; successful; thriving.*

born with a silver spoon in (his) mouth ∎ A moribund metaphor. *advantageous; auspicious; blessed; charmed; enchanted; favored; felicitous; flourishing; fortuitous;*

fortunate; golden; happy; in luck; lucky; propitious; prosperous; successful; thriving.

bottle up (inside) ∎ A moribund metaphor. *block; check; contain; control; curb; hide; hold back; repress; restrain; smother; stem; stifle; suppress.*

> I became more guilty and more frightened, and kept all this bottled up inside me, and naturally, inescapably, one night, when this woman had finished preaching, everything came roaring, screaming, crying out, and I fell to the ground before the altar.—James Baldwin, *The Fire Next Time*

bottomless pit ∎ A moribund metaphor. *abyss; hades; hell; inferno; netherworld; perdition.*

(the) bottom line ∎ A moribund metaphor. This is a bottomlessly ordinary term. People bewitched by words that have a trace of technicality to them are inclined to use it. In striving to sound technical, they manage to sound only typical. 1. *conclusion; consequence; culmination; decision; denouement; effect; end; outcome; result; upshot.* 2. *crux; essence; key; keynote; main point; salient point.* • The *bottom line* is that America can compete if the politicians are kept out of the picture. REPLACE WITH *upshot.* • The *bottom line* is that both kinds of water are generally safe. REPLACE WITH *conclusion.* • The *bottom line* is you get what you pay for. REPLACE WITH *main point.* • The *bottom line* for parents: choose gifts carefully. REPLACE WITH *keynote.* SEE ALSO **feedback; input; interface; output; parameters.**

bottom of the barrel ∎ A moribund metaphor. 1. *alluvium; debris; deposit; detritus; dregs; grounds; lees; precipitate; remains; residue; residuum; sediment; settlings; silt; wash.* 2. *close; completion; conclusion; end; ending; finale; finish; termination.* 3. *bums; deadbeats; derelicts; duds; failures; flobs; hobos; losers; pariahs; rabble; renegades; riffraff; scum; tramps; vagabonds; vagrants; washouts.*

bottom of the heap ∎ A moribund metaphor. *bottom; depths; nadir; pits; rock bottom.*

> You slip around the truth once, and then again, and one more time, and there you are, feeling, for a moment, that it was sudden, your arrival at the bottom of the heap.—Jane Hamilton, *A Map of the World*

bound and determined ∎ An inescapable pair. *bent on; determined; resolute; resolved.*

> While I'm not vain enough to buy a new winter coat—I will not spend hundreds of dollars on a piece of clothing I am bound and determined not to need a month from now—I am sufficiently self-conscious to leave the coat open, counting on a thick scarf to keep out the bitter damp.—Ayelet Waldman, *Love and Other Impossible Pursuits*

bow and scrape ∎ A moribund metaphor. *bootlick; bow; crawl; cringe; crouch; fawn; grovel; kowtow; slaver; stoop; toady; truckle.*

bowled over ∎ A moribund metaphor. *amazed; astonished; astounded; flabbergasted; shocked; staggered; stunned; surprised.*

brain drain ∎ An infantile phrase.

brand new ∎ An inescapable pair. • Did you forget he got himself a *brand new* car to drive around in? DELETE *brand.*

brass ring ∎ A moribund metaphor. *prize; success; triumph; trophy.*

bread and butter ∎ A moribund metaphor. 1. *food; keep; livelihood; living; subsistence; support; sustenance.* 2. *basis; center; core; essence; foundation; heart; hub; mainstay; nucleus; root; soul; spirit.* • Interfaces are the *bread and butter* of component technology. REPLACE WITH *core.*

bread buttered on both sides ∎ A moribund metaphor.

breadth and depth ∎ An inescapable pair. *ambit; area; breadth; compass; degree; extent; field; magnitude; range; reach; scope; sphere; sweep.*

break (his) back ∎ A moribund metaphor. *attempt; drudge; endeavor; essay; exert; grind; grub; labor; moil; slave; strain; strive; struggle; sweat; toil; travail; try; work.*

break down (the) barriers ∎ A moribund metaphor.

break (my) neck ∎ A moribund metaphor. *attempt; drudge; endeavor; essay; exert; grind; grub; labor; moil; slave; strain; strive; struggle; sweat; toil; travail; try; work.*

break out of the mold ∎ A moribund metaphor.

(it) breaks (my) heart ∎ A moribund metaphor. *desolate; disappoint; discourage; dishearten; dispirit; distress; sadden.*

break the back of ∎ A moribund metaphor. *beat; conquer; crush; defeat; overcome; rout; subdue; trounce; vanquish.* • We are all focused on *breaking the back of* the recession. REPLACE WITH *crushing.*

break the bank ∎ A moribund metaphor. *bankrupt; deplete; drain; exhaust; impoverish; pauperize; ruin.*

break the ice ∎ A moribund metaphor.

breathe (new) life into ∎ A moribund metaphor. *animate; arouse; enliven; exhilarate; inspire; inspirit; invigorate; revivify; spur; stimulate; vitalize; vivify.* • The Citizens for Limited Taxation petition would block school reform at the very time it is needed most to *breathe life into* our public schools. REPLACE WITH *invigorate.*

breathe (your) last (breath) ∎ A moribund metaphor. *be deceased; die; expire; perish.*

breathless anticipation ∎ An inescapable pair.

bright and early ∎ An inescapable pair.

(as) bright as a (new) button ∎ An insipid simile. 1. *beaming; bright; brilliant; burnished; dazzling; effulgent; gleaming; glistening; glittering; glossy; incandescent; luminous; lustrous; radiant; resplendent; shiny; sparkling.* 2. *able; adroit; alert; apt; astute; bright; brilliant; capable; clever; competent; discerning; enlightened; insightful; intelligent; judicious; keen; knowledgeable; learned; logical; luminous; perceptive; perspicacious; quick; quick-witted; rational; reasonable; sagacious; sage; sapient; sensible; sharp; shrewd; smart; sound; understanding; wise.*

(as) bright as a new penny ∎ An insipid simile. 1. *beaming; bright; brilliant; burnished; dazzling; effulgent; gleaming; glistening; glittering; glossy; incandescent; luminous; lustrous; radiant; resplendent; shiny; sparkling.* 2. *able; adroit; alert; apt; astute; bright; brilliant; capable; clever; competent; discerning; enlightened; insightful; intelligent; judicious; keen; knowledgeable; learned; logical; luminous; perceptive; perspicacious; quick; quick-witted; rational; reasonable; sagacious; sage; sapient; sensible; sharp; shrewd; smart; sound; understanding; wise.*

(as) bright as a new pin ∎ An insipid simile. 1. *beaming; bright; brilliant; burnished; dazzling; effulgent; gleaming; glistening; glittering; glossy; incandescent; luminous; lustrous; radiant; resplendent; shiny; sparkling.* 2. *able; adroit; alert; apt; astute; bright; brilliant; capable; clever; competent; discerning; enlightened; insightful; intelligent; judicious; keen; knowledgeable; learned; logical; luminous; perceptive; perspicacious; quick; quick-witted; rational; reasonable; sagacious; sage; sapient; sensible; sharp; shrewd; smart; sound; understanding; wise.*

(she) brightens up a room ∎ A moribund metaphor. *is beaming; is brilliant; is dazzling; is gleaming; is glowing; is incandescent; is luminescent; is luminous; is radiant; is resplendent; is shimmering; is sunny.* • When she walks into a room, she *brightens up the room.* REPLACE WITH *is incandescent.*

bright-eyed and bushy tailed ∎ A moribund metaphor. *active; adroit; alert; alive; animated; dynamic; eager; energetic; frisky; hearty; lively; nimble; peppy; perky; quick; ready; spirited; sprightly; spry; vibrant; vigorous; vivacious.*

bring (take) (her) down a notch (peg) ∎ A moribund metaphor. *abase; chasten; debase; decrease; deflate; degrade; demean; depreciate; depress; diminish; disgrace; dishonor; embarrass; humble; humiliate; lower; mortify; puncture; shame.*

bring (her) down from (her) high horse
∎ A moribund metaphor. *abase; chasten; debase; decrease; deflate; degrade; demean; depreciate; depress; diminish; disgrace; dishonor; embarrass; humble; humiliate; lower; mortify; puncture; shame.*

bring down the house ∎ A moribund metaphor. *acclaim; applaud; bellow; cheer; clamor; holler; howl; roar; scream; shout; vociferate; yell.*

bring home the bacon ∎ A moribund metaphor. *earn a living; earn money; prosper; succeed.*

bring to a close (a halt; an end; a stop) ∎ A wretched redundancy. *cease; close; complete; conclude; derail; discontinue; end; finish; halt; settle; stop; terminate.* • We are pleased to be able to *bring* this longstanding litigation *to a close.* REPLACE WITH *conclude.* • You might be contributing to *bringing* the nation's longest peacetime economic expansion *to a grinding halt.* REPLACE WITH *halting.* SEE ALSO **come to a close (a halt; an end; a stop); come to a screeching halt; grind to a halt.**

bring to a head ∎ A moribund metaphor. *cap; climax; conclude; consummate; crest; crown; culminate; peak.*

bring (come) to closure ∎ A torpid term. 1. *cease; close; complete; conclude; discontinue; end; finish; halt; stop.* 2. *conclude; decide; determine; establish; resolve; settle.*

bring (them) to (their) knees ∎ A moribund metaphor. *beat; conquer; cow; cripple; crush; defeat; disable; dispirit; enervate; enfeeble; humble; incapacitate; lame; make helpless; neutralize; oppress; overcome; overpower; overrun; overthrow; overwhelm; repress; subdue; subjugate; suppress; vanquish.* • A network of computers was *brought to its knees* by something out of our control that seemed to live in and even infect the system. REPLACE WITH *vanquished.*

bring to the table ∎ A moribund metaphor. *advance; bring up; broach; contribute; give; introduce; offer; present; proffer; propose; provide; raise; submit; suggest; tender.* • As a company that knows education, we thought we had something to *bring to the table.* REPLACE WITH *offer.*

broad in the beam ∎ A moribund metaphor. *hippy; platypygous.*

brought it home to (me) ∎ A moribund metaphor.

(as) brown as a berry ∎ An insipid simile. *beige; bronze; bronzed; brown; burnished; chestnut; copper; coppery; ecru; fawn; mahogany; ocherous; russet; sienna; sun-tanned; tan; tanned; tawny.*

(win) brownie points ∎ A moribund metaphor.

brutally honest ∎ An inescapable pair.

brute force ∎ An inescapable pair.

bucket of bolts ∎ A moribund metaphor.

build a better mousetrap (and the world will beat a path to your door) ∎ A popular prescription.

build bridges ∎ A moribund metaphor.

build bridges where there are walls ∎ A moribund metaphor.

build castles in Spain (the air) ∎ A moribund metaphor. *brood; daydream; dream; fantasize; imagine; meditate; muse; reflect.*

building blocks of ∎ A moribund metaphor.

bump in the road ∎ A moribund metaphor. *bar; barrier; block; blockage; check; deterrent; difficulty; encumbrance; handicap; hindrance; hurdle; impediment; interference; obstacle; obstruction.*

bumpy road (ahead) ∎ A moribund metaphor. *complication; difficulty; dilemma; mess; muddle; ordeal; pickle; plight; predicament; problem; quandary; trial; trouble.*

bunch of baloney ∎ A moribund metaphor. *balderdash; baloney; nonsense; rubbish.*

bundle of joy ∎ A moribund metaphor. *babe; baby; child; infant; neonate; newborn; nursling; suckling; toddler; tot; weanling.*

bundle of nerves ∎ A moribund metaphor. *agitated; anxious; eager; edgy; excitable; excited; fidgety; frantic; jittery; jumpy; nervous; ill at ease; on edge; restive; restless; skittish; uncomfortable; uneasy.*

burn a hole in (my) pocket ∎ A moribund metaphor.

burn (your) bridges (behind) (you) ∎ A moribund metaphor.

burning desire ∎ An inescapable pair. *ardor; eagerness; fervor; passion; vehemence; zeal.* • Suppose you sell group insurance to employers, and your prospect has ten employees and a *burning desire* to expand the business. REPLACE WITH *zeal.*

(it) burns (me) up ∎ A moribund metaphor. *acerbate; anger; annoy; bother; bristle; chafe; enrage; incense; inflame; infuriate; irk; irritate; madden; miff; provoke; rile; roil; vex.*

burn the candle at both ends ∎ A moribund metaphor. 1. *drudge; grind; grub; labor; moil; slave; strain; strive; struggle; sweat; toil; travail; work hard.* 2. *debilitate; deplete; drain; empty; enervate; exhaust; fatigue; overdo; overwork; sap; tire; wear out; weary.* 3. *be merry; carouse; carry on; celebrate; debauch; disport; frolic; party; play; revel; riot; roister; rollick; romp; skylark.*

burn the midnight oil ∎ A moribund metaphor. *drudge; grind; grub; labor; moil;*

slave; strain; strive; struggle; sweat; toil; travail; work hard; work long hours. • We are indebted to our wives and families for their patience while we *burned the midnight oil.* REPLACE WITH *worked long hours.*

bursting at the seams ∎ A moribund metaphor. 1. *aflame; agitated; animated; anxious; eager; ebullient; effervescent; enthusiastic; excitable; excited; fervent; fervid; frantic; frenzied; impassioned; impatient; lively; restless; spirited.* **2.** *abounding; brimful; brimming; bursting; chock-full; congested; crammed; crowded; dense; filled; full; gorged; jammed; jam-packed; overcrowded; overfilled; overflowing; packed; replete; saturated; stuffed; swarming; teeming.*

burst on (onto) the scene ∎ A moribund metaphor. *appear; arise; come forth; emerge; occur; originate; present itself; rise; surface; turn up.*

bur under (his) saddle ∎ A moribund metaphor. *affliction; annoyance; bane; bother; burden; curse; difficulty; inconvenience; irritant; irritation; load; nuisance; ordeal; pain; pest; plague; problem; torment; tribulation; trouble; vexation; weight; worry.*

bury (her) head in the sand ∎ A moribund metaphor. *cower; cringe; grovel; quail; recoil; shrink.* • When confronted with negative press, school officials ought not to *bury their heads in the sand.* REPLACE WITH *cower.*

bury the hatchet ∎ A moribund metaphor. *make peace.*

business as usual ∎ A torpid term. • All too many male-dominated workplaces still are doing *business as usual* and denying women equal pay and benefits. • In simple terms, it means *business as usual;* specifically, all business will be conducted today as it was yesterday. SEE ALSO **politics as usual**.

> The tile floor smelled strongly of antiseptic and faintly of cat pee: Business as usual.—Jo-Ann Mapson, *The Wilder Sisters*

business is business ∎ A quack equation.

bust (my) ass ∎ A moribund metaphor. *attempt; drudge; endeavor; essay; exert; grind; grub; labor; moil; slave; strain; strive; struggle; sweat; toil; travail; try; work.*

(as) busy as a beaver ∎ An insipid simile. *assiduous; busy; diligent; grinding; hardworking; indefatigable; industrious; inexhaustible; sedulous; slaving; tireless; toiling; unflagging; unrelenting; untiring.*

(as) busy as a bee ∎ An insipid simile. *assiduous; busy; diligent; grinding; hardworking; indefatigable; industrious; inexhaustible; sedulous; slaving; tireless; toiling; unflagging; unrelenting; untiring.*

butterflies in (her) stomach ∎ A moribund metaphor. 1. *agitated; anxious; eager; edgy; excitable; excited; fidgety; frantic; jittery; jumpy; nervous; ill at ease; on edge; restive; restless; skittish; uncomfortable; uneasy.* 2. *nauseated; nauseous; queasy; sick; squeamish.*

> Richard Ekstrom, the leader of the preliminary investigation, had butterflies in his stomach as he asked his team leader, Inspector Bublanski, to take a seat across from him.—Stieg Larsson, *The Girl Who Kicked the Hornet's Nest*

butter (them) up ∎ A moribund metaphor. *acclaim; applaud; celebrate; commend; compliment; extol; flatter; laud; praise.*

butter wouldn't melt in (her) mouth ∎ A moribund metaphor. *affected; artful; artificial; coy; crafty; cunning; deceitful; dishonest; demure; dissembling; dissimulating; duplicitous; fake; false; false-hearted; feigned; foxy; guileful; insincere; lying; mannered; mendacious; phony; plastic; sly; sneaky; tricky; two-faced; uncandid; underhanded; unfrank; unnatural; untrue; untruthful; wily.*

button (zip) your lip ∎ A moribund metaphor. 1. *be silent; be still; hush; keep quiet; quiet; silence.* 2. *be closed-mouthed; be quiet; be reticent; be silent; be speechless; be taciturn; be uncommunicative.*

buy a pig in a poke ∎ A moribund metaphor.

buy into ∎ A moribund metaphor. *accept; adopt; advocate; affirm; agree to; assent to; back; believe in; endorse; espouse; favor; further; hold; sanction; side with; support.* • When others witness your confidence in an activity, they are more likely to *buy into* your plans of action. REPLACE WITH *back.*

buy the farm ∎ A moribund metaphor. *be deceased; die; expire; perish.*

buy time ∎ A moribund metaphor. *defer; delay; hold off; hold up; postpone; put aside; put off; set aside; shelve; suspend; table; waive.*

by a hair's breadth ∎ A moribund metaphor. *barely; by a little; hardly; just; merely; narrowly; only just; scarcely.*

(won) by a landslide ∎ A moribund metaphor.

by a whisker ∎ A moribund metaphor. *barely; by a little; hardly; just; merely; narrowly; only just; scarcely.*

by fits and starts ∎ A moribund metaphor. *convulsively; erratically; fitfully; intermittently; irregularly; paroxysmally; randomly; spasmodically; sporadically; unevenly.*

by hook or (by) crook ∎ A moribund metaphor. *somehow; someway.*

(growing) by leaps and bounds ▮ A moribund metaphor. *abruptly; apace; briskly; fast; hastily; hurriedly; posthaste; promptly; quickly; rapidly; rashly; speedily; straightaway; swiftly; wingedly.*

by no (not by any) stretch of the imagination ▮ A moribund metaphor. *at no time; by no means; in no way; never; no; not; not at all; not ever; not in any way; not in the least.*

> Rubashov found that by no stretch of his imagination could he picture his neighbor's state of mind, in spite of all his practice in the art of 'thinking through others' minds'.—Arthur Koestler, *Darkness at Noon*

(go; pass) by the board ▮ A moribund metaphor. *abandoned; completed; concluded; disappeared; discarded; done; ended; finished; forfeited; gone (by); lost; over; passed; vanished.* • There was a little rain, sleet, and snow, but all that has *gone by the board.* REPLACE WITH *passed.*

(go) by the book ▮ A moribund metaphor. 1. *correctly; properly; rightly.* 2. *conservatively; conventionally; orthodoxly; predictably; traditionally.* • She's done everything *by the book.* REPLACE WITH *correctly.* • Olson dresses *by the book;* Boies wears black sneakers to court. REPLACE WITH *conservatively.*

by the same token ▮ A wretched redundancy. *also; and; as well; besides; beyond that (this); even; further; furthermore; in addition; likewise; moreover; more than that (this); similarly; still more; too; what is more.*

by the seat of (his) pants ▮ A moribund metaphor. *automatically; by impulse; by instinct; by intuition; by reflex; impulsively; instinctively; intuitively; reflexively; spontaneously; unthinkingly; viscerally.*

by the skin of (his) teeth ▮ A moribund metaphor. *barely; by a little; hardly; just; merely; narrowly; only just; scarcely.*

by the sweat of (his) brow ▮ A moribund metaphor. *arduously; backbreakingly; burdensomely; exhaustingly; fatiguingly; gruelingly; laboriously; onerously; strenuously; toilfully; toilsomely; toughly; wearisomely; with difficulty.*

by virtue of the fact that ▮ A wretched redundancy. *because; considering; for; in that; since.* • There are a lot of people who expect too little *by virtue of the fact that* that's all they've known. REPLACE WITH *because.* SEE ALSO **because of the fact that; considering the fact that; given the fact that; in consideration of the fact that; in view of the fact that; on account of the fact that.**

Cc

call a halt (an end; a stop) to ∎ A wretched redundancy. *cease; close; complete; conclude; derail; discontinue; end; finish; halt; settle; stop.* • Let's *call a halt to* this insanity. REPLACE WITH *end.* SEE ALSO **put a halt (an end; a stop) to**.

call a spade a spade ∎ A moribund metaphor. 1. *be aboveboard; be artless; be candid; be forthright; be frank; be genuine; be guileless; be honest; be ingenuous; be naive; be sincere; be straightforward; be truthful; be veracious; be veridical.* 2. *be blunt; clear; be direct; be explicit; be plain; be specific.*

call into question ∎ A wretched redundancy. *challenge; contradict; dispute; doubt; question.*

call it quits ∎ A moribund metaphor. *abandon; desert; forsake; leave; quit.*

call off the dogs ∎ A moribund metaphor.

call (out) on the carpet ∎ A moribund metaphor. *admonish; animadvert; berate; castigate; censure; chasten; chastise; chide; condemn; criticize; denounce; denunciate; discipline; excoriate; fulminate against; imprecate; impugn; inveigh against; objurgate; punish; rebuke; remonstrate; reprehend; reprimand; reproach; reprobate; reprove; revile; scold; swear at; upbraid; vituperate.* • Popular sentiment indicates that *calling the president on the carpet* is not a labor the people wish to bear. REPLACE WITH *rebuking the president.* • She *called Starr on the carpet* as well, notably for alleged leaks to the press. REPLACE WITH *upbraided Starr.*

callow youth ∎ An inescapable pair. *adolescent; artless; callow; green; guileless; immature; inexperienced; inexpert; ingenuous; innocent; juvenile; naive; raw; simple; undeveloped; unfledged; unskilled; unskillful; unsophisticated; untaught; untrained; unworldly; young; youthful.*

call the plays ∎ A moribund metaphor. *administer; boss; choose; command; control; decide; determine; dictate; direct; dominate; govern; in charge; in command; in control; manage; manipulate; master; order; overpower; oversee; predominate; prevail; reign over; rule; superintend.*

call the shots ∎ A moribund metaphor. *administer; boss; choose; command; control; decide; determine; dictate; direct; dominate; govern; in charge; in command; in control; manage; manipulate; master; order; overpower; oversee; predominate; prevail; reign over; rule; superintend.*

> It's neither true nor fair to say I'm to blame for her predicament, but I have a long history of letting Sylvia call the shots.—Dave King, *The Ha-Ha*

calm, cool, and collected ∎ An infantile phrase. *at ease; calm; collected; composed; controlled; cool; imperturbable; insouciant; nonchalant; placid; poised; relaxed; sedate; self-possessed; serene; tranquil; unemotional; unperturbed; unruffled.* • She seemed so *calm, cool, and collected* in the interview. REPLACE WITH *calm.*

(we) came, (we) saw, (we) conquered ∎ An infantile phrase.

can chew gum and think (walk) at the same time ∎ A moribund metaphor. *be able; be adept; be adroit; be ambidextrous; be capable; be competent; be deft; be dexterous; be nimble; be proficient; be skilled; be skillful.*

candor and frankness ∎ An inescapable pair. *candor; frankness; honesty; openness; sincerity; truth; truthfulness; veracity.*

(you) can (can't) have your cake and eat it too ∎ A popular prescription.

can I ask (tell) you something? ∎ A plebeian sentiment. This is a question asked by the ignorant, by the ill-bred, not the well mannered. • *Can I tell you something?* I don't really like to go out. DELETE *Can I tell you something?* • *Can I ask you something?* Do you want me to give you a check so you can take care of that? DELETE *Can I ask you something?* SEE ALSO **let me ask you something**.

(I) can take it or leave it ∎ An infantile phrase. *apathetic; cool; halfhearted; indifferent; insouciant; languid; laodicean; lukewarm; nonchalant; pococurante; tepid; unenthusiastic.*

(I) can't complain ∎ An infantile phrase. *all right; average; fair; fine; good; mediocre; not bad; passable; pretty good; tolerable; well.*

(we) can't help you if you don't want to be helped ∎ A popular prescription.

(he) can't see beyond (the end of) (his) nose ∎ A moribund metaphor. 1. *blind; eyeless; purblind; shortsighted; sightless; unseeing; unsighted; visionless.* 2. *addleheaded; bovine; cretinous; decerebrate; dense; dull; dull-witted; fatuous; fat-witted; half-witted; harebrained; hebetudinous; idiotic; ignorant;*

imbecilic; incogitant; insensate; mindless; moronic; muddled; nescient; obtuse; phlegmatic; slow; slow-witted; sluggish; thick; torpid; undiscerning; unintelligent; vacuous; witless.

can't see the forest (woods) for the trees ∎ A moribund metaphor. *nearsighted; myopic; purblind; shortsighted.*

> But, like many technical types, he lives and breathes minutiae and can't see the forest for the trees.—Nelson DeMille, *The General's Daughter*

(with) cap (hat) in hand ∎ A moribund metaphor. *deferentially; diffidently; humbly; modestly; respectfully; sheepishly; unassumingly; unpretentiously.*

captain of industry ∎ A moribund metaphor. *administrator; boss; brass; chief; commander; director; executive; foreman; head; headman; leader; manager; master; (high) muckamuck; officer; official; overseer; owner; president; principal; proprietor; superintendent; supervisor.*

capture the attention of ∎ A torpid term. *absorb; attract; beguile; bewitch; captivate; charm; enamor; engage; engross; enrapture; enthrall; entice; entrance; fascinate; mesmerize; occupy.* • The civil rights struggle *captured the attention of* the entire nation. REPLACE WITH *captivated.*

card up (his) sleeve ∎ A moribund metaphor.

(like) carrying coals to Newcastle ∎ An insipid simile. *barren; bootless; effete; feckless; feeble; fruitless; futile; impotent; inadequate; inconsequential; inconsiderable; ineffective; ineffectual; infertile; insignificant; inutile; meaningless; meritless; nugatory; null; of no value; pointless; powerless; profitless; purposeless; redundant; sterile; superfluous; trifling; trivial; unavailing; unimportant; unnecessary; unproductive; unprofitable; unserviceable; unworthy; useless; vain; valueless; weak; worthless.*

carry (his) own weight ∎ A moribund metaphor.

carry the ball ∎ A moribund metaphor.

carry the weight of the world on (my) shoulders ∎ A moribund metaphor.

carte blanche ∎ A foreign phrase.

carved (cast; fixed) in stone ∎ A moribund metaphor. 1. *assured; certain; decided; definite; determined; established; final; firm; fixed; resolved; set; settled; sure.* 2. *changeless; constant; eternal; everlasting; immutable; invariable; irreversible; irrevocable; permanent; rigid; stable; unalterable; unchangeable; unchanging; unending.* • The state's census count is not yet *fixed in stone.* REPLACE WITH *immutable.* • Your choice of per-server or per-seat licensing is not *cast in stone.*

REPLACE WITH *unalterable.*

cash in (their) chips ∎ A moribund metaphor. *be deceased; die; expire; perish.*

cash on the barrel ∎ A moribund metaphor.

cast a shadow over ∎ A moribund metaphor. 1. *becloud; cloak; darken; eclipse; mask; obscure; shroud; veil.* 2. *belittle; confound; degrade; demean; embarrass; humiliate; lower; shame.* SEE ALSO **hang like a cloud (over).**

cast in (our) lot with ∎ A moribund metaphor. *ally; collaborate; comply; concur; conspire; cooperate; join; unite; work together.*

cast into the pot ∎ A moribund metaphor.

castles in Spain (the air) ∎ A moribund metaphor. *apparition; caprice; chimera; delusion; dream; fanciful idea; fancy; fantasy; fluff; frivolity; hallucination; illusion; imagination; maggot; mirage; phantasm; vagary; vision; whim; whimsy.*

cast (his) net ∎ A moribund metaphor.

cast (your) pearls before swine ∎ A moribund metaphor.

cast the first stone ∎ A moribund metaphor.

catalyst for change ∎ A moribund metaphor. • These are the young people who will be the *catalysts for change* in their own communities in the coming decades.

catch as catch can ∎ A moribund metaphor. 1. *aimless; free; irregular; uncontrolled; unplanned.* 2. *by any means; however possible.*

catch (her) eye ∎ A moribund metaphor. *allure; attract; beguile; captivate; charm; enchant; enthrall; entice; fascinate; interest.*

catch forty winks ∎ A moribund metaphor. *doze; go to bed; nap; rest; retire; sleep; slumber.*

> There was one thing Stilton could do that Wally couldn't, and it would give him a nice edge in an hour or so—he could catch forty winks and get down there feeling a damn sight fresher than 'me laddo.'—John Lawton, *Bluffing Mr. Churchill*

catch in the act ∎ A moribund metaphor. *catch; decoy; ensnare; entrap; net; trap.*

catch some z's ∎ A moribund metaphor. *doze; go to bed; nap; rest; retire; sleep; slumber.*

catch the wave ∎ A moribund metaphor.

catch (him) with (his) pants down ∎ A moribund metaphor. *catch unawares; surprise.* • He isn't the first president to be *caught with his pants down*, nor will he be the last.

cat's got (your) tongue ∎ A moribund
metaphor. *be closed-mouthed; be quiet; be
reticent; be silent; be speechless; be taciturn;
be uncommunicative.*

caught in the crossfire ∎ A moribund
metaphor.

> He paused from this pattern only to whisper,
> when an innocent—and I must admit, quite
> plump—regular Joe got caught in the
> crossfire, "That should've been me!"—Marian
> Keyes, *Angels*

caught red-handed ∎ A moribund metaphor.

caught with (her) hand in the cookie
jar ∎ A moribund metaphor.

cautiously optimistic ∎ A torpid term.
*confident; encouraged; heartened; hopeful;
optimistic; rosy; sanguine. Optimistic* is a
perfectly vigorous word, but modified by
cautiously or *guardedly,* as it so often is, it
becomes valueless. *Cautiously optimistic*
is a phrase favored by poltroons and
politicians, most of whom make a point
of devaluing the meaning of their words.
• The retailer was *cautiously optimistic*
about its latest report. DELETE *cautiously.*
• When I realized that CBS was interested,
I became *cautiously optimistic.* REPLACE
WITH *hopeful.* • On the Rhode Island
waterfront, the fishermen are *cautious but
optimistic.* DELETE *but optimistic.* SEE
ALSO **guardedly optimistic**.

cease and desist ∎ An inescapable pair.
cease; desist; end; halt; stop.

celebrity ∎ A suspect superlative. As the
most popular books are sometimes the
least worthy of being read, so the most
public people are sometimes the least
worthy of being known.

If we must acknowledge these
creatures—these *celebrities*—let us better
understand them for who they are. All
dictionary definitions of *celebrity* should
include 1. a mediocrity; a vulgarian; a
coxcomb. 2. a scantly talented person who
through shameless self-aggrandizement
and utter inanity becomes widely known.
3. a repellent person. SEE ALSO **the rich
and famous**.

center around ∎ A wretched redundancy.
center on. • Concern will *center around*
military governments. REPLACE WITH
center on.

center of attention ∎ A suspect superlative.
cynosure. People who seek to be the *center
of attention* are forever peripheral to
themselves.

(take) center stage ∎ A moribund metaphor.

c'est la vie ∎ A foreign phrase. To this
popular French expression of resignation,
there are more than a few English-
language equivalents. SEE ALSO **such is
life; that's how (the way) it goes; that's how
(the way) the ball bounces; that's how (the
way) the cookie crumbles; that's life; that's
life in the big city; that's show biz; what are
you going to do; what can you do**.

chalk it up to experience ∎ A popular
prescription.

champing (chomping) at the bit ∎
A moribund metaphor. *anxious; ardent;
avid; craving; desiring; desirous; eager;
enthusiastic; fervent; fervid; frantic; frenzied;
impassioned; impatient; intent; itching; keen;
longing; pining; ready; vehement; yearning;
zealous.* • State corrections officials were
chomping at the bit to show not only that
the program was tightly managed but
also that it was benefiting offenders and
citizens alike. REPLACE WITH *eager.* • It
leaves me *chomping at the bit* to be able to
do something with these tapes. REPLACE
WITH *longing.*

change (shift; switch) gear ∎ A moribund
metaphor. *alter; begin again; begin anew;
change; convert; improve; metamorphose;
modify; reform; remake; remodel; rethink;
transform.*

> But the very thing I became aware of first
> was that time had shifted gear and was
> vibrating differently, and it was this that was
> the first assault on my own habitual pattern
> of substance.—Doris Lessing, *Briefing for a
> Descent into Hell*

change on a dime ∎ A moribund metaphor.
*be adaptable; be flexible; be malleable; be
versatile.* • He sees AmEx's program as an
example of what the smartest marketers
will be doing: creating rewards programs
that can *change on a dime* based on what
consumers tell them. REPLACE WITH *be
flexible.*

changing of the guard ∎ A moribund
metaphor.

charity begins at home ∎ A popular
prescription.

chart a new course ∎ A moribund metaphor.

cheap shot ∎ A moribund metaphor.

cheek by jowl ∎ A moribund metaphor.
*attached; close; inseparable; intimate; side
by side.*

chew (her) out ∎ A moribund metaphor.
*admonish; animadvert; belittle; berate;
castigate; censure; chasten; chastise; chide;
condemn; criticize; denounce; denunciate;
discipline; excoriate; fulminate against;
imprecate; impugn; inveigh against;
objurgate; punish; rebuke; remonstrate;
reprehend; reprimand; reproach; reprobate;
reprove; revile; scold; swear at; upbraid;
vituperate.*

chew the cud ∎ A moribund metaphor. *brood;
cerebrate; cogitate; consider; contemplate;
deliberate; excogitate; meditate; ponder;
reflect; ruminate; think.*

chew the fat (rag) ∎ A moribund metaphor. *babble; blab; cackle; chaffer; chat; chitchat; chatter; confabulate; converse; gossip; jabber; palaver; prate; prattle; rattle; talk.*

(that's) chicken feed ∎ A moribund metaphor. *frivolous; immaterial; inconsequential; inconsiderable; inferior; insignificant; minor; negligible; niggling; nugatory; petty; secondary; trifling; trivial; unimportant; worthless.*

chicken-or-egg (question) ∎ A moribund metaphor.

children should be seen and not heard ∎ A popular prescription.

(that's) child's play ∎ A moribund metaphor. *apparent; basic; clear; clear-cut; conspicuous; distinct; easily done; easy; effortless; elementary; evident; explicit; facile; limpid; lucid; manifest; obvious; patent; pellucid; plain; simple; simplicity itself; straightforward; translucent; transparent; unambiguous; uncomplex; uncomplicated; understandable; unequivocal; unmistakable.*

> This was child's play for him, and he got a dollar and seventy-five cents a day for it ….—Upton Sinclair, *The Jungle*

chill to the bone (marrow) ∎ A moribund metaphor. 1. *chill; cool; freeze; ice; refrigerate.* 2. *alarm; appall; benumb; daunt; frighten; horrify; intimidate; panic; paralyze; petrify; scare; shock; startle; terrify; terrorize.*

> The mere sight of that medley of wet nakedness chilled him to the bone.—James Joyce, *A Portrait of the Artist as a Young Man*

chink in (his) armor ∎ A moribund metaphor. *defect; deficiency; disadvantage; failing; fault; flaw; foible; fragility; frailness; frailty; handicap; limitation; shortcoming; susceptibility; susceptibleness; vulnerability; vulnerableness; weakness.*

chip on (her) shoulder ∎ A moribund metaphor. *animosity; bitterness; enmity; grievance; grudge; hostility; indignation; ill will; offense; rancor; resentment; spite; umbrage.*

chock full (of) ∎ A torpid term. *abounding; brimful; brimming; bursting; congested; crammed; crowded; dense; filled; full; gorged; jammed; jam-packed; overcrowded; overfilled; packed; replete; saturated; stuffed; swarming; teeming.* • Usually, when a new version of a computer operating system is released, it's *chock-full of* new features designed to make your tech life easier. REPLACE WITH *replete with.*

chrome dome ∎ An infantile phrase. *alopecic; bald; baldheaded; baldpated; glabrous; hairless; depilated; pilgarlic; smooth; tonsured.*

Cinderella story ∎ A moribund metaphor. *dream; fantasy.*

(as) clean as a hound's tooth ∎ An insipid simile. *antiseptic; clean; cleansed; disinfected; germ-free; hygienic; immaculate; sanitary; sanitized; scoured; scrubbed; spotless; stainless; sterile; unblemished; unsoiled; unspotted; unsullied; untarnished; washed.*

(as) clean as a whistle ∎ An insipid simile. *antiseptic; clean; cleansed; disinfected; germ-free; hygienic; immaculate; sanitary; sanitized; scoured; scrubbed; spotless; stainless; sterile; unblemished; unsoiled; unspotted; unsullied; untarnished; washed.*

clean bill of health ∎ A moribund metaphor. *blooming; doing well; energetic; fit; flourishing; good; hale; hardy; healthful; healthy; hearty; robust; sound; strong; vigorous; well; well-off.*

clean (his) clock ∎ A moribund metaphor. 1. *assail; assault; attack; batter; beat; cudgel; flagellate; flog; hit; lambaste; lash; lick; mangle; pound; pummel; strike; thrash; trounce.* 2. *beat; conquer; crush; defeat; outdo; overcome; overpower; overwhelm; prevail; quell; rout; succeed; triumph; trounce; vanquish; win.*

cleanliness is next to godliness ∎ A popular prescription.

clear a (major) hurdle ∎ A moribund metaphor. • The proposed sale and redevelopment of Lafayette Place *cleared a final hurdle* yesterday.

(as) clear as a bell ∎ An insipid simile. *audible; clarion; clear; distinct; plain; pure; sharp.*

(as) clear as crystal ∎ An insipid simile. *apparent; basic; clear; clear-cut; conspicuous; crystalline; distinct; easily done; easy; effortless; elementary; evident; explicit; facile; limpid; lucid; manifest; obvious; patent; pellucid; plain; simple; simplicity itself; straightforward; translucent; transparent; unambiguous; uncomplex; uncomplicated; understandable; unequivocal; unmistakable.*

(as) clear as day ∎ An insipid simile. *apparent; basic; clear; clear-cut; conspicuous; crystalline; distinct; easily done; easy; effortless; elementary; evident; explicit; facile; limpid; lucid; manifest; obvious; patent; pellucid; plain; simple; simplicity itself; straightforward; translucent; transparent; unambiguous; uncomplex; uncomplicated; understandable; unequivocal; unmistakable.*

(as) clear as mud ∎ An insipid simile. *ambiguous; blurred; blurry; cloudy; dim; fuzzy; hazy; indistinct; muddy; murky; nebulous; obfuscatory; obscure; opaque; unclear; vague.*

clear sailing ∎ A moribund metaphor. *apparent; basic; clear; clear-cut; conspicuous; distinct; easily done; easy; effortless;*

elementary; evident; explicit; facile; limpid; lucid; manifest; obvious; patent; pellucid; plain; simple; simplicity itself; straightforward; translucent; transparent; unambiguous; uncomplex; uncomplicated; understandable; unequivocal; unmistakable.

clear the air ∎ A moribund metaphor.

clear the decks ∎ A moribund metaphor.

clench like a fist ∎ A moribund metaphor. *clench; stiffen; tense; tighten.*

> I felt my body, my whole body, tense and clench as if it was a fist.—Gregory David Roberts, *Shantaram*

climbing the walls ∎ A moribund metaphor. *agitated; anxious; eager; edgy; excitable; excited; fidgety; frantic; jittery; jumpy; nervous; ill at ease; on edge; restive; restless; skittish; uncomfortable; uneasy.*

climb (move up) the ladder (of success) ∎ A moribund metaphor. *advance; flourish; progress; prosper; rise; succeed.*

clinging vine ∎ A moribund metaphor. (SEE) *clinging; dependent; subject; subordinate; subservient.*

cling like a limpet ∎ An insipid simile. *adhere; affix; attach; bind; cleave; cling; cohere; connect; fasten; fuse; hitch; hold; join; stick.*

clip (her) wings ∎ A moribund metaphor. *abase; chasten; debase; decrease; deflate; degrade; demean; depreciate; depress; diminish; disgrace; dishonor; embarrass; humble; humiliate; lower; mortify; puncture; shame.*

close (near) at hand ∎ A moribund metaphor. *accessible; at hand; close; close by; handy; near; nearby; neighboring; vicinal.*

close but no cigar ∎ An infantile phrase. *almost; just about; nearly.*

close (his) eyes to ∎ A moribund metaphor. *discount; disregard; ignore; snub.*

closely allied ∎ An inescapable pair.

closely guarded secret ∎ A torpid term.

> Each year He returned and incarnated Himself in a different leading citizen whose identity was always a closely guarded secret, and with His nondenominational mysteries He brought a playful glamour to the city.— Jonathan Franzen, *The Twenty-Seventh City*

close scrutiny ∎ An inescapable pair.

close (shut) the door on (to) ∎ A moribund metaphor. *ban; banish; bar; block; disallow; dismiss; eliminate; exclude; hinder; ignore; impede; obstruct; preclude; prevent; prohibit; proscribe; reject; rule out.*

clothes make the man ∎ A popular prescription.

clutch (grasp) at straws ∎ A moribund metaphor.

cock of the walk ∎ A moribund metaphor. *administrator; boss; brass; chief; commander; director; executive; foreman; head; headman; leader; magnate; manager; master; mogul; (high) muckamuck; notable; officer; official; overseer; patrician; personage; president; principal; ruler; superintendent; supervisor.*

cog in the wheel ∎ A moribund metaphor. *aide; apparatchik; assistant; cog; dependent; drudge; flunky; helper; hireling; inferior; junior; minion; secondary; servant; slave; subaltern; subordinate; underling; vassal.*

cold and calculating ∎ An inescapable pair.

> There was something cold and calculating about Elizabeth, small as she was.—Muriel Maddox, *Llantarnam*

(as) cold as a witch's tit ∎ An insipid simile. *algid; arctic; brumal; chilly; cold; cool; freezing; frigid; frosty; frozen; gelid; glacial; hibernal; hyperborean; ice-cold; icy; nippy; polar; rimy; wintry.*

(as) cold as ice ∎ An insipid simile. *algid; arctic; brumal; chilly; cold; cool; freezing; frigid; frosty; frozen; gelid; glacial; hibernal; hyperborean; ice-cold; icy; nippy; polar; rimy; wintry.*

(as) cold as marble ∎ An insipid simile. *algid; arctic; brumal; chilly; cold; cool; freezing; frigid; frosty; frozen; gelid; glacial; hibernal; hyperborean; ice-cold; icy; nippy; polar; rimy; wintry.*

cold enough to freeze the balls off a brass monkey ∎ A moribund metaphor. *algid; arctic; brumal; chilly; cold; cool; freezing; frigid; frosty; frozen; gelid; glacial; hibernal; hyperborean; ice-cold; icy; nippy; polar; rimy; wintry.*

(get) cold feet ∎ A moribund metaphor. *afraid; alarmed; apprehensive; cowardly; craven; diffident; fearful; frightened; pavid; pusillanimous; recreant; scared; timid; timorous; tremulous.* • When the woman heard that the story opened with the theft of the godparents' guns, she *got cold feet.* DELETE *became apprehensive.*

cold fish ∎ A moribund metaphor. *apathetic; callous; chilly; cold; cool; detached; dispassionate; distant; emotionless; frigid; glacial; hard; hardhearted; harsh; heartless; hostile; icy; impassive; indifferent; passionless; pitiless; reserved; unconcerned; unemotional; unfeeling; unfriendly; unresponsive.*

cold turkey ∎ A moribund metaphor.

collaborate together ∎ A wretched redundancy. *collaborate.* • Staff from the American and European sides *collaborate together* to make the journey and the home stay a rewarding experience. DELETE *together.*

collect (gather) dust ∎ A moribund metaphor. *fallow; idle; in abeyance; inactive; inoperative; set aside; unoccupied; unused.*

combine together ∎ A wretched redundancy. *combine.* • Look at each reviewer's comments separately or *combine* them *together* for a consolidated view. DELETE *together.*

come around ∎ A moribund metaphor. *agree; consent; feel as (we) do; support (us); think as (I) think.* • We believe that in the end the public is going to *come around.* REPLACE WITH *support us.*

come back to haunt ∎ A moribund metaphor. *haunt; recoil on; redound on; return to; revisit.*

> If Maggie Feller had learned one thing in her fourteen years of dealing with members of the opposite sex, it was this: your bad hookups will always come back to haunt you.—Jennifer Weiner, *In Her Shoes*

come clean ∎ A moribund metaphor. *acknowledge; admit; affirm; allow; avow; be forthright; be frank; be honest; be sincere; be straightforward; be truthful; be veracious; concede; confess; disclose; divulge; expose; grant; own; reveal; tell; uncover; unearth; unveil.* • It is time for the president to *come clean.* REPLACE WITH *be forthright.*

come forward (with) ∎ A moribund metaphor. *advance; broach; introduce; offer; present; propose; propound; submit; suggest; tender.* • Nobody has *come forward with* a good argument for any way to create more jobs and raise the incomes of working people without expanding trade. REPLACE WITH *proposed.* SEE ALSO **put forward.**

come full circle ∎ A moribund metaphor.

come hell or high water ∎ A moribund metaphor. *no matter what; regardless.*

(chickens) come home to roost ∎ A moribund metaphor.

come in from the cold ∎ A moribund metaphor. • Alternative medicine is *coming in from the cold.* REPLACE WITH *gaining respectability.*

(doesn't know enough to) come in out of the rain ∎ A moribund metaphor. 1. *addlebrained; addleheaded; addlepated; Boeotian; bovine; brainless; clueless; cretinous; decerebrate; dense; dim-witted; doltish; dull; dumb; dunderheaded; empty-headed; fatuous; fat-witted; harebrained; hebetudinous; ignorant; imbecilic; incogitant; insensate; ludicrous; mindless; moronic; muddled; nescient; obtuse; oxlike; phlegmatic; slow-witted; sluggish; stupid; torpid; unaware; unintelligent; unknowing; vacuous; witless.* 2. *adolescent; artless; callow; green; guileless; immature; inexperienced; inexpert; ingenuous; innocent; juvenile; naive; raw; simple; undeveloped; unfledged; unskilled; unskillful; unsophisticated; untaught; untrained; unworldly; young; youthful.*

> The little twerps haven't had sense enough to come in out of the rain, because Ariel can still hear their burps and the sounds of their voices, but not (as though she cares!) what they are saying to each other.—Pamela Carter Joern, *The Floor of the Sky*

come in through the back door ∎ A moribund metaphor.

come knocking (on my door) ∎ A moribund metaphor.

come on like gangbusters ∎ An insipid simile. 1. *assertive; commanding; dynamic; emphatic; energetic; forceful; intense; mighty; potent; powerful; strong; vehement; vigorous; virile.* 2. *authoritarian; authoritative; autocratic; bossy; despotic; dictatorial; dogmatic; domineering; imperious; iron-handed; lordly; overbearing; peremptory; tyrannical.*

come on strong ∎ A moribund metaphor. 1. *assertive; commanding; dynamic; emphatic; energetic; forceful; intense; mighty; potent; powerful; strong; vehement; vigorous; virile.* 2. *authoritarian; authoritative; autocratic; bossy; despotic; dictatorial; dogmatic; domineering; imperious; iron-handed; lordly; overbearing; peremptory; tyrannical.*

come out in the wash ∎ A moribund metaphor.

come out of left field ∎ A moribund metaphor. *be shocking; be startling; be surprising.* • His departure really *came out of left field.* REPLACE WITH *was surprising.*

come out of the closet ∎ A moribund metaphor.

come (crawl) out of the woodwork ∎ A moribund metaphor.

come out (up) smelling like a rose ∎ An insipid simile.

come out swinging ∎ A moribund metaphor. *aggressive; antagonistic; battling; bellicose; belligerent; combative; fighting; militant; pugnacious; truculent; warlike.*

comes (goes) with the territory (turf) ∎ A moribund metaphor. *is expected; is inescapable; is inevitable; is necessary; is unavoidable.* • He's got to understand that these questions *go with the territory.* REPLACE WITH *are inevitable.*

come to a boil ∎ A moribund metaphor. *cap; climax; conclude; consummate; crest; crown; culminate; peak.*

come to a close (a halt; an end; a stop) ∎ A wretched redundancy. *cease; close; complete; conclude; derail; discontinue; end; finish; halt; settle; stop; terminate.* • The days of easy credit, strong liquidity, and speculation are *coming to a close*. REPLACE WITH *ending*. SEE ALSO **bring to a close (a halt; an end; a stop); come to a screeching halt; grind to a halt**.

come to (find) a happy medium ∎ A moribund metaphor. *compromise*.

come to a head ∎ A moribund metaphor. *cap; climax; conclude; consummate; crest; crown; culminate; peak*.

come to a screeching halt ∎ A moribund metaphor. *cease; close; complete; conclude; derail; discontinue; end; finish; halt; settle; stop; terminate*. • It might be easier said than done, but if it doesn't change, and soon, the Cup run might *come to a screeching halt*. REPLACE WITH *end*. SEE ALSO **bring to a close (a halt; an end; a stop); grind to a halt**.

come to blows ∎ A moribund metaphor. *battle; brawl; clash; fight; grapple; jostle; make war; scuffle; skirmish; tussle; war; wrestle; wrangle*.

> Winnie said she believed at that moment it would come to blows, though she had never seen a man strike a woman, nor a woman strike a man for that matter.—Beth Gutcheon, *More Than You Know*

come to find out ∎ An infantile phrase. *ascertain; determine; discern; discover; find out; learn; realize*.

come to grips with ∎ A moribund metaphor. *accept; comprehend; cope with; deal with; face; handle; struggle with; understand*.

come to light ∎ A moribund metaphor. *appears; becomes apparent; becomes known; becomes visible; emerges; materializes; shows; surfaces*.

come to pass ∎ A moribund metaphor. *befall; come about; happen; occur; result; take place*.

come to terms with ∎ A torpid term. *accept; comprehend; cope with; deal with; face; handle; struggle with; understand*.

come to the end of the line (road) ∎ A moribund metaphor.

come up empty (handed) ∎ A moribund metaphor. *find nothing*.

come up roses ∎ A moribund metaphor.

(as) comfortable as an old shoe ∎ An insipid simile. *comfortable; cosy; habitable; homey; inhabitable; livable; safe; snug*.

coming (falling) apart at the seams ∎ A moribund metaphor. *breaking down; collapsing; crumbling; decaying; decomposing; degenerating; deteriorating; disintegrating; dissipating; dissolving; dying; ending; fading; failing; unraveling*. • How do you hold it together at work when your life is *coming apart at the seams*? REPLACE WITH *disintegrating*. • For the last year and a half it seems the world economy has been *coming apart at the seams*. REPLACE WITH *unraveling*.

(as) common as dirt ∎ An insipid simile. *average; basic; common; commonplace; customary; everyday; normal; omnipresent; ordinary; prevalent; quotidian; regular; standard; typical; ubiquitous; unexceptional; universal; unremarkable; usual; widespread; workaday*.

common courtesy ∎ A suspect superlative. If this expression is not heard as often as it once was, it's because courtesy is today not so common.

Genuine expressions of courtesy such as *please* and *thank you* (SEE) and *you're welcome* have been usurped by glib ones such as *have a nice day* and *I appreciate it* and *no problem*.

What's more, a vapid phrase like *how goes it* (SEE), or a vulgar one like *hey* (SEE), is more popular than an authentic *hello*.

The worsening of our speech accompanies the withering of our souls. SEE ALSO **(I) appreciate (it); have a good (nice) day (evening)**.

compare and contrast ∎ A wretched redundancy. *compare; contrast*. • Competition is essential to enable consumers to *compare and contrast* alternatives. REPLACE WITH *compare* or *contrast*.

(as) compared to what? ∎ An infantile phrase. SEE ALSO **everything's (it's all) relative; (as) opposed to what?**.

complete and utter ∎ A wretched redundancy. *absolute; compleat; complete; consummate; deadly; outright; perfect; thorough; thoroughgoing; total; unmitigated; unqualified; utter*. • She may be my boss, but she is also a *complete and utter* fool. REPLACE WITH *complete*.

component part ∎ A wretched redundancy. *component; part*. • Denial is a *component part* of dying. REPLACE WITH *component* or *part*.

comrades in arms ∎ A moribund metaphor.

concerted effort ∎ An inescapable pair.

conflicted ∎ A torpid term. *Conflicted* is a perfectly silly choice of words. It's as if to say having conflicting feelings about something—as common as that is—is more than that, more complicated or less explicable, and only a psychological-sounding term might adequately convey this.

People indefatigably mimic one another; *conflicted*, like so many other ridiculously popular terms, would have less appeal if people were more confident and inclined to think for themselves.

• Many such parents *feel conflicted* about segregating their children in special classes but think they have no alternative. REPLACE WITH *have conflicting feelings*.
• The single most important element to

a successful production of *Julius Caesar* is to see Brutus as a truly honorable, yet *conflicted* soul whose actions belie his intentions. REPLACE WITH *torn*. • My guess is that you have underlying and perhaps, *conflicted* feelings about the way this change occurred. REPLACE WITH *conflicting*.

And some people use *conflicted* to mean war-torn or embattled. • RONCO involvement in humanitarian demining in *conflicted* countries evolves from 20 years experience with worldwide development and humanitarian assistance contracts. REPLACE WITH *embattled*. • The war on drugs cannot alone explain why the U.S. is sending 60 Black Hawk and Huey helicopters to this *conflicted* nation. REPLACE WITH *war-torn*.

connect together ∎ A wretched redundancy. *connect*. • The next step was to *connect* these systems *together* into a system called APRS. DELETE *together*.

consensus of opinion ∎ A wretched redundancy. *consensus*. • The *consensus of opinion* is that newspaper endorsements are momentum builders. REPLACE WITH *consensus*.

considering the fact that ∎ A wretched redundancy. *because; considering; for; in that; since; when*. • I don't see how you can say you're not a prostitute *considering the fact that* you are paid for your time. REPLACE WITH *when*. SEE ALSO **because of the fact that; by virtue of the fact that; given the fact that; in consideration of the fact that; in view of the fact that; on account of the fact that**.

conspicuous by (his) absence ∎ A torpid term. • If I didn't sing about what I was going through, it would have been *conspicuous by its absence*.

contact ∎ An overworked word. *ask; call; inform; phone; query; question; reach; speak to; talk to; tell; write to*.

continue on ∎ A wretched redundancy. *continue*. • We're going to *continue on* with more of this. DELETE *on*.

continuing refrain ∎ An inescapable pair.

contrary to popular belief (opinion) ∎ A torpid term. • *Contrary to popular opinion*, a strong dollar does not attract foreign investment to U.S. stocks but to U.S. bonds.

conventional wisdom ∎ A suspect superlative. • Washington is in thrall at the moment to two competing *conventional wisdoms*.

conversation piece ∎ A plebeian sentiment. This is an annoying little term. That people might need an object whose purpose is mainly to stimulate conversation reveals just how infertile, just how fallow, our minds are.

convicted felon ∎ A wretched redundancy. *felon*. • You were a deputy sheriff and now you're a *convicted felon*? DELETE *convicted*.

cook (his) goose ∎ A moribund metaphor. 1. *afflict; blight; damage; impair; spoil; upset.* 2. *annihilate; assassinate; butcher; demolish; destroy; devastate; eradicate; exterminate; kill; massacre; murder; obliterate; pulverize; rack; ravage; raze; ruin; shatter; slaughter; slay; smash; undo; wrack; wreck.*

cooking the books ∎ A moribund metaphor. *deceit; deception; fraud.* • He engaged in a scheme of *cooking the books* to make his turn-around look real. REPLACE WITH *fraud*.

cook the books ∎ A moribund metaphor. *embezzle; falsify; peculate; pilfer; steal.*

(as) cool as a cucumber ∎ An insipid simile. *at ease; calm; collected; composed; controlled; cool; imperturbable; insouciant; nonchalant; placid; poised; relaxed; sedate; self-possessed; serene; tranquil; unemotional; unperturbed; unruffled.*

I'll be as cool as a cucumber, she decided, puzzling over the origin of that expression. Why a cucumber? Why not "cool as a carrot" Or "cool as a cabbage"? How about "cool as a corpse"?—Joy Fielding, *Lost*

cool customer ∎ A moribund metaphor. *at ease; calm; collected; composed; controlled; cool; imperturbable; insouciant; nonchalant; placid; poised; relaxed; sedate; self-possessed; serene; tranquil; unemotional; unperturbed; unruffled.*

cool (your) heels ∎ A moribund metaphor. *be patient; hold on; relax; wait.*

cooperate together ∎ A wretched redundancy. *cooperate*. • It's important that we *cooperate together* in order to resolve our problems. DELETE *together*.

cost a pretty penny ∎ A moribund metaphor. *costly; dear; expensive; high-priced; precious; priceless; valuable.*

(I) could (should) write a book ∎ A plebeian sentiment. If all those who proclaim *I could write a book*—or all those who are advised *You should write a book*—were to do so, we would be immersed (more than we already are) in the vengeful, petty, or everyday lamentations of hollow-headed homemakers, shameless celebrities, and failed or forgotten businesspeople. • *I could write a book* about the way parents pay high prices in raising a disabled child.

count (pinch) (my) pennies ∎ A moribund metaphor. *be cheap; be economical; be frugal; be miserly; be niggardly; be parsimonious; be stingy; be thrifty.*

course of action ∎ A wretched redundancy. *action; course; direction; intention; method;*

cover all the bases

move; plan; policy; procedure; route; scheme; strategy.

cover all the bases ∎ A moribund metaphor. *be comprehensive; be detailed; be exhaustive; be exacting; be fastidious; be methodical; be meticulous; be painstaking; be scrupulous; be systematic; be thorough; be thoroughgoing.*

> Delorme liked to do all the footwork, cover all the bases, and keep her supplementary reports up to the minute.—Giles Blunt, *By the Time You Read This*

cover a lot of ground ∎ A moribund metaphor.

cover (his) tracks ∎ A moribund metaphor.

crack the whip ∎ A moribund metaphor. 1. *bully; coerce; intimidate; menace; terrorize; threaten.* 2. *castigate; chastise; discipline; penalize; punish.*

crap shoot ∎ A moribund metaphor.

crash and burn ∎ A moribund metaphor. *be unsuccessful; bomb; break down; collapse; fail; fall short; falter; fizzle; flop; fold; founder; mess up; miscarry; misfire; not succeed; stumble; topple.*

(as) crazy as a coot ∎ An insipid simile. *batty; cracked; crazy; daft; demented; deranged; fey; foolish; goofy; insane; lunatic; mad; maniacal; neurotic; nuts; nutty; psychotic; raving; silly; squirrelly; touched; unbalanced; unhinged; unsound; wacky; zany.*

(as) crazy as a loon ∎ An insipid simile. *batty; cracked; crazy; daft; demented; deranged; fey; foolish; goofy; insane; lunatic; mad; maniacal; neurotic; nuts; nutty; psychotic; raving; silly; squirrelly; touched; unbalanced; unhinged; unsound; wacky; zany.*

> She was quite put out with him, it seemed, or else she was making her mind up that he was crazy as a loon—one of the two.— Barbara Kingsolver, *Prodigal Summer*

crazy like a fox ∎ An insipid simile. *artful; cagey; clever; conniving; crafty; cunning; foxy; guileful; shifty; shrewd; sly; smart; subtle; tricky; wily.*

crème de la crème ∎ A foreign phrase. *best; brightest; choice; choicest; elite; excellent; finest; first-class; first-rate; foremost; greatest; highest; matchless; nonpareil; optimal; optimum; outstanding; paramount; peerless; preeminent; premium; prominent; select; superior; superlative; top; unequaled; unexcelled; unmatched; unrivaled; unsurpassed.* • But I have the *crème de la crème* of celebrity users. REPLACE WITH *foremost.* • The following list contains the *crème de la crème* of online record retailers. REPLACE WITH *best.*

crisis ∎ An overworked word. We have a "crisis" for all occurrences. For example: *career crisis; crisis in the making; crisis in values; crisis of confidence; crisis proportions; crisis situation; crisis stage; current crisis; economic crisis; educational crisis; energy crisis; extinction crisis; family crisis; financial crisis; fiscal crisis; identity crisis; mid-life crisis; moral crisis; mounting crisis; national crisis; political crisis;* and even, incomprehensibly, *severe crisis.*

Surely, some of these crises are less than that. The terms we use to characterize events and emotions largely decide how we react to them. SEE ALSO **devastate**.

(shed) crocodile tears ∎ A moribund metaphor.

(as) crooked as a dog's hind legs ∎ An insipid simile.

(as) cross as a bear ∎ An insipid simile. *angry; bad-tempered; bilious; cantankerous; choleric; churlish; crabby; cranky; cross; curmudgeonly; disagreeable; dyspeptic; grouchy; gruff; grumpy; ill-humored; ill-tempered; irascible; irritable; mad; peevish; petulant; quarrelsome; short-tempered; splenetic; surly; testy; vexed.*

cross (my) fingers ∎ A moribund metaphor. *hope for; pray for; think positively; wish.*

cross (my) heart and hope to die ∎ A moribund metaphor. *affirm; asseverate; assert; attest; aver; avow; declare; pledge; promise; swear; testify; vow; warrant.*

cross swords ∎ A moribund metaphor. 1. *altercate; argue; disagree; dispute; feud; fight; quarrel; spat; squabble; wrangle.* 2. *battle; brawl; clash; fight; grapple; jostle; make war; scuffle; skirmish; tussle; war; wrestle.*

(we'll) cross that bridge when (we) come to it ∎ A moribund metaphor.

cross the line ∎ A moribund metaphor.

cross the Rubicon ∎ A moribund metaphor.

cross to bear ∎ A moribund metaphor. *affliction; burden; charge; cross; difficulty; encumbrance; hardship; hindrance; impediment; load; obstacle; obstruction; onus; oppression; ordeal; problem; trial; trouble; weight.*

crush like a bug ∎ An insipid simile. 1. *annihilate; assassinate; butcher; destroy; exterminate; kill; massacre; murder; slaughter; slay.* 2. *beat; conquer; crush; defeat; outdo; overcome; overpower; overwhelm; prevail; quell; rout; succeed; triumph; trounce; vanquish; win.*

> It was entirely possible that one song could destroy your life. Yes, musical doom could fall on a lone human form and crush it like a bug.—Jonathan Lethem, *The Fortress of Solitude*

cry (weep) like a baby ∎ An insipid simile. *cry; howl; shriek; sob; ululate; wail; weep; whimper; whine.*

> The next morning she found him gathering eggs in the henhouse, weeping like a baby.— Jennifer Haigh, *Baker Towers*

cry over spilt milk ∎ A moribund metaphor. *lament; mourn; sulk.*

crystal clear ∎ A moribund metaphor. *apparent; basic; clear; clear-cut; conspicuous; crystalline; distinct; easily done; easy; effortless; elementary; evident; explicit; facile; limpid; lucid; manifest; obvious; patent; pellucid; plain; simple; simplicity itself; straightforward; translucent; transparent; unambiguous; uncomplex; uncomplicated; understandable; unequivocal; unmistakable.* • What seems *crystal clear* to you, and perhaps to others, is not all that obvious to me. REPLACE WITH *obvious.*

cry (say) uncle ∎ A moribund metaphor. *abdicate; accede; acquiesce; bow; capitulate; cede; concede; give in; give up; quit; relinquish; retreat; submit; succumb; surrender; yield.*

cry wolf ∎ A moribund metaphor.

(not) (her) cup of tea ∎ A moribund metaphor. *bent; choice; leaning; pick; inclination; predilection; preference; propensity; tendency.* • Choosing a logo and letterhead design from a catalog may not be everyone's *cup of tea.* REPLACE WITH *preference.*

> In any case, Edwin always felt that Norman was more Marcia's friend than he was, more her cup of tea if anyone was.—Barbara Pym, *Quartet in Autumn*

curiosity killed the cat ∎ A popular prescription.

curse a blue streak ∎ A moribund metaphor. *anathematize; blaspheme; condemn; curse; cuss; damn; defile; desecrate; excoriate; execrate; fulminate; imprecate; swear at.*

cushion the blow ∎ A moribund metaphor. • We think that will help *cushion the blow* for some people.

cut and dried (dry) ∎ A moribund metaphor. 1. *common; commonplace; customary; everyday; normal; ordinary; quotidian; regular; routine; standard; typical; usual.* 2. *banal; bland; boring; deadly; dry; dull; everyday; flat; humdrum; insipid; jejune; lifeless; lusterless; mediocre; monotonous; prosaic; stale; tedious; tiresome; unexciting; uninteresting; vapid; watered-down.*

cut a rug ∎ A moribund metaphor. *dance.*

cut (her) dead ∎ A moribund metaphor. *disregard; ignore; snub.*

(as) cute as a button ∎ An insipid simile. *appealing; attractive; beautiful; becoming; captivating; comely; cute; dazzling; exquisite; fair; fetching; good-looking; gorgeous; handsome; lovely; nice-looking; pleasing; pretty; pulchritudinous; radiant; ravishing; seemly; stunning.*

cut (them) off at the pass ∎ A moribund metaphor.

cut off (my) nose to spite (my) face ∎ A moribund metaphor.

cut (its) own throat ∎ A moribund metaphor.

cut (her) teeth (on) ∎ A moribund metaphor. • Case majored in political science at Williams College and *cut his teeth* as a marketing executive at PepsiCo Inc. and Procter & Gamble.

cut the legs out from under ∎ A moribund metaphor.

cut the mustard ∎ A moribund metaphor. *fare well; flourish; meet expectations; prevail; progress; prosper; succeed; thrive; triumph; win.*

cutthroat competition ∎ An inescapable pair.

cut through red tape ∎ A moribund metaphor.

(the) cutting edge ∎ A moribund metaphor. *advanced; ground-breaking; innovative; inventive; new; original; pioneering; progressive; radical; revolutionary; unconventional.*

cut to pieces ∎ A moribund metaphor. 1. *annihilate; assassinate; butcher; destroy; exterminate; kill; massacre; murder; slaughter; slay.* 2. *beat; conquer; crush; defeat; outdo; overcome; overpower; overwhelm; prevail; quell; rout; succeed; triumph; trounce; vanquish; win.*

cut (costs) to the bone ∎ A moribund metaphor.

cut (stung) to the quick ∎ A moribund metaphor. *affront; crush; dash; devastate; hurt; injure; insult; offend; outrage; shatter; slap; slight; upset; wound.*

(could) cut (it) with a knife ∎ A moribund metaphor.

> Amid Grandfather and I was a silence you could cut with a scimitar.—Jonathan Safran Foer, *Everything Is Illuminated*

Dd

damaged goods ∎ A moribund metaphor.

dancing in the aisles (streets) ∎ A moribund metaphor. *be merry; carouse; carry on; celebrate; debauch; disport; frolic; party; play; revel; riot; roister; rollick; romp; skylark.*

(her) day in court ∎ A moribund metaphor.

day in (and) day out ∎ A moribund metaphor. *ceaseless; constant; continual; continuous; daily; diurnal; endless; eternal; everlasting; evermore; every day; frequent; interminable; nonstop; permanent; perpetual; persistent; recurrent; regular; repeated; unceasing; unremitting.*

> And the day in, day out routine of school— was that a sham, too, a cunning deception perpetrated to soften us up with rational expectations and foster nonsensical feelings of trust?—Philip Roth, *The Plot Against America*

day (moment) in the sun ∎ A moribund metaphor.

> I guess maybe my brother had his moment in the sun for the four years he was alive before Kate got diagnosed, but ever since then, we've been too busy looking over our shoulders to run headlong into growing up.—Jodi Picoult, *My Sister's Keeper*

days of wine and roses ∎ An infantile phrase.

dead and buried ∎ An inescapable pair. *ceased; completed; concluded; dead; deceased; defunct; done; ended; exanimate; expired; extinct; extinguished; finished; gone; inanimate; lifeless; no more; over; past; perished; stopped; terminated.*

dead and gone ∎ A wretched redundancy. *ceased; completed; concluded; dead; deceased; defunct; done; ended; exanimate; expired; extinct; extinguished; finished; gone; inanimate; lifeless; no more; over; past; perished; stopped; terminated.*

> Instead, they returned to Ireland when I was four, my brother, Malachy, three, the twins, Oliver and Eugene, barely one, and my sister, Margaret, dead and gone.—Frank McCourt, *Angela's Ashes*

(as) dead as a dodo ∎ An insipid simile. 1. *ceased; completed; concluded; dead; deceased; defunct; done; ended; exanimate; expired; extinct; extinguished; finished; gone; inanimate; lifeless; no more; over; perished; stopped; terminated.* 2. *antediluvian; antiquated; archaic; dead; obsolescent; obsolete; old; old-fashioned; outdated; outmoded; out of date; out of fashion; passé; superannuated.* 3. *beat; bushed; debilitated; depleted; drained; drowsy; enervated; exhausted; fatigued; groggy; sapped; sleepy; sluggish; slumberous; somnolent; soporific; spent; tired; weary; worn out.*

(as) dead as a doornail ∎ An insipid simile. 1. *ceased; completed; concluded; dead; deceased; defunct; done; ended; exanimate; expired; extinct; extinguished; finished; gone; inanimate; lifeless; no more; over; perished; stopped; terminated.* 2. *antediluvian; antiquated; archaic; dead; obsolescent; obsolete; old; old-fashioned; outdated; outmoded; out of date; out of fashion; passé; superannuated.* 3. *beat; bushed; debilitated; depleted; drained; drowsy; enervated; exhausted; fatigued; groggy; sapped; sleepy; sluggish; slumberous; somnolent; soporific; spent; tired; weary; worn out.*

> I settled on getting raised from the dead, since a big part of me still felt dead as a doornail.—Sue Monk Kidd, *The Secret Life of Bees*

dead body ∎ A wretched redundancy. *body.* • Their car was abandoned on a bridge, and *dead bodies* were nowhere to be found. DELETE *dead.*

dead duck ∎ A moribund metaphor.

deader than a doornail ∎ A moribund metaphor. 1. *ceased; completed; concluded; dead; deceased; defunct; done; ended; exanimate; expired; extinct; extinguished; finished; gone; inanimate; lifeless; no more; over; perished; stopped; terminated.* 2. *antediluvian; antiquated; archaic; dead; obsolescent; obsolete; old; old-fashioned; outdated; outmoded; out of date; out of fashion; passé; superannuated.* 3. *beat; bushed; debilitated; depleted; drained; drowsy; enervated; exhausted; fatigued; groggy; sapped; sleepy; sluggish; slumberous; somnolent; soporific; spent; tired; weary; worn out.*

dead in the water ∎ A moribund metaphor. *dead; dormant; dull; inactive; inanimate; indolent; inert; inoperative; languid; latent; lethargic; lifeless; listless; motionless; phlegmatic; quiescent; quiet; sluggish; stagnant; static; stationary; still; stock-still; torpid.* • The civil rights impulse from the

1960s is *dead in the water*. REPLACE WITH *listless*.

dead on arrival ∎ A moribund metaphor.

dead on (her) feet ∎ A moribund metaphor. *beat; bushed; debilitated; depleted; drained; drowsy; enervated; exhausted; fatigued; groggy; sapped; sleepy; sluggish; slumberous; somnolent; soporific; spent; tired; weary; worn out*.

dead ringer ∎ A moribund metaphor.

dead serious ∎ An inescapable pair.

dead to the world ∎ A moribund metaphor. 1. *asleep; dozing; napping; sleeping.* 2. *anesthetized; benumbed; comatose; insensate; insensible; insentient; oblivious; senseless; soporiferous; soporific; stuporous; unconscious.*

(as) deaf as a post ∎ An insipid simile. 1. *deaf; unhearing.* 2. *heedless; inattentive; oblivious; unmindful.*

deaf, dumb, and blind ∎ A moribund metaphor. *anesthetized; cataleptic; comatose; insensate; insensible; insentient; numb; sensationless; unconscious; unfeeling.*

deal a (crushing; devastating; major; serious) blow to ∎ A moribund metaphor. 1. *annihilate; assassinate; butcher; demolish; destroy; devastate; eradicate; exterminate; kill; massacre; murder; obliterate; pulverize; rack; ravage; raze; ruin; shatter; slaughter; slay; smash; undo; wrack; wreck.* 2. *beat; conquer; crush; defeat; outdo; overcome; overpower; overwhelm; prevail; quell; rout; succeed; triumph; trounce; vanquish; win.* Still another phrase favored by journalists *deal a (crushing; devastating; major; serious) blow to*, though it tries mightily to move us, leaves us unimpressed. Drained of any force it might once have had, this dimwitticism exhausts us precisely as much as it is exhausted. • Falling real estate values, the stock market crash, and changes in the rules under which S&Ls operate *dealt crushing blows to* the bank's success. • Most recently, it was Bennett who *dealt the most devastating blow* yet to Clinton's leadership.

(like) death warmed over ∎ An insipid simile. *anemic; ashen; blanched; bloodless; cadaverous; colorless; deathlike; doughy; haggard; lusterless; pale; pallid; pasty; peaked; sallow; sickly; wan; whitish.*

declare war (on) ∎ A moribund metaphor.

deepen the wound ∎ A moribund metaphor.

deeper in (into) the hole ∎ A moribund metaphor.

(has) deep pockets ∎ A moribund metaphor. *affluent; moneyed; opulent; prosperous; rich; wealthy; well-off; well-to-do.*

deep six ∎ (*v*) A moribund metaphor. *discard;*

eliminate; get rid of; jettison; reject; throw away; toss out.

definitely ∎ An overworked word. So popular is this word that we might well marvel at the assuredness of those who use it. But, of course, the overuse of *definitely* bespeaks carelessness more than it does confidence. SEE ALSO **100 (110) percent; absolutely; most assuredly; most (very) definitely.**

degree ∎ A torpid term. *Degree*—and the superfluity of phrases in which it is found—should be excised from almost all of our speech and writing. No sentence is made more compelling by the use of this word and its diffuse phrases. • I believe he has *a very high degree* of integrity and takes extreme pride in his workmanship. REPLACE WITH *a good deal.* • Increased employee morale would require *a lesser degree of* accuracy. REPLACE WITH *less.* • Their hopes are based, *to a large degree*, on signs that business activity is pulling out of its recent slowdown. REPLACE WITH *largely.* • *To a larger degree* than was expected, these economically stunted nations can count on help from the 12-nation organization. REPLACE WITH *More.* • Another realm in which schools of choice can and do differ is *the degree to which* the staff and parents are involved in the day-to-day operations of the school. REPLACE WITH *how much.* SEE ALSO **extent.**

> She knew she was sick but she didn't know the degree to which it was commonplace, a matter of spring flu, the usual malaise, passed from student to student and among faculty members.—Joyce Carol Oates, *Solstice*

déjà vu ∎ A foreign phrase.

déjà vu all over again ∎ An infantile phrase. • The police served him with a restraining order; it was *déjà vu all over again.*

delicate balance ∎ An inescapable pair.

den of iniquity ∎ A moribund metaphor.

den of thieves ∎ A moribund metaphor.

depart this life ∎ A moribund metaphor. *be deceased; die; expire; perish.*

desperately seeking ∎ An infantile phrase.

despite (in spite of) or (maybe; perhaps) because of (the fact that) ∎ An ineffectual phrase. These phrases sound as though they have the ring of respectability to them—that is, they sound intelligent—but since the phrases are formulaic (a staple among journalists and those who write like them) and the contribution they make to a sentence uncertain (*despite* virtually nullifies *because of*), they are actually disreputable—that is, they are dimwitted. • *Despite* his old-fashioned style, *or perhaps because of* it, Mansfield remains an extremely popular lecturer.

• *In spite of or, perhaps, because of the fact that* we humans are normally vision experts at a very young age, we have little intuition about how vision develops or how we accomplish seeing. • Excessive weight gain occurred during periods of this pregnancy *despite, or because of,* the mother's emotional problems. • Lately, she finds herself having a hard time falling asleep, *despite—or perhaps because of—*her exhaustion. • But this is what the harvest is all about, and *despite* the hard work, *or actually*, precisely *because of* it, a harvest wants to be celebrated. • They sustain a high level of motivation and achieve performance peak after performance peak *in spite of* (or *perhaps because of*) the lack of traditional supervision and rewards.

> Despite or perhaps because of the fact that he left us, he knows it's vital that he does nothing to undermine my self-confidence.—William Nicholson, *The Society of Others*

despite the fact that ❚ A TOP-TWENTY DIMWITTICISM. **A wretched redundancy.** *although; but; even if; even though; still; though; yet.* • Long a critic of exorbitant executive salaries, he agreed to a **4.7** percent raise, *despite the fact that* his company's profits doubled. REPLACE WITH *even though.* • *Despite the fact that* no serious adverse effects have been found, there are still risks. REPLACE WITH *Although.* SEE ALSO **in spite of the fact that; regardless of the fact that**.

devastate ❚ A TOP-TWENTY DIMWITTICISM. **An overworked word.** We can hardly wonder why so many of us are so easily *devastated.* This word is pervasive. Rarely are we *disconsolate*, rarely are we *flustered.* If only we would use more measured terms, we might feel less weak and woundable.

Consider these terms, all more moderate: *agitated; bothered; crestfallen; despondent; disappointed; discomposed; disconsolate; distressed; disturbed; downcast; downhearted; flustered; heartbroken; heartsick; perturbed; ruffled; unsettled; upset.* • When Glen was transferred to a city 100 miles away, I was *devastated.* REPLACE WITH *heartbroken.*

But if devastation it is, here are other terms that might relieve us of our reliance on this one: *atomized; crushed; demolished; desolate; destroyed; distraught; obliterated; overcome; overpowered; overwhelmed; prostrate; ravaged; ruined; shattered; undone.* • Dean and Jenna were *devastated* when she lost their baby. REPLACE WITH *shattered.* SEE ALSO **crisis**.

devil's disciple ❚ A moribund metaphor.

devil to pay ❚ A moribund metaphor.

develop steam ❚ A moribund metaphor.

dial down ❚ A moribund metaphor. *cut; decrease; diminish; lessen; reduce; shrink.*

• And while the report issued a call for increased emphasis on *dialing down* the radiation exposure with CT, the government may actually be out in front on this issue. REPLACE WITH *reducing.*

diametrically opposed ❚ An inescapable pair.

(the) dictionary defines ❚ An infantile phrase. • *Webster's New World Dictionary defines* investigate as "to search into; examine in detail; inquire into systematically." • *The dictionary defines* gratitude as "a feeling of thankful appreciation for favors or benefits received." SEE ALSO **as defined in (the dictionary)**.

(I thought I had) died and gone to heaven ❚ A moribund metaphor. *blissful; blithe; buoyant; cheerful; delighted; ecstatic; elated; enraptured; euphoric; exalted; excited; exhilarated; exultant; gay; glad; gleeful; good-humored; happy; intoxicated; jolly; jovial; joyful; joyous; jubilant; merry; mirthful; overjoyed; pleased; rapturous; thrilled.*

> Bram took a sip of his wine, smiled as his beautiful wife waltzed by in the arms of a half-pay officer whose expression told the world he felt as if he'd just died and gone to Heaven.—Kasey Michaels, *Then Comes Marriage*

die laughing ❚ A moribund metaphor.

die (wither) on the vine ❚ A moribund metaphor. *atrophy; be unsuccessful; bomb; break down; collapse; decay; fail; fall short; falter; fizzle; flop; flounder; fold; founder; languish; mess up; miscarry; miss; not succeed; shrivel; stumble; topple; wilt; wither.* • We believe Medicare is going to *wither on the vine* because we think people are going to voluntarily leave it. REPLACE WITH *founder.* • The history of computing is littered with great products that *withered on the vine*. REPLACE WITH *failed.*

different strokes for different folks ❚ A popular prescription.

digging (your) own grave ❚ A moribund metaphor.

dig in (his) heels ❚ A moribund metaphor. *be adamant; be balky; be bullheaded; be cantankerous; be contrary; be contumacious; be determined; be dogged; be firm; be headstrong; be inflexible; be intractable; be mulish; be obdurate; be obstinate; be ornery; be perverse; be refractory; be resistant; be resolute; be resolved; be rigid; be stubborn; be unyielding; be willful.* • By then, the auto industry was *digging in its heels*, and almost as soon as the law was approved, its provisions were called too stringent. REPLACE WITH *becoming resolute.*

dirt cheap ❚ A moribund metaphor. *cheap; economical; inexpensive; low-cost; low-*

priced; not costly.

dirty pool ■ A moribund metaphor.

dis (diss) ■ An infantile phrase. *belittle; criticize; defame; denigrate; dismiss; disparage; disregard; disrespect; malign; reject.* • The AARP *dissed* the GOP stand, with its statement that nothing in the proposed health care reform bills "would bring about the scenarios the RNC is concerned about." REPLACE WITH *dismissed.* • Sometimes the best way to *diss* an ex is by saying nothing at all. REPLACE WITH *disparage.* • So I guess I should apologize to Barry for insensitively *denigrating* him when he is a true artist whose work is worthy of great praise. REPLACE WITH *defaming.*

disappear (vanish) into thin air ■ A moribund metaphor. *disappear; disperse; dissolve; evaporate; fade; vanish; vaporize; volatilize.*

disappear (vanish) without a trace ■ A moribund metaphor. *disappear; disperse; dissolve; evaporate; fade; vanish; vaporize; volatilize.*

discretion is the better part of valor ■ A popular prescription.

dismal failure ■ An inescapable pair. • The mayor's attempt at improving the quality of life on Boston Common at night was a *dismal failure.*

divine intervention ■ An inescapable pair.

do a disappearing act ■ A moribund metaphor. *abscond; clear out; decamp; depart; desert; disappear; escape; exit; flee; fly; go; go away; leave; move on; part; pull out; quit; retire; retreat; run away; take flight; take off; vacate; vanish; withdraw.*

do a hatchet job on ■ A moribund metaphor. *asperse; badmouth; belittle; besmirch; bespatter; blacken; calumniate; defame; defile; denigrate; denounce; depreciate; deride; disparage; impugn; insult; libel; malign; profane; revile; scandalize; slander; slap; slur; smear; sully; taint; traduce; vilify; vitiate.*

do a job on ■ A moribund metaphor. 1. *blight; cripple; damage; deface; disable; disfigure; harm; hurt; impair; incapacitate; injure; lame; maim; mar; mess up; rack; ruin; sabotage; spoil; subvert; undermine; vitiate; wrack; wreck.* 2. *agitate; bother; disquiet; distress; disturb; fluster; jar; jolt; pain; perturb; ruffle; shake; trouble; unsettle; upset; wound.* SEE ALSO **do a number on**.

do all (everything) in (my) power ■ A torpid term. • I believe that Cashbuild has *done everything in its power* to cope with the changing South American environment.

do an about-face ■ A moribund metaphor. *apostatize; backtrack; flip-flop; recidivate; renege; reverse; tergiversate.* SEE ALSO **do**

a 180.

do (make) an end run around ■ A moribund metaphor. *avoid; bypass; circumvent; dodge; duck; elude; evade; go around; parry; sidestep; skirt.* • Trying to *do an end run around* the person responsible for making purchasing decisions isn't advisable. REPLACE WITH *sidestep.*

do a number on ■ A moribund metaphor. 1. *blight; cripple; damage; deface; disable; disfigure; harm; hurt; impair; incapacitate; injure; lame; maim; mar; mess up; rack; ruin; sabotage; spoil; subvert; undermine; vitiate; wrack; wreck.* 2. *agitate; bother; disquiet; distress; disturb; fluster; jar; jolt; pain; perturb; ruffle; shake; trouble; unsettle; upset; wound.* SEE ALSO **do a job on**.

do a 180 ■ A moribund metaphor. *apostatize; backtrack; flip-flop; recidivate; renege; reverse; tergiversate.* SEE ALSO **do an about-face**.

do as I say, not as I do ■ A popular prescription.

doctor, lawyer, Indian chief ■ A moribund metaphor.

dodge the bullet ■ A moribund metaphor.

(it) doesn't amount to a hill of beans ■ A moribund metaphor. *barren; bootless; effete; feckless; feeble; fruitless; futile; impotent; inadequate; inconsequential; inconsiderable; ineffective; ineffectual; infertile; insignificant; inutile; meaningless; meritless; nugatory; null; of no value; pointless; powerless; profitless; purposeless; sterile; trifling; trivial; unavailing; unimportant; unproductive; unprofitable; unserviceable; unworthy; useless; vain; valueless; weak; worthless.*

> I had too much to do, I told myself, to worry with last-minute, undoubtedly invalid last wills and testaments that probably wouldn't amount to a hill of beans.—Ann B. Ross, *Miss Julia Speaks Her Mind*

(money) doesn't grow on trees ■ A moribund metaphor. *exiguous; limited; inadequate; infrequent; meager; rare; scant; scanty; scarce; sparse; uncommon; unusual.*

doesn't have a clue ■ A moribund metaphor. *addlebrained; addleheaded; addlepated; Boeotian; bovine; brainless; clueless; cretinous; decerebrate; dense; dim-witted; doltish; dull; dumb; dunderheaded; empty-headed; fatuous; fat-witted; harebrained; hebetudinous; ignorant; imbecilic; incogitant; insensate; ludicrous; mindless; moronic; muddled; nescient; obtuse; oxlike; phlegmatic; slow-witted; sluggish; stupid; torpid; unaware; unintelligent; unknowing; vacuous; witless.*

doesn't have a snowball's chance in hell ■ A moribund metaphor. *impossible; unachievable; unattainable; unfeasible.*

doesn't have both oars in the water

doesn't have both oars in the water ■ A moribund metaphor. *batty; cracked; crazy; daft; demented; deranged; fey; foolish; goofy; insane; lunatic; mad; maniacal; neurotic; nuts; nutty; psychotic; raving; silly; squirrelly; strange; touched; unbalanced; unhinged; unsound; wacky; zany.*

doesn't have two nickels to rub together ■ A moribund metaphor. *bankrupt; broke; destitute; distressed; impecunious; impoverished; indigent; insolvent; needy; penniless; poor; poverty-stricken; underprivileged.*

doesn't hold water ■ A moribund metaphor. *baseless; captious; casuistic; casuistical; erroneous; fallacious; false; faulty; flawed; groundless; illogical; inaccurate; incorrect; invalid; irrational; jesuitical; mistaken; nonsensical; non sequitur; paralogistic; senseless; sophistic; sophistical; specious; spurious; unfounded; unreasonable; unsound; untenable; untrue; unveracious; wrong.*

doesn't know (her) ass from a hole in the wall ■ A moribund metaphor. 1. *addlebrained; addleheaded; addlepated; Boeotian; bovine; brainless; clueless; cretinous; decerebrate; dense; dim-witted; doltish; dull; dumb; dunderheaded; empty-headed; fatuous; fat-witted; harebrained; hebetudinous; ignorant; imbecilic; incogitant; insensate; ludicrous; mindless; moronic; muddled; nescient; obtuse; oxlike; phlegmatic; slow-witted; sluggish; stupid; torpid; unaware; unintelligent; unknowing; vacuous; witless.* 2. *deficient; inadequate; inapt; incapable; incompetent; ineffective; inefficacious; inept; lacking; not able; unable; unfit; unqualified; unsatisfactory; unskilled; wanting.*

doesn't know (his) ass from (his) elbow ■ A moribund metaphor. 1. *addlebrained; addleheaded; addlepated; Boeotian; bovine; brainless; clueless; cretinous; decerebrate; dense; dim-witted; doltish; dull; dumb; dunderheaded; empty-headed; fatuous; fat-witted; harebrained; hebetudinous; ignorant; imbecilic; incogitant; insensate; ludicrous; mindless; moronic; muddled; nescient; obtuse; oxlike; phlegmatic; slow-witted; sluggish; stupid; torpid; unaware; unintelligent; unknowing; vacuous; witless.* 2. *deficient; inadequate; inapt; incapable; incompetent; ineffective; inefficacious; inept; lacking; not able; unable; unfit; unqualified; unsatisfactory; unskilled; wanting.*

dog and pony show ■ A moribund metaphor.

dog days (of summer) ■ A moribund metaphor.

dog-eat-dog ■ A moribund metaphor. *barbarous; bloodthirsty; brutal; cold-blooded; compassionless; cruel; cutthroat; feral; ferocious; fierce; hard; hard-hearted; harsh; heartless; implacable; inexorable; inhuman; merciless; murderous; rancorous;* *relentless; ruthless; savage; uncompassionate; unmerciful; unrelenting; vicious; virulent; wild.*

dollars and sense ■ An infantile phrase.

dollars to doughnuts ■ A moribund metaphor. *be certain; be sure.*

> I had no place to stay, and dollars to doughnuts, sitting in front of me was a building with a vacant apartment.—Janet Evanovich, *Ten Big Ones*

don't count your chickens before they're hatched ■ A popular prescription.

don't cry over spilled milk ■ A popular prescription.

don't do anything I wouldn't do ■ An infantile phrase.

don't get mad, get even ■ A popular prescription. • Hillary, *don't get mad, get even*—write a book.

don't get me wrong ■ An infantile phrase. • I'm not trying to condone what I've done. *Don't get me wrong.* REPLACE WITH *Don't misunderstand me.* SEE ALSO **I hear you.**

don't give up the ship ■ A popular prescription. *carry on; continue; ensue; go on; keep up; persevere; persist; press on; proceed.*

don't hold (your) breath ■ A moribund metaphor.

don't knock it until you try it ■ A popular prescription.

don't rock the boat ■ A moribund metaphor.

don't see eye to eye ■ A moribund metaphor. *clash; conflict; differ; disagree; think differently.*

don't start anything you can't finish ■ A popular prescription.

doom and gloom ■ An inescapable pair.

doomed to failure ■ A torpid term. *damned; doomed; hopeless; ill-fated.*

do or die ■ A popular prescription.

do's and don'ts ■ *canon; codes; conventions; conventionality; customs; decorum; directives; etiquette; formula; formulary; guidelines; law; manners; policy; precepts; protocol; proprieties; regulations; rules; standards.*

(to) do the trick ■ A moribund metaphor. *be effective; be successful; be workable; succeed; work.*

dot the i's and cross the t's ■ A moribund metaphor. *be careful; be conscientious; be exact; be exacting; be fastidious; be finical; be finicky; be fussy; be meticulous; be nice; be painstaking; be particular; be picky; be precise; be punctilious; be scrupulous; be thorough.*

double-edge sword ∎ A moribund metaphor.

doubting Thomas ∎ A moribund metaphor. *cynic; disbeliever; doubter; skeptic.*

down and out ∎ A moribund metaphor. *bankrupt; broke; destitute; distressed; impecunious; impoverished; indigent; insolvent; needy; penniless; poor; poverty-stricken; underprivileged.*

down at the heels ∎ A moribund metaphor. 1. *dowdy; frowzy; messy; ragged; run-down; seedy; shabby; slipshod; sloppy; slovenly; tattered; threadbare; unkempt; untidy; worn.* 2. *bankrupt; broke; destitute; distressed; impecunious; impoverished; indigent; insolvent; needy; penniless; poor; poverty-stricken; underprivileged.*

down (out) for the count ∎ A moribund metaphor. 1. *asleep; napping; sleeping; slumbering; snoozing.* 2. *cataleptic; comatose; dormant; inactive; insensible; lifeless; out cold; passed out; unconscious; unresponsive.*

down in the dumps ∎ A moribund metaphor. *aggrieved; anhedonic; blue; cheerless; dejected; demoralized; depressed; despondent; disconsolate; discouraged; disheartened; dismal; dispirited; doleful; downcast; downhearted; dreary; forlorn; funereal; gloomy; glum; grieved; low; melancholy; miserable; morose; mournful; negative; pessimistic; plaintive; sad; sorrowful; unhappy; woebegone; woeful.*

down in the mouth ∎ A moribund metaphor. *aggrieved; anhedonic; blue; cheerless; dejected; demoralized; depressed; despondent; disconsolate; discouraged; disheartened; dismal; dispirited; doleful; downcast; downhearted; dreary; forlorn; funereal; gloomy; glum; grieved; low; melancholy; miserable; morose; mournful; negative; pessimistic; plaintive; sad; sorrowful; unhappy; woebegone; woeful.*

> Thought it was Nora, but when I opened the door, Lewis was standing there in his rumpled linen suit, looking a bit down in the mouth, not a trace of the bulldog in his face.—Richard B. Wright, *Clara Callan*

(go) down the drain ∎ A moribund metaphor. 1. *be misused; be squandered; be thrown way; be wasted.* 2. *break down; collapse; deteriorate; die; disappear; disintegrate; disperse; dissipate; dissolve; evaporate; fade; fail; finish; forfeit; go; lose; pass; scatter; vanish; vaporize; volatilize; waste.* • Without new revenue, our schools will *go down the drain.* REPLACE WITH *collapse.* 3. *annihilated; crushed; demolished; destroyed; obliterated; overturned; ravaged; ruined; scuttled; shattered; smashed; undone; wrecked.* • One major mistake and your career is *down the drain.* REPLACE WITH *ruined.*

down the hatch ∎ A moribund metaphor. *drink; gulp; guzzle; imbibe; quaff; swallow.*

(later on) down the line (path; pike; road) ∎ A wretched redundancy. *at length; before long; eventually; from now; in time; later; ultimately.* • Even though this knowledge might not seem essential right now, it just might prove invaluable *down the line.* REPLACE WITH *later.* • Two players will be added to the team *later, some months down the road.* REPLACE WITH *some months later.* • *Later on down the line,* we did in fact marry. REPLACE WITH *At length.*

(go) down the tubes ∎ A moribund metaphor. 1. *be despoiled; be destroyed; be devastated; be dissipated; be pillaged; be plundered; be ravaged; be ruined; break down; collapse; disintegrate; fail; fall short; flop; founder; miscarry; topple.* 2. *be misused; be squandered; be thrown way; be wasted.* • Her article points out a major reason why our country is *going down the tubes.* REPLACE WITH *foundering.* • All the money my parents spent on my braces *went down the tubes.* REPLACE WITH *was wasted.*

down to earth ∎ A moribund metaphor. *artless; common; earthly; everyday; genuine; guileless; mortal; mundane; natural; normal; plain; secular; staid; temporal; unaffected; unassuming; unpretentious; worldly.*

(come) down to the wire ∎ A moribund metaphor.

drag (their) feet ∎ A moribund metaphor. *arrest; balk; block; bridle; check; dawdle; defer; delay; detain; encumber; hamper; hesitate; hinder; hold up; impede; inhibit; obstruct; pause; postpone; put off; retard; stall; stay; stonewall; suspend.* • The regional Bells have *dragged their feet* in rolling out DSL services. REPLACE WITH *dawdled.*

drag into (through) the mud ∎ A moribund metaphor. *asperse; badmouth; belittle; besmirch; bespatter; blacken; calumniate; defame; defile; denigrate; denounce; depreciate; deride; disparage; impugn; insult; libel; malign; profane; revile; scandalize; slander; slap; slur; smear; sully; taint; traduce; vilify; vitiate.* • His name was *dragged through the mud* last week thanks to a Harvard Law School professor. REPLACE WITH *defamed.*

> He sat down again, trembling with rage; person after person was being dragged into the mud.—E. M. Forster, *A Passage to India*

drag (go) kicking and screaming ∎ A moribund metaphor. *antagonistically; defiantly; disagreeably; grudgingly; recalcitrantly; reluctantly; renitently; resistantly; resistingly; unconsentingly; unwillingly.*

draw a bead on ∎ A moribund metaphor. 1. *aim at; focus on; sight; train on.* 2.

admonish; animadvert; berate; castigate; censure; chasten; chastise; chide; condemn; criticize; denounce; denunciate; discipline; impugn; objurgate; punish; rebuke; remonstrate; reprehend; reprimand; reproach; reprobate; reprove; revile; scold; upbraid; vituperate.

draw a blank ∎ A moribund metaphor. 1. *be addleheaded; be bovine; be cretinous; be decerebrated; be dense; be dull; be dull-witted; be fatuous; be fat-witted; be half-witted; be harebrained; be hebetudinous; be idiotic; be ignorant; be imbecilic; be incogitant; be insensate; be mindless; be moronic; be muddled; be nescient; be obtuse; be phlegmatic; be slow; be slow-witted; be sluggish; be thick; be torpid; be undiscerning; be unintelligent; be vacuous; be witless.* 2. *be absent-minded; be forgetful; be lethean; be oblivious.* • A successful attorney, Caroline *draws a blank* when it comes to men. REPLACE WITH *is witless.*

draw a veil over ∎ A moribund metaphor. *adumbrate; becloud; befog; camouflage; cloak; cloud; conceal; cover; disguise; dissemble; enshroud; harbor; hide; keep secret; mask; obfuscate; obscure; overshadow; screen; shroud; suppress; veil; withhold.*

draw fire (from) ∎ A moribund metaphor.

draw in (his) horns ∎ A moribund metaphor. *back away; back down; back off; disengage; evacuate; fall back; recede; regress; retire; retreat; withdraw.*

draw in the reins ∎ A moribund metaphor. 1. *bridle; check; constrain; contain; control; curb; curtail; govern; harness; hold back; inhibit; limit; muzzle; regulate; rein in; repress; restrain; restrict; stem; stifle; suppress.* 2. *curtail; halt; stall; stay; stop.*

draw the line (at) ∎ A moribund metaphor.

draw the long bow ∎ A moribund metaphor. *elaborate; embellish; embroider; enhance; enlarge; exaggerate; hyperbolize; inflate; magnify; overdo; overreact; overstress; overstate; strain; stretch.*

dredge up dirt ∎ A moribund metaphor.

dressed to kill ∎ A moribund metaphor. *elaborately; elegantly; extravagantly; fashionably; flamboyantly; flashily; gaudily; lavishly; ostentatiously; profusely; richly; showily; smartly; stylishly.*

dribs and drabs ∎ An inescapable pair. *bits; chunks; crumbs; fragments; modicums; morsels; nuggets; particles; pieces; scraps; segments; shreds; snips; snippets; specks.*

drill down (into) ∎ A moribund metaphor. *delve (into); examine; explore; inspect; investigate; look (into); probe; scrutinize; search; study.* • As you *drill down* further into the results, you get to see more tightly refined sets of images based on what you choose. REPLACE WITH *delve.*

drink like a fish ∎ An insipid simile. *alcoholic; bibulous.*

drive a stake through the heart (of) ∎ A moribund metaphor. 1. *execute; kill; massacre; murder; slaughter; slay.* 2. *annihilate; demolish; destroy; eliminate; eradicate; exterminate; liquidate; obliterate; ravage; ruin; sack; wreck.* • The IRB's decision *drives a stake through the heart of* the myth peddled by Carey sympathizers inside and outside the Teamsters. REPLACE WITH *slays.*

drive a wedge between ∎ A moribund metaphor.

drive (me) bananas (crazy; nuts) ∎ A moribund metaphor. *annoy; badger; bedevil; bother; chafe; distress; disturb; exasperate; gall; grate; harass; harry; hassle; heckle; hector; hound; irk; irritate; nag; nettle; persecute; pester; plague; provoke; rankle; rile; roil; tease; torment; vex.*

drive into a ditch ∎ A moribund metaphor. *crush; damage; demolish; destroy; devastate; ravage; raze; ruin; shatter; slay; smash; spoil; trash; undo; wrack; wreck.* • These folks *drove* America's economy *into a ditch.* REPLACE WITH *ruined.*

drive (me) to drink ∎ A moribund metaphor. *annoy; badger; bedevil; bother; chafe; distress; disturb; exasperate; gall; grate; harass; harry; hassle; heckle; hector; hound; irk; irritate; nag; nettle; persecute; pester; plague; provoke; rankle; rile; roil; tease; torment; vex.*

drive (me) up the wall ∎ A moribund metaphor. *annoy; badger; bedevil; bother; chafe; distress; disturb; exasperate; gall; grate; harass; harry; hassle; heckle; hector; hound; irk; irritate; nag; nettle; persecute; pester; plague; provoke; rankle; rile; roil; tease; torment; vex.*

driving force ∎ A wretched redundancy. *drive; energy; force; impetus; motivation; power.*

drop (fall) by the wayside ∎ A moribund metaphor. 1. *abate; cease to be; diminish; disappear; dissolve; dwindle; fade; go away; recede; vanish.* 2. *be unsuccessful; fail; fall short; founder.* 3. *give in; give way; submit; succumb; surrender; yield.* • Social class distinctions have mostly *fallen by the wayside*, and scientists are now more likely to admit the collective nature of research. REPLACE WITH *disappeared.*

> Believe me in those days the girls were dropping by the wayside like seeds off a poppyseed bun and you learned to look at every day as a prize.—Barbara Kingsolver, *The Bean Trees*

drop-dead gorgeous ∎ A moribund metaphor. *attractive; beautiful; comely; exquisite; fair; fetching; good looking; gorgeous; handsome; lovely; pretty; pulchritudinous; ravishing.*

drop like a hot potato ∎ An insipid simile. *abandon; abdicate; desert; discard; ditch; drop; forgo; forsake; get rid of; give up; jettison; leave; quit; reject; relinquish; renounce; surrender; throw away; toss out; yield.*

drop like flies ∎ An insipid simile. *annihilate; decimate; demolish; slaughter.*

drop off the face of the earth ∎ A moribund metaphor. *disappear; vanish.*

drop the ball ∎ A moribund metaphor. *be unsuccessful; bomb; break down; collapse; fail; fall short; falter; fizzle; flop; fold; founder; mess up; miscarry; misfire; not succeed; stumble; topple.*

(as) drunk as a lord ∎ An insipid simile. *besotted; crapulous; drunk; inebriated; intoxicated; sodden; stupefied; tipsy.*

(as) drunk as a skunk ∎ An insipid simile. *besotted; crapulous; drunk; inebriated; intoxicated; sodden; stupefied; tipsy.*

(as) dry as a bone ∎ An insipid simile. *arid; dehydrated; desiccated; droughty; dry; exsiccated; parched; sear; shriveled; thirsty; wilted; withered.*

(as) dry as dust ∎ An insipid simile. *banal; barren; bland; boring; deadly; dreary; dry; dull; everyday; flat; humdrum; inanimate; insipid; jejune; lifeless; lusterless; mediocre; monotonous; prosaic; routine; spiritless; stale; tedious; tiresome; unexciting; uninteresting; vapid; wearisome.*

dubious distinction ∎ An inescapable pair. • Now the Cowboys are coming off a **34-0** shutout in Philadelphia while the Giants have the *dubious distinction* of being the first team to lose to Washington this season.

duck soup ∎ A moribund metaphor. *easily done; easy; effortless; elementary; facile; simple; simplicity itself; straightforward; uncomplex; uncomplicated.*

due to circumstances beyond (our) control ∎ An ineffectual phrase. Of those who use this phrase, we may remark that their speech is no more grammatical than their actions are genuine.
Due to, as often as not, should be *because of* or *owing to,* and only the similarly disingenuous would believe that *circumstances beyond our control* is an explanation rather than an evasion.
In the end, those who express themselves badly are less credible than those who express themselves well. • *Due to circumstances beyond our control,* no motel rooms are available in the area on June 25th, 26th, and 27th. • *Due to circumstances beyond our control,* the following items may not be available as advertised. SEE ALSO **due to popular demand**.

due to popular demand ∎ An ineffectual phrase. There is with this phrase, as with *due to circumstances beyond (our) control* (SEE), the same solecism and a similar suspicion. • *Due to popular demand,* The Magic Show will be held over another two weeks.

due to the fact that ∎ A wretched redundancy. *because; considering; for; in that; since.* • Requirements continue to decrease slowly *due to the fact that* activity generally decreases with age. REPLACE WITH *since.* • Could this be *due to the fact that* it is undecidable? REPLACE WITH *because.* SEE ALSO **attributable to the fact that; owing to the fact that.**

(as) dull as dishwater ∎ An insipid simile. 1. *addleheaded; bovine; cretinous; decerebrate; dense; dull; dull-witted; fatuous; fat-witted; half-witted; harebrained; hebetudinous; idiotic; ignorant; imbecilic; incogitant; insensate; mindless; moronic; muddled; nescient; obtuse; phlegmatic; slow; slow-witted; sluggish; thick; torpid; undiscerning; unintelligent; vacuous; witless.* 2. *banal; barren; bland; boring; deadly; dreary; dry; dull; everyday; flat; humdrum; inanimate; insipid; jejune; lifeless; lusterless; mediocre; monotonous; prosaic; routine; spiritless; stale; tedious; tiresome; unexciting; uninteresting; vapid; wearisome.*

(as) dumb as a stone ∎ An insipid simile. *addlebrained; addleheaded; addlepated; Boeotian; bovine; brainless; clueless; cretinous; decerebrate; dense; dim-witted; doltish; dull; dumb; dunderheaded; empty-headed; fatuous; fat-witted; harebrained; hebetudinous; ignorant; imbecilic; incogitant; insensate; ludicrous; mindless; moronic; muddled; nescient; obtuse; oxlike; phlegmatic; slow-witted; sluggish; stupid; torpid; unaware; unintelligent; unknowing; vacuous; witless.*

(as) dumb as dirt ∎ An insipid simile. *addlebrained; addleheaded; addlepated; Boeotian; bovine; brainless; clueless; cretinous; decerebrate; dense; dim-witted; doltish; dull; dumb; dunderheaded; empty-headed; fatuous; fat-witted; harebrained; hebetudinous; ignorant; imbecilic; incogitant; insensate; ludicrous; mindless; moronic; muddled; nescient; obtuse; oxlike; phlegmatic; slow-witted; sluggish; stupid; torpid; unaware; unintelligent; unknowing; vacuous; witless.* • Frankly, I think these allegations are simply *dumb as dirt.* REPLACE WITH *Boeotian.*

during (in; over) the course of ∎ A wretched redundancy. *during; in; over; throughout.* • *In the course of* a **30** minute conversation, she spoke about her married life and her plans for the future. REPLACE WITH *During.* • *Over the course of* a woman's life, she may experience a kaleidoscope of health concerns. REPLACE WITH *Throughout.*

during the period (time) that

> She had drunk a quantity of champagne, and during the course of her song she had decided, ineptly, that everything was very, very sad—she was not only singing, she was weeping too.—F. Scott Fitzgerald, *The Great Gatsby*

during the period (time) that ∎ A wretched redundancy. *while.* • *During the time that* we were with him, he called her several uncomplimentary names. REPLACE WITH *While.*

dust-up ∎ A moribund metaphor. *argument; dispute; fight; quarrel; scuffle; skirmish; tussle.*

dyed-in-the-wool ∎ A moribund metaphor. *ardent; constant; devoted; faithful; fixed; inflexible; intractable; inveterate; loyal; refractory; resolute; rigid; staunch; steadfast; unbending; unwavering; unyielding.*

dynamic duo ∎ An infantile phrase.

Ee

each and every (one) ∎ A wretched redundancy. *all; each; everybody; everyone.*
• Software developers have changed the way *each and every one* of us does business. REPLACE WITH *each.*

each one ∎ A wretched redundancy. *each.*
• The fact that these companies do have to compete for business gives *each one* an incentive to work harder and to lower prices. DELETE *one.* SEE ALSO **either one; neither one.**

each to his own ∎ A popular prescription.

eagle eyed ∎ A moribund metaphor. *alert; attentive; observant; vigilant; watchful.*

earn (his) stripes ∎ A moribund metaphor.

(as) easy as A B C ∎ An insipid simile. *apparent; basic; clear; clear-cut; conspicuous; distinct; easily done; easy; effortless; elementary; evident; explicit; facile; limpid; lucid; manifest; obvious; patent; pellucid; plain; simple; simplicity itself; straightforward; translucent; transparent; unambiguous; uncomplex; uncomplicated; understandable; unequivocal; unmistakable.*

(as) easy as 1 2 3 ∎ An insipid simile. *apparent; basic; clear; clear-cut; conspicuous; distinct; easily done; easy; effortless; elementary; evident; explicit; facile; limpid; lucid; manifest; obvious; patent; pellucid; plain; simple; simplicity itself; straightforward; translucent; transparent; unambiguous; uncomplex; uncomplicated; understandable; unequivocal; unmistakable.*

(as) easy as pie ∎ An insipid simile. *apparent; basic; clear; clear-cut; conspicuous; distinct; easily done; easy; effortless; elementary; evident; explicit; facile; limpid; lucid; manifest; obvious; patent; pellucid; plain; simple; simplicity itself; straightforward; translucent; transparent; unambiguous; uncomplex; uncomplicated; understandable; unequivocal; unmistakable.*
• It's *easy as pie* to strike up a conversation with the person sitting next to you. REPLACE WITH *easy.*

> It was easy as pie to slip back into my old self.—Laurie Colwin, *Goodbye Without Leaving*

easy on the eyes ∎ A moribund metaphor. *attractive; beautiful; comely; exquisite; fair; fetching; good looking; gorgeous; handsome; lovely; pretty; pulchritudinous; ravishing.*

> One of the four girls, the one in red, asked, "Will you be going, Michael?" An outsider, she was, but very easy on the eyes.—Anne Tyler, *The Amateur Marriage*

easy on the pocket(book) ∎ A moribund metaphor. *affordable; cheap; economical; inexpensive; low-cost; low-priced; reasonable.*

eat crow ∎ A moribund metaphor. *be abased; be chastened; be debased; be degraded; be demeaned; be disgraced; be dishonored; be embarrassed; be humbled; be humiliated; be lowered; be mortified; be shamed.*

eat dirt ∎ A moribund metaphor. *be abased; be chastened; be debased; be degraded; be demeaned; be disgraced; be dishonored; be embarrassed; be humbled; be humiliated; be lowered; be mortified; be shamed.*

eat, drink, and be merry ∎ A popular prescription. *be merry; carouse; carry on; celebrate; debauch; disport; frolic; party; play; revel; riot; roister; rollick; romp; skylark.*

eat, drink, and be merry, for tomorrow we die ∎ A popular prescription.

eat (your) heart out ∎ A moribund metaphor. *ache; agonize; grieve; hurt; lament; mourn; pine; sorrow; suffer; worry.*

eat (live) high off (on) the hog ∎ A moribund metaphor. *epicureanly; extravagantly; lavishly; lushly; luxuriantly; opulently; prodigally; profusely; sumptuously; very well.*

eat humble pie ∎ A moribund metaphor. *be abased; be chastened; be debased; be degraded; be demeaned; be disgraced; be dishonored; be embarrassed; be humbled; be humiliated; be lowered; be mortified; be shamed.*

> But telling my editors they were about to be fined several thousand dollars was not a prospect I relished. So I took a deep breath and ate humble pie.—Neely Tucker, *Love in the Driest Season*

eat (our) lunch ∎ A moribund metaphor. *beat (us); conquer (us); crush (us); defeat (us); outdo (us); overcome (us); overpower (us); overwhelm (us); quell (us); rout (us); trounce (us); vanquish (us).* • Meanwhile, China is *eating our lunch,* eviscerating our manufacturing base, with its mercantilist policy. REPLACE WITH *crushing us.* •

Chopp and the Democrats have been eating our lunch. REPLACE WITH *trouncing us.*

eat like a bird ∎ An insipid simile. *be abstemious; be ascetic.*

eat like a horse ∎ An insipid simile. 1. *be esurient; be famished; be gluttonous; be greedy; be hungry; be insatiable; be omnivorous; be rapacious; be ravenous; be starved; be starving; be voracious.* 2. *glut; gorge; overdo; overeat; overfeed; overindulge; sate; satiate; stuff; surfeit.*

eat like a pig ∎ An insipid simile. 1. *be esurient; be famished; be gluttonous; be greedy; be hungry; be insatiable; be omnivorous; be rapacious; be ravenous; be starved; be starving; be voracious.* 2. *glut; gorge; overdo; overeat; overfeed; overindulge; sate; satiate; stuff; surfeit.*

eat out of (the palm of) (her) hand ∎ A moribund metaphor. *abide by; acquiesce; comply with; conform; follow; obey; yield.*

eat (me) out of house and home ∎ A moribund metaphor. 1. *be esurient; be famished; be gluttonous; be greedy; be hungry; be insatiable; be omnivorous; be rapacious; be ravenous; be starved; be starving; be voracious.* 2. *glut; gorge; overdo; overeat; overfeed; overindulge; sate; satiate; stuff; surfeit.*

eat (him) (up) alive ∎ A moribund metaphor. 1. *consume; enclose; envelop; surround.* 2. *exploit; use.*

> We might had charged the stage to eat him up alive if he had been any more sly and enchanting and wise.—Philip Roth, *The Ghost Writer*

eat (her) words ∎ A moribund metaphor. *disavow; recant; repudiate; retract; take back; withdraw.*

ebb and flow ∎ A moribund metaphor. • Optimists try to attribute a linear progression to the *ebb and flow* of history.

effect ∎ An overworked word. For example: *chilling effect; cumulative effect; domino effect; dramatic effect; negative effect; snowball effect; sobering effect; trickle-down effect.* • LeBlanc's lawyers say that would *have a chilling effect on* fraud lawsuits brought by government employees. REPLACE WITH *discourage.* • You can learn how to free yourself from the *destructive effects* of negative people in your workplace. REPLACE WITH *detriment.* SEE ALSO **has an effect on**.

effective and efficient ∎ An inescapable pair. Businesspeople, in particular, seem unable to use the word *effective* without also using *efficient*. And though businesses endlessly plume themselves on how *effective and efficient* they are (and how *excellent* their products and services

are), this is rarely true. In the end, the dimwitted *effective and efficient* may mean to us all what it has come to mean to businesses: 1. shoddy and inept, 2. uncaring and purblind, 3. money-grubbing and malevolent.
 • For these methods, more *effective and efficient* methods are available. REPLACE WITH *effective* or *efficient.* • More than an audit, the study should evaluate the *efficiency and effectiveness* of social services and public works. REPLACE WITH *efficiency* or *effectiveness.* • The work place should be a safe environment where one can *effectively and efficiently* perform required duties. REPLACE WITH *effectively* or *efficiently.*

effectuate ∎ A torpid term. *bring about; carry out; cause; do; effect; execute; occasion.* SEE ALSO **eventuate**.

(with) egg on (my) face ∎ A moribund metaphor. *abashed; ashamed; chagrined; confused; discomfited; discomposed; disconcerted; embarrassed; flustered; humbled; humiliated; mortified; nonplused; perplexed; red-faced; shamed; shamefaced; sheepish; upset.* • Everybody likes to see Harvard *with egg on its face.* REPLACE WITH *embarrassed.*

egregious error ∎ An inescapable pair.

either one ∎ A wretched redundancy. *either.* • He doesn't care about *either one* of you. DELETE *one.* SEE ALSO *each one; neither one.*

(an) element ∎ A torpid term. • Proper validation is *an* essential *element.* DELETE *an element.* • Black turnout was especially low, and that was *a* key *element* to her victory. DELETE *a element.* SEE ALSO **(a) factor**.

elevate to an art form ∎ A moribund metaphor. • He would add to the gridlock, then compound the people's frustrations by *elevating* the blame game *to an art form.*

empty void ∎ A wretched redundancy. *emptiness; void.* • I know that without me around my mother got lonely and just needed someone to fill the *empty void.* REPLACE WITH *emptiness* or *void.*

enclosed herein (herewith) ∎ A wretched redundancy. *enclosed; here.* • *Enclosed herein* is the complete manuscript. REPLACE WITH *Here* or *Enclosed.*

enclosed please find ∎ A wretched redundancy. *enclosed is; here is.* • *Enclosed please find* materials that you might find useful prior to your arrival. REPLACE WITH *Enclosed are.* • *Enclosed please find* a listing of single family properties that are available for purchase by eligible buyers. REPLACE WITH *Here is.*

endangered species ∎ A moribund metaphor. • We all recognize that the nuclear family is an *endangered species.*

end of the line ∎ A moribund metaphor. *close; completion; conclusion; culmination; consummation; end; ending; finale; finish; fulfillment; termination.*

end on a high note ∎ A moribund metaphor.

end result ∎ A wretched redundancy. *result.* • The *end result* should be that all mothers and fathers would pay what they can afford. DELETE *end.*

enjoy (the moment) ∎ A popular prescription.

enjoy it while (you) can ∎ A popular prescription.

enough is enough ∎ A quack equation. Though often used to conclude an argument, *enough is enough* is the least compelling of summations. No one can argue *enough is enough* and expect to be persuasive. The phrase convinces us only that its user is as weary of reason as he is of what he complains about.

equally as ∎ A wretched redundancy. *as; equally.* • *Equally as* important, this program provides comprehensive preventive coverage. REPLACE WITH *As* or *Equally.*

ere ∎ A withered word. *before.* • So I avoided the hole and assumed it might likely be June *ere* it was patched. REPLACE WITH *before.*

ergo ∎ A withered word. *consequently; hence; therefore.*

establishment ∎ A torpid term. *business; club; company; firm; outlet; shop; store.* • You should park close to the entrance of the *establishment* you are shopping at. REPLACE WITH *store.*

et cetera (etc., etc. ; et cetera, et cetera) ∎ A grammatical gimmick. • I'm very outgoing and adaptable, *et cetera, et cetera.* DELETE *et cetera, et cetera.* • She told me he was everything she was looking for, *et cetera, et cetera.* DELETE *et cetera, et cetera.* • Dr. Holmes was a man of brilliant conversational gifts—one of the most notable of that noted circle which composed the "Saturday Club" in Boston—Longfellow, Emerson, Lowell, Whittier, Thoreau, Bayard Taylor, *etc., etc.* DELETE *etc., etc.*

When thoughts stumble and then stop, words, or at least intelligible words, do as well. As often as not, *et cetera* is a means of expressing, without having to admit to its meaning, all those words only dimly thought. SEE ALSO **blah, blah, blah; and so on, and so forth.**

etched in stone ∎ A moribund metaphor. 1. *assured; certain; decided; definite; determined; established; final; firm; fixed; resolved; set; settled; sure.* 2. *changeless; constant; eternal; everlasting; immutable; invariable; irreversible; irrevocable;*

permanent; rigid; stable; unalterable; unchangeable; unchanging; unending. • Nothing is *etched in stone* yet. REPLACE WITH *sure.*

et tu, Brute ∎ A foreign phrase.

even Steven ∎ An infantile phrase.

even the score ∎ A moribund metaphor.

eventuate ∎ A torpid term. *befall; come about; end; happen; occur; result; take place.* SEE ALSO **effectuate.**

ever and anon ∎ A withered word. *now and then; occasionally.*

everybody and (his) brother (mother) ∎ An infantile phrase. *all; everybody; everyone.* • *Everybody and their mother* is on line today. REPLACE WITH *Everybody.* • It's like *everybody and their brother* is having a hearing on Enron.

everybody talks about the weather, but nobody does anything about it ∎ An infantile phrase.

every cloud has a silver lining ∎ A popular prescription.

every effort is being made ∎ A suspect superlative. This phrase, disembodied though it is, serves to disarm people as it dismisses them. • *Every effort is being made* to find the perpetrators of this heinous crime. • *Every effort has been made* to make this verification as simple and painless as possible. • During this time, please be patient as *every effort is being made* to process your order in a timely manner. • First, we want to be sure that *every effort is being made* to spot, recover, preserve, identify and deliver any human remains to the families of the victims. SEE ALSO **that's interesting; that's nice.**

every nook and cranny ∎ A moribund metaphor. *all around; all over; all through; everyplace; everywhere; throughout.*

every single (solitary) ∎ A wretched redundancy. *every.* • *Every single solitary* night we see people dying. REPLACE WITH *Every.*

every step of the way ∎ A moribund metaphor. 1. *always; ceaselessly; constantly; continually; continuously; endlessly; eternally; everlastingly; evermore; forever; forevermore; frequently; interminably; nonstop; permanently; perpetually; persistently; recurrently; regularly; repeatedly; unceasingly; unremittingly.* 2. *all during; all over; all through; everywhere; throughout.*

everything but the kitchen sink ∎ A moribund metaphor. *aggregate; all; all things; entirety; everything; gross; lot; sum; total; totality; whole.*

everything happens for a reason ∎ A popular prescription.

everything's coming up roses ∎ An infantile phrase. *be auspicious; be encouraging; be good; be hopeful; be optimistic; be promising; be propitious; be rosy.*

everything's (it's all) relative ∎ An infantile phrase. SEE ALSO **(as) compared to what? (as) opposed to what?.**

everything under the sun ∎ A moribund metaphor. *all; all things; everything.* • I tried *everything under the sun* to get her to shape up. REPLACE WITH *everything.*

everything (it) will turn out for the best ∎ A popular prescription.

everything you always wanted to know about ... but were afraid to ask ∎ An infantile phrase.

every time (you) turn around ∎ A moribund metaphor. *always; ceaselessly; constantly; continually; continuously; endlessly; eternally; everlastingly; evermore; forever; forevermore; frequently; interminably; often; permanently; perpetually; persistently; recurrently; regularly; repeatedly; unceasingly; unremittingly.*

every Tom, Dick, and Harry ∎ A moribund metaphor. *all; citizenry; commonage; commonalty; common people; crowd; everybody; everyone; herd; hoi polloi; masses; mob; multitude; plebeians; populace; proletariat; public; rabble.* • I am not advocating that you tip *every Tom, Dick, and Harry.* REPLACE WITH *everyone.*

every trick in the book ∎ A moribund metaphor. • They're pulling *every trick in the book* to keep this amendment off the 1992 ballot.

excellence ∎ An overworked word. The word is overworked, and the concept undervalued. Too much, today, passes for *excellence.* Too much of our work is shoddy, too much of our wisdom, suspect, too much of our worth, unsure. • With your help, we will continue that tradition of *excellence.* SEE ALSO **pursue (strive for) excellence.**

excess verbiage ∎ A wretched redundancy. *verbiage.*

excruciating pain ∎ An inescapable pair. • This medication was initially prescribed to soothe the *excruciating pain* that I was suffering.

excuse me? ∎ An infantile phrase. No longer exclusively a polite way of signifying that you did not hear what a person has said, *excuse me* is also—especially among the young and stupidly egoistic—an impolite way of signifying that you did not like what a person has said. With an autocratic intonation, the person expresses hostility to what he hears. This phrase is particularly loathsome, for those who use it dare not

be openly angry or upset; they try to disguise their anger and arrogance behind a mantle of mannerliness. SEE ALSO **I'm sorry; thank you; whatever.**

expert opinion ∎ A suspect superlative.

expletive deleted ∎ An infantile phrase.

explore every avenue ∎ A moribund metaphor. *delve into; examine; explore; inspect; investigate; look into; probe; scrutinize; search; study.*

express (concern) ∎ A torpid term. Phrases like *express concern, express doubt, express opposition, express thanks* make any sentence instantly sodden. • Officials *express concern* about the slow pace of economic growth. REPLACE WITH *worry.* • House Democrats continue to *express anger* about the state's ethics and campaign finance laws. REPLACE WITH *fume.* • I want to *express my appreciation to* all of you who have lent us a hand in this endeavor. REPLACE WITH *thank.*

extend (hold out) the olive branch ∎ A moribund metaphor. *be accommodating; be agreeable; be conciliatory; be obliging; be peaceable; be propitiatory.*

extent ∎ A torpid term. Like *degree*, the word *extent*, along with the phrases in which it is found, is best avoided.

These are lifeless expressions, and it is listless people who use them. • In some cases, they've been transformed *to such an extent* that you can no longer recognize them. REPLACE WITH *so much.* • The study said that women, *to a greater extent* than men, manage by personal interactions with their subordinates. REPLACE WITH *more.* • Resources are always used *to the optimum extent.* REPLACE WITH *optimally.* • Sooner or later, we will see *to what extent* the central banks are prepared to back up words with actions. REPLACE WITH *how far.* • *The extent to which* these practices are seen as flowing in one direction, down from headquarters to subsidiaries, may influence *the extent to which* these practices are adopted and *to what extent* the behavior, beliefs, and values of the corporate culture are incorporated or even complied with. REPLACE WITH *How much, how much, and how much.* SEE ALSO **degree.**

extenuating circumstances ∎ A torpid term.

> It was a lovely apology for missing drinks the previous evening due to extenuating circumstances, you know, my job.—Michele Mitchell, *The Latest Bombshell*

(his) eyes are bigger than (his) stomach ∎ A moribund metaphor.

eyes are the windows of the soul ∎ A moribund metaphor.

(has) eyes in the back of (his) head
 ∎ A moribund metaphor. *alert; attentive;
aware; eagle-eyed; heedful; keen; observant;
perceptive; vigilant; wakeful; watchful.*

eyes (are) wide open ∎ A moribund
metaphor. *alert; attentive; aware; cognizant;
conscious; eagle-eyed; heedful; keen;
observant; perceptive; vigilant; wakeful;
watchful.*

Ff

fabulous ▮ An overworked word. As still another synonym for *very good* or *extremely pleasing*, *fabulous* is indeed overused. In its sense of *hard to believe* or *astounding*, it is now and again used, and in its sense of *like a fable* or *legendary*, it is woefully unused.

face the music ▮ A moribund metaphor. *pay*; *suffer*.

> Not to be a member of the communion of saints or gods or demigods or fathers or mothers or grandfathers or grandmothers or brothers or sisters or brethren of any kind, germane to me through consanguinity, affinity, or any other kind of linear or genitive or collateral bond. To face the music at last.—Edna O'Brien, *Night*

(a) factor ▮ A torpid term. • I think the TV show *was a contributing factor* to this tragedy. REPLACE WITH *contributed*. • They thought the biggest problem we were dealing with was a *jealousy factor*. REPLACE WITH *jealousy*. • The *key factor in* the decline appears to be the Irish-American voter's willingness to vote for candidates from other ethnic groups. REPLACE WITH *key to*. SEE ALSO **(an) element**. • The presence of a long umbilical cord *is a contributory factor* to the occurrence of nuchal cord. REPLACE WITH *contributes*.

facts and figures ▮ An inescapable pair.

facts and information ▮ A wretched redundancy. *data*; *facts*; *information*.

fade into the sunset ▮ A moribund metaphor. *disappear*; *disperse*; *dissolve*; *evaporate*; *fade*; *vanish*; *vaporize*; *volatilize*.

fade into the woodwork ▮ A moribund metaphor. *depart*; *disappear*; *disperse*; *dissolve*; *evaporate*; *fade*; *vacate*; *vanish*; *vaporize*; *volatilize*; *withdraw*. • It is easy to *fade into the woodwork* and never have to deal with those problems. REPLACE WITH *disappear*.

fading fast ▮ A moribund metaphor. *beat*; *bushed*; *debilitated*; *depleted*; *drained*; *drowsy*; *enervated*; *exhausted*; *fatigued*; *groggy*; *sapped*; *sleepy*; *sluggish*; *slumberous*; *somnolent*; *soporific*; *spent*; *tired*; *weary*; *worn out*.

fair and equitable ▮ An inescapable pair. *equitable*; *fair*; *just*. • The key to maintaining that system is ensuring that you are treated *fairly and equitably*.

REPLACE WITH *equitably* or *fairly*.

fair and square ▮ An inescapable pair. *aboveboard*; *creditable*; *equitable*; *fair*; *honest*; *honorable*; *just*; *lawful*; *legitimate*; *open*; *proper*; *reputable*; *respectable*; *right*; *square*; *straightforward*; *upright*; *veracious*; *veridical*.

fair game ▮ A moribund metaphor.

fair is fair ▮ A quack equation.

fair share ▮ A torpid term. *allocation*; *allotment*; *allowance*; *amount*; *apportionment*; *dole*; *lot*; *measure*; *part*; *piece*; *portion*; *quota*; *ration*; *share*. • We are setting out to get our *fair share* of the residential real estate mortgage business.

fair to middling ▮ A wretched redundancy. *average*; *common*; *fair*; *mediocre*; *middling*; *moderate*; *ordinary*; *passable*; *tolerable*.

fait accompli ▮ A foreign phrase.

fall between (through) the cracks ▮ A moribund metaphor. *be discounted*; *be disregarded*; *be elided*; *be forgotten*; *be ignored*; *be left out*; *be missed*; *be neglected*; *be omitted*; *be overlooked*; *be skipped*; *be slighted*; *be snubbed*; *elapse*; *end*; *fail*; *go by*; *lapse*; *slid*; *slip*. • Such a caring environment is particularly important for students who have few other sources of support and who might well *fall through the cracks* in a less personalized school setting. REPLACE WITH *be forgotten*. • Between groping for meaningful full-time employment and anguishing over the political state of our country, I've allowed some things to *fall between the cracks*. REPLACE WITH *lapse*.

fall flat on (its) face ▮ A moribund metaphor. *be unsuccessful*; *blunder*; *bomb*; *break down*; *bungle*; *collapse*; *fail*; *fall short*; *falter*; *fizzle*; *flop*; *fold*; *founder*; *mess up*; *miscarry*; *not succeed*; *stumble*; *topple*. • Some professional investors are betting the company will *fall flat on its face*. REPLACE WITH *fail*.

fall from grace) ▮ A moribund metaphor. *collapse*; *decline*; *downfall*; *failure*; *fall*; *misadventure*; *misfortune*; *offense*; *peccadillo*; *ruin*; *sin*; *transgression*; *wrongdoing*.

fall in (into) line (place) ▮ A moribund metaphor. *abide by*; *accede*; *accommodate*; *accord*; *acquiesce*; *adapt*; *adhere to*; *agree*; *be conventional*; *behave*; *be traditional*; *comply*; *concur*; *conform*; *correspond*;

follow; harmonize; heed; mind; obey; observe; submit; yield.

fall into (my) lap ∎ A moribund metaphor. • It just kind of *fell into my lap.*

fall on deaf ears ∎ A moribund metaphor. *discount; disregard; ignore.*

fall through the floor ∎ A moribund metaphor. *collapse; crash; decline; decrease; descend; dip; drop; ebb; fall; plummet; plunge; recede; sink; slide; slip; subside; topple; tumble.* • But Cellucci said the bond rating *fell through the floor* in the late 1980s during the fiscal crisis. REPLACE WITH *collapsed.*

fame and fortune ∎ A suspect superlative. SEE ALSO **the rich and famous**.

familiarity breeds contempt ∎ A popular prescription.

> When we first discussed my working on the books' pages, Nathan argued that, if I ever achieved my ambition to become the books editor, I would end up hating books. Familiarity bred contempt —Elizabeth Buchan, *Revenge Of The Middle-Aged Woman*

fan (fuel) the fire (flames) ∎ A moribund metaphor. *activate; agitate; animate; arouse; awaken; encourage; enkindle; enliven; exacerbate; excite; feed; foment; ignite; impassion; incite; inflame; intensify; invigorate; make worse; nourish; prod; provoke; rejuvenate; revitalize; revive; rouse; shake up; stimulate; stir up; vitalize; worsen.*

far and away ∎ A wretched redundancy. *by far; much.*

far and wide ∎ An inescapable pair. *all around; all over; all through; broadly; everyplace; everywhere; extensively; throughout; ubiquitously; universally; widely.* SEE ALSO **high and wide**; **left and right**.

far-reaching consequences (implications) ∎ An inescapable pair.

fascinating (good; interesting) stuff. ∎ An infantile phrase.

fashion statement ∎ A plebeian sentiment. Making a *fashion statement* is the concern of adolescents and addle-brained adults who have yet to fashion for themselves a sense of identity. Their habiliments interest them more than does their humanity.

People so intent on being fashionable make only misstatements. They but blither.

fast and furious ∎ An inescapable pair.

(as) fast as (her) legs can carry (her) ∎ An insipid simile. *abruptly; apace; at once; briskly; directly; expeditiously; fast; forthwith; hastily; hurriedly; immediately; instantaneously; instantly; posthaste; promptly; quickly; rapidly; rashly; right away; speedily; straightaway; swiftly; wingedly.*

fasten your seat belts ∎ A moribund metaphor.

faster than a speeding bullet, (more powerful than a locomotive, able to leap small buildings at a single bound) ∎ An infantile phrase.

fast track ∎ A moribund metaphor.

fast trigger finger ∎ A moribund metaphor.

(as) fat as a cow ∎ An insipid simile. *ample; big; bulky; chubby; chunky; colossal; corpulent; dumpy; enormous; fat; flabby; fleshy; gigantic; heavy; hefty; huge; immense; large; mammoth; massive; obese; plump; portly; pudgy; rotund; round; squat; stocky; stout.*

(as) fat as a pig ∎ An insipid simile. *ample; big; bulky; chubby; chunky; colossal; corpulent; dumpy; enormous; fat; flabby; fleshy; gigantic; heavy; hefty; huge; immense; large; mammoth; massive; obese; plump; portly; pudgy; rotund; round; squat; stocky; stout.*

fat cat ∎ A moribund metaphor. *billionaire; capitalist; financier; magnate; materialist; millionaire; mogul; multimillionaire; nabob; plutocrat; tycoon.*

fear and trembling ∎ An inescapable pair. *alarm; anxiety; apprehension; consternation; dismay; dread; fear; foreboding; fright; horror; panic; terror; trembling; trepidation.*

feast or famine ∎ An inescapable pair.

feather (their) nest ∎ A moribund metaphor. • He repeatedly denied allegations that he used his three years at the Denver-based thrift to *feather his own nest.*

feed (you) a line ∎ A moribund metaphor. *deceive; dissemble; distort; equivocate; falsify; fib; lie; misconstrue; mislead; misrepresent; pervert; prevaricate.*

feedback ∎ A torpid term. *answers; data; feelings; ideas; information; recommendations; replies; responses; suggestions; thoughts; views.* • Your *feedback* helps us continually improve. REPLACE WITH *suggestions.* • And as *feedback* is obtained, it is the duty of the firm's leaders to convey it to all members of the firm. REPLACE WITH *ideas.* SEE ALSO **(the) bottom line**; **input**; **interface**; **output**; **parameters**.

feeling no pain ∎ A moribund metaphor. *besotted; crapulous; drunk; inebriated; intoxicated; sodden; stupefied; tipsy.*

feeling (his) oats ∎ A moribund metaphor. *active; alive; animated; dynamic; energetic; exuberant; frisky; indefatigable; inexhaustible; invigorated; lively; peppy; spirited; sprightly; spry; tireless; unflagging; vibrant; vigorous; vivacious; zestful; zesty.*

feel the pinch ∎ A moribund metaphor.

feel the heat ∎ A moribund metaphor.

fell off a cliff ∎ A moribund metaphor. *crash; dive; drop; fall; plummet; plunge; topple; tumble.* • Sales *fell off a cliff* after the tax credit expired. REPLACE WITH *plummeted.* • North Texas home sales *fell off a cliff* in July. REPLACE WITH *plunged.*

fertile ground ∎ A moribund metaphor.

few and far between ∎ A wretched redundancy. *exiguous; limited; inadequate; infrequent; meager; rare; scant; scanty; scarce; sparse; uncommon; unusual.* • Role models are *few and far between* in those groups. REPLACE WITH *scarce.*

fiddle while Rome burns ∎ A moribund metaphor.

fight a losing battle ∎ A moribund metaphor.

fight fire with fire ∎ A moribund metaphor.

fight like cats and dogs ∎ An insipid simile (SEE moribund metaphors) 1. *altercate; argue; disagree; dispute; feud; fight; quarrel; spat; squabble; wrangle.* 2. *battle; brawl; clash; fight; grapple; jostle; make war; scuffle; skirmish; tussle; war; wrestle.*

filled to bursting (overflowing) ∎ A moribund metaphor. *abounding; brimful; brimming; bursting; chock-full; congested; crammed; crowded; dense; filled; full; gorged; jammed; jam-packed; overcrowded; overfilled; overflowing; packed; replete; saturated; stuffed; swarming; teeming.*

filled to the brim ∎ A moribund metaphor. *abounding; brimful; brimming; bursting; chock-full; congested; crammed; crowded; dense; filled; full; gorged; jammed; jam-packed; overcrowded; overfilled; packed; replete; saturated; stuffed; swarming; teeming.*

> I recall the scent of some kind of toilet powder—I believe she stole it from her mother's Spanish maid—a sweetish, lowly, musky perfume. It mingled with her own biscuit odor, and my senses were suddenly filled to the brim; a sudden commotion in a nearby bush prevented them from overflowing . . ..—Vladimir Nabokov, *Lolita*

fill in the blanks ∎ An infantile phrase.

fill (his) shoes ∎ A moribund metaphor.

fill the bill ∎ A moribund metaphor. 1. *be appropriate; be apt; be befitting; be felicitous; be fit; be fitting; be happy; be meet; be proper; be right; be seemly; be suitable; be suited.* 2. *be acceptable; be adequate; be qualified; be satisfactory; be sufficient.*

fill to capacity ∎ A wretched redundancy. *fill.* • Our free public facilities are *filled to capacity,* and there are long waiting lists for some programs. REPLACE WITH *filled.*

filthy lucre ∎ A moribund metaphor. *money; riches; wealth.*

final and irrevocable ∎ An inescapable pair. *final; firm; irrevocable; unalterable.*

final chapter ∎ A moribund metaphor. *close; completion; conclusion; consummation; culmination; denouement; end; ending; finale; finish; termination.*

final conclusion ∎ A wretched redundancy. • We have made no *final conclusions* on responsibility for the attacks in Kenya and Tanzania. DELETE *final.*

final culmination ∎ A wretched redundancy. *culmination.* • Owning a farm was the *final culmination* of all our efforts. DELETE *final.*

final decision ∎ A wretched redundancy. *decision.* • That's one of the things we have under consideration, but no *final decision* has been made. DELETE *final.*

finalize ∎ A torpid term. *complete; conclude; consummate; end; execute; finish; fulfill; made final; terminate.* • Delays in *finalizing* the state budget and its allocations to cities and towns make a special town meeting necessary. REPLACE WITH *completing.* SEE ALSO **utilize**.

finder's keepers, loser's weepers ∎ An infantile phrase.

find (some) middle ground ∎ A moribund metaphor. *compromise.*

fine and dandy ∎ An inescapable pair. *all right; excellent; fine; good; O.K.; well.* SEE ALSO **well and good**.

fine line ∎ A moribund metaphor. • There is a very *fine line* between vision and delusion.

fine weather for ducks ∎ A moribund metaphor. *rainy; wet.*

fingers on the pulse of ∎ A moribund metaphor.

fire (launch) a salvo ∎ A moribund metaphor.

(all) fired (hopped, psyched) up ∎ A moribund metaphor. *afire; aflame; anxious; ardent; burning; eager; enthusiastic; excited; fanatic; fanatical; fervent; fervid; fiery; impassioned; inflamed; intense; perfervid; keen; passionate; vehement; zealous.*

fire in (his) belly ∎ A moribund metaphor. *ambitious; ardent; determined; dogged; driven; eager; enthusiastic; fervent; impassioned; motivated; passionate; persistent; pushy; resolute; strong-willed.*

firmly establish ∎ An inescapable pair. Adverbs often modify other words needlessly. Here, *firmly* is superfluous, for *establish* means "to make firm." • The play *firmly established* him as a dramatist. DELETE *firmly.*

first and foremost ∎ A TOP-TWENTY DIMWITTICISM. A wretched redundancy. *chief; chiefly; first; foremost; initial; initially; main; mainly; most important;*

mostly; primarily; primary; principal; principally. • *First and foremost* these people must have a commitment to public service. REPLACE WITH *Most important*. SEE ALSO **first and most important**.

first and most important ∎ A wretched redundancy. *chief; chiefly; first; foremost; initial; initially; main; mainly; most important; mostly; primarily; primary; principal; principally.* SEE ALSO **first and foremost**.

first begin (start) ∎ A wretched redundancy. *begin; start.* • When we *first started* exploring the idea, we didn't even know if it was possible to do. DELETE *first*.

first line of defense ∎ A moribund metaphor.

first of all ∎ A wretched redundancy. *first.* • *First of all*, I am delighted about our progress in that area. REPLACE WITH *First*. SEE ALSO **second of all**.

first (highest; number-one; top) priority ∎ A TOP-TWENTY DIMWITTICISM. A torpid term. Nothing that is soulful, little that is genuine can be said using these expressions, so when a U.S. cardinal drearily sermonizes "The protection of children must be our *number-one priority*," we are hardly convinced that this is his or the church's principal concern. When we read, in some corporate promotional piece, "Your satisfaction is our *number-one priority*," we are likewise, and for good reason, suspicious. Mechanical expressions like *first (highest; number-one; top) priority* defy tenderness, resist compassion, and counter concern. SEE ALSO **reach epidemic proportions**.

fish or cut bait ∎ A moribund metaphor.

(bigger; other) fish to fry ∎ A moribund metaphor.

> Now, I wish I could remember Daddy's reply to all her nagging, but I had bigger fish to fry that weekend and didn't much care that Missy had inexplicably fallen in love with her own uncle ....—Janis Owens, *The Schooling of Claybird Catts*

(as) fit as a fiddle ∎ An insipid simile. *athletic; beefy; brawny; energetic; fit; good; hale; hardy; healthful; healthy; hearty; husky; lanky; lean; manly; muscular; powerful; robust; shapely; sinewy; slender; solid; sound; stalwart; stout; strong; sturdy; thin; trim; vigorous; virile; well; well-built.*

fit for a king ∎ A moribund metaphor. *august; awe-inspiring; distinguished; elegant; eminent; exalted; exquisite; extraordinary; extravagant; glorious; grand; great; impressive; kingly; luxurious; magnificent; majestic; monarchical; nobel; opulent; princely; regal; royal; sovereign; splendid; stately; sumptuous.*

fitting and proper ∎ An inescapable pair. *appropriate; apt; befitting; felicitous; fit; fitting; happy; meet; proper; right; seemly; suitable; suited.* • And it is generally regarded as *fitting and proper* for women to do this. REPLACE WITH *fitting*.

fit to be tied ∎ A moribund metaphor. *angry; cross; enraged; fuming; furious; incensed; indignant; infuriated; irate; mad; outraged; raging; wrathful.*

fix (her) wagon ∎ A moribund metaphor. 1. *castigate; censure; chasten; chastise; chide; criticize; discipline; penalize; punish; rebuke; reprove; scold.* 2. *spank.*

flaming inferno ∎ An infantile phrase. *blaze; conflagration; fire; inferno.*

flash in the pan ∎ A moribund metaphor. *brief; ephemeral; evanescent; fleeting; momentary; short; short-lived; short-term; temporary; transient; transitory.*

(as) flat as a board ∎ An insipid simile. *even; flat; flush; horizontal; level; plane; smooth.*

(as) flat as a pancake ∎ An insipid simile. *even; flat; flush; horizontal; level; plane; smooth.*

flat on (his) back ∎ A moribund metaphor. *afflicted; ailing; crippled; debilitated; defenseless; disabled; diseased; feeble; fragile; helpless; ill; incapacitated; indisposed; infirm; not (feeling) well; sick; sickly; unhealthy; unwell; valetudinarian; weak.*

(my) (own) flesh and blood ∎ A moribund metaphor. 1. *brother; child; daughter; father; kin; mother; parent; relative; sibling; sister; son.* 2. *depth; reality; substance.*

flight of fancy ∎ A moribund metaphor. *caprice; chimera; crotchet; daydream; delusion; dream; fancy; fantasy; hallucination; humor; illusion; imagination; notion; phantasm; vagary; whim; whimsy.*

flip (her) lid ∎ A moribund metaphor. *bellow; bluster; clamor; explode; fulminate; fume; holler; howl; rage; rant; rave; roar; scream; shout; storm; thunder; vociferate; yell.*

(on the) flip side (of the coin) ∎ A moribund metaphor. 1. *antithesis; contrary; converse; opposite; reverse.* 2. *but; in contrast; conversely; however; inversely; whereas; yet.*

(whatever) floats (your) boat ∎ A moribund metaphor. *absorbs (you); amuses (you); arouses (you); diverts (you); engages (you); entertains (you); excites (you); fascinates (you); inspires (you); interests (you); motivates (you); rouses (you); stimulates (you); stirs (you).* • I am an artiste of sorts, dance, music, poetry, art, theatre all *float my boat*. REPLACE WITH *inspire me*.

flotsam and jetsam ∎ An inescapable pair. 1. *debris; litter; rack; refuse; rubbish;*

rubble; wrack; wreckage. **2.** *bits; fragments; modicums; odds and ends; particles; pieces; remnants; scraps; shreds; snippets; trifles.* **3.** *itinerants; rovers; tramps; vagabonds; vagrants; wanderers.*

flowing with milk and honey ∎ A moribund metaphor.

fly (ride) below (under) the radar (of) ∎ A moribund metaphor. **1.** *disregarded; hidden; ignored; imperceptible; indiscernible; invisible; overlooked; undetectable; undetected; unheard of; unknown; unnoticeable; unnoticed; unobserved; unperceived; unrevealed; unseen.* **2.** *discreet; inconspicuous; self-effacing; unassuming; understated; unobtrusive.* • The sport isn't exactly *riding under the radar* in the United States anymore, thanks in large part to Lance Armstrong's dominant reign in the Tour de France. REPLACE WITH *unnoticed.* • *Flying under the radar* are the Russians, who may just be warming up for the medal round. REPLACE WITH *Unassuming.*

fly-by-night ∎ A moribund metaphor. *irresponsible; undependable; unreliable; untrustworthy.*

fly by the seat of (his) pants ∎ A moribund metaphor. *be extemporaneous; be instinctive; be spontaneous; impromptu; improvise.* • Administrators who *fly by the seat of their pants* typically rely on trial and error because there are no overarching objectives and guidelines. REPLACE WITH *are instinctive.*

flying high ∎ A moribund metaphor. **1.** *advantageous; auspicious; blessed; charmed; enchanted; favored; felicitous; flourishing; fortuitous; fortunate; golden; happy; in luck; lucky; propitious; prosperous; successful; thriving.* **2.** *blissful; blithe; buoyant; cheerful; delighted; ecstatic; elated; enraptured; euphoric; exalted; excited; exhilarated; exultant; gay; glad; gleeful; good-humored; happy; intoxicated; jolly; jovial; joyful; joyous; jubilant; merry; mirthful; overjoyed; pleased; rapturous; thrilled.*

fly in the face of ∎ A moribund metaphor. *buck; challenge; contradict; defy; disobey; dispute; disregard; flout; go against; ignore; militate against; neglect; oppose; overlook; resist; violate.* • This is nonsensical and *flies in the face of* history and basic economic principles. REPLACE WITH *contradicts.*

fly in the ointment ∎ A moribund metaphor. *bar; barrier; block; blockage; catch; check; deterrent; difficulty; encumbrance; handicap; hindrance; hitch; hurdle; impediment; interference; obstacle; obstruction; rub; snag.*

fly off the handle ∎ A moribund metaphor. *bellow; blow up; bluster; clamor; explode; fulminate; fume; holler; howl; rage; rant; rave; roar; scream; shout; storm; thunder; vociferate; yell.* • To tell the truth, investors

are *flying off the handle* everywhere you look. REPLACE WITH *howling.* • Meditation makes me a much calmer person; I don't *fly off the handle* so much. REPLACE WITH *rant.*

fly the coop ∎ A moribund metaphor. *abscond; clear out; decamp; depart; desert; disappear; escape; exit; flee; fly; go; go away; leave; move on; part; pull out; quit; retire; retreat; run away; take flight; take off; vacate; vanish; withdraw.*

> So poor Bridget, it's all mapped out, and the only alternative would be to fly the coop, but she isn't the type.—Adrian McKinty, *Dead I Well May Be*

fly (too) close to the sun ∎ A moribund metaphor. *chance; dare; endanger; gamble; hazard; imperil; jeopardize; make bold; peril; risk; venture.*

foaming (frothing) at the mouth ∎ A moribund metaphor. *be angry; be berserk; be convulsive; be crazed; be delirious; be demented; be demoniac; be deranged; be enraged; be feral; be ferocious; be fierce; be frantic; be frenzied; be fuming; be furious; be hysterical; be infuriated; be in hysterics; be insane; be incensed; be irate; be mad; be maddened; be maniacal; be murderous; be possessed; be rabid; be raging; be ranting; be raving; be savage; be seething; be wild; be wrathful.*

focus attention (concentration) on ∎ A wretched redundancy. *concentrate on; focus on.* • Microsoft has always *focused its attention on* software products and software standards. REPLACE WITH *focused on.* • It is hardly magic to *focus concentration on* success instead of failure. REPLACE WITH *concentrate on.* SEE ALSO **focus effort (energy) on.**

focus effort (energy) on ∎ A wretched redundancy. *concentrate on; focus on.* • This downsizing will cut our expenses and allow us to *focus our efforts on* serving our customers. REPLACE WITH *focus on.* • Owners can *focus their energy on* expanding the business to a point where it can function outside of a "nurtured" environment. REPLACE WITH *focus on.* SEE ALSO **focus attention (concentration) on.**

focus in on ∎ A wretched redundancy. *focus on.* • I have to *focus in on* what I want to accomplish. DELETE *in.*

fold (their) tent ∎ A moribund metaphor. *abscond; clear out; decamp; depart; desert; disappear; escape; exit; flee; fly; go; go away; leave; move on; part; pull out; quit; retire; retreat; run away; take flight; take off; vacate; vanish; withdraw.*

follow in (her) footsteps ∎ A moribund metaphor.

follow suit ∎ A moribund metaphor. *copy; do*

as much; follow; imitate; mimic. • NYNEX is expected to *follow suit* in the near future. REPLACE WITH *do as much.* • When American Airlines slashed fares, TWA *followed suit.* REPLACE WITH *did as much.*

follow the crowd ∎ A moribund metaphor. *abide by; accede; accommodate; accord; acquiesce; adapt; adhere to; agree; be conventional; behave; be traditional; comply; concur; conform; correspond; follow; harmonize; heed; mind; obey; observe; submit; yield.*

follow your instincts ∎ A popular prescription.

food for thought ∎ A moribund metaphor. SEE ALSO **(it's) something to think about**.

food for worms ∎ A moribund metaphor. *dead; deceased; defunct; exanimate; expired; extinct; extinguished; finished; gone; inanimate; lifeless; no more; perished; terminated.*

fools rush in where angels fear to tread ∎ A popular prescription.

footloose and fancy free ∎ A moribund metaphor. *at liberty; autonomous; free; independent; self-reliant; unattached; unbound; unconfined; unconstrained; unencumbered; unentangled; unfettered; uninhibited; unrestrained; unrestricted; unshackled; untied.*

footprints in the sands of time ∎ A moribund metaphor.

foot the bill ∎ A moribund metaphor. *pay (for).*

> To argue would mean she was offering to foot the bill, something she had done so often over their years of living together that it had become expected of her.—Amy Tan, *The Bonesetter's Daughter*

for all intents and purposes ∎ A wretched redundancy. *effectively; essentially; in effect; in essence; practically; virtually.* • *For all intents and purposes,* the civil rights acts of 1964 and 1965 signified the demise of official segregation in the United States. REPLACE WITH *In effect.* SEE ALSO **for all practical purposes; to all intents and purposes; to all practical purposes**.

for all practical purposes ∎ A wretched redundancy. *effectively; essentially; in effect; in essence; practically; virtually.* • Services are, *for all practical purposes,* sold as products to end users, so the distinction between services and goods is artificial at best. REPLACE WITH *essentially.* SEE ALSO **for all intents and purposes; to all intents and purposes; to all practical purposes**.

for all (he was) worth ∎ A moribund metaphor.

for a song ∎ A moribund metaphor. *cheaply; economically; inexpensively.*

> A real beauty, with wood-spoke wheels and navy mohair upholstery. He was getting it for a song, from a widow who'd never learned to drive her husband's car.—Anita Shreve, *Sea Glass*

for better or for worse ∎ A torpid term.

> But the family room, the only room where any of us has ever spent any time, has always been, for better or for worse, the ultimate reflection of our true inclinations.—Dave Eggers, *A Heartbreaking Work of Staggering Genius*

forever and a day ∎ A moribund metaphor. *always; ceaselessly; constantly; continually; continuously; endlessly; eternally; everlastingly; evermore; forever; forevermore; immortally; indefinitely; interminably; permanently; perpetually; persistently; unceasingly; unremittingly.*

for every action there's an equal and opposite reaction ∎ A popular prescription.

for every negative there is a positive ∎ A popular prescription.

for everything there is a season ∎ A popular prescription.

forewarn ∎ A wretched redundancy. *warn.* • *Forewarn* your clients that they might be stared at by locals. REPLACE WITH *Warn.* SEE ALSO **advance warning; warn in advance**.

forewarned is forearmed ∎ A quack equation.

for free ∎ A wretched redundancy. *free.*

forgive and forget ∎ A popular prescription.

fork in the road ∎ A moribund metaphor.

formative years ∎ A torpid term. *adolescence; childhood; immaturity; juvenility.*

forsooth ∎ A withered word. *actually; indeed; in fact; in faith; in reality; in truth; truly.*

(it's) for the birds ∎ A moribund metaphor. 1. *absurd; asinine; childish; comical; farcical; fatuous; flighty; foolhardy; foolish; frivolous; giddy; idiotic; immature; inane; laughable; ludicrous; nonsensical; preposterous; ridiculous; senseless; silly.* 2. *barren; bootless; effete; feckless; feeble; fruitless; futile; impotent; inadequate; inconsequential; inconsiderable; ineffective; ineffectual; infertile; insignificant; inutile; meaningless; meritless; nugatory; null; of no value; pointless; powerless; profitless; purposeless; sterile; trifling; trivial; unavailing; unimportant; unproductive; unprofitable; unserviceable; unworthy; useless; vain; valueless; weak; worthless.*

for the (simple) fact that ∎ A wretched redundancy. *because; considering; for; in that; since.* • Women received some assistance in the colonial period *for the simple fact that* American Protestants strongly favored "peaceable" and intact families. REPLACE WITH *because.* SEE ALSO **for the (simple) reason that.**

for the most part ∎ A wretched redundancy. *almost all; chiefly; commonly; generally; greatly; in general; largely; mainly; most; mostly; most often; much; nearly all; overall; normally; typically; usually.* • The search for solutions to these crises has focused *for the most part* on the legal system. REPLACE WITH *largely.*

for (with) the purpose of -ing ∎ A wretched redundancy. *for (-ing); so as to; to.* • These analyses have been used *for the purpose of criticizing* the shortcomings of Western management. REPLACE WITH *for criticizing* or *to criticize.* • The other was the development in 1923 of a comparison microscope that could be used *for the purpose of determining* whether or not a bullet found at the scene of a crime was fired by a particular gun. REPLACE WITH *for determining* or *to determine.*

for the (simple) reason that ∎ A wretched redundancy. *because; considering; for; in that; since.* • Polls dominate political discourse *for the simple reason that* "Everyone else has an opinion; the pollster has a fact." REPLACE WITH *because.* SEE ALSO **for the (simple) fact that.**

for your information ∎ An ineffectual phrase. • *For your information,* he loves me, and I love him. DELETE *For your information.*

forward progress ∎ A torpid term. • It is our sincere goal to achieve *forward progress* and business growth for our clients based on their potential and capacity. USE *progress.* • Overall the new Zunes and the expanded feature set are certainly *forward progress* in Microsoft's attempt to establish a competing mp3 player brand. USE *progress.* • This move should allow us to start producing Biodiesel and generating revenue by the end of this year with comparatively minor overhead costs while concurrently enabling well-planned, *forward progress* to continue on the larger Biofuel facility. USE *progress.* • Just when we think we're making *forward progress,* we find out things aren't running the way we thought they would or that the numbers that are generating just don't seem right or they're off by a lot. USE *progress.*

> In a football game, *forward progress* may be sensibly described as "the location to which a ball carrier's forward momentum carries him before he is tackled," but used elsewhere it is thoroughly nonsensical: *to progress* means "to advance, to move forward."

foul up (gum up; screw up) the works ∎ A moribund metaphor. 1. *agitate; confuse; disorder; disorganize; disquiet; disrupt; disturb; fluster; jar; jinx; jolt; jumble; mix up; muddle; perturb; rattle; ruffle; shake up; stir up; unnerve; unsettle; upset.* 2. *blight; cripple; damage; disable; harm; hurt; impair; incapacitate; lame; mar; mess up; rack; ruin; sabotage; spoil; subvert; undermine; vitiate; wrack; wreck.*

free and easy ∎ An inescapable pair. *casual; carefree; easygoing; informal; insouciant; lighthearted; nonchalant; relaxed; untroubled.*

free and gratis ∎ An infantile phrase. *free.*

(as) free as a bird ∎ An insipid simile. *autonomous; free; independent; self-reliant; unattached; unbound; unconfined; unconstrained; unencumbered; unentangled; unfettered; uninhibited; unrestrained; unrestricted; unshackled; untied.*

(as) free as the wind ∎ An insipid simile. *autonomous; free; independent; self-reliant; unattached; unbound; unconfined; unconstrained; unencumbered; unentangled; unfettered; uninhibited; unrestrained; unrestricted; unshackled; untied.*

free gift ∎ A wretched redundancy. *gift.* • With every renewal, you will receive a *free gift.* DELETE *free.*

(no) free lunch ∎ A moribund metaphor.

free ride ∎ A moribund metaphor.

freezing cold ∎ An inescapable pair. *algid; arctic; brumal; chilly; cold; cool; freezing; frigid; frosty; frozen; gelid; glacial; hibernal; hyperborean; ice-cold; icy; nippy; polar; rimy; wintry.*

(as) fresh as a daisy ∎ An insipid simile. *active; alive; animated; blooming; dynamic; energetic; fresh; healthy; hearty; lively; peppy; refreshed; rested; rosy; ruddy; spirited; sprightly; spry; vibrant; vigorous; vivacious.*

fret and fume ∎ An inescapable pair.

frighten by (his) own shadow ∎ A moribund metaphor. *alarm; appall; benumb; daunt; frighten; horrify; intimidate; panic; paralyze; petrify; scare; shock; startle; terrify; terrorize; unnerve.*

frighten (scare) out of (her) wits ∎ A moribund metaphor. *alarm; appall; benumb; daunt; frighten; horrify; intimidate; panic; paralyze; petrify; scare; shock; startle; terrify; terrorize; unnerve.*

frighten the life out of ∎ A moribund metaphor. *alarm; appall; benumb; daunt; frighten; horrify; intimidate; panic; paralyze; petrify; scare; shock; startle; terrify; terrorize; unnerve.*

(go) from a simmer to a hard boil ∎ A moribund metaphor.

from A to Z ∎ A moribund metaphor. 1. *all*

during; all over; all through; throughout. **2.** *altogether; completely; entirely; fully; perfectly; quite; roundly; thoroughly; totally; unreservedly; utterly; wholly.*

from beginning to end ∎ A moribund metaphor. **1.** *always; ceaselessly; constantly; continually; continuously; endlessly; eternally; everlastingly; evermore; forever; forevermore; frequently; interminably; nonstop; permanently; perpetually; persistently; recurrently; regularly; repeatedly; unceasingly; unremittingly.* **2.** *all during; all over; all through; throughout.* **3.** *altogether; completely; entirely; fully; perfectly; quite; roundly; thoroughly; totally; unreservedly; utterly; wholly.*

from (the) cradle to (the) grave ∎ A moribund metaphor. **1.** *always; ceaselessly; constantly; continually; continuously; endlessly; eternally; everlastingly; evermore; forever; forevermore; frequently; interminably; nonstop; permanently; perpetually; persistently; recurrently; regularly; repeatedly; unceasingly; unremittingly.* **2.** *all during; all over; all through; throughout.*

from darkness to light ∎ A moribund metaphor.

> No longer a pariah, you were now a desired guest at parties, where you were supposed to speak eloquently about the struggle, to tear up and talk about the walk from the darkness into the light.—Lisa Fugard, *Skinner's Drift*

from dawn to (until) dusk ∎ A moribund metaphor. *all day; all the time; always; ceaselessly; constantly; continually; continuously; endlessly; eternally; everlastingly; evermore; forever; forevermore; frequently; interminably; nonstop; permanently; perpetually; persistently; recurrently; regularly; repeatedly; unceasingly; unremittingly.* • She has to put up with this kind of stuff *from dawn to dusk.* REPLACE WITH *endlessly.*

from hence ∎ A wretched redundancy. *hence.*

from pillar to post ∎ A moribund metaphor. • You can't let your convictions be shaken, or you'll jump *from pillar to post* the moment times become difficult.

from rags to riches ∎ A moribund metaphor.

from soup to nuts ∎ A moribund metaphor. *all; all things; everything.*

from start to finish ∎ A moribund metaphor. **1.** *always; ceaselessly; constantly; continually; continuously; endlessly; eternally; everlastingly; evermore; forever; forevermore; frequently; interminably; nonstop; permanently; perpetually; persistently; recurrently; regularly; repeatedly; unceasingly; unremittingly.*

2. *all during; all over; all through; throughout.*

from stem to stern ∎ A moribund metaphor. **1.** *all during; all over; all through; throughout.* **2.** *altogether; completely; entirely; fully; perfectly; quite; roundly; thoroughly; totally; unreservedly; utterly; wholly.*

from the bottom (depths) of (my) heart ∎ A moribund metaphor. *earnestly; fervently; genuinely; heartily; honestly; sincerely; unreservedly; wholeheartedly.*

from the frying pan into the fire ∎ A moribund metaphor.

(straight) from the horses mouth ∎ A moribund metaphor.

from the word *go* ∎ An infantile phrase.

> Even my life so far has been plain. More Daisy than Elizabeth from the word go.—Meg Rosoff, *How I Live Now*

from tip to toe ∎ A moribund metaphor. **1.** *all during; all over; all through; throughout.* **2.** *altogether; completely; entirely; fully; perfectly; quite; roundly; thoroughly; totally; unreservedly; utterly; wholly.*

from top to bottom ∎ A moribund metaphor. **1.** *all during; all over; all through; throughout.* **2.** *altogether; completely; entirely; fully; perfectly; quite; roundly; thoroughly; totally; unreservedly; utterly; wholly.*

from whence ∎ A wretched redundancy. *whence.* • The dolphins were judged sufficiently healthy to be taken back to the sea *from whence* they came. DELETE *from.* • And it all boiled over on talk radio— *from whence* it moved into the nation's high schools and junior highs and into late-night television. DELETE *from.*

front and center ∎ An inescapable pair. *foremost; high; leading; main; major; prominent; salient; top.*

> John and I used to talk about how the current phase of the moon as well as the names of trees and flowers and birds—at least the local ones!—should be front and center in people's brains; maybe such a connection to nature would help to make us more civilized.—Elizabeth Berg, *The Year of Pleasures*

fuel the fire of ∎ A moribund metaphor. **1.** *fire; ignite; inflame; kindle.* **2.** *galvanize; goad; incite; induce; needle; poke; prod; prompt; provoke; spur; stimulate; urge.* **3.** *activate; animate; arouse; electrify; energize; enliven; excite; inspirit; invigorate; motivate; quicken; stimulate; stir; vitalize; vivify.*

full capacity ∎ A wretched redundancy. *capacity.* • Buses are running closer to *full capacity* than at any time since the strike

full frontal assault

began. DELETE *full*.

full frontal assault ∎ A moribund metaphor.

full of (herself) ∎ A moribund metaphor. *egocentric; egoistic; egotistic; egotistical; narcissistic; self-absorbed; selfish; solipsistic.*

full of beans ∎ A moribund metaphor. 1. *active; alive; animated; bouncy; dynamic; energetic; exuberant; frisky; indefatigable; inexhaustible; invigorated; lively; peppy; perky; spirited; sprightly; spry; tireless; unflagging; vibrant; vigorous; vivacious; zestful; zesty.* 2. *amiss; astray; deceived; deluded; erring; erroneous; fallacious; false; faulty; inaccurate; incorrect; incredible; in error; misguided; misinformed; mislead; mistaken; not correct; not right; unbelievable; wrong.*

full of holes ∎ A moribund metaphor. 1. *defective; faulty; flawed; impaired; imperfect; marred; tainted.* 2. *baseless; captious; casuistic; casuistical; erroneous; fallacious; false; faulty; flawed; groundless; illogical; inaccurate; incorrect; invalid; irrational; jesuitic; jesuitical; mistaken; nonsensical; non sequitur; paralogistic; senseless; sophistic; sophistical; specious; spurious; unfounded; unreasonable; unsound; untenable; untrue; unveracious; wrong.*

full of hot air ∎ A moribund metaphor. 1. *aggrandizing; blustering; boasting; bragging; coloring; crowing; elaborating; embellishing; embroidering; exaggerating; fanfaronading; gloating; hyperbolizing; magnifying; overstating; swaggering.* 2. *amiss; astray; deceived; deluded; erring; erroneous; fallacious; false; faulty; inaccurate; incorrect; in error; misguided; misinformed; mislead; mistaken; not correct; not right; wrong.*

full of piss and vinegar ∎ A moribund metaphor. *active; alive; animated; dynamic; energetic; hearty; indefatigable; inexhaustible; lively; peppy; spirited; sprightly; spry; tireless; unflagging; vibrant; vigorous; vivacious.*

full of vim and vigor ∎ A moribund metaphor. *active; alive; animated; dynamic; energetic; hearty; indefatigable; inexhaustible; lively; peppy; spirited; sprightly; spry; tireless; unflagging; vibrant; vigorous; vivacious.*

full plate ∎ A moribund metaphor. *booked; busy; employed; engaged; involved; obligated; occupied.*

full potential ∎ A wretched redundancy. *potential.* • Youngsters with talents that range from mathematical to musical are not challenged to work to their *full potential.* DELETE *full*.

(at) full speed (ahead) ∎ A moribund metaphor. *abruptly; apace; at once; briskly; directly; expeditiously; fast; forthwith; hastily; hurriedly; immediately; instantaneously; instantly; posthaste; promptly; quickly; rapidly; rashly; right away; speedily; straightaway; swiftly; wingedly.*

(at) full steam (ahead) ∎ A moribund metaphor. *abruptly; apace; at once; briskly; directly; expeditiously; fast; forthwith; hastily; hurriedly; immediately; instantaneously; instantly; posthaste; promptly; quickly; rapidly; rashly; right away; speedily; straightaway; swiftly; wingedly.*

G g

gain a foothold ∎ A moribund metaphor.

gain an advantage over ∎ A torpid term. *beat; conquer; crush; defeat; outdo; overcome; overpower; overwhelm; prevail; quell; rout; succeed; triumph; trounce; vanquish; win.*

gain steam ∎ A moribund metaphor.

game plan ∎ A moribund metaphor. *action; course; direction; intention; method; move; plan; policy; procedure; route; scheme; strategy.*

game, set, and match ∎ A moribund metaphor.

garden variety ∎ A moribund metaphor. *average; common; commonplace; customary; everyday; fair; mediocre; middling; normal; ordinary; passable; plain; quotidian; regular; routine; simple; standard; tolerable; typical; uneventful; unexceptional; unremarkable; usual; workaday.*

gather together ∎ A wretched redundancy. *gather.* • This summer's training provided all 1,500 youth an opportunity to *gather together* from around the country and to develop their skills and knowledge. DELETE *together.*

(I) gave (him) the best years of (my) life ∎ A plebeian sentiment.

gaze into a crystal ball ∎ A moribund metaphor. *anticipate; augur; divine; envision; forebode; forecast; foreknow; foresee; foretell; predict; prognosticate; prophesy; vaticinate.*

general consensus ∎ A wretched redundancy. *consensus.* • The *general consensus* is that house prices have hit bottom. DELETE *general.*

(as) gentle as a lamb ∎ An insipid simile. *affable; agreeable; amiable; amicable; compassionate; friendly; gentle; good-hearted; good-natured; humane; kind; kind-hearted; kindly; personable; pleasant; tender; tolerant.*

gentleman ∎ A suspect superlative. Slipshod usage has reduced *gentleman* to a vulgarism. Common or crude people say *gentleman* when *man* would serve; though *gentleman* may sound dignified, it is actually dimwitted. Moreover, any man who doesn't, in revulsion, quiver at being called a *gentleman* is likely in jeopardy of becoming as vulgar as the word. • I am seeking a professional *gentleman* with diversified interests. REPLACE WITH *man.* • One *gentleman* told me it is a fantasy

world and not to believe everything I hear. REPLACE WITH *man.* SEE ALSO **lady**.

get (our) act together ∎ An infantile phrase. • They don't have the luxury of five years to *get their act together.*

get (has) a fix on ∎ A moribund metaphor. *ascertain; assess; comprehend; determine; evaluate; learn; understand.*

get (has) a handle on ∎ A moribund metaphor. 1. *cope with; deal with.* 2. *ascertain; assess; comprehend; determine; evaluate; learn; understand.*

get a life ∎ An infantile phrase.

get a rise out of ∎ A moribund metaphor. *acerbate; anger; annoy; bother; bristle; chafe; enrage; exasperate; gall; incense; inflame; infuriate; irk; irritate; madden; miff; pique; provoke; rile; roil; vex.*

get away with murder ∎ A moribund metaphor.

get (my) back up ∎ A moribund metaphor. *acerbate; anger; annoy; bother; bristle; chafe; enrage; exasperate; gall; incense; inflame; infuriate; irk; irritate; madden; miff; pique; provoke; rile; roil; vex.*

get (his) dander up ∎ A moribund metaphor. *acerbate; anger; annoy; bother; bristle; chafe; enrage; exasperate; gall; incense; inflame; infuriate; irk; irritate; madden; miff; pique; provoke; rile; roil; vex.*

get down to brass tacks ∎ A moribund metaphor.

get (put) (all) (your) ducks in a row ∎ A moribund metaphor. *arrange; categorize; classify; order; organize; prepare; ready; sort.*

> Everywhere they're smoothing down imperfections, putting hairs in place, putting ducks in a row, replacing divots.—Jonathan Lethem, *Motherless Brooklyn*

get (their) feet wet ∎ A moribund metaphor.

get (your) foot in the door ∎ A moribund metaphor.

get (my) goat ∎ A moribund metaphor. *acerbate; anger; annoy; bother; bristle; chafe; enrage; incense; inflame; infuriate; irk; irritate; madden; miff; provoke; rile; roil; vex.* • "In denial" is one of those politically correct terms that *gets my goat.* REPLACE WITH *infuriates me.*

get (her) hackles up ∎ A moribund

get (your) house in order

metaphor. *acerbate; anger; annoy; bother; bristle; chafe; enrage; incense; inflame; infuriate; insult; irk; irritate; madden; miff; offend; provoke; rile; roil; vex.*

get (your) house in order ∎ A moribund metaphor.

get in (my) hair ∎ A moribund metaphor. *annoy; badger; bedevil; bother; chafe; distress; disturb; gall; grate; harass; harry; hassle; heckle; hector; hound; irk; irritate; nag; nettle; persecute; pester; plague; provoke; rankle; rile; roil; tease; torment; vex.*

get into the act ∎ A moribund metaphor.

get in touch with (your) feelings ∎ A popular prescription. *be aware; be cognizant; be conscious; be insightful; be mindful; be perceptive; be sensitive.*

get off (my) back ∎ A moribund metaphor.

get (it) off (your) chest ∎ A moribund metaphor. *acknowledge; admit; affirm; allow; avow; concede; confess; disclose; divulge; expose; grant; own; reveal; tell; uncover; unearth; unveil.*

get off on the wrong foot ∎ A moribund metaphor.

get off the dime ∎ A moribund metaphor. 1. *be certain; be decided; be decisive; be determined; be positive; be resolute; be sure.* 2. *budge; move; stir.*

get off the ground ∎ A moribund metaphor. *begin; commence; embark on; inaugurate; initiate; introduce; launch; originate; start.* • Like all true entrepreneurs, they were eager to *get* another project *off the ground.* REPLACE WITH *launch.*

get on (my) nerves ∎ A moribund metaphor. *annoy; badger; bedevil; bother; chafe; distress; disturb; gall; grate; harass; harry; hassle; heckle; hector; hound; irk; irritate; nag; nettle; persecute; pester; plague; provoke; rankle; rile; roil; tease; torment; vex.*

get on the stick ∎ A moribund metaphor. *be active; be lively; move; stir.*

get (go) on with (my) life ∎ A popular prescription. SEE ALSO **put (it) behind (us)**.

get out of Dodge ∎ A moribund metaphor. *abscond; clear out; decamp; depart; desert; disappear; escape; exit; flee; fly; go; go away; leave; move on; part; pull out; quit; retire; retreat; run away; take flight; take off; vacate; vanish; withdraw.* • The most sensible thing to do was *get out of Dodge.* REPLACE WITH *leave.*

get (it) out of (your) system ∎ A moribund metaphor. *acknowledge; admit; affirm; allow; avow; concede; confess; disclose; divulge; expose; grant; own; reveal; tell; uncover; unearth; unveil.*

(don't) get (your) panties in a bunch ∎ A moribund metaphor. 1. *agitated; anxious; aroused; displeased; disquieted; excited; flustered; perturbed; troubled; upset; worried.* 2. *acerbated; angered; annoyed; bothered; disturbed; exasperated; galled; irked; irritated; miffed; nettled; provoked; rankled; riled; roiled; upset; vexed.*

get (your) skates on ∎ A moribund metaphor. *accelerate; advance; bestir; bustle; charge; dash; go faster; hasten; hurry; quicken; run; rush; speed up; sprint.*

get the ax ∎ A moribund metaphor. *canned; discharged; dismissed; fired; let go; ousted; released; sacked; terminated.*

get (start) the ball rolling ∎ A moribund metaphor. *begin; commence; embark on; inaugurate; initiate; introduce; launch; originate; start.*

get the better of ∎ A moribund metaphor. 1. *beat; conquer; crush; defeat; outdo; overcome; overpower; overwhelm; prevail; quell; rout; succeed; triumph; trounce; vanquish; win.* 2. *outmaneuver; outsmart; outwit.*

> My body had got the better of me and could no longer be trusted.—Christina Schwarz, *Drowning Ruth*

get (give) the bum's rush ∎ A moribund metaphor. *chuck; eject; expel; fling; throw out.*

(I) get the picture ∎ A moribund metaphor. *appreciate; apprehend; comprehend; discern; fathom; grasp; know; perceive; realize; recognize; see; understand.*

get the word out ∎ A moribund metaphor. *advertise; announce; broadcast; disseminate; proclaim; promote; promulgate; publicize; publish; trumpet.*

(let's) get this show on the road ∎ A moribund metaphor. *begin; commence; embark; inaugurate; initiate; launch; originate; start.*

get to the bottom of (this) ∎ A moribund metaphor. *appreciate; apprehend; comprehend; discern; fathom; grasp; know; perceive; realize; recognize; see; understand.*

get under (my) skin ∎ A moribund metaphor. *acerbate; anger; annoy; bother; bristle; chafe; disturb; exasperate; gall; grate; irk; irritate; miff; nettle; provoke; rankle; rile; roil; upset; vex.*

get-up-and-go ∎ A moribund metaphor. *ambition; bounce; dash; drive; dynamism; élan; energy; enthusiasm; initiative; liveliness; motivation; spirit; verve; vigor; vim; vitality; vivacity; zeal.*

(full of) get up and go ∎ A moribund metaphor. 1. *active; alive; animated; dynamic; energetic; exuberant; frisky; indefatigable; inexhaustible; invigorated; lively; peppy; spirited; sprightly; spry; tireless; unflagging; vibrant; vigorous; vivacious; zestful; zesty.* 2. *ambitious; assiduous; busy; determined; diligent; hard-working; industrious; motivated; perseverant; persevering; persistent; sedulous.*

get up on the wrong side of the bed ∎ A moribund metaphor. *bad-tempered; cantankerous; crabby; cranky; cross; disagreeable; grouchy; ill-humored; ill-natured; ill-tempered; irascible; irritable; quarrelsome; peevish; petulant; splenetic; sullen; surly; testy.*

get (her) walking papers ∎ A moribund metaphor. *canned; discharged; dismissed; fired; let go; ousted; released; sacked; terminated.*

get wind of ∎ A moribund metaphor. *ascertain; become aware of; discover; find out; hear about; learn.*

get (our) wires crossed ∎ A moribund metaphor. *baffle; befuddle; bewilder; confound; confuse; disconcert; flummox; mix up; muddle; nonplus; perplex; puzzle.*

(it'll) get worse before it gets better ∎ A plebeian sentiment. • Things will *get worse* at the bank *before they get better.*

gild (paint) the lily ∎ A moribund metaphor. *overdo; overstate.*

gird (up) (one's) loins ∎ A moribund metaphor. *bolster; brace; fortify; harden; prepare; reinforce; shore up; steel; strengthen.*

give (her) a bum steer ∎ A moribund metaphor. *bamboozle; befool; beguile; betray; bilk; bluff; cheat; con; deceive; defraud; delude; dupe; feint; fool; gyp; hoodwink; lead astray; misdirect; misguide; misinform; mislead; spoof; swindle; trick.*

give (her) a dose (taste) of (her) own medicine ∎ A moribund metaphor.

give and take ∎ An inescapable pair. *collaboration; cooperation; exchange; reciprocity.*

give (them) an inch and (they'll) take a mile ∎ A moribund metaphor.

give (them) a piece of (his) mind ∎ A moribund metaphor. *admonish; animadvert; berate; castigate; censure; chasten; chastise; chide; condemn; criticize; denounce; denunciate; discipline; impugn; objurgate; punish; rebuke; remonstrate; reprehend; reprimand; reproach; reprobate; reprove; revile; scold; upbraid; vituperate.*

> She didn't come down to give them a piece of her mind because it was no use fighting; they were sometimes able to get me some small job or other, through the influence of Jimmy's uncle Tambow, who delivered the vote of his relatives in the ward and was a pretty big wheel in Republican ward politics.—Saul Bellow, *The Adventures of Augie March*

give (him) a run for (his) money ∎ A moribund metaphor.

give away the store ∎ A moribund metaphor.

give (her) a wide berth (to) ∎ A moribund

metaphor. *avoid; bypass; circumvent; dodge; elude; evade; shun; sidestep; skirt.*

give birth (to) ∎ A moribund metaphor. *bring about; cause; effect; generate; inaugurate; initiate; introduce; occasion; produce; provoke; result in.*

give credit where credit is due ∎ A popular prescription.

give (my) eyeteeth (right arm) for ∎ A moribund metaphor.

give it a rest ∎ A moribund metaphor. 1. *be silent; be still; hush; keep quiet; quiet; silence.* 2. *cease; close; complete; conclude; derail; desist; discontinue; end; finish; halt; quit; settle; stop; terminate.*

give it a shot (whirl) ∎ A moribund metaphor. *aim; attempt; endeavor; essay; exert; labor; moil; strain; strive; struggle; toil; try hard; undertake; work at.*

give it (take) (your) best shot ∎ A moribund metaphor. *aim; attempt; endeavor; essay; exert; labor; moil; strain; strive; struggle; toil; try; try hard; undertake; work at; work hard.*

> It was all very well to tell yourself, as he had been doing for years, that all you could do was give it your best shot.—Jane Smiley, *Moo*

given the fact that ∎ A wretched redundancy. *because; considering; for; in that; since; when.* • *Given the fact that* all kibbutz youth were inducted into the army and commingled with tens of thousands of potential mates from outside their kibbutz before they got married, the rate of **200** marriages from within the same kibbutz is far more than could be expected by chance. REPLACE WITH *Since.* • I'd be interested in being a guest, but I gather you can't even consider it *given the fact that* I live in Cancun. REPLACE WITH *since.* SEE ALSO **because of the fact that; by virtue of the fact that; considering the fact that; in consideration of the fact that; in view of the fact that; on account of the fact that.**

give rise to ∎ A moribund metaphor. *bring about; cause; effect; generate; inaugurate; initiate; introduce; occasion; produce; provoke; result in.*

(it) gives (me) something to do ∎ A plebeian sentiment. SEE ALSO **(it) keeps (me) busy; (it) keeps (me) out of trouble; (it's) something to do.**

give (him) the back of (my) hand ∎ A moribund metaphor. *abuse; affront; disdain; insult; offend; outrage; scorn; slap.*

give (her) the brush (brush-off) ∎ A moribund metaphor. *abuse; affront; avoid; disdain; disregard; ignore; insult; neglect; offend; outrage; overlook; rebuff; reject; scorn; shun; sidestep; slap; slight; slur; skirt;*

give (him) the business

sneer; snub; spurn.

give (him) the business ∎ A moribund metaphor. *admonish; animadvert; berate; castigate; censure; chasten; chastise; chide; condemn; criticize; denounce; denunciate; discipline; impugn; objurgate; punish; rebuke; remonstrate; reprehend; reprimand; reproach; reprobate; reprove; revile; scold; upbraid; vituperate.*

give (him) the cold shoulder ∎ A moribund metaphor. *abuse; affront; avoid; disdain; disregard; ignore; insult; neglect; offend; outrage; overlook; rebuff; reject; scorn; shun; sidestep; slap; slight; slur; skirt; sneer; snub; spurn.*

give the devil his due ∎ A moribund metaphor.

give (her) the pink slip ∎ A moribund metaphor. *discharge; dismiss; fire; lay off; sack; suspend; terminate; throw out.*

give (him) the runaround ∎ A moribund metaphor. *avoid; dodge; doubletalk; equivocate; evade; fence; hedge; palter; prevaricate; quibble; shuffle; sidestep; tergiversate; waffle.*

give (him) the third degree ∎ A moribund metaphor. *catechize; cross-examine; examine; grill; inquire; interrogate; pump; question; quiz; test.*

give the thumbs down (sign) ∎ A moribund metaphor. *decline; deny; disallow; disapprove; forbid; nix; prohibit; proscribe; refuse; reject; rule out; say no; turn down; veto.*

give the thumbs up (sign) ∎ A moribund metaphor. *accredit; affirm; allow; approve; authorize; back; bless; certify; countenance; endorse; favor; permit; ratify; sanction; support.*

give (me) the time of day ∎ A moribund metaphor. *be affable; be approachable; be cordial; be friendly; be genial; be pleasant; be polite; be receptive; be responsive; be sociable.*

> In about an hour, I would be sitting across the table from the most attractive woman who had ever stooped so low as to give me the time of day.—Don Keith, *The Forever Season*

give up the ghost ∎ A moribund metaphor. *be deceased; die; expire; perish.*

gloom and doom ∎ An inescapable pair.

go against the grain (of) ∎ A moribund metaphor. *buck; challenge; contradict; defy; disobey; dispute; disregard; flout; go against; ignore; neglect; oppose; overlook; resist; violate.* • Does the message *go against the grain* of corporate philosophy? REPLACE WITH *flout.*

> It is not in our makeup to intervene. This goes against the grain, is entirely out of our character.—Kate Walbert, *Our Kind*

go ahead, make my day ∎ An infantile phrase.

go belly up ∎ A moribund metaphor. *break down; collapse; disintegrate; fail; fall short; flop; founder; miscarry; topple.* • All the biotech start-ups in the Bioventures portfolio would likely *go belly up* if the veterinary school is shut down. REPLACE WITH *fail.*

God is love ∎ A quack equation.

go downhill ∎ A moribund metaphor. *decay; decline; degenerate; destroy; deteriorate; disintegrate; ebb; erode; fade; fall off; languish; lessen; plummet; ruin; wane; weaken; wither; worsen.* • The bad news is that during the second night, everybody's performance *went downhill*. REPLACE WITH *deteriorated.*

go for the gold ∎ An infantile phrase.

go for the gusto ∎ An infantile phrase.

go forward ∎ A TOP-TWENTY DIMWITTICISM. A torpid term. **1.** *advance; continue; develop; go on; grow; happen; improve; increase; make headway; make progress; move on; occur; proceed; progress; take place.* **2.** *shall; will;* DELETE.
• The way in which this is drafted will allow those takeovers to *go forward*, which would allow for a greater efficiency and productivity. REPLACE WITH *proceed.* • It is still our expectation that the summit will *go forward* and be productive. REPLACE WITH *occur.* • We look forward to *going forward*. REPLACE WITH *proceeding.*
Going forward is replacing auxiliary verbs like *will* and *shall*, which to the politicians and businesspeople who now rely on *going forward*, do not convey futurity as effectively. *Going forward*, to these dimwitted thinkers, seems to reveal the future more forcefully; yet distinctions in tense, mood, and voice may be forfeited along with a subtle, yet indispensable, sense of what it means to be human.
• This highlights perhaps the greatest risk to the economy *going forward*. • We need to train more Iraqi troops *going forward*. • I can't wait to share ideas about what we can do *going forward*. • *Going forward*, as the company has more mature branches, its profit margins should benefit and widen a bit more. • The company will continue to face challenges *going forward*. • This is an excellent opportunity for both companies and we look forward to maintaining positive momentum *going forward*.
SEE ALSO **a step forward; a step (forward) in the right direction; move forward; move (forward) in the right direction; proceed forward.**

going, going, gone ∎ An infantile phrase.

going great guns ∎ A moribund metaphor.

going on (19) ∎ An infantile phrase. • I'm *69 going on 70.* • I've been there 5 years, *going* *on 6 years.*

Elizabeth Costello is a writer, born in 1928, which makes her sixty-six years old, going on sixty-seven.—J. M. Coetzee, *Elizabeth Costello*

going to hell in a handbasket ∎
A moribund metaphor. *collapse; corrode; crumble; decay; decline; degenerate; destroy; deteriorate; disintegrate; ebb; erode; fade; fail; fall off; fester; flag; languish; lessen; plummet; putrefy; regress; rot; ruin; stagnate; ulcerate; wane; weaken; wither; worsen.* •
The typical reaction people seem to have is that public education is *going to hell in a handbasket.* REPLACE WITH *deteriorating.*

going (have) to live with that for the rest of my life ∎ A plebeian sentiment.

go (send; throw) into a tailspin ∎ A
moribund metaphor. 1. *be unsuccessful; bomb; break down; collapse; fail; fall short; falter; fizzle; flop; fold; founder; mess up; miscarry; not succeed; stagger; stumble; topple; totter.*
2. *be ailing; be anxious; be unhealthy; be ill; be sick; be sickly; be unwell.*

go into orbit ∎ A moribund metaphor.
1. *be delighted; be ecstatic; be elated; be enraptured; be euphoric; be exalted; be excited; be exhilarated; be exultant; be gay; be glad; be gleeful; be good-humored; be happy; be intoxicated; be jolly; be jovial; be joyful; be joyous; be jubilant; be merry; be mirthful; be overjoyed; be pleased; be rapturous; be thrilled.* 2. *be angry; be annoyed; be enraged; be exasperated; be furious; be incensed; be infuriated; be irate; be irked; be irritated; be mad; be raging; be wrathful.*

golden opportunity ∎ An inescapable pair.
• We have a *golden opportunity* to prevent this cycle from continuing.

go (run) like the wind ∎ An insipid simile.
abruptly; apace; at once; briskly; directly; expeditiously; fast; forthwith; hastily; hurriedly; immediately; instantaneously; instantly; posthaste; promptly; quickly; rapidly; rashly; right away; speedily; straightaway; swiftly; wingedly.

(has) gone with the wind ∎ A moribund
metaphor. 1. *be forgotten; dead; disappeared; dissolved; evaporated; past; vanished.* • I
would retain some of what I read, and then it would very likely *be gone with the wind.* REPLACE WITH *vanish.* 2.
ephemeral; evanescent; fleeting; flitting; fugacious; fugitive; short-lived; transient; transitory; volatile.

good and sufficient ∎ An inescapable pair.
adequate; good; satisfactory; sufficient.

(as) good as gold ∎ An insipid simile.
best; excellent; exceptional; fine; finest; first-class; first-rate; good; great; optimal; optimum; superior; superlative.

good, bad, and (or) indifferent ∎ A torpid

term. • We really don't know what the effect will be; it could be *good, bad, or indifferent.*

good egg ∎ A moribund metaphor. *agreeable; decent; ethical; forthright; honest; just; moral; righteous; straight; trustworthy; upright; virtuous.*

good riddance to bad rubbish ∎ An
infantile phrase.

good (great) stuff ∎ When we need to use the word *stuff* to describe something we like, something we also call *good* or *great*, we might wonder if we have lost all sense of what is likable.

Stuff best describes the nondescript and uneventful, the poor, the ordinary, and the pathetic.

good things come in small packages ∎
A popular prescription.

go off half-cocked ∎ A moribund metaphor.
careless; emotional; foolhardy; hasty; headlong; heedless; impulsive; incautious; indiscreet; precipitate; rash; reckless; thoughtless; unmindful; unthinking.

go off the deep end ∎ A moribund
metaphor. 1. *be careless; be emotional; be foolhardy; be hasty; be headlong; be heedless; be impulsive; be incautious; be indiscreet; be precipitate; be rash; be reckless; be thoughtless; be unmindful; be unthinking.*
2. *acerbate; anger; annoy; bother; bristle; chafe; enrage; incense; inflame; infuriate; irk; irritate; madden; miff; provoke; rile; roil; vex.*

go (her) one better ∎ A moribund metaphor.
beat; best; better; defeat; eclipse; exceed; excel; outclass; outdo; outflank; outmaneuver; outpace; outperform; outplay; outrank; outrival; outsmart; outstrip; outthink; outwit; overcome; overpower; overshadow; prevail; rout; surpass; top; triumph; trounce; vanquish; whip; win.

goose egg ∎ A moribund metaphor. *cipher; naught; zero.*

(his) goose is cooked ∎ A moribund metaphor.

go overboard ∎ A moribund metaphor.
exaggerate; hyperbolize; overdo; overreact; overstress; overstate.

go (send) over the edge ∎ A moribund
metaphor. 1. *be unsuccessful; bomb; break down; collapse; fail; fall short; falter; fizzle; flop; fold; founder; mess up; miscarry; not succeed; stumble; topple.* 2. *be ailing; be anxious; be unhealthy; be ill; be sick; be sickly; be unwell.* 3. *acerbate; anger; annoy; bother; bristle; chafe; enrage; incense; inflame; infuriate; irk; irritate; madden; miff; provoke; rile; roil; vex.*

Jack is their guide: young and irreverent, thank God. Reverence would send Paul over the edge.—Julia Glass, *Three Junes*

go (head) south ∎ A moribund metaphor. 1. *collapse; crash; decline; decrease; descend; dip; drop; ebb; fail; fall; plummet; plunge; recede; regress; retire; sink; slide; slip; subside; topple; tumble.* 2. *cease; end; halt; quit; stop.* • And it is possible that the market may *go south* before the shares can be offered. REPLACE WITH *fall.* • Obviously, any of these could cause your spirits to *go south* temporarily. REPLACE WITH *ebb.* • He expressed some concern for her job if the relationship should *go south.* REPLACE WITH *fail.* • If the economy hadn't *gone south* on us, we would have had airline service earlier this year. REPLACE WITH *collapsed.*

go the extra mile ∎ A moribund metaphor. • Average citizens who regularly *go the extra mile* to make this a better world are everywhere.

go their separate ways ∎ A moribund metaphor. *break up; divorce; part; separate; split up.*

go the way of all flesh ∎ A moribund metaphor. *be deceased; die; expire; perish.*

go the way of the dinosaur ∎ A moribund metaphor. *become extinct; cease to exist; disappear; vanish.*

go the whole hog ∎ An infantile phrase. *do completely; do entirely; do fully; do thoroughly; do totally; do utterly; do wholly; do wholeheartedly.*

> Perhaps it was that if I was going to have a predawn wedding in a crimson dress, I might as well go the whole hog and be hovering at an unsuspecting witness's bedside as he woke.—Suzannah Dunn, *The Queen of Subtleties*

go through the ceiling (roof) ∎ A moribund metaphor. *bellow; bluster; clamor; explode; fulminate; fume; holler; howl; rage; rant; rave; roar; scream; shout; storm; thunder; vociferate; yell.*

go through the mill ∎ A moribund metaphor.

go (shoot) through the roof ∎ A moribund metaphor. *ascend; balloon; billow; bulge; climb; escalate; expand; go up; grow; improve; increase; inflate; mount; multiply; rise; skyrocket; soar; surge; swell.* • Some people thought it was an extravagance at a time when billings aren't exactly *going through the roof.* REPLACE WITH *soaring.* • My quality of life has *gone through the roof* since he quit his job. REPLACE WITH *improved immeasurably.*

go to bat for ∎ A moribund metaphor. *abet; advance; advocate; aid; assist; back; bolster; champion; defend; espouse; fight for; further; help; support; uphold.* • All I want to say is that it is easier to *go to bat for* people when they recognize they're wrong. REPLACE WITH *defend.*

go toe to toe with ∎ A moribund metaphor. *battle; compete; contend; fight; struggle; vie.*

(we) got off on the wrong foot ∎ A moribund metaphor.

go to pieces ∎ A moribund metaphor. *decay; decline; degenerate; destroy; deteriorate; disintegrate; ebb; erode; fade; fall off; languish; lessen; ruin; wane; weaken; wither; worsen.*

go to pot ∎ A moribund metaphor. *decay; decline; degenerate; destroy; deteriorate; disintegrate; ebb; erode; fade; fall off; languish; lessen; ruin; wane; weaken; wither; worsen.*

go to (her) reward ∎ A moribund metaphor. *be deceased; die; expire; perish.*

go (run) to seed ∎ A moribund metaphor. *decay; decline; degenerate; deteriorate; devitalize; disintegrate; ebb; erode; fade; fall off; languish; lessen; ruin; wane; weaken; wither; worsen.*

go to the dogs ∎ A moribund metaphor. *decay; decline; degenerate; destroy; deteriorate; disintegrate; ebb; erode; fade; fall off; languish; lessen; ruin; wane; weaken; wither; worsen.*

go to the mat (for) ∎ A moribund metaphor. 1. *battle; brawl; clash; fight; grapple; jostle; scuffle; skirmish; tussle; war; wrestle.* 2. *advocate; aid; assist; back; champion; defend; espouse; help; protect; shield; support; uphold.* 3. *argue; dispute; fight; quarrel; wrangle.*

go up in flames ∎ A moribund metaphor. *annihilate; break down; crumble; demolish; destroy; deteriorate; die; disintegrate; dissolve; end; eradicate; exterminate; obliterate; pulverize; rack; ravage; raze; ruin; shatter; smash; undo; wrack; wreck.*

go up (the chimney) in smoke ∎ A moribund metaphor. *annihilate; break down; crumble; demolish; destroy; deteriorate; die; disappear; disintegrate; dissipate; dissolve; end; eradicate; evaporate; exterminate; fade; obliterate; pulverize; rack; ravage; raze; ruin; shatter; smash; undo; vanish; vaporize; volatilize; wrack; wreck.* • Everything I worked for over the last ten years is *going up in smoke.* REPLACE WITH *evaporating.*

go with the flow ∎ A moribund metaphor. *abide by; accede to; accept; accommodate; acquiesce; adapt to; adhere to; adjust to; agree to; assent; be agreeable; be complacent; be conventional; bend; be resigned; be traditional; bow; comply with; concede to; concur; conform; consent to; fit; follow; reconcile; submit; succumb; yield.* • We have to go *go with the flow.* REPLACE WITH *acquiesce.*

grab the brass ring ∎ A moribund metaphor. *be successful; be triumphant; be victorious; prevail; succeed; triumph; win.*

> Craps was a safer bet than flicks. Not wanting just to survive, but to win, I handicapped my chances. One thing was for sure, I wasn't gonna grab the brass ring in Vegas.—Robert Evans, *The Kid Stays in the Picture*

(as) graceful as a swan ■ An insipid simile. *agile; graceful; limber; lissome; lithe; lithesome; nimble; supple.*

grace (us) with (his) presence ■ A torpid term. • Most of these essays first appeared in *The New Yorker*, which Liebling *graced with his presence* between 1935 and 1963.

(like) Grand Central Station ■ An insipid simile. 1. *abounding; brimful; brimming; bursting; chock-full; congested; crammed; crowded; dense; filled; full; gorged; jammed; jam-packed; overcrowded; overfilled; overflowing; packed; replete; saturated; stuffed; swarming; teeming.* 2. *busy; hectic.*

(pure) gravy ■ A moribund metaphor. 1. *benefit; earnings; gain; money; proceeds; profit.* 2. *a benefit; a bonus; a dividend; a gift; a gratuity; a lagniappe; an extra; a perk; a perquisite; a pourboire; a premium; a tip.*

> And he'd like being told the good news. He'd smile, maybe. Anything you win for nothing, anything that falls into your lap, it's all gravy, right?—Joyce Carol Oates, *Blonde*

gravy train ■ A moribund metaphor.

grease (her) palm with silver ■ A moribund metaphor. 1. *bribe; induce; pay; suborn.* 2. *compensate; pay; recompense; tip.*

grease the skids ■ A moribund metaphor. *arrange; get ready; organize; prepare; set up.*

great ■ A suspect superlative. *Great expectations* often turn out to be slight realizations, and *great stuff* is seldom more than stuff.

Great is also, of course, a hugely overworked word. Consider this laughable sentence: • When I think of their golf course, the first word that comes to mind is *great*.

Alternatives to the quotidian *great* include *consequential; considerable; consummate; distinguished; eminent; excellent; exceptional; exemplary; exquisite; extraordinary; fine; flawless; grand; ideal; illustrious; impeccable; imposing; impressive; magnificent; marvelous; matchless; momentous; nonpareil; notable; noteworthy; perfect; preeminent; remarkable; select; splendid; superb; superior; superlative; supreme; transcendent; weighty; wonderful.*

(go) great guns ■ A moribund metaphor. *abruptly; briskly; expeditiously; fast; hastily; hurriedly; posthaste; promptly; quickly; rapidly; speedily; straightaway; swiftly; wingedly.*

green around the gills ■ A moribund metaphor. 1. *afflicted; ailing; diseased; ill; indisposed; infirm; not (feeling) well; sick; sickly; suffering; unhealthy; unsound; unwell; valetudinarian.* 2. *nauseated; nauseous; queasy; sick; squeamish; vomiting.*

(as) green as grass ■ An insipid simile. 1. *aquamarine; emerald; green; greenish; teal; verdant; virescent.* 2. *adolescent; artless; awkward; callow; green; guileless; immature; inexperienced; inexpert; ingenuous; innocent; juvenile; naive; raw; simple; undeveloped; unfledged; unseasoned; unskilled; unskillful; unsophisticated; untaught; untrained; unworldly; young; youthful.*

green-eyed monster ■ A moribund metaphor. *envy; jealousy.*

green light ■ A moribund metaphor. *allowance; approval; assent; authority; authorization; blessing; consent; freedom; leave; liberty; license; permission; permit; power; sanction; warrant.* Like *red light*, the expression *green light* appeals to people who grasp the meaning of colorful visuals and expressive pictures more easily than they do polysyllabic words and complicated thoughts. Some people upgrade simple or straightforward ideas to unintelligible ones; others degrade substantive or nuanced ideas to unsophisticated ones. *Green light* is an example of the latter, but both tactics suggest an insincere mind, an unknowable heart.

• The Baby Bells—which already have *the green light* to go into just about any other venture—have railed against the remaining restrictions since they were imposed. REPLACE WITH *permission*. • The FBI was given *the green light* by the Justice Department to continue its investigation. REPLACE WITH *authorization*. • Why would we be surprised when others take that message as *a green light* to lie, cheat, steal, and do whatever will benefit them? REPLACE WITH *permission*. SEE ALSO **red light**.

greenlight ■ A moribund metaphor. *allow; approve; authorize; certify; endorse; license; okay; permit; ratify; sanction.* • The company does have an oil spill plan for the Gulf that was *green-lighted* last year by the federal government. REPLACE WITH *approved*. • It may have been *greenlighted* by Osama bin Laden himself. REPLACE WITH *authorized*. • The council also greenlighted several other personnel moves, including multiple police and City Attorney's Office promotions. REPLACE WITH *endorsed*. • Despite those significant drawbacks, Vagelos green-lighted the project and the trials showed immediate success. REPLACE WITH *okayed*.

green with envy ■ A moribund metaphor. *covetous; desirous; envious; grudging; jealous; resentful.*

grim reaper ■ A moribund metaphor. *death.*

grin and bear it ▮ A popular prescription.

grind to a halt ▮ A moribund metaphor. *cease; close; complete; conclude; end; finish; halt; settle; stop; terminate.* • Once it becomes apparent that no payment is forthcoming, construction activity can quickly *grind to a halt.* REPLACE WITH *halt.*

grist for the mill ▮ A moribund metaphor.

gross exaggeration ▮ An inescapable pair. *embellishment; exaggeration; hyperbole; overstatement.*

(get in on the) ground floor ▮ A moribund metaphor.

ground zero ▮ A moribund metaphor.

grow (spread) like a cancer ▮ An insipid simile. *augment; breed; duplicate; grow; increase; metastasize; multiply; mushroom; procreate; proliferate; propagate; reproduce; snowball; spread; swell.*

gruesome twosome ▮ An infantile phrase.

guardedly optimistic ▮ A torpid term. *confident; encouraged; heartened; hopeful; optimistic; rosy; sanguine.* • Firefighters are *guardedly optimistic* that they have the blaze under control. DELETE *guardedly.* • We're *guardedly optimistic* that this synthetic compound may work. DELETE *guardedly.* SEE ALSO **cautiously optimistic**.

guardian angel ▮ A suspect superlative. *liberator; redeemer; rescuer; savior.*

guesstimate ▮ An infantile phrase. *appraisal; assessment; estimate; estimation; guess; impression; opinion.* • If you would like a *guesstimate* of time required for your site, we would be happy to give you one. REPLACE WITH *estimate.* • Yet with just a few moments of thought you can make a surprisingly good *guesstimate.* REPLACE WITH *guess.* • They were asked to guess what the contents were and *guesstimate* how many objects were in the envelope. REPLACE WITH *guess. Guesstimate* is a perfectly ridiculous merger that people who are uncomfortable with using *guess* will turn to. Most of us prefer knowing to not knowing, or at least we prefer letting others believe we are knowledgeable. *Guesstimate,* these people reason, adds intelligence and respectability to their wild *guess,* their unsubstantiated *estimate.*

(as) guilty as sin ▮ An insipid simile. *at fault; blamable; blameful; blameworthy; censurable; condemnable; culpable; guilty; in error; reprehensible.*

Hh

hale and hearty ∎ An inescapable pair. *energetic; fine; fit; good; hale; healthful; healthy; hearty; robust; sound; strong; vigorous; well.*

(anyone with) half a brain ∎ A moribund metaphor.

half a loaf is better than none ∎ A moribund metaphor.

half-baked (idea) ∎ A moribund metaphor. *bad; blemished; defective; deficient; faulty; flawed; ill-conceived; imperfect; inadequate; incomplete; inferior; malformed; poor; unsound.*

(go at it) hammer and tongs ∎ A moribund metaphor. *actively; aggressively; dynamically; emphatically; energetically; fast; ferociously; fervently; fiercely; forcefully; frantically; frenziedly; furiously; hard; intensely; intently; mightily; passionately; powerfully; robustly; savagely; spiritedly; strenuously; strongly; vehemently; viciously; vigorously; violently; wildly; with vigor.*

> He'd always been of the hammer-and-tongs school. She taught him sexual stealth, the occasional necessity of stillness.—Ian McEwan, *Amsterdam*.

handed to (her) on a silver platter ∎ A moribund metaphor.

hand and (in) glove ∎ A moribund metaphor. *amiable; amicable; attached; brotherly; chummy; close; confidential; devoted; familiar; friendly; inseparable; intimate; loving; thick.*

(goes) hand in hand ∎ A moribund metaphor. *be indissoluble; be indivisible; be inseparable; be together.*

> New churches were established in the surrounding villages and a few schools with them. From the very beginning religion and education went hand in hand.—Chinua Achebe, *Things Fall Apart*.

hand over fist ∎ A moribund metaphor. *apace; briskly; expeditiously; fast; hastily; hurriedly; posthaste; quickly; rapidly; speedily; swiftly; wingedly.*

(my) hands are tied ∎ A moribund metaphor.

handwriting (is) on the wall ∎ A moribund metaphor. *divination; foreboding; forewarning; indication; omen; portent; prediction; premonition; presage;*
presentiment; sign; signal; warning.

hang (hold) (on) by a thread ∎ A moribund metaphor. • The small towns in western Massachusetts are *holding on by a thread.*

hang fire ∎ A moribund metaphor. *be delayed; be slow.* 2. *be undecided; be unsettled.*

hang (your) hat on ∎ A moribund metaphor.

hang (our) hats ∎ A moribund metaphor. *dwell; inhabit; live; reside; stay.*

> It is not the same as Hoving Road where we all once hung our hats, but things change in ways none of us can expect, no matter how damn much we know or how smart and good-intentioned each of us is or thinks he is.—Richard Ford, *The Sportswriter*

hang in there ∎ A moribund metaphor. *carry on; get along; manage; succeed.* • Even though profits remain down, most firms are still *hanging in there.* REPLACE WITH *succeeding.* • I'm *hanging in there.* REPLACE WITH *managing.*

hang like a cloud (over) ∎ An insipid simile. 1. *becloud; cloak; darken; eclipse; mask; obscure; shroud; veil.* 2. *belittle; confound; degrade; demean; embarrass; humiliate; lower; shame.* • Their parents' divorce *hangs like a cloud over* their lives. REPLACE WITH *beclouds.* • There is nothing that Jesus does not understand about the heartache that *hangs like a cloud over* the history of our lives. REPLACE WITH *darkens.* • The aftermath of the bitter July incident *hangs like a cloud over* professors, students, and administrators alike. REPLACE WITH *embarrasses.* SEE ALSO **cast a shadow (over)**.

hang on every word ∎ A moribund metaphor. *attend to; hark; hear; hearken; heed; listen; pay attention; pay heed.*

hang over (our) heads ∎ A moribund metaphor. *hang over; impend; loom; menace; overhang; overshadow; threaten; tower over.*

(these things) happen to other people, not to (me) ∎ A plebeian sentiment.

(as) happy as a clam (at high tide) ∎ An insipid simile. *blissful; blithe; buoyant; cheerful; delighted; ecstatic; elated; enraptured; euphoric; exalted; excited; exhilarated; exultant; gay; glad; gleeful; good-humored; happy; intoxicated; jolly; jovial; joyful; joyous; jubilant; merry; mirthful; overjoyed; pleased; rapturous; thrilled.*

(as) happy as a lark

(as) happy as a lark ▮ An insipid simile. *blissful; blithe; buoyant; cheerful; delighted; ecstatic; elated; enraptured; euphoric; exalted; excited; exhilarated; exultant; gay; glad; gleeful; good-humored; happy; intoxicated; jolly; jovial; joyful; joyous; jubilant; merry; mirthful; overjoyed; pleased; rapturous; thrilled.*

> They are happy as larks, they shine with their luck, their joy.—Audrey Niffenegger, *The Time Traveler's Wife*

(as) happy as Larry ▮ An insipid simile. *blissful; blithe; buoyant; cheerful; delighted; ecstatic; elated; enraptured; euphoric; exalted; excited; exhilarated; exultant; gay; glad; gleeful; good-humored; happy; intoxicated; jolly; jovial; joyful; joyous; jubilant; merry; mirthful; overjoyed; pleased; rapturous; thrilled.*

happy camper ▮ An infantile phrase. *blissful; blithe; buoyant; cheerful; delighted; ecstatic; elated; enraptured; euphoric; exalted; excited; exhilarated; exultant; gay; glad; gleeful; good-humored; happy; intoxicated; jolly; jovial; joyful; joyous; jubilant; merry; mirthful; overjoyed; pleased; rapturous; thrilled.* • The six families who bought in to the project, all at full price, are not *happy campers* these days. REPLACE WITH *pleased.*

hard and fast (rule) ▮ A moribund metaphor. *absolute; binding; certain; defined; dogmatic; entrenched; established; exact; exacting; fast; firm; fixed; hard; immutable; inflexible; invariable; permanent; resolute; rigid; set; severe; solid; steadfast; strict; stringent; unalterable; unbending; uncompromising; unyielding.* • Events are happening too quickly in Eastern Europe to make *hard and fast* plans at this point. REPLACE WITH *firm.*

(as) hard as a rock ▮ An insipid simile. 1. *adamantine; firm; granitelike; hard; petrified; rock-hard; rocklike; rocky; solid; steellike; steely; stonelike; stony.* 2. *athletic; beefy; brawny; burly; firm; fit; hale; hardy; hearty; husky; manly; mighty; muscular; powerful; puissant; robust; rugged; sinewy; solid; stalwart; stout; strapping; strong; sturdy; tough; vigorous; virile; well-built.* 3. *constant; dependable; determined; faithful; fast; firm; fixed; inexorable; inflexible; loyal; obdurate; resolute; resolved; rigid; solid; stable; staunch; steadfast; steady; stern; tenacious; unflinching; unwavering; unyielding.*

(as) hard as nails ▮ An insipid simile. 1. *athletic; beefy; brawny; burly; firm; fit; hale; hardy; hearty; husky; manly; mighty; muscular; powerful; puissant; robust; rugged; sinewy; solid; stalwart; stout; strapping; strong; sturdy; tough; vigorous; virile; well-built.* 2. *constant; dependable; determined; faithful; fast; firm; fixed; inexorable; inflexible; loyal; obdurate; resolute; resolved; rigid; solid; stable; staunch; steadfast; steady; stern; tenacious; unflinching; unwavering; unyielding.*

hard (tough) nut to crack ▮ A moribund metaphor. 1. *arduous; backbreaking; burdensome; difficult; exhausting; fatiguing; hard; herculean; laborious; not easy; onerous; severe; strenuous; toilful; toilsome; tough; troublesome; trying; wearisome.* 2. *impenetrable; incomprehensible; inexplicable; inscrutable; mysterious; obscure; unexplainable; unfathomable; ungraspable; unintelligible; unknowable.*

hard (rough) on the eyes ▮ A moribund metaphor. *coarse; homely; ill-favored; plain; ugly; unattractive; unbeautiful; uncomely; unsightly.*

hard (tough) row to hoe ▮ A moribund metaphor. *arduous; backbreaking; burdensome; difficult; exhausting; fatiguing; hard; herculean; laborious; not easy; onerous; severe; strenuous; toilful; toilsome; tough; troublesome; trying; wearisome.*

hard to believe ▮ A torpid term. *beyond belief; beyond comprehension; doubtful; dubious; farfetched; implausible; improbable; incomprehensible; inconceivable; incredible; inexplicable; questionable; remote; unbelievable; unimaginable; unlikely; unrealistic.*

hard (tough) to swallow ▮ A moribund metaphor. 1. *beyond belief; beyond comprehension; doubtful; dubious; farfetched; implausible; improbable; incomprehensible; inconceivable; incredible; inexplicable; questionable; remote; unbelievable; unimaginable; unlikely; unrealistic.* 2. *disagreeable; distasteful; indigestible; unpalatable; unpleasant.*

has a bun in the oven ▮ A moribund metaphor. be *anticipating;* be *enceinte;* be *expectant;* be *expecting;* be *gravid;* be *parturient;* be *pregnant;* be *with child.*

has a finger in every pie ▮ A moribund metaphor.

has a heart as big as all outdoors ▮ An insipid simile. *beneficent; benevolent; compassionate; big-hearted; generous; good-hearted; humane; kind; kind-hearted; kindly; sensitive; sympathetic; understanding.*

has a heart of gold ▮ A moribund metaphor. *beneficent; benevolent; compassionate; big-hearted; generous; good-hearted; good-natured; humane; kind; kind-hearted; kindly; sensitive; sympathetic; understanding.*

has a heart of stone ▮ A moribund metaphor. *apathetic; callous; chilly; cold; cool; detached; dispassionate; distant; emotionless; frigid; glacial; hard; hardhearted; harsh; heartless; hostile; icy; impassive; indifferent; passionless; pitiless; reserved; unconcerned; unemotional; unfeeling; unfriendly; unresponsive.*

has an effect on ▪ A wretched redundancy. *acts on; affects; bears on; influences; sways; works on.* • That's one of the problems that *has an effect on* everyone's quality of life. REPLACE WITH *affects.* SEE ALSO **effect**.

has an impact on ▪ A wretched redundancy. *acts on; affects; bears on; influences; sways; works on.* • That too *had an impact on* the jury. REPLACE WITH *swayed.* SEE ALSO **impact**.

has a swelled head ▪ A moribund metaphor. *arrogant; cavalier; conceited; disdainful; egocentric; egotistic; egotistical; haughty; lofty; pompous; pretentious; proud; narcissistic; self-centered; self-important; self-satisfied; supercilious; superior; vain.*

has both feet on the ground ▪ A moribund metaphor. *businesslike; careful; cautious; circumspect; expedient; judicious; politic; practical; pragmatic; prudent; realistic; reasonable; sensible; utilitarian.*

has (his) hands full ▪ A moribund metaphor. *booked; busy; employed; engaged; involved; obligated; occupied.*

has (him) in the palm of (my) hand ▪ A moribund metaphor. *be in charge; be in command; be in control.*

has the patience of Job ▪ A moribund metaphor. *accepting; accommodating; acquiescent; complacent; complaisant; compliant; cowed; deferential; docile; dutiful; easy; forbearing; gentle; humble; long-suffering; meek; mild; obedient; passive; patient; prostrate; quiet; reserved; resigned; stoical; submissive; subservient; timid; tolerant; tractable; unassuming; uncomplaining; yielding.*

has to do with ▪ A wretched redundancy. *concerns; deals with; is about; pertains to; regards; relates to.* • The most recent academy committee mission *has to do with* climate-monitoring satellites. REPLACE WITH *concerns.*

has two left feet ▪ A moribund metaphor. *awkward; blundering; bumbling; bungling; clumsy; gawky; gauche; ham-handed; heavy-handed; inapt; inept; lubberly; lumbering; maladroit; uncoordinated; uncouth; ungainly; ungraceful; unhandy; unskillful; unwieldy.*

hat in hand ▪ A moribund metaphor. *diffidently; humbly; meekly; modestly; respectfully; unassumingly.*

haul (rake) over the coals ▪ A moribund metaphor. *admonish; animadvert; berate; castigate; censure; chasten; chastise; chide; condemn; criticize; denounce; denunciate; discipline; excoriate; fulminate against; imprecate; impugn; inveigh against; objurgate; punish; rebuke; remonstrate; reprehend; reprimand; reproach; reprobate; reprove; revile; scold; swear at; upbraid; vituperate.*

have a conniption (fit) ▪ A moribund metaphor. *bellow; bluster; clamor; explode; fulminate; fume; holler; howl; rage; rant; rave; roar; scream; shout; storm; thunder; vociferate; yell.*

have a frog in (your) throat ▪ A moribund metaphor. *be croaky; be grating; be gravelly; be guttural; be hoarse; be husky; be throaty.*

have a good (fantastic; nice) day (evening) ▪ A plebeian sentiment. We are bovine creatures who find that formulas rather than feelings suit us well enough; indeed, they suit us mightily. How pleasant it is not to have to think of a valid sentiment when a vapid one does so nicely; how effortless to rely on triteness rather than on truth.

Dimwitticisms veil our true feelings and avert our real thoughts. SEE ALSO **common courtesy**.

have a hemorrhage A ▪ moribund metaphor. *bellow; bluster; clamor; explode; fulminate; fume; holler; howl; rage; rant; rave; roar; scream; shout; storm; thunder; vociferate; yell.*

have (take) a listen ▪ An infantile phrase. *listen.* As inane as it is insulting, *have (take) a listen* obviously says nothing that *listen* alone does not. Journalists and media personalities who use this offensive phrase ought to be silenced; businesspeople, dismissed; public officials, pilloried.

• But some fans will take a walk and *take a listen* to the sales pitch, intrigued by such generous offers and possibility of making such a huge profit. REPLACE WITH *listen.*
• It has been far too long since I have had the opportunity to hear the Seneca Chamber Orchestra, so I went over to Christ Church United Methodist to *have a listen,* and boy, has it grown. REPLACE WITH *listen.* • *Take a listen* and decide for yourself. REPLACE WITH *Listen.* • But first we will *take a listen* to attorney Frederic Woocher arguing against the law. REPLACE WITH *listen.*

have (me) by the ears ▪ A moribund metaphor. *clasp; cleave (to); clench; clutch; grab; grasp; grip; hold; secure; seize.*

> In spite of the recent falls in the value of the Nasdaq index and the value of Amazon stock, the new technology had the city by the ears . . .—Salman Rushdie, *Fury*

(you) have to learn to walk before (you) can run ▪ A popular prescription.

(you) have to love (yourself) before (you) can love another ▪ A popular prescription.

(you) have (your) whole life ahead of (you) ▪ A popular prescription.

(stand) head and shoulders above (the rest) ▪ A moribund metaphor. *abler;*

better; exceptional; greater; higher; more able (accomplished; adept; capable; competent; qualified; skilled; talented); outstanding; standout; superior; superlative. • By now, a few names should clearly be *heads and shoulders above* all others. REPLACE WITH *better than.*

head for the hills ∎ A moribund metaphor. *abscond; clear out; decamp; depart; desert; disappear; escape; exit; flee; fly; go; go away; leave; move on; part; pull out; quit; retire; retreat; run away; take flight; take off; vacate; vanish; withdraw.*

head in the clouds and feet on the ground ∎ A moribund metaphor.

head into the home stretch ∎ A moribund metaphor.

head on the block ∎ A moribund metaphor.

head over heels ∎ A moribund metaphor. *altogether; ardently; completely; deeply; earnestly; entirely; fervently; fully; intensely; passionately; perfectly; quite; roundly; thoroughly; totally; unreservedly; utterly; wholly; zealously.*

head over heels (in love) ∎ A moribund metaphor. *besotted; crazed; haunted; infatuated; lovesick; mad; obsessed; possessed; smitten.*

> Even in his Mammon days, he always leaned to the general while I tumbled head over heels into the particular; he loved ideas and I personalities; he was all for argument and I yearned for gossip.—Louis Auchincloss, *The Rector of Justin*

(as) healthy as a horse ∎ An insipid simile. *athletic; beefy; brawny; energetic; fine; fit; good; hale; hardy; hearty; healthful; healthy; husky; lanky; lean; manly; muscular; powerful; robust; shapely; sinewy; slender; solid; sound; stalwart; strong; sturdy; thin; trim; vigorous; virile; well; well-built.*

heap dirt (scorn) on ∎ A moribund metaphor. *asperse; badmouth; belittle; besmirch; bespatter; blacken; calumniate; defame; defile; denigrate; denounce; depreciate; deride; disparage; impugn; insult; libel; malign; profane; revile; scandalize; slander; slap; slur; smear; sully; taint; traduce; vilify; vitiate.*

hear by (via) the grapevine ∎ A moribund metaphor.

heart and soul ∎ A moribund metaphor. 1. *altogether; completely; entirely; fully; perfectly; quite; roundly; thoroughly; totally; unreservedly; utterly; wholly.* 2. *earnestly; fervently; genuinely; heartily; honestly; sincerely; unreservedly; wholeheartedly.*

(my) heart bleeds for (you) ∎ A moribund metaphor. *commiserate; empathize; feel bad; feel sorry; pity; sympathize.*

(his) heart is in the right place ∎ A moribund metaphor. *be well-intentioned.*

(you) hear what I'm saying? ∎ An ineffectual phrase. • She's the one who did it, not me. *You hear what I'm saying?* DELETE *You hear what I'm saying?* SEE ALSO **(you) know what I mean? (you) know what I'm saying; (you) know what I'm telling you? (do) you know?.**

(I) hear you ∎ An infantile phrase. *appreciate; apprehend; comprehend; grasp; see; understand.*

heaven on earth ∎ A moribund metaphor. *ambrosial; angelic; beatific; blissful; delightful; divine; enchanting; glorious; godlike; godly; heavenly; joyful; magnificent; resplendent; splendid; sublime.*

(as) heavy as lead ∎ An insipid simile. *bulky; heavy; hefty; weighty.*

heavy (tough) going ∎ A moribund metaphor. *arduous; backbreaking; burdensome; difficult; exhausting; fatiguing; hard; herculean; laborious; not easy; onerous; severe; strenuous; toilful; toilsome; tough; troublesome; trying; wearisome.*

Heinz 57 ∎ A moribund metaphor. *assorted; diverse; hybrid; mixed; motley; varied; variegated; various.*

(through) hell and high water ∎ A moribund metaphor. *adversity; affliction; calamity; catastrophe; difficulty; distress; hardship; misadventure; misfortune; ordeal; trial; tribulation; trouble; woe.*

hell (hellbent) for leather ∎ A moribund metaphor. *breakneck; brisk; fast; hasty; hurried; immediate; madcap; prompt; quick; rapid; rash; speedy; swift; wild; winged.* • Connors clearly thought that he had more to gain by pursuing his *hell-for-leather* expansion in the region.

hell has no fury like (a woman scorned) ∎ An insipid simile.

hell on earth ∎ A moribund metaphor. *chthonian; chthonic; hellish; impossible; infernal; insufferable; insupportable; intolerable; painful; plutonic; sulfurous; unbearable; uncomfortable; unendurable; unpleasant; stygian; tartarean.* • Being a stepmother is *hell on earth.* REPLACE WITH *hellish.* SEE ALSO **a living hell.**

hell on wheels ∎ A moribund metaphor. 1. *boisterous; disorderly; feral; obstreperous; rambunctious; riotous; roistering; rowdy; uncontrolled; undisciplined; unrestrained; unruly; untamed; wild.* 2. *angry; bad-tempered; bilious; cantankerous; choleric; churlish; crabby; cranky; cross; curmudgeonly; disagreeable; dyspeptic; grouchy; gruff; grumpy; ill-humored; ill-tempered; irascible; irritable; mad; peevish; petulant; quarrelsome; short-tempered; splenetic; surly; testy; vexed.*

hem and haw ∎ An inescapable pair. *dally; dawdle; hesitate; vacillate; waver.*

hemorrhage red ink ∎ A moribund metaphor.

(right) here and now ∎ An inescapable pair. *currently; now; nowadays; presently; the present; today.*

here's the thing ∎ An ineffectual phrase. • *Here's the thing*, whoever is mayor must be able to work with the community. DELETE *Here's the thing.* • *Here's the thing*, men don't even know that we're different. DELETE *Here's the thing.* SEE ALSO **that's the thing; the thing about (of) it is; the thing is.**

here, there, and everywhere ∎ A wretched redundancy. *all over; everywhere; omnipresent; ubiquitous.*

here today, gone tomorrow ∎ An infantile phrase. *brief; ephemeral; evanescent; fleeting; flitting; fugacious; fugitive; impermanent; momentary; passing; short; short-lived; temporary; transient; transitory; volatile.* • I still love it even though nothing is as *here today, gone tomorrow* as a job in TV. REPLACE WITH *fleeting.* • In politics, issues that are *here today are gone tomorrow.* REPLACE WITH *are ephemeral.*

here to stay ∎ An infantile phrase. *constant; deep-rooted; enduring; entrenched; established; everlasting; fixed; lasting; long-lived; permanent; secure; stable; unending.* • They questioned whether ability grouping is *here to stay.* REPLACE WITH *permanent.*

hero ∎ A TOP-TWENTY DIMWITTICISM. A suspect superlative. Seldom someone who strives valorously to achieve a noble goal, *hero* has come to mean anyone who simply does his job or, perhaps, doing it, dies. As often, *hero* is used to describe a person who behaves ethically or suitably—merely, as he was told or taught.

Only comic book characters and cartoon creatures, today, define the word well. • The brother of former POW Jessica Lynch is calling his sister a *hero.* • A two-year-old boy who dialed **999** after his mother suffered an epileptic fit was today hailed a "little *hero*" by police in England. • Juventus goal *hero* David Trezeguet says his teammates are confident they can reach the Champions League final after last night's **2-1** defeat by Real Madrid. • A Brazilian bulldozer driver has become a national *hero* after refusing to knock down a house shared by a single mother and her seven children. • A male nurse who died of SARS was yesterday given a *hero's* funeral attended by Chief Executive Tung Chee-hwa.

hey ∎ An infantile phrase. As a substitute for *hello* or *hi*, *hey* is a cheerless one. • You have a sharp mind for business and know how to relate to those who are self-employed or who work in unconventional careers (because, *hey*, you're part of the group!).

hide (their) heads in the sand ∎ A moribund metaphor. *brush aside; avoid; discount; disregard; dodge; duck; ignore; neglect; omit; pass over; recoil from; shrink from; shun; shy away from; turn away from; withdraw from.* • Even when informed of the problem, some denominations are continuing to *hide their heads in the sand.*

(neither) hide nor (or) hair ∎ A moribund metaphor. *nothing; sign; soupçon; trace; vestige.*

(left) high and dry ∎ An inescapable pair. *abandoned; alone; deserted; forgotten; helpless; left; powerless; stranded.*

> His voice trailed off, he didn't know where; it left him high and dry, just staring at Ikmen like a fool.—Barbara Nadel, *Belshazzar's Daughter*

high and low ∎ An inescapable pair. *all around; all over; all through; broadly; everyplace; everywhere; extensively; throughout; ubiquitously; universally; widely.* SEE ALSO **far and wide; left and right.**

high and mighty ∎ An inescapable pair. *arrogant; cavalier; conceited; condescending; contemptuous; despotic; dictatorial; disdainful; dogmatic; domineering; haughty; imperious; insolent; lofty; overbearing; overweening; patronizing; pompous; pretentious; scornful; self-important; supercilious; superior; vainglorious.*

(as) high as a kite ∎ An insipid simile. 1. *agitated; aroused; ebullient; effusive; enthused; elated; excitable; excited; exhilarated; expansive; impassioned; inflamed; overwrought; stimulated.* 2. *besotted; crapulous; drunk; inebriated; intoxicated; sodden; stupefied; tipsy.*

high (top) man on the totem pole ∎ A moribund metaphor. *administrator; boss; brass; chief; commander; director; executive; foreman; head; headman; leader; manager; master; (high) muckamuck; officer; official; overseer; president; principal; superintendent; supervisor.*

(give) high marks ∎ A moribund metaphor.

high on the hog ∎ A moribund metaphor. *extravagantly; lavishly; luxuriantly.* A moribund metaphor. • It's the state officials who are living *high on the hog.* REPLACE WITH *extravagantly.*

high-water mark ∎ A moribund metaphor.

highway robbery ∎ A moribund metaphor.

high, wide, and handsome ∎ A moribund metaphor. *carefree; stylish.*

hindsight is 20/20 ∎ A quack equation.

hired gun ∎ A moribund metaphor. 1. *assassin; killer; mercenary; murderer.* 2. *adviser; authority; consultant; counselor; expert; guru; specialist.*

hit (him) like a hammer

hit a home run ▪ A moribund metaphor. *advance; fare well; flourish; prevail; progress; prosper; succeed; thrive; triumph; win.*

hit (strike; touch) a nerve ▪ A moribund metaphor.

hit (him) (straight) between the eyes ▪ A moribund metaphor. *amaze; astonish; astound; awe; dazzle; dumbfound; flabbergast; overpower; overwhelm; shock; startle; stun; stupefy; surprise.*

hit (rock) bottom ▪ A moribund metaphor. *bankrupt; broke; destitute; distressed; impecunious; impoverished; indigent; insolvent; penniless; poor; poverty-stricken.*

hitch (your) wagon to a star ▪ A moribund metaphor. *be ambitious; be determined; be motivated; be striving.*

hit (close to) home ▪ A moribund metaphor.

hit (him) like a hammer ▪ An insipid simile. *fiercely; forcibly; hard; intensely; powerfully; severely; violently.*

> As he walked in the door, the smell of the market hit Andy like a hammer.—James Wesley Rawles, *Survivors*

hit (me) like a ton of bricks ▪ An insipid simile. *amaze; astonish; astound; awe; confound; daze; dazzle; dumbfound; flabbergast; overpower; overwhelm; shock; stagger; startle; stun; stupefy; surprise.* • The report *hit Congress like a ton of bricks.* REPLACE WITH *overwhelmed Congress.*

hit or miss ▪ A moribund metaphor. *aimless; arbitrary; capricious; casual; erratic; haphazard; incidental; inconsistent; infrequent; irregular; lax; loose; occasional; odd; offhand; random; sporadic; uncontrolled; unplanned.*

hit over the head ▪ A moribund metaphor.

hit pay dirt ▪ A moribund metaphor. *flourish; get rich; prevail; prosper; succeed; thrive; triumph; win.*

hit the ceiling ▪ A moribund metaphor. *bellow; bluster; clamor; explode; fulminate; fume; holler; howl; rage; rant; rave; roar; scream; shout; storm; thunder; vociferate; yell.*

hit the ground running ▪ A moribund metaphor. • I get up in the morning and *hit the ground running.*

hit the hay ▪ A moribund metaphor. *doze; go to bed; nap; rest; retire; sleep; slumber.*

hit the jackpot ▪ A moribund metaphor. *flourish; get rich; prevail; prosper; succeed; thrive; triumph; win.*

hit the nail (squarely) on the head ▪ A moribund metaphor. *be correct; be right.*

hit the road ▪ A moribund metaphor. *abscond; clear out; decamp; depart; desert; disappear; escape; exit; flee; fly; go; go away; leave; move on; part; pull out; quit; retire; retreat; run away; take flight; take off; vacate; vanish; withdraw.*

hit the roof ▪ A moribund metaphor. 1. *be angry; be annoyed; be enraged; be exasperated; be furious; be incensed; be infuriated; be irate; be irked; be irritated; be mad; be raging; be wrathful.* 2. *bellow; bluster; clamor; explode; fulminate; fume; holler; howl; rage; rant; rave; roar; scream; shout; storm; thunder; vociferate; yell.* • He *hit the roof.* REPLACE WITH *became enraged.*

> Salvation had finally arrived, I saw that at once, but as soon as Sophie heard I wanted to remarry she hit the roof. 'You're not fit to marry anyone,' she said.—Susan Howatch, *The High Flyer*

hit the sack ▪ A moribund metaphor. *doze; go to bed; nap; rest; retire; sleep; slumber.*

hit the skids ▪ A moribund metaphor. *decay; decline; degenerate; destroy; deteriorate; disintegrate; ebb; erode; fade; fall off; languish; lessen; ruin; wane; weaken; wither; worsen.*

hit (him) while (he's) down ▪ A moribund metaphor.

(as) hoarse as a crow ▪ An insipid simile. *grating; gravelly; gruff; guttural; harsh; hoarse; rasping; raspy; throaty.*

hoist with (his) own petard ▪ A moribund metaphor.

(can't) hold a candle (to) ▪ A moribund metaphor. 1. *compare; equal; equate; liken; match; measure up; meet; rival.* 2. *be inferior.* • Various third-party utilities are available to improve this situation, but only one of them *holds a candle to* the NetWare SALVAGE utility. REPLACE WITH *rivals.* • When it comes to hosting wackos, the oft-maligned Web can't *hold a candle to* AM radio. REPLACE WITH *compare to.*

hold a gun to ▪ A moribund metaphor. *coerce; command; compel; constrain; demand; dictate; force; insist; make; order; pressure; require.*

hold all the cards ▪ A moribund metaphor. *administer; boss; command; control; dictate; direct; dominate; govern; in charge; in command; in control; manage; manipulate; master; order; overpower; oversee; predominate; prevail; reign over; rule; superintend.*

hold (keep; play) (cards) close to the chest (vest) ▪ A moribund metaphor. *clandestine; cloaked; closed; concealed; confidential; covert; furtive; hidden; masked; mysterious; private; secretive; secret; shrouded; sly; stealthy; surreptitious; veiled.* • If police have any leads, they are keeping them *close to the vest.* REPLACE WITH *secret.*

hold (their) feet to the fire ∎ A moribund metaphor. *coerce; command; compel; constrain; demand; enforce; force; goad; impel; importune; incite; induce; insist; instigate; make; oblige; press; pressure; prod; push; require; spur; urge.* • The task now for those senators who truly support reform is to *hold their colleagues' feet to the fire* and bring this bill up again and again. REPLACE WITH *pressure their colleagues.* • He campaigns by movement-building: helping candidates, running ads to promote tax cuts, and *holding congressional Republicans' feet to the fire.* REPLACE WITH *prodding congressional Republicans.*

hold (your) fire ∎ A moribund metaphor. 1. *be silent; be still; hush; keep quiet; quiet; silence.* 2. *be closed-mouthed; be quiet; be reticent; be silent; be speechless; be taciturn; be uncommunicative.*

hold (their) ground ∎ A moribund metaphor. 1. *hold fast; stand firm.* 2. *assert; command; decree; dictate; insist; order; require.*

hold (my) hand ∎ A moribund metaphor. *accompany; escort; guide.* • The intent of this text is to *hold your hand* through the learning process. REPLACE WITH *guide you.*

hold (her) head up (high) ∎ A moribund metaphor. *be proud; show self-respect.*

hold on for dear life ∎ A torpid term. *clutch; grab; grasp; hold; seize.*

hang (hold) on to your hat ∎ A moribund metaphor. *be careful; be cautious; be prepared; be wary; look out; take heed; watch out.*

hem and haw ∎ A moribund metaphor. *be indecisive; be uncertain; dally; dawdle; hesitate; vacillate.*

hold the fort ∎ A moribund metaphor. 1. *defend; guard; protect.* 2. *look after.*

hold the phone ∎ A moribund metaphor. *be patient; hold on; pause; slow down; wait.*

hold the purse strings ∎ A moribund metaphor. *administer; boss; command; control; dictate; direct; dominate; govern; in charge; in command; in control; manage; manipulate; master; order; overpower; oversee; predominate; prevail; reign over; rule; superintend.*

hold (my) breath ∎ A moribund metaphor. *agitated; anxious; eager; edgy; excitable; excited; fidgety; frantic; jittery; jumpy; nervous; ill at ease; on edge; restive; restless; skittish; uncomfortable; uneasy.*

> Still, though I'd already unlatched the door for her, I felt unprepared for her arrival, needing to back away and sit again in my leather chair. I was holding my breath, waiting for her to go away.—Elizabeth Rosner, *The Speed of Light*

hold (your) tongue ∎ A moribund metaphor.

1. *be silent; be still; hush; keep quiet; quiet; silence.* 2. *be closed-mouthed; be quiet; be reticent; be silent; be speechless; be taciturn; be uncommunicative.*

hold true ∎ A wretched redundancy. *hold.* • What *holds true* for them may not *hold true* for others. DELETE *true.*

hold water ∎ A moribund metaphor. *hold; is true; is valid.* • We have to ask if the ancient ideas of the roles of bonds still *hold water.* REPLACE WITH *hold.*

hold your horses ∎ A moribund metaphor. *be patient; calm down; hang on; hold on; pause; slow down; wait.*

home free ∎ A moribund metaphor. *guarded; protected; safe; secure; sheltered; shielded; undamaged; unharmed; unhurt; unscathed.*

home is where the heart is ∎ A popular prescription.

homely as a mud fence ∎ An insipid simile. *coarse; homely; ill-favored; plain; ugly; unattractive; unbeautiful; uncomely; unsightly.*

(as) honest as the day is long ∎ An insipid simile. *aboveboard; blunt; candid; direct; earnest; faithful; forthright; frank; genuine; honest; reliable; sincere; straightforward; trustworthy; truthful; upright; veracious; veridical.*

> On this occasion, in each of their three written references, all four of the candidates were described as hardworking, reliable, loyal and as honest as the day is long.—Dick Francis, *Under Orders*

honest truth ∎ A wretched redundancy. *honesty; truth.* • If you want the *honest truth,* I am in love with him. REPLACE WITH *truth.*

honestly and truly ∎ An inescapable pair. • I *honestly and truly* believed he was the best I could hope for. REPLACE WITH *honestly* or *truly.*

honesty is the best policy ∎ A popular prescription.

hook, line, and sinker ∎ A moribund metaphor. *altogether; completely; entirely; fully; perfectly; roundly; quite; thoroughly; totally; unreservedly; utterly; wholly.*

hoot and holler ∎ An inescapable pair. *bay; bawl; bellow; blare; caterwaul; clamor; cry; holler; hoot; howl; roar; screak; scream; screech; shout; shriek; shrill; squawk; squeal; vociferate; wail; whoop; yell; yelp; yowl.*

hope and expect (expectation) ∎ A wretched redundancy. *hope; expect (expectation); trust.* • I *hope and expect* you'll be seeing a lot more of this. REPLACE WITH *expect* or *hope.*

hope and pray ∎ An inescapable pair. • I *hope and pray* that in future features of this sort, the *Globe* puts the emphasis where it belongs.

hope for the best ∎ A popular prescription. *be confident; be encouraged; be heartened; be hopeful; be optimistic; be positive; be rosy; be sanguine.*

hope for the best but expect the worst ∎ A popular prescription. • Since governments can never know how stable the oil-exporting countries are, governments of importing countries should *hope for the best but prepare for the worst.*

(just) hope (it'll) go away ∎ A popular prescription.

hopeless romantic ∎ An inescapable pair.

hopes and dreams ∎ An inescapable pair.

hope springs eternal ∎ A popular prescription. *confident; encouraged; heartened; hopeful; optimistic; rosy; sanguine.*

hopping mad ∎ An inescapable pair. *agitated; alarmed; angry; annoyed; aroused; choleric; enraged; fierce; fuming; furious; incensed; inflamed; infuriated; irate; irritable; mad; maddened; raging; splenetic.*

hornet's nest ∎ A moribund metaphor. *complexity; complication; difficulty; dilemma; entanglement; imbroglio; labyrinth; maze; muddle; perplexity; plight; predicament; problem; puzzle; quagmire; tangle.* • Senator Dodd called the jurisdictional issue a *hornet's nest* but said he was ready to tackle it. REPLACE WITH *imbroglio.*

horse of a different (another) color ∎ A moribund metaphor. *aberrant; abnormal; anomalistic; anomalous; atypical; bizarre; curious; deviant; different; distinct; distinctive; eccentric; exceptional; extraordinary; fantastic; foreign; grotesque; idiosyncratic; independent; individual; individualistic; irregular; novel; odd; offbeat; original; peculiar; puzzling; quaint; queer; rare; remarkable; separate; singular; uncommon; unconventional; unexampled; unique; unnatural; unorthodox; unparalleled; unprecedented; unusual; weird.*

hot air ∎ A moribund metaphor. *aggrandizement; bluster; boasting; braggadocio; bragging; bravado; crowing; elaboration; embellishment; embroidery; exaggeration; fanfaronade; gasconade; gloating; hyperbole; overstatement; rodomontade; swaggering.*

hot and bothered ∎ An inescapable pair. *agitated; anxious; aroused; bothered; displeased; disquieted; disturbed; excited; flustered; perturbed; troubled; upset; worried.*

hot and heavy ∎ An inescapable pair. *aggressive; dynamic; emphatic; energetic; ferocious; fervent; fierce; forceful; frantic; frenzied; furious; intense; mighty; passionate; powerful; robust; savage;* *spirited; strenuous; strong; vehement; vicious; vigorous; violent.*

(as) hot as fire ∎ An insipid simile. *aflame; blazing; blistering; boiling; burning; fiery; flaming; heated; hot; ovenlike; roasting; scalding; scorching; searing; simmering; sizzling; steaming; sweltering; torrid; tropical; warm.*

(as) hot as hades (hell) ∎ An insipid simile. *aflame; blazing; blistering; boiling; burning; fiery; flaming; heated; hot; ovenlike; roasting; scalding; scorching; searing; simmering; sizzling; steaming; sweltering; torrid; tropical; warm.*

hot little hands ∎ A moribund metaphor.

hotly contested ∎ An inescapable pair.

hot potato ∎ A moribund metaphor. *card; character; eccentric; exception; original.*

hot ticket ∎ A moribund metaphor. *card; character; eccentric; exception; original.*

hot to trot ∎ A moribund metaphor. 1. *concupiscent; horny; lascivious; lecherous; lewd; libidinous; licentious; lustful; prurient.* 2. *anxious; eager; impatient; ready; willing.*

hot under the collar ∎ A moribund metaphor. *agitated; alarmed; angry; annoyed; aroused; choleric; enraged; fierce; fuming; furious; incensed; inflamed; infuriated; irate; irritable; mad; maddened; raging; splenetic.*

how could this have happened? ∎ A plebeian sentiment.

how did (I) get into this? ∎ A plebeian sentiment.

how goes it? (how's it going? how you doing?) ∎ An ineffectual phrase. These phrases are uttered by the unalert and inert. *How goes it? how's it going?* and *how you doing?* are gratuitous substitutes for a gracious *hello.*

how much (do) you want to bet? ∎ An infantile phrase.

hue and cry ∎ An inescapable pair. *clamor; commotion; din; hubbub; noise; outcry; protest; racket; shout; tumult; uproar.*

huff and puff ∎ An inescapable pair. 1. *blow; breathe heavily; gasp; huff; pant; puff; wheeze.* 2. *bellow; bluster; clamor; explode; fulminate; fume; holler; howl; rage; rant; rave; roar; scream; shout; storm; thunder; vent; vociferate; yell.*

> Finally as she stood there huffing and puffing, while he was near apoplectic, she would agree to a compromise.—J. P. Donleavy, *The Saddest Summer of Samuel S*

huge throng ∎ A wretched redundancy. *throng.* • A *huge throng* of young people attended the concert. DELETE *huge.*

hugs and kisses ∎ An inescapable pair.

human nature being what it is ∎ An ineffectual phrase (SEE) • *Human nature being what it is,* most of us would rather speak our own mind than listen to what someone else says. DELETE *Human nature being what it is.* • *Human nature being what it is,* when people place demands on others, their initial reaction is to rebel. DELETE *Human nature being what it is.* • *Human nature being what it is,* getting an extra day made everybody slow down. DELETE *Human nature being what it is.*

(my) humble abode ∎ An infantile phrase. • I recently had the opportunity to visit CMD's headquarters in Boulder, Colorado, not far from my *humble abode.* REPLACE WITH *home.*

hung the moon ∎ A moribund metaphor. *astonishing; astounding; extraordinary; marvelous; outstanding; remarkable; spectacular; startling; stunning; wonderful; wondrous.* • He thinks his mama *hung the moon.* REPLACE WITH *is extraordinary.*

(as) hungry as a bear ∎ An insipid simile. *esurient; famished; gluttonous; greedy; hungry; insatiable; omnivorous; rapacious; ravenous; starved; starving; voracious.*

(as) hungry as a horse ∎ An insipid simile. *esurient; famished; gluttonous; greedy; hungry; insatiable; omnivorous; rapacious; ravenous; starved; starving; voracious.*

hunt with the hounds and run with the hares ∎ A moribund metaphor.

hurdle to clear ∎ A moribund metaphor. *bar; barrier; block; blockage; check; deterrent; difficulty; encumbrance; handicap; hindrance; hurdle; impediment; interference; obstacle; obstruction.*

hurl insults ∎ A moribund metaphor.

hustle and bustle ∎ An inescapable pair. *activity; bustle; chaos; commotion; flurry; hubbub; hustle; stir; turmoil.* • Macau presents a restful alternative to the *hustle and bustle* of Hong Kong. REPLACE WITH *hustle.*

> As John Morgan walked through the hustle and bustle of the Emergency Room on his way to the small, staff locker room, he shook his head. It always amazed him that so many people could have so many crazy things happen to them in the middle of the night.—Sean Hanzelik, *The Letters*

Ii

I can't believe I'm telling you this ◗ A plebeian sentiment. Only the foolish or the unconscious, unaware of or ambivalent about the words they use or why they use them, can exclaim *I can't believe I'm telling you this.* Language use, the essence of being human, entails certain responsibilities—care and consciousness among them; otherwise, it's all dimwitted. SEE ALSO **I don't know why I'm telling you this**.

I can't get no satisfaction ◗ An infantile phrase.

icing on the cake ◗ A moribund metaphor. *a benefit; a bonus; a dividend; a gift; a gratuity; a lagniappe; an extra; a perk; a perquisite; a pourboire; a premium; a tip.* • Accreditation is still only *icing on the cake* and does not guarantee a department any rewards beyond the recognition of peers. REPLACE WITH *a perquisite.*

> Dr. Pierce and Deena had returned to our Sunday school class, buoying my spirits. And several of the alumni from the Live Free or Die class had stopped attending, which was icing on the cake.—Philip Gulley, *Life Goes On: A Harmony Novel*

idle rich ◗ An inescapable pair.

I don't know ◗ A plebeian sentiment. • New passion is sweet, but after you know someone for a while, it fades. *I don't know.* • I know who I am—I have a good sense of that—but I will never know you, or anyone else, as well. *I don't know.*
For a person to conclude his expressed thoughts and views with *I don't know* would nullify all he seemed to know if it weren't that *I don't know* is less an admission of not knowing than it is an apology for presuming to.

I don't know if (whether) I'm coming or going ◗ A moribund metaphor. *baffled; befuddled; bewildered; confounded; confused; disconcerted; flummoxed; mixed up; muddled; perplexed; puzzled.*

I don't know, what do you want to do? ◗ An infantile phrase.

I don't know why I'm telling you this ◗ A plebeian sentiment. SEE ALSO **I can't believe I'm telling you this.**

I (just) don't think about it ◗ A plebeian sentiment. SEE ALSO **you think too much.**

if and when ◗ A wretched redundancy. *if;*

when. • *If and when* a conflict should arise, it should be taken care of as soon as possible to protect the harmonious environment. REPLACE WITH *If* or *when.* SEE ALSO **if, as, and when; when and if; when and whether; when, as, and if; whether and when.**

if, as, and when ◗ A wretched redundancy. *if; when.* SEE ALSO **if and when; when and if; when, as, and if; when and whether; whether and when.**

if at first you don't succeed (try, try again) ◗ A popular prescription.

I feel (understand) your pain ◗ The people who spout about how empathic they are (*I feel your pain; I know how you feel*) are often the same people who have scant notion of what it is to be sensitive, kindhearted, even responsive. The emphasis is on showing empathy, which we do more for our own welfare than for others'; it's socially obligatory to be, or pretend to be, empathic. Ultimately, empathy will be thought no more highly of than sympathy now is. SEE ALSO **I'm sorry.**

if it ain't broke, don't fix it ◗ A popular prescription.

if it feels good, it can't be bad ◗ A popular prescription.

if it isn't one thing, it's another ◗ A plebeian sentiment. SEE ALSO **it's one thing after another.**

if it's (not) meant to be, it's (not) meant to be ◗ A popular prescription.

if it sounds too good to be true, it (probably) is ◗ A popular prescription.

if the shoe fits (wear it) ◗ A moribund metaphor.

if the truth be (were) known (told) ◗ An ineffectual phrase.

if you can't beat them, join them ◗ A popular prescription.

if you can't say something nice, don't say anything ◗ A plebeian sentiment. SEE ALSO **be nice.**

if you can't stand the heat, stay out of the kitchen ◗ A popular prescription.

if you don't know, I'm not going to tell you ◗ An infantile phrase.

ignorance is bliss ◗ A plebeian sentiment.

I (I've) got to (have to) tell you (something) ∎ An ineffectual phrase. Like *I'll tell you (something)*, *I'll tell you what*, *I'm telling you*, and *let me tell you (something)*, *I (I've) got to (have to) tell you (something)* is a mind-numbing expression spoken only by people who are unaware of how foolish they sound—and of how foolish they are. These are the same people who are wont to begin other sentences with *Look* or *Listen, Hey* or *Okay*. A phrase that's rarely written is a phrase that should be seldom spoken. • *I got to tell you*, he was the only person I could discuss my frustrations with. DELETE *I got to tell you*. • *I've got to tell you something*, I'm so proud of you. DELETE *I've got to tell you something*. • *I have to tell you*, the emerging country rates are up 21 percent. DELETE *I have to tell you*.

I just work here ∎ A plebeian sentiment.

I'll bet you any amount of money ∎ An infantile phrase.

ill-gotten gains ∎ An inescapable pair.

I'll tell you (something) ∎ An ineffectual phrase. This phrase—like *I got to (have to) tell you (something)*; *I'll tell you what*; *I'm telling you*; *let me tell you (something)*—is mouthed by unimpressive men and irritating women, the one no more able, no more elegant than the other. • You got off easy, *I'll tell you*. DELETE *I'll tell you*. • *I'll tell you something*, they look like the greatest team ever. DELETE *I'll tell you something*. • *I'll tell you something,* if it doesn't work out, you've always got a job here. DELETE *I'll tell you something*. • The publisher got a sharp letter from me, *I'll tell you*. DELETE *I'll tell you*. SEE ALSO **I got to (have to) tell you (something)**; **I'll tell you what**; **I'm telling you**; **let me tell you (something)**.

I'll tell you what ∎ An ineffectual phrase. • *I'll tell you what*, let's pause for a commercial and then you can tell us your story. DELETE *I'll tell you what*. • *I'll tell you what*, I'm not bitter against women, but I sure judge them quicker now. DELETE *I'll tell you what*. SEE ALSO **I got to (have to) tell you (something)**; **I'll tell you (something)**; **I'm telling you**; **let me tell you (something)**.

I love (him) but I'm not in love with (him) ∎ A popular prescription. The need to distinguish between loving someone and being *in* love with someone is fundamentally false. That there are different kinds of love is nothing that any discerning person has to be reminded of. Some who make such a distinction may do so to ease their conscience, to absolve themselves for not loving someone who likely loves them and whom they surely feel gratitude or obligation to. In these instances, saying *I love (him) but I'm not in love with (him)* is simply a way of feeling good about having made someone feel bad.

Love, like few other words, ought not to be trifled with. • *I love him but I'm not in love with him.* REPLACE WITH *I love him.* SEE ALSO **be nice; excuse me?**.

I'm bored (he's boring) ∎ A plebeian sentiment. Being boring is preferable to being bored. The boring are often thoughtful and imaginative; the bored, thoughtless and unimaginative.

We would do well to shun those who whine about how bored they are or how boring another is. It's they, these bored ones, who in their eternal quest for entertainment and self-oblivion are most suited to causing trouble, courting turmoil, and coercing talk. SEE ALSO **(it) keeps (me) busy**.

I mean ∎ A grammatical gimmick. Elliptical for "what I mean to say," *I mean* is said by those who do not altogether know what they mean to say. • Nobody deserves to die like that. *I mean*, he didn't stand a chance. DELETE *I mean*. • *I mean*, being in the entertainment field is not easy; *I mean*, I work hard at my job and still have performances to give. DELETE *I mean*. • I enjoy the outdoors; *I mean*, how can you live here and not enjoy it? DELETE *I mean*. • *I mean*, if you were in the movies or on TV, *I mean*, many more people would be interested. DELETE *I mean*.

imitation is the sincerest form of flattery ∎ A popular prescription.

I'm not perfect (you know) ∎ A plebeian sentiment. Even though *(I'm) a perfectionist* (SEE) is a suspect superlative—meaning that people who proclaim this do not easily disabuse themselves of the notion of being perfect—*I'm not perfect (you know)* is a plebeian sentiment—meaning that people who proclaim this all too easily excuse themselves for being imperfect. • I have some deep-seated anger. Hey, *I'm not perfect, you know.* SEE ALSO **(I'm) a perfectionist; nobody's perfect**.

I'm not stupid (you know) ∎ A plebeian sentiment. • *I'm not stupid, you know*; I'm 24 years old, and I've been around.

impact (on) (*v*) ∎ An overworked word. *act on; affect; bear on; influence; sway; work on.* • Let's look at two important trends that may *impact* the future of those languages. REPLACE WITH *influence*. • Everybody's district is *impacted* in a different way. REPLACE WITH *affected*. SEE ALSO **has an impact on**.

implement ∎ An overworked word. *accomplish; achieve; carry out; complete; execute; fulfill; realize.*

I'm not a lawyer (doctor; expert; scientist) but ∎ An infantile phrase. DELETE. Nonlawyers (like nondoctors and other nonprofessionals) use this dimwitted

I'm sorry

phrase to be excused from, rather than be accused of, the inaccuracy of their comments and suggestions. Better they be still. • *I'm not a lawyer, but* I would think you would edit and republish the will. DELETE *I'm not a lawyer, but.* • *I'm not a scientist, but* the report the FDA used as its basis seemed awfully weak in actual numbers. DELETE *I'm not a scientist, but.* • *I'm not a writer, but* I can find things. DELETE *I'm not a writer, but.*

I'm sorry ∎ A plebeian sentiment. No simple apology, the plebeian *I'm sorry* pretends to soothe while it actually scolds. Even though it may seem like an apology—often for something that requires nothing of the sort—*I'm sorry* is said, unapologetically, in a tone of resentment.

Traditionally, a woman's emotion—for women have been, more than men, reluctant to express anger, bare and unbounded—resentment more and more of late finds favor with men and women alike.

• Nine years old is too young to be left alone, *I'm sorry.* • I have to disagree. *I'm sorry.* • I know you guys are going to blow up after I'm done talking, but *I'm sorry.* SEE ALSO **excuse me?; nice; thank you.**

I'm sorry ∎ A plebeian sentiment. *I'm sorry,* uttered, invariably, when people hear another speak of some difficulty, ought to annoy whomever it is said to. This is the height of dimwitted English, for the people who say *I'm sorry*—an expression precisely as untrue as it is trite—likely have no more empathy in their hearts than there are syllables in the sentence. SEE ALSO **I feel (understand) your pain.**

I'm telling you ∎ An ineffectual phrase. • It has more twists and turns than Route 66, *I'm telling you.* DELETE *I'm telling you.* • *I'm telling you,* there are people who take this seriously. DELETE *I'm telling you.* SEE ALSO **I got to (have to) tell you (something); I'll tell you (something); I'll tell you what; let me tell you (something).**

in a big (major) way ∎ A torpid term. *acutely; a great deal; badly; consumedly; enormously; exceedingly; extremely; greatly; hugely; immensely; intensely; largely; mightily; prodigiously; seriously; strongly; very much.* • He wants to meet me *in a big way.* REPLACE WITH *very much.* • It hurt me *in a big way.* REPLACE WITH *badly.* SEE ALSO **in the worst way.**

> The photographer had barked "Smile!" I'd overcompensated in a big way.—Susan Isaacs, *After All These Years*

in a bind ∎ A moribund metaphor. *at risk; endangered; hard-pressed; imperiled; in a bind; in a dilemma; in a fix; in a jam; in a predicament; in a quandary; in danger; in difficulty; in jeopardy; in peril; in trouble; jeopardized.*

in (the) absence of ∎ A wretched redundancy. *absent; having no; lacking; minus; missing; not having; with no; without.* • *In the absence of* these articulated linkages, changes introduced will be difficult to monitor. REPLACE WITH *Absent.*

in a class by (itself) ∎ A moribund metaphor. *different; exceptional; extraordinary; incomparable; inimitable; matchless; nonpareil; notable; noteworthy; novel; odd; original; peculiar; peerless; remarkable; singular; special; strange; uncommon; unequaled; unexampled; unique; unmatched; unparalleled; unrivaled; unusual; without equal.*

(head) in a (the) cloud(s) ∎ A moribund metaphor. *absent; absent-minded; absorbed; abstracted; bemused; captivated; daydreaming; detached; distracted; distrait; dreamy; engrossed; enraptured; faraway; fascinated; immersed; inattentive; in thought; lost; mesmerized; oblivious; preoccupied; rapt; spellbound.*

> It brought it all back to me. Celia Langley. Celia Langley standing in front of me, her hands on her hips and her head in a cloud.—Andrea Levy, *Small Island*

in a delicate condition ∎ A moribund metaphor. *anticipating; enceinte; expectant; expecting; gravid; parturient; pregnant; with child.*

in a dog's age ∎ A moribund metaphor.

in advance of ∎ A wretched redundancy. *ahead of; before.* • *In advance of* introducing our guest, let me tell you why he's here. REPLACE WITH *Before.* SEE ALSO **in advance of; previous to; subsequent to.**

in a (the) family way ∎ A moribund metaphor. *anticipating; enceinte; expectant; expecting; gravid; parturient; pregnant; with child.*

in a (blue) funk ∎ A moribund metaphor. *aggrieved; anhedonic; blue; cheerless; dejected; demoralized; depressed; despondent; disconsolate; discouraged; disheartened; dismal; dispirited; doleful; downcast; downhearted; dreary; forlorn; funereal; gloomy; glum; grieved; low; melancholy; miserable; morose; mournful; negative; pessimistic; plaintive; sad; sorrowful; unhappy; woebegone; woeful.*

in a good mood ∎ A torpid term. *blissful; blithe; buoyant; cheerful; cheery; content; contented; delighted; elated; excited; gay; glad; gleeful; happy; jolly; joyful; joyous; merry; pleased; sanguine; satisfied.* SEE ALSO **positive feelings.**

in a heartbeat ∎ A moribund metaphor. *abruptly; apace; at once; briskly; directly; expeditiously; fast; forthwith; hastily; hurriedly; immediately; instantaneously; instantly; posthaste; promptly; quickly;*

rapidly; rashly; right away; speedily; straightaway; swiftly; wingedly.

> Bless me, father, for I have sinned, I have lied to my husband, left him never knowing he will have a child, and would do it all again in a heartbeat.—Ann Patchett, *Patron Saint of Liars*

in a jam ∎ A moribund metaphor. *at risk; endangered; hard-pressed; imperiled; in a bind; in a dilemma; in a fix; in a jam; in a predicament; in a quandary; in danger; in difficulty; in jeopardy; in peril; in trouble; jeopardized.*

in a lather ∎ A moribund metaphor. *agitated; distraught; disturbed; excited; nervous; shaken; uneasy; upset.*

in a manner of speaking ∎ A wretched redundancy. *as it were; in a sense; in a way; so to speak.* • Your contractor is correct *in a manner of speaking.* REPLACE WITH *in a sense.*

in and of itself (themselves) ∎ A wretched redundancy. *as such; in itself (in themselves).* • This trend is interesting *in and of itself* but is also quite instructive. REPLACE WITH *in itself.* • All the benefits are worthwhile *in and of themselves,* but they have the additional benefit of translating into improved cost efficiency. REPLACE WITH *in themselves.*

in a New York minute ∎ An insipid simile. *abruptly; apace; at once; briskly; directly; expeditiously; fast; forthwith; hastily; hurriedly; immediately; instantaneously; instantly; posthaste; promptly; quickly; rapidly; rashly; right away; speedily; straightaway; suddenly; swiftly; wingedly.* • Then again, if the Knicks lose, those deals could dry up *in a New York minute.* REPLACE WITH *instantly.*

in a nutshell ∎ A moribund metaphor. *briefly; concisely; in brief; in short; in sum; succinctly; tersely.*

> One thing leads to another; that is, houses lead to commodes, and then commodes lead to houses, which lead to land, which leads to dairy cattle, which lead to cheese, which leads to pizza pies, which lead to manicotti and veal Parmesan, which lead to wine, which leads to love, which leads to babies, houses, and commodes. That was Gordon Baldwin in a nutshell.—Jane Smiley, *Good Faith*

in any way, shape, form, or fashion ∎ An infantile phrase. *at all; in any way; in some way; in the least; somehow; someway.* That anyone uses this expression is wondrous. To discerning listeners and readers, *in any way, shape, form, or fashion,* as well as similar assemblages, is as rickety as it is ridiculous.
• If students are asked to leave the University, their return certainly should not be celebrated *in any way, shape, form, or fashion.* DELETE *in any way, shape, form, or fashion.* • Do you feel being on television will help you *in any way, shape, or form?* REPLACE WITH *somehow.* • That control is no longer there, not *in any way, shape, or form.* REPLACE WITH *at all.* • He wants something that doesn't resemble the landmark *in any way, shape, or fashion.* REPLACE WITH *in the least.* SEE ALSO **in every way, shape, and (or) form; in no way, shape, form, or fashion.**

in a pickle ∎ A moribund metaphor. *at risk; endangered; hard-pressed; imperiled; in a bind; in a dilemma; in a fix; in a jam; in a predicament; in a quandary; in danger; in difficulty; in jeopardy; in peril; in trouble; jeopardized.*

> Well, if he was in a pickle in regard to his followers, why the hell should she make it easy for him?—Susan Isaacs, *Red, White and Blue*

in a pig's eye ∎ A moribund metaphor. *at no time; by no means; hardly; in no way; never; no; not at all; not ever; not in any way; not in the least; scarcely; unlikely.*

(stuck) in a rut ∎ A moribund metaphor. *bogged down; caught; cornered; enmeshed; ensnared; entangled; entrapped; netted; mired; snared; stuck; trapped.*

in a (constant) state of flux ∎ A torpid term. *capricious; changeable; erratic; ever-changing; fluid; variable.*

in a timely fashion (manner; way) ∎ A wretched redundancy. *in time; promptly; quickly; rapidly; right away; shortly; soon; speedily; swiftly; timely.* • He believes in getting the job done *in a timely fashion* and is very committed to achieving that goal.

(off) in a world of (his) own ∎ A moribund metaphor. *absent; absent-minded; absorbed; abstracted; bemused; captivated; daydreaming; detached; distracted; distrait; dreamy; engrossed; enraptured; faraway; fascinated; immersed; inattentive; lost; mesmerized; oblivious; preoccupied; rapt; spellbound.*

in (her) birthday suit ∎ A moribund metaphor. *bare; disrobed; naked; nude; stripped; unclothed; uncovered; undressed.*

in close (near) proximity to ∎ A wretched redundancy. *accessible (to); adjacent (to); bordering; at hand; close (to); close by; handy; near; nearby; neighboring; not far from; vicinal.* • Cities were born out of the desire and necessity of human beings to live and work *in close proximity to* each other. REPLACE WITH *close to.* • In those cases, the verb will be in agreement with the subject that is *closest in proximity to* the verb. REPLACE WITH *closest to.*

in (the) clover ∎ A moribund metaphor. *affluent; moneyed; opulent; prosperous; rich;*

successful; wealthy; well-off; well-to-do.

in cold blood ∎ A moribund metaphor. *deliberately; intentionally; knowingly; mindfully; on purpose; premeditatively; willfully.*

in connection with ∎ A wretched redundancy. *about; as for; as to; concerning; for; in; of; on; over; regarding; respecting; to; toward; with.* • The police wanted to talk to him *in connection with* a fur store robbery. REPLACE WITH *about.* • *In connection with* the hiring incidents, this was the first time he denied any wrongdoing. REPLACE WITH *Concerning.*

in consideration of the fact that ∎ A wretched redundancy. *because; considering; for; in that; since.* • *In consideration of the fact that* we have to have something submitted by January 15, we have get to started on this. REPLACE WITH *Since.* SEE ALSO **because of the fact that; considering the fact that; by virtue of the fact that; given the fact that; in view of the fact that; on account of the fact that**.

in (my) corner ∎ A moribund metaphor.

incredible ∎ An overworked word. 1. *beyond belief; beyond comprehension; doubtful; dubious; implausible; imponderable; improbable; incomprehensible; inconceivable; inexplicable; questionable; unfathomable; unimaginable; unthinkable.* 2. *astonishing; astounding; breathtaking; extraordinary; fabulous; fantastic; marvelous; miraculous; overwhelming; prodigious; sensational; spectacular; wonderful; wondrous.* Like the platitudinous *unbelievable* (SEE), this word is very much overused.

One of the hallmarks of dimwitted language is the unimaginativeness of those who use it. We would do well to try to distinguish ourselves through our speech and writing rather than rely on the words and phrases that so many others are wont to use. Those who speak as others speak, inescapably, think as others think. • But that someone would shoot a two-year-old child is *incredible.* REPLACE WITH *unimaginable.* • All these people are *incredibly* brave. REPLACE WITH *astonishingly.*

incumbent upon ∎ A torpid term. *binding; compelling; compulsory; essential; imperative; mandatory; necessary; obligatory; required; requisite; urgent.*

in (his) cups ∎ A moribund metaphor. *besotted; crapulous; drunk; inebriated; intoxicated; sodden; stupefied; tipsy.*

indebtedness ∎ A torpid term. *debt.*

indelible impression ∎ An inescapable pair. To describe something considered unforgettable with a cliché—an unoriginal, a forgettable, phrase—is indeed dimwitted. • The tundra will make an *indelible impression* on you. • War has made an *indelible impression* on international art movements, as well as on Australian art.

> It was never published, but I saw it once and it made an indelible impression on my mind.— Sherwood Anderson, *Winesburg, Ohio*

in-depth analysis ∎ An inescapable pair.

indicate ∎ A torpid term. *Indicate* has virtually devoured every word that might be used instead of it.

More designative words include *acknowledge; admit; affirm; allow; announce; argue; assert; avow; bespeak; betoken; claim; confess; comment; concede; contend; declare; disclose; divulge; expose; feel; hint; hold; imply; insinuate; intimate; maintain; make known; mention; note; point out; profess; remark; reveal; say; show; signal; signify; state; suggest; tell; uncover; unearth; unveil.* • He *indicated* that he would be fine. REPLACE WITH *said.* • People have provided us with documents that *indicate* that veterans were exposed. REPLACE WITH *reveal.* • They have *indicated* that they do not understand the managed competition proposals and don't want to. REPLACE WITH *confessed.* • Last week's decision of the Federal Reserve Board *indicated* that minority-lending records will be an issue for many years to come. REPLACE WITH *signaled.*

individual(s) (*n*) ∎ A torpid term. *anybody; anyone; everybody; everyone; man; men; people; person; somebody; someone; those; woman; women; you.* • This *individual* needs to be stopped. REPLACE WITH *woman.* • He seemed like a friendly enough *individual.* REPLACE WITH *person.*

in due course (time) ∎ A torpid term. *at length; eventually; in time; ultimately; yet.*

in each others' pocket ∎ A moribund metaphor. 1. *indissoluble; indivisible; inseparable; involved; together.* 2. *dependent; reliant.*

in every way, shape, form, or fashion ∎ An infantile phrase. *altogether; completely; entirely; fully; quite; roundly; thoroughly; in all ways; in every way; perfectly; totally; unreservedly; utterly; wholly.* • For centuries, since the first African ancestors were brought here, whites have tried to imitate blacks *in every way, shape, form, or fashion* and I'm tired of it. REPLACE WITH *in all ways.* • He supports her *in every way, shape, and form.* REPLACE WITH *thoroughly.* SEE ALSO **in any way, shape, form, or fashion; in no way, shape, form, or fashion**.

in excess of ∎ A wretched redundancy. *above; better than; beyond; faster than; greater than; larger than; more than; over; stronger than.* • *In excess of* 10 candidates wanted to make the town of Andover both their profession and their home. REPLACE WITH *More* *than.* • Police said Mr. Howard was driving *in excess of* 90 miles per hour. REPLACE WITH *faster than.*

in extremis ∎ A foreign phrase. *decaying; declining; deteriorating; disintegrating; dying; ebbing; expiring; fading; failing; near death; sinking; waning.*

inextricably tied ∎ An inescapable pair. • In good times and in bad, our future and our fortunes are *inextricably tied* together.

in fine fettle ∎ A moribund metaphor. *energetic; fine; fit; good; hale; hardy; healthful; healthy; hearty; robust; sound; strong; trim; vigorous; well.*

in for a rude awakening (shock) ∎ A torpid term. • The companies that still think the only ones who are going to make it are Caucasian males are *in for a rude awakening.*

In for a (pleasant) surprise ∎ A torpid term. • If she had set out to write a story about a spoiled brat, she was *in for a surprise.*

in full swing ∎ A moribund metaphor.

in harm's way ∎ A moribund metaphor. *exposed; insecure; obnoxious; unguarded; unprotected; unsafe; unsheltered; unshielded; vulnerable.*

in high dudgeon ∎ A moribund metaphor. *bitterly; grudgingly; resentfully.*

in high gear ∎ A moribund metaphor. *abruptly; apace; briskly; directly; expeditiously; fast; hastily; hurriedly; immediately; instantaneously; instantly; posthaste; promptly; quickly; rapidly; rashly; speedily; swiftly; wingedly.*

> Rosemary was in high gear. She was mounting a campaign to woo the chairman of the committee that would vote the bill out to the full Senate or decide to let it die ignominiously.—Marge Piercy, *The Third Child*

in hot water ∎ A moribund metaphor. *at risk; endangered; hard-pressed; imperiled; in danger; in difficulty; in jeopardy; in peril; in trouble; jeopardized.*

in its (their) entirety ∎ A wretched redundancy. *all; complete; completely; entire; entirely; every; full; fully; roundly; whole; wholly.* • This would leave Wednesday, either partially or *in its entirety,* for coordination. REPLACE WITH *entirely.*

inject (new) life into ∎ A moribund metaphor. *animate; energize; enliven; inspirit; invigorate; vitalize.*

in less than no time ∎ A moribund metaphor. *abruptly; apace; at once; briskly; directly; expeditiously; fast; forthwith; hastily; hurriedly; immediately; instantaneously; instantly; posthaste; promptly; quickly; rapidly; rashly; right*

away; speedily; straightaway; suddenly; swiftly; unexpectedly; wingedly.

(keep) (us) in line ∎ A moribund metaphor. *acquiescent; amenable; behaving; biddable; compliant; docile; dutiful; in conformity; law abiding; obedient; pliant; submissive; tame; tractable; yielding.*

in loco parentis ∎ A foreign phrase.

in (our) midst ∎ A wretched redundancy. *amid; among.* • There are growing numbers of crazy people *in our midst.* REPLACE WITH *among us.*

in nature ∎ A wretched redundancy. • He said the diaries are personal *in nature.* DELETE *in nature.* • Laws governing freedom to protest politically obviously are political *in nature.* DELETE *in nature.*

(as) innocent as a newborn babe (child) ∎ An insipid simile. *artless; guileless; ingenuous; innocent; naïve; simple.*

in nothing (no time) flat ∎ A torpid term. *abruptly; apace; at once; briskly; directly; expeditiously; fast; forthwith; hastily; hurriedly; immediately; instantaneously; instantly; posthaste; promptly; quickly; rapidly; rashly; right away; speedily; straightaway; suddenly; swiftly; unexpectedly; wingedly.*

in no way, shape, form, or fashion ∎ An infantile phrase. *at no time; by no means; in no way; never; no; not; not at all; not ever; not in any way; not in the least.* • The gas contributed *in no way, shape, or form* to the fire. REPLACE WITH *not at all.* • *In no way, shape, or form* did she resemble a 63-year-old woman. REPLACE WITH *In no way.* • *In no way, shape, form, or fashion* was there any wrongdoing or misappropriation of funds. REPLACE WITH *Never.* SEE ALSO **in any way, shape, form, or fashion; in every way, shape, and (or) form**.

in one ear and out the other ∎ A moribund metaphor. *forgetful; heedless; inattentive; lethean; neglectful; negligent; oblivious; remiss; thoughtless; unmindful; unthinking.*

> I hand them over, glad to be relieved of them. Maybe she'll understand them better than I. Anchee's explanations, I'm afraid, went in one ear and out the other.—Dennis Danvers, *The Watch*

(get) in on the ground floor ∎ A moribund metaphor.

in over (my) head ∎ A moribund metaphor. 1. *overburdened; overextended; overloaded; overwhelmed.* 2. *in arrears; in debt.*

(he's) in (his) own world ∎ A moribund metaphor. *self-absorbed; self-involved; solipsistic.*

in point of fact ∎ A wretched redundancy.

actually; *indeed*; *in fact*; *in faith*; *in reality*; *in truth*; *truly*. • *In point of fact,* we do all the wrong things, and we have for years. REPLACE WITH *In fact*. • *In point of fact*, Krakatoa is west of Java, but east apparently sounded better to Hollywood. REPLACE WITH *Actually*. • There aren't, *in point of fact*, one or two buildings; there are two exactly. DELETE *in point of fact*.

input ∎ A TOP-TWENTY DIMWITTICISM. A torpid term. *data*; *feelings*; *ideas*; *information*; *recommendations*; *suggestions*; *thoughts*; *views*. • We would appreciate *input* from anyone who has knowledge in the above areas. REPLACE WITH *information*. • Of course, discretion must be used in evaluating their *inputs* since sales reps are biased toward lowering prices and pushing volume. REPLACE WITH *suggestions*. SEE ALSO **(the) bottom line**; **feedback**; **interface**; **output**; **parameters**.

inquiring minds (want to know) ∎ An infantile phrase.

in (with) reference to ∎ A wretched redundancy. *about*; *as for*; *as to*; *concerning*; *for*; *in*; *of*; *on*; *over*; *regarding*; *respecting*; *to*; *toward*; *with*. • *With reference to* the latest attempt to forge statehood for the District of Columbia, I favor our ancestors' concept that the District ought to be an entity unto itself. REPLACE WITH *As for*.

in (with) regard to ∎ A wretched redundancy. *about*; *as for*; *as to*; *concerning*; *for*; *in*; *of*; *on*; *over*; *regarding*; *respecting*; *to*; *toward*; *with*. • *With regard to* the *StataQuest*, I am expecting the first six chapters sometime this week. REPLACE WITH *Regarding*.

in (high) relief ∎ A moribund metaphor. *clearly*; *conspicuously*; *distinctly*; *manifestly*; *markedly*; *noticeably*; *obviously*; *perceptibly*; *plainly*; *prominently*; *unmistakably*; *visibly*.

in (with) respect to ∎ A wretched redundancy. *about*; *as for*; *as to*; *concerning*; *for*; *in*; *of*; *on*; *over*; *regarding*; *respecting*; *to*; *toward*; *with*. • Some history *with respect to* the origins and evolution of the AS/400 will then be discussed. REPLACE WITH *on*.

in seventh heaven ∎ A moribund metaphor. *blissful*; *blithe*; *buoyant*; *cheerful*; *delighted*; *ecstatic*; *elated*; *enraptured*; *euphoric*; *exalted*; *excited*; *exhilarated*; *exultant*; *gay*; *glad*; *gleeful*; *good-humored*; *happy*; *intoxicated*; *jolly*; *jovial*; *joyful*; *joyous*; *jubilant*; *merry*; *mirthful*; *overjoyed*; *pleased*; *rapturous*; *thrilled*.

in short order ∎ A torpid term. *abruptly*; *apace*; *at once*; *briskly*; *directly*; *expeditiously*; *fast*; *forthwith*; *hastily*; *hurriedly*; *immediately*; *instantaneously*; *instantly*; *posthaste*; *promptly*; *quickly*; *rapidly*; *rashly*; *right away*; *speedily*; *straightaway*; *swiftly*; *wingedly*.

in short supply ∎ A torpid term. *exiguous*; *inadequate*; *meager*; *rare*; *scant*; *scanty*; *scarce*; *sparse*; *uncommon*; *unusual*.

inside (and) out ∎ A moribund metaphor. *altogether*; *completely*; *entirely*; *fully*; *perfectly*; *quite*; *roundly*; *thoroughly*; *totally*; *unreservedly*; *utterly*; *wholly*.

in spite of the fact that ∎ A wretched redundancy. *although*; *but*; *even if*; *even though*; *still*; *though*; *yet*. • This is true *in spite of the fact that* a separate symbol has been designated for input and output operations. REPLACE WITH *even though*. SEE ALSO **despite the fact that**; **regardless of the fact that**.

> Right away after the move I longed for it, in spite of the fact that I'd been in a conspicuous position, the kid of a proselytizing socialist schoolteacher and a city-slicker piano-playing mother.—Jane Hamilton, *Disobedience*

in (within) striking distance ∎ A moribund metaphor.

integral part ∎ An inescapable pair. This is another example of one word modifying another to little or no purpose.

integrate together ∎ A wretched redundancy. *integrate*. • The cost of the transmitters can be significantly reduced if all the lasers can be *integrated together* on a single substrate. DELETE *together*.

interesting ∎ An overworked word. *absorbing*; *alluring*; *amusing*; *arresting*; *bewitching*; *captivating*; *charming*; *curious*; *diverting*; *enchanting*; *engaging*; *engrossing*; *entertaining*; *enthralling*; *enticing*; *exciting*; *fascinating*; *gripping*; *intriguing*; *invigorating*; *inviting*; *pleasing*; *provocative*; *refreshing*; *riveting*; *spellbinding*; *stimulating*; *taking*; *tantalizing*. Not only An overworked word, *interesting* is also a worsened one, for it connotes uninteresting as often as it denotes interesting. SEE ALSO **that's interesting**.

interface ∎ A torpid term. SEE ALSO **(the) bottom line**; **feedback**; **input**; **output**; **parameters**.

in terms of ∎ A TOP-TWENTY DIMWITTICISM. A wretched redundancy. This phrase is most often a plodding replacement for words like *about*; *as for*; *as to*; *concerning*; *for*; *in*; *of*; *on*; *regarding*; *respecting*; *through*; *with*. And with some slight thought, the phrase frequently can be pared from a sentence. • *In terms of* what women need to know about men, I have learned a lot. REPLACE WITH *Regarding*. • A key element *in terms of* quality health care is going to be having the best *in terms of the* education and continuing educational abilities to train the best in this country. REPLACE WITH *of*; DELETE *in terms of the*. • For further information, you would want to read outside sources that analyze *your* competitors in terms of their products. REPLACE WITH *your competitors' products.*

intestinal fortitude ∎ An infantile phrase. *boldness; bravery; courage; daring; determination; endurance; fearlessness; firmness; fortitude; grit; guts; hardihood; hardiness; intrepidity; mettle; nerve; perseverance; resolution; resolve; spirit; spunk; stamina; steadfastness; tenacity.* • It takes a little luck and a lot of *intestinal fortitude* to break into a game. REPLACE WITH *daring.* • Voters will need *intestinal fortitude* to make it to election day. REPLACE WITH *fortitude.*

in the affirmative ∎ A wretched redundancy. *affirmatively; favorably; positively; yes.* • The answer is *in the affirmative.* REPLACE WITH *yes.*

in the altogether ∎ A moribund metaphor. *bare; disrobed; naked; nude; stripped; unclothed; uncovered; undressed.*

in the arms of Morpheus ∎ A moribund metaphor. *asleep; dozing; dreaming; napping; sleeping; slumbering; unconscious.*

in the back of (my) mind ∎ A moribund metaphor. *subconsciously; subliminally.* • I always knew, *in the back of my mind*, that something was bothering him. REPLACE WITH *subconsciously.*

(it's) in the bag ∎ A moribund metaphor. *assured; certain; definite; guaranteed; incontestable; incontrovertible; indisputable; indubitable; positive; secure; sure; unquestionable.*

in the ballpark of ∎ A moribund metaphor. *about; around; close to; more or less; near; nearly; or so; roughly; some.* • Estimates put the cost of each TAO work time gained or lost *in the ballpark of* $3 million per year. REPLACE WITH *around.* SEE ALSO **in the neighborhood of; in the vicinity of.**

in the black ∎ A moribund metaphor. *debt-free; debtless.*

in the blink of an eye ∎ A moribund metaphor. *abruptly; apace; at once; briskly; directly; expeditiously; fast; forthwith; hastily; hurriedly; immediately; instantaneously; instantly; posthaste; promptly; quickly; rapidly; rashly; right away; speedily; straightaway; suddenly; swiftly; unexpectedly; wingedly.* • Self-indulgent, run-on sentences will *earn you a rejection slip in the blink of an eye.* REPLACE WITH *quickly earn you a rejection slip.*

> He said things he didn't believe, about how we will all be transformed in the blink of an eye, about how we will all be reunited in heaven, where there is neither suffering nor death, anymore.—Haven Kimmel, *The Solace of Early Evening*

in the buff ∎ A moribund metaphor. *bare; disrobed; naked; nude; stripped; unclothed; uncovered; undressed.*

in (on) the cards ∎ A moribund metaphor. *certain; destined; expected; fated; foreordained; foreseeable; imminent; impending; liable; likely; possible; probable; ordained; prearranged; predestined; predetermined; predictable; sure.* • I think that kind of complexity is not *in the cards.* REPLACE WITH *likely.*

in the chips ∎ A moribund metaphor. *affluent; moneyed; opulent; prosperous; rich; wealthy; well-off; well-to-do.*

in the clear ∎ A moribund metaphor. 1. *absolved; acquitted; blameless; clear; excused; exonerated; faultless; guiltless; inculpable; innocent; irreproachable; unblamable; unblameworthy; vindicated.* 2. *guarded; protected; safe; secure; sheltered; shielded.* 3. *debt-free; debtless.*

in the closet ∎ A moribund metaphor. *clandestine; concealed; confidential; covert; hidden; private; secret; secluded; shrouded; surreptitious; undercover; unspoken; veiled.*

in the cold light of reason ∎ A moribund metaphor.

(keep) in the dark ∎ A moribund metaphor. *ignorant; incognizant; insensible; mystified; nescient; unacquainted; unadvised; unapprised; unaware; unenlightened; unfamiliar; uninformed; uninitiated; uninstructed; unintelligent; unknowing; unschooled; untaught; unversed.* • They told me everything; I was never *kept in the dark.* REPLACE WITH *uninformed.*

in the dead of night ∎ A moribund metaphor.

> Some of it she told him anyway, that it was extremely urgent she communicate with a friend in Tijuana, that quite possibly it was a matter of life and death, which is why she had taken it upon herself to wake him in the dead of night and for that, together with the breaking of his window, she had apologized profusely.—Kem Nunn, *Tijuana Straits*

in the depths of depression (despair) ∎ A moribund metaphor. *aggrieved; anhedonic; blue; cheerless; dejected; demoralized; depressed; despondent; disconsolate; discouraged; disheartened; dismal; dispirited; doleful; downcast; downhearted; dreary; forlorn; funereal; gloomy; glum; grieved; low; melancholy; miserable; morose; mournful; negative; pessimistic; plaintive; sad; sorrowful; unhappy; woebegone; woeful.*

in the distant future ∎ A wretched redundancy. *at length; eventually; finally; in the end; in time; later; one day; over the (months); over time; someday; sometime; ultimately; with time.* • A similar agreement with Mexico could result in a true North American common market *in the distant future.* REPLACE WITH *one* *day*. SEE ALSO **in the immediate future**; **in the near future**; **in the not-too-distant future**.

in the doghouse ∎ A moribund metaphor. *in disfavor*; *in disgrace*.

in the doldrums ∎ A moribund metaphor. 1. *dead*; *dormant*; *dull*; *immobile*; *immovable*; *inactive*; *inanimate*; *indolent*; *inert*; *inoperative*; *languid*; *latent*; *lethargic*; *lifeless*; *listless*; *motionless*; *phlegmatic*; *quiescent*; *quiet*; *sluggish*; *stagnant*; *static*; *stationary*; *still*; *stock-still*; *torpid*; *unresponsive*. 2. *aggrieved*; *anhedonic*; *blue*; *cheerless*; *dejected*; *demoralized*; *depressed*; *despondent*; *disconsolate*; *discouraged*; *disheartened*; *dismal*; *dispirited*; *doleful*; *downcast*; *downhearted*; *dreary*; *forlorn*; *funereal*; *gloomy*; *glum*; *grieved*; *low*; *melancholy*; *miserable*; *morose*; *mournful*; *negative*; *pessimistic*; *plaintive*; *sad*; *sorrowful*; *unhappy*; *woebegone*; *woeful*.

in the driver's seat ∎ A moribund metaphor. *administer*; *boss*; *command*; *control*; *dictate*; *direct*; *dominate*; *govern*; *in charge*; *in command*; *in control*; *manage*; *manipulate*; *master*; *order*; *overpower*; *oversee*; *predominate*; *prevail*; *reign over*; *rule*; *superintend*. • Buyers are most definitely *in the driver's seat*. REPLACE WITH *in charge*. • Unlike traditional pension plans, which your employer controls, 401(k) plans put you *in the driver's seat*. REPLACE WITH *in control*.

(down) in the dumps ∎ A moribund metaphor. *aggrieved*; *anhedonic*; *blue*; *cheerless*; *dejected*; *demoralized*; *depressed*; *despondent*; *disconsolate*; *discouraged*; *disheartened*; *dismal*; *dispirited*; *doleful*; *downcast*; *downhearted*; *dreary*; *forlorn*; *funereal*; *gloomy*; *glum*; *grieved*; *low*; *melancholy*; *miserable*; *morose*; *mournful*; *negative*; *pessimistic*; *plaintive*; *sad*; *sorrowful*; *unhappy*; *woebegone*; *woeful*.

in the event (that) ∎ A wretched redundancy. *if*; *should*. • *In the event* you think I am overreacting, let me call attention to the realities of the contemporary workplace. REPLACE WITH *If* or *Should*.

in the final (last) analysis ∎ A wretched redundancy. *in the end*; *ultimately*.

in the first place ∎ A wretched redundancy. *first*. • *In the first place*, I don't want to, and *in the second place*, I can't afford to. REPLACE WITH *First*; *second*. SEE ALSO **in the second place**.

in the flesh ∎ A moribund metaphor. 1. *alive*. 2. *in person*; *present*.

in the fullness of time ∎ A moribund metaphor. *at length*; *eventually*; *in time*; *ultimately*; *yet*.

> Here in the fullness of time would lie Kaiser himself.—Evelyn Waugh, *The Loved One*

in the heat of battle ∎ A moribund metaphor.

in the heat of the moment ∎ A moribund metaphor.

in the immediate future ∎ A wretched redundancy. *at once*; *at present*; *before long*; *currently*; *directly*; *immediately*; *in a (week)*; *next (month)*; *now*; *presently*; *quickly*; *shortly*; *soon*; *straightaway*; *this (month)*. • I will, *in the immediate future*, contact my fellow mayor in New York and ask him to make a decision. REPLACE WITH *this week*. SEE ALSO **in the distant future**; **in the near future**; **in the not-too-distant future**.

in (on) the issue (matter; subject) of ∎ A wretched redundancy. *about*; *as for*; *as to*; *concerning*; *for*; *in*; *of*; *on*; *over*; *regarding*; *respecting*; *to*; *toward*; *with*. • This state used to be a leader *on the issue of* health reform. REPLACE WITH *in*. • *On the matter of* quality in teaching, he proposed a more symbiotic relationship between classroom time and research. REPLACE WITH *As for*.

in the know ∎ A moribund metaphor. 1. *able*; *adept*; *apt*; *capable*; *competent*; *conversant*; *deft*; *dexterous*; *experienced*; *expert*; *familiar*; *practiced*; *proficient*; *seasoned*; *skilled*; *skillful*; *veteran*. 2. *adroit*; *astute*; *bright*; *brilliant*; *clever*; *discerning*; *effective*; *effectual*; *efficient*; *enlightened*; *insightful*; *intelligent*; *judicious*; *keen*; *knowledgeable*; *learned*; *logical*; *luminous*; *perceptive*; *perspicacious*; *quick*; *rational*; *reasonable*; *sagacious*; *sage*; *sapient*; *sensible*; *sharp*; *shrewd*; *smart*; *sound*; *understanding*; *wise*.

(live) in the lap of luxury ∎ A moribund metaphor. *affluent*; *moneyed*; *opulent*; *prosperous*; *rich*; *wealthy*; *well-off*; *well-to-do*.

in (over) the long run (term) ∎ A wretched redundancy. *at length*; *eventually*; *finally*; *in the end*; *in time*; *later*; *long-term*; *one day*; *over the (months)*; *over time*; *someday*; *sometime*; *ultimately*; *with time*. • *In the long run*, that may be the most important thing. REPLACE WITH *Over time*. SEE ALSO **in (over) the short run (term)**.

in the market for ∎ A moribund metaphor. *able to afford*; *desire*; *looking for*; *need*; *ready to buy*; *require*; *seeking*; *want*; *wish for*.

in the midst of ∎ A wretched redundancy. *amid*; *among*; *between*; *encircled by*; *encompassed by*; *in*; *inside*; *in the middle of*; *surrounded by*. • The United States, *in the midst of* increasing tension over Korea, is softening its tone on China. REPLACE WITH *amid*. • My profound conviction is that anytime we are together, Christ is *in the midst of* us. REPLACE WITH *among*.

in the money ∎ A moribund metaphor. *affluent*; *moneyed*; *opulent*; *prosperous*; *rich*; *wealthy*; *well-off*; *well-to-do*.

in the near future ∎ A wretched redundancy.

before long; directly; eventually; in time; later; one day; presently; quickly; shortly; sometime; soon. • I'm looking forward to the possibility that you might review my work *in the near future.* REPLACE WITH *soon.* SEE ALSO **in the distant future; in the immediate future; in the not-too-distant future**.

in the neighborhood of ❚ A wretched redundancy. *about; around; close to; more or less; near; nearly; or so; roughly; some.* • The rebels may have killed *in the neighborhood of* ten people. REPLACE WITH *close to.* SEE ALSO **in the ballpark of; in the vicinity of**.

in the not-too-distant future ❚ A wretched redundancy. *before long; directly; eventually; in time; later; one day; presently; quickly; shortly; sometime; soon.* • *In the not-too-distant future,* Americans will have the telephone equivalent of a superhighway to every home and business. REPLACE WITH *Before long.* SEE ALSO **in the distant future; in the immediate future; in the near future**.

in the not-too-distant past ❚ A wretched redundancy. *before; earlier; formerly; not long ago; once; recently.* • *In the not-too-distant past,* women were expected to be home, be nice, be sexy, and be quiet. REPLACE WITH *Not long ago.* SEE ALSO **in the past; in the recent past**.

in the offing ❚ A moribund metaphor. *approaching; at hand; close; coming; expected; forthcoming; imminent; impending; looming; near; nearby.*

in the past ❚ A wretched redundancy. • I'm just saying what we did do *in the past.* DELETE *in the past.* • We can remember *in the past* when we sometimes had two or three representatives. DELETE *in the past.* SEE ALSO **in the not-too-distant past; in the recent past**.

in the picture ❚ A moribund metaphor. SEE ALSO **not in the picture**.

in the pink ❚ A moribund metaphor. *energetic; fine; fit; good; hale; hardy; healthful; healthy; hearty; robust; sound; strong; vigorous; well.*

in the pipeline ❚ A moribund metaphor.

in the process of -ing ❚ A wretched redundancy. *as; while;* DELETE. Even though *in the process of* seems to add significance to what is being said—and to who is saying it—it plainly subtracts from both. • The hurricane is *in the process of* making a slow turn to the northeast. DELETE *in the process of.* • I'm *in the process of* going on a lot of interviews. DELETE *in the process of.* • The office is still *in the process of* collecting facts. DELETE *in the process of.*

> In the process of taking his jacket off, the Artiste thrust his thick chest forward.—Tom Wolfe, *A Man in Full*

in (within) the realm of possibility ❚ A wretched redundancy. *believable; conceivable; conjecturable; doable; feasible; imaginable; likely; plausible; possible; practicable; supposable; thinkable; workable.* • Appointment of a "civilian" generalist public administrator possessing some public safety background is also *within the realm of possibility.* REPLACE WITH *possible.* • I'm afraid it is *within the realm of possibility* that that many warheads may be missing. REPLACE WITH *conceivable.*

in the recent past ❚ A wretched redundancy. *before; earlier; formerly; lately; not long ago; of late; once; recent; recently.* • *In the recent past,* such performers were on the fringes of American culture. REPLACE WITH *Recently.* SEE ALSO **in the not-too-distant past; in the past**.

in the red ❚ A moribund metaphor. *in arrears; in debt.*

in the right direction ❚ A torpid term. • Furthermore, when onerous regulations are brought to the attention of senior officials, the government has taken steps *in the right direction.* REPLACE WITH *to make them less unwieldy.*

in the right place at the right time ❚ An infantile phrase. SEE ALSO **in the wrong place at the wrong time**.

in the saddle ❚ A moribund metaphor. *administer; boss; command; control; dictate; direct; dominate; govern; in charge; in command; in control; manage; manipulate; master; order; overpower; oversee; predominate; prevail; reign over; rule; superintend.*

in the same boat ❚ A moribund metaphor.

> They might all be in the same boat—sharing a comparatively small plot of land—but that didn't mean it was necessary to socialize.—Katie Fforde, *Wild Designs*

in the second place ❚ A wretched redundancy. *second.* • *In the second place,* I sincerely believe that the merger has given it another chance to become the quality institution these students deserve. REPLACE WITH *Second.* SEE ALSO **in the first place**.

in (over) the short run (term) ❚ A wretched redundancy. *at present; before long; currently; directly; eventually; in time; later; next (month); now; one day; presently; quickly; shortly; short-term; sometime; soon; this (month).* • I hope we're able to do something about this *in the short term.* REPLACE WITH *soon.* SEE ALSO **in (over) the long run (term)**.

in the soup ❚ A moribund metaphor. *at risk; endangered; hard-pressed; imperiled; in a bind; in a dilemma; in a fix; in a jam; in a predicament; in a quandary; in danger; in difficulty; in jeopardy; in peril; in trouble;*

jeopardized.

in the spotlight ▮ A moribund metaphor.
celebrated; eminent; famous; illustrious; prominent; renowned.

in the swim ▮ A moribund metaphor.
absorbed; active; busy; employed; engaged; engrossed; immersed; involved; occupied; preoccupied; wrapped up in.

in the swing of things ▮ A moribund
metaphor. *in step; in sync; in tune.*

in the thick of (it) ▮ A moribund metaphor.
1. *amid; among; encircled; encompassed; in the middle; surrounded.* 2. *absorbed; active; busy; employed; engaged; engrossed; immersed; involved; occupied; preoccupied; wrapped up in.*

in the trenches ▮ A moribund metaphor.

in the twinkling (wink) of an eye ▮
A moribund metaphor. *abruptly; apace; at once; briskly; directly; expeditiously; fast; forthwith; hastily; hurriedly; immediately; instantaneously; instantly; posthaste; promptly; quickly; rapidly; rashly; right away; speedily; straightaway; suddenly; swiftly; unexpectedly; wingedly.*

> It actually struck the Minister-President
> on the shoulder as he stooped over his
> dying servant, then falling between his feet
> exploded with a terrific concentrated violence,
> striking him dead to the ground, finishing the
> wounded man and practically annihilating the
> empty sledge in the twinkling of an eye.—
> Joseph Conrad, *Under Western Eyes*

in the vicinity of ▮ A wretched redundancy.
about; around; close to; more or less; near; nearly; or so; roughly; some. • The final
phase prohibits smoking anywhere *in the vicinity of* the main building's entrance.
REPLACE WITH *near.* • The public puts
its approval of Clinton's conduct *in the vicinity of* 70 percent. REPLACE WITH
around. SEE ALSO **in the ballpark of; in the neighborhood of.**

in the wake of ▮ A moribund metaphor. *after; behind; ensuing; following; succeeding.* SEE
ALSO **(hot) on the heels of; reach epidemic proportions.**

in the wastebasket ▮ A moribund metaphor.
abandoned; discarded; dismissed; jettisoned; rejected; repudiated; thrown out; tossed out.

in the way of ▮ A TOP-TWENTY
DIMWITTICISM. A wretched redundancy.
• They don't think they'll meet much *in the way of* resistance. DELETE *in the way of.* • The result is a staggering investment
in foreign-oriented training with little *in the way of* return on investment. DELETE
in the way of. • They didn't have much
in the way of money. DELETE *in the way of.* • The result is that this disorganized
interview usually provides little *in the way of* valuable information. DELETE *in the*

way of.

in the worst (possible) way ▮ A
torpid term. *acutely; a great deal; badly; consumedly; exceedingly; extremely; greatly; hugely; immensely; intensely; mightily; prodigiously; seriously; very much.* • The
Eagles want to win *in the worst way.*
REPLACE WITH *very much.* SEE ALSO **in a big way.**

**in the wrong place at the wrong
time ▮** An infantile phrase. An ascription
of meaningfulness for those who
unhappily speak it, it is an accidence to
meaninglessness for those who sadly hear
it. Along with *in the right place at the right time* (SEE), this phrase is evidence of what
reason has been reduced to. • That little
girl was just *in the wrong place at the wrong time.*

in this day and age ▮ A moribund metaphor.
at present; currently; now; presently; these days; today. • *In this day and age,* we need
to train medical students to see beyond the
front door of the hospital and to see the
broader issues. REPLACE WITH *Today.*

in (their) time of need ▮ A torpid term. •
The ultimate beneficiaries are those who
turn to the Clinic *in their time of need.*

in two shakes (of a lamb's tail) ▮
A moribund metaphor. *abruptly; apace; at once; briskly; directly; expeditiously; fast; forthwith; hastily; hurriedly; immediately; instantaneously; instantly; posthaste; promptly; quickly; rapidly; rashly; right away; speedily; straightaway; suddenly; swiftly; unexpectedly; wingedly.*

in view of the fact that ▮ A wretched
redundancy. *because; considering; for; in that; since.* • *In view of the fact that* you couldn't
pay your bills, you became a prostitute?
REPLACE WITH *Because.* SEE ALSO
**because of the fact that; considering the
fact that; by virtue of the fact that; given
the fact that; in consideration of the fact
that; on account of the fact that.**

(a lot of) irons in the fire ▮ A moribund
metaphor. 1. *assignments; chores; duties; involvements; jobs; projects; responsibilities; tasks.* 2. *possibilities; potentialities; prospects.*

I second that emotion ▮ An infantile
phrase.

I shall return ▮ An infantile phrase.

(money) isn't everything ▮ A popular
prescription. • Price is important, but *price isn't everything.*

**it doesn't take (you don't have to be)
a rocket scientist (an Einstein; a PhD)
to ▮ (know)** An infantile phrase. We can be
reasonably certain that the people who use
this expression are not rocket scientists, not
Einsteins, not PhDs. We can be less certain
that the people who use this phrase are

not dull-witted, not obtuse, not brainless. • *It doesn't take a rocket scientist to* see that a brutal police attack on a peaceful march is unacceptable and outrageous. • *It doesn't take a rocket scientist to* understand that high standards and a quality education should rank over diversity. • *It doesn't take an Einstein to* know that when kids see Mark McGwire they're going to head to the mall and buy the supplements. • *It doesn't take a rocket scientist to* figure out what's going on here. • *It doesn't take a PhD to* realize that the problem with the lagoon is what it contains—trash and polluted water. SEE ALSO **alive and kicking**.

it felt (seemed) like a lifetime ▮ An insipid simile. SEE ALSO **it felt (seemed) like an eternity**.

it felt (seemed) like an eternity ▮ An insipid simile. • Although it took 10 hours to convince the man to come down, *it felt like an eternity*. SEE ALSO **it felt (seemed) like a lifetime**.

it has been brought to (my) attention ▮ An ineffectual phrase. • *It has been brought to my attention* that we have no record of your order. REPLACE WITH *I have been told*. SEE ALSO **it has come to (my) attention**.

it has come to (my) attention ▮ An ineffectual phrase. • *It has come to our attention* that the number 3 is very popular. REPLACE WITH *We have learned*. • *It has come to my attention that* your deposit was received too late to be disbursed to your creditors this month. DELETE *It has come to my attention that*. SEE ALSO **it has been brought to (my) attention**.

it is important to note (that) ▮ An ineffectual phrase. Attachments like *it is important to note (that)* and *it is interesting to note (that)* suggest that whatever follows them is probably not so important or interesting. Only people who mistrust the import or interest of their own statements use phrases like these—clear signals that their meaning is likely without merit, their message likely without allure. • *It is important to note that* you can change these settings for any document. DELETE *It is important to note that*. SEE ALSO **it is interesting to note (that)**; **it is significant to note (that)**.

it is important to realize (that) ▮ An ineffectual phrase. • *It is important to realize that* analogical reasoning is used to explain and clarify, whereas causal reasoning is used to prove. DELETE *It is important to realize that*.

it is important to remember (that) ▮ An ineffectual phrase. • *It is important to remember that* all three phases are important to your success. DELETE *It is important to remember that*.

it is important to understand (that) ▮ An ineffectual phrase. • *It is important to understand that* turning the grid lines on and off changes only the display on the monitor and not the printout. DELETE *It is important to understand that*. SEE ALSO **you have to understand (that)**.

it is interesting to note (that) ▮ An ineffectual phrase. • *It is interesting to note that* although the sex hormone makes men more subject to baldness than women, it is more acceptable for women to wear wigs. DELETE *It is interesting to note that*. • *It is interesting to note that* in America bylines were largely an outcome of false reporting in another war, the Civil War. DELETE *It is interesting to note that*. SEE ALSO **it is important to note (that)**; **it is significant to note (that)**.

(so) ... it isn't (even) funny ▮ An infantile phrase. • We've got so much overcapacity in the securities business *it isn't funny*. • I'm so sick of her *it isn't funny*.

it isn't over till it's over ▮ A popular prescription.

it is significant to note (that) ▮ An ineffectual phrase. • *It is significant to note that* the original database has not been altered. DELETE *It is significant to note that*. SEE ALSO **it is important to note (that)**; **it is interesting to note (that)**.

it is what it is ▮ A quack equation. Must we mouth all that is obvious? If we could but halve our silly sententiousness, we might double the time we spend thinking, feeling, and wondering.

it is worth noting (that) ▮ An ineffectual phrase. • *It is worth noting that* he regarded her as "one of the finest writers of fiction." DELETE *It is worth noting that*.

it just happened ▮ An infantile phrase. As an explanation for how circumstances or incidents unfold, none is more puerile. And though we might excuse children such a sentiment, it is rarely they who express it.

It just happened is a phrase used by those too slothful or too fearful to know what has happened. • It wasn't something I planned; *it just happened*. • What can I say? *it just happened*. SEE ALSO **because (that's why)**; **whatever happens happens**.

it makes you (stop and) think ▮ A plebeian sentiment.

it must (should) be mentioned (that) ▮ An ineffectual phrase. • *It should be mentioned that* hiperspace is used by authorized programs only. DELETE *It should be mentioned that*.

it must (should) be noted (that) ▮ An ineffectual phrase. • *It should be noted that* not all parents require an extensive interview. DELETE *It should be noted that*. • In terms of who conducts investigations,

it must (should) be pointed out (that)

it should be noted that patrol personnel also may be used as investigators. DELETE *it should be noted that.*

it must (should) be pointed out (that)
▮ An ineffectual phrase. • *It should be pointed out that* when you send this type of letter you must follow through with the filing in the court, or it can be looked on as a threat. DELETE *It should be pointed out that.*

it must (should) be realized (that) ▮ An
ineffectual phrase. • *It should be realized that* uncoupling is complete when the partners have defined themselves and are defined by others as separate and independent of each other. DELETE *It should be realized that.*

it must (should) be understood
(that) ▮ An ineffectual phrase. • *It should be understood that* a quitting concern assumption would be clearly disclosed on the financial statement. DELETE *It should be understood that.*

it never ends ▮ A plebeian sentiment.

it never rains, but it pours ▮ A moribund metaphor.

I told you (so) ▮ An infantile phrase.

it's a bird, it's a plane, (it's Superman)
▮ An infantile phrase.

it's a dirty job, but someone's got to do it ▮ A popular prescription.

it's a dream come true ▮ A moribund metaphor. • To be mentioned in the same sentence as Bette Davis—*it's a dream come true.*

it's a free country ▮ An infantile phrase. This expression is one that only fettered thinkers could possibly use. One of the difficulties with dimwitticisms is that, because they are so familiar, people will most often use them thoughtlessly. Manacled as people are to these well-worn phrases, original thoughts and fresh words are often unreachable. • If owners of eating establishments want to allow smoking, let them do so—*it's a free country.* • *It's a free country.* It's what makes America great. • *It's a free country,* and no one tells me what to say!

it's a jungle (out there) ▮ A moribund metaphor.

it's all good ▮ An infantile phrase. Have we not had enough of this idiotic optimism? It's *not* all good. Global warming, Al-qaeda, the Middle East, North Korea, China, cancer, heart disease, AIDS, obesity everywhere, lack of health care, genocide, malnutrition, man's inhumanity to man, corporate greed, celebrities. It is not all good.

It may be that optimists live longer than pessimists, but it's far better to die sooner knowing the truth than it is to live longer denying it.

it's all Greek to me ▮ An infantile phrase. *abstract; abstruse; ambiguous; arcane; blurred; blurry; cloudy; confusing; cryptic; deep; dim; esoteric; impenetrable; inaccessible; incoherent; incomprehensible; indecipherable; indistinct; muddy; murky; nebulous; obscure; puzzling; recondite; unclear; unfathomable; unintelligible; vague.*

it's a long story ▮ A torpid term. *It's a long story*—cipher for *I don't want to tell you*—is a mannerly expression that we use to thwart the interest of a person in whom we are not much interested. SEE ALSO **that's for me to know and you to find out**.

it's always darkest just before dawn ▮ A popular prescription.

it's always something ▮ A plebeian sentiment.

it's an art ▮ A suspect superlative. • Parallel parking is not easy; *it's an art.* • Creating a seamless event involves skill and experience; *it's an art.* • Congress is involved with changing the bankruptcy system; *it's an art* with no exact formula. • Admissions is not a precise science, *it's an art.*

it's a nice place to visit but I wouldn't want to live there ▮ A popular prescription.

it's a two-way street ▮ A moribund metaphor.

it's a whole different ballgame ▮ A moribund metaphor.

it's better than nothing ▮ A popular prescription.

it's better to have loved and lost than never to have loved at all ▮ A popular prescription.

it's like a death in the family ▮ An insipid simile.

it's like losing a member of the family ▮ An insipid simile.

it's more fun than a barrel of monkeys ▮ A moribund metaphor. *amusing; comical; entertaining; funny; hilarious; humorous; hysterical; riotous; risible; side-splitting.*

it's not over till (until) it's over ▮ A quack equation. People say *it's not over till (until) it's over* in earnest, as if it were a weighty remark, a solemn truth when, of course, it's nothing but dimwitted. We might have an occasional insight, even a revelation, if we didn't persistently speak, and think in terms of, this kind of rubbish. • But *it isn't over till it's over*, and right now we have a statement from Dubai Ports World and little else.

it's not over till (until) the fat lady sings ▮ An infantile phrase.

it's (been) one of those days ❚ A plebeian sentiment.

it's one thing after another ❚ A plebeian sentiment. SEE ALSO **if it isn't one thing, it's another**.

it's the same old story ❚ A torpid term.

it's what's inside that counts ❚ A popular prescription.

it takes all kinds ❚ A popular prescription.

it takes one to know one ❚ An infantile phrase.

it takes two ❚ A popular prescription.

it takes two to tango ❚ A popular prescription.

it was a dark and stormy night ❚ An infantile phrase.

it will all come out in the wash ❚ A moribund metaphor.

it works both ways ❚ A popular prescription.

Jj

(made) (her) jaw drop ▌ A moribund metaphor. *amaze; astonish; astound; awe; confound; dumbfound; flabbergast; jar; jolt; overwhelm; shock; start; startle; stun; stupefy; surprise.* • There are a couple levels that are truly inspired, though there's nothing that will *make your jaw drop.* REPLACE WITH *astound you.* • But Jabra, a company that usually doesn't let us down with its Bluetooth headsets, has rolled out a model that *made our jaw drop.* REPLACE WITH *stunned us.*

> She found herself living again a moment at her mother's funeral, which at the time had made her jaw drop with amazement.—Rebecca West, *Sunflower*

(has) (his) jaw set ▌ A moribund metaphor. *be determined; be firm; be fixed; be inexorable; be inflexible; be obdurate; be resolute; be resolved; be rigid; be tenacious; be unflinching; be unwavering; be unyielding.* • Both Frist and Delay seem to *have their jaws set* on this one. REPLACE WITH *be firm.*

(Dr.) Jekyll-(Mr.) Hyde (personality) ▌ A moribund metaphor. *capricious; changeable; erratic; fickle; fitful; flighty; fluctuating; haphazard; inconsistent; inconstant; intermittent; irregular; mercurial; occasional; random; sometime; spasmodic; sporadic; unpredictable; unsettled; unstable; unsteady; vacillating; volatile; wavering; wayward.*

je ne sais quoi ▌ A foreign phrase.

John Hancock ▌ A moribund metaphor. *signature.*

Johnny-come-lately ▌ A moribund metaphor. *climber; latecomer; newcomer; parvenu; upstart.*

joie de vivre ▌ A foreign phrase.

join at the hip ▌ A moribund metaphor. *indissoluble; indivisible; inseparable; together.*

join forces ▌ A moribund metaphor. *ally; collaborate; comply; concur; conspire; cooperate; join; unite; work together.*

join together ▌ A wretched redundancy. *join.* • ASA *joins* a powerful job scheduler *together* with select elements of automated operations to create a unique software system. DELETE *together.*

judge not, lest you be judged ▌ A popular prescription.

juggling act ▌ A moribund metaphor.

jump all over ▌ A moribund metaphor. *admonish; anathematize; berate; blame; castigate; censure; chastise; chide; condemn; criticize; curse; decry; denounce; execrate; imprecate; inculpate; indict; rebuke; reprimand; reproach; reprove; scold; upbraid.*

jump down (her) throat ▌ A moribund metaphor. *admonish; animadvert; berate; castigate; censure; chasten; chastise; chide; condemn; criticize; denounce; denunciate; discipline; excoriate; fulminate against; imprecate; impugn; inveigh against; objurgate; punish; rebuke; remonstrate; reprehend; reprimand; reproach; reprobate; reprove; revile; scold; swear at; upbraid; vituperate.*

jump for joy ▌ A moribund metaphor. *be blissful; be blithe; be buoyant; be cheerful; be delighted; be ecstatic; be elated; be enraptured; be euphoric; be exalted; be excited; be exhilarated; be exultant; be gay; be glad; be gleeful; be good-humored; be happy; be intoxicated; be jolly; be jovial; be joyful; be joyous; be jubilant; be merry; be mirthful; be overjoyed; be pleased; be rapturous; be thrilled.*

jump from the frying pan into the fire ▌ A moribund metaphor.

jump in with both feet ▌ A moribund metaphor.

> I wanted to jump in with both feet, but something stopped me.—Jessica Speart, *Coastal Disturbance*

jumping-off point ▌ A moribund metaphor.

jump on the bandwagon ▌ A moribund metaphor. *be included; be involved; enlist; enroll; join; sign up; take part.* • Once everyone in an industry has learned about something that works, there's a tendency to *jump on the bandwagon.*

jump out at you ▌ A moribund metaphor. *appears; becomes apparent; becomes known; becomes visible; emerges; materializes; shows; surfaces.*

jump out of (her) skin ▌ A moribund metaphor. *be amazed; be astonished; be astounded; be awed; be flabbergasted; be jarred; be jolted; be overwhelmed; be shocked; be started; be startled; be stunned; be stupefied; be surprised.*

jump ship ∎ A moribund metaphor. *abandon; desert; forsake; leave; quit.*

jump the gun ∎ A moribund metaphor.

jump through hoops ∎ A moribund metaphor.

(the) jury is still out ∎ A moribund metaphor. *be arguable; be debatable; be disputable; be doubtful; be dubious; be in doubt; be moot; be open; be questionable; be uncertain; be unclear; be undecided; be undetermined; be unknown; be unresolved; be unsettled; be unsolved; be unsure.*
  Still another way to express not knowing or being undecided, *the jury is still out,* used figuratively, is as foolish a phrase as it is a meaning. Any sentence in which this dimwitticism is used is sentenced to being forgettable.

> If the jury is still out on women police, then the jury is still out on Tobe. Still out, after all these months, and still hollering for transcripts of the judge's opening address.—Martin Amis, *Night Train*

just exactly ∎ A wretched redundancy. *exactly; just.* • *Just exactly* what do you mean? REPLACE WITH *Just* or *Exactly.*

just recently ∎ A wretched redundancy. *just; recently.* • I *just recently* completed my bachelor's degree. REPLACE WITH *just* or *recently.*

just what the doctor ordered ∎ A moribund metaphor. *be exactly right; be great; be ideal; be just right; be perfect; be wonderful.*

just when you thought it was safe to ∎ An infantile phrase.

121

K k

keep a (the) lid on ∎ A moribund metaphor. *bridle; check; constrain; contain; control; curb; curtail; govern; harness; hold back; inhibit; limit; muzzle; rein in; repress; restrain; restrict; stem; stifle; suppress.* • Its leaders have said they cannot *keep a lid on* popular anger if the government does not begin to respond to citizens' demands. REPLACE WITH *restrain.*

> Buster had declined, of course, but there was talk that he got some of his employees to join and keep the lid on things.—Loraine Despres, *The Scandalous Summer of Sissy LeBlanc*

keep a low profile ∎ A moribund metaphor.

keep an ear to the ground ∎ A moribund metaphor. *be alert; be attentive; be awake; be aware; be eagle-eyed; be heedful; be informed; be keen; be observant; be vigilant; be wakeful; be watchful.*

keep an eye out for ∎ A moribund metaphor. *be alert; be attentive; be awake; be aware; be eagle-eyed; be heedful; be informed; be keen; be observant; be vigilant; be wakeful; be watchful; hunt; look for; search.*

keep a stiff upper lip ∎ A moribund metaphor. *be brave; be courageous; be determined; be resolute.*

keep (them) at arm's length ∎ A moribund metaphor. • In some cases, you need to *keep hurtful people at arm's length* so they can't continue hurting you.

keep a tight rein on ∎ A moribund metaphor. *bridle; check; constrain; contain; control; curb; curtail; govern; harness; hold back; inhibit; limit; muzzle; regulate; rein in; repress; restrain; restrict; stem; stifle; suppress.*

keep a watchful eye on ∎ A moribund metaphor. *be alert; be attentive; be awake; be aware; be eagle-eyed; be heedful; be informed; be keen; be observant; be vigilant; be wakeful; be watchful.*

keep body and soul together ∎ A moribund metaphor. *endure; exist; keep alive; live; manage; subsist; survive.*

keep (your) chin up ∎ A moribund metaphor. *be brave; be courageous; be determined; be resolute.*

keep (his) cool ∎ A moribund metaphor. *be calm; be composed; be patient; be self-possessed; be tranquil.*

keep (our) distance ∎ A moribund metaphor. *be aloof; be chilly; be cool; be reserved; be standoffish; be unamiable; be unamicable; be uncompanionable; be uncongenial; be unfriendly; be unsociable; be unsocial.*

keep (his) eye on the ball ∎ A moribund metaphor. 1. *be alert; be attentive; be awake; be aware; be eagle-eyed; be heedful; be observant; be vigilant; be wakeful; be watchful.* 2. *be able; be adroit; be apt; be astute; be bright; be brilliant; be capable; be clever; be competent; be discerning; be effective; be effectual; be efficient; be enlightened; be insightful; be intelligent; be judicious; be keen; be knowledgeable; be learned; be logical; be luminous; be perceptive; be perspicacious; be quick; be rational; be reasonable; be sagacious; be sage; be sapient; be sensible; be sharp; be shrewd; be smart; be sound; be understanding; be wise.*

keep (your) eyes (open) peeled ∎ A moribund metaphor. *be alert; be attentive; be awake; be aware; be eagle-eyed; be heedful; be observant; be vigilant; be wakeful; be watchful.*

keep (its) finger on the pulse of ∎ A moribund metaphor. • The Chinese government has been able to *keep its finger on the pulse of* technology acquisition activities.

keep (your) fingers crossed ∎ A moribund metaphor. *hope for; pray for; think positively; wish.*

keep (me) glued to (my) seat ∎ A moribund metaphor.

keep (my) head above water ∎ A moribund metaphor. *be solvent; exist; live; subsist; survive.*

keep (your) head on (your) shoulders ∎ A moribund metaphor. *be calm; be composed; be patient; be self-possessed; be tranquil.*

keep in check ∎ A moribund metaphor. *bridle; check; constrain; contain; control; curb; curtail; govern; harness; hold back; inhibit; limit; muzzle; regulate; rein in; repress; restrain; restrict; stem; stifle; suppress.*

keep (your) nose clean ∎ A moribund metaphor. *behave.*

keep (your) nose to the grindstone ∎ A popular prescription. *drudge; grind; grub; labor; moil; slave; strain; strive; struggle; sweat; toil; travail; work hard.*

keep on a short leash ∎ A moribund metaphor. *bridle; check; constrain; contain; control; curb; curtail; govern; harness; hold back; inhibit; limit; muzzle; regulate; rein in; repress; restrain; restrict; stem; stifle; suppress.*

keep (your) pants (shirt) on ∎ A moribund metaphor. *be calm; be composed; be patient; be self-possessed; be tranquil; calm down; hold on; wait.*

(it) keeps (me) busy ∎ A plebeian sentiment. SEE ALSO **(he's) boring; (it) gives (me) something to do; (it) keeps (me) out of trouble; (it's) something to do.**

(it) keeps (me) going ∎ A plebeian sentiment.

keep smiling ∎ A plebeian sentiment. *Keep smiling* is insisted on by ghoulish brutes who would rob us of our gravity, indeed, steal us from ourselves.

(it) keeps (me) out of trouble ∎ A plebeian sentiment. (SEE) SEE ALSO **(it) gives (me) something to do; (it) keeps (me) busy; (it's) something to do.**

keep the ball rolling ∎ A moribund metaphor. *continue; go on; keep on; move on; persevere; persist; proceed.*

keep the faith ∎ A popular prescription. *be confident; be encouraged; be heartened; be hopeful; be optimistic; be positive; be sanguine.*

keep the home fires burning ∎ A moribund metaphor.

keep the wolves at bay ∎ A moribund metaphor.

keep under (his) hat ∎ A moribund metaphor. *camouflage; cloak; conceal; cover; disguise; enshroud; harbor; hide; keep secret; mask; screen; shroud; suppress; veil; withhold.*

keep under lock and key ∎ A moribund metaphor. 1. *confine; detain; hold; imprison; intern; jail; lock up; restrain.* 2. *lock up; protect; secure.*

keep up appearances ∎ A plebeian sentiment.

> She desired children, decorum, an establishment; she desired to avoid waste, she desired to keep up appearances.—Ford Madox Ford, *The Good Soldier*

keep up with the Joneses ∎ A plebeian sentiment.

kick the bucket ∎ A moribund metaphor. *be deceased; die; expire; perish.*

> So when I put my phone to my ear and heard her choke out "He's gone" who could blame me for thinking that Dad had kicked the bucket and that now it was only her and me.—Marian Keyes, *The Other Side of the Story*

kick up (our) heels ∎ A moribund metaphor. *be merry; carouse; carry on; cavort; celebrate; debauch; disport; frolic; gambol; party; play; revel; riot; roister; rollick; romp; skylark.*

kill (them) by inches ∎ A moribund metaphor. *afflict; agonize; crucify; excruciate; harrow; martyr; persecute; rack; torment; torture.*

kill the goose that lays the golden egg ∎ A moribund metaphor.

kill two birds with one stone ∎ A moribund metaphor.

kill (her) with kindness ∎ A moribund metaphor.

kind (and) gentle ∎ An inescapable pair. *affable; agreeable; amiable; amicable; compassionate; friendly; gentle; good-hearted; good-natured; humane; kind; kind-hearted; personable; pleasant; tender; tolerant.*

(a) ... kind (sort; type) of thing ∎ A grammatical gimmick. • It was *a* spur-of-the-moment *kind of thing.* DELETE *a ... kind of thing.* • It's *a* very upsetting *sort of thing.* DELETE *a ... sort of thing.* • It's difficult to find a person to commit to in terms of a long-term relationship *type of thing.* DELETE *type of thing.*

kiss and make up ∎ A moribund metaphor. *make up; reconcile; reunite.*

> You have to be careful when criticizing a friend's partner because the second they kiss and make up, *you* are the baddie who slagged off the love of her life.—Anna Maxted, *Running in Heels*

kiss and tell ∎ A moribund metaphor.

kiss (him) goodbye ∎ A moribund metaphor. *abandon; abdicate; cede; desert; forfeit; forgo; give up; lose (out on); relinquish; renounce; sacrifice; surrender; waive; yield.* • Without a new government-funded convention center, Boston will *kiss major gatherings and tourist events goodbye.* REPLACE WITH *forfeit major gatherings and tourist events.*

kiss of death ∎ A moribund metaphor.

kith and kin ∎ An inescapable pair. *acquaintances; family; friends; kin; kindred; kinfolk; kinsman; kith; relatives.*

knee-high to a grasshopper ∎ A moribund metaphor. 1. *diminutive; dwarfish; elfin; elfish; lilliputian; little; miniature; minikin; petite; pygmy; short; small; teeny; tiny.* 2. *young; youthful.*

knee-jerk reaction ∎ A moribund metaphor. *automatic; habitual; instinctive; inveterate; mechanical; perfunctory; reflex; spontaneous; unconscious; unthinking.*

knight in shining armor ∎ A moribund metaphor.

knock-down, drag-out fight ∎ A moribund metaphor. 1. *altercation; argument; disagreement; discord; disputation; dispute; feud; fight; misunderstanding; quarrel; rift; row; spat; squabble.* 2. *battle; brawl; clash; fight; grapple; jostle; make war; scuffle; skirmish; tussle; war; wrestle.*

knock (me) down with a feather ∎ A moribund metaphor. *amaze; astonish; astound; awe; dazzle; dumbfound; flabbergast; overpower; overwhelm; shock; startle; stun; stupefy; surprise.*

knock (throw) for a loop ∎ A moribund metaphor. *amaze; astonish; astound; awe; dazzle; dumbfound; flabbergast; overpower; overwhelm; shock; startle; stun; stupefy; surprise; unnerve; unsettle.*

knock off (his) feet ∎ A moribund metaphor. *amaze; astonish; astound; awe; dazzle; dumbfound; flabbergast; overpower; overwhelm; shock; startle; stun; stupefy; surprise.*

knock on wood ∎ A moribund metaphor. *hope for; pray for; think positively; wish.*

knock (himself) out ∎ A moribund metaphor. *aim; attempt; endeavor; essay; exert; exhaust; labor; moil; strain; strive; struggle; toil; try hard; undertake; work at.*

knock-out punch ∎ A moribund metaphor.

knock (her) socks off ∎ A moribund metaphor. 1. *amaze; astonish; astound; awe; dazzle; dumbfound; flabbergast; overpower; overwhelm; shock; startle; stun; stupefy; surprise.* 2. *beat; better; conquer; defeat; exceed; excel; outclass; outdo; outflank; outmaneuver; outperform; outplay; overcome; overpower; prevail; rout; succeed; surpass; top; triumph; trounce; vanquish; whip; win.*

knock the bottom out of ∎ A moribund metaphor. *belie; confute; contradict; controvert; counter; debunk; deny; disprove; discredit; dispute; expose; invalidate; negate; rebut; refute; repudiate.*

knock the spots off ∎ A moribund metaphor. *beat; better; conquer; defeat; exceed; excel; outclass; outdo; outflank; outmaneuver; outperform; outplay; overcome; overpower; prevail; rout; succeed; surpass; top; triumph; trounce; vanquish; whip; win.*

know for a fact ∎ An infantile phrase. • *I know for a fact that he was there with her.* DELETE *for a fact.* • *I'm sure they do; I know for a fact they do.* DELETE *for a fact.*

(don't) know ... from Adam ∎ A moribund metaphor. *unacquainted; unconversant; unfamiliar; unknown.*

(know) ... inside (and) out ∎ A moribund metaphor. *completely; comprehensively; deeply; exhaustively; expertly; fully; in depth; in detail; profoundly; thoroughly; well.*

They came here because they *knew* this place. They knew it inside and out.—Zadie Smith, *White Teeth*

knowledge is power ∎ A quack equation.

know all the angles ∎ A moribund metaphor. 1. *able; adept; apt; capable; competent; deft; dexterous; experienced; expert; practiced; proficient; seasoned; skilled; skillful; veteran.* 2. *adroit; astute; bright; brilliant; clever; discerning; effective; effectual; efficient; enlightened; insightful; intelligent; judicious; keen; knowledgeable; learned; logical; luminous; perceptive; perspicacious; quick; rational; reasonable; sagacious; sage; sapient; sensible; sharp; shrewd; smart; sound; understanding; wise.*

(you) know something? ∎ An ineffectual phrase. • *You know something?* I'm going to do whatever is in my power to end this relationship. DELETE *You know something?.* • *You know something?* I never loved you either. DELETE *You know something?.* SEE ALSO **(you) know what?.**

know what's what ∎ An infantile phrase. 1. *able; adept; apt; capable; competent; deft; dexterous; experienced; expert; practiced; proficient; seasoned; skilled; skillful; veteran.* 2. *adroit; astute; bright; brilliant; clever; discerning; effective; effectual; efficient; enlightened; insightful; intelligent; judicious; keen; knowledgeable; learned; logical; luminous; perceptive; perspicacious; quick; rational; reasonable; sagacious; sage; sapient; sensible; sharp; shrewd; smart; sound; understanding; wise.*

(you) know what? ∎ An ineffectual phrase. • *You know what?* When we return, you'll meet her mother. DELETE *You know what?.* • *She broke up with me, and you know what?,* I've got a career now, which is good. DELETE *you know what?.* SEE ALSO **(you) know something?.**

(you) know what I mean? ∎ An ineffectual phrase. • *Some people have to work at it more than others. Know what I mean?* DELETE *Know what I mean?* • *How can you not be depressed if you don't remember things. You know what I mean?* DELETE *You know what I mean?* SEE ALSO **(you) hear what I'm saying? (you) know what I'm saying? (you) know what I'm telling you? (do) you know?.**

(you) know what I'm saying? ∎ An ineffectual phrase. • *It was an association that wasn't based on any fact. You know what I'm saying?* DELETE *You know what I'm saying?* • *I want a girl that's real. You know what I'm saying?* DELETE *You know what I'm saying?* SEE ALSO **(you) hear what I'm saying? (you) know what I mean? (you) know what I'm telling you? (do) you know?.**

(you) know what I'm telling you? ∎ An ineffectual phrase. • *I don't know; I can't think of the words. You know what I'm* *telling you?* DELETE *You know what I'm telling you?* • I like to be with a woman who has the same mindset as I do. *You know what I'm telling you?* DELETE *You know what I'm telling you?* SEE ALSO **(you) hear what I'm saying? (you) know what I mean? (you) know what I'm saying? (do) you know?**.

knuckle under ▮ A moribund metaphor. *abdicate; accede; acquiesce; bow; capitulate; cede; concede; give in; give up; quit; relinquish; retreat; submit; succumb; surrender; yield.*

kudos ▮ A foreign phrase.

L l

lack of ∎ A torpid term. Whatever happened to our negative words, to the prefixes *dis-, il-, im-, in-, ir-, mis-, non-,* and *un-*? No doubt many people say *absence of* or *lack of* because they know so few negative forms of the words that follow these phrases. These people will say *lack of moderation* instead of *immoderation* and *absence of pleasure* instead of *displeasure*.

Others subscribe to society's oral imperative that all things negative be left unsaid. To these people, *lack of respect* is somehow preferable to, and more positive than, *disrespect*. • These reports by the media reflect a *lack of sensitivity* to basic human decency. REPLACE WITH *insensitivity*. • It was her *lack of judgment* that lost us the sale. REPLACE WITH *misjudgment*. SEE ALSO **absence of; less than (enthusiastic)**.

lady ∎ A suspect superlative. *Lady* has become a pejorative term. No longer does it suggest a cultured, sophisticated woman; rather, it suggests a woman hopelessly common, forever coarse. • If you wanted to sweep one of these *ladies* off her feet, what would you do? REPLACE WITH *women*. • I am a *lady*, and I like to be treated as such. REPLACE WITH *well-bred woman*. • I have a question for both of you *ladies*. DELETE *ladies*. SEE ALSO **class; gentleman**.

land on (her) feet ∎ A moribund metaphor. *come through; continue; endure; hold on; persevere; persist; remain; survive.*

landslide victory ∎ A moribund metaphor.

last but (by) no means least ∎ An infantile phrase. This term, like *last but not least*, needs to be retired. It's a drab, depressing formula used by forlorn people, by team players (SEE) and troglodytes alike, by hacks and hirelings all.

last but not least ∎ An infantile phrase.

> They were concerned for the newcomer, and they were concerned for themselves; midwives, barber-surgeons, nannies, priest and, last but not least, solicitors crowded around the event in droves.—Peter Esterhazy, *Celestial Harmonies*

lasting ∎ An overworked word. For example: *lasting consequence; lasting contribution; lasting impact; lasting impression; lasting lesson; lasting peace.*

last nail in (his) coffin ∎ A moribund metaphor.

last of the Mohicans ∎ An infantile phrase.

laughing (my) head off ∎ A moribund metaphor. *cachinnate; cackle; chortle; chuckle; convulse; guffaw; hoot; howl; laugh; roar; shriek.*

laughing on the outside and crying on the inside ∎ A moribund metaphor.

laughter is the best medicine ∎ A popular prescription.

launching pad (for) ∎ A moribund metaphor. *base; beginning; foundation; springboard; start*

laundry list ∎ A moribund metaphor. *blacklist; catalog; checklist; directory; inventory; list; listing; litany; record; register; roll; roster.*

> It said, simply and quickly, that Raymond Lilly, convicted felon, had been released from police custody in the matter of the several slayings, followed by a list of the dead. It was quite a laundry list of names.—Harry Connolly, *Child of Fire*

lavishly illustrated ∎ An inescapable pair.

law of the jungle ∎ A moribund metaphor.

(don't) lay a finger (hand) on ∎ A moribund metaphor. *caress; feel; finger; fondle; handle; pat; paw; pet; rub; stroke; touch.*

lay an egg ∎ A moribund metaphor. *abort; blunder; bomb; fail; fall short; falter; flop; flounder; go wrong; miscarry; not succeed; slip; stumble; trip.*

lay at (their) door ∎ A moribund metaphor. *accredit to; ascribe to; assign to; associate to; attribute to; blame on; charge to; connect with; correlate to; credit to; equate to; impute to; link to; relate to; trace to.*

lay a trap for ∎ A moribund metaphor. *catch; decoy; ensnare; entrap; net; trap.*

lay at the door (feet) of ∎ A moribund metaphor. *accredit to; ascribe to; assign to; associate to; attribute to; blame on; charge to; connect with; correlate to; credit to; equate to; impute to; link to; relate to; trace to.* • It doesn't seem that all this volatility can be *laid at the feet of* foreigners. REPLACE WITH *blamed on*.

lay (put) (your) cards on the table ∎ A moribund metaphor. *be aboveboard; be candid; be forthright; be frank; be honest; be open; be straightforward; be truthful.*

lay down the law ∎ A moribund metaphor. 1. *assert; command; decree; dictate; insist; order; require.* 2. *admonish; berate; castigate; censure; chastise; chide; condemn; criticize; decry; rebuke; reprimand; reproach; reprove; scold; upbraid.*

lay (spread) it on thick ∎ A moribund metaphor. 1. *elaborate; embellish; embroider; enhance; enlarge; exaggerate; hyperbolize; inflate; magnify; overdo; overreact; overstress; overstate; strain; stretch.* 2. *acclaim; applaud; celebrate; commend; compliment; congratulate; eulogize; extol; flatter; hail; laud; panegyrize; praise; puff; salute.*

lay (it) on the line ∎ A moribund metaphor. *be aboveboard; be candid; be forthright; be frank; be honest; be open; be straightforward; be truthful.*

lay (her) out in lavendar ∎ A moribund metaphor. *admonish; animadvert; berate; castigate; censure; chasten; chastise; chide; condemn; criticize; denounce; denunciate; discipline; excoriate; fulminate against; imprecate; impugn; inveigh against; lecture; objurgate; punish; rebuke; remonstrate; reprehend; reprimand; reproach; reprobate; reprove; revile; scold; swear at; upbraid; vituperate.*

lay the groundwork (for) ∎ A moribund metaphor. *arrange; groom; make ready; plan; prepare; prime; ready.*

lead (her) by the nose ∎ A moribund metaphor. *administer; boss; command; control; dictate; direct; dominate; domineer; govern; in charge; in command; in control; manage; manipulate; master; misuse; order; overpower; oversee; predominate; prevail; reign over; rule; superintend; tyrannize; use.*

lead down the garden path ∎ A moribund metaphor. *bamboozle; befool; beguile; bilk; bluff; cheat; con; deceive; defraud; delude; dupe; feint; fool; gyp; hoodwink; lead astray; misdirect; misguide; misinform; mislead; spoof; swindle; trick; victimize.*

leader of the pack ∎ A moribund metaphor. 1. *administrator; boss; brass; chief; commander; director; executive; foreman; head; headman; leader; manager; master; (high) muckamuck; officer; official; overseer; president; principal; superintendent; supervisor.* 2. *aristocrat; dignitary; eminence; lord; luminary; magnate; mogul; notable; patrician; personage; ruler; sovereign; worthy.*

(put) lead in your pencil ∎ A moribund metaphor. *energy; force; life; power; punch; spirit; strength; verve; vigor; vim; vitality; zest.*

leak like a sieve ∎ An insipid simile. 1. *leaky; permeable.* 2. *forgetful; heedless; inattentive; lethean; neglectful; negligent; oblivious; remiss; thoughtless; unmindful; unthinking.*

lean and hungry (look) ∎ A moribund metaphor.

lean and mean ∎ An inescapable pair.

leaps off the page ∎ A moribund metaphor.

learn the ropes ∎ A moribund metaphor.

> She was left sitting until a slight, sparrow-like woman, with bright fringed hair and round blue eyes, came past and remarked warningly that she should keep her eyes open and learn the ropes.—Doris M. Lessing, *Martha Quest*

leave a bad taste in (my) mouth ∎ A moribund metaphor.

leave a little (a lot; much; something) to be desired ∎ A torpid term. *be deficient; be inadequate; be insufficient; be lacking; be substandard; be wanting.* • In the area of health, the U.S. position *leaves much to be desired.* REPLACE WITH *is sickly.* • The plan was great; it was the execution that *left a little to be desired.* REPLACE WITH *was not.* • Sorry about that, my handwriting *leaves something to be desired.* REPLACE WITH *is scarcely legible.*

leave holding the bag ∎ A moribund metaphor. *abandon; depart from; desert; exclude; forsake; leave; quit; withdraw from.*

leave (out) in the cold ∎ A moribund metaphor. *abandon; ban; banish; bar; desert; exclude; exile; forsake; ostracize; shut out.*

leave (him) in the dust ∎ A moribund metaphor. *beat; best; better; defeat; eclipse; exceed; excel; outclass; outdo; outflank; outmaneuver; outpace; outperform; outplay; outrank; outrival; outsmart; outstrip; outthink; outwit; overcome; overpower; overshadow; prevail; rout; surpass; top; triumph; trounce; vanquish; whip; win.* • It is here where Homo sapiens *leaves* other species *in the dust,* and the hands usually make it possible. REPLACE WITH *surpasses.*

leave (hanging) in the lurch ∎ A moribund metaphor. *abandon; depart from; desert; exclude; forsake; leave; quit; withdraw from.* • We don't want to *leave* parents *hanging in the lurch.* REPLACE WITH *abandon.*

> Today, Jorie has once again left her poor friend Charlotte in the lurch, with no explanations or apologies.—Alice Hoffman, *Blue Diary*

leave no stone unturned ∎ A moribund metaphor. *analyze; canvass; comb; examine; explore; filter; forage; hunt; inspect; investigate; look for; probe; quest; ransack; rummage; scour; scrutinize; search; seek; sieve; sift; winnow.*

leave the door (wide) open (for) ∎ A moribund metaphor. • The remainder of the majority *left the door open for* a return to capital punishment.

leave well enough alone ∎ A popular
prescription.

left and right ∎ An inescapable pair. *all
around; all over; all through; broadly;
everyplace; everywhere; extensively;
throughout; ubiquitously; universally;
widely.* SEE ALSO **far and wide; high and
low.**

leg to stand on ∎ A moribund metaphor.

lend a (helping) hand (to) ∎ A moribund
metaphor. *aid; assist; benefit; favor; help;
oblige; succor.* • During this holiday season,
it is fitting for all of us to be thinking of
lending a helping hand to those in need.
REPLACE WITH *aiding.* • These writers
believe it's their mission to *lend a hand*
wherever there is a need. REPLACE WITH
help.

lend an ear ∎ A moribund metaphor. *attend
to; heed; listen; note.*

leopards don't lose their spots ∎ A
moribund metaphor.

less is more ∎ A quack equation.

less than (enthusiastic) ∎ A torpid term.
• When Fred told his wife about the
unbelievable opportunity, he was shocked
at her *less than enthusiastic* response.
REPLACE WITH *unenthusiastic.* • The
response from their neighbors has been
less than hospitable. REPLACE WITH
inhospitable. SEE ALSO **absence of; lack of.**

let bygones be bygones ∎ A popular
prescription.

let go of the past ∎ A popular prescription.

let grass grow under (your) feet ∎ A
moribund metaphor. *be idle; be inactive; be
lazy; be unemployed; be unoccupied; dally;
dawdle; delay; hesitate; linger; loaf; loiter;
loll; lounge; pause; relax; repose; rest; tarry;
unwind; wait; waste time.*

let (take) (her) hair down ∎ A moribund
metaphor. *be casual; be free; be informal;
be loose; be natural; be open; be relaxed; be
unbound; be unconfined; be unrestrained; be
unrestricted.*

let (him) have it with both barrels ∎ A
moribund metaphor. *admonish; animadvert;
berate; castigate; censure; chasten; chastise;
chide; condemn; criticize; denounce;
denunciate; discipline; excoriate; fulminate
against; imprecate; impugn; inveigh against;
objurgate; punish; rebuke; remonstrate;
reprehend; reprimand; reproach; reprobate;
reprove; revile; scold; swear at; upbraid;
vituperate.*

let it all hang out ∎ A moribund metaphor.
*acknowledge; admit; affirm; allow; avow;
concede; confess; disclose; divulge; expose;
grant; own; reveal; tell; uncover; unearth;
unveil.*

let it be ∎ A popular prescription.

let me ask you something ∎ An ineffectual
phrase. • *Let me ask you something,* is
there anything about school that you like?
DELETE *Let me ask you something.* • *Let me
ask you something:* What would you think
if I met three women tonight? DELETE *Let
me ask you something.* SEE ALSO **can I ask
(tell) you something?.**

let me tell you (something) ∎ An
ineffectual phrase. Of course the people who
use this phrase seldom enunciate *let me;*
they mutter *lemme,* an inauspicious sign,
we might reasonably believe, of what is
to come. *Let me tell you (something)* is a
vulgarity, very nearly an insult. It unveils a
person, only crudely consciousness of what
he utters, who has as much respect for the
language as he does for his listeners.
• This is really class, *let me tell you.*
DELETE *let me tell you.* • It's been one of
those days, *let me tell you.* DELETE *let me
tell you.* • *Let me tell you,* there is nothing
scarier than being in hurricane force winds
and hearing huge clangs and thumps and
shattering of glass or metal. DELETE *Let
me tell you.* SEE ALSO **I got to (have to) tell
you (something); I'll tell you (something); I'll
tell you what; I'm telling you.**

let nature take its course ∎ A popular
prescription.

let sleeping dogs lie ∎ A popular
prescription. *avoid; discount; disregard; dodge;
duck; ignore; neglect; omit; pass over; shun;
shy away from; turn away from; withdraw
from.*

let the cat out of the bag ∎ A moribund
metaphor. *reveal secrets.*

let the chips fall where they may ∎ A
moribund metaphor.

let there be no mistake ∎ A torpid term.
SEE ALSO **make no mistake (about it).**

let your fingers do the walking ∎ An
infantile phrase.

let your mind run wild ∎ A moribund
metaphor.

level the playing field ∎ A moribund
metaphor. *balance; equalize; even out; level;
make equal; make fair; make level.* • The
chief aim of the bill is to *level the playing
field* so that challengers and incumbents
will have an equal opportunity to get their
message across. • We're not out to hurt
anybody, we're just out to *level the playing
field.* SEE ALSO **a level playing field.**

level to the ground ∎ A moribund metaphor.
*annihilate; assassinate; butcher; demolish;
destroy; devastate; eradicate; exterminate;
kill; massacre; murder; obliterate; pulverize;
rack; ravage; raze; ruin; shatter; slaughter;
slay; smash; undo; wrack; wreck.*

lick (his) chops (lips) ∎ A moribund metaphor. *exult; gloat; rejoice.*

lick into shape ∎ A moribund metaphor. *drill; instruct; perfect; train.*

lick (your) wounds ∎ A moribund metaphor.

lie down on the job ∎ A moribund metaphor. *be idle; be inactive; be lazy; be unemployed; be unoccupied; dally; dawdle; linger; loaf; loiter; loll; lounge; malinger; tarry.*

lie like a rug ∎ An insipid simile. *deceive; dissemble; distort; equivocate; falsify; fib; lie; misconstrue; mislead; misrepresent; pervert; prevaricate.*

> He had the press, he had the money, and he would lie like a rug in order to manipulate people into helping him.—Diane Jessup, *The Dog Who Spoke With Gods*

lie low ∎ A moribund metaphor. 1. *be closed-mouthed; be quiet; be reticent; be silent; be speechless; be still; be taciturn; be uncommunicative; keep quiet.* 2. *disappear; hide; hole up.*

lie through (his) teeth ∎ A moribund metaphor. *deceive; dissemble; distort; equivocate; falsify; fib; lie; misconstrue; mislead; misrepresent; pervert; prevaricate.*

life begins at forty ∎ A popular prescription.

life goes on ∎ A popular prescription.

life in a fishbowl ∎ A moribund metaphor.

life in the fast lane ∎ A moribund metaphor.

life is a cabaret ∎ A moribund metaphor.

life is for the living ∎ A popular prescription.

life isn't (always) fair ∎ A popular prescription.

life is short ∎ A quack equation.

(live a) life of luxury ∎ A moribund metaphor. *affluent; moneyed; opulent; prosperous; rich; wealthy; well-off; well-to-do.*

lift a finger ∎ A moribund metaphor. *aid; assist; benefit; favor; help; oblige; succor.*

light a fire under ∎ A moribund metaphor. *arouse; awaken; excite; galvanize; goad; impel; incite; induce; motivate; prompt; provoke; push; rouse; spur; stimulate; stir; urge.* • May the bishops' counsel encourage those husbands already living their words and *light a fire under* those dozing. REPLACE WITH *rouse.*

(as) light as a feather ∎ An insipid simile. *airy; buoyant; delicate; ethereal; feathery; gaseous; gauzy; gossamer; light; lightweight; slender; slight; sylphid; thin; vaporous; weightless.*

(as) light as air ∎ An insipid simile. *airy; buoyant; delicate; ethereal; feathery; gaseous; gauzy; gossamer; light; lightweight; slender;* slight; sylphid; thin; vaporous; weightless.

light at the end of the tunnel ∎ A moribund metaphor. *anticipation; expectancy; expectation; hope; hopefulness; optimism; possibility; promise; prospect; sanguinity.* • When the opportunity arose that he could work for the government, we saw *light at the end of the tunnel.* REPLACE WITH *possibility.*

like a bolt from (out of) the blue ∎ A moribund metaphor. *bombshell; shock; surprise; thunderbolt; thunderclap.*

(know) (her) like a book ∎ An insipid simile. *altogether; completely; entirely; fully; perfectly; quite; roundly; thoroughly; totally; unreservedly; utterly; wholly.*

(built) like a brick shithouse ∎ An insipid simile. *durably; firmly; robustly; solidly; strongly; sturdily; well.*

(works) like a charm ∎ An insipid simile. *accurately; easily; exactly; excellently; faultlessly; flawlessly; flowingly; impeccably; indefectibly; methodically; perfectly; precisely; regularly; smoothly; systematically; well.*

like a deer caught in the headlights ∎ An insipid simile. *afraid; alarmed; anxious; apprehensive; fearful; frightened; panicky; scared; terrified; timid; timorous.* • Tom looked *like a deer caught in the headlights.* REPLACE WITH *terrified.*

> Mark was fiddling with a brightly colored train, but, every so often, he glanced up at the television with the fascination of a rabbit caught in the headlights.—Elizabeth Buchan, *Revenge of the Middle-Aged Woman*

(take to it) like a duck to water ∎ An insipid simile. *easily; effortlessly; fluently; naturally; smoothly; with ease.*

(fits) like a glove ∎ An insipid simile. *accurately; easily; exactly; excellently; faultlessly; flawlessly; flowingly; impeccably; indefectibly; methodically; perfectly; precisely; regularly; smoothly; systematically; well.* • By having a single, reliable technology solution that fits all of our companies *like a glove*, we are delivering the best technology at the best price to our associates. REPLACE WITH *faultlessly.*

like a hole in the head ∎ An insipid simile. *by no means; hardly; in no way; not at all; not in any way; not in the least; scarcely.*

> Kate needed water like a hole in the head. Whisky: that might just help.—Judith Cutler, *Power on Her Own*

(go over) like a lead balloon ∎ An insipid simile. *badly; poorly; unsatisfactorily; unsuccessfully.*

like clockwork

like clockwork ▌ An insipid simile. *accurately; easily; exactly; excellently; faultlessly; flawlessly; flowingly; impeccably; indefectibly; methodically; perfectly; precisely; regularly; smoothly; systematically; well.*

like comparing dollars to doughnuts ▌ A moribund metaphor. *different; discordant; discrepant; dissimilar; dissonant; divergent; incommensurable; incommensurate; incomparable; incompatible; incongruent; incongruous; inconsistent; inconsonant; inharmonious; unlike.*

like crazy (mad) ▌ An insipid simile. 1. *actively; aggressively; dynamically; emphatically; energetically; ferociously; fervently; fiercely; forcefully; frantically; frenziedly; furiously; hard; intensely; intently; mightily; passionately; powerfully; robustly; savagely; spiritedly; strenuously; strongly; vehemently; viciously; vigorously; violently; wildly; with vigor.* 2. *ardently; devotedly; eagerly; enthusiastically; fervently; fervidly; passionately; spiritedly; zealously.* 3. *hastily; hurriedly; posthaste; promptly; quickly; rapidly; speedily; swiftly; very fast; wingedly.* • He is also eating *like crazy.* REPLACE WITH *zealously.*

like hell ▌ An insipid simile. 1. *actively; aggressively; dynamically; emphatically; energetically; ferociously; fervently; fiercely; forcefully; frantically; frenziedly; furiously; hard; intensely; intently; mightily; passionately; powerfully; robustly; savagely; spiritedly; strenuously; strongly; vehemently; viciously; vigorously; violently; wildly; with vigor.* 2. *ardently; devotedly; eagerly; enthusiastically; fervently; fervidly; passionately; spiritedly; zealously.* 3. *hastily; hurriedly; posthaste; promptly; quickly; rapidly; speedily; swiftly; very fast; wingedly.*

(selling) like hotcakes ▌ An insipid simile. *briskly; fast; hurriedly; quickly; rapidly; speedily; swiftly; well; wingedly.* • Their current album is selling *like hotcakes.* REPLACE WITH *swiftly.*

> I translate Breteuil because it's easy and because it sells like hot cakes in any language.—Iris Murdoch, *Under the Net*

like (as if) it's going out of fashion (style) ▌ An insipid simile. 1. *abundantly; amply; bountifully; copiously; generously; in abundance; lavishly; plentifully; profusely; prolifically.* 2. *actively; aggressively; dynamically; emphatically; energetically; ferociously; fervently; fiercely; forcefully; frantically; frenziedly; furiously; hard; intensely; intently; mightily; passionately; powerfully; robustly; savagely; spiritedly; strenuously; strongly; vehemently; viciously; vigorously; violently; wildly; with vigor.* 3. *hastily; hurriedly; posthaste; promptly; quickly; rapidly; speedily; swiftly; very fast; wingedly.* • I've been taking aspirin *like it's going out of style.* REPLACE WITH *aggressively.* SEE ALSO **like there's no tomorrow**.

like (someone) kicked me in the stomach ▌ A moribund metaphor. 1. *nauseated; nauseous; queasy; sick; squeamish.* 2. *afflicted; ailing; diseased; ill; indisposed; infirm; not (feeling) well; sick; sickly; suffering; unhealthy; unsound; unwell; valetudinarian.*

> I stood up quickly and felt like someone had kicked me in the stomach.—Karen Arsenault, *The Broken Teaglass*

like (a streak of; greased) lightning ▌ An insipid simile. *abruptly; apace; at once; briskly; directly; expeditiously; fast; forthwith; hastily; hurriedly; immediately; instantaneously; instantly; posthaste; promptly; quickly; rapidly; rashly; right away; speedily; straightaway; swiftly; wingedly.*

(works) like magic ▌ An insipid simile. *amazingly; astonishingly; astoundingly; extraordinarily; inexplicably; magically; miraculously; mysteriously; phenomenally; remarkably; wondrously.*

like nobody's business ▌ An insipid simile. 1. *beautifully; brilliantly; consummately; dazzlingly; excellently; exceptionally; expertly; exquisitely; extraordinarily; fabulously; flawlessly; grandly; magnificently; marvelously; perfectly; remarkably; splendidly; superbly; superlatively; supremely; transcendently; very well; wonderfully; wondrously.* 2. *actively; aggressively; dynamically; emphatically; energetically; ferociously; fervently; fiercely; forcefully; frantically; frenziedly; furiously; hard; intensely; intently; mightily; passionately; powerfully; robustly; savagely; spiritedly; strenuously; strongly; vehemently; viciously; vigorously; violently; wildly; with vigor.* • Here was the one and only Kronos Quartet in town again, playing—as always—*like nobody's business.* REPLACE WITH *superbly.* • He can play the piano *like nobody's business.* REPLACE WITH *beautifully.*

like seeing (looking) ... through rose-colored glasses ▌ A moribund metaphor. *hopeful; optimistic; pollyanna; pollyannaish; positive; roseate; sanguine; upbeat.* • Life then becomes *like seeing the world through rose-colored glasses*: beautiful and warm. REPLACE WITH *polyannaish.*

(sounds) like something out of a novel ▌ An insipid simile.

> Bluey had started by thinking they were like something out of a novel herself, the sort of novel set in another, intriguing age and society.—Joanna Trollope, *The Men and the Girls*

like the back of (my) hand ∎ An insipid simile. *altogether; completely; entirely; fully; perfectly; quite; roundly; thoroughly; totally; unreservedly; utterly; wholly.*

like there's no tomorrow ∎ An insipid simile. 1. *actively; aggressively; dynamically; emphatically; energetically; ferociously; fervently; fiercely; forcefully; frantically; frenziedly; furiously; hard; intensely; intently; mightily; passionately; powerfully; robustly; savagely; spiritedly; strenuously; strongly; vehemently; viciously; vigorously; violently; wildly; with vigor.* 2. *hastily; hurriedly; posthaste; promptly; quickly; rapidly; speedily; swiftly; very fast; wingedly.* SEE ALSO **like it's going out of style**.

like the shifting sands ∎ An insipid simile. *brief; ephemeral; evanescent; fleeting; flitting; fugacious; fugitive; impermanent; momentary; passing; short; short-lived; temporary; transient; transitory; volatile.*

like watching paint dry ∎ An insipid simile. *banal; barren; bland; boring; deadly; dreary; dry; dull; everyday; flat; humdrum; inanimate; insipid; jejune; lifeless; lusterless; mediocre; monotonous; prosaic; routine; spiritless; stale; tedious; tiresome; unexciting; uninteresting; vapid; wearisome.*

like water ∎ An insipid simile. *abundantly; copiously; freely; generously; liberally; profusely; unreservedly.*

> It might seem strange that a successful Hollywood lady would go for a nomadic gent who ran through passports like water, could spout off funny if lewd phrases in thirty languages, and never would be financially secure.—David Baldacci, *The Christmas Train*

like water (rolling) off a duck's back ∎ An insipid simile . *to no avail; with no result; without effect.*

(spread) like wildfire ∎ An insipid simile. 1. *briskly; fast; hastily; hurriedly; quickly; promptly; rapidly; speedily; swiftly.* 2. *actively; aggressively; dynamically; emphatically; energetically; ferociously; fervently; fiercely; forcefully; frantically; frenziedly; furiously; hard; intensely; intently; mightily; passionately; powerfully; robustly; savagely; spiritedly; strenuously; strongly; vehemently; viciously; vigorously; violently; wildly; with vigor.*

line of fire ∎ A moribund metaphor.

lines are drawn ∎ A moribund metaphor.

lining (his) pockets ∎ A moribund metaphor.

link together ∎ A wretched redundancy. *link.* • This business will *link together* the telephone, the television, and the computer. DELETE *together*.

(my) lips are sealed ∎ A moribund metaphor.

liquid refreshment ∎ An infantile phrase. *beverage; drink; refreshment.*

litany of complaints ∎ A moribund metaphor.

literary event ∎ A suspect superlative.

little old lady from Dubuque ∎ A moribund metaphor. *boor; bumpkin; commoner; common man; common person; conventional person; peasant; philistine; pleb; plebeian; vulgarian; yokel.* • By the time the contest was over, *little, old ladies in Dubuque* could probably discourse on the subject.

lit to the gills ∎ A moribund metaphor. *besotted; crapulous; drunk; inebriated; intoxicated; sodden; stupefied; tipsy.*

lit up like a Christmas tree ∎ An insipid simile.

live and learn ∎ A popular prescription.

live and let live ∎ A popular prescription.

live as though each day were your last ∎ A popular prescription.

live dangerously ∎ A popular prescription.

live each day to the fullest ∎ A popular prescription.

live for the moment ∎ A popular prescription.

live happily ever after ∎ A suspect superlative.

live high off (on) the hog ∎ A moribund metaphor.

live in a pigsty ∎ A moribund metaphor.

live one day at a time ∎ A popular prescription.

lives and breathes ∎ A moribund metaphor. *abounds with; emanates; exudes; is itself; oozes; overflows with; radiates; reeks of; teems with.* • Pop diva Lady gaga *lives and breathes* shock value. REPLACE WITH *exudes.*

live wire ∎ A moribund metaphor. *card; character; eccentric; exception; original.*

(learn to) live with it ∎ A popular prescription.

loaded for bear ∎ A moribund metaphor. 1. *eager; prepared; primed; ready; set.* 2. *angry; bad-tempered; bilious; cantankerous; choleric; churlish; crabby; cranky; cross; curmudgeonly; disagreeable; dyspeptic; grouchy; gruff; grumpy; ill-humored; ill-tempered; irascible; irritable; mad; peevish; petulant; quarrelsome; riled; roiled; short-tempered; splenetic; surly; testy; vexed.*

lo and behold ∎ A withered word.

location, location, location ∎ An infantile phrase.

lock horns with ∎ A moribund metaphor. *battle; brawl; clash; fight; grapple; jostle;*

make war; scuffle; skirmish; tussle; war; wrestle.

lock, stock, and barrel ∎ A moribund metaphor. *aggregate; all; all things; entirety; everything; gross; lot; sum; total; totality; whole.*

long and hard ∎ A torpid term. *aggressively; dynamically; emphatically; energetically; ferociously; fervently; fiercely; forcefully; frantically; frenziedly; furiously; hard; intensely; intently; mightily; passionately; powerfully; robustly; savagely; spiritedly; strenuously; strongly; vehemently; viciously; vigorously; violently; wildly; with vigor.* • The compromise would be a partial victory for Baybanks, which has fought *long and hard* against the legislation. REPLACE WITH *mightily.*

long in the tooth ∎ A moribund metaphor. *aged; aging; ancient; antediluvian; antique; archaic; elderly; hoary; hoary-headed; old; patriarchal; prehistoric; seasoned; superannuated.*

> Notice these are all attractive, smart, funny women who happen to be a little long in the tooth.—Patricia Gaffney, *The Saving Graces*

long overdue ∎ An inescapable pair. • This legislation is *long overdue.*

long road ahead ∎ A moribund metaphor.

(a) long shot ∎ A moribund metaphor. *doubtful; dubious; farfetched; implausible; improbable; remote; unlikely; unrealistic.* • Something that might happen is *a longer shot* than something that may happen. REPLACE WITH *less likely.*

long time no see ∎ An infantile phrase.

look a fright ∎ A moribund metaphor. *disheveled; dowdy; frowzy; messy; ragged; run-down; scruffy; seedy; shabby; sloppy; slovenly; tattered; tousled; unkempt; untidy.*

(don't) look a gift horse in the mouth ∎ A popular prescription.

look before you leap ∎ A popular prescription. *be careful; be cautious; be circumspect; be prudent; be safe; be wary.*

look down (her) nose (at) ∎ A moribund metaphor. *contemn; deride; despise; detest; disdain; jeer at; laugh at; mock; ridicule; scoff at; scorn; shun; slight; sneer; snub; spurn.*

look into a crystal ball ∎ A moribund metaphor. *forecast; foreshadow; foretell; portend; predict; prefigure; presage; prognosticate; prophesy.*

look like a drowned rat ∎ An insipid simile. *bedraggled; drenched; dripping; saturated; soaked; sopping; wet.*

look over (our) shoulders ∎ A moribund metaphor. *be anxious; be apprehensive; be fearful; be frightened; be insecure; be*

nervous; be panicky; be scared; be timid; be timorous; be uneasy.

looks aren't everything ∎ A popular prescription.

(she) looks like a million bucks (dollars) ∎ An insipid simile. 1. *appealing; attractive; beautiful; becoming; captivating; comely; cute; dazzling; exquisite; fair; fetching; good-looking; gorgeous; handsome; lovely; nice-looking; pleasing; pretty; pulchritudinous; radiant; ravishing; seemly; stunning.* 2. *energetic; fine; fit; good; hale; hardy; healthful; healthy; hearty; robust; sound; strong; vigorous; well.* 3. *affluent; moneyed; opulent; prosperous; rich; successful; wealthy; well-off; well-to-do.*

look the other way ∎ A moribund metaphor. *brush aside; avoid; discount; disregard; dodge; duck; ignore; neglect; omit; pass over; recoil from; shrink from; shun; shy away from; turn away from; withdraw from.*

look what the tide brought in ∎ A moribund metaphor.

look who's talking ∎ An infantile phrase.

look what (who) the cat dragged in ∎ A moribund metaphor.

loose cannon ∎ A moribund metaphor. *capricious; changeable; erratic; fickle; fluctuating; inconsistent; inconstant; mercurial; unpredictable; unstable; unsteady; variable; volatile; wavering.*

lose (her) head (over) ∎ A moribund metaphor. 1. *alarm; appall; benumb; daunt; frighten; horrify; intimidate; panic; paralyze; petrify; scare; shock; startle; terrify; terrorize.* 2. *infatuated.*

lose (his) marbles (mind) ∎ A moribund metaphor. *batty; cracked; crazy; daft; demented; deranged; fey; foolish; goofy; insane; lunatic; mad; maniacal; neurotic; nuts; nutty; psychotic; raving; silly; squirrelly; touched; unbalanced; unhinged; unsound; wacky; zany.*

> I'd had older men look at me that way since I'd lost my baby fat, but they usually didn't lose their marbles over me when I was wearing my royal blue parka and yellow elephant bell-bottoms—Alice Sebold, *The Lovely Bones*

lose steam ∎ A moribund metaphor.

lost in the shuffle ∎ A moribund metaphor. *be discounted; be disregarded; be forgotten; be ignored; be neglected; be omitted; be passed over; be shunned.* • There is so much to teach that is writing related, that sometimes the writing itself can *get lost in the shuffle.* REPLACE WITH *be neglected.*

loud and clear ∎ An inescapable pair. *apparent; audible; clear; conspicuous; definite; distinct; emphatic; evident; explicit; graphic; lucid; manifest; obvious;*

patent; pellucid; plain; sharp; translucent; transparent; unambiguous; uncomplex; uncomplicated; understandable; unequivocal; unmistakable; vivid.

love and cherish ∎ An inescapable pair.

love conquers all ∎ A popular prescription.

love is blind ∎ A quack equation.

love it or leave it ∎ An infantile phrase.

love moves mountains ∎ A moribund metaphor.

low blow ∎ A moribund metaphor. *dishonorable; foul; inequitable; unconscientious; underhanded; unethical; unfair; unjust; unprincipled; unscrupulous; unsportsmanlike.*

lower the boom ∎ A moribund metaphor. 1. *admonish; animadvert; berate; castigate; censure; chasten; chastise; chide; condemn; criticize; denounce; denunciate; discipline; excoriate; fulminate against; imprecate; impugn; inveigh against; objurgate; punish; rebuke; remonstrate; reprehend; reprimand; reproach; reprobate; reprove; revile; scold; swear at; upbraid; vituperate.* 2. *abort; annul; arrest; cancel; cease; check; conclude; derail; discontinue; end; halt; nullify; quash; quell; revoke; squelch; stop; suspend; terminate.*

lowest common denominator ∎ A torpid term. For some—copycat journalists, delicate marketing people, and feeble-minded social scientists perhaps—*lowest common denominator* is a long-winded, short-sighted way of avoiding more telling words.
 • Instead of disseminating the best in our culture, television too often panders to the *lowest common denominator*. REPLACE WITH *worst*. • If you fear making anyone mad, then you ultimately probe for the *lowest common denominator* of human achievement. REPLACE WITH *nadir*. • In that environment, each show tried to appeal to the *lowest common denominator*. REPLACE WITH *masses*. • The J.D. InterPrizes' *lowest common denominator* design concept allows for the widest possible viewing audience. REPLACE WITH *readily accessible*. • So movies must imitate the familiar and be pitched to the *lowest common denominator,* causing most of them to be flat, stale and familiar. REPLACE WITH *dull-minded*.

low (man) on the totem pole ∎ A moribund metaphor. *inferior; junior; lesser; low ranking; minor; second rate; secondary; subordinate.* • If you're a freshman member, regardless of what party you're in, you're *low on the totem pole* to be sure. REPLACE WITH *low ranking*.

> Everyone in Emerson House had a job of some sort, and as low man on the totem pole Cal got the job nobody else wanted: dishwasher.—Orland Outland, *Different People*

Mm

(as) mad as a hatter ∎ An insipid simile. *batty; cracked; crazy; daft; demented; deranged; fey; foolish; goofy; insane; lunatic; mad; maniacal; neurotic; nuts; nutty; psychotic; raving; silly; squirrelly; touched; unbalanced; unhinged; unsound; wacky; zany.*

(as) mad as a hornet ∎ An insipid simile. *angry; berserk; convulsive; crazed; delirious; demented; demoniac; deranged; enraged; feral; ferocious; fierce; frantic; frenzied; fuming; furious; hysterical; infuriated; in hysterics; insane; incensed; irate; mad; maddened; maniacal; murderous; possessed; rabid; raging; ranting; raving; savage; seething; wild; wrathful.*

> She always wanted to get to the game in time to hear the National Anthem, and she'd get mad as a hornet at Irv when he'd insist they leave early to beat the bridge traffic if the game was in hand one way or the other.—Pam Houston, *Sight Hound*

(as) mad as a March hare ∎ An insipid simile. *batty; cracked; crazy; daft; demented; deranged; fey; foolish; goofy; insane; lunatic; mad; maniacal; neurotic; nuts; nutty; psychotic; raving; silly; squirrelly; touched; unbalanced; unhinged; unsound; wacky; zany.*

(as) mad as a wet hen ∎ An insipid simile. *angry; berserk; convulsive; crazed; delirious; demented; demoniac; deranged; enraged; feral; ferocious; fierce; frantic; frenzied; fuming; furious; hysterical; infuriated; in hysterics; insane; incensed; irate; mad; maddened; maniacal; murderous; possessed; rabid; raging; ranting; raving; savage; seething; wild; wrathful.*

(he) made (me) an offer (I) couldn't refuse ∎ An infantile phrase. • We'd still be here today if Bally's hadn't *made us an offer we couldn't refuse.*

(you) made my day ∎ A plebeian sentiment. Often a response to being complimented, *you made my day* appeals to the mass of people who rely on others for their opinion of themselves.

And if they embrace others' approval, so they bow to their criticism.

made of money ∎ A moribund metaphor. *affluent; moneyed; opulent; prosperous; rich; successful; wealthy; well-off; well-to-do.*

magic bullet ∎ A moribund metaphor. *answer; solution.*

major ∎ An overworked word. For example: *major blow; major breakthrough; major commitment; major concern; major consideration; major defeat; major disaster; major new writer; major opportunity; major player; major ramifications; major road block; major setback; major thrust.*

make a clean breast of ∎ A moribund metaphor. *acknowledge; admit; affirm; allow; avow; concede; confess; disclose; divulge; expose; grant; own; reveal; tell; uncover; unearth; unveil.*

make a concerted effort ∎ A wretched redundancy. *aim; attempt; endeavor; essay; labor; moil; seek; strive; toil; try; undertake; venture; work.* • True change will come only when those in power *make a concerted effort* to promote large numbers of women and blacks to high-status jobs. REPLACE WITH *try.*

make a conscious attempt (effort) ∎ A wretched redundancy. *aim; attempt; endeavor; essay; labor; moil; seek; strive; toil; try; undertake; venture; work.* • We *made a conscious effort* not to do what most companies do. REPLACE WITH *strived.* • Wash your hands and *make conscious attempts* not to touch your face, nose, and eyes. REPLACE WITH *try.*

make a conscious choice (decision) ∎ A wretched redundancy. *Make a conscious choice* means no more than *choose,* and *make a conscious decision* no more than *decide.* Of course, this phrase suggests that those who use it may not otherwise be conscious of what they choose or decide, or even, it could be, do or say. • We *made a conscious decision* that this sort of legal terrorism would not affect the way we operate. REPLACE WITH *decided.* • They *made a conscious choice* not to have any bedroom scenes in this movie. REPLACE WITH *chose.* SEE ALSO **make an informed choice (decision).**

make a decision ∎ A wretched redundancy. *conclude; decide; determine; resolve.* • It's difficult to *make a decision* at this time. REPLACE WITH *decide.* • If he *made a decision* not to use protection, he should *make a decision* to support the child. REPLACE WITH *resolved* and *resolve.*

make a determination ∎ A wretched redundancy. *conclude; decide; determine; resolve.* • We want the SJC to look at it and *make a determination* to clearly state what is permissible and impermissible. REPLACE

WITH *determine.*

make a difference (about; on) ▮ A
suspect superlative. Many of us speak of
making a difference, some of us strive to
make a difference, but few of us—despite
the popularity of the phrase—succeed in
making a difference. 1. *be climacteric; be
consequential; be considerable; be critical; be
crucial; be effective; be effectual; be helpful;
be important; be significant; be useful; be
vital; count; matter.* 2. *act on; affect; bear
on; influence; sway; work on.* 3. *aid; assist;
help.* • She is part of a great tradition in
U.S. society, in which ordinary individuals
voice their concerns in order to *make a
difference about* issues that matter to them.
REPLACE WITH *influence.* • You need to
have a sense of humor and to recognize
that there's hope, not only despair, in the
world—and you need to know that you
can *make a difference.* REPLACE WITH *be
helpful.* • Your answers are important, and
they do *make a difference.* REPLACE WITH
matter.

make a federal case out of ▮ A moribund
metaphor. *elaborate; embellish; embroider;
enhance; enlarge; exaggerate; hyperbolize;
inflate; magnify; overdo; overreact;
overstress; overstate; strain; stretch.*

make a getaway ▮ A moribund metaphor.
*abscond; clear out; decamp; depart; desert;
disappear; escape; exit; flee; fly; go; go away;
leave; move on; part; pull out; quit; retire;
retreat; run away; take flight; take off;
vacate; vanish; withdraw.*

make a monkey out of ▮ A moribund
metaphor. *abase; chasten; debase; degrade;
demean; deride; disgrace; dishonor; dupe;
embarrass; humble; humiliate; mock;
mortify; ridicule; shame.*

> You make a monkey out of one of them and
> he jumps on your back and stays there for
> life, but let one make a monkey out of you
> and all you can do is kill him or disappear.—
> Flannery O'Connor, *Everything That Rises
> Must Converge*

make a mountain out of a molehill ▮
A moribund metaphor. *elaborate; embellish;
embroider; enhance; enlarge; exaggerate;
hyperbolize; inflate; magnify; overdo;
overreact; overstress; overstate; strain;
stretch.*

make an informed choice (decision) ▮
A wretched redundancy. *choose; decide.* SEE
ALSO **make a conscious choice (decision).**

make a pig of (myself) ▮ A moribund
metaphor. *cloy; cram; glut; gorge; overdo;
overeat; overfeed; overindulge; sate; satiate;
stuff; surfeit.*

make a quick exit ▮ A moribund metaphor.
*abscond; clear out; decamp; depart; desert;
disappear; escape; exit; flee; fly; go; go away;
leave; move on; part; pull out; quit; retire;*
*retreat; run away; take flight; take off;
vacate; vanish; withdraw.*

make a silk purse out of a sow's ear ▮
A moribund metaphor.

make (raise) a stink ▮ A moribund
metaphor. *bellow; bemoan; bluster; carp;
clamor; complain; criticize; explode;
fulminate; fume; gripe; grouse; grumble;
holler; howl; lament; moan; object; protest;
rage; rant; rave; roar; scream; shout; storm;
thunder; vociferate; yell; whine.*

> What did trouble him was that he might
> not lie enough or in the right way to suit
> Washington, and that some eager beaver, or
> numbskull, or stooge might raise a stink that
> would cost Benny his job.—Patricia Highsmith,
> *Tales of Natural and Unnatural Catastrophes*

make (my) blood boil ▮ A moribund
metaphor. *acerbate; anger; annoy; bother;
bristle; chafe; enrage; incense; inflame;
infuriate; irk; irritate; madden; miff;
provoke; rile; roil; vex.*

make (both) ends meet ▮ A moribund
metaphor. *economize; endure; exist; live;
manage; subsist; survive.* • Older people are
having a tough enough time trying to *make
ends meet.* REPLACE WITH *survive.*

make eyes at ▮ A moribund metaphor. *flirt.*

make false statements ▮ A wretched
redundancy. *lie.* • The indictment alleges
that he *made false statements* to the FEC
and obstructed proceedings. REPLACE
WITH *lied.*

make (my) flesh creep ▮ A moribund
metaphor. *alarm; appall; disgust; frighten;
horrify; nauseate; panic; repel; repulse;
revolt; scare; shock; sicken; startle; terrify.*

make (my) hair stand on end ▮ A
moribund metaphor. *alarm; appall; disgust;
frighten; horrify; nauseate; panic; repel;
repulse; revolt; scare; shock; sicken; startle;
terrify.*

make hay while the sun shines ▮ A
moribund metaphor. *capitalize on; exploit; take
advantage.*

make heads or tails of ▮ A moribund
metaphor. *appreciate; apprehend;
comprehend; discern; fathom; grasp;
know; make sense of; perceive; realize;
recognize; see; understand.* • His failures
in punctuation make it almost impossible
to *make heads or tails of* his convoluted
sentences. REPLACE WITH *understand.*

make it big ▮ A moribund metaphor. *prevail;
succeed; triumph; win.*

make mincemeat (out) of ▮ A moribund
metaphor. *crush; defeat; demolish; destroy;
devastate; hammer; obliterate; overpower;
overwhelm; rack; ravage; rout; ruin; shatter;
slaughter; smash; thrash; undo; wrack;
wreck.*

make no bones (about it)

make no bones (about it) ∎ A moribund metaphor. *avidly; eagerly; enthusiastically; heartily; promptly; readily; unconditionally; unhesitatingly; unreservedly; unwaveringly; wholeheartedly.*

> She made no bones about accepting her client's invitation to dine, and showed no surprise when he confidentially murmured that he had a little proposition to put before her.—Dorothy L. Sayers, *Strong Poison*

make no mistake (about it) ∎ An ineffectual phrase. • *Make no mistake about it*, if we were to leave, other nations would leave, too, and chaos would resume. • *Make no mistake*, Jacksonville is not a bad team. • *Make no mistake about it*, this impeachment issue has become a battle for who controls the Republican party. SEE ALSO **let there be no mistake**.

make (raise) objection ∎ A moribund metaphor. *bemoan; carp; complain; gripe; grouse; grumble; lament; moan; object; protest; whine.*

make (yourself) scarce ∎ An infantile phrase. *abscond; clear out; decamp; depart; desert; disappear; escape; exit; flee; fly; go; go away; leave; move on; part; pull out; quit; retire; retreat; run away; take flight; take off; vacate; vanish; withdraw.*

make (me) see red ∎ A moribund metaphor. *acerbate; anger; annoy; bother; bristle; chafe; enrage; incense; inflame; infuriate; irk; irritate; madden; miff; provoke; rile; roil; vex.*

(try to) make the best (most) of it ∎ A popular prescription.

make the feathers (fur) fly ∎ A moribund metaphor. *battle; brawl; clash; fight; grapple; jostle; make war; scuffle; skirmish; tussle; war; wrestle; wrangle.*

> When the flying fur from the divorce settled, I found myself with a grown daughter, a full-time university job (after years of part-time teaching), a modest securities portfolio, and an entire future to invent.—Frances Mayes, *Under the Tuscan Sun*

make the grade ∎ A moribund metaphor. 1. *accomplish; achieve; make good; succeed.* 2. *be able; be accomplished; be adept; be adequate; be capable; be competent; be deft; be equal to; be equipped; be fitted; be proficient; be qualified; be skilled; be skillful; be suited; measure up.*

make up (his) mind ∎ A wretched redundancy. *choose; conclude; decide; determine; pick; resolve; select; settle.*

make tracks ∎ A moribund metaphor. *abscond; clear out; decamp; depart; desert; disappear; escape; exit; flee; fly; go; go away; leave; move on; part; pull out; quit; retire; retreat; run away; take flight; take off; vacate; vanish; withdraw.*

make waves ∎ A moribund metaphor. *agitate; disrupt; disturb; perturb; rattle; ruffle; shake up; stir up; unsettle.*

many of my closest friends (are) ∎ A plebeian sentiment. • *Many of my closest friends* are Italian.

marching orders ∎ A moribund metaphor.

mass exodus ∎ A wretched redundancy. *exodus.*

maybe, maybe not ∎ An infantile phrase.

maybe yes, maybe no ∎ An infantile phrase.

may (might) possibly ∎ A wretched redundancy. *may (might).* • *I might possibly* be there when you are. DELETE *possibly.*

mea culpa ∎ A foreign phrase.

meal ticket ∎ A moribund metaphor.

meaningful ∎ An overworked word. So elusive is meaning in our lives that we think we must modify scores of words with the word *meaningful.* Though we may struggle not to believe that emptiness is all, attaching *meaningful* to words like *action, change, dialogue, discussion, experience* is no sound solution. *Meaningful* describes that which has meaning, and derides that which has none. SEE ALSO **significant**.

(...) means never having to say you're sorry ∎ An infantile phrase.

meat and potatoes ∎ A moribund metaphor. *basal; basic; elementary; essential; fundamental; primary; rudimentary.*

(as) meek as a lamb ∎ An insipid simile. *accepting; accommodating; acquiescent; complacent; complaisant; compliant; cowed; deferential; docile; dutiful; easy; forbearing; gentle; humble; long-suffering; meek; mild; obedient; passive; patient; prostrate; quiet; reserved; resigned; stoical; submissive; subservient; timid; tolerant; tractable; unassuming; uncomplaining; yielding.*

(as) meek as Moses ∎ An insipid simile. *accepting; accommodating; acquiescent; complacent; complaisant; compliant; cowed; deferential; docile; dutiful; easy; forbearing; gentle; humble; long-suffering; meek; mild; obedient; passive; patient; prostrate; quiet; reserved; resigned; stoical; submissive; subservient; timid; tolerant; tractable; unassuming; uncomplaining; yielding.*

> Having embarrassed himself, he went in, meek as Moses, to the Judge.—Carson McCullers, *Clock Without Hands*

meet (him) halfway ∎ A moribund metaphor. *compromise.*

meeting of (the) minds ∎ A moribund metaphor. *accord; accordance; agreement; common view; compatibility; concord; concordance; concurrence; consensus;*

harmony; unanimity; understanding; unison; unity. • We're talking to him to see if we can have *meeting of minds.* REPLACE WITH *agreement.*

meet (his) Waterloo ∎ A moribund metaphor. *be beaten; be conquered; be crushed; be defeated; be outdone; be overcome; be overpowered; be overwhelmed; be quelled; be routed; be trounced; be vanquished.*

(go to) meet your maker ∎ A moribund metaphor. *die; expire.*

me, myself, and I ∎ An infantile phrase.

mend fences ∎ A moribund metaphor. *reconcile.* • Please continue to tell your readers it's never too late to try to *mend those fences.* REPLACE WITH *reconcile.*

meteoric rise ∎ An inescapable pair. • His approach has struck a chord with the American people—hence his unprecedented and *meteoric rise* to prominence.

Mickey-Mouse ∎ An infantile phrase. *inferior; poor; second-class; second-rate; shoddy; subordinate; substandard.*

middle-of-the-road ∎ A moribund metaphor. **1.** *average; common; conservative; conventional; everyday; mediocre; middling; normal; ordinary; quotidian; second-rate; standard; traditional; typical; uneventful; unexceptional; unremarkable; usual.* **2.** *careful; cautious; circumspect; prudent; safe; wary.*

might makes right ∎ A popular prescription.

milk the last drop out of ∎ A moribund metaphor.

millstone around (my) neck ∎ A moribund metaphor. *burden; duty; encumbrance; hardship; hindrance; impediment; obligation; obstacle; obstruction; onus; responsibility.*

mind like a steel trap ∎ An insipid simile. *adroit; astute; bright; brilliant; clever; discerning; enlightened; insightful; intelligent; judicious; keen; knowledgeable; learned; logical; luminous; perceptive; perspicacious; quick; rational; reasonable; sagacious; sage; sapient; sensible; sharp; shrewd; smart; sound; understanding; wise.*

mind (your) P's and Q's ∎ A moribund metaphor. *be accurate; be careful; be exact; be meticulous; be particular; be precise.*

mindset ∎ An overworked word. *attitude; bent; bias; cast; disposition; habit; inclination; leaning; outlook; penchant; perspective; point of view; position; predilection; predisposition; prejudice; proclivity; slant; stand; standpoint; temperament; tendency; view; viewpoint; way of thinking.* • You don't have these huge organizations built on patronage anymore, but the *mindset* is still there. REPLACE WITH *predisposition.* • What we are doing is changing people's *mindset.* REPLACE WITH *views.* • The report is critical of the *mindset* of those in charge of the pipeline. REPLACE WITH *attitude.*

mind the store ∎ A moribund metaphor.

mirabile dictu ∎ A foreign phrase.

miracle of miracles ∎ An infantile phrase. *astonishingly; astoundingly; breathtakingly; extraordinarily; fabulously; fantastically; marvelously; miraculously; overwhelmingly; prodigiously; sensationally; spectacularly; wonderfully; wondrously.* • *Miracle of miracles,* it works because of two things: Keanu Reeves and theology. REPLACE WITH *Miraculously.* • *Miracle of miracles,* in our second at-bat, with the brace strapped on tight, we homered against the Mets. REPLACE WITH *Amazingly.* • I was cleaning the house the other day, and, *miracle of miracles,* my kids were actually helping. REPLACE WITH *astonishingly.*

> And maybe if she closed her eyes she could see a time—miracle of miracles—when Helen Bober was enrolled here, not just a stranger on the run, pecking at a course or two at night, and tomorrow morning back at Levenspiel's Louisville Panties and Bras.—Bernard Malamud, *The Assistant*

misery loves company ∎ A popular prescription.

(didn't) miss a beat ∎ A moribund metaphor. *be indecisive; be uncertain; falter; hesitate; vacillate; waver.*

> Bess didn't miss a beat. She looked up, looked Christine straight in the eye and said, "Chris, don't go cutting the fool."—Nancy Bartholomew, *Stand by Your Man*

mission accomplished ∎ An infantile phrase.

miss the boat ∎ A moribund metaphor. **1.** *be deprived of; forego; forfeit; give up; lose out; miss out; sacrifice; surrender.* **2.** *erroneous; false; inaccurate; incorrect; mistaken; misunderstand; not understand; wrong.* • If we define success in terms of material things, we *miss the boat.* REPLACE WITH *lose out.* • One way to do that in a reply brief is to acknowledge your adversary's opposition papers explicitly, but insist that your opponent is still *missing the boat.* REPLACE WITH *wrong.*

mix and mingle ∎ An inescapable pair. *associate; consort; hobnob; fraternize; keep company; mingle; mix; socialize.*

mixed bag ∎ A moribund metaphor.

> Usually he was entertained by Tokyo Station, the mixed bag of commuters in three-piece suits and farmers in cone-shaped hats of straw.—Martin Cruz Smith, *December 6*

moan and groan ∎ An inescapable pair. *bawl; bemoan; bewail; blubber; cry; groan;*

moan; snivel; sob; wail; weep; whimper; whine.

modus operandi ∎ A foreign phrase.

modus vivendi ∎ A foreign phrase.

Monday morning quarterback(ing) ∎ A moribund metaphor.

money can't buy everything ∎ A popular prescription.

(like) money in the bank ∎ An insipid simile. *absolute; assured; certain; definite; guaranteed; sure; sure-fire.*

money is the root of all evil ∎ A popular prescription.

money (making) machine ∎ A moribund metaphor.

money talks ∎ A moribund metaphor.

money to burn ∎ A moribund metaphor.

monkey on (my) back ∎ A moribund metaphor. 1. *addiction; fixation; habit; obsession.* 2. *complication; difficulty; dilemma; mess; muddle; ordeal; pickle; plight; predicament; problem; quandary; trial; trouble.*

monkey see, monkey do ∎ An infantile phrase.

mop (wipe) the floor with ∎ A moribund metaphor. 1. *assail; assault; attack; batter; beat; cudgel; flagellate; flog; hit; lambaste; lash; lick; mangle; pound; pummel; strike; thrash; trample; trounce.* 2. *beat; conquer; crush; defeat; outdo; overcome; overpower; overwhelm; prevail; quell; rout; subdue; succeed; triumph; trounce; vanquish; win.*
• Amazon.com has *mopped the floor with* barnesandnoble.com. REPLACE WITH *routed.*

more is better ∎ A quack equation.

more preferable ∎ A wretched redundancy. *preferable.* • While the patient is still at risk to hemorrhage during that time, waiting may be *more preferable* to surgery. DELETE *more.*

more than (I) bargained for ∎ A torpid term.

more ... than you could shake a stick at ∎ A moribund metaphor. *countless; dozens of; hundreds of; incalculable; inestimable; innumerable; many; numerous; scores of; thousands of; untold.* • He had *more* women in his life *than you could shake a stick at.* REPLACE WITH *untold.*

more times than I care to admit ∎ A torpid term.

> I've been married twice, done in more times than I care to admit.—Sue Grafton, *E Is for Evidence*

most assuredly ∎ An infantile phrase.

assuredly; certainly; decidedly; definitely; positively; surely; undoubtedly; unequivocally; unhesitatingly; unquestionably. • The customer will *most assuredly* notify the maitre d' if he or she is expecting someone else. REPLACE WITH *certainly.* SEE ALSO **100 (110) percent; absolutely; definitely; most (very) definitely.**

most (very) definitely ∎ An infantile phrase. It is irredeemably dimwitted to say *most definitely* when the more moderate, indeed, the more civilized *certainly, I (am), indeed; just so, quite right, surely, that's right,* or *yes* will do. • And you feel your daughter was unjustly treated?
Most definitely. REPLACE WITH *I do.*
• So whoever you meet has to accommodate your needs?
Very definitely. REPLACE WITH *Yes.*
• So when you're sitting around, you are the only white person there?
Most definitely. REPLACE WITH *Just so.*
As a synonym for words like *assuredly; certainly; decidedly; definitely; positively; surely; undoubtedly; unequivocally; unhesitatingly; unquestionably;* the phrase *most definitely* is ridiculously redundant.
• Getting this magazine out is a labor of love, but it is *most definitely* labor. REPLACE WITH *decidedly.* • Colder weather is *most definitely* on the way. REPLACE WITH *unquestionably.*
• Would you do it again?
Most definitely. REPLACE WITH *Unhesitatingly.* SEE ALSO **100 (110) percent; absolutely; definitely; most assuredly.**

motivating force ∎ A wretched redundancy. *drive; energy; force; impetus; motivation; power.*

motley crew ∎ An inescapable pair.

move forward ∎ A TOP-TWENTY DIMWITTICISM. A torpid term. *advance; continue; develop; go on; grow; happen; improve; increase; make headway; make progress; move on; occur; proceed; progress; take place.*
Politicos and spokespeople endlessly spout fuzzy phrases like *move forward* and *go forward* and *proceed forward* and even *move forward in the right direction.* Pellucid words like *advance, further, improve, proceed,* and *progress* seem to completely elude their intellects. These useless expressions are spoken and written by people who seem unable to remember that the English language has both a present and a future tense. *Going forward, moving forward,* and the like are used instead of, or along with, present- or future-tense expressions. This may mean that, before long, people will not easily be able to distinguish between the present and the future, or that they may not be able to think in terms of the future. Already, there is evidence of this, for many of us are without imagination and foresight.
• I believe that it was contact with the United States that has *moved* the

process of economic reform *forward*, and hopefully some day will *move* the process of political reform *forward*. REPLACE WITH *advanced* and *advance*. • What we need is to empower the city in order to *move* it *forward*. REPLACE WITH *improve*. • As the company *moves forward*, it's very important that we hold on to those values. REPLACE WITH *grows*. • Serious hurdles remain to make this workable and complete, but this agreement today gives us a way to *move forward*. REPLACE WITH *proceed*. • Even if Congress decides they want to play politics this year, we can *move forward and* make progress. DELETE *move forward and*. • Using these components as our groundwork, we can now *move forward and* examine how to apply them in your Web application. DELETE *move forward and*.

And here is a truly ludicrous example: • As the year *moves forward*, we will see more *forward movement* in global and domestic environmental issues. REPLACE WITH *advances* and *progress*. SEE ALSO **a step forward; a step (forward) in the right direction; go forward; move (forward) in the right direction; proceed forward**.

move heaven and earth ∎ A moribund metaphor. *aim; attempt; endeavor; essay; exert; exhaust; labor; moil; strain; strive; struggle; toil; try hard; undertake; work at.*

> Even then I begged my grandfather to see that my testimony was published; but the Michaelises also belong to those old families that move heaven and earth to keep their names out of the papers.—Thornton Wilder, *Theophilus North*

move (forward) in the direction (of) -ing ∎ A torpid term. *advance; continue; develop; go on; grow; happen; improve; increase; make headway; make progress; move on; occur; proceed; progress; take place.* • We've decided to *move in the direction of helping* the claimants make an educated choice. REPLACE WITH *help*.

move (forward) in the right direction ∎ A torpid term. *advance; continue; develop; go on; grow; happen; improve; increase; make headway; make progress; move on; occur; proceed; progress; take place.*

Only the least eloquent speakers use *move forward* or *move forward in the right direction*. These expressions are wholly unable to move us. They dull our minds and immobilize our actions.

• I know the company will resolve its problems and *move forward in the right direction*. REPLACE WITH *grow*. • All the numbers are looking pretty good and *moving in the right direction*. REPLACE WITH *increasing*. • We are *moving in the right direction*, and I want to keep *moving in the right direction*. REPLACE WITH *making progress* and *making progress*.

Often, formulaic phrases like *move in the right direction* are simply bluster, as in this nearly nonsensical sentence: • I'm ready, willing, and able to bring people together and get everybody *moving in the right direction forward*.

Like slander and excessive swearing, *move (forward) in the right direction* exposes a person of questionable character and certain inarticulacy. SEE ALSO **a step forward; a step (forward) in the right direction; go forward; move forward; proceed forward**.

move it or lose it ∎ An infantile phrase.

move mountains ∎ A moribund metaphor. *aim; attempt; endeavor; essay; exert; exhaust; labor; moil; strain; strive; struggle; toil; try hard; undertake; work at.*

mover and shaker ∎ A moribund metaphor. 1. *administrator; boss; brass; chief; commander; director; executive; foreman; head; headman; leader; manager; master; (high) muckamuck; officer; official; overseer; president; principal; superintendent; supervisor.* 2. *aristocrat; dignitary; eminence; lord; luminary; magnate; mogul; notable; patrician; personage; ruler; sovereign; worthy.*

move the ball forward ∎ A moribund metaphor. *advance; further; proceed; progress.*

moving target ∎ A moribund metaphor.

(make) much ado about nothing ∎ An infantile phrase. *elaborate; embellish; embroider; enhance; enlarge; exaggerate; hyperbolize; inflate; magnify; overdo; overestimate; overrate; overreact; overstress; overstate; strain; stretch.* • If you think this discussion about apostrophes is *much ado about nothing*, tell that to the Apostrophe Protection Society. REPLACE WITH *overstated*.

muck and mire ∎ An inescapable pair.

muddy the waters ∎ A moribund metaphor. *becloud; blur; complicate; confuse; muddy; obscure.*

> Still, Swenson can't muddy the waters by asking him to look at two books.—Francine Prose, *Blue Angel*

muscle in on ∎ A moribund metaphor. *break in; encroach; infiltrate; intrude; penetrate; pierce.*

music to (my) ears ∎ A moribund metaphor.

(a) must have ∎ An infantile phrase. *compulsory; critical; essential; imperative; important; indispensable; mandatory; necessary; needed; obligatory; required; requisite; vital.* • His book is a student's friend, a professional's ally, a *must-have* reference. REPLACE WITH *indispensable*. • No application has yet emerged to make a miniaturized computer a *must-have*. REPLACE WITH *essential*. • Microsoft

(a) must see

Services for NetWare is *a must-have* for any administrator who is managing a network that includes both types of users. REPLACE WITH *vital*. • This software is *a must have* in any web marketing company's toolbox. REPLACE WITH *mandatory*. SEE ALSO **a (absolute) must**; **(a) must (miss)**; **(a) must see**; **a (definite) plus**.

(a) must see ∎ An infantile phrase. 1. *compulsory; critical; essential; imperative; important; indispensable; mandatory; necessary; needed; obligatory; required; requisite; vital*. 2. *compelling; powerful*. • This is *must-see* TV. REPLACE WITH *compelling*. • It is the *must-see* event of the season. REPLACE WITH *obligatory*. SEE ALSO **a (absolute) must**; **(a) must (miss)**; **(a) must have**; **a (definite) plus**.

mutual admiration society ∎ An infantile phrase. *affinity with*.

mutually exclusive ∎ An inescapable pair. A phrase from the thoughtless person's formulary, *mutually exclusive* reduces the readability of any sentence in which it is used. *Mutually exclusive* screams a fallow imagination, a barren intellect, a cowering spirit.
• It has managed to prove that Islam and democracy are not *mutually exclusive*.
• Being selective and being aggressive are not *mutually exclusive*. • The two wildly different stories that jurors will be presented with in some ways are not *mutually exclusive*. • As Ferrari, Pegoretti and Cipollini all prove, a powerful engine and a sexy profile are not *mutually exclusive*.

my way or the highway ∎ A moribund metaphor. *immovable; inflexible; intractable; intransigent; obdurate; rigid; uncompromising; unbending; unmalleable; unyielding*. • We can't engage in *my way or the highway* attitudes. REPLACE WITH *intransigent*. • Coughlin is that old school, Bill Parcells, *my way or the highway* type. He won't bend at all. REPLACE WITH *intractable*.

Nn

nagging doubts ∎ An inescapable pair.

nail (their) colors (flag) to the mast ∎ A moribund metaphor.

(like) nailing jelly to a tree (the wall) ∎ An insipid simile. *barren; bootless; effete; feckless; feeble; fruitless; futile; impotent; inadequate; inconsequential; inconsiderable; ineffective; ineffectual; infertile; insignificant; inutile; meaningless; meritless; nugatory; null; of no value; pointless; powerless; profitless; sterile; trifling; trivial; unavailing; unimportant; unproductive; unprofitable; unserviceable; unworthy; useless; vain; valueless; weak; worthless.*

nail (him) to the wall ∎ A moribund metaphor. 1. *admonish; anathematize; berate; blame; castigate; censure; chastise; chide; condemn; criticize; curse; decry; denounce; execrate; imprecate; inculpate; indict; rebuke; reprimand; reproach; reprove; scold; upbraid.* 2. *beat; better; conquer; defeat; exceed; excel; outclass; outdo; outflank; outmaneuver; outperform; outplay; overcome; overpower; prevail; rout; succeed; surpass; top; triumph; trounce; vanquish; whip; win.*

> But if he was a bad guy, I'd nail him to the wall.—Jane Heller, *Lucky Stars*

(as) naked as a jaybird ∎ An insipid simile. *bare; disrobed; naked; nude; stripped; unclothed; uncovered; undressed.*

(my) name is mud ∎ A moribund metaphor.

name of the game ∎ A moribund metaphor. *basis; center; core; crux; essence; gist; heart; kernel; pith; substance.*

(as) narrow as an arrow ∎ An insipid simile. *asthenic; attenuated; bony; cachectic; emaciated; gaunt; lank; lanky; lean; narrow; rail-thin; scraggy; scrawny; skeletal; skinny; slender; slight; slim; spare; spindly; svelte; sylphid; thin; trim; wispy.*

national pastime ∎ A moribund metaphor. *baseball.*

neat and tidy ∎ An inescapable pair. *neat; orderly; tidy.*

(as) neat as a pin ∎ An insipid simile. *methodical; neat; ordered; orderly; organized; systematic; tidy; trim; well-organized.*

necessary evil ∎ A torpid term. • Their staunch refusal to concede that new taxes are, at the least, a *necessary evil*, could shut them out of the budget process altogether.

(a) necessary prerequisite ∎ A wretched redundancy. *necessary; prerequisite.* • An understanding of expressions is *a necessary prerequisite* to learning any command language. DELETE *necessary.* • The transfer of information is *a necessary prerequisite* for the effective transfer of technology. DELETE *a prerequisite.*

necessary requirement ∎ A wretched redundancy. *necessary; requirement.* • Because of the labor problems that we have been having with the police patrolmen's union, we will be unable to meet the *necessary requirements* by the deadline. DELETE *necessary.*

necessity is the mother of invention ∎ A popular prescription.

neck and neck ∎ A moribund metaphor. *abreast; close; equal; tied.*

> Up till a moment ago we were neck and neck but then my peel broke and I had to refind my purchase.—Janni Visman, *Yellow*

(our) neck of the woods ∎ A moribund metaphor. *area; community; country; county; district; domain; environment; environs; locale; locality; milieu; neighborhood; part; region; section; sector; surroundings; territory; vicinity; zone.*

> Now, they don't read a lot of books in this neck of the woods.—Will Ferguson, *Happiness*

need(s) and want(s) ∎ An inescapable pair.

negative (*n*) ∎ A torpid term. *burden; deterrence; deterrent; disadvantage; drawback; encumbrance; frailty; hardship; hindrance; liability; limitation; obstacle; onus; shortcoming; weakness.* • I don't see how it's a *negative* to the United States to be supporting a democratic government. REPLACE WITH *disadvantage.* SEE ALSO **positive**.

negative effect (impact) ∎ A torpid term. SEE ALSO **positive effect (impact)**. • The committee is concerned with both short-term and long-term *negative effects*. REPLACE WITH *disruptions.* • Imaging helps to overcome the *negative effects* produced by generalizations. REPLACE WITH *inaccuracies.*

negative feelings ∎ A torpid term. This expression tells us how little we listen to how we feel. In our quest for speed and efficiency, we have forfeited our feelings.

The niceties of emotion—*anger, animosity, anxiety, depression, despair, displeasure, disquiet, distrust, fear, frustration, fury, gloom, grief, guilt, hatred, hopelessness, hostility, ill will, insecurity, jealousy, malice, melancholy, rage, resentment, sadness, shame, sorrow, stress,* and so on—have been sacrificed to a pointless proficiency. • It was reported that IAM headquarters failed to renew a $1 million bond that matured in June, due to their *negative feelings* toward El Al's actions. REPLACE WITH *displeasure.* • *Negative feelings* can trigger a cascade of stress hormones that accelerate the heart rate, shut down the immune system, and encourage blood clotting. REPLACE WITH *Resentment or anger.* • But *those negative feelings* can work against you if they render you unwilling or unable to act the next time you face a major decision. REPLACE WITH *anger and embarrassment.* • Though little is known about the effects of negative emotions on your heart, there are a few theories about why *negative feelings* can do so much damage. SEE ALSO **positive feelings**.

neither a borrower nor a lender be ∎ A popular prescription.

neither fish nor fowl ∎ A moribund metaphor. *indefinite; indeterminate; indistinct; undefined; undetermined.*

neither here nor there ∎ A moribund metaphor. *extraneous; immaterial; impertinent; inapplicable; irrelevant.*

neither one ∎ A wretched redundancy. *neither.* • *Neither one* of these choices is exclusive of the other. DELETE *one.* SEE ALSO **each one; either one**.

ne plus ultra ∎ A foreign phrase.

nerves of steel ∎ A moribund metaphor. *bold; brave; courageous; dauntless; fearless; intrepid; stouthearted; unafraid.*

nest egg ∎ A moribund metaphor. *assets; finances; funds; resources; savings.*

never (not) in a million years ∎ An infantile phrase. *at no time; by no means; in no way; never; no; not; not at all; not ever; not in any way; not in the least.* • I would never have imagined—*not in a million years*—feeling compelled to come to the defense of that grande dame of the administration, the president's wife. DELETE *not in a million years.*

never in my wildest dreams ∎ An infantile phrase. *at no time; by no means; in no way; never; no; not; not at all; not ever; not in any way; not in the least.* • *Never in my wildest dreams* did I imagine that Pinochet would be arrested here in London. DELETE *in my wildest dreams.*

never say die ∎ A popular prescription.

never say never ∎ A popular prescription.

new and improved ∎ A suspect superlative.

new and innovative ∎ An inescapable pair. *innovative; new.* • We used some *new and innovative* manufacturing techniques. REPLACE WITH *innovative* or *new.*

new deck (pack) of cards ∎ A moribund metaphor.

(the) new kid on the block ∎ A moribund metaphor. • Being *the new kid on the block* does not excuse them from their responsibilities.

(like) new wine in old bottles ∎ An insipid simile.

nice ∎ An overworked word. *affable; agreeable; amiable; amicable; companionable; compassionate; congenial; cordial; delightful; friendly; genial; good; good-hearted; good-natured; humane; kind; kind-hearted; likable; neighborly; personable; pleasant; pleasing; sociable; tender; tolerant.*

The word *nice* we might reserve for its less well-known definitions of *fastidious* and *subtle.*

(as) nice as pie ∎ An insipid simile. *affable; agreeable; amiable; amicable; companionable; compassionate; congenial; cordial; delightful; friendly; genial; good; good-hearted; good-natured; humane; kind; kind-hearted; likable; neighborly; personable; pleasant; pleasing; sociable; tender; tolerant.*

> And then once more her eyes glaze, her body deadens, and she cries out again and again, 'Who are you? Who are you? Who are you?' and she is crying and this time I simply want to escape this strange circle, and I get up and hastily pull on my clothes, and the Conga all the time saying, as nice as pie, genuinely upset, 'But why? Why are you going?'—Richard Flanagan, *Gould's Book of Fish*

nice work if you can get it ∎ A plebeian sentiment.

nickel-and-dime ∎ A moribund metaphor. 1. *cheap; economical; inexpensive; low-cost; low-priced.* 2. *cheap; frugal; miserly; niggardly; parsimonious; stingy; thrifty.* 3. *inconsequential; insignificant; minor; negligible; paltry; petty; small; small-time; trifling; trivial; unimportant.* • The banks were shoveling money into every *nickel-and-dime* developer that walked in. REPLACE WITH *insignificant.*

nickel-and-dime (him) to death ∎ A moribund metaphor. • Many governors have begun to *nickel-and-dime taxpayers to death* with fees, fines, tolls, and excise taxes. SEE ALSO **to death**.

(like) night and day ∎ An insipid simile. *antipodal; antipodean; antithetical; contrary; converse; diametric; diametrical; different; inverse; opposite; reverse.*

nip and tuck ∎ A moribund metaphor.

nip (it) in the bud ∎ A moribund metaphor. *abort; annul; arrest; balk; block; cancel; check; contain; crush; derail; detain; end; extinguish; foil; frustrate; halt; hinder; impede; neutralize; nullify; obstruct; prevent; quash; quell; repress; restrain; retard; squash; squelch; squish; stall; stay; stifle; stop; subdue; suppress; terminate; thwart.* • Another reader in California has found a sure-fire method for *nipping travel stress in the bud.* REPLACE WITH *squelching travel stress.*

nipping at (your) heels ∎ A moribund metaphor.

> Then he ran off behind his brother, as if embarrassment were nipping at his heels.—Patricia Jones, *Red on a Rose*

no big deal ∎ An infantile phrase. *inappreciable; inconsequential; inconsiderable; insignificant; minor; negligible; niggling; nugatory; petty; trifling; trivial; unimportant; unsubstantial.*

nobody but nobody ∎ An infantile phrase. *nobody; nobody at all; none; no one; no one at all.*

nobody's perfect ∎ A popular prescription. SEE ALSO **(I'm) a perfectionist; I'm not perfect (you know).**

no easy task ∎ A torpid term. *arduous; backbreaking; burdensome; difficult; exhausting; fatiguing; hard; herculean; laborious; not easy; onerous; severe; strenuous; toilful; toilsome; tough; troublesome; trying; wearisome.* • Getting this place ready has been *no easy task.* REPLACE WITH *backbreaking.*

no great shakes ∎ A moribund metaphor. 1. *average; common; commonplace; customary; everyday; fair; mediocre; middling; normal; ordinary; passable; quotidian; regular; routine; standard; tolerable; typical; uneventful; unexceptional; unremarkable; usual.* 2. *inappreciable; inconsequential; inconsiderable; insignificant; minor; negligible; niggling; nugatory; petty; trifling; trivial; unimportant; unsubstantial.*

no guts, no glory ∎ A popular prescription.

no holds barred ∎ A moribund metaphor. *candidly; explicitly; openly; overtly; without restraint.*

no ifs, ands, ors, or buts ∎ An infantile phrase. SEE ALSO **period.**

no man is an island ∎ A popular prescription.

non compos mentis ∎ A foreign phrase. *batty; cracked; crazy; cretinous; daft; demented; deranged; insane; lunatic; mad; maniacal; neurotic; nuts; nutty; psychotic; raving; squirrelly; touched; unbalanced; unhinged; unsound.*

none of the above ∎ An infantile phrase. •

Do you want to talk to me or argue with me?
None of the above. REPLACE WITH *Neither.* SEE ALSO **all of the above.**

no news is good news ∎ A quack equation. • There is a new breed of progressive administrators who do not believe that *no news is good news.*

no offense (intended) ∎ An infantile phrase.

> And I say that with no offence to the good people of Sydney intended.—Nick Hornby, *A Long Way Down*

(every) nook and cranny ∎ A moribund metaphor. *complexities; details; fine points; intricacies; minutiae; niceties; particulars.* • There is lots of time in which to explore the *nooks and crannies* of virtually any topic on AM radio. REPLACE WITH *intricacies.*

no pain, no gain ∎ A popular prescription.

no picnic ∎ A moribund metaphor. 1. *arduous; backbreaking; burdensome; difficult; exhausting; fatiguing; hard; herculean; laborious; not easy; onerous; severe; strenuous; toilful; toilsome; tough; troublesome; trying; wearisome.* 2. *disagreeable; distasteful; objectionable; unlikable; unpleasant.*

no problem ∎ An infantile phrase. 1. *you're welcome.* 2. *not at all; not in the least.* 3. *my pleasure.* 4. *I'd be glad to; I'd be happy to.* 5. *it's O.K.; that's all right.* 6. *easy; easily; effortlessly; readily.* • Thanks very much.
No problem. REPLACE WITH *You're welcome.* • Can you do it?
No problem. REPLACE WITH *Easily.* SEE ALSO **common courtesy.**

no pun intended ∎ An infantile phrase.

north (of) ∎ A moribund metaphor. *above; beyond; more than; over; upwards (of).* • But the answer is *north of* 50,000 companies whose fortunes are pretty directly tied to the Big Three. REPLACE WITH *more than.* • This cartoon, which runs a shade *north of* twenty minutes, revolves around this tiny child angel. REPLACE WITH *over.*

nose out of joint ∎ A moribund metaphor. 1. *acerbated; angry; annoyed; bothered; cross; displeased; enraged; furious; grouchy; incensed; inflamed; infuriated; irate; irked; irritated; mad; miffed; peeved; provoked; riled; roiled; testy; upset; vexed.* 2. *covetous; desirous; envious; grudging; jealous; resentful.*

(it's) no skin off (my) nose ∎ A moribund metaphor.

no small feat (task) ∎ A torpid term. *arduous; backbreaking; burdensome; difficult; exhausting; fatiguing; hard; herculean; laborious; not easy; onerous;*

(I'm) no spring chicken

severe; strenuous; toilful; toilsome; tough; troublesome; trying; wearisome.

(I'm) no spring chicken ∎ A moribund metaphor. *aged; aging; ancient; antediluvian; antique; archaic; elderly; hoary; hoary-headed; old; patriarchal; prehistoric; seasoned; superannuated.*

no strings attached ∎ A moribund metaphor. *unconditionally; unreservedly.*

no sweat ∎ A moribund metaphor. *easily done; easy; effortless; elementary; facile; simple; simplicity itself; straightforward; uncomplex; uncomplicated.*

not a Chinaman's chance ∎ A moribund metaphor. 1. *doubtful; dubious; farfetched; implausible; improbable; remote; unlikely; unrealistic.* 2. *hopeless; impossible; impracticable; impractical; infeasible; unrealizable; unworkable.*

not a ghost of a chance ∎ A moribund metaphor. 1. *doubtful; dubious; farfetched; implausible; improbable; remote; unlikely; unrealistic.* 2. *hopeless; impossible; impracticable; impractical; infeasible; unrealizable; unworkable.*

not a hope in hell ∎ A moribund metaphor. 1. *doubtful; dubious; farfetched; implausible; improbable; remote; unlikely; unrealistic.* 2. *hopeless; impossible; impracticable; impractical; infeasible; unrealizable; unworkable.*

not all (what) (it's) cracked up to be ∎ A torpid term. *deficient; disappointing; discouraging; dissatisfying; inadequate; inapt; incapable; incompetent; ineffective; inferior; insufficient; lacking; unfit; unqualified; unsatisfactory; wanting.*

not a mean bone in (her) body ∎ A moribund metaphor. *affable; agreeable; amiable; amicable; compassionate; friendly; gentle; good-hearted; good-natured; humane; kind; kind-hearted; personable; pleasant; tender; tolerant.*

not a snowball's chance in hell ∎ A moribund metaphor. 1. *doubtful; dubious; farfetched; implausible; improbable; remote; unlikely; unrealistic.* 2. *hopeless; impossible; impracticable; impractical; infeasible; unrealizable; unworkable.*

not by a long shot ∎ A moribund metaphor. *at no time; by no means; in no way; never; no; not; not at all; not ever; not in any way; not in the least.*

notch in (his) belt ∎ A moribund metaphor. *accomplishment; achievement; attainment; success; triumph.*

I think he married her to put a notch in his belt. I mean, an enemy who's sleeping with your daughter has a certain advantage over you.—Rachel Kushner, *Telex from Cuba*

not for all the tea in China ∎ A moribund

metaphor. *at no time; by no means; in no way; never; no; not; not at all; not ever; not in any way; not in the least.*

not for anything in the world ∎ A moribund metaphor. *at no time; by no means; in no way; never; no; not; not at all; not ever; not in any way; not in the least.*

not for love or money ∎ A moribund metaphor. *at no time; by no means; in no way; never; no; not; not at all; not ever; not in any way; not in the least.*

not for the world ∎ A moribund metaphor. *at no time; by no means; in no way; never; no; not; not at all; not ever; not in any way; not in the least.*

nothing could be further from the truth ∎ A torpid term. 1. *by no means; in no way; never; no; not; not at all; not ever; nothing of the sort; not in any way; not in the least.* 2. *be amiss; be astray; be deceived; be deluded; be erring; be erroneous; be fallacious; be false; be faulty; be inaccurate; be incorrect; be in error; be misguided; be misinformed; be mislead; be mistaken; be not correct; be not right; be untrue; be wrong.*

You would think that anyone who uses this phrase—anyone, that is, whose words or actions were being questioned or whose honor was being impugned—would choose to speak more eloquently. You would think that unfair or inaccurate accusations would elicit profound and persuasive expressions of denial. When they do not, as they certainly do not when a person resorts to *nothing could be further from the truth,* we have to wonder who is telling the truth and who is not. Formulaic responses like this may make us doubt the sincerity of those who use them • The premise put forth by the administration that employment must be sacrificed to protect the environment *could not be further from the truth.* REPLACE WITH *is erroneous.* • I know there will be Republicans who will try to say that because I'm not with you today in Chicago that I'm trying to distance myself from you, but *nothing could be further from the truth.* REPLACE WITH *they are mistaken.* • W. R. Grace makes use of my "model citizen" sound bite as though it were some sort of blanket absolution. *Nothing could be further from the truth.* REPLACE WITH *It is not.*

They had been credited with attempting to stir up rebellion among the animals on neighbouring farms. Nothing could be further from the truth!—George Orwell, *Animal Farm*

nothing lasts forever ∎ A popular prescription.

nothing to sneeze at ∎ A moribund metaphor. *consequential; considerable; meaningful; momentous; significant; substantial; weighty.* • Two hundred thousand jobs is *nothing to sneeze at.*

REPLACE WITH *considerable*.

nothing to write home about ▮ A moribund metaphor. 1. *average; common; commonplace; customary; everyday; fair; mediocre; middling; normal; ordinary; passable; quotidian; regular; standard; tolerable; typical; uneventful; unexceptional; unexciting; unremarkable; usual; workaday.* 2. *banal; barren; bland; boring; deadly; dreary; dry; dull; everyday; flat; humdrum; inanimate; insipid; jejune; lifeless; lusterless; mediocre; monotonous; prosaic; routine; spiritless; stale; tedious; tiresome; unexciting; uninteresting; vapid; wearisome.*

nothing ventured, nothing gained ▮ A popular prescription.

not in (this) lifetime ▮ A moribund metaphor. *at no time; by no means; in no way; never; no; not; not at all; not ever; not in any way; not in the least.*

not in (out of) the picture ▮ A moribund metaphor. Some metaphors—so bloodless have they become—accommodate many different meanings. *Not in (out of) the picture* is one of them, for this pale expression could easily mean *dead* or *departed*, conceivably mean *forgotten* or *forgettable*, or imaginably mean *unmentionable* or *nameless*. SEE ALSO **in the picture**.

not on your life ▮ A moribund metaphor. *at no time; by no means; in no way; never; no; not; not at all; not ever; not in any way; not in the least.*

not what (it) used to be ▮ A torpid term. *deficient; disappointing; discouraging; dissatisfying; inadequate; inapt; incapable; incompetent; ineffective; inferior; insufficient; lacking; unfit; unqualified; unsatisfactory; wanting.*

not with a bang but with a whimper ▮ An infantile phrase.

not worth a continental ▮ A moribund metaphor. *barren; bootless; effete; feckless; feeble; fruitless; futile; impotent; inadequate; inconsequential; inconsiderable; ineffective; ineffectual; infertile; insignificant; inutile; meaningless; meritless; nugatory; null; of no value; pointless; powerless; profitless; sterile; trifling; trivial; unavailing; unimportant; unproductive; unprofitable; unserviceable; unworthy; useless; vain; valueless; weak; worthless.*

not worth a (tinker's) damn ▮ A moribund metaphor. *barren; bootless; effete; feckless; feeble; fruitless; futile; impotent; inadequate; inconsequential; inconsiderable; ineffective; ineffectual; infertile; insignificant; inutile; meaningless; meritless; nugatory; null; of no value; pointless; powerless; profitless; sterile; trifling; trivial; unavailing; unimportant; unproductive; unprofitable; unserviceable; unworthy; useless; vain; valueless; weak; worthless.*

not worth a plugged nickel ▮ A moribund metaphor. *barren; bootless; effete; feckless; feeble; fruitless; futile; impotent; inadequate; inconsequential; inconsiderable; ineffective; ineffectual; infertile; insignificant; inutile; meaningless; meritless; nugatory; null; of no value; pointless; powerless; profitless; sterile; trifling; trivial; unavailing; unimportant; unproductive; unprofitable; unserviceable; unworthy; useless; vain; valueless; weak; worthless.*

not worth a straw ▮ A moribund metaphor. *barren; bootless; effete; feckless; feeble; fruitless; futile; impotent; inadequate; inconsequential; inconsiderable; ineffective; ineffectual; infertile; insignificant; inutile; meaningless; meritless; nugatory; null; of no value; pointless; powerless; profitless; sterile; trifling; trivial; unavailing; unimportant; unproductive; unprofitable; unserviceable; unworthy; useless; vain; valueless; weak; worthless.*

not worth (his) salt ▮ A moribund metaphor. *barren; bootless; effete; feckless; feeble; fruitless; futile; impotent; inadequate; inconsequential; inconsiderable; ineffective; ineffectual; infertile; insignificant; inutile; meaningless; meritless; nugatory; null; of no value; pointless; powerless; profitless; sterile; trifling; trivial; unavailing; unimportant; unproductive; unprofitable; unserviceable; unworthy; useless; vain; valueless; weak; worthless.*

> If a local Bruglione could not influence the city he lived in, he was not worth his salt.—Mario Puzo, *The Last Don*

not worth the paper it's written (printed) on ▮ A moribund metaphor. *barren; bootless; effete; feckless; feeble; fruitless; futile; impotent; inadequate; inconsequential; inconsiderable; ineffective; ineffectual; infertile; insignificant; inutile; meaningless; meritless; nugatory; null; of no value; pointless; powerless; profitless; sterile; trifling; trivial; unavailing; unimportant; unproductive; unprofitable; unserviceable; unworthy; useless; vain; valueless; weak; worthless.* • I say to you that the governor's budget is *not worth the paper it's written on*. REPLACE WITH *useless*. • He went on to say that he did not believe in the United States Constitution, and that it was *not worth the paper it's printed on*. REPLACE WITH *nugatory*.

no use crying over spilt milk ▮ A popular prescription.

no way ▮ An infantile phrase. *at no time; by no means; in no way; never; no; not; not at all; not ever; not in any way; not in the least.*

no way José ▮ An infantile phrase. *at no time; by no means; in no way; never; no; not; not at all; not ever; not in any way; not in the least.*

now it's my time (turn) ▮ A plebeian

sentiment. • I've done my family duty and brought up my children, and *now it's my turn*.

now you see it, now you don't ∎ An infantile phrase.

null and void ∎ An inescapable pair. *abolished; annulled; canceled; countermanded; invalid; null; nullified; recalled; repealed; rescinded; revoked; void; withdrawn; worthless*. • We aren't sure what the terms of the deal are, or what may be expected of them, or what may make them *null and void*. REPLACE WITH *invalid*.

(her) number is up ∎ A moribund metaphor.

> Ach, just my luck! Then the old fellow's number is up.—Isaac Babel, *Red Cavalry*

number-one ∎ A moribund metaphor. *chief; foremost; leading; main; primary; prime; principal*.

number one (two) ∎ A wretched redundancy. *first (second)*. • *Number one*, I don't feel that qualifies her as black. *Number two*, a person's color shouldn't be worn on their sleeve. REPLACE WITH *First; Second*.

nuts and bolts ∎ A moribund metaphor. *basics; essentials; facts; foundation; fundamentals; principles*. • In this text, we explore the *nuts and bolts* of radio production. REPLACE WITH *essentials*.

nuttier than a fruitcake ∎ A moribund metaphor. *batty; cracked; crazy; daft; demented; deranged; fey; foolish; goofy; insane; lunatic; mad; maniacal; neurotic; nuts; nutty; psychotic; raving; silly; squirrelly; touched; unbalanced; unhinged; unsound; wacky; zany*.

(as) nutty as a fruitcake ∎ An insipid simile. *batty; cracked; crazy; daft; demented; deranged; fey; foolish; goofy; insane; lunatic; mad; maniacal; neurotic; nuts; nutty; psychotic; raving; silly; squirrelly; touched; unbalanced; unhinged; unsound; wacky; zany*.

Oo

object of one's affection ∎ An infantile phrase. *admirer; beau; beloved; boyfriend (girlfriend); companion; darling; dear; flame; infatuate; inamorato (inamorata); lover; paramour; steady; suiter; swain; sweetheart; wooer.* SEE ALSO **significant other**.

obscene ∎ An overworked word. *abhorrent; abominable; accursed; appalling; atrocious; awful; beastly; blasphemous; detestable; disagreeable; disgusting; dreadful; execrable; frightening; frightful; ghastly; grisly; gruesome; hateful; horrendous; horrible; horrid; horrifying; indecent; indelicate; inhuman; insulting; loathsome; monstrous; obnoxious; odious; offensive; repellent; repugnant; repulsive; revolting; tasteless; terrible; terrifytng; unspeakable; unutterable; vulgar.* • Certain levels of expenditure are *obscene* and do a great injustice to our concept of social justice. REPLACE WITH *offensive*. • It's an *obscene* scenario that's being played out. REPLACE WITH *unspeakable*.

obviate the need for ∎ A wretched redundancy. *obviate.* • If indicated, create a limited-access, safe unit to *obviate the need for* activity restriction. DELETE *the need for*.

oceans of ink ∎ A moribund metaphor.

> Those journalists who professed science, at war with those who professed wit, spilled oceans of ink in this memorable campaign. —Jules Verne, *Twenty Thousand Leagues Under the Seas*

of biblical (epic) proportions ∎ A moribund metaphor. *colossal; elephantine; enormous; epical; gargantuan; giant; gigantic; great; grand; huge; immense; impressive; legendary; mammoth; massive; monstrous; prodigious; stupendous; titanic; tremendous; vast.* • It has been called *a comeback of epic proportions.* REPLACE WITH *an epical comeback.* • He created a landmark television character whose suffering was *of biblical proportions.* REPLACE WITH *prodigious.*

> As if she'd made a cosmic announcement, her last word was followed by a trumpet blast of Biblical proportions that shook the windows.—Jill Churchill, *The Merchant of Menace*

(woman) of easy virtue ∎ A moribund metaphor. *dissolute; immoral; licentious; loose; promiscuous; wanton.*

off and running ∎ A moribund metaphor.

off base ∎ A moribund metaphor. *amiss; astray; deceived; deluded; erring; erroneous; fallacious; false; faulty; inaccurate; incorrect; in error; misguided; misinformed; mislead; mistaken; not correct; not right; wrong.* • Given all the uncertainty surrounding the nation's economic future, no one is prepared to say the administration is *off base.* REPLACE WITH *incorrect.*

off (her) rocker ∎ A moribund metaphor. *batty; cracked; crazy; daft; demented; deranged; fey; foolish; goofy; insane; lunatic; mad; maniacal; neurotic; nuts; nutty; psychotic; raving; silly; squirrelly; touched; unbalanced; unhinged; unsound; wacky; zany.*

off the beaten path (track) ∎ A moribund metaphor. 1. *aberrant; abnormal; anomalistic; anomalous; atypical; bizarre; curious; deviant; different; distinct; distinctive; eccentric; exceptional; extraordinary; fantastic; foreign; grotesque; idiosyncratic; independent; individual; individualistic; irregular; novel; odd; offbeat; original; peculiar; queer; strange; uncommon; unconventional; unexampled; unique; unnatural; unorthodox; unusual; weird.* 2. *inaccessible; isolated; remote; secluded; unreachable.* • A lot of smaller towns of 800 to 3,000 people are *off the beaten path.* REPLACE WITH *remote.*

off the cuff ∎ A moribund metaphor. *extemporaneous; extempore; impromptu; improvised; spontaneous; unprepared; unprompted; unrehearsed.*

(go) off the deep end ∎ A moribund metaphor. *batty; cracked; crazy; daft; demented; deranged; fey; foolish; goofy; insane; lunatic; mad; maniacal; neurotic; nuts; nutty; psychotic; raving; silly; squirrelly; touched; unbalanced; unhinged; unsound; wacky; zany.*

(let) off the hook ∎ A moribund metaphor. *absolve; acquit; clear; condone; exculpate; excuse; exonerate; forgive; overlook; pardon; remit; vindicate.* • Confronting sexual issues is so taboo in most African culture that rapists are frequently *let off the hook* because few families will endure the public shame of acknowledging the abuse. REPLACE WITH *acquitted.* • But as news events in the scandal coverage ebb, the media have had to find new ways to *let Clinton off the hook.* REPLACE WITH *absolve Clinton.* • Now she's calling for

Nicaragua and Honduras to be *let off the hook* for at least two years. REPLACE WITH *excused*.

off the mark ∎ A moribund metaphor. *false; imprecise; inaccurate; incorrect; inexact; wrong.*

off the record ∎ A moribund metaphor. *classified; confidential; personal; private; privy; restricted; secret.*

off the top of (my) head ∎ A moribund metaphor. *extemporaneous; extempore; impromptu; improvised; spontaneous; unprepared; unprompted; unrehearsed.*

off the wall ∎ A moribund metaphor. *aberrant; abnormal; anomalistic; anomalous; atypical; bizarre; curious; deviant; different; distinct; distinctive; eccentric; exceptional; extraordinary; fantastic; foreign; grotesque; idiosyncratic; independent; individual; individualistic; irregular; novel; odd; offbeat; original; peculiar; puzzling; quaint; queer; rare; remarkable; separate; singular; strange; uncommon; unconventional; unexampled; unique; unorthodox; unparalleled; unprecedented; unusual; weird.*

off to the races ∎ A moribund metaphor.

(goes) off track ∎ A moribund metaphor. *amiss; astray; deceived; deluded; erring; erroneous; fallacious; false; faulty; inaccurate; incorrect; in error; misguided; misinformed; mislead; mistaken; not correct; not right; wrong.*

> An intelligent and beautiful girl from a loving family grows up in Orangetown, Ontario, her mother's a writer, her father's a doctor, and then she goes off the track.—Carol Shields, *Unless*

off (her) trolley ∎ A moribund metaphor. *batty; cracked; crazy; daft; demented; deranged; fey; foolish; goofy; insane; lunatic; mad; maniacal; neurotic; nuts; nutty; psychotic; raving; silly; squirrelly; touched; unbalanced; unhinged; unsound; wacky; zany.*

oftentimes ∎ A wretched redundancy. *frequently; often; repeatedly.* • *Oftentimes*, this results in overloading the office staff with the added responsibility of planning the company's meetings and events. REPLACE WITH *Often*.

(time is) of the essence ∎ A torpid term. *critical; crucial; essential; important; key; significant; vital.*

> Time was of the essence—not only because of what those rival companies were up to, but also (and the Rani lowered her voice mysteriously) for Other Reasons.—Aldous Huxley, *Island*

of the first water ∎ A moribund metaphor. *best; brightest; choice; choicest; elite; excellent; finest; first-class; first-rate;*

foremost; greatest; highest; highest quality; matchless; nonpareil; optimal; optimum; outstanding; paramount; peerless; preeminent; premium; prominent; select; superior; superlative; top; unequaled; unexcelled; unmatched; unrivaled; unsurpassed.

off (his) trolley ∎ A moribund metaphor. *batty; cracked; crazy; daft; demented; deranged; fey; foolish; goofy; insane; lunatic; mad; maniacal; neurotic; nuts; nutty; psychotic; raving; silly; squirrelly; touched; unbalanced; unhinged; unsound; wacky; zany.*

ofttimes ∎ A withered word. *frequently; often; repeatedly.*

of two minds ∎ A moribund metaphor. *ambivalent; confused; divided; indecisive; in doubt; irresolute; neutral; torn; uncertain; uncommitted; undecided; unsure.*

old adage ∎ A wretched redundancy. *adage.* • The *old adage* "The first half of our lives is ruined by our parents and the last half by our children" need not be and should not be. DELETE *old*.

old and decrepit ∎ An inescapable pair.

(as) old as Adam ∎ An insipid simile. *aged; aging; ancient; antediluvian; antique; archaic; elderly; hoary; hoary-headed; old; patriarchal; prehistoric; seasoned; superannuated; venerable.*

(as) old as time ∎ An insipid simile. *aged; aging; ancient; antediluvian; antique; archaic; elderly; hoary; hoary-headed; old; patriarchal; prehistoric; seasoned; superannuated; venerable.*

> The family! Here was the old blackmail tactic, old as Time.—Joyce Carol Oates, *The Tattooed Girl*

old-boy network ∎ A moribund metaphor.

old cliché ∎ A wretched redundancy. *cliché.* • Working for these guys I feel like the *old cliché* "a cog in the wheel." DELETE *old*.

old enough to know better ∎ An infantile phrase.

old enough to know better but young enough not to care ∎ An infantile phrase.

oldest story in the book ∎ A moribund metaphor.

old habits never die ∎ A popular prescription.

> Old habits never die. And when you've once been in the business of granting wishes, the impulse never quite leaves you.—Joanne Harris, *Chocolat*

old hat ∎ A moribund metaphor. 1. *antediluvian; antiquated; archaic; dead; obsolescent; obsolete; old; old-fashioned;*

outdated; outmoded; out of date; out of fashion; passé; superannuated. **2.** banal; barren; bland; boring; deadly; dreary; dry; dull; everyday; flat; humdrum; inanimate; insipid; jejune; lifeless; lusterless; mediocre; monotonous; prosaic; routine; spiritless; stale; tedious; tiresome; unexciting; uninteresting; vapid; wearisome.

old maxim ∎ A wretched redundancy. *maxim.* • A number of studies indicate that, in deciding what punishment is appropriate for different crimes, individuals typically rely on an *old maxim*: Let the punishment fit the crime. DELETE *old.*

old saw ∎ A wretched redundancy. *saw.* • The claim is similar to the *old saw* from the tobacco industry, now proven false, that there is no direct link between cancer and smoking. DELETE *old.*

old saying ∎ A wretched redundancy. *saying.* • The *old saying* "A picture is worth a thousand words" is usually true. DELETE *old.*

old wives' tale ∎ A moribund metaphor.

on a ... basis ∎ A wretched redundancy. • Meat production is the major use of goats *on a worldwide basis.* REPLACE WITH *worldwide.* • I am tortured *on a daily basis.* REPLACE WITH *daily.* • I see him for my treatment *on a regular basis.* REPLACE WITH *regularly.* • You meet the students *on a weekly basis.* REPLACE WITH *weekly.* • We should look at these issues *on a case-by-case basis.* REPLACE WITH *case by case.*

on account of the fact that ∎ A wretched redundancy. *because; considering; for; given; in that; since.* • The former Beatle refused the award *on account of the fact that* he believes he is too young to receive it and does not want to be perceived as a washed-up has been. REPLACE WITH *because.* SEE ALSO **because of the fact that; considering the fact that; by virtue of the fact that; given the fact that; in view of the fact.**

on a collision course ∎ A moribund metaphor.

on a different wavelength ∎ A moribund metaphor. *conflict; differ; disagree; disharmonize; feel differently; think unalike.*

on a dime ∎ A moribund metaphor. *cheaply; economically; inexpensively.* • When it comes to interior design or decorating *on a dime,* you've got hundreds of tips and tricks to share with readers. REPLACE WITH *economically.*

(working) on all cylinders ∎ A moribund metaphor. **1.** *able; adept; apt; capable; competent; conversant; deft; dexterous; experienced; expert; familiar; practiced; proficient; seasoned; skilled; skillful; veteran.* **2.** *adroit; astute; bright; brilliant; clever; discerning; effective; effectual; efficient; enlightened; insightful; intelligent; judicious;* keen; knowledgeable; learned; logical; luminous; perceptive; perspicacious; quick; rational; reasonable; sagacious; sage; sapient; sensible; sharp; shrewd; smart; sound; understanding; wise.* • This rapid growth cycle is a challenge opportunity and needs good *people working on all cylinders* to take advantage of it. REPLACE WITH *capable people.*

on all fours (with) ∎ A moribund metaphor. *analogous (to); equal (to); equivalent (to); identical (to).* • There's no circumstance in history that fits identically *on all fours* with subsequent circumstances. DELETE *on all fours.*

on an even keel ∎ A moribund metaphor. *balanced; even; firm; fixed; stable; steadfast; steady; unfaltering; unwavering.*

on a ... note ∎ A wretched redundancy. • *On a personal note,* I would not be all that appalled if my children were to perform well only 99 percent of the time. REPLACE WITH *Personally.*

on a roll ∎ A moribund metaphor. *doing well; flourishing; prospering; succeeding; thriving.*

on a scale of 1 to 10 ∎ An infantile phrase. The popularity of this phrase is further evidence of the delight some people have with numbers and counting and the distaste they have for words and concepts. Of course, their fondness for numbers may not go much beyond the count of 10—so too, perhaps, the number of words in their vocabulary. • *On a scale of 1 to 10,* how much does uncertainty surrounding laws and regulations in [COUNTRY] increase the risk of equities in that country? • *On a scale of 1 to 10,* just how good a student are you? • *On a scale of 1 to 10* (1 being the lowest, 10 being the highest) please rank the usefulness and intuitiveness of the website's navigational elements. • How would you rank your programming skills (in your best language) *on a scale of 1 to 10,* with 1 being lowest and 10 being highest? SEE ALSO **(for) a laugh; avid reader.**

on a shoestring ∎ A moribund metaphor. *cheaply; economically; inexpensively.*

> He had been everywhere and he knew everything about traveling on a shoestring.— Laura Kalpakian, *Steps and Exes: A Novel of Family*

on automatic pilot ∎ A moribund metaphor. *automatic; habitual; mechanical; routine.*

(come) on board ∎ A moribund metaphor. • Some doctors are starting to *come on board,* but many haven't got a clue what's going on. REPLACE WITH *take alternative medicine seriously.*

on both sides (either side) of the equation ∎ A moribund metaphor. • I believe there is little trust *on either side*

on both sides of the fence

of the equation. • Merrills tempers the super-cycle view to some extent however, by suggesting simply that there are risks *on either side of the equation.* • There is already a writer and producer attached to our first project, working *on both sides of the equation*—game and movie. • I have likewise seen the disconnect between people of color and law enforcement—the misconceptions *on both sides of the equation.*

on both sides of the fence ∎ A moribund metaphor. *ambivalent; divided; indecisive; in doubt; irresolute; neutral; torn; uncertain; uncommitted; undecided; unsure.*

once bitten (burned), twice shy ∎ A popular prescription.

once (and) for all ∎ A torpid term. *conclusively; decisively; finally.* • Our broken judicial confirmation process must *be fixed once and for all.* REPLACE WITH *finally be fixed.*

once in a blue moon ∎ A moribund metaphor. *hardly; infrequently; not often; occasionally; rarely; scarcely; seldom; sporadically; uncommonly.*

once in a lifetime (opportunity) ∎ A moribund metaphor. *different; exceptional; extraordinary; incomparable; inimitable; matchless; nonpareil; notable; noteworthy; novel; odd; original; peculiar; peerless; rare; remarkable; singular; special; strange; uncommon; unequaled; unexampled; unique; unmatched; unparalleled; unrivaled; unusual; without equal.* • This is a *once in a lifetime* opportunity. REPLACE WITH *singular.*

once upon a time ∎ An infantile phrase.

on cloud nine ∎ A moribund metaphor. *blissful; blithe; buoyant; cheerful; delighted; ecstatic; elated; enraptured; euphoric; exalted; excited; exhilarated; exultant; gay; glad; gleeful; good-humored; happy; intoxicated; jolly; jovial; joyful; joyous; jubilant; merry; mirthful; overjoyed; pleased; rapturous; thrilled.*

on (our) doorstep ∎ A moribund metaphor. *approaching; at hand; close; coming; expected; forthcoming; imminent; impending; looming; near; nearby.*

(the) one and only ∎ A wretched redundancy. *one; only; sole.* • In the early days of any business, the *one and only* thing you understand is that the customer is king. REPLACE WITH *one* or *only.*

one and the same ∎ A wretched redundancy. *identical; one; the same.* • Are you saying that submission and competition are *one and the same*? REPLACE WITH *the same.* • Some people believe that marketing and advertising are *one and the same.* REPLACE WITH *identical.*

on easy street ∎ A moribund metaphor.

affluent; moneyed; opulent; prosperous; rich; wealthy; well-off; well-to-do.

one big, happy family ∎ A suspect superlative.

one foot in and one foot out ∎ A moribund metaphor. *ambivalent; divided; indecisive; irresolute; torn; uncertain; uncommitted; undecided; unsure.*

(put) one foot in front of the other ∎ A moribund metaphor.

one foot in the grave ∎ A moribund metaphor. *decaying; declining; deteriorating; disintegrating; dying; ebbing; expiring; fading; failing; moribund; near death; sinking; very ill; waning.*

> She only used to marvel how so old and flabby a man, with one foot in the grave, came to be possessed of so fertile an imagination.—Esther Singer Kreitman, *Deborah*

one for the books ∎ A moribund metaphor. *different; exceptional; extraordinary; incomparable; inimitable; matchless; nonpareil; notable; noteworthy; novel; odd; original; peculiar; peerless; remarkable; singular; special; strange; uncommon; unequaled; unexampled; unique; unmatched; unparalleled; unrivaled; unusual; without equal.*

one good turn deserves another ∎ A popular prescription.

one hundred (100) percent ∎ An infantile phrase. *absolutely; altogether; categorically; completely; entirely; fully; perfectly; positively; quite; roundly; thoroughly; totally; unconditionally; unreservedly; utterly; wholly.* • I agree with you *one hundred percent.* REPLACE WITH *unreservedly.*

one in a million ∎ A moribund metaphor. *different; exceptional; extraordinary; incomparable; inimitable; matchless; nonpareil; notable; noteworthy; novel; odd; original; peculiar; peerless; remarkable; singular; special; strange; uncommon; unequaled; unexampled; unique; unmatched; unparalleled; unrivaled; unusual; without equal.* • One teacher commented that Philip is *one in a million.* REPLACE WITH *peerless.*

one man's meat is another man's poison ∎ A popular prescription.

one man's trash is another man's treasure ∎ A popular prescription.

one of a kind ∎ A torpid term. *different; exceptional; extraordinary; incomparable; inimitable; matchless; nonpareil; notable; noteworthy; novel; odd; original; peculiar; peerless; remarkable; singular; special; strange; uncommon; unequaled; unexampled; unique; unmatched; unparalleled; unrivaled; unusual; without equal.*

one size fits all ∎ An infantile phrase.

procrustean. • We do not advocate a *one-size-fits-all* approach in making decisions about how students should be educated. REPLACE WITH *procrustean.*

one step at a time ∎ A popular prescription.

(well) one thing led to another ∎ A grammatical gimmick.

one-two punch ∎ A moribund metaphor.

one-way street ∎ A moribund metaphor.

one-way ticket to ∎ A moribund metaphor.

on firm (solid) ground ∎ A moribund metaphor. *firm; solid; sound; stable; sturdy.*

ongoing ∎ A TOP-TWENTY DIMWITTICISM. An overworked word. *Ongoing* has superseded practically all of its synonyms. We have *ongoing basis; ongoing care; ongoing commitment; ongoing destruction; ongoing discussions; ongoing education; ongoing effort; ongoing investigation; ongoing plan; ongoing process; ongoing program; ongoing relationship; ongoing service; ongoing support;* and so many more.

Consider these synonyms: *ceaseless; constant; continual; continuing; continuous; endless; enduring; incessant; lifelong; long-lived; nonstop; progressing; unbroken; unceasing; unremitting.* • With this new rehabilitation center, patients will no longer have to travel outside the community to receive the *ongoing* care they need. DELETE *ongoing.* • Establishing paternity also may force more women into *ongoing* relationships with fathers who are abusive or violent. REPLACE WITH *lifelong.*

(up) on (her) high horse ∎ A moribund metaphor. *arrogant; cavalier; condescending; contemptuous; despotic; dictatorial; disdainful; dogmatic; domineering; haughty; imperious; insolent; lofty; overbearing; overweening; patronizing; pompous; pretentious; scornful; self-important; supercilious; superior; vainglorious.*

on ice ∎ A moribund metaphor. *in abeyance; on hold; pending; stalled; suspended.*

on (its) last legs ∎ A moribund metaphor. 1. *decaying; declining; deteriorating; disappearing; disintegrating; dying; ebbing; expiring; fading; failing; moribund; near death; sinking; vanishing; waning.* 2. *beat; bushed; debilitated; depleted; drained; drowsy; enervated; exhausted; fatigued; groggy; sapped; sleepy; sluggish; slumberous; somnolent; soporific; spent; tired; weary; worn out.* • The battle for a smoke-free environment is hardly *on its last legs.* REPLACE WITH *moribund.*

(high) on (my) list of priorities ∎ A torpid term.

> You were living with Amanda in New York and marriage wasn't high on your list of priorities, although on Amanda's it was.—Jay McInerney, *Bright Lights, Big City*

only the strong survive ∎ A popular prescription.

on (his) part ∎ A wretched redundancy. *among; by; for; from; of; -s.* • I think this is really irresponsible *on your part.* REPLACE WITH *of you.* • I guess this is selfish *on my part.* REPLACE WITH *of me.* • It's an incredible sacrifice *on her part and her family's part.* REPLACE WITH *from her and her family.* • This single one-page assignment made the point that Wilder's attitudes toward Native Americans and toward African Americans are problematic, and made it better than any amount of lecturing *on my part* could have done. REPLACE WITH *I.* SEE ALSO **on the part of.**

> All but Lucia, that is to say, whose throne had, quite unintentionally on Olga's part, been quite pulled smartly from under her, and her scepter flew in one direction, and her crown in another.—E. F. Benson, *Lucia in London*

on pins and needles ∎ A moribund metaphor. *agitated; anxious; apprehensive; disquieted; distressed; disturbed; edgy; fretful; ill at ease; impatient; in suspense; nervous; on edge; restive; restless; troubled; uneasy; unquiet; unsettled; worried.* • Democrats—already *on pins and needles* over the release of Clinton's grand jury testimony—were scrambling yesterday with how to cope over the second tape. REPLACE WITH *uneasy.*

on (her) plate ∎ A moribund metaphor. *awaiting (her); before (her); pending.*

on safe ground ∎ A moribund metaphor. *guarded; protected; safe; secure; sheltered; shielded.*

on shaky ground ∎ A moribund metaphor. *indefensible; shaky; unsound; unsustainable.*

on speaking terms ∎ A wretched redundancy. *speaking.*

> For reasons they could no longer define clearly, Colin and Mary were not on speaking terms.—Ian McEwan, *The Comfort of Strangers*

(right) on target ∎ A moribund metaphor. *accurate; correct; exact; perfect; precise; proper; right; (exactly; just) so; true; veracious.*

on tenterhooks ∎ A moribund metaphor. *agitated; anxious; apprehensive; disquieted; distressed; disturbed; edgy; fretful; ill at ease; impatient; in suspense; nervous; on edge; restive; restless; troubled; uneasy; unquiet; unsettled; worried.*

> Mick sat on tenterhooks, leaning forward in his chair, glaring at her almost hysterically: and whether he was more anxious out of vanity for her to say Yes! or whether he was more panic-stricken for fear she *should* say Yes!—who can tell?—D. H. Lawrence, *Lady Chatterley's Lover*

on the back burner ■ A moribund metaphor. *deferred; delayed; in abeyance; on hold; pending; postponed; stalled; suspended.* • The planned training center in Hanover, NJ, has been *on the back burner* because of the recession and the club's focus on getting Red Bull Arena completed. REPLACE WITH *delayed.* • The free trade agreement between Colombia and the U.S. will remain *on the back burner* because President Barack Obama's priority is passing healthcare reform. REPLACE WITH *in abeyance.* SEE ALSO **place (put) on the back burner**.

on the ball ■ A moribund metaphor. 1. *alert; attentive; awake; aware; eagle-eyed; heedful; observant; vigilant; wakeful; watchful.* 2. *able; adroit; apt; astute; bright; brilliant; capable; clever; competent; discerning; effective; effectual; efficient; enlightened; insightful; intelligent; judicious; keen; knowledgeable; learned; logical; luminous; perceptive; perspicacious; quick; rational; reasonable; sagacious; sage; sapient; sensible; sharp; shrewd; smart; sound; understanding; wise.*

on the basis of ■ A wretched redundancy. *after; based on; because of; by; due to; for; from; in; on; owing to; through; via; with.* • NABCO chooses material for this site *on the basis of* its timely and useful content. REPLACE WITH *based on.* • Exemption from IRB review and approval is determined *on the basis of* the risks associated with the study. REPLACE WITH *by.* • There shall be no discrimination against any individual *on the basis of* ethnic group, race, religion, gender, sexual orientation, age, or record of public offense. REPLACE WITH *because of.*

on the blink ■ A moribund metaphor. *broken; defective; in disrepair; not working; not functioning; out of order.*

on the brink of ■ A moribund metaphor. *about to; (very) close (to); (very) near (to).*

(right) on the button ■ A moribund metaphor. *accurate; correct; exact; irrefutable; precise; right; true.*

on the chopping block ■ A moribund metaphor. *at risk; endangered; imperiled; in danger; in jeopardy; in peril; in trouble; jeopardized.*

(ride) on the coattails of ■ A moribund metaphor.

on the cuff ■ A moribund metaphor. *on credit.*

on the cutting (leading) edge ■ A moribund metaphor. *first; forefront; foremost; leading; vanguard.*

on the day ■ A torpid term. *today;* DELETE. • He scored 16 points *on the day.* REPLACE WITH *today.* • The euro was flat *on the day* at 133.85 yen after it rose nearly 0.6 percent on Wednesday. REPLACE WITH *today.*

• Even late in the fourth set, I was up a break to take it into a fifth set, and I just didn't quite play the big points as well as he did *on the day.* DELETE *on the day.* Sports writers, known for mismanaging words, and financial analysts, known for mismanaging money, are especially fond of the expression *on the day.*

on the dot ■ A moribund metaphor. *exactly (at); on time; precisely (at); promptly (at); punctually (at).*

They must be clean and neat about their persons and clothes and show up promptly—on the dot—and in good condition for the work every day.—Theodore Dreiser, *An American Tragedy*

on the drawing board ■ A moribund metaphor. • The university now has seven new schools *on the drawing board.*

on the edge of (their) seats ■ A moribund metaphor. *absorb; arrest; bewitch; captivate; charm; curious; divert; enchant; engage; engross; entertain; enthrall; entice; excite; fascinate; intrigue; rivet; spellbind; stimulate; tantalize.* • People are *on the edge of their seats* about this report. REPLACE WITH *fascinated.*

on the fast track ■ A moribund metaphor.

(sit) on the fence ■ A moribund metaphor. *ambivalent; divided; impartial; indecisive; irresolute; neutral; noncommittal; torn; uncertain; uncommitted; undecided; unsettled; unsure.*

on the firing line ■ A moribund metaphor.

on the fly ■ A moribund metaphor. *ad-lib; extemporize; improvise.*

on the fritz ■ A moribund metaphor. *broken; defective; in disrepair; not working; not functioning; out of order.*

on the front burner ■ A moribund metaphor. *cardinal; chief; dominant; foremost; head; important; leading; main; paramount; predominant; primary; principal; prominent; topmost; uppermost.* • Preserving Yellowstone is probably a priority for most Americans, but at the moment it's not *on anyone's front burner.* REPLACE WITH *paramount.* • While lawmakers continue their work, the governor is visiting schools across the state to keep the issue *on the front burner.* REPLACE WITH *predominant.* SEE ALSO **place (put) on the front burner**.

on the front lines ■ A moribund metaphor.

on the go ■ A moribund metaphor. *absorbed; active; busy; employed; engaged; engrossed; going; immersed; involved; moving; occupied; preoccupied; wrapped up in.*

(hot) on the heels of ■ A moribund metaphor. *after; behind; ensuing; following; succeeding.* SEE ALSO **in the wake of**.

on the horizon ∎ A moribund metaphor. *approaching; at hand; close; coming; expected; forthcoming; imminent; impending; near; nearby.*

(caught) on the horns of a dilemma ∎ A moribund metaphor. *at risk; endangered; hard-pressed; imperiled; in a bind; in a dilemma; in a fix; in a jam; in a predicament; in a quandary; in danger; in difficulty; in jeopardy; in peril; in trouble; jeopardized.*

(take it) on the lam ∎ A moribund metaphor. *abscond; clear out; decamp; depart; desert; disappear; escape; exit; flee; fly; go; go away; leave; move on; part; pull out; quit; retire; retreat; run away; take flight; take off; vacate; vanish; withdraw.*

on the level ∎ A torpid term. *aboveboard; creditable; equitable; fair; genuine; honest; honorable; just; lawful; legitimate; open; proper; reputable; respectable; right; sincere; square; straightforward; truthful; upright; veracious; veridical.*

on the loose ∎ A torpid term. *at large; at liberty; free; loose; unattached; unbound; unconfined; unrestrained; unrestricted.*

on the mark ∎ A moribund metaphor. *accurate; correct; exact; precise; right; true.*

on the mend ∎ A torpid term. *ameliorating; amending; coming round; convalescent; convalescing; gaining strength; getting better; healing; improving; looking up; meliorating; mending; rallying; recovering; recuperating; refreshing; renewing; reviving; strengthening.*

(right) on the money ∎ A moribund metaphor. *accurate; correct; exact; fact; irrefutable; precise; right; true.* • I think it was *right on the money.* REPLACE WITH *irrefutable.*

on the nose ∎ A moribund metaphor. *accurate; correct; exact; irrefutable; precise; right; true.*

> As usual, he gives me two hours with him, what will be two hours on the nose.—Binnie Kirshenbaum, *A Disturbance in One Place*

(on the) other side of the coin ∎ A moribund metaphor. 1. *antithesis; contrary; converse; opposite; reverse.* 2. *but; in contrast; conversely; however; inversely; whereas; yet.* • *On the other side of the coin,* if you're astute you can occasionally buy them at big discounts. REPLACE WITH *But.*

on the part of ∎ A TOP-TWENTY DIMWITTICISM. A wretched redundancy. *among; by; for; from; of; -s. On the part of* is a preposition phrase that apparently appeals to bombastic men and women who may not fully consider what they say, for they certainly do not consider how they say it. People use *on the part of* when they're too lazy to think of the proper, a

better word—most often a two- to four-letter, monosyllabic preposition. This is a thoughtless person's phrase. • As a result, and following vigorous lobbying *on the part of* CFS victims, the disease is now called chronic fatigue immunodeficiency syndrome. REPLACE WITH *by.* • Open-ended questions require much more effort *on the part of* the person answering them. REPLACE WITH *from.* • There is some cultural resistance *on the part of* some U.S. racial and ethnic groups to government-sponsored contraceptive programs. REPLACE WITH *from.* • *Misconduct on the part of the police* sometimes also violates the criminal law. REPLACE WITH *Police misconduct.* • It has also sometimes been attributed to an attitude *on the part of* health counselors that the poor are charity cases who should be satisfied with whatever they get since they are probably not paying for their own care. REPLACE WITH *among.* • If we are to get over the current crisis, *sacrifices on the part of everyone will have to be made.* REPLACE WITH *everyone will have to make sacrifices.* • Exhaustive questions reduce the *frustration on the part of the respondents.* REPLACE WITH *respondents' frustrations.* SEE ALSO **on (his) part.**

on the Q.T. ∎ A moribund metaphor. *clandestinely; confidentially; covertly; furtively; mysteriously; in private; in secret; privately; quietly; secludedly; secretly; slyly; stealthily; surreptitiously; undercover.*

on the razor's edge ∎ A moribund metaphor. *at risk; endangered; hard-pressed; imperiled; in danger; in difficulty; in jeopardy; in peril; in trouble; jeopardized.*

(start) on the right foot ∎ A moribund metaphor. *auspiciously; favorably; positively; propitiously; well.*

on the right track ∎ A moribund metaphor. *on target; on track.*

on the road ∎ A moribund metaphor. *traveling.*

on the road to recovery ∎ A moribund metaphor. *ameliorating; amending; coming round; convalescent; convalescing; feeling better; gaining strength; getting better; healing; improving; looking up; meliorating; mending; rallying; recovering; recuperating; refreshing; renewing; reviving; strengthening.* • His wife has been ill, but she's *on the road to recovery.* REPLACE WITH *improving.*

on the rocks ∎ A moribund metaphor. *at risk; collapsing; endangered; failing; foundering; imperiled; in danger; in difficulty; in jeopardy; in peril; in trouble; jeopardized.* • Our marriage is *on the rocks.* REPLACE WITH *imperiled.*

on the ropes ∎ A moribund metaphor. 1. *at risk; endangered; hard-pressed; imperiled; in danger; in difficulty; in jeopardy; in peril; in* *trouble; jeopardized.* **2.** *defenseless; helpless; impotent; powerless.*

on the same page ∎ A moribund metaphor. *agree; concur; feel similarly; harmonize; be in accord; be in agreement; be in harmony; like-minded; match; mesh; think alike. On the same page* is spoken or written by pawns and puppets who cannot think for themselves, who rely on others for how they should speak and what they should think; who prize the ease of agreement more than they do the entanglement of dissent; who turn few pages and read fewer books.

• I believe we're all *on the same page.* REPLACE WITH *thinking alike.* • It gives us direction—everybody is *on the same page,* everybody knows where we want to get and how we want to get there. REPLACE WITH *in harmony.* • He usually gets his way, but we're usually *on the same page.* REPLACE WITH *in agreement.* • You have to be a serious writer to become a published author; if you *are on the same page,* we'd like to hear from you. REPLACE WITH *agree.*

> He figured since Franklin hadn't responded to the idea with a gasp or an indignant speech they were on the same page.—Bill Fitzhugh, *Fender Benders*

on the same wavelength ∎ A moribund metaphor. *agree; concur; feel similarly; harmonize; be in accord; be in agreement; be in harmony; like-minded; match; mesh; think alike.*

> He was the typical teacher on the same wavelength as his kids, since he himself didn't look a day over thirty, and the best part of it was that he wasn't some half-ass.—Zoe Valdes, *Dear First Love*

on the ... side ∎ A wretched redundancy. • Tuesday will be *on the chilly side.* REPLACE WITH *chilly.* • She is *on the thin side.* REPLACE WITH *thin.* • That means the 550,000 estimate is probably *on the low side.* REPLACE WITH *low.*

on the sly ∎ A torpid term. *clandestinely; confidentially; covertly; furtively; mysteriously; in private; in secret; privately; quietly; secludedly; secretly; slyly; stealthily; surreptitiously; undercover.*

on the spot ∎ A torpid term. **1.** *at once; directly; forthwith; immediately; instantly; momentarily; promptly; right away; straightaway; summarily; without delay.* **2.** *at risk; endangered; hard-pressed; imperiled; in danger; in difficulty; in jeopardy; in peril; in trouble; jeopardized.*

on the spur of the moment ∎ A wretched redundancy. *impetuously; impulsively; spontaneously; suddenly; unexpectedly; without warning.*

on the table ∎ A TOP-TWENTY DIMWITTICISM. A moribund metaphor. *before us; being considered; being discussed; considerable; discussable; under discussion.* Whoever speaks this expression speaks words scarcely worth hearing. Whoever writes this expression writes words scarcely worth reading. There are words that stir, words that persuade, words that compel; the expression *on the table* is not and is never among them.

• A healthy dialog on value systems when there is no pressing issue *on the table* may help clear the air. REPLACE WITH *before us.* • There is nothing that is not *on the table.* REPLACE WITH *being considered.* • The White House could withdraw his nomination but say that option isn't *on the table.* REPLACE WITH *being discussed.*

(out) on the town ∎ A moribund metaphor. *be merry; carouse; carry on; celebrate; debauch; disport; frolic; party; play; revel; riot; roister; rollick; romp; skylark.*

on the up-and-up ∎ A torpid term. *aboveboard; creditable; equitable; fair; honest; honorable; just; lawful; legitimate; open; proper; reputable; respectable; right; sincere; square; straightforward; upright; veracious; veridical.*

on the warpath ∎ A moribund metaphor. **1.** *angry; bad-tempered; bilious; cantankerous; choleric; churlish; crabby; cranky; cross; curmudgeonly; disagreeable; dyspeptic; grouchy; gruff; grumpy; ill-humored; ill-tempered; irascible; irritable; mad; peevish; petulant; quarrelsome; riled; roiled; short-tempered; splenetic; surly; testy; vexed.* **2.** *aggressive; antagonistic; arguing; argumentative; battling; bellicose; belligerent; bickering; brawling; clashing; combative; contentious; fighting; militant; pugnacious; quarrelsome; querulous; squabbling; truculent; warlike; wrangling.*

on the wings of the wind ∎ A moribund metaphor. *abruptly; apace; at once; briskly; directly; expeditiously; fast; forthwith; hastily; hurriedly; immediately; instantaneously; instantly; posthaste; promptly; quickly; rapidly; rashly; right away; speedily; straightaway; swiftly; wingedly.*

(start) on the wrong foot ∎ A moribund metaphor. *adversely; inauspiciously; negatively; unfavorably; unpropitiously.*

on the wrong track ∎ A moribund metaphor. *amiss; astray; deceived; deluded; erring; erroneous; fallacious; false; faulty; inaccurate; incorrect; in error; misguided; misinformed; mislead; mistaken; not correct; not right; wrong.*

(skate) on thin ice ∎ A moribund metaphor. *chance; dare; endanger; gamble; hazard; imperil; jeopardize; make bold; peril; risk; venture.*

(keep) on (his) toes ∎ A moribund metaphor.

be alert; be attentive; be awake; be aware; be heedful; be prepared; be ready; be vigilant; be wakeful.

(sitting) on top of the world ∎ A moribund metaphor. 1. *advantageous; auspicious; blessed; charmed; enchanted; favored; felicitous; flourishing; fortuitous; fortunate; golden; in luck; lucky; propitious; prosperous; successful; thriving.* 2. *blissful; blithe; buoyant; cheerful; delighted; ecstatic; elated; enraptured; euphoric; exalted; excited; exhilarated; exultant; gay; glad; gleeful; good-humored; happy; intoxicated; jolly; jovial; joyful; joyous; jubilant; merry; mirthful; overjoyed; pleased; rapturous; thrilled.*

onward and upward ∎ An inescapable pair.

open and aboveboard ∎ A moribund metaphor. *aboveboard; creditable; equitable; fair; honest; honorable; just; lawful; legitimate; open; proper; reputable; respectable; right; square; straightforward; upright; veracious; veridical.*

open (up) a Pandora's box ∎ A moribund metaphor.

open (my) eyes (to) ∎ A moribund metaphor. *introduce.* • My classes *opened my eyes to* the countless possibilities in my field. USE *introduced me to.*

open the door for (on; to) ∎ A moribund metaphor. *bring about; cause; create; effect; generate; inaugurate; initiate; introduce; lead to; occasion; produce; provoke; result in; usher in.* • This breakthrough could *open the door to* a wide range of new varieties of important crops. REPLACE WITH *result in.* • Human embryo cells have been isolated and grown in the test tube for the first time, a development that could *open the door to* new drug therapies. REPLACE WITH *lead to.*

open the floodgates ∎ A moribund metaphor.

operative ∎ A torpid term. • The *operative* philosophy is spelled out early on: Winning is the most important thing in life.

opportunity knocks only once ∎ A popular prescription.

(as) opposed to what? ∎ An infantile phrase. SEE ALSO **(as) compared to what?; everything's (it's all) relative**.

opposites attract ∎ A popular prescription.

or anything ∎ A grammatical gimmick. • I didn't go beat her up, *or anything.* DELETE *or anything.* • Not to be rude *or anything,* but I don't think we should talk to each other. DELETE *or anything.* SEE ALSO **or anything like that**.

or anything like that ∎ A grammatical gimmick. • He wasn't my first boyfriend *or anything like that.* DELETE *or anything like that.* • He didn't go out and say, "Who goes there?" *or anything like that.* DELETE *or anything like that.* • I really apologize if I was inappropriate or upset you *or anything like that.* DELETE *or anything like that.* SEE ALSO **or anything**.

or (a; the) lack thereof ∎ A torpid term. • He was ousted because the majority of voters believe he didn't do a good job as mayor—not because of his skin color, but because of his merit *or lack thereof.*

or something ∎ A grammatical gimmick. As there are phrases that help us begin sentences, like *I'll tell you (something),* so there are phrases that help us end them. *Or something, or something like that, or something or other* extricate us from having to conclude our thoughts clearly. Said as a person's thoughts end, but before his words do, *or something,* like its many relations, is a thoughtless phrase that reminds us only of our trembling humanity.
• This is like something I'd wear in third grade, *or something.* DELETE *or something.* • It makes you mad when they make them sound like they're vicious people—that if you walk the street, they're going to grab you *or something.* DELETE *or something.*
SEE ALSO **or something like that; or something or other**.

> The guy in Sydney must be asleep at the switch. Or something.—Phil Rosette, *The Freya Project*

or something like that ∎ A grammatical gimmick. • Why couldn't they have shot him in his arm or leg *or something like that?* DELETE *or something like that.* SEE ALSO **or something; or something or other**.

or something or other ∎ A grammatical gimmick. • We might go to the movies *or something or other.* DELETE *or something or other.* SEE ALSO **or something; or something like that**.

or what ∎ A grammatical gimmick. • Did you see an opportunity for escape, or plan it for a long time, *or what?* DELETE *or what.*
• Was he being vulgar *or what?* DELETE *or what.* • Did you make enough money so you can retire *or what?* REPLACE WITH *or not.*

or whatever ∎ A grammatical gimmick.
• They say he corrupted my mind *or whatever.* DELETE *or whatever.* • Is it a good thing, is it a bad thing, is it useless, *or whatever?* DELETE *or whatever.* • She just wants the extra attention, *or whatever.* DELETE *or whatever.* • You can call this arrogance or way too much self-assurance *or whatever.* DELETE *or whatever.* • The percent remembered is the same whether the audience is a business audience, a college audience, a PTA audience, *or whatever.* DELETE *or whatever.*

or words to that effect ∎ A grammatical gimmick.

out and out

out and out ∎ A torpid term. *absolute;
compleat; complete; consummate; deadly;
outright; perfect; thorough; thoroughgoing;
total; unmitigated; unqualified; utter.*

out at the elbows ∎ A moribund metaphor.
1. *disheveled; dowdy; frowzy; messy; ragged;
run-down; seedy; shabby; slipshod; sloppy;
slovenly; tattered; threadbare; unkempt;
untidy; worn.* 2. *bankrupt; broke; destitute;
distressed; impecunious; impoverished;
indigent; insolvent; needy; penniless; poor;
poverty-stricken; underprivileged.*

out for blood ∎ A moribund metaphor.
revengeful; ruthless; vengeful; vindictive.

out in left field ∎ A moribund metaphor. 1.
*amiss; astray; confused; deceived; deluded;
erring; erroneous; fallacious; false; faulty;
inaccurate; incorrect; in error; misguided;
misinformed; mislead; mistaken; not
correct; not right; uninformed; wrong.* 2.
*ignorant; incognizant; insensible; nescient;
unacquainted; unadvised; unapprised;
unaware; unenlightened; unfamiliar;
unintelligent; unknowing; unschooled;
untaught; unversed.* • On this issue,
feminists are truly *out in left field.*
REPLACE WITH *misguided.*

(they're) out in the cold ∎ A moribund
metaphor. *abandoned; alone; assailable;
attackable; defenseless; deserted; exposed;
forsaken; obnoxious; penetrable; pregnable;
stranded; undefended; unguarded;
unprotected; unshielded; vulnerable.*

out in the sun too much ∎ A moribund
metaphor. *bewildered; confounded; confused;
dazed; mixed up; muddled; perplexed.*

out like a light ∎ An insipid simile.
1. *asleep; dozing; napping; sleeping.*
2. *anesthetized; benumbed; comatose;
insensate; insensible; insentient; oblivious;
senseless; soporiferous; soporific; stuporous;
unconscious.*

out of a clear blue sky ∎ A moribund
metaphor. *by surprise; suddenly;
unexpectedly; without warning.*

out of circulation ∎ A moribund metaphor. 1.
*broken; defective; in disrepair; not working;
not functioning; out of order.* 2. *afflicted;
ailing; diseased; ill; indisposed; infirm;
not (feeling) well; sick; sickly; suffering;
unhealthy; unsound; unwell; valetudinarian.*

out of commission ∎ A moribund metaphor.
1. *broken; defective; in disrepair; not working;
not functioning; out of order.* 2. *afflicted;
ailing; diseased; ill; indisposed; infirm;
not (feeling) well; sick; sickly; suffering;
unhealthy; unsound; unwell; valetudinarian.*

out of gas ∎ A moribund metaphor. *beat;
bushed; debilitated; depleted; drained;
drowsy; enervated; exhausted; fatigued;
groggy; sapped; sleepy; sluggish; slumberous;
somnolent; soporific; spent; tired; weary;
worn out.*

out of harm's way ∎ A moribund metaphor.
*guarded; protected; safe; secure; sheltered;
shielded; undamaged; unharmed; unhurt;
unscathed.*

out of it ∎ A moribund metaphor. *ignorant;
incognizant; insensible; nescient;
unacquainted; unadvised; unapprised;
unaware; unenlightened; unfamiliar;
uninformed; unintelligent; unknowing;
unschooled; untaught; unversed.*

out of kilter ∎ A moribund metaphor. 1.
askew; awry; cockeyed; misaligned; skewed.
2. *shaky; unbalanced; unsettled; unsound;
unstable; wobbly.* 3. *broken; defective; in
disrepair; not working; not functioning; out
of order.*

> In a further aside, I should just like to add
> here that I have observed in my sixty-four
> years that passion both erodes and enhances
> character in equal measure, and not slowly
> but instantly, and in such a manner that
> what is left is not in balance but is thrown
> desperately out of kilter in both directions.—
> Anita Shreve, *All He Ever Wanted*

out of line ∎ A moribund metaphor. 1.
*improper; inappropriate; inapt; indecorous;
unbefitting; uncalled for; unfit; unfitting;
unsuitable; unsuited.* 2. *boisterous;
contrary; contumacious; disobedient;
disorderly; fractious; insubordinate;
misbehaving; obstreperous; rebellious;
recalcitrant; refractory; rowdy; uncontrolled;
undisciplined; unruly.*

out of reach ∎ A moribund metaphor. 1.
*inaccessible; remote; unapproachable;
unreachable.* 2. *impossible; impracticable;
improbable; unfeasible; unlikely; unworkable.*

out of sorts ∎ A moribund metaphor. *angry;
annoyed; cheerless; cross; dejected; depressed;
despondent; discouraged; dispirited;
displeased; downcast; enraged; furious;
gloomy; glum; grouchy; irate; irritated; mad;
morose; peevish; riled; roiled; sad; testy;
troubled; uneasy; unhappy; upset; vexed;
worried.*

out of sync ∎ A moribund metaphor. 1.
askew; awry; cockeyed; misaligned; skewed.
2. *shaky; unbalanced; unsettled; unsound;
unstable; wobbly.* 3. *broken; defective; in
disrepair; not working; not functioning; out
of order.*

out of the blue ∎ A moribund metaphor. *by
surprise; suddenly; unexpectedly; without
warning.*

**out of the frying pan and into the fire
∎** A moribund metaphor. *aggravate; complicate;
exacerbate; heighten; increase; intensify;
irritate; make worse; worsen.*

out of the game ∎ A moribund metaphor.

out of the realm of possibility ∎
A wretched redundancy. *implausible;
imponderable; impossible; impracticable;*

inconceivable; infeasible; not likely; unbelievable; unconjecturable; unimaginable; unsupposable; unthinkable; unworkable. • It's not *out of the realm of possibility* that he wants to embarrass the president. REPLACE WITH *unthinkable.*

out of the running ▪ A moribund metaphor. *noncontender; not competing; not contending.*

out of the woods ▪ A moribund metaphor. *guarded; protected; safe; secure; sheltered; shielded; undamaged; unharmed; unhurt; unscathed.*

out of thin air ▪ A moribund metaphor.

out of this world ▪ A moribund metaphor. *consummate; distinguished; eminent; excellent; exceptional; exemplary; exquisite; extraordinary; fabulous; fantastic; flawless; grand; great; ideal; illustrious; magnificent; marvelous; matchless; nonpareil; perfect; preeminent; remarkable; splendid; superb; superior; superlative; supreme; terrific; transcendent; tremendous; wonderful; wondrous.*

out of whack ▪ A moribund metaphor. 1. *askew; awry; cockeyed; misaligned; skewed.* 2. *shaky; unbalanced; unsettled; unsound; unstable; wobbly.* 3. *broken; defective; in disrepair; not working; not functioning; out of order.*

(create) out of (the) whole cloth ▪ A moribund metaphor. *fabricated; fake; false; falsified; fictional; fictitious; forged; invented; made-up; untrue.*

> She considered that she had created this man out of whole cloth, had thought him up, and she was sure that she could do a better job if she had to do it again.—John Steinbeck, *The Moon Is Down*

(go) out on a limb ▪ A moribund metaphor. 1. *at risk; endangered; hard-pressed; imperiled; in a bind; in a dilemma; in a fix; in a jam; in a predicament; in a quandary; in danger; in difficulty; in jeopardy; in peril; in trouble; jeopardized.* 2. *abandoned; alone; assailable; attackable; defenseless; deserted; exposed; forsaken; obnoxious; penetrable; pregnable; stranded; undefended; unguarded; unprotected; unshielded; vulnerable.* 3. *be adventuresome; be adventurous; be bold; be daring.*

output ▪ A torpid term. SEE ALSO **(the) bottom line; feedback; input; interface; parameters**.

out the window ▪ A TOP-TWENTY DIMWITTICISM. A moribund metaphor. 1. *abandoned; discarded; dismissed; jettisoned; rejected; repudiated; thrown out; tossed out.* 2. *dead; disappeared; dissolved; dispersed; evaporated; finished; forfeited; gone; inapplicable; inappropriate; inoperative; insignificant; irrelevant; lost; no longer applicable (apply); over; passed; scattered;*

unimportant; vanished. • It's just that old rules are *out the window*, like most of last year's assumptions about Europe. REPLACE WITH *inapplicable.* • It's 1999 in America, a land where common sense *went out the window* long ago. REPLACE WITH *was jettisoned.*

out to lunch ▪ A moribund metaphor. 1. *absent-minded; absorbed; abstracted; bemused; daydreaming; distrait; dreamy; faraway; lost; preoccupied.* 2. *forgetful; heedless; inattentive; lethean; neglectful; oblivious; unmindful.* 3. *ignorant; incognizant; insensible; nescient; unacquainted; unadvised; unapprised; unaware; unenlightened; unfamiliar; unintelligent; unknowing; unschooled; untaught; unversed.* 4. *amiss; astray; confused; deceived; deluded; erring; erroneous; fallacious; false; faulty; inaccurate; incorrect; in error; misguided; misinformed; mislead; mistaken; not correct; not right; uninformed; wrong.*

(put) out to pasture ▪ A moribund metaphor. *discharge; dismiss; fire; lay off; let go; release; retire; sack; set aside; shelve.* A moribund metaphor. • Motors Inc. said Joe will be *put out to pasture* when it introduces next year's lineup of vehicles. REPLACE WITH *retired.*

over a barrel ▪ A moribund metaphor. *defenseless; helpless; impotent; powerless.*

over and done with ▪ A wretched redundancy. *completed; concluded; done; ended; finished; over; passed; through.* • But in reality, it is the same old story, one we'd like to think of as *over and done with.* REPLACE WITH *concluded.*

over (my) dead body ▪ A moribund metaphor. *at no time; by no means; in no way; never; no; not; not at all; not ever; not in any way; not in the least*

overplay (his) hand ▪ A moribund metaphor.

(go) over the edge ▪ A moribund metaphor. *batty; cracked; crazy; daft; demented; deranged; fey; foolish; goofy; insane; lunatic; mad; maniacal; neurotic; nuts; nutty; psychotic; raving; silly; squirrelly; touched; unbalanced; unhinged; unsound; wacky; zany.*

over the hill ▪ A moribund metaphor. *aged; aging; ancient; antediluvian; antique; archaic; elderly; hoary; hoary-headed; old; patriarchal; prehistoric; seasoned; superannuated; venerable.*

over the moon ▪ A moribund metaphor. *blissful; blithe; buoyant; cheerful; delighted; ecstatic; elated; enraptured; euphoric; exalted; excited; exhilarated; exultant; gay; glad; gleeful; good-humored; happy; intoxicated; jolly; jovial; joyful; joyous; jubilant; merry; mirthful; overjoyed; pleased; rapturous; thrilled.*

over the transom

> Over breakfast, expecting her to be over the moon, Paul had told her that she could give her notice in at the nursery, he'd fix her up a half share in a smart little business with the girlfriend of a friend of his.—Elizabeth Young, *Asking for Trouble*

over the transom ∎ A moribund metaphor. *unasked (for)*; *unsolicited*; *unsought*.

overworked and understaffed ∎ An inescapable pair.

owing to the fact that ∎ A wretched redundancy. *because*; *considering*; *for*; *in that*; *since*. • *Owing to the fact that* many companies are members of more than one EDI system, it is helpful if they all change in recognizable ways. REPLACE WITH *Since*. SEE ALSO **attributable to the fact that**; **due to the fact that**.

> In the past she and I had seldom spoken to each other, owing to the fact that her 'one remaining joy'—her charming little Karl—had never succeeded in kindling into flame those sparks of maternity which are supposed to grow in great numbers upon the altar of every respectable female heart ....—Katherine Mansfield, *In a German Pension*

Pp

pack a punch (wallop) ∎ A moribund metaphor. *cogent; convincing; dynamic; effective; effectual; emotional; energetic; ferocious; fierce; forceful; formidable; gripping; hard-hitting; herculean; impassioned; inspiring; intense; lively; mighty; moving; passionate; persuasive; potent; powerful; strong; vehement; vigorous; vital.* • No doubt hurricane Bonnie is still *packing a punch.* REPLACE WITH *mighty.*

packed in (trapped) like sardines (in a can) ∎ An insipid simile. *abounding; brimful; brimming; bursting; chock-full; congested; crammed; crowded; dense; filled; full; gorged; jammed; jam-packed; overcrowded; overfilled; overflowing; packed; replete; saturated; stuffed.*

> She gave me a rather disparaging look and took out a tin of Golden Virginia, which she opened to reveal a layer of tiny neat joints packed in like sardines.—Kate Atkinson, *Emotionally Weird*

pack to the gills ∎ A moribund metaphor. *abounding; brimful; brimming; bursting; chock-full; congested; crammed; crowded; dense; filled; full; gorged; jammed; jam-packed; overcrowded; overfilled; overflowing; packed; replete; saturated; stuffed; swarming; teeming.* • Maybe we'll visit the Museum of Science, which will surely be *packed to the gills* and most unpleasant. REPLACE WITH *overcrowded.*

pack to the rafters ∎ A moribund metaphor. *abounding; brimful; brimming; bursting; chock-full; congested; crammed; crowded; dense; filled; full; gorged; jammed; jam-packed; overcrowded; overfilled; overflowing; packed; replete; saturated; stuffed; swarming; teeming.*

pack up and leave ∎ A moribund metaphor. *abscond; clear out; decamp; depart; desert; disappear; escape; exit; flee; fly; go; go away; leave; move on; part; pull out; quit; retire; retreat; run away; take flight; take off; vacate; vanish; withdraw.*

paddle (my) own canoe ∎ A moribund metaphor. *be autonomous; be free; be independent; be self-reliant; be self-sufficient.*

pain and suffering ∎ An inescapable pair. *agony; anguish; distress; grief; misery; pain; suffering; torment; worry.*

painfully shy ∎ An inescapable pair. *afraid; apprehensive; bashful; coy; demure; diffident; distant; fearful; humble; introverted; meek; modest; pavid; quiet; reserved; reticent; retiring; sheepish; shrinking; shy; timid; timorous; tremulous; unassuming; unobtrusive; unsociable; unsocial; withdrawn.*

paint a (rosy) picture of ∎ A moribund metaphor. *delineate; demonstrate; depict; describe; document; draw; evince; illustrate; indicate; paint; picture; portray; present; report; represent; reveal; show.* • The document will *paint a picture of* the nation's worsening financial system and warn that many large banks are near insolvency. REPLACE WITH *describe.* • Together, they *paint a picture of* hard times ahead. REPLACE WITH *portray.*

paint (himself) into a corner ∎ A moribund metaphor. *at bay; catch; corner; enmesh; ensnare; entangle; entrap; net; snare; trap.*

paint the town red ∎ A moribund metaphor. *be merry; carouse; carry on; celebrate; debauch; disport; frolic; party; play; revel; riot; roister; rollick; romp; skylark.*

paint with a broad brush ∎ A moribund metaphor. *generalize; universalize.*

pair of (two) twins ∎ A wretched redundancy. *twins.* • There were *two twins* at the mall who came up to him and asked him out. DELETE *two.*

(as) pale as death ∎ An insipid simile. *anemic; ashen; blanched; bloodless; cadaverous; colorless; deathlike; doughy; haggard; lusterless; pale; pallid; pasty; peaked; sallow; sickly; wan; whitish.*

> Her skin had turned as pale as death, after she'd been stuck in that blasted compartment of hers with a shade that only went up halfway, while the train rattled and shook, rattled and shook, day after day after day across the country.—John Sedgwick, *The Education of Mrs. Bemis*

(as) pale as a ghost ∎ An insipid simile. *anemic; ashen; blanched; bloodless; cadaverous; colorless; deathlike; doughy; haggard; lusterless; pale; pallid; pasty; peaked; sallow; sickly; wan; whitish.*

parameter ∎ An overworked word. 1. *boundary; guideline; guidepost; limit; limitation; perimeter.* 2. *characteristic; factor.* • At this time, potential funding *parameters* may change in a variety of ways. REPLACE WITH *characteristics.* • We would like to send you our most recent catalog to see if any of our books fit within your reviewing *parameters*. REPLACE WITH *guidelines*. SEE ALSO (the) **bottom line**; **feedback**; **input**; **interface**; **output**.

pardon my French ∎ An infantile phrase.

par excellence ∎ A foreign phrase. *incomparable*; *preeminent*.

par for the course ∎ A moribund metaphor. The people who say *par for the course* are *average*; *common*; *commonplace*; *customary*; *everyday*; *mediocre*; *middling*; *normal*; *ordinary*; *quotidian*; *regular*; *routine*; *standard*; *typical*; *uneventful*; *unexceptional*; *unremarkable*; *usual* users of the English language.

  Though sports and even the word *sports* may make us imagine action and excitement, sports metaphors are among the most prosaic expressions available to us. Those who use them are precisely as dull and uninspired as are their words. • That is *par for the course* for foreign businesses here, which have descended upon the Soviet Union much as they descended upon China. REPLACE WITH *normal*. • It's *par for the course* for this administration to blame all of its troubles on someone else. REPLACE WITH *customary*.

> I'd heard of cleaning ladies with filthy houses, and of divorced marriage counselors, so maybe this was par for the course.—Susan Coll, *Rockville Pike*

part and parcel ∎ An inescapable pair. ∎ *component*; *element*; *factor*; *part*; *portion*.

parting is such sweet sorrow ∎ A popular prescription.

parting of the ways ∎ A moribund metaphor. *altercation*; *argument*; *conflict*; *disagreement*; *discord*; *disputation*; *dispute*; *feud*; *fight*; *misunderstanding*; *quarrel*; *rift*; *row*; *spat*; *squabble*.

partner in crime ∎ A moribund metaphor. *abettor*; *accessory*; *accomplice*; *affiliate*; *ally*; *assistant*; *associate*; *co-conspirator*; *cohort*; *collaborator*; *colleague*; *compatriot*; *compeer*; *comrade*; *confederate*; *consort*; *co-worker*; *crony*; *partner*; *peer*.

part of the landscape ∎ A moribund metaphor. *average*; *common*; *conventional*; *customary*; *everyday*; *expected*; *familiar*; *habitual*; *natural*; *normal*; *ordinary*; *regular*; *routine*; *standard*; *usual*; *traditional*; *typical*. • In the Bay Area, bad traffic's *part of the landscape*. REPLACE WITH *expected*. • When does an exotic species become *part of the landscape*? REPLACE WITH *familiar*.

pass (away; on) ∎ A torpid term. *death*; *decease*; *die*; *expire*; *perish*. • I was blessed to have been raised by two wonderful, loving parents (both of them have *passed*). REPLACE WITH *died*. • The holiday season can be a very difficult time following the *passing* of a loved one.

REPLACE WITH *death*. • Former Knoxville Ice Bears defenseman Paul Lynch, who was a member of the 2008 SPHL Championship team, has *passed away* unexpectedly. REPLACE WITH *died*. • He decided to go back and pursue the chemo and finish out some of the end-of-life things before he *passed*. REPLACE WITH *died*. • Always quotable even after *passing*. REPLACE WITH *dying*.

pass the buck ∎ A moribund metaphor. *ascribe*; *assign*; *attribute*; *impute*.

pass the time of day ∎ A moribund metaphor. *babble*; *blab*; *cackle*; *chaffer*; *chat*; *chitchat*; *chatter*; *confabulate*; *converse*; *gossip*; *jabber*; *palaver*; *prate*; *prattle*; *rattle*; *talk*.

pass with flying colors ∎ A moribund metaphor. *ace*; *do well*; *excel*; *shine*.

past experience ∎ A wretched redundancy. *experience*. • I know from *past experience* that a lot of you are not going to like what I have to say. DELETE *past*.

past history ∎ A wretched redundancy. *history*. • We did not anticipate that the town would attempt to live off of its *past history*. DELETE *past*.

past (his) prime ∎ A torpid term. *aged*; *aging*; *ancient*; *antediluvian*; *antique*; *archaic*; *elderly*; *hoary*; *hoary-headed*; *old*; *patriarchal*; *prehistoric*; *seasoned*; *superannuated*; *venerable*.

past the point of no return ∎ A moribund metaphor.

> Until that last time, when I knew I had to go, when I knew that if I told my son I'd broken my nose, blacked my eyes, split my lip, by walking into the dining-room door in the dark, that I would have gone past some point of no return.—Anna Quindlen, *Black and Blue*

(as) patient as Job ∎ An insipid simile. *accepting*; *accommodating*; *acquiescent*; *complacent*; *complaisant*; *compliant*; *cowed*; *deferential*; *docile*; *dutiful*; *easy*; *forbearing*; *gentle*; *humble*; *long-suffering*; *meek*; *mild*; *obedient*; *passive*; *patient*; *prostrate*; *quiet*; *reserved*; *resigned*; *stoical*; *submissive*; *subservient*; *timid*; *tolerant*; *tractable*; *unassuming*; *uncomplaining*; *yielding*.

pat on the back ∎ A moribund metaphor. *acclaim*; *accolade*; *acknowledgment*; *applause*; *appreciation*; *approval*; *compliment*; *congratulation*; *felicitation*; *homage*; *honor*; *plaudits*; *praise*; *recognition*; *tribute*. • The selections are a nice *pat on the back* for our talented staff around the world. REPLACE WITH *compliment*. • To me, it's *a pat on the back* for hard work well done. REPLACE WITH *an acknowledgment*.

pat (myself) on the back ∎ A moribund metaphor. *acclaim*; *applaud*; *celebrate*; *cheer*;

commend; compliment; congratulate; extol; flatter; hail; honor; laud; plume; praise; puff; salute; self-congratulate. • After *patting himself on the back,* he incidentally points out that many other people may have had something to do with it. REPLACE WITH *congratulating himself.*

pave the way (for) ▌ A moribund metaphor. 1. *arrange; groom; make ready; plan; prepare; prime; ready.* 2. *bring about; cause; create; effect; generate; inaugurate; initiate; introduce; lead to; occasion; produce; provoke; result in; usher in.* • Chartering all schools *paves the way* for a new way to organize public education. REPLACE WITH *prepares.*

pay (their) debt to society ▌ A moribund metaphor.

pay (my) dues ▌ A moribund metaphor.

pay the fiddler (piper) ▌ A moribund metaphor. *pay; suffer.*

pay the price ▌ A moribund metaphor. *pay; suffer.*

pay the ultimate price ▌ Like other euphemisms, other ludicrous expressions for death and dying, *pay the ultimate price*—for *be executed; be killed; be murdered; die*—diminishes death, often an avenging, merciless death. There is no reverence for the dead, or for death, in this dimwitted expression. SEE ALSO **pass; pass away.**

pay through the nose ▌ A moribund metaphor. *costly; dear; excessive; exorbitant; expensive; high-priced.*

peace and harmony ▌ A wretched redundancy. *harmony; peace.* • I want there to be *peace and harmony* between us. REPLACE WITH *harmony* or *peace.*

> When Ada reached the story's conclusion, and the old lovers after long years together in peace and harmony had turned to oak and linden, it was full dark.—Charles Frazier, *Cold Mountain*

peace and quiet ▌ An inescapable pair. *calm; calmness; composure; equanimity; peace; peacefulness; poise; quiet; quietude; repose; rest; serenity; silence; stillness; tranquility.*

peaches and cream (complexion) ▌ A moribund metaphor.

pea in (my) shoe ▌ A moribund metaphor. *affliction; annoyance; bane; bother; burden; curse; difficulty; inconvenience; irritant; irritation; load; nuisance; ordeal; pain; pest; plague; problem; torment; tribulation; trouble; vexation; weight; worry.*

peaks and valleys ▌ A moribund metaphor. *alterations; changes; erraticism; fluctuations; fortuitousness; inconstancies; shifts; uncertainties; vacillations; variations; vicissitudes.*

peanut gallery ▌ An infantile phrase. *audience; spectators; viewers.*

pearls of wisdom ▌ A moribund metaphor. *acumen; astuteness; erudition; insight; intelligence; perspicacity; sagacity; wisdom.* • In addition to the $50,000 fee, his *pearls of wisdom* will cost three first-class airplane tickets. REPLACE WITH *insights.*

pearly whites ▌ A moribund metaphor. *teeth.*

> Then I saw him out of the corner of my eye, a little flash of pearly whites, a curl of chestnut hair, jawbones that could cut glass, and an entourage bigger than the crowd at my last birthday party.—Eric Garcia, *Cassandra French's Finishing School for Boys*

pencil pusher ▌ A moribund metaphor. 1. *assistant; clerk; office worker; recorder; scribe; secretary; typist.* 2. *drudge; menial; scullion; toiler.*

penny pinching ▌ A moribund metaphor. *cheap; economical; frugal; miserly; niggardly; parsimonious; stingy; thrifty.*

people are who (what) they are ▌ A quack equation.

people who live in glass houses shouldn't throw stones ▌ A popular prescription.

(as) per (your request) ▌ A torpid term. *according to; as.* Quintessentially dimwitted, *(as) per (your request)* is used by brainless people who cannot manage to sustain an original thought. These are the people who rely on ready-made phrases and formulas; the people who unquestioningly do as they're told; the people who join mass movements because they themselves cannot bear the burden of making decisions; the people who hate on instruction and fear forever.
• *As per your request,* you have been unsubscribed. REPLACE WITH *As you requested.* • Enclosed are chapters 1 through 6, *as per your request.* REPLACE WITH *as you requested.* • *As per usual,* he refuses to choose between his chief of staff and his chief of budget. REPLACE WITH *As usual.* • *Per our discussion,* please substitute the version developed in the earlier tool for all but the last two sentences of this. REPLACE WITH *As we discussed.* • OPEC crude production in the first half of 1989 was supposed to be 18.5 million b/d, *as per* the November 1988 agreement. REPLACE WITH *as stated in.* • *As per* the Semiconductor Industry Association, U.S. manufacturers accounted for nearly $137 billion in revenues during the year 1997. REPLACE WITH *According to.*

perception is reality ▌ A quack equation. Perception is too often purblind for there to be much reality to this quack equation. Still, it is a formula, uttered by mountebanks and managers alike, that has done much to disturb the life and livelihood of people.

perchance ∎ A withered word. 1. *conceivably*; *feasibly*; *maybe*; *perhaps*; *possibly*. 2. *accidentally*; *by chance*.

perennially popular ∎ An inescapable pair.

period ∎ An infantile phrase. • The lesson of the women's movement is clearly that no one makes it on their own. *Period*. DELETE *period*. • I know some professional, single women who would not date married men. *Period*. DELETE *period*. SEE ALSO **no ifs, ands, or buts**.

period of time ∎ A TOP-TWENTY DIMWITTICISM. A wretched redundancy. *period*; *time*; *while*. • I've been wanting to watch this movie for a long *period of time*. REPLACE WITH *time*. • Over a considerable *period of time*, this therapy gradually provides immunization. REPLACE WITH *period*.

> He enjoyed these exercises in increasing intimacy and was warmed by the knowledge that he would be able to remain for a period of time in the vicinity of the natural references that would move him.—Jane Urquhart, *A Map of Glass*

perish the thought ∎ An infantile phrase.

> Perish the thought—such dark thoughts were too cynical and bleak to entertain.—Robert Traver, *Anatomy of a Murder*

persona non grata ∎ A foreign phrase. *undesirable*.

(as) phony (queer) as a three-dollar bill ∎ An insipid simile. *artificial*; *bogus*; *counterfeit*; *ersatz*; *fake*; *false*; *feigned*; *fictitious*; *forged*; *fraudulent*; *imitation*; *mock*; *phony*; *pseudo*; *sham*; *simulated*; *spurious*; *synthetic*.

phony baloney ∎ An infantile phrase. *artificial*; *bogus*; *counterfeit*; *ersatz*; *fake*; *false*; *feigned*; *fictitious*; *forged*; *fraudulent*; *imitation*; *mock*; *phony*; *pseudo*; *sham*; *simulated*; *spurious*; *synthetic*.

physician, heal thyself ∎ A popular prescription.

pick and choose ∎ An inescapable pair. *choose*; *cull*; *decide*; *determine*; *elect*; *pick*; *select*. • For years, we could *pick and choose* where our students worked. REPLACE WITH *select*.

pick of the litter ∎ A moribund metaphor. *best*; *choice*; *elite*; *excellent*; *finest*; *first-class*; *first-rate*; *foremost*; *greatest*; *highest*; *matchless*; *nonpareil*; *optimal*; *optimum*; *outstanding*; *paramount*; *peerless*; *preeminent*; *premium*; *prominent*; *select*; *superior*; *superlative*; *top*; *unequaled*; *unexcelled*; *unmatched*; *unrivaled*; *unsurpassed*.

pick up speed ∎ A moribund metaphor. *accelerate*; *advance*; *bestir*; *bustle*; *hasten*; *hurry*; *precipitate*; *quicken*; *rush*; *speed up*.

pick up steam ∎ A moribund metaphor. 1. *accelerate*; *advance*; *bestir*; *bustle*; *hasten*; *hurry*; *precipitate*; *quicken*; *rush*; *speed up*. 2. *advance*; *awaken*; *better*; *expand*; *flourish*; *gain*; *gain strength*; *grow*; *heal*; *improve*; *increase*; *pick up*; *progress*; *prosper*; *rally*; *recover*; *recuperate*; *refresh*; *renew*; *revive*; *rouse*; *strengthen*; *thrive*.

pick up (take) the ball (and run with it) ∎ A moribund metaphor. *activate*; *bring about*; *cause*; *create*; *effect*; *enter on*; *generate*; *inaugurate*; *initiate*; *instigate*; *introduce*; *lead to*; *occasion*; *produce*; *provoke*; *usher in*.

pick up the pace ∎ A moribund metaphor. *accelerate*; *advance*; *bestir*; *bustle*; *charge*; *dash*; *go faster*; *hasten*; *hurry*; *quicken*; *run*; *rush*; *speed up*; *sprint*.

> Today, I'm running behind Greta, who picks up the pace just as we hit the twisted growth at the base of the mountain.—Jodi Picoult, *Vanishing Acts*

pick up the pieces ∎ A moribund metaphor.

pick up the tab ∎ A moribund metaphor. *pay (for)*.

picture of health ∎ A moribund metaphor. *fit*; *good*; *hale*; *hardy*; *healthful*; *healthy*; *hearty*; *robust*; *sound*; *strong*; *well*.

picture perfect ∎ A moribund metaphor. *absolute*; *beautiful*; *consummate*; *excellent*; *exemplary*; *exquisite*; *faultless*; *flawless*; *ideal*; *impeccable*; *lovely*; *magnificent*; *matchless*; *nonpareil*; *model*; *peerless*; *perfect*; *pretty*; *pure*; *sublime*; *superb*; *supreme*; *transcendent*; *ultimate*; *unblemished*; *unequaled*; *unexcelled*; *unrivaled*; *unsurpassed*; *untarnished*.

pièce de résistance ∎ A foreign phrase.

(a) piece of cake ∎ A moribund metaphor. *apparent*; *basic*; *clear*; *clear-cut*; *conspicuous*; *distinct*; *easily done*; *easy*; *effortless*; *elementary*; *evident*; *explicit*; *facile*; *limpid*; *lucid*; *manifest*; *obvious*; *patent*; *pellucid*; *plain*; *simple*; *simplicity itself*; *straightforward*; *translucent*; *transparent*; *unambiguous*; *uncomplex*; *uncomplicated*; *understandable*; *unequivocal*; *unmistakable*. Evoking only the silliest of images, *a piece of cake* ought to tell us that those who use this expression have nothing serious to say, and perhaps little thoughtful to think.
 • Choosing the menu for the wedding reception isn't always *a piece of cake*. REPLACE WITH *easy*. • Setting up a Palm device to use GoType! is *a piece of cake*. REPLACE WITH *simplicity itself*. • At my high school, preparing for college is not *a piece of cake*. REPLACE WITH *effortless*.

> Her job at UGP is a piece of cake, a lot of financial paper shuffling and occasional simultaneous interpreting of meetings between the polite and cold Swiss men in dark suits who run the front office and the hostile and sneering Arabs—known, I regret to say, as "towel heads"—who secretly control everything.—Katharine Weber, *Objects in Mirror Are Closer Than They Appear*

(a) piece of the action ∎ An infantile phrase. • Similar to the U.S. model, it will give companies the capital and technology they need while giving employees a *piece of the action* and establishing a constituency for capitalism.

(a) piece (slice) of the pie ∎ A moribund metaphor.

(a) piece of the puzzle ∎ A moribund metaphor. *clue; hint; inkling; pointer; sign.*

(a) piece of work ∎ A moribund metaphor. *aberrant; abnormal; anomalistic; anomalous; atypical; bizarre; curious; deviant; different; distinct; distinctive; eccentric; exceptional; extraordinary; fantastic; foreign; grotesque; idiosyncratic; independent; individual; individualistic; irregular; novel; odd; offbeat; original; peculiar; puzzling; quaint; queer; rare; remarkable; separate; singular; strange; uncommon; unconventional; unexampled; unique; unnatural; unorthodox; unparalleled; unprecedented; unusual; weird.*

pie in the sky ∎ A moribund metaphor. *artificial; capricious; chimeric; chimerical; delusive; dreamy; fanciful; fantastical; fictitious; frivolous; hallucinatory; illusory; imaginary; maggoty; phantasmal; phantasmic; unreal; whimsical.* • The only alternatives to testing she proposes are scarcely more than *pie in the sky.* REPLACE WITH *illusory.* • Other predictions were laughably *pie-in-the-sky.* REPLACE WITH *chimerical.*

pillar of society (the church; the community) ∎ A suspect superlative. It is the pillars of society—whether powerful, knowledgeable, or moneyed—who are often the most wobbly among us.

Few who have power do not misapply it, few who have knowledge do not misuse it, and few who have money do not misspend it.

For these reasons and others, before long and before others, pillars totter and then topple.

• But beware—you'll be going up against the well-informed dealer who might be viewed as *a pillar of the community.*

pillar (tower) of strength ∎ A moribund metaphor. *constant; dependable; determined; faithful; fast; firm; fixed; inexorable; inflexible; loyal; obdurate; reliable; resolute; resolved; rigid; solid; stable; staunch; steadfast; steady; stern; strong; supportive; tenacious; true; trustworthy; trusty; unflinching; unwavering; unyielding.*

pin (his) ears back ∎ A moribund metaphor. **1.** *beat; better; cap; defeat; exceed; excel; outclass; outdo; outflank; outmaneuver; outperform; outplay; outrank; outsmart; outthink; outwit; overcome; overpower; prevail over; surpass; top; triumph over; trounce; whip; win out.* **2.** *admonish; animadvert; berate; castigate; censure; chasten; chastise; chide; condemn; criticize; denounce; denunciate; discipline; impugn; objurgate; punish; rebuke; remonstrate; reprehend; reprimand; reproach; reprobate; reprove; revile; scold; upbraid; vituperate.*

pin the blame on ∎ A moribund metaphor. *accuse; blame; censure; charge; condemn; criticize; implicate; incriminate; inculpate; rebuke; reprimand; reproach; reprove; scold.*

place (put) on the back (front) burner ∎ A moribund metaphor. Like many dimwitticisms, *place (put) on the front burner* and *place (put) on the back burner* are silly expressions that make us question the seriousness and commitment of whoever uses them. These childish images fight against eloquence and thwart persuasion. • Illegal immigration needs to be *put on the front burner.* • He has insisted that the issue of global poverty be *put on the front burner* of human-rights concerns. SEE ALSO **on the front burner; on the back burner.**

> Everyone involved reported to him, and everything they reported was put on the front burner.—Tom Clancy, *Shadow Warriors*

place the blame on (her) shoulders ∎ A moribund metaphor. *accuse; blame; censure; charge; condemn; criticize; implicate; incriminate; inculpate; rebuke; reprimand; reproach; reprove; scold.*

plain and simple ∎ An inescapable pair. *apparent; basic; clear; clear-cut; conspicuous; distinct; easily done; easy; effortless; elementary; evident; explicit; facile; limpid; lucid; manifest; obvious; patent; pellucid; plain; simple; simplicity itself; straightforward; translucent; transparent; unambiguous; uncomplex; uncomplicated; understandable; unequivocal; unmistakable.*

(as) plain as a pikestaff ∎ An insipid simile. *apparent; basic; clear; clear-cut; conspicuous; distinct; easily done; easy; effortless; elementary; evident; explicit; facile; limpid; lucid; manifest; obvious; patent; pellucid; plain; simple; simplicity itself; straightforward; translucent; transparent; unambiguous; uncomplex; uncomplicated; understandable; unequivocal; unmistakable.*

(as) plain as day ∎ An insipid simile. *apparent; basic; clear; clear-cut; conspicuous; distinct; easily done; easy; effortless; elementary; evident; explicit; facile; limpid; lucid; manifest; obvious; patent; pellucid; plain; simple; simplicity itself; straightforward; translucent; transparent;*

(as) plain as the nose on (your) face

unambiguous; uncomplex; uncomplicated; understandable; unequivocal; unmistakable.

> To a person that knew B. from hill's foot, it was just as plain as day that if that card laid on there in the office, Mr. Brightman would miss that important meeting in St. Louis in the morning.—Kate Chopin, *A Vocation and a Voice*

(as) plain as the nose on (your) face
■ An insipid simile. *apparent; basic; clear; clear-cut; conspicuous; distinct; easily done; easy; effortless; elementary; evident; explicit; facile; limpid; lucid; manifest; obvious; patent; pellucid; plain; simple; simplicity itself; straightforward; translucent; transparent; unambiguous; uncomplex; uncomplicated; understandable; unequivocal; unmistakable.*

plain (smooth) sailing ■ A moribund metaphor. *apparent; basic; clear; clear-cut; conspicuous; distinct; easily done; easy; effortless; elementary; evident; explicit; facile; limpid; lucid; manifest; obvious; patent; pellucid; plain; simple; simplicity itself; smooth; straightforward; translucent; transparent; unambiguous; uncomplex; uncomplicated; understandable; unequivocal; unmistakable.*

plain vanilla ■ A moribund metaphor. *basic; common; conservative; conventional; customary; general; normal; ordinary; quotidian; regular; routine; standard; traditional; typical; uncreative; undaring; unimaginative; usual.* • He was uninterested in staying now that the bank has been limited to *plain vanilla* banking. REPLACE WITH *basic.*

plan ahead ■ A wretched redundancy. *plan.* • It's important that you *plan ahead* for your retirement. DELETE *ahead.*

plan for the worst, but hope for the best ■ A popular prescription.

plan of action ■ A torpid term. *action; course; direction; intention; method; move; plan; policy; procedure; route; scheme; strategy.*

plans and specifications ■ A wretched redundancy. *plans; specifications.* • Allowed expenditures include architectural and engineering services and related costs for *plans and specifications* for the renovation. USE *plans* or *specifications.*

play ball ■ A moribund metaphor. *agree; assent; collaborate; comply; concur; conspire; cooperate; join in; participate; work together.*

play both ends against the middle ■ A moribund metaphor.

play (your) cards right ■ A moribund metaphor.

play cat and mouse ■ A moribund metaphor. *fool; tease.*

play catch up ■ A moribund metaphor.

play (his cards) close to the chest (vest) ■ A moribund metaphor. *be clandestine; be confidential; be covert; be furtive; be mysterious; be private; be secretive; be secret; be sly; be stealthy; be surreptitious.*

play cupid ■ A moribund metaphor.

play fast and loose (with) ■ A moribund metaphor. *be careless; be dishonest; be disloyal; be false; be undependable; be unpredictable; be unreliable; be untrue; be untrustworthy.*

play games (with) ■ A moribund metaphor. *confuse; deceive; trick.*

play hardball ■ A moribund metaphor. *be demanding; be hard-hitting; be harsh; be rough; be severe; be stern; be strict; be tough.*

play hard to get ■ A moribund metaphor. *be coy; be fickle.*

play (raise) havoc with ■ A moribund metaphor. *disturb; mess up; devastate; rack; ravage; ruin; shatter; smash; undo; upset; wrack; wreck.*

play hell (the devil) with ■ A moribund metaphor. *disturb; mess up; devastate; rack; ravage; ruin; shatter; smash; undo; upset; wrack; wreck.*

play hide and seek ■ A moribund metaphor.

(like) playing Russian roulette ■ An insipid simile. • Licensees who sell on Sundays in violation of state law are *playing Russian roulette* with their licenses.

(will it) play in Peoria ■ A moribund metaphor.

play it by ear ■ A moribund metaphor. *ad-lib; extemporize; improvise.*

play musical chairs ■ A moribund metaphor.

play out ■ A torpid term. 1. *carry out; execute; perform; play.* 2. *develop; evolve; unfold.* • We will report to you how all this *plays out.* REPLACE WITH *unfolds.*

play possum ■ A moribund metaphor.

> On other occasions, I had learned at great cost that it is always wiser, with grownups and with a crowd, to play possum, as if beneath the snout of a fierce animal.—Albert Memmi, *The Pillar of Salt*

play second fiddle ■ A moribund metaphor. *be ancillary; be inferior; be lesser; be lower; be middling; be minor; be second; be secondary; be second-rate; be subordinate; be subservient; be substandard.*

play the field ■ A moribund metaphor. *date.*

play the fool ■ A moribund metaphor. *be silly; clown; fool around; mess around.*

play the game ■ A moribund metaphor. *abide by; accommodate; accord; acquiesce;*

act fairly; adapt; adhere to; agree; behave; comply; concur; conform; correspond; follow; harmonize; heed; mind; obey; observe; submit; yield.

play the waiting game ∎ A moribund metaphor. *be patient; wait.*

play to the crowd ∎ A moribund metaphor. *perform; play up; posture; show off.*

play (your) trump card ∎ A moribund metaphor.

play with fire ∎ A moribund metaphor. *chance; dare; endanger; gamble; hazard; imperil; jeopardize; make bold; peril; risk; venture.*

pleasant surprise ∎ An inescapable pair.

(as) pleased as Punch ∎ An insipid simile. *blissful; buoyant; cheerful; delighted; elated; excited; gay; glad; gladdened; gleeful; good-humored; gratified; happy; jolly; jovial; joyful; joyous; jubilant; merry; mirthful; pleased; tickled.*

pleasingly plump ∎ An inescapable pair. *ample; big; bulky; chubby; chunky; colossal; corpulent; dumpy; enormous; fat; flabby; fleshy; gigantic; heavy; hefty; huge; immense; large; mammoth; massive; obese; plump; portly; pudgy; rotund; round; squat; stocky; stout.*

plow new ground ∎ A moribund metaphor. **1.** *arrange; groom; make ready; plan; prepare; prime; ready.* **2.** *bring about; cause; create; effect; generate; inaugurate; initiate; introduce; lead to; occasion; produce; provoke; result in; usher in.*

(5:00) p.m. ... (in the) afternoon (evening) ∎ A wretched redundancy. *(5:00) p.m.; (in the) afternoon (evening).* • The city school legislature was called to order at *2 p.m.* on a Monday *afternoon.* DELETE *afternoon.*

poetry in motion ∎ A moribund metaphor. *agile; graceful; limber; lissome; lithe; lithesome; nimble; supple.*

point the finger (of blame) at ∎ A moribund metaphor. *accuse; blame; censure; charge; condemn; criticize; implicate; incriminate; inculpate; rebuke; reprimand; reproach; reprove; scold.* • When the problem is that severe, regulators have to *point the finger at* someone. REPLACE WITH *blame.*

poke (her) nose into ∎ A moribund metaphor. *encroach; entrench; infringe; interfere; intrude; invade; meddle; pry; tamper; trespass.*

politics as usual ∎ A torpid term. This is but a euphemism, a politic phrase, for words like *cheating; deceit; deceitfulness; deception; dishonesty; duplicity; falsehood; fraudulence; lying; mendacity; perfidy; self-interest; selfishness; tergiversation; treachery* or *backbiting; bad-mouthing; calumny;*

cruelty; defamation; denigration; infighting; insult; malevolence; malice; meanness; nastiness; slander; slur; spite; spitefulness; viciousness; vilification; vindictiveness. • In the course of this election, there has been too much *politics as usual.* REPLACE WITH *dishonesty.* • Democrats have been somewhat more restrained than Republicans in returning to *politics as usual,* apparently because they don't want to be seen as undermining Bush during wartime. REPLACE WITH *backbiting.*

pomp and circumstance ∎ An inescapable pair. *array; ceremony; circumstance; dazzle; display; fanfare; grandeur; magnificence; ostentation; pageantry; panoply; parade; pomp; resplendence; ritual; show; spectacle; splendor.*

(as) poor as a churchmouse ∎ An insipid simile. *bankrupt; broke; destitute; distressed; impecunious; impoverished; indigent; insolvent; needy; penniless; poor; poverty-stricken; underprivileged.*

(as) poor as sin ∎ An insipid simile. *bankrupt; broke; destitute; distressed; impecunious; impoverished; indigent; insolvent; needy; penniless; poor; poverty-stricken; underprivileged.*

> They would be poor as sin on his military pay, and then Teddy would just get himself killed and leave her stranded in California with nothing—or worse, with a baby.—Maile Meloy, *Liars and Saints*

poor cousin to ∎ A moribund metaphor. • Independent TV stations were once viewed as *poor cousins to* networked-owned stations and affiliates.

pose no immediate (imminent) danger (threat) ∎ A torpid term. • And though the radioactive fuel may *pose no immediate threat,* the canisters continue to deteriorate.

positive (*n*) ∎ A torpid term. *advantage; asset; benefit; gain; good; strength.* SEE ALSO **negative**.

positive effect (impact) ∎ A torpid term. • The breakup doesn't undo any of the *positive effects,* and it doesn't mean I revert to the way I was 10 years ago. REPLACE WITH *goodness.* • A small but growing number of school programs on problem solving show *positive effects* in preventing depression. REPLACE WITH *success.* • It's a defeat for minority children who can't afford to attend private schools through grade 6, thus missing out on the *positive effect* of a private school education. REPLACE WITH *benefit.* SEE ALSO **negative effect (impact)**.

positive feelings ∎ A torpid term. As the following variety of synonyms shows, *positive feelings* is a pulpous expression that arouses only our inattention: *affection; approval; blissfulness; courage; delectation;*

delight; ecstasy; enjoyment; fondness; friendliness; friendship; generosity; goodwill; happiness; hope; joy; kindness; lightheartedness; like; liking; love; loyalty; merriment; passion; peace; pleasure; rapture; relish; respect; warmth. • I feel she may have *positive feelings* for me, and I'd like to know for sure. REPLACE WITH *affection*. • The goal is to capture the *positive feelings* about making special purchases. REPLACE WITH *delectation*. • The better in touch you are with your *positive feelings* for each other, the less likely you are to act contemptuous of your spouse when you have a difference of opinion. REPLACE WITH *fondness and admiration*. SEE ALSO **in a good mood; negative feelings**.

pot of gold ▌ A moribund metaphor. *affluence; fortune; money; opulence; prosperity; riches; treasure; wealth.*

pound the pavement ▌ A moribund metaphor. *hunt; look for; quest; ransack; rummage; scour; search; seek.*

pouring (down) rain ▌ A wretched redundancy. *pouring; raining; storming.*

pour oil on troubled waters ▌ A moribund metaphor. *allay; alleviate; appease; assuage; calm; compose; ease; mitigate; mollify; pacify; palliate; quiet; relieve; soothe; still; tranquilize.*

pour (rub) salt on (our) wounds ▌ A moribund metaphor. *aggravate; complicate; exacerbate; heighten; increase; intensify; irritate; make worse; worsen.*

practice makes perfect ▌ A popular prescription.

practice what (you) preach ▌ A popular prescription.

praise (them) to the skies ▌ A moribund metaphor. *acclaim; applaud; celebrate; commend; compliment; congratulate; eulogize; extol; flatter; hail; laud; panegyrize; praise; puff; salute.*

preaching to the choir (chorus) ▌ A moribund metaphor.

precarious position ▌ An inescapable pair.

pretty ▌ An overworked word. *adequately; amply; enough; fairly; moderately; quite; rather; reasonably; somewhat; sufficiently; tolerably.*
 • She's a *pretty* bright woman. REPLACE WITH *reasonably*. • We're suffering some *pretty* devastating effects right now. DELETE *pretty*.
 Pretty, in these senses, proclaims its users have a vocabulary of little more than disyllabic words. For a person who says *pretty* also says *little* and *logy, really* and *leery, input* and *impact*. And with so few words, only so much can be known, only so much can be conveyed.

(as) pretty as a picture ▌ An insipid simile. *appealing; attractive; beautiful;*

becoming; captivating; comely; cute; dazzling; exquisite; fair; fetching; good-looking; gorgeous; handsome; lovely; nice-looking; pleasing; pretty; pulchritudinous; radiant; ravishing; seemly; stunning.

prevailing winds of ▌ A moribund metaphor.

previous to ▌ A torpid term. *before.* • *Previous to* meeting her, I showed no interest in women. REPLACE WITH *Before*. SEE ALSO **in advance of; previous to; subsequent to.**

prick (puncture) (his) balloon ▌ A moribund metaphor. *abase; chasten; debase; decrease; deflate; degrade; demean; depreciate; depress; diminish; disgrace; dishonor; embarrass; humble; humiliate; lower; mortify; puncture; shame.*

prick up (her) ears ▌ A moribund metaphor. *attend to; hark; hear; hearken; heed; listen; pay attention; pay heed.*

> I pricked up my ears, for it was positively the first time I had ever heard a foreign tongue.— Willa Cather, *My Antonia*

pride and joy ▌ An inescapable pair.

prim and proper ▌ An inescapable pair.

primrose path ▌ A moribund metaphor.

prince charming ▌ An infantile phrase.

princely price ▌ An inescapable pair. *costly; dear; excessive; exorbitant; expensive; high-priced.*

prioritize ▌ A torpid term. *arrange; classify; list; order; place; put; rank; rate.* • He *prioritizes* this relationship above all his "after high school plans," such as going to college. REPLACE WITH *ranks*.

prior to ▌ A torpid term. *before.*
 • Select only the cells to be printed *prior to* selecting the Print command. REPLACE WITH *before*. • Certain verbs in English require the use of a pronoun *prior to* and after an infinitive phrase. REPLACE WITH *before*. SEE ALSO **in advance of; previous to; subsequent to.**

prize(d) possession ▌ An inescapable pair. • In an era of spiraling costs, a good indirect cost rate is a *prized possession*.

proactive ▌ A TOP-TWENTY DIMWITTICISM. A torpid term. 1. *anticipatory; involved; participatory.* 2. *aggressive; assertive; enterprising.* • To educate parents to take this more *proactive* role in the education of their children, the board has authorized the creation of a parent-controlled Family Education Resources Center. REPLACE WITH *participatory*. • It is vital to obtain sell-through information from retailers so that you can take *proactive* steps to get a new order. REPLACE WITH *aggressive*. • A school needs a PR person to develop a *proactive* approach that anticipates problems before they develop. REPLACE WITH *enterprising*.

• Smaller, specialty firms, such as Bath & Body Works, or apparel stores, such as Bloomingdale's, Nordstrom, and Canada's famed Harry Rosen, teach their employees to *proactively* ask customers if they need assistance. DELETE *proactively*.

proceeded to ∎ A torpid term. • The team *proceeded to develop* the recently generated ideas into a concrete curriculum. REPLACE WITH *developed*. • He then *proceeded to declare* his undying love for me. REPLACE WITH *declared*.

proceed forward ∎ A torpid term. *advance; continue; develop; go on; grow; happen; improve; increase; make headway; make progress; move on; occur; proceed; progress; take place.* • Reducing operating losses in this business will give us increased flexibility to *proceed forward* with other endeavors. REPLACE WITH *proceed*. SEE ALSO **a step forward; a step (forward) in the right direction; go forward; move forward; move (forward) in the right direction.**

(as) proud as a peacock ∎ An insipid simile. *arrogant; cavalier; conceited; disdainful; egocentric; egotistic; egotistical; haughty; lofty; pompous; pretentious; prideful; proud; narcissistic; self-centered; self-important; self-satisfied; supercilious; superior; vain.*

proud parent ∎ An inescapable pair.

pull a fast one ∎ A moribund metaphor. *bamboozle; befool; beguile; bilk; bluff; cheat; con; deceive; defraud; delude; dupe; feint; fool; gyp; hoodwink; lead astray; misdirect; misguide; misinform; mislead; spoof; swindle; trick; victimize.*

pull a rabbit out of the hat ∎ A moribund metaphor. *be creative; be ingenious; be inventive; be resourceful.*

pull (yank) (her) chain ∎ A moribund metaphor. *bamboozle; befool; beguile; bilk; bluff; cheat; con; deceive; defraud; delude; dupe; feint; fool; gyp; hoodwink; jest; joke; kid; lead astray; misdirect; misguide; misinform; mislead; rib; spoof; swindle; tease; trick; trifle with.*

pull (my) leg ∎ A moribund metaphor. *bamboozle; befool; beguile; bilk; bluff; cheat; con; deceive; defraud; delude; dupe; feint; fool; gyp; hoodwink; jest; joke; kid; lead astray; misdirect; misguide; misinform; mislead; rib; spoof; swindle; tease; trick; trifle with.*

(like) pulling teeth ∎ An insipid simile. *arduous; backbreaking; burdensome; difficult; exhausting; fatiguing; hard; herculean; laborious; not easy; onerous; severe; strenuous; toilful; toilsome; tough; troublesome; trying; wearisome.* • Getting these people to level with reporters is often *like pulling teeth*. REPLACE WITH *arduous*.

pull no punches ∎ A moribund metaphor. *be blunt; be candid; be direct; be forthright; be frank; be open; be outspoken; be straightforward.*

pull (it) off ∎ A moribund metaphor. *accomplish; bring about; do; carry out; perform; succeed.*

pull out all the stops ∎ A moribund metaphor. *aim; attempt; endeavor; essay; exert; exhaust; labor; moil; strain; strive; struggle; toil; try hard; undertake; work at.*

pull strings ∎ A moribund metaphor.

pull the plug (on) ∎ A moribund metaphor. *abandon; abort; annul; arrest; ban; cancel; cease; check; conclude; derail; desert; desist; discontinue; end; forsake; halt; invalidate; leave; quit; repeal; rescind; revoke; stop; suspend; terminate; withdraw.* • Organizers say they'll *pull the plug* on the parade if a gay and lesbian group is allowed to participate. REPLACE WITH *cancel*. • Cellucci *pulled the plug on* the PAC last summer after learning it was being organized by inmates at some of the states' toughest prisons. REPLACE WITH *banned*.

> He thought about it, wondering if he really could pull the plug.—Christopher Bram, *Lives of the Circus Animals*

pull the rug out from under ∎ A moribund metaphor. *capsize; founder; invert; overset; overthrow; overturn; reverse; sink; tip; topple; tumble; upend; upset.*

> For once the big dick of the law and government would not pull the rug out from under me.—Tim Miller, *Shirts & Skin*

pull the wool over (his) eyes ∎ A moribund metaphor. *bamboozle; befool; beguile; bilk; bluff; cheat; con; deceive; defraud; delude; dupe; fake; feign; feint; fool; gyp; hoodwink; lead astray; lie; misdirect; misguide; misinform; mislead; misrepresent; pretend; spoof; swindle; trick; victimize.* • You also have a built-in B.S. detector, and you can tell if someone is attempting to *pull the wool over your eyes*. REPLACE WITH *mislead you*.

pull (yourself) up by (your) own bootstraps ∎ A moribund metaphor.

pull up stakes ∎ A moribund metaphor. *abscond; clear out; decamp; depart; desert; disappear; escape; exit; flee; fly; go; go away; leave; move on; part; pull out; quit; retire; retreat; run away; take flight; take off; vacate; vanish; withdraw.*

(can't) punch (his) way out of a paper bag ∎ A moribund metaphor. *ham-fisted; inadequate; incapable; incompetent; ineffective; ineffectual; inefficacious; inept; lacking; not able; unable; unfit; unqualified; unskilled; useless; wanting.*

pure and simple ∎ An inescapable pair. *basic; elementary; fundamental; pure; simple; straightforward; uncomplicated.*

(as) pure as the driven snow ∎ An insipid simile. 1. *decent; ethical; exemplary; good; honest; honorable; just; moral; pure; righteous; straight; upright; virtuous; wholesome.* 2. *celibate; chaste; immaculate; maidenly; modest; snowy; spotless; stainless; unblemished; unsoiled; untarnished; virgin; virginal; virtuous.*

pursuant to ∎ A torpid term. *according to; by; following; under.*

pursue (strive for) excellence ∎ A suspect superlative. • *Striving for excellence* is not just a goal but a way of life. • The recipients had to prepare brief statements on what inspires them to *strive for excellence.* SEE ALSO **excellence.**

push and shove ∎ An inescapable pair. *bulldoze; drive; propel; push; shove; thrust.*

(when) push comes to shove ∎ A moribund metaphor.

push the envelope ∎ A moribund metaphor. 1. *be adventuresome; be adventurous; be bold; be daring.* 2. *beat; exceed; outdo; outstrip; surpass; top.*

   Like thousands of English idioms, *push the envelope* helps ensure that any article, any book in which it appears is mediocre and unmemorable.

   Literature does not allow worn metaphors like this; bestsellers demand them.

> I push the envelope and put my right hand gently, softly, on his upper arm, inches away from his chin.—Alix Strauss, *The Joy of Funerals*

push the panic button ∎ A moribund metaphor. *be alarmed; be anxious; be excited; be frightened; be jumpy; be nervous; be panicky; be panic-stricken; be scared; be unnerved.*

push the right buttons ∎ A moribund metaphor.

pushed (me) to the wall ∎ A moribund metaphor. 1. *coerced; compelled; constrained; dictated; enforced; enjoined; forced; made; ordered; pressed; pressured; required.* 2. *at bay; caught; cornered; enmeshed; ensnared; entangled; entrapped; netted; snared; trapped.*

put a bug in (his) ear ∎ A moribund metaphor. *allude to; clue; connote; cue; hint; imply; indicate; insinuate; intimate; prompt; suggest; tip off.*

put a damper on ∎ A moribund metaphor. *check; dampen; deaden; depress; discourage; hinder; impede; inhibit; obstruct; repress; restrain.*

put a gun to (my) head ∎ A moribund metaphor. *coerce; command; compel; constrain; demand; dictate; enforce; enjoin; force; insist; make; order; pressure; require.* • Nobody *put a gun to your head.* REPLACE WITH *forced you.*

put a halt (an end; a stop) to ∎ A wretched redundancy. *cease; close; complete; conclude; derail; discontinue; end; finish; halt; settle; stop.* • It's time we *put a stop to* all the violence. REPLACE WITH *stop.* SEE ALSO **call a halt (an end; a stop) to.**

put a lid on (it) ∎ A moribund metaphor. 1. *abandon; abort; annul; arrest; ban; cancel; cease; check; conclude; desert; desist; discontinue; end; forsake; halt; leave; quit; stop; suspend; terminate.* 2. *censor; hush up; muffle; quash; smother; squash; squelch; stifle.* 3. *be closed-mouthed; be quiet; be reticent; be silent; be speechless; be still; be taciturn; be uncommunicative; hush (up); keep quiet; shut up.* • *Put a lid on it.* REPLACE WITH *Be quiet.*

(don't) put all (your) eggs in one basket ∎ A moribund metaphor.

put a sock in (it) ∎ A moribund metaphor. *be closed-mouthed; be quiet; be reticent; be silent; be speechless; be still; be taciturn; be uncommunicative; hush (up); keep quiet; shut up.* • *Put a lid on it.* REPLACE WITH *Be quiet.*

> I listened patiently to all this minutiae, never once wishing he'd put a sock in it.—Jane Heller, *Female Intelligence*

put a spin on ∎ A moribund metaphor.

put (it) behind (us) ∎ A moribund metaphor. • She is eager to testify before the grand jury and to *put this part of the investigation behind her.* SEE ALSO **get (go) on with (my) life.**

put (his) best foot forward ∎ A moribund metaphor.

put (your) finger on ∎ A moribund metaphor. *ascertain; detect; discern; discover; distinguish; find out; identify; know; learn; locate; make out; note; notice; perceive; pick out; pinpoint; place; point out; realize; recall; recognize; recollect; remember; see; specify; spot; think of.*

> She tried to put her finger on what it was that she liked about him and couldn't.—Larry McMurtry, *Moving On*

put (her) foot down ∎ A moribund metaphor. 1. *hold fast; stand firm.* 2. *assert; command; decree; dictate; insist; order; require.* 3. *deny; disallow; forbid; prohibit; refuse; reject.* • I *put my foot down.* REPLACE WITH *refused.*

put (his) foot in (his) mouth ∎ A moribund metaphor.

put forward ∎ A torpid term. *advance; broach; introduce; offer; present; propose; propound; submit; suggest; tender.* • There is speculation that he opposed Moynihan's plan so he could *put forward* his own. REPLACE WITH *propose.* SEE ALSO **come forward (with)**.

put (his) head in the lion's mouth ∎ A moribund metaphor. *chance; dare; endanger; gamble; hazard; imperil; jeopardize; make bold; peril; risk; venture.*

put (our) heads together ∎ A moribund metaphor. *collaborate; conspire; cooperate; work together.*

put (your) house (back) in order ∎ A moribund metaphor. *correct; rectify; redress; remedy; restore; right.* • Ravaged by losses after it lost direction in a period of rapid growth, Phoenix is attempting to *put its house back in order.* REPLACE WITH *right itself.*

put in a plug for ∎ A moribund metaphor. *acclaim; applaud; celebrate; commend; compliment; congratulate; eulogize; extol; flatter; hail; laud; panegyrize; praise; puff; salute.*

put (him) in bad light ∎ A moribund metaphor.

put in cold storage ∎ A moribund metaphor. *defer; delay; forget; hold off; hold up; ignore; pigeonhole; postpone; procrastinate; put aside; put off; set aside; shelve; suspend; table; waive.*

put in motion ∎ A moribund metaphor. *begin; commence; embark; inaugurate; initiate; launch; originate; start; undertake.*

put (her) in (her) place ∎ A moribund metaphor. *abase; chasten; debase; decrease; deflate; degrade; demean; depreciate; depress; diminish; disgrace; dishonor; embarrass; humble; humiliate; lower; mortify; puncture; shame.*

> Whenever he first spoke, whatever he said, one of us would have to put him in his place.—Karen Joy Fowler, *The Jane Austen Book Club*

put (yourself) in (her) place ∎ A moribund metaphor. *be sorry for; commiserate; empathize; feel for; feel sorry for; identify with; pity; sympathize; understand.*

put (myself) in (his) shoes ∎ A moribund metaphor. *be sorry for; commiserate; empathize; feel for; feel sorry for; identify with; pity; sympathize; understand.*

put (your) life on the line ∎ A moribund metaphor. *chance; dare; endanger; gamble; hazard; imperil; jeopardize; make bold; peril; risk; venture.*

put money on ∎ A moribund metaphor. *bet; gamble; wager.*

put (his) neck on the line ∎ A moribund metaphor. *chance; dare; endanger; gamble; hazard; imperil; jeopardize; make bold; peril; risk; venture.*

put new life into ∎ A moribund metaphor. *animate; energize; enliven; inspire; inspirit; invigorate; refresh; reinvigorate; rejuvenate; revitalize; revive; rouse; stimulate; stir; vitalize.*

put on airs ∎ A moribund metaphor. *be affected; be arrogant; be conceited; be condescending; be contumelious; be disdainful; be egotistic; be egotistical; be haughty; be high-handed; be magisterial; be overbearing; be pompous; be pretentious; be proud; be prideful; be self-important; be snobbish; be supercilious; be superior.*

put on an act ∎ A moribund metaphor. *affect; fake; feign; make believe; pretend; simulate.*

put (her) on a pedestal ∎ A moribund metaphor. *adore; cherish; esteem; eulogize; exalt; extol; glorify; honor; idealize; idolize; laud; love; panegyrize; prize; revere; treasure; venerate; worship.*

put one over on (her) ∎ A moribund metaphor. *bamboozle; befool; beguile; bilk; bluff; cheat; con; deceive; defraud; delude; dupe; feint; fool; gyp; hoodwink; lead astray; misdirect; misguide; mislead; spoof; swindle; trick; victimize.*

put on hold ∎ A torpid term. *defer; delay; forget; hold off; hold up; ignore; pigeonhole; postpone; procrastinate; put aside; put off; set aside; shelve; suspend; table; waive.* • The agreement had been scheduled to go into effect on Tuesday, after being *put on hold* for 30 days. REPLACE WITH *delayed.*

put on ice ∎ A moribund metaphor. *defer; delay; forget; hold off; hold up; ignore; pigeonhole; postpone; procrastinate; put aside; put off; set aside; shelve; suspend; table; waive.*

put (us) on the map ∎ A moribund metaphor. • At the time analysts thought Ames was just the tonic Zayre needed, and the deal *put the 30-year-old Ames on the map.*

put (it) on the table ∎ A moribund metaphor. *disclose; discuss; divulge; expose; make known; relate; release; reveal; tell; unveil.* • The president hasn't *put a single specific on the table.* REPLACE WITH *disclosed.*

put on (my) thinking cap ∎ A moribund metaphor. *brood over; cogitate on; consider; contemplate; deliberate on; dwell on; excogitate on; meditate on; mull over; ponder; reflect on; study; think about.*

put (it) out of (its) misery ∎ A moribund metaphor. 1. *destroy; kill; murder; slay.* 2. *cease; close; end; finish; halt; shut off; stop; terminate; turn off.*

> She applied the parking brake, gently put the engine out of its misery, then held on for dear life as it convulsed, sputtered, and died with a sigh.—Rob Kean, *The Pledge*

put out to pasture

put out to pasture ∎ A moribund metaphor. 1. *cast off; discard; dismiss; drop; dump; eliminate; exclude; expel; jettison; lay aside; reject; retire; set aside; shed.* 2. *ax; discharge; dismiss; fire; let go; retire.* • Playing a hot-blooded parent helps you feel like you haven't yet been *put out to pasture.* REPLACE WITH *dismissed.*

put (his) pants on one leg at a time ∎ A moribund metaphor. *average; common; commonplace; conservative; conventional; customary; everyday; mediocre; middling; normal; ordinary; quotidian; regular; routine; standard; traditional; typical; uneventful; unexceptional; unremarkable; usual.*

put pen to paper ∎ A moribund metaphor. *author; compose; indite; inscribe; jot down; pen; scrabble; scratch; scrawl; scribble; scribe; write.*

put (your) shoulder to the wheel ∎ A moribund metaphor. *drudge; grind; grub; labor; moil; slave; strain; strive; struggle; sweat; toil; travail; work hard.*

put (your) stamp of approval on ∎ A moribund metaphor. *approve of; authorize; certify; endorse; sanction.* • To portray our community as *putting a stamp of approval on* the execution is inaccurate. REPLACE WITH *approving of.*

put that in your pipe and smoke it ∎ A moribund metaphor.

put the brakes on ∎ A moribund metaphor. *abandon; abort; arrest; block; bridle; cancel; cease; check; conclude; control; curb; derail; desert; desist; discontinue; disturb; end; forsake; halt; interrupt; leave; obstruct; quit; repress; restrain; stop; suppress; suspend; terminate.* • The parent's problems with its retail divisions effectively *put the brakes on* the project and helped stall other downtown projects as well. REPLACE WITH *stopped.* • It *put the brakes on* the decline of political talk radio. REPLACE WITH *checked.*

put the cart before the horse ∎ A moribund metaphor. *backward; counterclockwise; inside-out; inverted; reversed; upside-down.*

put the best face on ∎ A moribund metaphor. • In the aftermath, AT&T management tried to *put the best face on* an embarrassing and costly mix-up.

put the fear of God into (them) ∎ A torpid term. *alarm; appall; benumb; daunt; frighten; horrify; intimidate; panic; paralyze; petrify; scare; shock; startle; terrify; terrorize.*

put the finger on ∎ A moribund metaphor. *betray; deliver up; inform on; turn in.*

put the finishing (last) touches on ∎ A moribund metaphor. *complete; conclude; end; finalize; finish; wrap up.*

put the genie back in the bottle ∎ A moribund metaphor.

put the kibosh on ∎ A moribund metaphor. *abort; annul; arrest; balk; block; bridle; cancel; check; derail; detain; end; foil; frustrate; halt; harness; neutralize; nullify; restrain; retard; stall; stay; stop; terminate; thwart.*

put the screws to ∎ A moribund metaphor. *bulldoze; bully; coerce; compel; constrain; demand; drive; enforce; enjoin; goad; force; impel; incite; intimidate; make; necessitate; obligate; oblige; order; press; pressure; prod; require; threaten; tyrannize; urge.*

put the skids on ∎ A moribund metaphor. *abandon; abort; arrest; cancel; cease; check; conclude; derail; desert; desist; discontinue; end; forsake; halt; leave; quit; stop; suspend; terminate.*

put through (her) paces ∎ A moribund metaphor. *catechize; cross-examine; examine; grill; inquire; interrogate; pump; question; quiz; test.*

put through the wringer ∎ A moribund metaphor. *catechize; cross-examine; examine; grill; inquire; interrogate; pump; question; quiz; test.*

put together the pieces of the puzzle ∎ A moribund metaphor. *clear up; decipher; disentangle; explain; explicate; figure out; resolve; solve; unravel; untangle; work out.*

put (them) to the test ∎ A torpid term. *catechize; cross-examine; examine; grill; inquire; interrogate; pump; question; quiz; test.*

put two and two together ∎ Instead of *putting two and two together*, we might think better, less simply, perhaps, if we were to try to *comprehend, conclude, construe, decipher, deduce, discern, draw, fathom, figure out, gather, grasp, imagine, infer, interpret, perceive, realize, reason, see, surmise,* or *understand.* The words we express define the world we experience.

(like) putty in (my) hands ∎ An insipid simile. *accommodating; acquiescent; adaptable; agreeable; amenable; complacent; complaisant; compliant; deferential; docile; ductile; elastic; flexible; malleable; manageable; moldable; obedient; obliging; persuasible; pliant; responsive; submissive; tractable; trained; yielding.*

put up or shut up ∎ An infantile phrase.

Qq

queer fish ▪ A moribund metaphor. *aberrant; abnormal; anomalistic; anomalous; atypical; bizarre; curious; deviant; different; distinct; distinctive; eccentric; exceptional; extraordinary; fantastic; foreign; grotesque; idiosyncratic; independent; individual; individualistic; irregular; novel; odd; offbeat; original; peculiar; puzzling; quaint; queer; rare; remarkable; separate; singular; strange; uncommon; unconventional; unexampled; unique; unnatural; unorthodox; unparalleled; unprecedented; unusual; weird.*

(a) question mark ▪ A torpid term. *enigma; mystery; puzzle; question; uncertain; uncertainty; unknown; unsure.* • But that's still *a question mark.* REPLACE WITH *unknown.* • But what happens thereafter is *a question mark,* especially since Disney has a longer history with Hasbro's arch-rival Mattel Inc. REPLACE WITH *uncertain.*

(as) quick and dirty ▪ An inescapable pair. *crude; haphazard; improvised; makeshift; provisional; slapdash; temporary; tentative.*

(as) quick as a bunny ▪ An insipid simile. *brisk; expeditious; fast; fleet; hasty; hurried; immediate; instant; instantaneous; prompt; quick; rapid; speedy; spry; sudden; swift; winged.*

(as) quick as a flash ▪ An insipid simile. *brisk; expeditious; fast; fleet; hasty; hurried; immediate; instant; instantaneous; prompt; quick; rapid; speedy; spry; sudden; swift; winged.*

(as) quick as a wink ▪ An insipid simile. *brisk; expeditious; fast; fleet; hasty; hurried; immediate; instant; instantaneous; prompt; quick; rapid; speedy; spry; sudden; swift; winged.*

> I showed her everything, and she got a job quick as a wink in my same factory, in a section where they made flexible mounts for the fifty-calibers.—Nancy E. Turner, *The Water and the Blood*

(as) quick as lightning ▪ An insipid simile. *brisk; expeditious; fast; fleet; hasty; hurried; immediate; instant; instantaneous; prompt; quick; rapid; speedy; spry; sudden; swift; winged.*

quick on (his) feet ▪ A moribund metaphor. 1. *brisk; expeditious; fast; fleet; hasty; hurried; immediate; instant; instantaneous; prompt; quick; rapid; speedy; spry; sudden; swift; winged.* 2. *able; adroit; alert; apt; astute; bright; brilliant; capable; clever; competent; discerning; enlightened; insightful; intelligent; judicious; keen; knowledgeable; learned; logical; luminous; perceptive; perspicacious; quick; rational; reasonable; sagacious; sage; sapient; sensible; sharp; shrewd; smart; sound; understanding; wise; witty.*

quick on the draw ▪ A moribund metaphor. *fast; fast-acting; quick; rapid; speedy; swift.*

quid pro quo ▪ A foreign phrase.

(as) quiet as a mouse ▪ An insipid simile. *dumb; hushed; motionless; mum; mute; noiseless; quiet; reticent; silent; speechless; stationary; still; stock-still; subdued; taciturn; unmoving; voiceless; wordless.*

quiet desperation ▪ An inescapable pair.

> There was a look of quiet desperation on her face, just weeks into this new life, one she hadn't wanted.—Kathleen Cambor, *In Sunlight, in a Beautiful Garden*

quit the scene ▪ A torpid term. *abscond; clear out; decamp; depart; desert; disappear; escape; exit; flee; fly; go; go away; leave; move on; part; pull out; quit; retire; retreat; run away; take flight; take off; vacate; vanish; withdraw.*

quit while (you're) ahead ▪ A popular prescription.

quote, unquote ▪ An infantile phrase. *as it were; so-called; so to speak; such as it is.* • It's too soon in the *quote, unquote* relationship for that. REPLACE WITH *so-called.* • I was referred to them by a friend of mine, *quote, unquote.* REPLACE WITH *as it were.*

Rr

(gone to) rack (wrack) and ruin ∎ An inescapable pair. *broken down; crumbly; decayed; deteriorated; dilapidated; run-down; shabby.*

rack (wrack) (my) brains ∎ A moribund metaphor. *endeavor; exert; labor; moil; slave; strain; strive; struggle; toil; try; work.*

radiantly happy ∎ An inescapable pair. *blissful; blithe; buoyant; cheerful; delighted; ecstatic; elated; enraptured; euphoric; exalted; excited; exhilarated; exultant; gay; glad; gleeful; good-humored; happy; intoxicated; jolly; jovial; joyful; joyous; jubilant; merry; mirthful; overjoyed; pleased; rapturous; thrilled.*

> And both were radiantly happy because of old times' sake.—Theodore Dreiser, *An American Tragedy*

raid the cookie jar ∎ A moribund metaphor. *filch; pilfer; pinch; purloin; rob; steal; take; thieve.*

raining cats and dogs ∎ A moribund metaphor. *pouring; raining; storming.*

raining pitchforks ∎ A moribund metaphor. *pouring; raining; storming.*

rain on (your) parade ∎ A moribund metaphor. 1. *depress; disappoint; discourage; dishearten; disillusion; dispirit; disturb; upset.* 2. *blight; cripple; damage; disable; disrupt; disturb; harm; hurt; impair; incapacitate; lame; mar; mess up; rack; ruin; sabotage; spoil; subvert; undermine; vitiate; wrack; wreck.* • I didn't want to dampen Paul's enthusiasm and I didn't have the heart to *rain on his parade* by telling him I knew Dr. Harris. REPLACE WITH *disillusion him.*

> It would have been wrong to rain on her parade at that moment, but even more irresponsible to encourage her.—Wang Anyi, *The Song of Everlasting Sorrow*

(come) rain or shine ∎ A moribund metaphor. *no matter what; regardless.*

raise a (red) flag ∎ A moribund metaphor. *alert; apprise; caution; forewarn; inform; notify; signal; warn.*

raise Cain ∎ A moribund metaphor. 1. *bellow; bluster; clamor; complain; criticize; explode; fulminate; fume; holler; howl; object; protest; rage; rant; rave; roar; scream; shout; storm; thunder; vociferate; yell.* 2. *be merry;*

carouse; carry on; celebrate; debauch; disport; frolic; party; play; revel; riot; roister; rollick; romp; skylark.

raise (some) eyebrows (of) ∎ A moribund metaphor. *amaze; astonish; astound; awe; dumbfound; flabbergast; jar; jolt; shock; start; startle; stun; stupefy; surprise.* • An executive at one financial institution that participated in the bailout said Goldman Sachs's dual role *raised the eyebrows of* some participants. REPLACE WITH *surprised.*

raise hell ∎ A moribund metaphor. 1. *bellow; bemoan; bluster; carp; clamor; complain; criticize; explode; fulminate; fume; gripe; grouse; grumble; holler; howl; lament; moan; object; protest; rage; rant; rave; roar; scream; shout; storm; thunder; vociferate; yell; whine.* 2. *be merry; carouse; carry on; celebrate; debauch; disport; frolic; party; play; revel; riot; roister; rollick; romp; skylark.*

raise the dead ∎ A moribund metaphor. *be merry; carouse; carry on; celebrate; debauch; disport; frolic; party; play; revel; riot; roister; rollick; romp; skylark.*

raise the flag ∎ A moribund metaphor. *be delighted; be elated; be glad; be overjoyed; be pleased; celebrate; cheer; exult; glory; jubilate; rejoice; triumph.*

raise the hackles ∎ A moribund metaphor. *acerbate; anger; annoy; bother; bristle; chafe; enrage; incense; inflame; infuriate; insult; irk; irritate; madden; miff; nettle; offend; provoke; rile; roil; vex.*

raise the roof ∎ A moribund metaphor. 1. *bellow; bluster; clamor; complain; explode; fulminate; fume; holler; howl; object; protest; rage; rant; rave; roar; scream; shout; storm; thunder; vociferate; yell.* 2. *be merry; carouse; carry on; celebrate; debauch; disport; frolic; party; play; revel; riot; roister; rollick; romp; skylark.*

raison d'être ∎ A foreign phrase.

rake over the coals ∎ A torpid term. *admonish; animadvert; berate; castigate; censure; chasten; chastise; chide; condemn; criticize; denounce; denunciate; discipline; impugn; objurgate; punish; rebuke; remonstrate; reprehend; reprimand; reproach; reprobate; reprove; revile; scold; upbraid; vituperate.*

rally 'round the flag ∎ A moribund metaphor.

rank and file ∎ A moribund metaphor. *all; citizenry; commonage; commonalty;*

common people; crowd; everybody; everyone; followers; herd; hoi polloi; laborers; masses; mob; multitude; plebeians; populace; proletariat; public; rabble; workers.

rant and rave ∎ An inescapable pair. *bellow; bluster; clamor; explode; fulminate; fume; holler; howl; rage; rant; rave; roar; scream; shout; storm; thunder; vent; vociferate; yell.*

rap (his) knuckles ∎ A moribund metaphor. *admonish; animadvert; berate; castigate; censure; chasten; chastise; chide; condemn; criticize; denounce; denunciate; discipline; impugn; objurgate; punish; rebuke; remonstrate; reprehend; reprimand; reproach; reprobate; reprove; revile; scold; upbraid; vituperate.*

rara avis ∎ A foreign phrase. *aberrant; abnormal; anomalistic; anomalous; atypical; bizarre; curious; deviant; different; distinct; distinctive; eccentric; exceptional; extraordinary; fantastic; foreign; grotesque; idiosyncratic; independent; individual; individualistic; irregular; novel; odd; offbeat; original; peculiar; puzzling; quaint; queer; rare; remarkable; separate; singular; strange; uncommon; unconventional; unexampled; unique; unnatural; unorthodox; unparalleled; unprecedented; unusual; weird.*

rarely (seldom) ever ∎ A wretched redundancy. *rarely (seldom).* • We are brothers, but we *rarely ever* speak. DELETE *ever.*

rat race ∎ A moribund metaphor.

(like) rats abandoning a ship ∎ An insipid simile.

rattle (their) cage ∎ A moribund metaphor. 1. *agitate; disquiet; disturb; excite; stir up; trouble; upset; work up.* 2. *goad; incite; inflame; needle; provoke; rouse; spur.* 3. *acerbate; anger; annoy; bother; bristle; chafe; enrage; incense; inflame; infuriate; insult; irk; irritate; madden; miff; nettle; offend; provoke; rile; roil; vex.*

> Never, *never* had she met anyone who could rattle her cage with such quick thoroughness.—Susan Anderson, *Obsessed*

rave reviews ∎ A suspect superlative. • The new LapLink for Windows is already getting *rave reviews* from both industry experts and users like you. • But it turned out *Maximumrocknroll* gave it a *rave review.* • In 1995, CeCe got *rave reviews* for her solo debut.

raving lunatic ∎ An inescapable pair.

reach epidemic proportions ∎ A torpid term. This phrase and journalistic junk of its kind—for example, *(breathe; heave) a collective sigh of relief* (SEE); *an uphill battle (fight)* (SEE); *deal a (crushing; devastating; major; serious) blow to* (SEE); *first (number-one; top) priority* (SEE); *grind to a halt* (SEE); *in the wake of; send a message (signal)* (SEE);

shocked (surprised) and saddened (dismayed) (SEE); *weather the storm (of)* (SEE)—ensure the writers of them will never be seriously read, and the readers of them never thoroughly engaged.
• The availability of guns on the street has *reached epidemic proportions.* • Dog bites among children are reportedly *reaching epidemic proportions.*

reach for the sky ∎ A moribund metaphor. *exceed; excel; outclass; outdo; outrival; outshine; outstrip; shine; stand; surpass.*

reach out and touch (someone) ∎ An infantile phrase.

> She sat in silence for a long moment, afraid he would reach out and touch her.—Tim Farrington, *The Monk Downstairs*

reach the end of (our) rope (tether) ∎ A moribund metaphor. *exhausted; frazzled; harassed; stressed; stressed out; tense; weary; worn out.*

read between the lines ∎ A moribund metaphor. *assume; conclude; conjecture; deduce; gather; guess; hypothesize; imagine; infer; presume; speculate; suppose; surmise; theorize; venture.*

read it and weep ∎ An infantile phrase.

read (her) like a (an open) book ∎ An insipid simile. *empathize; identify with; know; sympathize; understand.*

read my lips ∎ An infantile phrase.

read (him) the riot act ∎ A moribund metaphor. *admonish; animadvert; berate; castigate; censure; chasten; chastise; chide; condemn; criticize; denounce; denunciate; discipline; excoriate; fulminate against; imprecate; impugn; inveigh against; objurgate; punish; rebuke; remonstrate; reprehend; reprimand; reproach; reprobate; reprove; revile; scold; swear at; upbraid; vituperate.*

ready, willing, and able ∎ An infantile phrase. • She described her client as being *ready, willing, and able* to testify. REPLACE WITH *willing.* • We have a lot of social problems that need to be addressed, and I'm *ready, willing, and able* to do that. REPLACE WITH *ready.*

re- again ∎ A wretched redundancy. *re-.* • I divorced him, and then I *remarried again.* DELETE *again.* • We missed the first ten minutes of his talk, so he *repeated* it *again* for us. DELETE *again.*

real ∎ An overworked word. For example: *real contribution; real difference; real obvious; real possibility; real progress; real tragedy.*

reality check ∎ An infantile phrase.

real, live ∎ An infantile phrase.

really ■ An overworked word. If such an intensive is needed at all, alternatives to the word *really* include *consumedly*; *enormously*; *especially*; *exceedingly*; *exceptionally*; *extraordinarily*; *extremely*; *genuinely*; *particularly*; *remarkably*; *specially*; *truly*; *uncommonly*; *very*.

Often, however, such highlighting seems only to moderate the value of our statements. • At the *London Review* we take serious pride in our role as one of the *really* significant participants in the international exchange of ideas and information. DELETE *really*. • He did a *really* good job of convincing us to buy. DELETE *really*. • This speechlessness is *really* affecting his moods, his behavior, and his mental state. DELETE *really*. SEE ALSO **very**.

really? ■ An infantile phrase. SEE ALSO **you're kidding**; **you've got to be kidding**.

really (and) truly ■ An infantile phrase. • I *really and truly* love being in love. DELETE *really and truly*. • Do you *really truly* believe that your mom thinks you're a whore? DELETE *really*. • They *really and truly* thought I would never make it. DELETE *really and*. • She was, *really and truly,* only following orders. DELETE *really and truly*. • *Star* magazine is reporting that not only is Demi Moore *really and truly* pregnant with Ashton Kutcher's child, she's having a boy! DELETE *really and truly*.

> There I was with my parents and my sister and a serving plate layered with skewers of shish kabob, and I thought I was going to be ill. Really and truly ill.—Chris Bohjalian, *Before You Know Kindness*

rear (its) (ugly) head ■ A moribund metaphor. *appear*; *emerge*; *materialize*; *surface*. • That hypocritical axiom, "Do as I say, not as I do" seems to have *reared its ugly head* on the editorial pages of the *Globe* once again. • None of us knows for sure whether there is another problem in this volatile environment which could *rear its ugly head* soon.

reasonable facsimile ■ An inescapable pair.

(the) reason (why) is because ■ A wretched redundancy. *because*; *reason is (that)*. • One of *the reasons why* people keep this to themselves *is because of* the stigma. REPLACE WITH *the reasons ... is*.

(the) reason why ■ A wretched redundancy. *reason*. • There is a *reason why* she is the way she is. DELETE *why*. • The researchers are not certain as to the *reason why*. DELETE *why*.

receive back ■ A wretched redundancy. *receive*. • DPL now communicates with Excel, sending the input values and *receiving back* the output value Profit. DELETE *back*.

reckless abandon ■ An inescapable pair.

record-breaking ■ A wretched redundancy. *record*. • We'll take a look at some *record-breaking* snowfalls. REPLACE WITH *record*. SEE ALSO **all-time record**; **record-high**.

record-high ■ A wretched redundancy. *record*. • In Concord, it was a *record-high* 12 degrees. REPLACE WITH *record*. SEE ALSO **all-time record**; **record-breaking**.

(as) red as a beet ■ An insipid simile. 1. *beet-red*; *blood-red*; *burgundian*; *burgundy*; *cardinal*; *carmine*; *cerise*; *cherry*; *crimson*; *fire-engine-red*; *maroon*; *purple*; *purplish*; *red*; *reddish*; *rose*; *rose-colored*; *rosy*; *rubefacient*; *rubescent*; *rubicund*; *rubied*; *rubiginous*; *ruby*; *ruddy*; *rufescent*; *rufous*; *russet*; *sanguine*; *sanguineous*; *scarlet*; *vermilion*; *wine*; *wine-colored*. 2. *abashed*; *ashamed*; *blushing*; *chagrined*; *confused*; *discomfited*; *discomposed*; *disconcerted*; *embarrassed*; *flushed*; *flustered*; *mortified*; *nonplused*; *perplexed*; *red-faced*; *shamed*; *shamefaced*; *sheepish*.

(as) red as a cherry ■ An insipid simile. 1. *beet-red*; *blood-red*; *burgundian*; *burgundy*; *cardinal*; *carmine*; *cerise*; *cherry*; *crimson*; *fire-engine-red*; *maroon*; *purple*; *purplish*; *red*; *reddish*; *rose*; *rose-colored*; *rosy*; *rubefacient*; *rubescent*; *rubicund*; *rubied*; *rubiginous*; *ruby*; *ruddy*; *rufescent*; *rufous*; *russet*; *sanguine*; *sanguineous*; *scarlet*; *vermilion*; *wine*; *wine-colored*. 2. *abashed*; *ashamed*; *blushing*; *chagrined*; *confused*; *discomfited*; *discomposed*; *disconcerted*; *embarrassed*; *flushed*; *flustered*; *mortified*; *nonplused*; *perplexed*; *red-faced*; *shamed*; *shamefaced*; *sheepish*.

(as) red as a rose ■ An insipid simile. 1. *beet-red*; *blood-red*; *burgundian*; *burgundy*; *cardinal*; *carmine*; *cerise*; *cherry*; *crimson*; *fire-engine-red*; *maroon*; *purple*; *purplish*; *red*; *reddish*; *rose*; *rose-colored*; *rosy*; *rubefacient*; *rubescent*; *rubicund*; *rubied*; *rubiginous*; *ruby*; *ruddy*; *rufescent*; *rufous*; *russet*; *sanguine*; *sanguineous*; *scarlet*; *vermilion*; *wine*; *wine-colored*. 2. *abashed*; *ashamed*; *blushing*; *chagrined*; *confused*; *discomfited*; *discomposed*; *disconcerted*; *embarrassed*; *flushed*; *flustered*; *mortified*; *nonplused*; *perplexed*; *red-faced*; *shamed*; *shamefaced*; *sheepish*.

(as) red as a ruby ■ An insipid simile. 1. *beet-red*; *blood-red*; *burgundian*; *burgundy*; *cardinal*; *carmine*; *cerise*; *cherry*; *crimson*; *fire-engine-red*; *maroon*; *purple*; *purplish*; *red*; *reddish*; *rose*; *rose-colored*; *rosy*; *rubefacient*; *rubescent*; *rubicund*; *rubied*; *rubiginous*; *ruby*; *ruddy*; *rufescent*; *rufous*; *russet*; *sanguine*; *sanguineous*; *scarlet*; *vermilion*; *wine*; *wine-colored*. 2. *abashed*; *ashamed*; *blushing*; *chagrined*; *confused*; *discomfited*; *discomposed*; *disconcerted*; *embarrassed*; *flushed*; *flustered*; *mortified*; *nonplused*; *perplexed*; *red-faced*; *shamed*; *shamefaced*; *sheepish*.

red herring ∎ A moribund metaphor. *decoy; distraction; diversion; lure; ploy, trick.*

red in the face ∎ A moribund metaphor. *abashed; ashamed; blushing; chagrined; confused; discomfited; discomposed; disconcerted; embarrassed; flushed; flustered; mortified; nonplused; perplexed; red-faced; shamed; shamefaced; sheepish.*

> They laughed together understandingly; then, bending forward, he kissed her hastily on the cheek and went out, leaving her red in the face as if she were a young lass.—Catherine Cookson, *The Glass Virgin*

red-letter day ∎ A moribund metaphor.

red light ∎ A moribund metaphor. *ban; disallowance; enjoinment; exclusion; interdiction; prohibition; proscription; veto.* SEE ALSO **green light**.

red tape ∎ A moribund metaphor. *bureaucracy; formalities; paperwork; procedures; regulations; rules.*

refer back ∎ A wretched redundancy. *refer.* • *Refer back* to Chapter 4. DELETE *back*.

reflect back ∎ A wretched redundancy. *reflect.* • Part of the energy is *reflected back* into medium 1 as a reflected ray, and the remainder passes into medium 2 as a refracted ray. DELETE *back*.

regardless of the fact that ∎ A wretched redundancy. *although; but; even if; even though; still; though; yet.* • *Regardless of the fact that* these products are low in sucrose, they still contain energy from other nutrients. REPLACE WITH *Though*. SEE ALSO **despite the fact that; in spite of the fact that.**

(as) regular as clockwork ∎ An insipid simile. *cyclic; established; fixed; habitual; periodic; recurrent; recurring; regular; repetitive; rhythmic; rhythmical.*

> And week after week, regular as clockwork, LaShawndra comes over and raids Mother's kitchen like it's the Piggly Wiggly.—Tina McElroy Ansa, *You Know Better*

reinvent the wheel ∎ A moribund metaphor.

relate back ∎ A wretched redundancy. *relate.* • Like the Chicago School, anomie theory *relates back* to the European sociology of the 1800s. DELETE *back*.

relic of the past ∎ A wretched redundancy. *relic.* • The very idea of a single, domestic market has become a *relic of the past*. REPLACE WITH *relic*.

(it) remains to be seen ∎ A TOP-TWENTY DIMWITTICISM. A torpid term. *I don't know; (it's) not (yet) known; (that's) uncertain; (that's) unclear; (it's) unknown.* This phrase is often euphemistic for *(I) don't know* and similar admissions.

• So much *remains to be seen*. REPLACE WITH *is unknown*. • *It remains to be seen* whether dietary soybeans can protect women against breast cancer. REPLACE WITH *We do not know*. • How the French public, fond of both cigarettes and alcohol, will respond *remains to be seen*. REPLACE WITH *is not yet known*. SEE ALSO **your guess is as good as mine; (just have to) wait and see.**

remedy the situation ∎ A torpid term. Like all torpid terms, *remedy the situation* neither moves nor motivates us; its use practically ensures that nothing will be righted, nothing remedied.

An ill we might be moved to correct, a problem we might be inspired to solve, but a situation we might never be roused to remedy.

• If the decisions actually turn out to hamper civil rights enforcement, obviously I would want to take steps to *remedy the situation*. • To *remedy the situation*—and make the process fairer, the SEC should require that voting be strictly confidential. • One issue has been bothering management for quite a while, but they feel somewhat helpless to *remedy the situation*. • The report again called on the government to *remedy this intolerable situation*. SEE ALSO **(a) situation.**

reminisce about the past ∎ A wretched redundancy. *reminisce.* • She's now 89 years old and she spends most of her time *reminiscing about the past*. DELETE *about the past*.

remove the cotton from (my) ears ∎ A moribund metaphor.

repay back ∎ A wretched redundancy. *repay.* • She is *repaying* her debt *back* to society. DELETE *back*.

replace back ∎ A wretched redundancy. *replace.* • When a change needs to be made, a developer reserves that file from the library, makes the change, and then *replaces* it *back*. DELETE *back*.

reports of (my) death are greatly exaggerated ∎ An infantile phrase.

represent(s) ∎ A torpid term. Increasingly, *represents* is being used for a sad, simple *is* (and *represent* for *are*).

• The budgeted capacity level *represents* the level of expected business activity under normal operating conditions. REPLACE WITH *is*. • Newstar and BASYS currently *represent* the major newsroom computer systems in the broadcasting field. REPLACE WITH *are*. • Radiosurgery *represents* a major step forward in our ability to treat tumors that previously have been untreatable. REPLACE WITH *is*. • I think Ginger, Patty, and I *represent* three very hardworking, committed faculty members. REPLACE WITH *are*.

respond back ∎ A wretched redundancy. *respond.* • The OPP will review each request and *respond back* within ten business days. DELETE *back.*

rest and relaxation ∎ An inescapable pair. *calm; calmness; leisure; peace; peacefulness; quiet; quietude; relaxation; repose; rest; serenity; stillness; tranquility.*

rest on (her) laurels ∎ A moribund metaphor.

restore back ∎ A wretched redundancy. *restore.* • The new Undo feature allows you to *restore* the disk *back* to its original state. DELETE *back.*

retreat back ∎ A wretched redundancy. *retreat.* • We face tough times and I hope we can learn to work together and not *retreat back* to some of our regretful attitudes of the past. DELETE *back.*

return back ∎ A wretched redundancy. *return.* • When SEU is exited, the user will be *returned back* to the Programmer Menu. DELETE *back.*

revenge is sweet ∎ A quack equation.

revert back ∎ A wretched redundancy. *revert.* • Scientists speculate that the rapid spread of the disease may be due to farmland *reverting back* to woodland. DELETE *back.* • Not knowing what to do, I would *revert right back* to my old eating habits. DELETE *right back.*

revolving door policy ∎ A moribund metaphor.

(as) rich as Croesus ∎ An insipid simile. *affluent; moneyed; opulent; prosperous; rich; wealthy; well-off; well-to-do.*

richly deserves ∎ An inescapable pair. • Instead of vilifying him, we should be giving him the encouragement and support he *richly deserves.*

rich man, poor man, beggarman, thief ∎ A moribund metaphor. • It doesn't matter whether you are *rich man, poor man, beggar, or thief*, if you are black, there's an artificial ceiling on your ambition.

ride herd on ∎ A moribund metaphor. *control; direct; guard; manage; mind; watch over.*

ride off into the sunset ∎ A moribund metaphor. *abscond; clear out; decamp; depart; desert; disappear; escape; exit; flee; fly; go; go away; leave; move on; part; pull out; quit; retire; retreat; run away; take flight; take off; vacate; vanish; withdraw.*

ride on (her) coattails ∎ A moribund metaphor.

ride out the storm ∎ A moribund metaphor.

ride roughshod over ∎ A moribund metaphor. *boss; browbeat; brutalize; bully; dictate; domineer; enslave; master; oppress; overpower; overrule; reign over; repress; rule;* *subjugate; suppress; tyrannize.*

(as) right as rain ∎ An insipid simile. 1. *accurate; correct; exact; irrefutable; precise; right; true.* 2. *fit; good; hale; hardy; healthful; healthy; hearty; robust; sound; strong; well.*

(what's) right is right ∎ A quack equation.

right off the bat ∎ A moribund metaphor. *abruptly; apace; at once; briskly; directly; expeditiously; fast; forthwith; hastily; hurriedly; immediately; instantaneously; instantly; posthaste; promptly; quickly; rapidly; rashly; right away; speedily; straightaway; swiftly; wingedly.*

(on the) right track ∎ A moribund metaphor.

ring a bell ∎ A moribund metaphor. *be familiar; remind; sound familiar.*

ring down the curtain (on) ∎ A moribund metaphor. *cease; close; complete; conclude; discontinue; end; finish; halt; settle; stop.*

ringing endorsement ∎ An inescapable pair.

ringing off the hook ∎ A moribund metaphor. *ceaselessly; constantly; continually; continuously; nonstop; perpetually; steadily.* • The phones are *ringing off the hook.* REPLACE WITH *constantly ringing.*

rip (tear) to shreds ∎ A moribund metaphor. *demolish; destroy; devastate; obliterate; rack; ravage; ruin; shatter; smash; undo; wrack; wreck.*

rise from the ashes ∎ A moribund metaphor. *regenerate; rekindle; renew; restart; revitalize; revive; rise anew.*

rise to the bait ∎ A moribund metaphor. *get angry; react; rejoin; respond; retort.*

> My job was to look respectfully attentive without rising to his bait —Gail Godwin, *Queen of the Underworld*

road less traveled ∎ A moribund metaphor.

road to ruin ∎ A moribund metaphor. • To permit lying is a step down the *road to ruin.*

roar (in) like a lion ∎ An insipid simile. *growl; roar.*

rob Peter to pay Paul ∎ A moribund metaphor.

rock the boat ∎ A moribund metaphor. *agitate; confuse; disorder; disorganize; disquiet; disrupt; disturb; fluster; jar; jolt; jumble; mess up; mix up; muddle; perturb; rattle; ruffle; shake up; stir up; trouble; unnerve; unsettle; upset.*

(positive) role model ∎ A torpid term. *archetype; example; exemplar; good example; good man (woman); guide; hero; ideal; inspiration; model; paragon; prototype.*

rolling in money ∎ A moribund metaphor.

affluent; moneyed; opulent; prosperous; rich; wealthy; well-off; well-to-do.

roll (turn) over in (his) grave ▪ A moribund metaphor. 1. *alarm; amaze; astonish; jolt; shock; surprise.* 2. *acerbated; angered; annoyed; bothered; distress; disturbed; exasperated; galled; irked; irritated; miffed; nettled; provoked; rankled; riled; roiled; upset; vexed.*

roll in the aisles ▪ A moribund metaphor. *cachinnate; cackle; chortle; chuckle; convulse; guffaw; hoot; howl; laugh; roar; shriek; whoop.*

roll out the red carpet ▪ A moribund metaphor. *esteem; honor; respect; venerate; welcome.*

roll up (her) sleeves ▪ A moribund metaphor. *drudge; grind; grub; labor; moil; slave; strain; strive; struggle; sweat; toil; travail; work hard.*

roll with the punches ▪ A moribund metaphor. *abide by; accede to; accept; accommodate; acquiesce; adapt to; adhere to; adjust to; agree to; assent; be agreeable; be complacent; be conventional; bend; be resigned; be traditional; how; comply with; concede to; concur; conform; consent to; fit; follow; reconcile; submit; succumb; yield.*

romantic interlude ▪ A suspect superlative. *intercourse; love-making; sex.*

Rome wasn't built in a day ▪ A popular prescription.

root cause ▪ A wretched redundancy. *cause; origin; reason; root; source.* • It does not truly solve the problem of rising health care costs since it does not address the *root cause* of the problem. REPLACE WITH *root.*

rootin', tootin', shootin' ▪ An infantile phrase.

rotten apple ▪ A moribund metaphor. *bastard; blackguard; cad; charlatan; cheat; cheater; fake; fraud; impostor; knave; mountebank; phony; pretender; quack; rascal; rogue; scoundrel; swindler; undesirable; villain.*

rotten to the core ▪ A moribund metaphor. *bad; base; contemptible; corrupt; crooked; deceitful; despicable; dishonest; evil; immoral; iniquitous; malevolent; mean; miserable; nefarious; pernicious; praetorian; rotten; sinister; underhanded; unethical; untrustworthy; venal; vicious; vile; wicked.*

rough and ready ▪ An inescapable pair.

rough and tumble ▪ A moribund metaphor. *boisterous; disorderly; raucous; riotous; rough; tempestuous; tumultuous; turbulent; uproarious; violent; wild.*

rough around the edges ▪ A moribund metaphor. 1. *bad-mannered; boorish; coarse; crude; ill-mannered; loutish; oafish; rough; rude; uncouth; uncultured; unrefined; unsophisticated; vulgar.* 2. *imperfect; incomplete; unfinished.*

rousing success ▪ An inescapable pair.

rub elbows (shoulders) with ▪ A moribund metaphor. *associate; be involved with; consort; fraternize; frequent; hobnob; keep company; mingle; mix; see; socialize.*

rub (me) the wrong way ▪ A moribund metaphor. 1. *acerbate; anger; annoy; chafe; gall; grate; irk; irritate; miff; nettle; provoke; rankle; rile; roil; upset; vex.* 2. *affront; agitate; bother; disrupt; disturb; fluster; insult; jar; offend; perturb; rattle; ruffle; shake up; stir up; trouble; unnerve; unsettle; upset.* • I wouldn't want to do anything that would *rub her the wrong way.* REPLACE WITH *annoy her.*

ruffle (her) feathers ▪ A moribund metaphor. *affront; agitate; bother; disrupt; disturb; fluster; insult; jar; offend; perturb; rattle; ruffle; shake up; stir up; trouble; unnerve; unsettle; upset.*

rules and regulations ▪ An inescapable pair. *regulations; rules.* • You may have a player that's disappointed, but we're adhering to our *rules and regulations.* REPLACE WITH *regulations* or *rules.*

rules are made to be broken ▪ A popular prescription.

rule the roost ▪ A moribund metaphor. *administer; be in charge; be in command; be in control; boss; command; control; dictate; direct; dominate; govern; lead; manage; manipulate; master; order; overpower; oversee; predominate; preponderate; prevail; reign over; rule; superintend.* • High school football no longer *rules the roost.* REPLACE WITH *predominates.*

> Each of the stories Ma told us about Papa reinforced the message that he was the boss, that he ruled the roost, that what he said went.—Wally Lamb, *I Know This Much Is True*

rule with an iron fist (hand) ▪ A moribund metaphor. *authoritarian; authoritative; autocratic; cruel; despotic; dictatorial; dogmatic; domineering; hard; harsh; imperious; iron-handed; lordly; oppressive; overbearing; peremptory; repressive; rigorous; severe; stern; strict; tough; tyrannical.*

run a tight ship ▪ A moribund metaphor. *controlled; ordered; organized; structured.*

run circles (rings) around ▪ A moribund metaphor. *beat; better; cap; defeat; exceed; excel; outclass; outdo; outflank; outmaneuver; outperform; outplay; outrank; outsmart; outstrip; outthink; outwit; overcome; overpower; prevail over; surpass; top; triumph over; trounce; whip; win out.*

run (it) into the ground ▪ A moribund metaphor.

running on empty ▪ A moribund metaphor. *be exhausted; be fatigued; be spent; be tired; be weary; be worn out.*

running on fumes ▮ A moribund metaphor. *beat; bushed; drowsy; exhausted; fatigued; sleepy; spent; tired; weary; worn-out.*

run off at the mouth ▮ A moribund metaphor. *babbling; blathering; chatty; facile; fluent; garrulous; glib; jabbering; logorrheic; long-winded; loquacious; prolix; talkative; verbose; voluble; windy.*

run of the mill ▮ A moribund metaphor. *average; common; commonplace; customary; everyday; fair; mediocre; middling; normal; ordinary; passable; plain; quotidian; regular; routine; simple; standard; tolerable; typical; uneventful; unexceptional; unremarkable; usual; workaday.*

run out of steam ▮ A moribund metaphor. *be exhausted; be fatigued; conclude; decline; deteriorate; die; droop; dwindle; end; expire; fade; fail; finish; flag; languish; perish; quit; regress; stop; tire; weaken; wear out.* • Market rallies within ongoing bear markets tend to *run out of steam* as soon as the market climbs back up to the vicinity of its 200-day moving average. REPLACE WITH *languish.*

(money) runs through (his) fingers ▮ A moribund metaphor.

run the gauntlet ▮ A moribund metaphor. *bear; endure; experience; face; suffer; undergo.*

run the show ▮ A moribund metaphor. *administer; boss; command; control; dictate; direct; dominate; govern; in charge; in command; in control; manage; manipulate; master; order; overpower; oversee; predominate; prevail; reign over; rule; superintend.*

> He had called me sir more than enough times for me to have no hallucinations about who was running the show, and so I did leave, and, as I say, that was the end of it.—Philip Roth, *The Human Stain*

run with the pack ▮ A moribund metaphor. *abide by; accede to; accept; accommodate; acquiesce; adapt to; adhere to; adjust to; agree to; assent; be agreeable; be complacent; be conventional; bend; be resigned; be traditional; bow; comply with; concede to; concur; conform; consent to; fit; follow; reconcile; submit; succumb; yield.*

run with the hare and hunt with the hounds ▮ A moribund metaphor.

Ss

sacred cow ❚ A moribund metaphor.

sacrificial lamb ❚ A moribund metaphor. *sacrifice; victim.*

safe and sound ❚ An inescapable pair. *all right; unharmed; uninjured; safe.*

> They were going to pray that he come home safe and sound, with a minimum of mosquito bites.—William Kowalski, *The Adventures of Flash Jackson*

safe haven ❚ A wretched redundancy. *asylum; haven; refuge; sanctuary; shelter.* • Massachusetts, which likes to think of itself as a liberal mecca, is no *safe haven*. REPLACE WITH *haven.*

safety net ❚ A moribund metaphor.

said ❚ A withered word. *that; the; these; this; those;* DELETE. • Therefore, the relative pronouns used to introduce clauses will retain *said* function. REPLACE WITH *this.*

sail (too) close to the wind ❚ A moribund metaphor. *chance; dare; endanger; gamble; hazard; imperil; jeopardize; make bold; peril; risk; venture.*

sail under false colors ❚ A moribund metaphor. *bamboozle; befool; beguile; belie; bilk; bluff; cheat; color; con; deceive; defraud; delude; disguise; dissemble; dissimulate; dupe; fake; falsify; feign; feint; fool; gyp; hoodwink; lead astray; masquerade; misdirect; misguide; misinform; mislead; misrepresent; pretend; simulate; spoof; swindle; trick.*

(the) same ❚ A torpid term. *it; one; them.* • Gemini critique partners are eager to assist, but steel yourself against their tendency to fire off suggestions without consideration of your emotional reaction to *the same.* REPLACE WITH *them.* • Provide access aisle for first accessible parking space that lacks *same.* REPLACE WITH *it.*

(the) same but different ❚ An infantile phrase. SEE ALSO **same difference**.

sans ❚ A withered word. *bereft; lacking; without.* • He has a reckless streak, as revealed in his tendency to go swimming *sans* suit. REPLACE WITH *without a.* • Using this button will allow you to see what the dialog box will look like to the user, *sans* any personal or company information that you'll eventually add to it. REPLACE WITH *without.*

save ❚ A withered word. *but; except.* • The room was quiet during his performance, *save* when he would take a deep breath and let out some of it. REPLACE WITH *except.* • In 1990, the Emirate of Kuwait—tiny in all respects *save* its role in oil affairs—was invaded by fellow OPEC and Arab League member Iraq. REPLACE WITH *but.*

saved by the bell ❚ An infantile phrase.

save (it) for a rainy day ❚ A moribund metaphor.

save (his) neck (skin) ❚ A moribund metaphor.

save your breath ❚ A moribund metaphor. *be quiet; be silent; be still; hush; keep quiet; keep still.*

(as) scarce (scarcer) as hen's teeth ❚ An insipid simile. *exiguous; inadequate; meager; rare; scant; scanty; scarce; sparse; uncommon; unusual.*

scare the (living) daylights out of (me) ❚ A moribund metaphor. *alarm; appall; benumb; daunt; frighten; horrify; intimidate; panic; paralyze; petrify; scare; shock; startle; terrify; terrorize.*

scare the pants off (me) ❚ A moribund metaphor. *alarm; appall; benumb; daunt; frighten; horrify; intimidate; panic; paralyze; petrify; scare; shock; startle; terrify; terrorize.*

scare to death ❚ A moribund metaphor. *alarm; appall; benumb; daunt; frighten; horrify; intimidate; panic; paralyze; petrify; scare; shock; startle; terrify; terrorize.* SEE ALSO **to death**.

school of hard knocks ❚ A moribund metaphor.

(just) scratch the surface ❚ A moribund metaphor.

scream and yell ❚ An inescapable pair. *bay; bawl; bellow; blare; caterwaul; clamor; cry; holler; hoot; howl; roar; screak; scream; screech; shout; shriek; shrill; squawk; squeal; vociferate; wail; whoop; yell; yelp; yowl.* • If parents are *screaming and yelling* at each other, that causes fear in children. REPLACE WITH *yelling.* • It's very flattering that women *scream and yell* when you walk on stage. REPLACE WITH *scream.* SEE ALSO **yell and scream**.

scream (yell) at the top of (my) lungs ❚ A moribund metaphor. *bay; bawl; bellow; blare; caterwaul; clamor; cry; holler; hoot;*

scream (yell) bloody murder

howl; roar; screak; scream; screech; shout; shriek; shrill; squawk; squeal; vociferate; wail; whoop; yell; yelp; yowl.

scream (yell) bloody murder ❚ A moribund metaphor. 1. *bay; bawl; bellow; blare; caterwaul; clamor; cry; holler; hoot; howl; roar; screech; shout; shriek; shrill; squawk; squeal; vociferate; wail; whoop; yell; yelp; yowl.* 2. *clamor; complain; explode; fulminate; fume; fuss; gripe; grumble; holler; howl; object; protest; rage; rant; rave; remonstrate; roar; scream; shout; storm; thunder; vociferate; yell.* • The Jones lawyers would have *screamed bloody murder*, and rightly so. REPLACE WITH *protested.*

screech to a halt ❚ A moribund metaphor. *cease; close; complete; conclude; derail; discontinue; end; finish; halt; settle; stop.* • Work in 535 congressional offices *screeched to a halt.* REPLACE WITH *ceased.*

second banana ❚ A moribund metaphor. *aide; assistant; associate; inferior; junior; minion; secondary; subordinate; underling.* • Murphy's greatest political need is to convince the public that she is a leader, and not just the governor's long-suffering *second banana.*

second of all ❚ A wretched redundancy. *second.* • *Second of all*, you're going to get hurt if you continue this behavior. REPLACE WITH *Second.* SEE ALSO **first of all**.

second to none ❚ A torpid term. *best; different; exceptional; extraordinary; finest; first; greatest; highest; incomparable; inimitable; matchless; nonpareil; notable; noteworthy; novel; odd; optimal; optimum; original; outstanding; peculiar; peerless; remarkable; singular; special; strange; superlative; uncommon; unequaled; unexampled; unique; unmatched; unparalleled; unrivaled; unusual; without equal.*

see eye to eye ❚ A moribund metaphor. *agree; concur; think alike.* • We *see eye to eye* on most all matters. REPLACE WITH *agree.*

seeing is believing ❚ A quack equation.

seek and you shall find ❚ A popular prescription.

see red ❚ A moribund metaphor. *acerbate; anger; annoy; bother; bristle; chafe; enrage; incense; inflame; infuriate; irk; irritate; madden; miff; provoke; rile; roil; vex.*

see the glass half empty ❚ A moribund metaphor. *cynical; dark; despairing; doubtful; gloomy; hopeless; morbid; pessimistic; sullen.*

see the light ❚ A moribund metaphor. *appreciate; apprehend; comprehend; discern; fathom; grasp; know; make sense of; perceive; realize; recognize; see; understand.*

see the light of day ❚ A moribund metaphor. 1. *be actualized; be carried out; be implemented; be initiated; be instituted; be realized; be undertaken.* • The proposal will never *see the light of day.* REPLACE WITH *be realized.* 2. *be accomplished; be achieved; be completed; be consummated; be executed; be finished; be fulfilled.*

seething mass of humanity ❚ A moribund metaphor.

self-fulfilling prophecy ❚ A torpid term. • If retailers think negatively and pessimistically in terms of Christmas, it's going to be a *self-fulfilling prophecy.*

sell (him) a bill of goods ❚ A moribund metaphor. *cheat; deceive; defraud; dupe; fool; lie to; swindle; trick; victimize.* • We realize that we've been *sold a bill of goods.* REPLACE WITH *swindled.*

sell (him) down the river ❚ A moribund metaphor. *betray; deliver up; inform on; turn in.*

send a (loud) message (signal) ❚ A torpid term. This phrase is a favorite among journalists and politicians—scrawlers and stammerers—who are accustomed to expressing themselves with dead and indifferent words. And from such words, only the faintest of feelings and the shallowest of thoughts can be summoned.
 • The patent system that protects new drugs from competition *sends a message* to pharmaceutical companies: if you invest enough money and come up with a hit, you can make a killing. REPLACE WITH *says.* • We want to *send a message* that this kind of behavior will not be tolerated. REPLACE WITH *make clear.* • The police department *sent out a message* that we would not allow such looting to occur again. REPLACE WITH *made it known.* • By agreeing to act now, we are *sending a signal* that we do not want this plan to fail. REPLACE WITH *announcing.* • I think the MFA, by hosting this exhibit, is *sending the wrong message to* the public. REPLACE WITH *misguiding.* • A triple-spaced term paper *sends the loud message* that the writer probably has very little to say. REPLACE WITH *proclaims.* SEE ALSO **reach epidemic proportions**.

send chills (shivers) down (my) spine
❚ A moribund metaphor. 1. *agitate; disquiet; disrupt; disturb; fluster; jar; jolt; perturb; rattle; ruffle; shake up; stir up; trouble; unnerve; unsettle; upset.* 2. *alarm; appall; benumb; daunt; frighten; horrify; intimidate; panic; paralyze; petrify; scare; shock; startle; terrify; terrorize.*

send (them) packing ❚ A moribund metaphor. *discard; dismiss; discharge.*

send shock waves (through) ❚ A moribund metaphor. *agitate; arouse; astound; bother; confuse; discomfit; disconcert; disquiet; disrupt; disturb; excite; jolt; shock; startle;*

stimulate; stir; stun; unsettle; upset. • When Swiss pharmaceutical giant Roche Holding Ltd. announced that it would buy 60 percent of Genentech Inc., it *sent shock waves through* the biotechnology community. REPLACE WITH *shocked*.

send up a trial balloon ∎ A moribund metaphor. *assess; check; explore; inspect; investigate; look into; probe; test; try.*

separate and distinct ∎ A redundancy. *distinct; separate.* • Nor are the stages *separate and distinct;* they may occur at the same time. REPLACE WITH *distinct*.

separate and independent ∎ A wretched redundancy. *independent; separate.* • Since the audio and video in an Interactive Multipoint videoconference travel over *separate and independent* paths, the audio must be delayed to synchronize it with the video. REPLACE WITH *separate*.

separate out ∎ A wretched redundancy. *separate.* • I don't think you can *separate out* those two things. DELETE *out*. • Our objective was to *separate out* the NLR from the continuum emission by subtracting the different filter images. DELETE *out*. • One of the things that became very clear to us early on was that you simply can't *separate out* issues like curriculum and teachers' professional development and learning and instruction. DELETE *out*.

separate the men from the boys ∎ A moribund metaphor. *choose; cull; differentiate; discriminate; distinguish; divide; filter; isolate; pick; screen; segregate; select; separate; sieve; sift; sort; strain; weed out; winnow.*

separate the sheep from the goats ∎ A moribund metaphor. *choose; cull; differentiate; discriminate; distinguish; divide; filter; isolate; pick; screen; segregate; select; separate; sieve; sift; sort; strain; weed out; winnow.*

separate the wheat from the chaff ∎ A moribund metaphor. *choose; cull; differentiate; discriminate; distinguish; divide; filter; isolate; pick; screen; segregate; select; separate; sieve; sift; sort; strain; weed out; winnow.*

serious reservations ∎ An inescapable pair.

set in concrete ∎ A moribund metaphor. *eternal; everlasting; firm; immutable; invariable; irreversible; irrevocable; permanent; rigid; stable; unalterable; unchangeable; unchanging.*

set (her) teeth on edge ∎ A moribund metaphor. 1. *acerbate; anger; annoy; bristle; chafe; enrage; incense; inflame; infuriate; irk; irritate; madden; miff; nettle; offend; provoke; rile; roil; vex.* 2. *agitate; bother; disconcert; disturb; fluster; perturb; unnerve; upset.*

The music runs clear up my spine and sets my teeth on edge.—Michael Lee West, *Crazy Ladies*

set the record straight ∎ A torpid term. • There are a lot of things I can do in my book in terms of *setting the record straight.* • EPA believes it's time to *set the record straight* about an indisputable fact: secondhand smoke is a real and preventable health risk.

set the stage (for) ∎ A moribund metaphor. *arrange; groom; make ready; plan; prepare; prime; ready.*

set the wheels in motion ∎ A moribund metaphor. *begin; commence; embark; inaugurate; initiate; launch; originate; start; undertake.*

set the world on fire ∎ A moribund metaphor. *amaze; animate; awe; beguile; captivate; charm; dazzle; electrify; enchant; engross; enthrall; entrance; excite; exhilarate; fascinate; hypnotize; impress; intoxicate; mesmerize; thrill; overwhelm; rivet.*

settle the score ∎ A moribund metaphor.

seventh heaven ∎ A moribund metaphor. *bliss; delight; ecstasy; joy; rapture.*

shake to its foundations ∎ A moribund metaphor. *agitate; disquiet; disrupt; disturb; fluster; jar; jerk; jolt; perturb; quake; quiver; rattle; ruffle; shake up; shudder; stir up; unnerve; unsettle; tremble; upset.*

shaking in (his) boots ∎ A moribund metaphor. 1. *afraid; alarmed; apprehensive; cowardly; craven; diffident; faint-hearted; fearful; frightened; pavid; pusillanimous; recreant; scared; terror-stricken; timid; timorous; tremulous.* 2. *jittery; jumpy; nervous; quivering; shaking; shivering; shivery; shuddering; skittish; trembling.*

shaking like a leaf ∎ An insipid simile. 1. *jittery; jumpy; nervous; quivering; shaking; shivering; shivery; shuddering; skittish; trembling.* 2. *afraid; alarmed; apprehensive; cowardly; craven; diffident; faint-hearted; fearful; frightened; pavid; pusillanimous; recreant; scared; terror-stricken; timid; timorous; tremulous.*

shank's mare ∎ A moribund metaphor. *by foot.*

share and share alike ∎ A popular prescription.

(as) sharp as a razor ∎ An insipid simile. *able; adroit; apt; astute; bright; brilliant; capable; clever; competent; discerning; enlightened; insightful; intelligent; judicious; keen; knowledgeable; learned; logical; luminous; perceptive; perspicacious; quick; rational; reasonable; sagacious; sage; sapient; sensible; sharp; shrewd; smart; sound; understanding; wise.*

(as) sharp as a tack

(as) sharp as a tack ∎ An insipid simile.
1. *dapper; neat; smart; trim; well dressed; well groomed.* 2. *able; adroit; apt; astute; bright; brilliant; capable; clever; competent; discerning; enlightened; insightful; intelligent; judicious; keen; knowledgeable; learned; logical; luminous; perceptive; perspicacious; quick; rational; reasonable; sagacious; sage; sapient; sensible; sharp; shrewd; smart; sound; understanding; wise.*

shed (throw) light on ∎ A moribund metaphor. *clarify; clear up; describe; disentangle; elucidate; enlighten; explain; explicate; illume; illuminate; interpret; make clear; make plain; reveal; simplify.*

> But he had little faith that Dohmler would throw much light on the matter; he himself was the incalculable element involved.— F. Scott Fitzgerald, *Tender is the Night*

shift (swing) into high gear ∎ A moribund metaphor. • The lawyer is *shifting into high gear,* summoning all his persuasive powers for a rhetorical flourish that will dazzle the jury and save his client a multimillion-dollar court award.

shine a (bright) light (spotlight) in (on) ∎ A moribund metaphor. 1. *bare; betray; disclose; divulge; expose; give away; reveal; show; tell; uncover; unearth; unveil.* 2. *clarify; clear up; elucidate; enlighten; illume; illuminate.* 3. *delve into; explore; investigate; look at; search; survey.* • Here at CNN, we're happy to be able to *shine a light on* this. REPLACE WITH *expose.* • We *shined a light in* every corner of his life. REPLACE WITH *explored.*

ship of fools ∎ A moribund metaphor.

(like) (two) ships passing in the night ∎ An insipid simile.

> She became a ship passing in the night—an emblem of the loneliness of human life, an occasion for queer confidences and sudden appeals for sympathy.—Virginia Woolf, *The Voyage Out*

(my) ship to come in ∎ A moribund metaphor.

shocked (surprised) and saddened (dismayed) ∎ A torpid term. These are formulas that people—especially spokespeople and journalists it seems—use to express indignation. And, as formulas, the *shock and sadness,* the *shock and dismay,* the *shock and outrage* is scarcely heartfelt.
• Gilda Radner's death from cancer *shocked and saddened* Hollywood. • I was *shocked and saddened* by the news of his death. • Shoppers and shop owners were also *shocked and saddened* by Mr. Stuart's suicide. • Relatives were *shocked and dismayed* by what they saw today. • When Kissinger was selected instead of the banking mogul, Rockefeller's staff were *shocked and dismayed.* • Sullivan says she is *surprised and saddened* by the recent turn of events. • We are *saddened and outraged* by the tragic death of a young man just starting to fulfill his life promise. • We are terribly *shocked and dismayed;* Ed was an active and important member of our community who will be missed by his colleagues. • Needless to say, my dear husband was, and is, *shocked and saddened.* • I am *shocked and saddened* by these allegations. • I want to begin by saying that Hillary and I are profoundly *shocked and saddened* by the tragedy today in Littleton. • The man who was at the heart of the Cape Verdean neighborhood leaves behind a wife, five children, and a *shocked and saddened* community.

A newspaper editor who has just learned of the mutilation of one of his female reporters in a strife-torn country remarks he is *saddened and distressed* by her death. This is the same soulless formula; anyone who has not surrendered to this dimwitticism would surely have said it differently. SEE ALSO **reach epidemic proportions**.

> Shocked and surprised as I was I agreed without hesitation, prompted both by curiosity as to his own feelings and a desire to discuss the transaction which concerned the child.— Lawrence Durrell, *Justine*

shoot down ∎ A moribund metaphor. *belie; confute; contradict; controvert; counter; debunk; deny; disprove; discredit; dispute; expose; invalidate; negate; rebut; refute; repudiate.*

shoot from the hip ∎ A moribund metaphor. 1. *be aboveboard; be artless; be blunt; be candid; be direct; be forthright; be frank; be genuine; be guileless; be honest; be ingenuous; be naive; be outspoken; be sincere; be straightforward.* 2. *hasty; headlong; heedless; hot-headed; impetuous; impulsive; incautious; precipitate; rash; reckless; thoughtless; unthinking.* • Congress is feeling very ambivalent, there are very complicated questions of government here, and these *shoot-from-the-hip* folks already have their opinion locked in cement. REPLACE WITH *incautious.*

shoot full of holes ∎ A moribund metaphor. *belie; confute; contradict; controvert; counter; debunk; deny; disprove; discredit; dispute; expose; invalidate; negate; rebut; refute; repudiate.*

(like) shooting fish in a barrel ∎ An insipid simile. *easily done; easy; effortless; elementary; facile; simple; simplicity itself; straightforward; uncomplex; uncomplicated.*

shoot the breeze (bull) ∎ A moribund metaphor. *babble; blab; cackle; chaffer; chat; chitchat; chatter; confabulate; converse; gossip; jabber; palaver; prate; prattle; rattle;*

182

talk. • He would come down every couple of weeks just to *shoot the breeze.* REPLACE WITH *chat.*

shoot the messenger ∎ A moribund metaphor.

shoot the works ∎ A moribund metaphor.

shop till you drop ∎ A moribund metaphor.

short and sweet ∎ An inescapable pair. *brief; compact; concise; condensed; curt; laconic; pithy; short; succinct; terse.*

short and to the point ∎ A torpid phrase. *brief; compact; concise; condensed; curt; laconic; pithy; short; succinct; terse.*

short end of the stick ∎ A moribund metaphor.

shot heard around the world ∎ A moribund metaphor.

shot (himself) in the foot ∎ A moribund metaphor.

shot to hell ∎ A moribund metaphor. 1 *demolished; destroyed; devastated; obliterated; racked; ruined; shattered; smashed; wracked; wrecked.* 2. *damaged; decayed; decrepit; deteriorated; dilapidated; ragged; shabby; shopworn; tattered; worn.*

(stand) shoulder to shoulder ∎ A moribund metaphor. *collaborate; comply; concur; conspire; cooperate; work together.*

shout (it) from the housetops (rooftops) ∎ A moribund metaphor. *advertise; announce; broadcast; cry out; declaim; disseminate; exclaim; proclaim; promulgate; publicize; publish; shout; trumpet; yell.*

shove down (their) throats ∎ A moribund metaphor. *bulldoze; bully; coerce; compel; constrain; demand; drive; enforce; enjoin; goad; force; impel; incite; intimidate; make; necessitate; obligate; oblige; order; press; pressure; prod; require; threaten; tyrannize; urge.*

show me a ... and I'll show you a ... ∎ An infantile phrase. • *Show me a* person who's lived a normal, conventional life, *and I'll show you a* dullard.

shrinking violet ∎ A moribund metaphor. *diffident; quiet; reserved; retiring; self-effacing; shy; timid.*

shut (his) eyes to ∎ A moribund metaphor. *brush aside; avoid; discount; disregard; dodge; duck; ignore; neglect; omit; pass over; recoil from; shrink from; shun; shy away from; turn away from; withdraw from.*

sick and tired (of) ∎ An inescapable pair. 1. *annoyed; bored; discouraged; disgusted; exasperated; exhausted; fatigued; fed up; impatient; irked; irritated; sick; sickened; tired; wearied; weary.* 2. *cloyed; glutted; gorged; jaded; sated; satiated; surfeited.* • I'm *sick and tired* of seeing the welfare bashing in the newspaper. REPLACE WITH *weary.* • No matter how desperate and *sick and*

tired and lonely I felt, I was also vibrant and alive. REPLACE WITH *discouraged.*

(as) sick as a dog ∎ An insipid simile. 1. *afflicted; ailing; diseased; ill; indisposed; infirm; not (feeling) well; sick; sickly; suffering; unhealthy; unsound; unwell; valetudinarian.* 2. *nauseated; nauseous; queasy; sick; squeamish; vomiting.*

sick to death ∎ A moribund metaphor. *annoyed; bored; discouraged; disgusted; exasperated; exhausted; fatigued; fed up; impatient; irked; irritated; sick; sickened; tired; wearied; weary.* SEE ALSO **to death**.

signed, sealed, and delivered ∎ A moribund metaphor. *completed; concluded; consummated; ended; executed; finished; fulfilled; made final; terminated.*

significant ∎ An overworked word. For example: *significant development; significant effect; significant impact; significant progress.* SEE ALSO **meaningful**.

significant other ∎ A torpid term. The use of this dispassionate expression will likely result in a bloodless relationship with whomever it is used to describe. Any one of the following words is a far better choice: *admirer; beau; beloved; boyfriend (girlfriend); companion; confidant; darling; dear; dearest; familiar; family member; flame; friend; husband (wife); inamorata (inamorato); infatuate; intimate; love; lover; paramour; partner; spouse; steady; suitor; swain; sweetheart.*

• Whether it be with instructors, *significant others,* children, or bosses, you practice the art of gentle persuasion continually. REPLACE WITH *spouses.* • My *significant other* is always calling me a spoil sport because I won't compromise on things. REPLACE WITH *lover.* • Men trying to use it to cheat on their *significant others* should know that a pager number will work on a woman for only a short time. REPLACE WITH *girlfriends or wives.* • I am being stalked by a former *significant other.* REPLACE WITH *boyfriend.* SEE ALSO **object of one's affection**.

silence is golden ∎ A quack equation.

(as) silent as the dead (grave) ∎ An insipid simile. *dumb; hushed; mum; mute; noiseless; quiet; reticent; silent; speechless; still; stock-still; taciturn; voiceless; wordless.*

(as) silly as a goose ∎ An insipid simile. *absurd; asinine; childish; comical; farcical; fatuous; flighty; foolhardy; foolish; frivolous; giddy; idiotic; immature; inane; laughable; ludicrous; nonsensical; ridiculous; senseless; silly.*

silver lining ∎ A moribund metaphor.

simultaneously at the same time ∎ A wretched redundancy. *at the same time; simultaneously.* • This machine does four welds *simultaneously at the same time.* REPLACE WITH *at the same time* or *simultaneously.* SEE ALSO **while at the same time; while simultaneously**.

(a) sine qua non ∎ A foreign phrase. *critical essential; indispensable; necessary; requisite; vital.* • A comprehensive neurologic assessment is *a sine qua non* in assessing cases of cerebral palsy. REPLACE WITH *indispensable.*

sing a different tune ∎ A moribund metaphor. *differ; disagree; feel differently; be in conflict; be in disagreement; think unalike.*

singe (your) wings ∎ A moribund metaphor. *be harmed; be injured; be wounded.*

sing for (her) supper ∎ A moribund metaphor.

sing from the same hymn (song) sheet ∎ A moribund metaphor. *agree; concur; feel similarly; harmonize; be in accord; be in agreement; be in harmony; like-minded; match; mesh; think alike.*

single best (biggest; greatest; highest; largest; most) ∎ A wretched redundancy. *best (most).* This expression is a good example of how people pay scant attention to what they say or write. Idiom or no, superlatives like *best* and *most* need not be qualified by the word *single.* People attend more to what others say—copying, as they do, one another's words—than to what they themselves say.
• The *single most* important problem is discrimination among one another. DELETE *single.* • Good records are the *single best* way to avoid having deductions disallowed in the event you are audited. DELETE *single.* • The *single biggest* issue is the cost of upgrading a substandard system. DELETE *single.* • The school committee and the superintendent place student safety as their *single highest* priority. DELETE *single.*

sing like a bird ∎ An insipid simile. *dulcet; harmonious; melodic; melodious; pleasant-sounding; sonorous; sweet.*

sing (his) praises ∎ A torpid term. *acclaim; applaud; celebrate; commend; compliment; congratulate; eulogize; extol; flatter; hail; laud; panegyrize; praise; puff; salute.*

sing the blues ∎ A moribund metaphor. 1. *be aggrieved; be anhedonic; be blue; be cheerless; be dejected; be demoralized; be depressed; be despondent; be disconsolate; be discouraged; be disheartened; be dismal; be dispirited; be doleful; be downcast; be downhearted; be dreary; be forlorn; be funereal; be gloomy; be glum; be grieved; be low; be melancholy; be miserable; be morose; be mournful; be negative; be pessimistic; be plaintive; be sad;* be sorrowful; be unhappy; be woebegone; be woeful.* 2. *bemoan; carp; complain; gripe; grouse; grumble; lament; moan; object; protest; whine.*

sing the same tune ∎ A moribund metaphor. *agree; concur; feel similarly; harmonize; be in accord; be in agreement; be in harmony; like-minded; match; mesh; think alike.*

(enough to) sink a ship ∎ A moribund metaphor. *a big (Brobdingnagian; colossal; enormous; gargantuan; giant; gigantic; grand; great; huge; immense; large; massive; monstrous; prodigious; tremendous; vast) amount; a great deal; a lot.*

sink or swim ∎ A moribund metaphor.

sink (my) teeth into ∎ A moribund metaphor. 1. *absorb; engage; engross; immerse; involve; plunge; submerge.* 2. *brood over; cogitate on; consider; contemplate; deliberate on; dwell on; excogitate on; meditate on; mull over; ponder; reflect on; study; think about.*
• If you can *sink your teeth into* a good role, and the end result is anything like what you hope it's going to be, it's really satisfying. • Rarely does a recording of such grace and elegance also offer so much to *sink your teeth into.*

> She can't get into it. It's not at all like sinking your teeth into a foreign language.—Nancy Zafris, *The Metal Shredders*

sit on (her) duff ∎ A moribund metaphor. *be idle; be inactive; be lazy; be unemployed; be unoccupied; dally; dawdle; loaf; loiter; loll; lounge; relax; repose; rest.*

sit on (their) hands ∎ A moribund metaphor. *be idle; be inactive; be lazy; be unemployed; be unoccupied; dally; dawdle; loaf; loiter; loll; lounge; relax; repose; rest.*

sit on the fence ∎ A moribund metaphor. *be ambivalent; be divided; be indecisive; be in doubt; be irresolute; be neutral; be torn; be uncertain; be uncommitted; be undecided; be unsure.* • If you're *sitting on the fence* or your answer is yes, you're in luck. REPLACE WITH *undecided.*

sit tight ∎ A moribund metaphor. *be patient; hold on; wait.*

sitting on a gold mine ∎ A moribund metaphor.

(a) situation ∎ An overworked word. For example: *crisis situation; difficult situation; life-threatening situation; push-pull situation; no-lose situation; no-win situation; open-ended situation; problematic situation; sad situation; tragic situation; win-win situation.* • It's really *a pathetic situation.* DELETE *a situation.* • If there is an emergency *situation,* then that person can exit as well. DELETE *situation.* • It's nice to be *in a situation where you are* recognized for the work you're doing. DELETE *in a situation where you are.* • The *air conditioning situation* is currently under repair. DELETE *situation* or REPLACE WITH *air conditioner*. • The network approach *is a win-win situation for* all involved. REPLACE WITH *benefits*. SEE ALSO **remedy the situation**.

(sit) with (his) head in (his) hands ∎ A moribund metaphor. *brood; despair; despond; mope.*

(it's) six of one, half dozen of the other ∎ A moribund metaphor. *either; either way; it doesn't matter; no matter.*

skate on thin ice ∎ A moribund metaphor. *chance; dare; endanger; gamble; hazard; imperil; jeopardize; make bold; peril; risk; venture.*

skeletons in the closet (cupboard) ∎ A moribund metaphor. *secret; surprise.*

(all) skin and bones ∎ A moribund metaphor. *asthenic; attenuated; bony; cachectic; emaciated; gaunt; lank; lanky; lean; narrow; rail-thin; scraggy; scrawny; skeletal; skinny; slender; slight; slim; spare; spindly; svelte; sylphid; thin; trim; wispy.*

(as) skinny as a stick ∎ An insipid simile. *asthenic; attenuated; bony; cachectic; emaciated; gaunt; lank; lanky; lean; narrow; rail-thin; scraggy; scrawny; skeletal; skinny; slender; slight; slim; spare; spindly; svelte; sylphid; thin; trim; wispy.*

slap on the wrist ∎ A moribund metaphor. *admonish; animadvert; berate; castigate; censure; chastise; chide; condemn; criticize; denounce; discipline; objurgate; punish; rebuke; remonstrate; reprehend; reprimand; reproach; reprobate; reprove; revile; scold; upbraid; vituperate.* • When the story proved false, Oliver and Smith were fired, but Arnett was *slapped on the wrist* and retained by CNN. REPLACE WITH *chided*.

sleep like a log ∎ An insipid simile. *doze; nap; rest; sleep; slumber.*

sleep like a top ∎ An insipid simile. *doze; nap; rest; sleep; slumber.*

sleep the sleep of the just ∎ A moribund metaphor. *doze; nap; rest; sleep; slumber.*

slice of life ∎ A moribund metaphor.

slim and trim ∎ An inescapable pair. *asthenic; attenuated; bony; cachectic; emaciated; gaunt; lank; lanky; lean; narrow; rail-thin; scraggy; scrawny; skeletal; skinny; slender; slight; slim; spare; spindly; svelte; sylphid; thin; trim; wispy.*

slings and arrows ∎ A moribund metaphor. 1. *assault; attack; blow.* 2. *adversity; bad luck; calamity; catastrophe; hardship; ill fortune; misadventure; mischance; misfortune; mishap; reversal; setback.*

slip of the lip (tongue) ∎ A moribund metaphor. *blunder; error; gaffe; mistake; slip.*

> It sometimes happens that when you make a slip of the tongue you don't want to correct it. You try to pretend that what you said was what you meant.—V. S. Naipaul, *Half a Life*

slipped (my) mind ∎ A moribund metaphor. *be forgetful; be heedless; be inattentive; be lethean; be neglectful; be negligent; be oblivious; be remiss; be thoughtless; be unmindful; be unthinking.*

> An appointment was made with a counselor but the day came and went and they both pretended it had slipped their minds.—Kevin Guilfoile, *Cast of Shadows*

(as) slippery as an eel ∎ An insipid simile. 1. *elusive; ephemeral; evanescent; evasive; fleeting; fugitive; passing; short-lived; slippery; volatile.* 2. *crafty; cunning; deceitful; dishonest; foxy; shifty; slick; tricky; wily.*

slippery character (customer) ∎ A moribund metaphor. *bastard; blackguard; cad; charlatan; cheat; cheater; fake; fraud; impostor; knave; mountebank; phony; pretender; quack; rascal; rogue; scoundrel; swindler; undesirable; villain.*

slippery slope ∎ A moribund metaphor. *debility; decay; decline; degeneration; deterioration; regression; weakening.* • There are concerns that this will only be the beginning of *a slippery slope*. REPLACE WITH *a decline*.

slip through (our) fingers ∎ A moribund metaphor. *abscond; clear out; decamp; depart; desert; disappear; escape; exit; flee; fly; go; go away; leave; move on; part; pull out; quit; retire; retreat; run away; take flight; take off; vacate; vanish; withdraw.*

slip through the cracks ∎ A moribund metaphor. *discount; disregard; elide; exclude; forget; ignore; leave out; miss; neglect; omit; overlook; pass over; skip; slight.*

> All shiny and idealistic, but the truth is, some people slip through the cracks in the care department, and cash for a bottle or a fix is what they need to get themselves through a cold, damp night like this one.—Marcia Muller, *Locked In*

slow and steady wins the race ∎ A popular prescription.

(as) slow as molasses (in January) ∎ An insipid simile. *crawling; dallying; dawdling; deliberate; dilatory; faltering; hesitant; laggardly; lagging; leisurely; methodical; plodding; procrastinating; slothful; slow; slow-paced; sluggardly; sluggish; snaillike; systematic; tardy; tortoiselike; unhurried.*

slow(ly) but sure(ly) ∎ An inescapable pair.

slower than molasses (in January) ∎ A moribund metaphor. *crawling; dallying;*

smack dab in the middle of

dawdling; deliberate; dilatory; faltering; hesitant; laggardly; lagging; leisurely; methodical; plodding; procrastinating; slothful; slow; slow-paced; sluggardly; sluggish; snaillike; systematic; tardy; tortoiselike; unhurried.

smack dab in the middle of ▪ An infantile phrase. • It puts readers *smack dab in the middle of* the action.

small potatoes ▪ A moribund metaphor. *immaterial; inappreciable; inconsequential; inconsiderable; insignificant; meaningless; minor; negligible; niggling; nugatory; petty; trifling; trivial; unimportant; unsubstantial.* • And 10,000 cases is *no small potatoes.* REPLACE WITH *not insignificant.*

> Near the beginning of the walk were the relatively small potatoes.—Glenn Beck, *The Overton Window*

(as) smart as a whip ▪ An insipid simile. *able; adroit; alert; apt; astute; bright; brilliant; capable; clever; competent; discerning; enlightened; intelligent; judicious; keen; knowledgeable; learned; logical; luminous; perceptive; perspicacious; quick; quick-witted; rational; reasonable; sagacious; sage; sapient; sensible; sharp; shrewd; smart; sound; understanding; wise.*

smart cookie ▪ A moribund metaphor. *able; adroit; apt; astute; bright; brilliant; capable; clever; competent; discerning; enlightened; intelligent; judicious; keen; knowledgeable; learned; logical; luminous; perceptive; perspicacious; quick; rational; reasonable; sagacious; sage; sapient; sensible; sharp; shrewd; smart; sound; understanding; wise.*

smell a rat ▪ A moribund metaphor.

smell fishy ▪ A moribund metaphor. *doubtful; dubious; questionable; shady; shaky; suspect; suspicious.*

smoke and mirrors ▪ A moribund metaphor. *artfulness; artifice; chicanery; cover-up; cozenage; craftiness; cunning; deceit; deceiving; deception; dissembling; dissimulation; duplicity; feigning; fraud; guile; pretense; shamming; trickery; wile.*

smokes like a chimney ▪ An insipid simile.

smoking gun ▪ A moribund metaphor. *evidence; proof.*

(as) smooth as glass ▪ An insipid simile. 1. *burnished; even; glassy; glossy; greasy; lustrous; oily; polished; satiny; silky; sleek; slick; slippery; smooth; velvety.* 2. *apparent; basic; clear; clear-cut; conspicuous; distinct; easily done; easy; effortless; elementary; evident; explicit; facile; limpid; lucid; manifest; obvious; patent; pellucid; plain; simple; simplicity itself; smooth; straightforward; translucent; transparent; unambiguous; uncomplex; uncomplicated; understandable; unequivocal; unmistakable.*

(as) smooth as silk ▪ An insipid simile. 1. *burnished; even; glassy; glossy; greasy; lustrous; oily; polished; satiny; silky; sleek; slick; slippery; smooth; velvety.* 2. *apparent; basic; clear; clear-cut; conspicuous; distinct; easily done; easy; effortless; elementary; evident; explicit; facile; limpid; lucid; manifest; obvious; patent; pellucid; plain; simple; simplicity itself; smooth; straightforward; translucent; transparent; unambiguous; uncomplex; uncomplicated; understandable; unequivocal; unmistakable.*

smooth (her) feathers ▪ A moribund metaphor. *allay; appease; assuage; calm; comfort; compose; conciliate; console; moderate; modulate; mollify; pacify; placate; propitiate; quiet; soften; soothe; still; temper; tranquilize.*

snake in the grass ▪ A moribund metaphor. *animal; barbarian; beast; brute; degenerate; fiend; knave; lout; monster; rake; rascal; reptile; rogue; ruffian; savage; scamp; scoundrel; villain.*

> In plain English, I didn't at all relish the notion of helping his inquiries, when those inquiries took him (in the capacity of snake in the grass) among my fellow-servants.—Wilkie Collins, *The Moonstone*

snatch victory from the jaws of defeat ▪ A moribund metaphor.

snow job ▪ A moribund metaphor. *deception; dishonesty.*

(as) snug as a bug in a rug ▪ An insipid simile. *comfortable; cosy; habitable; homey; inhabitable; livable; safe; snug.*

(as) sober as a judge ▪ An insipid simile. 1. *dignified; earnest; formal; grave; pensive; reserved; sedate; self-controlled; self-restrained; serious; severe; sober; solemn; somber; staid; stern; strict; subdued; thoughtful.* 2. *abstemious; sober; teetotal; temperate.*

social butterfly ▪ A moribund metaphor. *fin-lover; gadabout; pleasure-seeker.*

(as) soft as velvet ▪ An insipid simile. *delicate; downy; feathery; fine; fluffy; satiny; silken; silky; smooth; soft; velvety.*

soft landing ▪ A moribund metaphor. • The airline industry's problem is trying to determine whether this is a *soft landing* for the economy or a recession.

soft touch ▪ A moribund metaphor.

(as) solid as a rock ▪ An insipid simile. 1. *adamantine; firm; granitelike; hard; petrified; rock-hard; rocklike; rocky; solid; steellike; steely; stonelike; stony.* 2. *athletic; beefy; brawny; burly; firm; fit; hale; hardy; hearty; husky; manly; mesomorphic; mighty; muscular; powerful; puissant; robust; rugged; sinewy; solid; stalwart; stout; strapping; strong; sturdy; tough; vigorous; virile; well-built.* 3. *constant;*

dependable; determined; faithful; fast; firm; fixed; inexorable; inflexible; loyal; obdurate; resolute; resolved; rigid; solid; stable; staunch; steadfast; steady; stern; strong; tenacious; unflinching; unwavering; unyielding.

some of my best friends are ∎ A plebeian sentiment.

(thirty)-something ∎ An infantile phrase. • But they're not the typical self-absorbed, *30-something* crowd. • If you give a speech on social security, your purpose will vary for audiences made up of *twenty-something, forty-something,* or *seventy-something* individuals.

(there's) something in the wind ∎ A moribund metaphor.

(there's) something rotten in the state of Denmark ∎ A moribund metaphor.

(like) something out of a (Norman Rockwell painting) ∎ An insipid simile. • Li River cruises can take your clients past dreamlike rock formations; they *look like something out of a Salvador Dali painting.*

(it's) something to do ∎ A plebeian sentiment. SEE ALSO **(it) gives (me) something to do; (it) keeps (me) busy; (it) keeps (me) out of trouble**.

(it's) something to look forward to ∎ A plebeian sentiment. Those who use this phrase acknowledge the future appeals to them more than does the present, as they do the apparent pallor of their lives.

(it's) something to think about ∎ A plebeian sentiment. SEE ALSO **food for thought**.

song and dance ∎ A moribund metaphor. 1. *pattern; routine.* 2. *deception; dissimulation; duplicity; equivocation; evasion; excuse; fabrication; falsehood; fib; invention; lie; mumbo-jumbo; nonsense; prevarication.*

son of a gun ∎ A moribund metaphor. *brute; degenerate; fiend; knave; lout; rake; rascal; rogue; ruffian; scamp; scoundrel; villain.*

sooner rather than later ∎ A torpid term. 1. *before long; presently; shortly; soon.* 2. *abruptly; apace; at once; briskly; directly; expeditiously; fast; forthwith; hastily; hurriedly; immediately; instantaneously; instantly; posthaste; promptly; quickly; rapidly; rashly; right away; speedily; straightaway; swiftly; wingedly.* • These people will die unless help arrives *sooner rather than later.* REPLACE WITH *soon.* • That, more than BSE or foot and mouth disease, is why McDonald's is pushing so hard to get an animal ID system in place *sooner rather than later.* REPLACE WITH *swiftly.*

sorely missed ∎ An inescapable pair. Let us not die only to have it said we will be *sorely missed.* We should prefer silence to such insipidity. More disturbing still is that we should be spoken of so blandly, so, indeed, badly. This is hardly the wording of a tribute, hardly an encomium. • He is going to be *sorely missed* by his teammates. • He will be *sorely missed* by those of us who were privileged to call him our friend. • He will be *sorely missed* by his family, fiends and neighbors.

sound and fury ∎ An infantile phrase.

> It seemed a poor catch, for all their sound and fury, and Mr. Murphy would be glad to let them have it.—Kevin Baker, *Dreamland*

(as) sound as a bell ∎ An insipid simile. 1. *cogent; convincing; intelligent; judicious; just; logical; prudent; rational; reasonable; sensible; sound; telling; valid; well-founded; well-grounded; wise.* 2. *athletic; beefy; brawny; energetic; fit; good; hale; hardy; healthful; healthy; hearty; lanky; lean; manly; mesomorphic; muscular; powerful; robust; shapely; sinewy; slender; solid; sound; stalwart; strong; sturdy; thin; trim; vigorous; virile; well; well-built.*

(as) sound as a dollar ∎ An insipid simile. 1. *cogent; convincing; intelligent; judicious; just; logical; prudent; rational; reasonable; sensible; sound; telling; valid; well-founded; well-grounded; wise.* 2. *athletic; beefy; brawny; energetic; fit; good; hale; hardy; healthful; healthy; hearty; lanky; lean; manly; mesomorphic; muscular; powerful; robust; shapely; sinewy; slender; solid; sound; stalwart; strong; sturdy; thin; trim; vigorous; virile; well; well-built.*

(she) sounds like a broken record ∎ An insipid simile.

(as) sour as vinegar ∎ An insipid simile.

sour grapes ∎ A moribund metaphor. *bile; bitterness; resentment; umbrage.*

sour note ∎ A moribund metaphor.

so what else is new? ∎ An infantile phrase.

sow the seeds of ∎ A moribund metaphor. *circulate; disseminate; distribute; propagate; sow; spread.*

sow (his) wild oats ∎ A moribund metaphor. *be dissolute; be licentious; be wild; have sex.*

spare the rod and spoil the child ∎ A popular prescription.

speaks volumes ∎ A moribund metaphor.

(she's) special ∎ A suspect superlative.

(that) special someone ∎ A suspect superlative. *admirer; amorist; beau; boyfriend; flame; gallant; girlfriend; inamorata; inamorato; lover; paramour; steady; suitor; swain; sweetheart; wooer.* • I still haven't met *that special someone,* but I am confident it will happen soon.

speed bump ∎ A moribund metaphor. *barrier;*

difficulty; hindrance; impediment; obstacle; obstruction; problem.

> Because every day, no matter how cheerful, how innocuous, always contains within it some little speed bump of anger or hate, some wrong place, wrong time hell-is-other-people moment of despair.—Sarah Vowel, *Take the Cannoli*

spick and span ∎ An inescapable pair. *antiseptic; clean; cleansed; disinfected; germ-free; hygienic; immaculate; neat; orderly; sanitary; sanitized; scoured; scrubbed; spotless; spruce; stainless; sterile; tidy; unblemished; unsoiled; unspotted; unsullied; untarnished; washed.*

> He was secretly orderly and in person spick and span—his friends declared that they had never seen his hair rumpled.—F. Scott Fitzgerald, *The Beautiful and Damned*

spilled milk ∎ A moribund metaphor.

spill (his) guts ∎ A moribund metaphor. *broadcast; confess; disclose; divulge; expose; make known; proclaim; publicize; reveal; talk; tell; uncover; unearth; unveil.*

> Nor do I covet the mute commiseration of friends who *don't know what to say* and so leave me to spill my guts by way of making conversation.—Lionel Shriver, *We Need to Talk About Kevin*

spill the beans ∎ A moribund metaphor. *confess; disclose; divulge; leak; make known; reveal; tell.*

spinning (my) wheels ∎ A moribund metaphor. *mired; stalled; stuck.*

spit and image (spitting image) ∎ An inescapable pair. *clone; copy; counterpart; doppelgänger; double; duplicate; exact likeness; match; twin.*

spit and polish ∎ A moribund metaphor.

spoil rotten ∎ A moribund metaphor. *coddle; gratify; humor; indulge; mollycoddle; overindulge; overprotect; pamper; spoil.*

spot on ∎ A moribund metaphor. *accurate; correct; exact; perfect; precise; proper; right; (exactly; just) so; true; veracious.*

spread (himself) too thin ∎ A moribund metaphor.

sprout up like mushrooms ∎ An insipid simile. *breed; multiply; proliferate; propagate; reproduce; spread.*

(on the) spur of the moment ∎ A moribund metaphor. *abrupt; extemporaneous; extempore; immediate; impromptu; improvised; impulsive; instant; quick; rash; spontaneous; sudden; unexpected; unprepared; unprompted; unrehearsed.*

square peg in a round hole ∎ A moribund metaphor. *aberrant; abnormal; anomalistic; anomalous; atypical; bizarre; curious; deviant; different; distinct; distinctive; eccentric; exceptional; extraordinary; fantastic; foreign; grotesque; idiosyncratic; independent; individual; individualistic; irregular; novel; odd; offbeat; original; peculiar; puzzling; quaint; queer; rare; remarkable; separate; singular; uncommon; unconventional; unexampled; unique; unnatural; unorthodox; unparalleled; unprecedented; unusual; weird.*

squeaky clean ∎ A moribund metaphor. *high-minded; moralistic; principled; strait-laced; upright; upstanding.*

stab (her) in the back ∎ A moribund metaphor. 1. *assail; attack; badmouth; complain; criticize; denounce; knock; put down.* 2. *abuse; harm; hurt; injure; maltreat; mistreat; wound.* • If I stop trusting people because they may *stab me in the back*, I could miss out on some valuable and enriching friendships. REPLACE WITH *mistreat me.*

stack the cards (deck) ∎ A moribund metaphor. • While such efforts must invariably fail, the climate of distrust and fear *stacks the deck* against individuals who must move into a hostile environment.

(old) stamping (stomping) ground ∎ A moribund metaphor. *hangout; haunt; neighborhood; rendezvous; residence.*

stamp of approval ∎ A moribund metaphor. *approval; authorization; certification; endorsement; sanction.*

stand (their) ground ∎ A moribund metaphor. 1. *hold fast; persevere; persist; stand firm; stick with.* 2. *be adamant; be balky; be bullheaded; be cantankerous; be contrary; be contumacious; be dogged; be headstrong; be inflexible; be intractable; be mulish; be obdurate; be obstinate; be ornery; be perverse; be refractory; be resolute; be rigid; be stubborn; be unyielding; be willful.*

stand on (his) own two feet ∎ A moribund metaphor. *assured; confident; independent; self-assured; self-confident; self-contained; self-governing; self-reliant; self-ruling; self-sufficient; self-supporting; sure.*

stand on the sidelines ∎ A moribund metaphor. • Surgeons who have been *standing on the sidelines* are beginning to take up the procedure themselves.

stand out from (in) the crowd (pack) ∎ A moribund metaphor. *aberrant; abnormal; anomalistic; anomalous; atypical; bizarre; curious; deviant; different; distinct; distinctive; eccentric; exceptional; extraordinary; fantastic; foreign; grotesque; idiosyncratic; independent; individual; individualistic; irregular; novel; odd; offbeat; original; peculiar; puzzling; quaint; queer; rare; remarkable; separate; singular; strange;*

uncommon; unconventional; unexampled; unique; unnatural; unorthodox; unparalleled; unprecedented; unusual; weird.

stand (stick) out like a sore thumb

∎ An insipid simile. *apparent; arresting; blatant; conspicuous; evident; flagrant; glaring; gross; manifest; noticeable; observable; obtrusive; obvious; outstanding; patent; prominent; salient.*

(his) star is on the rise ∎ A moribund metaphor.

(has) stars in her eyes ∎ A moribund metaphor. *dreamy; happy; idealistic; optimistic; starry-eyed.*

start the ball rolling ∎ A moribund metaphor. *begin; commence; enter on; initiate.*

start with a clean slate ∎ A moribund metaphor. *begin anew; start afresh; start over.*

state of siege ∎ A moribund metaphor.

staying power ∎ A moribund metaphor. *determination; durability; endurance; firmness; fortitude; permanence; permanency; perseverance; resolution; resolve; spunk; stability; stamina; steadfastness; tenacity.*

stay on target ∎ A moribund metaphor.

stay the course ∎ A moribund metaphor. *advance; continue; go on; grow; make progress; move on; occur; press on; proceed; progress.*
• Maeng says she knows that West Point, the oldest military academy in the country, will be challenging; however, she plans to *stay the course.* • The congressman wants to *stay the course* until the farm bill comes up for its scheduled review in a few years. • If parents *stay the course* and recognize God's confidence and trust in their parenting skills, then life will be fine throughout the world.

> There was nothing to do but patch himself up as well as he could, stay the course, *not be depressed.*—Jonathan Franzen, *The Corrections*

(as) steady as a rock ∎ An insipid simile. *constant; dependable; determined; faithful; fast; firm; fixed; inexorable; inflexible; loyal; obdurate; reliable; resolute; resolved; rigid; solid; stable; staunch; steadfast; steady; stern; strong; supportive; tenacious; true; trustworthy; trusty; unflinching; unwavering; unyielding.*

steal the show ∎ A moribund metaphor.

steal (her) thunder ∎ A moribund metaphor.

steer clear (of) ∎ A moribund metaphor. *avoid; bypass; circumvent; dodge; elude; evade; shun; sidestep; skirt.* • It was a signal to the new mayor to *steer cleer of* divisiveness and cliquishness. REPLACE WITH *shun.*

steer wrong ∎ A moribund metaphor. *beguile; betray; deceive; lead astray; misdirect; misguide; mislead.* • I trust that you won't *steer* them *wrong.* REPLACE WITH *mislead.*

stem the flow ∎ A moribund metaphor. *abort; arrest; block; check; curb; decelerate; delay; end; halt; hamper; hinder; impede; obstruct; plug; quash; quell; retard; slow; squash; stay; stem; stop; suspend; terminate.*

stem the tide ∎ A moribund metaphor. *abort; arrest; block; check; curb; decelerate; delay; end; halt; hamper; hinder; impede; obstruct; plug; quash; quell; retard; slow; squash; stay; stem; stop; suspend; terminate.* • But twenty years of effort have failed to *stem the tide of* environmental degradation. REPLACE WITH *retard.*

> It was the inability to speak openly about them, and thus to devise ways and means to stem the tide until they could re-form their ranks.—Lawrence Durrell, *Constance*

step on (his) toes ∎ A moribund metaphor. *abuse; affront; anger; annoy; bother; displease; harm; hurt; insult; irk; irritate; offend; outrage; provoke; rile; roil; slap; slight; smart; trouble; upset; vex; wound.* • During his five months as acting mayor, he *stepped on many people's toes.* REPLACE WITH *offended many people.*

step up to the plate ∎ A moribund metaphor. 1. *aim for; attempt; endeavor; engage; participate; pursue; seek; strive for; try.* 2. *advance; appear; approach; come forth; come forward; emerge; rise; show; surface; transpire.* 3. *act; perform; speak; talk.* 4. *be accountable; be answerable; be responsible.* • Rumors of an imminent buyout circulated, but no one *stepped up to the plate.* REPLACE WITH *came forward.* • Industry is *stepping up to the plate on* this. REPLACE WITH *pursuing.* • Because his public presence has been tainted greatly, she's going to have to *step up to the plate* and do more. REPLACE WITH *come forward.*

stewed to the gills ∎ A moribund metaphor. *besotted; crapulous; drunk; inebriated; intoxicated; sodden; stupefied; tipsy.*

stew in (her) own juice ∎ A moribund metaphor. *brood; fret; mope; stew; worry.*

stick in (eat at) (his) craw (throat) ∎ A moribund metaphor. *acerbate; anger; annoy; bother; bristle; chafe; enrage; envenom; exacerbate; gall; incense; inflame; infuriate; insult; irk; irritate; madden; miff; nettle; offend; provoke; rankle; rile; roil; vex.* • And when Bethenny Frankel gets wind of this, it's going to *stick in her craw* something fierce! REPLACE WITH *anger her.* • That's not to say that a loss or imperfection doesn't *eat at his craw*; it does. REPLACE WITH *offend him.*

stick (your) neck out

stick (your) neck out ∎ A moribund metaphor. *chance; dare; endanger; gamble; hazard; imperil; jeopardize; make bold; peril; risk; venture.* • They do not *stick their necks out* to initiate change—they are followers. REPLACE WITH *venture.*

sticks and stones will break my bones, but words will never hurt me ∎ An infantile phrase.

stick to (your) guns ∎ A moribund metaphor. 1. *hold fast; persevere; persist; stand firm; stick with.* 2. *be adamant; be balky; be bullheaded; be cantankerous; be contrary; be contumacious; be dogged; be headstrong; be inflexible; be intractable; be mulish; be obdurate; be obstinate; be ornery; be perverse; be refractory; be resolute; be rigid; be stubborn; be unyielding; be willful.*

stick to (your) ribs ∎ A moribund metaphor. *fill; sate; satiate; satisfy.*

stick to the knitting ∎ A moribund metaphor.

sticky wicket ∎ A moribund metaphor. *affliction; annoyance; bane; bother; burden; curse; difficulty; inconvenience; irritant; irritation; load; nuisance; ordeal; pain; pest; problem; tribulation; trouble; vexation; weight; worry.*

(as) stiff as a board ∎ An insipid simile. 1. *firm; inelastic; inflexible; rigid; stiff; unbending; unmalleable; unpliable; unyielding.* 2. *awkward; ceremonious; constrained; formal; precise; priggish; prim; proper; prudish; punctilious; puritanical; reserved; starched; stiff; stilted; strait-laced; stuffy; unrelaxed; uptight.*

still and all ∎ A wretched redundancy. *even so; still; yet.* • *Still and all,* I love her. REPLACE WITH *Even so* or *Still.*

(as) still as a mouse ∎ An insipid simile. *dead; dormant; dull; immobile; immovable; inactive; inanimate; indolent; inert; inoperative; languid; latent; lethargic; lifeless; listless; motionless; noiseless; phlegmatic; quiescent; quiet; silent; sluggish; soundless; stagnant; static; stationary; still; stock-still; torpid; unresponsive.*

(as) still as death ∎ An insipid simile. *dead; dormant; dull; immobile; immovable; inactive; inanimate; indolent; inert; inoperative; languid; latent; lethargic; lifeless; listless; motionless; noiseless; phlegmatic; quiescent; quiet; silent; sluggish;*

soundless; stagnant; static; stationary; still; stock-still; torpid; unresponsive.

still kicking ∎ A moribund metaphor. *alive; animate; breathing; live; living.*

still waters run deep ∎ A popular prescription.

stink like hell ∎ An insipid simile. *reek; smell; stink.*

stir up a hornet's nest ∎ A moribund metaphor. SEE ALSO *hornet's nest.*

stitch in time ∎ A moribund metaphor.

stop and smell the flowers (roses) ∎ A moribund metaphor. *be idle; be inactive; be lazy; be unemployed; be unoccupied; dally; dawdle; loaf; loiter; loll; lounge; relax; repose; rest.*

stop (him) (dead) in (his) tracks ∎ A moribund metaphor. *arrest; check; freeze; halt; hold; immobilize; restrain; stop.*

stop the world I want to get off ∎ An infantile phrase.

storm brewing ∎ A moribund metaphor.

(the) story of (my) life ∎ A plebeian sentiment. • I've always felt like an outcast; it's *the story of my life.*

straddle the fence ∎ A moribund metaphor. *ambivalent; divided; indecisive; in doubt; irresolute; neutral; torn; uncertain; uncommitted; undecided; unsure.*

(as) straight as an arrow ∎ An insipid simile. 1. *direct; lineal; linear; straight.* 2. *decent; ethical; exemplary; good; honest; honorable; just; moral; pure; righteous; straight; upright; virtuous; wholesome.*

straight from the horse's mouth ∎ A moribund metaphor.

straight from the shoulder ∎ A moribund metaphor. *bluntly; candidly; directly; forthrightly; frankly; man to man; openly; outspokenly; plainly; straightforwardly; unambiguously; unequivocally.*

straight shooter ∎ A moribund metaphor. *decent; ethical; forthright; honest; just; moral; righteous; straight; trustworthy; upright; virtuous.*

strange ∎ An overworked word. *aberrant; abnormal; anomalistic; anomalous; atypical; bizarre; curious; deviant; different; distinct; distinctive; eccentric; exceptional; extraordinary; fantastic; foreign; grotesque; idiosyncratic; independent; individual; individualistic; irregular; novel; odd; offbeat; original; peculiar; puzzling; quaint; queer; rare; remarkable; separate; singular; uncommon; unconventional;*

unexampled; unique; unnatural; unorthodox; unparalleled; unprecedented; unusual; weird. SEE ALSO **weird.**

strange bedfellows ▌ A moribund metaphor.

stretch the point (truth) ▌ A moribund metaphor. *elaborate; embellish; embroider; enhance; enlarge; exaggerate; hyperbolize; inflate; magnify; overdo; overstress; overstate; strain; stretch.*

strike (touch) a chord ▌ A moribund metaphor. *be familiar; remind; sound familiar.* • These words *struck a familiar chord* with many of the 6,000 conference participants.

strike gold ▌ A moribund metaphor.

strike while the iron is hot ▌ A moribund metaphor. *capitalize on; exploit.*

strings attached ▌ A moribund metaphor. *conditions; limitations; preconditions; prerequisites; provisions; qualifications; requirements; stipulations; terms.*

stroll down memory lane ▌ A moribund metaphor. *be nostalgic; recall; recollect; remember; reminisce; think back.*

(as) strong as a horse ▌ An insipid simile. *athletic; beefy; brawny; burly; energetic; fit; hale; hardy; healthful; healthy; hearty; husky; manly; mesomorphic; mighty; muscular; powerful; puissant; robust; rugged; sinewy; solid; sound; stalwart; stout; strapping; strong; sturdy; vigorous; virile; well-built.*

(as) strong as a lion ▌ An insipid simile. *athletic; beefy; brawny; burly; energetic; fit; hale; hardy; healthful; healthy; hearty; husky; manly; mesomorphic; mighty; muscular; powerful; puissant; robust; rugged; sinewy; solid; sound; stalwart; stout; strapping; strong; sturdy; vigorous; virile; well-built.*

(as) strong as an ox ▌ An insipid simile. *athletic; beefy; brawny; burly; energetic; fit; hale; hardy; healthful; healthy; hearty; husky; manly; mesomorphic; mighty; muscular; powerful; puissant; robust; rugged; sinewy; solid; sound; stalwart; stout; strapping; strong; sturdy; vigorous; virile; well-built.*

(as) stubborn as a mule ▌ An insipid simile. *adamant; balky; bullheaded; cantankerous; contrary; contumacious; dogged; headstrong; inflexible; intractable; mulish; obdurate; obstinate; ornery; perverse; refractory; resolute; rigid; stubborn; unyielding; willful.*

stuff and nonsense ▌ An inescapable pair. *absurdity; fatuousness; folly; foolishness; ludicrousness; nonsense; preposterousness; ridiculousness; rubbish; silliness.*

stuff to the gills ▌ A moribund metaphor. *abounding; brimful; brimming; bursting; chock-full; congested; crammed; crowded; dense; filled; full; gorged; jammed; jam-packed; overcrowded; overfilled; overflowing;*

packed; replete; saturated; stuffed; swarming; teeming.

(major) stumbling block ▌ A moribund metaphor. *barrier; hindrance; hurdle; impediment; obstacle; obstruction.* • Modernization of the Chinese HRM system is fraught with significant *stumbling blocks.*

stupid ▌ An overworked word. This epithet, along with others as common, is much overused. Let's do our best to convince *stupid* people that they are by calling them, instead, *addlebrained; addleheaded; addlepated; Boeotian; bovine; cretinous; decerebrate; doltish; dull-witted; dunderheaded; fatuous; fat-witted; harebrained; hebetudinous; imbecilic; incogitant; insensate; ludicrous; moronic; muddled; nescient; obtuse; oxlike; pedestrian; phlegmatic; sluggish; torpid; vacuous; witless.*

(as) sturdy as an oak ▌ An insipid simile. *athletic; beefy; brawny; burly; energetic; fit; hale; hardy; healthful; healthy; hearty; husky; manly; mesomorphic; mighty; muscular; powerful; puissant; robust; rugged; sinewy; solid; sound; stalwart; stout; strapping; strong; sturdy; vigorous; virile; well-built.*

subsequent to ▌ A torpid term. *after; following.* • *Subsequent to* the initiation of the Ethics Committee investigation, the senator took back some tapes in my possession which I had not yet transcribed. REPLACE WITH *Following.* SEE ALSO **in advance of; previous to; subsequent to.**

such is life ▌ A plebeian sentiment. SEE ALSO **that's how (the way) it goes; that's how (the way) the ball bounces; that's how (the way) the cookie crumbles; that's life; that's life in the big city; that's show biz; what are you going to do; what can you do.**

suck the life out of ▌ A moribund metaphor. *bleed dry; deplete; drain; exhaust; sap; suck dry.*

suddenly and without warning ▌ A wretched redundancy. *impetuously; impulsively; spontaneously; suddenly; unexpectedly; without warning.*

sufficient enough ▌ A wretched redundancy. *enough; sufficient.* • Just tell them your new number, and that should be *sufficient enough.* REPLACE WITH *sufficient* or *enough.* SEE ALSO **adequate enough.**

sugar and spice ▌ A moribund metaphor.

sum and substance ▌ An inescapable pair. *basis; center; core; crux; essence; gist; heart; kernel; pith; substance; sum.*

(as) sure as death ▌ An insipid simile. *assured; certain; destined; established; fated; fixed; foreordained; ineluctable; inescapable; inevitable; inexorable; irresistible; irreversible; irrevocable; ordained; prearranged; predestined; predetermined; sure; unalterable; unavoidable; unchangeable;*

(as) sure as death and taxes

unpreventable; unstoppable.

(as) sure as death and taxes ∎ An insipid simile. *assured; certain; destined; established; fated; fixed; foreordained; ineluctable; inescapable; inevitable; inexorable; irresistible; irreversible; irrevocable; ordained; prearranged; predestined; predetermined; sure; unalterable; unavoidable; unchangeable; unpreventable; unstoppable.*

survival of the fittest ∎ A popular prescription.

swallow (her) pride ∎ A moribund metaphor. *abase; chasten; debase; degrade; demean; disgrace; dishonor; embarrass; humble; humiliate; lower; mortify; shame.*

swan song ∎ A moribund metaphor. *farewell; good-bye.*

swear by all that's holy ∎ A moribund metaphor. *affirm; asseverate; assert; attest; aver; avow; declare; pledge; promise; swear; testify; vow; warrant.*

swear like a sailor (trooper) ∎ An insipid simile. *abusive; blackguardly; coarse; crude; fescennine; foul-mouthed; indecent; lewd; obscene; profane; ribald; scurrilous; thersitical; vulgar.*

swear on a stack of bibles ∎ A moribund metaphor. *affirm; asseverate; assert; attest; aver; avow; declare; pledge; promise; swear; testify; vow; warrant.*

sweat bullets ∎ A moribund metaphor. 1. *excrete; exude; ooze; perspire; sweat; swelter; wilt.* 2. *be afraid; be agitated; be anxious; be apprehensive; be distraught; be distressed; be fearful; be fretful; be impatient; be nervous; be panicky; be tense; be uneasy; be worried.* 3. *drudge; grind; grub; labor; moil; slave; strain; strive; struggle; sweat; toil; travail; work hard.*

sweep off (her) feet ∎ A moribund metaphor. *amaze; astonish; astound; awe; dazzle; dumbfound; flabbergast; overpower; overwhelm; shock; startle; stun; stupefy; surprise.*

sweep (it) under the (carpet) rug ∎ A moribund metaphor. 1. *brush aside; avoid; discount; disregard; dodge; duck; ignore; neglect; omit; pass over; recoil from; shrink from; shun; shy away from; turn away from; withdraw from.* 2. *camouflage; cloak; conceal; cover; disguise; enshroud; harbor; hide; keep secret; mask; screen; shroud; suppress; veil; withhold.* • The strategy was to *sweep it under the rug.* REPLACE WITH *ignore it.*

sweep (it) under the table ∎ A moribund metaphor. 1. *brush aside; avoid; discount; disregard; dodge; duck; ignore; neglect; omit; pass over; recoil from; shrink from; shun; shy away from; turn away from; withdraw from.* 2. *camouflage; cloak; conceal; cover; disguise; enshroud; harbor; hide; keep secret; mask; screen; shroud; suppress; veil; withhold.* • We see the word *anti-Semitism* every day in our secular newspapers, but the word *anti-Catholic* is *swept under the table.* REPLACE WITH *brushed aside.*

(as) sweet as honey ∎ An insipid simile. 1. *honeyed; luscious; saccharine; sugary; sweet; sweetened; syrupy.* 2. *agreeable; ambrosial; beguiling; celestial; charming; delectable; delicious; delightful; divine; enchanting; engaging; enjoyable; fun; heavenly; glorious; gratifying; inviting; joyful; joyous; luscious; pleasant; pleasing; pleasurable.*

(as) sweet as pie ∎ An insipid simile. 1. *honeyed; luscious; saccharine; sugary; sweet; sweetened; syrupy.* 2. *agreeable; ambrosial; beguiling; celestial; charming; delectable; delicious; delightful; divine; enchanting; engaging; enjoyable; fun; heavenly; glorious; gratifying; inviting; joyful; joyous; luscious; pleasant; pleasing; pleasurable.*

sweeten the pot ∎ A moribund metaphor. *add to; augment; enhance; improve; increase; supplement.*

sweeter than honey ∎ A moribund metaphor. 1. *honeyed; luscious; saccharine; sugary; sweet; sweetened; syrupy.* 2. *agreeable; ambrosial; beguiling; celestial; charming; delectable; delicious; delightful; divine; enchanting; engaging; enjoyable; fun; heavenly; glorious; gratifying; inviting; joyful; joyous; luscious; pleasant; pleasing; pleasurable.*

sweetness and light ∎ A moribund metaphor. *agreeable; ambrosial; beguiling; celestial; charming; delectable; delicious; delightful; divine; enchanting; engaging; enjoyable; fun; heavenly; glorious; gratifying; inviting; joyful; joyous; luscious; pleasant; pleasing; pleasurable.*

sweet smell of success ∎ A moribund metaphor.

(as) swift as an arrow ∎ An insipid simile. *brisk; expeditious; fast; fleet; hasty; hurried; immediate; instant; instantaneous; prompt; quick; rapid; speedy; spry; sudden; swift; winged.*

swim against the current (tide) ∎ A moribund metaphor. 1. *drudge; grind; grub; labor; moil; slave; strain; strive; struggle; sweat; toil; travail; work hard.* 2. *battle; fight; tussle; wrestle.*

swim like a fish ∎ An insipid simile.

swim upstream ∎ A moribund metaphor.

swim with the tide ∎ A moribund metaphor. *abide by; accede to; accept; accommodate; acquiesce; adapt to; adhere to; adjust to; agree to; assent to; be agreeable; be complacent; be conventional; bend; be resigned; be traditional; bow; comply with; concede to; concur; conform; consent to; fit; follow; reconcile; submit; succumb; yield.*

tabula rasa ∎ A foreign phrase.

take a back seat (to) ∎ A moribund metaphor. 1. *be ancillary; be inferior; be lesser; be lower; be minor; be second; be secondary; be subordinate; be subservient.* 2. *be diffident; be humble; be meek; be self-effacing.* • Just a few years after this work, machine learning *took a back seat* to expert knowledge systems. REPLACE WITH *became subordinate.* • As in most races for most offices, issues have *taken a back seat* to personality, image, footwork, money, and most important, field organization. REPLACE WITH *became ancillary.* • Power based on expertise frequently *takes a back seat* to power based on position. REPLACE WITH *is second.*

> Would she never see the day when she didn't have to take a back seat to a man's feelings?—Madalyn Reese, *No Place to Hide*

take a bath ∎ A moribund metaphor. *lose money.*

take a beating ∎ A moribund metaphor. 1. *be beaten; be conquered; be crushed; be defeated; be outdone; be overcome; be overpowered; be overwhelmed; be quelled; be routed; be trounced; be vanquished.* 2. *be assailed; be assaulted; be attacked; be battered; be beaten; be cudgeled; be flagellated; be flogged; be hit; be lambasted; be lashed; be licked; be mangled; be pounded; be pummeled; be struck; be thrashed; be trounced.*

take a breather ∎ An infantile phrase. *be idle; be inactive; be lazy; be unemployed; be unoccupied; dally; dawdle; loaf; loiter; loll; lounge; relax; repose; rest.*

> She stops to take a breather, picks up the ringing phone.—Kate Moses, *Wintering*

take a dim view of ∎ A moribund metaphor. *deprecate; disapprove; dislike; frown on; object; protest.*

take a fancy (shine) to ∎ A moribund metaphor. *delight in; enjoy; fancy; like; relish.*

take a front seat (on) ∎ A moribund metaphor. *be dominant; be principal; be supreme; dominate; lead; prevail; reign; rise above; rule; surmount; triumph.* • There are protection rights that, according to law, *take a front seat.* REPLACE WITH *prevail.* • America's position in North Korea and Afghanistan will *take a front seat on* this weekend's Sunday morning talk shows. REPLACE WITH *dominate.*

> Yesterday she was ready to pick up the phone, call Jeff, and tell him off for all he was worth. This morning, family took a front seat.—Margaret Johnson-Hodge, *Warm Hands*

take a gander (at) ∎ An infantile phrase. *gaze; glance; glimpse; look; observe; stare; watch.*

take a haircut ∎ A moribund metaphor. *lose money.* • He suggested what has been plain for some time—that holders of $1.7 billion in junk bonds would probably *take a haircut.* REPLACE WITH *lose money.*

take a hit ∎ A moribund metaphor. *be assailed; be assaulted; be attacked; be battered; be beaten; be cudgeled; be flagellated; be flogged; be hit; be lambasted; be lashed; be licked; be mangled; be pounded; be pummeled; be struck; be thrashed; be trounced.*

take a leaf (page) out of (their) book ∎ A moribund metaphor. *copy; duplicate; emulate; follow; imitate; mimic.*

take a load off (your) mind ∎ A moribund metaphor. *acknowledge; admit; affirm; allow; avow; concede; confess; disclose; divulge; expose; grant; own; reveal; tell; uncover; unearth; unveil.*

take a long, hard look (at) ∎ A torpid term. *analyze; assay; check out; delve into; examine; investigate; probe; scrutinize; study.* • We need leaders with the will and the determination to *take a long, hard look at* the structure of our government. REPLACE WITH *examine.*

take a nose dive ∎ A moribund metaphor. *collapse; crash; dive; drop; fall; nose-dive; plummet; plunge.*

take a powder ∎ A moribund metaphor. *abscond; clear out; decamp; depart; desert; disappear; escape; exit; flee; fly; go; go away; leave; move on; part; pull out; quit; retire; retreat; run away; take flight; take off; vacate; vanish; withdraw.*

take a turn for the better ∎ A moribund metaphor. *ameliorate; amend; come round; convalesce; gain strength; get better; heal; improve; look up; meliorate; mend; rally; recover; recuperate; refresh; regain strength; renew; revive; strengthen.*

take a turn for the worse ∎ A moribund metaphor. *decay; decline; degenerate; deteriorate; disintegrate; ebb; erode; fade; fall off; languish; lessen; wane; weaken; wither; worsen.*

take (my) ball (toys) and go home

take (my) ball (toys) and go home ∎ An infantile phrase.

take (your) breath away ∎ A moribund metaphor. *amaze; astonish; astound; awe; dazzle; dumbfound; flabbergast; overpower; overwhelm; shock; startle; stun; stupefy; surprise.*

take by storm ∎ A moribund metaphor. 1. *conquer; defeat; overcome; overwhelm; prevail; quell; rout; seize; storm; subdue; triumph; vanquish.* 2. *amaze; animate; awe; beguile; captivate; charm; dazzle; electrify; enchant; engross; enthrall; entrance; excite; exhilarate; fascinate; hypnotize; impress; intoxicate; mesmerize; thrill; overwhelm; rivet.* • In the two years since it was introduced as the newest drug for depression, Prozac has *taken* the mental health community *by storm.* REPLACE WITH *captivated.*

> What I had thought to take by storm fell into my hands as simply as fruit from a tree.—Peter De Vries, *The Blood of the Lamb*

take each day as it comes ∎ A popular prescription.

take exception to ∎ A wretched redundancy. *challenge; demur; disagree with; disapprove of; dispute; find fault with; object to; oppose; protest; question; resent.* • I *take exception to* your analysis of his difficulties. REPLACE WITH *disagree with.* SEE ALSO **take issue with.**

take (him) for a ride ∎ A moribund metaphor. *bamboozle; befool; beguile; bilk; bluff; cheat; con; deceive; defraud; delude; dupe; feint; fool; gyp; hoodwink; lead astray; misdirect; misguide; misinform; mislead; spoof; swindle; trick; victimize.*

take (my) hat off to ∎ A moribund metaphor. *acclaim; applaud; commend; compliment; congratulate; extol; hail; laud; praise.*

take (a lot of) heat ∎ A moribund metaphor.

take into account ∎ A wretched redundancy. *allow for; consider; contemplate; examine; inspect; investigate; look at; ponder; provide for; regard; scrutinize; study; think over; weigh.* • The character of the army is also an important factor to be *taken into account.* REPLACE WITH *considered.* SEE ALSO **take into consideration.**

take into consideration ∎ A wretched redundancy. *allow for; consider; contemplate; examine; inspect; investigate; look at; ponder; provide for; regard; scrutinize; study; think over; weigh.* • All this will be *taken into consideration*, and financial analysis will be done. REPLACE WITH *examined.* SEE ALSO **take into account.**

take issue with ∎ A wretched redundancy. *challenge; demur; disagree with; disapprove of; dispute; find fault with; object to; oppose; protest; question; resent.* • Some *take issue*

with the state requiring people to use seat belts. REPLACE WITH *object to.* SEE ALSO **take exception to.**

take it as it comes ∎ A popular prescription.

(I) take it (that) back ∎ An infantile phrase. 1. *be incorrect; be in error; be misguided; be misinformed; be mislead; be mistaken; be not right; be wrong.* 2. *disavow; recant; renounce; repudiate; retract; withdraw.* • Joanie is in third place; no, I *take it back*—it's another runner. REPLACE WITH *I'm wrong.* • I always wanted to be with someone more respectable; not respectable, I *take that back*, professional. REPLACE WITH *I retract that.*

take it one day (step) at a time ∎ A popular prescription.

take it on the chin ∎ A moribund metaphor. 1. *be beaten; be conquered; be crushed; be defeated; be flattened; be outdone; be overcome; be overpowered; be trampled; be trounced; be vanquished.* 2. *abide; accept; bear; brook; endure; stand; stomach; suffer; take; tolerate; withstand.*

take (her) life in (her) hands ∎ A moribund metaphor. *chance; dare; endanger; gamble; hazard; imperil; jeopardize; make bold; peril; risk; venture.*

take (his) lumps ∎ A moribund metaphor. • We fought our way back to profitability after *taking our lumps.*

take (their) medicine ∎ A moribund metaphor.

taken aback ∎ A moribund metaphor. *amazed; astonished; astounded; flabbergasted; shocked; staggered; stunned; surprised.*

take off the table ∎ A moribund metaphor. *dismiss; not consider; reject; set aside; shelve.* • I don't think we should ever *take* a nuclear response *off the table.*

take the bait ∎ A moribund metaphor.

> I almost take the bait and then decide, no, if I start talking about the boss, taking him apart, it will never quit.—Louise Erdrich, *Tales of Burning Love*

take the bit between (in) (her) teeth ∎ A moribund metaphor. *defy; disobey; rebel; resist; revolt; take charge; take control.*

take the bitter with the sweet ∎ A popular prescription.

take the bull by the horns ∎ A moribund metaphor. *challenge; confront; defy.*

take the cake ∎ A moribund metaphor. 1. *be best; be finest; be first; be first-rate; be outstanding; win.* 2. *be absurd; be disgraceful; be inane; be lowest; be outrageous; be poorest; be preposterous; be ridiculous; be worst.* • I am accustomed to being shocked by John Ellis, but "Beyond manifest destiny" *takes the cake*. REPLACE WITH *is outrageous*.

take the high road ∎ A moribund metaphor. 1. *be beneficent; be benevolent; be broad-minded; be charitable; be civil; be courteous; be gracious; be high-minded; be kind; be liberal; be magnanimous; be noble*. 2. *be decent; be ethical; be exemplary; be good; be honest; be honorable; be just; be moral; be pure; be respectful; be righteous; be straight; be upright; be virtuous; be wholesome*.

take the money and run ∎ A moribund metaphor. *abscond; clear out; decamp; depart; desert; disappear; escape; exit; flee; fly; go; go away; leave; make off; move on; part; pull out; quit; retire; retreat; run away; steal away; take flight; take off; vacate; vanish; withdraw*.

take the plunge ∎ A moribund metaphor. *dive in; do it; jump in*.

take the wind out of (his) sails ∎ A moribund metaphor. 1. *abase; chasten; debase; decrease; deflate; degrade, demean; depreciate; depress; diminish; disgrace; dishonor; embarrass; humble; humiliate; lower; mortify; puncture; shame*. 2. *arrest; balk; block; bridle; check; curb; derail; detain; end; foil; frustrate; halt; harness; hold up; impede; inhibit; obstruct; restrain; retard; slow; stall; stay; stop; suppress; terminate; thwart*.

(to) take this opportunity (to) ∎ An ineffectual phrase. On the podium and before others, people speak what they're expected to say. Alone and on their deathbeds, they moan that no one knew who they were. *(To) take this opportunity (to)* is one of the phrases that people learn to mimic before they know to moan. • I would like *to take this opportunity* to apologize to my family and friends. DELETE *to take this opportunity*. • I'd like *to take this opportunity* to renew our commitment to you—to provide you with superior service. DELETE *to take this opportunity*. • Let me *take this opportunity to* thank our most inspirational guest. DELETE *take this opportunity to*. • As we wind down the current year, I would like to *take this opportunity to* thank you for your hard work on the Tech Communications Workshop this past academic year. DELETE *take this opportunity to*.

take to (his) heels ∎ A moribund metaphor. *abscond; clear out; decamp; depart; desert; disappear; escape; exit; flee; fly; go; go away; leave; move on; part; pull out; quit; retire; retreat; run away; take flight; take off; vacate; vanish; withdraw*.

take (him) to task ∎ A torpid term. *admonish; animadvert; berate; blame; castigate; censure; chasten; chastise; chide; condemn; criticize; denounce; denunciate; discipline; impugn; objurgate; punish; rebuke; remonstrate; reprehend; reprimand;*

reproach; reprobate; reprove; revile; scold; upbraid; vituperate. • In polite, carefully chosen words, the auditors *take management to task* for a multitude of sins. REPLACE WITH *censure*.

take (her) to the cleaners ∎ A moribund metaphor.

take (them) to the woodshed ∎ A moribund metaphor. *admonish; animadvert; berate; castigate; censure; chasten; chastise; chide; condemn; criticize; denounce; denunciate; discipline; excoriate; fulminate against; imprecate; impugn; inveigh against; objurgate; punish; rebuke; remonstrate; reprehend; reprimand; reproach; reprobate; reprove; revile; scold; swear at; upbraid; vituperate*.

take with a grain (pinch) of salt ∎ A moribund metaphor. *be suspicious; be wary; disbelieve; distrust; doubt; have doubts; have misgivings; have reservations; mistrust; question; suspect; wonder*. • But this pane's data should be *taken with a grain of salt*. REPLACE WITH *doubted*.

> But Tim Paddy hinted that this story should be taken with a pinch of salt.—William Trevor, *Fools of Fortune*

(like) taking candy from a baby ∎ An insipid simile. *apparent; basic; clear; clear-cut; conspicuous; distinct; easily done; easy; effortless; elementary; evident; explicit; facile; limpid; lucid; manifest; obvious; patent; pellucid; plain; simple; simplicity itself; straightforward; translucent; transparent; unambiguous; uncomplex; uncomplicated; understandable; unequivocal; unmistakable*.

> It was a situation tailor-made for Eden, who would've considered it just slightly more challenging than taking candy from a baby and then pushing the buggy off a cliff.— Antoinette Stockenberg, *Safe Harbor*

(like) taking lambs to the slaughter ∎ An insipid simile.

(tell) tales out of school ∎ A moribund metaphor. • A lot of people thought they were *telling tales out of school*.

> I oughtn't to tell tales out of school but it's a long time ago now and I'm glad Sarah has found happiness, but in those days it was well-known in Pankot that Susan was always pinching her elder sister's young men ....—Paul Scott, *Staying On*

talk a blue streak ∎ A moribund metaphor. *babbling; blathering; chatty; facile; fluent; garrulous; glib; jabbering; logorrheic; long-winded; loquacious; prolix; talkative; verbose; voluble; windy*.

talk (my) ear (head) off ∎ A moribund metaphor. *babbling; blathering; chatty; facile;*

talk is cheap

fluent; garrulous; glib; jabbering; logorrheic; long-winded; loquacious; prolix; talkative; verbose; voluble; windy.

talk is cheap ∎ A quack equation.

talk (speak) out of both sides of (his) mouth ∎ A moribund metaphor. *be ambivalent; be indecisive; be irresolute; be uncertain; be unsure; be wishy-washy; dodge; doubletalk; equivocate; evade; fence; hedge; palter; prevaricate; quibble; shuffle; sidestep; tergiversate; waffle.*

(he) talks a good game ∎ A moribund metaphor.

talk through (his) hat ∎ A moribund metaphor. *babble; blather; jabber; prate; prattle.*

talk turkey ∎ A moribund metaphor.

tan (warm) (her) hide ∎ A moribund metaphor. *spank.*

tar and feather ∎ A moribund metaphor. *admonish; animadvert; berate; castigate; censure; chasten; chastise; chide; condemn; criticize; denounce; denunciate; discipline; impugn; objurgate; punish; rebuke; remonstrate; reprehend; reprimand; reproach; reprobate; reprove; revile; scold; upbraid; vituperate.*

tar (him) with the same brush ∎ A moribund metaphor.

teach (me) the ropes ∎ A moribund metaphor. *coach; educate; initiate; instruct; teach; train; tutor.*

team player ∎ A suspect superlative. This term is much favored by those in the business world for an employee who thinks just as others do and behaves just as he is expected to. A *team player* is a person who has not the spirit to think for or be himself.

Of course, nothing new, nothing innovative is likely to be realized by insisting, as the business world does, on objectivity and consensus.

A team player is often no more than a *bootlicker*; no more than a *fawner,* a *flatterer,* a *follower*; no more than a *lackey,* a *minion,* a *stooge*; no more than a *sycophant,* a *toady,* a *yes-man.* • Mulvey, whose termination is perhaps the most striking—he was one of the bank's stellar performers—was not regarded as a *team player.*

tear (out) (my) hair ∎ A moribund metaphor. 1. *acerbated; angry; annoyed; bothered; cross; displeased; enraged; furious; grouchy; incensed; inflamed; infuriated; irate; irked; irritated; mad; miffed; peeved; provoked; riled; roiled; testy; upset; vexed.* 2. *agitated; anxious; apprehensive; distraught; distressed; fearful; frustrated; nervous; panicky; stressed; stressful; tense; tormented; troubled; uneasy; worried.*

teeter on the brink (of) ∎ A moribund metaphor.

tell it like it is ∎ An infantile phrase. *be blunt; be candid; be forthright; be frank; be honest; be open; be truthful.* • He's not whining; he's just *telling it like it is.* REPLACE WITH *being honest.* • These videos may be informative and *tell it like it is* but are far too explicit and do not belong in a coed classroom. REPLACE WITH *truthful.*

tell it to the Marines ∎ A moribund metaphor.

tell (her) off ∎ A torpid term. *admonish; animadvert; berate; castigate; censure; chasten; chastise; chide; condemn; criticize; denounce; denunciate; discipline; impugn; objurgate; punish; rebuke; remonstrate; reprehend; reprimand; reproach; reprobate; reprove; revile; scold; upbraid; vituperate.*

tell (them) where to get off ∎ A torpid term. *admonish; animadvert; berate; castigate; censure; chasten; chastise; chide; condemn; criticize; denounce; denunciate; discipline; impugn; objurgate; punish; rebuke; remonstrate; reprehend; reprimand; reproach; reprobate; reprove; revile; scold; upbraid; vituperate.*

tempest in a teapot ∎ A moribund metaphor.

terra firma ∎ A foreign phrase.

terrific ∎ An overworked word. *Terrific* means *causing terror* or *terrifying*, but of late, it means only *very bad* or, annoyingly, *very good.* • I have a *terrific* stomachache. REPLACE WITH *very bad.* • We had a *terrific* time at the party. REPLACE WITH *very good.* SEE ALSO **awesome; awful.**

test the waters ∎ A moribund metaphor.

thank goodness it's Friday ∎ An infantile phrase.

thanks but no thanks ∎ An infantile phrase. *thanks; thanks all the same; thanks anyway; thanks just the same.*

thank you ∎ A plebeian sentiment. Even *thank you*—once a sure sign of civility— becomes part of the plebeian patois when it is spoken mechanically.

Only a spectacularly thoughtless person would thank others for having been abused or berated by them, for having been refused or rejected by them. SEE ALSO **excuse me?; I'm sorry.**

thank you for having me ∎ A torpid term. *my pleasure; thank you; you're welcome.* Elliptical for *thank you for having me on your show*—or *program*—*thank you for having me* is further evidence of how thoughtless we have become. Nearly every guest on a radio or television or Internet program will conclude his interview with this automatic, imitative term, as though it were obligatory.

thank(ing) you in advance ∎ A plebeian sentiment. These phrases are more than plebeian, they are impudent. Only the lowbred or harebrained would presume to thank another for something while requesting it of him. • We *thank you in advance* for your understanding in this situation. • *Thank you in advance* for taking the time to help us. • *Thanks in advance* for your cooperation. • I have contacted the folks at ArtistDirect as well, and wanted to *thank you in advance* for your compliance in this matter.

And now variations of this phrase are being used in other, even more facile and sillier, constructions: • If I offend any man, woman, beast, or anything in between, *I apologize in advance.* • He apologizes in advance* to those with a more normal sense of humor.

thank you so (so) much ∎ An infantile phrase. Instead of the genuine sounding *thank you*, many people are using, almost exclusively, the fulsome-sounding *thank you so much*. That those who use the expression do not understand and cannot hear the artificiality of *thank you so much* is a marvel, and suggests that people do not pay attention to what they or others say. Speech, even the rudimentary words of politeness and civility, is becoming increasingly perfunctory and insincere. And we, increasingly blithe and unaware.

And some people, uncertain of the meaning and sincerity of their *Thank you so much*, are doubly annoying and infantile when they say *Thank you so so much.*

that makes two of us ∎ An infantile phrase. *as I do; I do too; neither do I; no more do I; nor do I; so do I.*

that's for me to know and you to find out ∎ An infantile phrase. SEE ALSO **it's a long story**.

that's how (the way) it goes ∎ A plebeian sentiment. *That's how (the way) it goes* and other expressions of resignation are often spoken by some people and rarely, if at all, spoken by others.

It is dimwitted people who are too often resigned when they should be complaining, too often resigned when they should be demanding, too often resigned when they should be raging. SEE ALSO **such is life; that's how (the way) the ball bounces; that's how (the way) the cookie crumbles; that's life; that's life in the big city; that's show biz; what are you going to do; what can you do**.

> The window was open so the skinny bird flew in. Flappity-flap with its frazzled black wings. That's how it goes.—Bernard Malamud, *Idiots First*

that's how (the way) the ball bounces ∎ A plebeian sentiment. SEE ALSO **such is life; that's how (the way) it goes; that's how (the way) the cookie crumbles; that's life; that's life in the big city; that's show biz;**

what are you going to do; what can you do.

that's how (the way) the cookie crumbles ∎ A plebeian sentiment. SEE ALSO **such is life; that's how (the way) it goes; that's how (the way) the ball bounces; that's life; that's life in the big city; that's show biz; what are you going to do; what can you do**.

that's interesting ∎ A plebeian sentiment. *That's interesting*, like *that's nice* (SEE), is most often a witless response to what a person has said. As such, it is no more than an acknowledgment of having been bored, an admission of not having listened, or a confession of having nothing clever to say. SEE ALSO **every effort is being made; interesting**.

that's life ∎ A plebeian sentiment. SEE ALSO **such is life; that's how (the way) it goes; that's how (the way) the ball bounces; that's how (the way) the cookie crumbles; that's life in the big city; that's show biz; what are you going to do; what can you do**.

that's life in the big city ∎ A plebeian sentiment. SEE ALSO **such is life; that's how (the way) it goes; that's how (the way) the ball bounces; that's how (the way) the cookie crumbles; that's life; that's show biz; what are you going to do; what can you do**.

that's nice ∎ A plebeian sentiment. This phrase is used to dismiss what a person has said. *That's nice* is a perfunctory response that, though it suggests interest in a person, actually reveals indifference to the person. SEE ALSO **every effort is being made; that's interesting**.

that's show biz ∎ A plebeian sentiment. SEE ALSO **such is life; that's how (the way) it goes; that's how (the way) the ball bounces; that's how (the way) the cookie crumbles; that's life; that's life in the big city; what are you going to do; what can you do**.

that's the thing ∎ An ineffectual phrase. SEE ALSO **here's the thing; the thing about (of) it is; the thing is**.

that's what it's all about ∎ A popular prescription. • It's the little things, not the big things—like playing with my son—*that's what it's all about.*

that's where (you) enter the picture ∎ A moribund metaphor.

that would be ∎ An infantile phrase. *That would be* is a mindless excrescence.
• So, how much carbon does a typical car add to the atmosphere each year, anyway? "*That would be*" about 30 pounds. DELETE "*That would be.*"
• Who is the tour guide? "*That would be*" me. DELETE "*That would be.*"
• In a state that still flies the Confederate battle flag on its statehouse grounds, could a Democratic governor grant clemency to a white man convicted of killing a black

man? "*That would be*" a big no. DELETE "*That would be.*"

• Do you recognize the handwriting and initials?

"*That would be*" my handwriting. "*That would be*" my initials. Use "*That is*"; "*These are.*"

• What is the first storm of the season? "*That would be*" Arthur. DELETE "*That would be.*"

• Who sat back here?

Oh "*that would be*" Charles Thomas. DELETE "*that would be.*"

the ABCs of ▪ A moribund metaphor. *basics; basis; elements; essentials; foundation; fundamentals; principles; rudiments.* • The program will discuss *the ABCs of* eating right. REPLACE WITH *fundamentals.*

the Achilles heel of ▪ A moribund metaphor. *defect; deficiency; disadvantage; failing; fault; flaw; foible; fragility; frailness; frailty; handicap; limitation; shortcoming; susceptibility; susceptibleness; vulnerability; vulnerableness; weakness.*

the agony and the ecstasy ▪ A moribund metaphor.

the almighty dollar ▪ A moribund metaphor.

the alpha and omega of ▪ A moribund metaphor.

the American dream ▪ A suspect superlative. • *The American dream* has become a nightmare.

the apple doesn't fall far from the tree ▪ A popular prescription.

the apple of (my) eye ▪ A moribund metaphor. *hero; idol; star.*

the awkward age ▪ A moribund metaphor. *adolescence.*

the ax fell ▪ A moribund metaphor.

the ball's in (your) court ▪ A moribund metaphor. • I think, nationally, *the ball is* definitely *in our court* now.

the best and (the) brightest ▪ A suspect superlative. *best; brightest; choice; choicest; elite; excellent; finest; first-class; first-rate; foremost; greatest; highest; matchless; nonpareil; optimal; optimum; outstanding; paramount; peerless; preeminent; premium; prominent; select; superior; superlative; top; unequaled; unexcelled; unmatched; unrivaled; unsurpassed.* • He decried the "cult of efficiency" into which have fallen so many of *the best and brightest* of the conservative young. REPLACE WITH *the brightest.* • Bandied about were the names of several of *the best and brightest* of the next generation. REPLACE WITH *the elite.*

the best defense is a good offense ▪ A popular prescription.

the best (that) money can buy ▪ A suspect superlative.

(in) the best of all (possible) worlds ▪ A suspect superlative. *best; choice; elite; excellent; finest; first-class; first-rate; foremost; greatest; highest; ideal; matchless; nonpareil; optimal; optimum; outstanding; paramount; peerless; preeminent; premium; prominent; select; superior; superlative; supreme; top; unequaled; unexcelled; unmatched; unrivaled; unsurpassed.* • *In the best of all possible worlds,* test procedures for which neither type of error is possible could be developed. REPLACE WITH *ideally.*

the best (greatest) thing since sliced bread ▪ A moribund metaphor.

the best things in life are free ▪ A popular prescription.

(she's) the best thing that ever happened to (me) ▪ A plebeian sentiment.

the bigger the better ▪ A quack equation.

the bigger they are, the harder they fall ▪ A popular prescription.

the big picture ▪ A moribund metaphor. • Let's not make decisions without looking at *the big picture.*

the blind leading the blind ▪ A moribund metaphor.

the bloom is off the rose ▪ A moribund metaphor.

the bottom fell out ▪ A moribund metaphor. *break down; break up; collapse; crash; crumple; disintegrate; end; fail; fall apart; fold; stop.* • He elected to stop financing condominium projects nearly two years before *the bottom fell out* of that business.

the bread always falls on the buttered side ▪ A moribund metaphor.

the calm before the storm ▪ A moribund metaphor.

the cards (deck) are stacked against (him) ▪ A moribund metaphor.

the cat's out of the bag ▪ A moribund metaphor.

(look) (like) the cat that (ate) swallowed the canary ▪ An insipid simile. 1. *complacent; gleeful; pleased; self-satisfied; smug; thrilled.* • On the day after an election in which President Clinton was supposed to have been chastened, many of the faces at the White House looked *like the cat that swallowed the canary.* REPLACE WITH *complacent.*

the child is father of the man ▪ A popular prescription.

the clock is ticking ▪ A moribund metaphor.

the coast is clear ▪ A moribund metaphor.

the cook's tour ▪ A moribund metaphor.

the cream of the crop ▪ A moribund

metaphor. *best; brightest; choice; choicest; elite; excellent; finest; first-class; first-rate; foremost; greatest; highest; matchless; nonpareil; optimal; optimum; outstanding; paramount; peerless; preeminent; premium; prominent; select; superior; superlative; top; unequaled; unexcelled; unmatched; unrivaled; unsurpassed.*

(see) the cup (glass) half empty ∎ A moribund metaphor. *(be) despairing; (be) downbeat; (be) hopeless; (be) negative; (be) pessimistic.*

(see) the cup (glass) half full ∎ A moribund metaphor. *(be) cheerful; (be) hopeful; (be) optimistic; (be) pollyanna; (be) pollyannaish; (be) positive; (be) roseate; (be) sanguine; (be) upbeat.* • I tend to *see the cup as half full,* and look for that positive outlook in those I surround myself with. REPLACE WITH *be optimistic.*

the devil finds work for idle hands to do ∎ A popular prescription.

the devil take the hindmost ∎ A moribund metaphor.

the die is cast ∎ A moribund metaphor.

the dog days of summer ∎ A moribund metaphor. *boiling; hot; humid; scorching; sizzling; sweltering.*

(when) the dust settles ∎ A moribund metaphor.

the early bird catches the worm ∎ A popular prescription.

the end justifies the means ∎ A popular prescription.

the exception, not (rather than) the rule ∎ A torpid term. *aberrant; abnormal; anomalistic; anomalous; atypical; bizarre; curious; deviant; different; distinct; distinctive; eccentric; exceptional; extraordinary; fantastic; foreign; grotesque; idiosyncratic; independent; individual; individualistic; irregular; notable; noteworthy; novel; odd; offbeat; original; peculiar; puzzling; quaint; queer; rare; remarkable; separate; singular; strange; uncommon; unconventional; unexampled; unique; unnatural; unorthodox; unparalleled; unprecedented; unusual; weird.*
  Most people find it easier to mimic a repeatedly used phrase like this—however wordy and inexact, however obtuse and tedious—than to remember a rarely used word like *aberrant* or *anomalous.* • Today, in region after region, single-town school districts are *the exception, not the rule.* REPLACE WITH *exceptional.* • Arrest or issuing a citation is *the exception, not the rule.* REPLACE WITH *atypical.*

the exception that proves the rule ∎ An infantile phrase.

the exception to the rule ∎ A torpid term. *aberrant; abnormal; anomalistic; anomalous; atypical; bizarre; curious;*

deviant; different; distinct; distinctive; eccentric; exceptional; extraordinary; fantastic; foreign; grotesque; idiosyncratic; independent; individual; individualistic; irregular; notable; noteworthy; novel; odd; offbeat; original; peculiar; puzzling; quaint; queer; rare; remarkable; separate; singular; strange; uncommon; unconventional; unexampled; unique; unnatural; unorthodox; unparalleled; unprecedented; unusual; weird.

the face that launched a thousand ships ∎ A moribund metaphor.

the (plain; simple) fact is (that) ∎ An ineffectual phrase. • *The fact is* at least the governor is trying. DELETE *The fact is.* • *The simple fact is* we are now spending nearly $1 trillion on health care. DELETE *The simple fact is.* • *The plain fact is* American women are buying guns like they've never bought them before. DELETE *The plain fact is.*

the (simple) fact of the matter is ∎ An ineffectual phrase. • *The fact of the matter is* the police took the children from you. DELETE *The fact of the matter is.* • Despite her behavior, *the simple fact of the matter is* I still love her. DELETE *the simple fact of the matter is.* SEE ALSO **the truth of the matter is**.

the fact remains (that) ∎ An ineffectual phrase. • We call this campaign a "snoozer," but *the fact remains* both candidates did behave responsibly. DELETE *the fact remains.* • Whether one prefers the proverb's optimism or Euripides' pessimism, *the fact remains that* the way in which investigations are conducted can have a significant impact on the outcome of any case. DELETE *the fact remains that.*

the fact that ∎ An ineffectual phrase. • *The fact that* many more computers are in communication with one another increases concern that users' privacy will be violated. REPLACE WITH *That.* • *The fact that* she was rather attractive did not escape their notice. REPLACE WITH *That.*

the family that prays together stays together ∎ A popular prescription.

the fat's in the fire ∎ A moribund metaphor.

the feeling's mutual ∎ An infantile phrase.

the final (last) frontier ∎ A moribund metaphor.

(that's) the final (last) straw ∎ A moribund metaphor.

the first step is always the hardest ∎ A popular prescription.

the four corners of the earth (world) ∎ *all over; everyplace; everywhere; throughout (the land); universally.* A moribund metaphor. • These changes will affect our American patients as well as those who come to the

the (date) from hell

clinic from *the four corners of the world*.

the (date) from hell ∎ A moribund metaphor.

the genie is out of the bottle ∎ A moribund metaphor.

the genuine article ∎ A moribund metaphor. *actual; authentic; genuine; legitimate; pure; real; sterling; true; unadulterated; unalloyed; veritable.*

> He had constantly to be reassured. *Was this the genuine article? Was this the real guaranteed height of a Good Time?*—Christopher Isherwood, *Goodbye to Berlin*

the good, (the) bad, and (the) ugly ∎ An infantile phrase. • Teach yourself to open up more and share with your readership by forcing yourself to look at *the good, bad, and ugly* of your life.

the good doctor ∎ An infantile phrase. • I think everything *the good doctor* has said is hogwash.

the good news is (that) ∎ An infantile phrase. • *The good news is that* most students report that speaking gets easier as the term progresses.

the good old days ∎ A suspect superlative. *antiquity; history; the past; yesterday.* • We're going back to *the good old days* on gas prices.

(kill) the goose that lays the golden egg ∎ A moribund metaphor.

the grass is (always) greener (on the other side of) ∎ A popular prescription.

the great American novel ∎ A suspect superlative.

the great beyond ∎ A moribund metaphor. *afterlife; eternity; everlastingness.*

the hand that rocks the cradle (rules the world) ∎ A popular prescription.

the have-nots ∎ A moribund metaphor. *bankrupt; broke; destitute; distressed; impecunious; impoverished; indigent; insolvent; needy; penniless; poor; poverty-stricken; underprivileged.* • You, me, and many others can afford to pay a little more for health insurance if it gives some to the *have-nots.* REPLACE WITH *indigent.*

the haves ∎ A moribund metaphor. *affluent; comfortable; moneyed; opulent; privileged; prosperous; rich; wealthy; well-off; well-to-do.*

the heat is on ∎ A moribund metaphor. *be coerced; be compelled; be forced; be pressured.*

the hell out of it ∎ A moribund metaphor. *assiduously; diligently; grindingly; indefatigably; industriously; inexhaustibly; relentlessly; sedulously; tirelessly; unflaggingly; unrelentingly; untiringly.* • I hope you market *the hell out of it.* REPLACE WITH *it assiduously.*

(down) the home stretch ∎ A moribund metaphor.

the honeymoon is over ∎ A moribund metaphor.

the hostess with the mostess ∎ An infantile phrase.

the jury is still out ∎ A moribund metaphor. *be arguable; be debatable; be disputable; be doubtful; be dubious; be in doubt; be moot; be open; be questionable; be uncertain; be unclear; be undecided; be undetermined; be unknown; be unresolved; be unsettled; be unsolved; be unsure.* • *The jury is still out* on how the Medicare cuts will actually be carried out.

the (whole) kit and caboodle ∎ A moribund metaphor. *aggregate; all; all things; entirety; everything; gross; lot; sum; total; totality; whole.*

the land of milk and honey ∎ A moribund metaphor.

the land of nod ∎ A moribund metaphor. *sleep; slumber.*

the law is the law ∎ A quack equation.

the lesser of two evils ∎ A torpid term.

the less said, the better ∎ A popular prescription.

(live) the life of Reilly ∎ A moribund metaphor. 1. *be affluent; be moneyed; be opulent; be prosperous; be rich; be wealthy; be well-off; be well-to-do.* 2. *be extravagant; be lavish; be lush; be luxuriant; be sumptuous; be very well.* • It was *the life of Reilly*, but something was missing.

the light at the end of the tunnel ∎ A moribund metaphor. *anticipation; expectancy; expectation; hope; hopefulness; optimism; possibility; promise; prospect; sanguinity.* • That's when *the light at the end of the tunnel* for the immediate future went out.

the lion's share ∎ A moribund metaphor. *almost all; most; much; nearly all.* • The company was late to develop HMOs, and it let competitors grab *the lion's share* of the market. REPLACE WITH *most.*

the little boy's (girl's) room ∎ An infantile phrase. *bathroom; lavatory; restroom; toilet.*

(like) the little engine (that could) ∎ An insipid simile.

the little woman ∎ An infantile phrase. *consort; helpmate; helpmeet; mate; spouse; wife.*

the long and (the) short of (it) ∎ A wretched redundancy. *basis; center; core; crux; essence; gist; heart; kernel; pith; substance.*

the main event ∎ A moribund metaphor.

the man in the street ∎ A moribund metaphor. *citizen; commoner; everyman; pleb; plebeian; vulgarian.*

the manner (means; mechanism; method; procedure; process) by (in) which ▮ A wretched redundancy. These magisterial-sounding phrases should be replaced by one of the least stately of words: *how*. • I'm not going to discuss *the methods by which* we achieved that. REPLACE WITH *how*. • The philosophical methodology specifies *the procedure by which* concepts will be used to construct a theory. REPLACE WITH *how*. • It does less well in explaining *the process by which* a particular firm decides to implement a price change. REPLACE WITH *how*. • Virtually all of them have been critical of *the manner in which* the administration dealt with the situation. REPLACE WITH *how*.

the man who came to dinner ▮ An infantile phrase.

the medium is the message ▮ A quack equation.

the meek shall inherit the earth ▮ A popular prescription.

the men in white coats ▮ A moribund metaphor.

the Midas touch ▮ A moribund metaphor.

the milk of human kindness ▮ A moribund metaphor. *commiseration; compassion; sympathy; understanding*.

the more the merrier ▮ A quack equation.

the more things change, the more they stay the same ▮ A popular prescription.

thence ▮ A withered word. 1. *from that place; from there*. 2. *from that time*. 3. *hence; therefore; thus*. • Saudi Arabia pumps some crude through the IPSA pipeline to the Red Sea and *thence* through the Suez canal. REPLACE WITH *from there*.

the only good (cat) is a dead (cat) ▮ A quack equation.

the opening (latest) salvo ▮ A moribund metaphor.

the pen is mightier than the sword ▮ A moribund metaphor.

the pits ▮ A moribund metaphor. 1. *abhorrent; abominable; appalling; atrocious; awful; beastly; detestable; disagreeable; disgusting; dreadful; frightening; frightful; ghastly; grisly; gruesome; horrendous; horrible; horrid; horrifying; inhuman; loathsome; objectionable; obnoxious; odious; offensive; repellent; repugnant; repulsive; revolting; terrible; terrifying; unspeakable; unutterable*. 2. *calamitous; deplorable; depressing; distressing; disturbing; grievous; lamentable; unfortunate; upsetting; sad; tragic; woeful*.

the point of no return ▮ A moribund metaphor.

(like) the pot calling the kettle black ▮ An insipid simile.

the power of the purse ▮ A moribund metaphor.

the promised land ▮ A moribund metaphor. *Eden; El Dorado; Elysian Fields; Elysium; heaven; kingdom come; nirvana; paradise; utopia; Valhalla*.

the proof of the pudding (is in the eating) ▮ A popular prescription.

the quick and the dead ▮ A moribund metaphor.

the real McCoy ▮ A moribund metaphor. *actual; authentic; genuine; legitimate; pure; real; sterling; true; unadulterated; unalloyed; veritable*. • When you are talking about classical scholarship, he is *the real McCoy*.

there are no words to describe (express) ▮ A plebeian sentiment. There are many more words than people seem to think, and far more is expressible with them than people seem to imagine.

Those who depend on dimwitticisms to convey thought and feeling are more apt to believe *there are no words to describe* ..., for these people are, necessarily, most frustrated by the limits of language.

Dimwitticisms do permit us to describe our most universal feelings, our most banal thoughts, but they prevent us from describing more individual feelings, more brilliant thoughts. These are reserved for a language largely unknown to everyday speakers and writers. SEE ALSO **words cannot describe (express)**.

there are other fish in the sea ▮ A moribund metaphor.

there are two sides to every (question) story ▮ A popular prescription.

thereby hangs a tale ▮ A torpid term.

there's a first time for everything ▮ A popular prescription.

there's a new sheriff in town ▮ An infantile phrase.

there's a time and a place for everything ▮ A popular prescription.

there's more than one way to skin a cat ▮ A popular prescription.

there's no accounting for taste ▮ A popular prescription.

there's no fool like an old fool ▮ A popular prescription.

there's no (such thing as a) free lunch ▮ A popular prescription.

there's no going back ▮ A popular prescription.

there's no harm in trying ▮ A popular prescription.

there's no place like home ▮ A popular prescription.

there's no rest for the weary ∎ A popular prescription.

there's nothing new under the sun ∎ A popular prescription.

there's no time like the present ∎ A popular prescription. • They say *there's no time like the present* and that's never been truer.

there's nowhere to go but up ∎ A popular prescription.

there's safety (strength) in numbers ∎ A popular prescription.

(and) the rest is history ∎ An infantile phrase.

the rich and famous ∎ A suspect superlative. *The rich and famous* infatuate only foolish people, who are as boring to themselves as they are barren of themselves. • It has become a summer hideaway for *the rich and famous*. SEE ALSO **celebrity; fame and fortune**.

(a case of) the right hand not knowing what the left hand is doing ∎ A moribund metaphor.

the road to hell is paved with good intentions ∎ A popular prescription.

the rock of Gibraltar ∎ A moribund metaphor. 1. *beefy; brawny; burly; energetic; firm; fit; hale; hardy; healthful; healthy; hearty; husky; manly; mighty; muscular; powerful; puissant; robust; rugged; sinewy; solid; sound; stalwart; stout; strapping; strong; sturdy; tough; vigorous; virile; well-built.* 2. *constant; dependable; determined; faithful; fast; firm; fixed; inexorable; inflexible; loyal; obdurate; resolute; resolved; rigid; solid; stable; staunch; steadfast; steady; stern; strong; tenacious; unflinching; unwavering; unyielding.*

> Under normal circumstances he's the Rock of Gibraltar to most women, but in all the years Jay had known me, he had never seen me cry.—Rosemarie A. D'Amico, *Options*

the roof fell in ∎ A moribund metaphor. *break down; break up; collapse; crash; crumple; disintegrate; end; fail; fall apart; fold; stop.*

(money is) the root of all evil ∎ A popular prescription.

the rule rather than the exception ∎ A torpid term. *basic; common; commonplace; conventional; customary; general; normal; ordinary; quotidian; regular; routine; standard; typical; uneventful; unexceptional; unremarkable; usual.* • New advertising campaigns costing $5 million or even $10 million are becoming *the rule rather than the exception*. REPLACE WITH *common*.

the rules of the game ∎ A moribund metaphor.

the rules of the road ∎ A moribund metaphor.

the salt of the earth ∎ A moribund metaphor.

the second American Revolution ∎ A moribund metaphor.

(plant) the seeds of ∎ A moribund metaphor.

(cost) the shirt off (my) back ∎ A moribund metaphor.

the shoe is on the other foot ∎ A moribund metaphor.

the short end of the stick ∎ A moribund metaphor.

the show must go on ∎ A popular prescription.

the silent majority ∎ A moribund metaphor. *all; citizenry; commonage; commonalty; common people; crowd; everybody; everyone; followers; herd; hoi polloi; masses; mob; multitude; plebeians; populace; proletariat; public; rabble.*

the $64,000 question ∎ An infantile phrase. • That's *the $64,000 question* for a number of people.

the sky's the limit ∎ A moribund metaphor.

the slings and arrows of outrageous fortune ∎ A moribund metaphor.

the sooner the better ∎ A quack equation.

the sound and the fury ∎ A moribund metaphor.

the specter of ∎ A moribund metaphor. • The Troika's standard response to all who raised *the specter of* diminished social services has been insult, invective, and ire.

the squeaky wheel gets the grease ∎ A popular prescription.

the staff of life ∎ A moribund metaphor. *bread.*

the stage has been set ∎ A moribund metaphor. • *The stage has been set* for a contract that will have to contain genuine reforms.

the straight and narrow (path) ∎ A moribund metaphor. *decent; ethical; exemplary; good; honest; honorable; just; moral; pure; righteous; straight; upright; virtuous; wholesome.*

the straw that broke the camel's back ∎ A moribund metaphor.

the stuff dreams (legends) are made of ∎ A moribund metaphor.

the stuff of (legends) ∎ A moribund metaphor. • His mumbo-jumbo about the war on terror was *the stuff of* prime time television. • The abuse of this child truly is *the stuff of* nightmares. • Lance Armstrong's record seventh win of the

Tour de France is *the stuff of* true legends.
• Being in the Hambletonian is *the stuff of*
dreams—and obituaries.

**the summer (winter) of (our)
discontent** ∎ A moribund metaphor.

the sun, the moon, and the stars ∎ A
moribund metaphor.

(a case of) the tail wagging the dog ∎
A moribund metaphor. backward; in reverse.

the temper of our time ∎ A moribund
metaphor.

the thin end of the wedge ∎ A moribund
metaphor.

the thing about (of) it is ∎ An ineffectual
phrase. • *The thing about it is* it's
humiliating and destructive to the psyche
to be hit. DELETE *The thing about it is.* •
The thing about it is what they say or do
has no influence on what I do. DELETE
The thing about it is. • *The thing about it
is* I could never tell her anything. DELETE
The thing about it is. SEE ALSO **here's the
thing; that's the thing; the thing is**.

the thing is ∎ An ineffectual phrase. • *The
thing is* we know sexual orientation is
discovered prior to adolescence. DELETE
The thing is. • *The thing is* I work two
jobs, and when I get home I want to relax.
DELETE *The thing is.* • But *the thing is,*
there's always someone who knows where
they are. DELETE *the thing is.* SEE ALSO
**here's the thing; that's the thing; the thing
about (of) it is**.

the three musketeers ∎ An infantile phrase.

the thrill of a lifetime ∎ A moribund
metaphor. *amazing; astounding; awe-
inspiring; breathtaking; elating; exciting;
exhilarating; fabulous; gripping;
magnificent; marvelous; splendid; stunning;
superb; thrilling; wonderful; wondrous.*

the tide of ∎ A moribund metaphor. SEE
ALSO **a barrage of**.

the time has come ∎ A torpid term. •
The time has come to recognize that
personal diaries must be accorded greater
protection than business records.

the time will come ∎ A torpid term.

the toast of the town ∎ A moribund
metaphor.

the truth of the matter is ∎ An ineffectual
phrase. • *The truth of the matter is* half
of the people who get married end up
divorced. DELETE *The truth of the matter
is.* • *The truth of the matter is,* I don't
understand it, but I'm against it. DELETE
The truth of the matter is. SEE ALSO **the
fact of the matter is**.

the truth will set you free ∎ A popular
prescription.

the twelfth of never ∎ An infantile phrase.

the walking dead ∎ A moribund metaphor.

the wave of the future ∎ A moribund
metaphor.

**the way to a man's heart is through
his stomach** ∎ A popular prescription.

the weak link (in the chain) ∎ A moribund
metaphor.

**the wheels are falling off the
wagon** ∎ A moribund metaphor. *breaking
down; collapsing; crumbling; decaying;
decomposing; degenerating; deteriorating;
disintegrating; dissipating; dissolving; dying;
ending; fading; failing; unraveling.*

the whole ball of wax ∎ A moribund
metaphor. *aggregate; all; all things; entirety;
everything; gross; lot; sum; total; totality;
whole.*

**the whole is greater than the sum of
its parts** ∎ A popular prescription.

the whole nine yards ∎ A moribund
metaphor. *aggregate; all; all things; entirety;
everything; gross; lot; sum; total; totality;
whole.* • You've won the Sony TV, the
VCR, the stereo system, the camcorder,
the whole nine yards. REPLACE WITH
everything.

the whole shebang ∎ A moribund metaphor.
*aggregate; all; all things; entirety; everything;
gross; lot; sum; total; totality; whole.*

the whole shooting match ∎ A moribund
metaphor. *aggregate; all; all things; entirety;
everything; gross; lot; sum; total; totality;
whole.*

the why and (the) wherefore ∎ A
wretched redundancy. *aim; cause; design;
end; goal; intent; intention; motive; object;
objective; purpose; reason.*

the wolf at the door ∎ A moribund
metaphor. 1. *creditor; taxman.* 2. *bandit;
crook; outlaw; robber; thief; thug.*

the wonderful world of ∎ A moribund
metaphor.

the (F)-word ∎ An infantile phrase. • Many
men have trouble with *the C-word.*
REPLACE WITH *commitment.* • During
the holidays, many people write and ask
about *the D-word,* depression. DELETE
the D-word. • Nearly everyone involved
with the contract was using *the H-word,*
"historic," to describe it. DELETE *the
H-word.* • Journalists agonized over asking
about the *"A" word.* REPLACE WITH
affair. • For most middle-aged women,
the M-word is not a laughing matter.
REPLACE WITH *menopause.* • The see-
through Clinton has three schemes in his
playbook to divert us all from *the "M"
word.* REPLACE WITH *Monica.*

the world is (his) oyster ∎ A moribund
metaphor.

(and) the world will beat a path to (your) door

(and) the world will beat a path to (your) door ∎ A moribund metaphor.

(looks) the worse for wear ∎ A moribund metaphor. 1. *broken-down; crumbly; damaged; decayed; decrepit; depleted; deteriorated; dilapidated; dingy; dirty; exhausted; filthy; flimsy; foul; frayed; grimy; grubby; grungy; ragged; ramshackle; rickety; seedy; shabby; shaky; soiled; sordid; sullied; squalid; tattered; tired; tottering; unclean; unsound; used up; washed-out; worn; worn-out.* 2. *aged; aging; elderly; hoary; old; seasoned.*

the worst of all (possible) worlds ∎ A moribund metaphor.

the wrong side of the tracks ∎ A moribund metaphor.

the yin and the yang ∎ A moribund metaphor.

thick and fast ∎ An inescapable pair.

(as) thick as molasses ∎ An insipid simile. *concentrated; congealed; gelatinous; gluey; glutinous; gooey; gummy; inspissated; jellied; jellified; jellylike; mucilaginous; sticky; thick; viscid; viscous.*

(as) thick as thieves ∎ An insipid simile. *amiable; amicable; attached; brotherly; chummy; close; confidential; devoted; familiar; friendly; inseparable; intimate; loving; thick.*

(as) thin as a reed ∎ An insipid simile. *asthenic; attenuated; bony; cachectic; emaciated; gaunt; lank; lanky; lean; narrow; rail-thin; scraggy; scrawny; skeletal; skinny; slender; slight; slim; spare; spindly; svelte; sylphid; thin; trim; wispy.*

(as) thin as a rail ∎ An insipid simile. *asthenic attenuated; bony; cachectic; emaciated; gaunt; lank; lanky; lean; narrow; rail-thin; scraggy; scrawny; skeletal; skinny; slender; slight; slim; spare; spindly; svelte; sylphid; thin; trim; wispy.*

(a) thing ∎ An overworked word. • The mind is *an* amazing *thing.* DELETE *an thing.* • It's *a* very important *thing.* DELETE *a thing.* • We have won the battle, but the war is *an* ongoing *thing.* DELETE *an thing.* • I think that change is *a* good *thing.* DELETE *a thing.* • You do this by comparing something your listeners know a lot about with something they know little or nothing about in order to make the unfamiliar *thing* clear. DELETE *thing.*

think outside the box ∎ A torpid term. *be clever; be creative; be innovative; be inventive; be original.*

  Think outside the box is an uninspired, hackneyed way of saying *be clever, be creative, be inventive.* People who use this phrase nicely illustrate the antithesis of what it means.

thinly veiled ∎ An inescapable pair.

this and that ∎ A grammatical gimmick.

this can't be happening (to me) ∎ A plebeian sentiment.

this is the first day of the rest of your life ∎ A popular prescription.

this is to inform you that ∎ An ineffectual phrase. • *This is to inform you that* your credit application has been approved and your account is now open. DELETE *This is to inform you that.* SEE ALSO **(please) be advised that; (please) be informed that**.

thorn in (my) flesh (side) (of) ∎ A moribund metaphor. *affliction; annoyance; bane; blight; bother; burden; curse; difficulty; inconvenience; irritant; irritation; load; nuisance; ordeal; pain; pest; plague; problem; torment; tribulation; trouble; vexation; weight; worry.* • Inventory collateral valuations have been a *thorn in the side of* the agricultural industry for years. REPLACE WITH *bane to.*

those who can, do; those who can't, teach ∎ A popular prescription.

three sheets to the wind ∎ A moribund metaphor. *besotted; crapulous; drunk; inebriated; intoxicated; sodden; stupefied; tipsy.*

three strikes and you're out ∎ An infantile phrase.

thrilled to death ∎ A moribund metaphor. *blissful; blithe; buoyant; cheerful; delighted; ecstatic; elated; enraptured; euphoric; exalted; excited; exhilarated; exultant; gay; glad; gleeful; good-humored; happy; intoxicated; jolly; jovial; joyful; joyous; jubilant; merry; mirthful; overjoyed; pleased; rapturous; thrilled.* SEE ALSO **to death.**

> Eveline was thrilled to death, but they got Eric Egstrom to come along too, on account of Frenchmen having such a bad reputation.— John Dos Passos, *The 42nd Parallel*

thrills and chills ∎ An inescapable pair.

(is) through the roof ∎ A moribund metaphor. *astronomical; enormous; exceptional; extraordinary; extreme; great; huge; immense; massive; prodigious; sky-high; vast.* • The talent this year is *through the roof.* REPLACE WITH *prodigious.*

through thick and thin ∎ A moribund metaphor.

throw (a dog) a bone ∎ A moribund metaphor.

throw (her) a curve ∎ A moribund metaphor. *bamboozle; befool; beguile; bilk; bluff; cheat; con; deceive; defraud; delude; dupe; feint; fool; gyp; hoodwink; lead astray; misdirect; misguide; misinform; mislead; spoof; swindle; trick; victimize.*

throw a monkey wrench into (the works) ∎ A moribund metaphor. 1. *agitate; complicate; confound; confuse; disorder; disorganize; disquiet; disrupt; disturb; fluster; jar; jinx; jolt; jumble; mix up; muddle; muddy; obfuscate; perturb; rattle; ruffle; shake up; stir up; thwart; trouble; unnerve; unsettle; upset.* 2. *blight; cripple; damage; disable; harm; hurt; impair; incapacitate; lame; mar; mess up; rack; ruin; sabotage; spoil; subvert; undermine; vitiate; wrack; wreck.* • Koulis's lawyers are hoping to *throw a wrench into* the case by convincing others it was not drugs that caused her death after all. REPLACE WITH *disrupt.*

throw a wet blanket on ∎ A moribund metaphor. *bridle; check; constrain; contain; curb; curtail; dampen; discourage; foil; harness; hinder; impede; inhibit; obstruct; quell; repress; restrain; restrict; retard; stifle; subdue; suppress; thwart; weaken.* SEE ALSO **throw cold water on.**

throw caution to the wind ∎ A moribund metaphor. 1. *be adventuresome; be adventurous; be audacious; be bold; be brave; be courageous; be daring; be dauntless; be fearless; be intrepid; be mettlesome; be plucky; be stalwart; be unafraid; be valiant; be valorous; be venturesome.* 2. *be careless; be foolhardy; be hasty; be heedless; be impetuous; be incautious; be precipitate; be* rash; be reckless; be thoughtless.

throw cold water on ∎ A moribund metaphor. *bridle; check; constrain; contain; curb; curtail; dampen; discourage; foil; harness; hinder; impede; inhibit; obstruct; quell; repress; restrain; restrict; retard; stifle; subdue; suppress; thwart; weaken.* SEE ALSO **throw a wet blanket on.**

throw down the gauntlet (glove) ∎ A moribund metaphor. *affront; brave; call; challenge; confront; dare; defy; encounter; face; meet.*

throw dust in (your) eyes ∎ A moribund metaphor. *bamboozle; befool; beguile; bilk; bluff; cheat; con; deceive; defraud; delude; dupe; feint; fool; gyp; hoodwink; lead astray; misdirect; misguide; misinform; mislead; spoof; swindle; trick; victimize.*

throw enough dirt, and some will stick ∎ A moribund metaphor.

throw for a loop ∎ A moribund metaphor. *amaze; astonish; astound; awe; dazzle; dumbfound; flabbergast; overpower; overwhelm; shock; startle; stun; stupefy; surprise.*

throw (toss) (his) hat in the ring ∎ A moribund metaphor. 1. *enlist; enroll; enter; join; run; sign on; sign up.* 2. *commence; begin; enter into; start; undertake.*

throw (toss) in the sponge (towel) ∎ A moribund metaphor. *abdicate; accede; acquiesce; bow; capitulate; cede; concede; give in; give up; quit; relinquish; retreat; submit; succumb; surrender; yield.* • The bloated bureaucracy remains unscathed, spending continues uncontrolled, and the House leadership has *thrown in the towel* to the governor. REPLACE WITH *acquiesced.* • If I get any more overwhelmed, I'm going to *throw in the towel.* REPLACE WITH *quit.*

throw (them) off the scent ∎ A moribund metaphor. *bamboozle; befool; beguile; bilk; bluff; cheat; con; hoodwink; lead astray; deceive; defraud; delude; dupe; feint; fool; gyp; misdirect; misguide; misinform; mislead; spoof; swindle; trick.*

throw out the baby with the bath water ∎ A moribund metaphor.

throw (toss) out the window ∎ A moribund metaphor. *abandon; chuck; discard; dismiss; dump; jettison; reject; repudiate; throw out; toss out.* • Everything I tried to teach them about getting along and togetherness has been *thrown out the window.* REPLACE WITH *jettisoned.*

throw the book at ∎ A moribund metaphor. *admonish; animadvert; berate; castigate; censure; chasten; chastise; chide; condemn; criticize; denounce; denunciate; discipline; excoriate; fulminate against; imprecate; impugn; inveigh against; objurgate; penalize; punish; rebuke; remonstrate; reprehend; reprimand; reproach; reprobate; reprove;*

throw (them) to the dogs (wolves)

revile; scold; swear at; upbraid; vituperate.

throw (them) to the dogs (wolves) ∎
A moribund metaphor. 1. *forfeit; sacrifice; surrender.* 2. *endanger; imperil; jeopardize.*

> I remember his ex-partner at the hospital saying he'll be thrown to the hounds, and I can only hope he's wrong, that the guards will look out for one of their own, though I feel like I'm lying to myself thinking this.—Andre Dubus III, *House of Sand and Fog*

throw (him) under the bus ∎ A moribund metaphor. 1. *betray.* 2. *forfeit; sacrifice; surrender.* It looks as though the District of Columbia was *thrown under the bus* to get a political deal. REPLACE WITH *sacrificed.*

> Why would he throw her under the bus like that? Of all the people in the room she thought he would have been the one she could count on.—Glen Inglis, *Broken Heroes*

throw (his) weight around ∎ A moribund metaphor. *awe; browbeat; bully; frighten; intimidate; menace; push around; scare; threaten; torment.*

thumb (his) nose (at) ∎ A moribund metaphor. *contemn; deride; despise; detest; disdain; jeer at; laugh at; mock; ridicule; scoff at; scorn; shun; slight; sneer; snub; spurn.* • We burden our own banks with record keeping and reporting while offshore bankers *thumb their noses at* us. REPLACE WITH *mock.*

> He's breaking the rules, under their noses, thumbing his nose at them, getting away with it.—Margaret Atwood, *The Handmaid's Tale*

(turn) thumbs down ∎ A moribund metaphor. *decline; deny; disallow; disapprove; forbid; nix; prohibit; proscribe; refuse; reject; rule out; say no; turn down; veto.*

thunderous applause ∎ An inescapable pair.

tickled pink ∎ A moribund metaphor. *blissful; buoyant; cheerful; delighted; elated; excited; gay; glad; gladdened; gleeful; good-humored; gratified; happy; jolly; jovial; joyful; joyous; jubilant; merry; mirthful; pleased; tickled.*

tickled to death ∎ A moribund metaphor. *blissful; buoyant; cheerful; delighted; elated; excited; gay; glad; gladdened; gleeful; good-humored; gratified; happy; jolly; jovial; joyful; joyous; jubilant; merry; mirthful; pleased; tickled.* SEE ALSO **to death.**

tied to (her) apron strings ∎ A moribund metaphor. *clinging; dependent; subject; subordinate; subservient.*

tie the knot ∎ A moribund metaphor. *marry; wed.*

tie up loose ends ∎ A moribund metaphor. *complete; conclude; end; finalize; finish; wrap up.*

> Stanley asked if he needed to tie up loose ends. Stanley watched him, waiting for an answer, and Spooner tried to decide if he needed to tie up the loose end.—Pete Dexter, *Spooner*

(as) tight as a drum ∎ An insipid simile. *firm; snug; strained; stretched; taut; tense; tight.*

tighten (our) belts ∎ A moribund metaphor. *reduce costs; save money.* • We are constantly looking for ways to *tighten our belts.* REPLACE WITH *save money.*

tighten the screws ∎ A moribund metaphor. *coerce; command; compel; constrain; demand; dictate; enforce; enjoin; force; insist; make; order; press; pressure; push.*

(talk) till (I'm) blue in the face ∎ A moribund metaphor. *always; ceaselessly; constantly; continually; continuously; endlessly; eternally; everlastingly; evermore; forever; forevermore; immortally; indefinitely; interminably; permanently; perpetually; persistently; unceasingly; unremittingly.*

till (until) (her) dying days ∎ A moribund metaphor. *always; ceaselessly; constantly; continually; continuously; endlessly; eternally; everlastingly; evermore; forever; forevermore; immortally; indefinitely; interminably; permanently; perpetually; persistently; unceasingly; unremittingly.*

till (until) hell freezes over ∎ A moribund metaphor. *always; ceaselessly; constantly; continually; continuously; endlessly; eternally; everlastingly; evermore; forever; forevermore; immortally; indefinitely; interminably; permanently; perpetually; persistently; unceasingly; unremittingly.*

till (until) it's coming out (of) (my) ears ∎ A moribund metaphor. *excessively; exorbitantly; extravagantly; immoderately; in excess; inordinately; profligately; unrestrainedly.*

till kingdom come ∎ A moribund metaphor. *always; ceaselessly; constantly; continually; continuously; endlessly; eternally; everlastingly; evermore; forever; forevermore; immortally; indefinitely; interminably; permanently; perpetually; persistently; unceasingly; unremittingly.*

> I let out a great bellow such as cattle do and would have gone on bellowing till Kingdom Come had not some sinner taken my ear and turned me to look under Johnson's devilish table.—Jeanette Winterson, *Sexing the Cherry*

till (until) the cows come home ∎ A moribund metaphor. *always; ceaselessly; constantly; continually; continuously; endlessly; eternally; everlastingly; evermore; forever; forevermore; immortally; indefinitely; interminably; permanently; perpetually; persistently; unceasingly;*

unremittingly. • You can press Escape *until the cows come home*, and it will do nothing. REPLACE WITH *unceasingly.*

tilt at windmills ∎ A moribund metaphor.

time and effort ∎ An inescapable pair. • He still puts a lot of *time and effort* into his commercials.

time and energy ∎ An inescapable pair. • Boiling water also is cheaper than buying bottled water, but it takes more *time and energy.*

time and tide wait for no man ∎ A popular prescription.

time flies when you're having fun ∎ A popular prescription.

time heals all wounds ∎ A popular prescription.

time is a great healer ∎ A popular prescription.

time is money ∎ A quack equation.

time period ∎ A wretched redundancy. *period; time.* • Would you go along with this for a *time period*? REPLACE WITH *period* or *time.*

time was when ∎ A torpid term. *before; earlier; formerly; long ago; once; previously.*

time will tell ∎ A moribund metaphor. • We have made many changes in attitude and practice, and only *time will tell* whether these are for the ultimate good or merely more mischief.

tip (my) hat to ∎ A moribund metaphor. 1. *acknowledge; flag; greet; hail; recognize; salute; wave to; welcome.* 2. *acclaim; applaud; cheer; commend; compliment; congratulate; hail; praise; salute; support; toast.* • I *tip my hat to* Mayor Menino for having the vision to see that Boston does not require a professional football team to remain a world-class city. REPLACE WITH *salute.* • I'd also like to *tip my hat to* Jeff Staples for his fast editing and feedback. REPLACE WITH *acknowledge.*

tip of the iceberg ∎ A moribund metaphor. *beginning; commencement; foundation; inauguration; inception; least of it; onset; start.* The monstrous and omnipresent *tip of the iceberg*, like so many other dimwitted usages, alerts us to an inarticulate speaker, a tentative writer. • We have just seen the *tip of the iceberg* of corporations that have loaded up with too much debt and gone broke because of the merger and takeover wars. REPLACE WITH *beginning.* • I feel these issues and programs are just the *tip of the iceberg.* REPLACE WITH *start.*
And here are a couple of examples no less than wonderful: • It's difficult to tell whether my study is the iceberg and the tip is yet to be found, or whether my study was the *tip of the iceberg.* • These attacks are only the *tip of the iceberg*; they are the part of the iceberg that is visible above the water, in clear view—but as everyone knows, the largest part of the iceberg, and possibly the most dangerous, lies beneath the surface of the water and is difficult to detect.

tip the scales ∎ A moribund metaphor.

(as) tired as a dog ∎ An insipid simile. *beat; bushed; debilitated; depleted; drained; drowsy; enervated; exhausted; fatigued; groggy; sapped; sleepy; sluggish; slumberous; somnolent; soporific; spent; tired; weary; worn out.*

to all intents and purposes ∎ A wretched redundancy. *effectively; essentially; in effect; in essence; practically; virtually.* • To all intents and purposes, you were dating two women at a time. REPLACE WITH *In effect.* SEE ALSO **for all intents and purposes; for all practical purposes; to all intents and purposes; to all practical purposes.**

to all practical purposes ∎ A wretched redundancy. *effectively; essentially; in effect; in essence; practically; virtually.* • The ruling Unionist party is, *to all practical purposes*, a Protestant party. REPLACE WITH *in essence.* SEE ALSO **for all intents and purposes; for all practical purposes; to all intents and purposes.**

to a T ∎ A moribund metaphor. *accurately; correctly; exactly; faultlessly; flawlessly; ideally; just right; perfectly; precisely; rightly; strictly; to perfection; unerringly; very well.*

> Like all Whiting males, C.B. was a short man who disliked drawing attention to the fact, so the low-slung Spanish architecture suited him to a T.—Richard Russo, *Empire Falls*

to beat the band ∎ A moribund metaphor. *actively; aggressively; dynamically; emphatically; energetically; fast; ferociously; fervently; fiercely; forcefully; frantically; frenziedly; furiously; hard; intensely; intently; mightily; passionately; powerfully; robustly; savagely; spiritedly; strenuously; strongly; vehemently; viciously; vigorously; violently; wildly; with vigor.* • When you wake up, it should be snowing *to beat the band.* REPLACE WITH *mightily.*

to burn ∎ A moribund metaphor. 1. *enormous; great; huge; immense; large; massive; monstrous; prodigious; tremendous; vast.* 2. *excessive; exorbitant; extreme; immoderate; inordinate; undue.* • And Mrs. Dole has *Southern charm to burn.* REPLACE WITH *immense Southern charm.*

today is the first day of the rest of (your) life ∎ A popular prescription.

to death ∎ A moribund metaphor. *consumedly; enormously; exceedingly; excessively; exorbitantly; extraordinarily; extremely; greatly; hugely; immensely;*

to each (his) own

immoderately; inordinately; intemperately; intensely; mightily; prodigiously; unreasonably; unrestrainedly; very much. • I love him *to death.* REPLACE WITH *prodigiously.*

And as if *to death* were not persuasive enough: • The DoD and VA appeared content to study Gulf War illnesses *literally to death.* REPLACE WITH *unrestrainedly.*

to each (his) own ▪ A popular prescription.

to err is human ▪ A popular prescription.

to err is human, to forgive divine ▪ A popular prescription.

toe the line (mark) ▪ A moribund metaphor. *abide by; accede; accommodate; accord; acquiesce; adapt; adhere to; agree; behave; comply; concur; conform; correspond; follow; harmonize; heed; mind; obey; observe; submit; yield.*

(leveraged) to (their) eyebrows ▪ A moribund metaphor.

(smell) to high heaven ▪ A moribund metaphor. *decidedly; mightily; greatly; forcefully; hugely; powerfully; strongly; terribly; tremendously.*

to make a long story short ▪ A torpid term. *briefly; concisely; in brief; in short; in sum; succinctly; tersely.*

(with) tongue in cheek ▪ A moribund metaphor. *facetiously; humorously; in fun; in jest; in play; jocosely; jokingly; kiddingly; playfully; teasingly.*

(set) tongues wagging ▪ A moribund metaphor. *babble; blab; cackle; chaffer; chat; chitchat; chatter; confabulate; converse; gossip; jabber; palaver; prate; prattle; rattle; talk.*

too big for (his) breeches ▪ A moribund metaphor. *arrogant; cavalier; condescending; contemptuous; despotic; dictatorial; disdainful; dogmatic; domineering; haughty; imperious; insolent; lofty; overbearing; overweening; patronizing; pompous; pretentious; scornful; self-important; supercilious; superior; vainglorious.*

(she's) too good for (him) ▪ A suspect superlative.

too hot to handle ▪ A moribund metaphor.

(you) took the words (right) out of (my) mouth ▪ A moribund metaphor.

too many chiefs (and not enough Indians) ▪ A moribund metaphor.

too many cooks spoil the broth (brew) ▪ A popular prescription.

too smart for (his) own good ▪ A plebeian sentiment.

(fight) tooth and nail ▪ A moribund metaphor. *actively; aggressively; dynamically; emphatically; energetically; ferociously; fervently; fiercely; forcefully; frantically;*

frenziedly; furiously; hard; intensely; intently; mightily; passionately; powerfully; robustly; savagely; spiritedly; strenuously; strongly; vehemently; viciously; vigorously; violently; wildly; with vigor. • Bank of Boston, the state's largest bank, lobbied *tooth and nail* against the interstate law. REPLACE WITH *intensely.*

toot (your) own horn ▪ A moribund metaphor. *acclaim; applaud; bluster; boast; brag; celebrate; cheer; commend; compliment; congratulate; crow; extol; flatter; gloat; hail; honor; laud; praise; puff; salute; self-congratulate; strut; swagger.* • Engineers are the world's worst at *tooting their own horn.* REPLACE WITH *applauding themselves.* • Even so, the group president of Lucent Technologies' Global Service Provider business division isn't the type to *toot her own horn.* REPLACE WITH *boast.*

top brass ▪ A moribund metaphor. *administrator; boss; brass; chief; commander; director; executive; foreman; head; headman; leader; manager; master; (high) muckamuck; officer; official; overseer; president; principal; superintendent; supervisor.*

toss and turn ▪ An inescapable pair.

> Heaven knew how he missed her and how many nights he remained awake tossing and turning while thinking about her.—Ha Jin, *Waiting*

to tell you the truth ▪ An ineffectual phrase.

(march) to the beat of a different drummer ▪ A moribund metaphor. *aberrant; abnormal; anomalistic; anomalous; atypical; bizarre; curious; deviant; different; distinct; distinctive; eccentric; exceptional; extraordinary; fantastic; foreign; grotesque; idiosyncratic; independent; individual; individualistic; irregular; novel; odd; offbeat; original; peculiar; puzzling; quaint; queer; rare; remarkable; separate; singular; strange; uncommon; unconventional; unexampled; unique; unnatural; unorthodox; unparalleled; unprecedented; unusual; weird.*

to the bone ▪ A moribund metaphor. *altogether; completely; entirely; fully; perfectly; quite; roundly; thoroughly; totally; unreservedly; utterly; wholly.*

to the ends (far reaches) of the earth ▪ A moribund metaphor. 1. *always; ceaselessly; constantly; continually; continuously; endlessly; eternally; everlastingly; evermore; forever; forevermore; frequently; interminably; nonstop; permanently; perpetually; persistently; recurrently; regularly; repeatedly; unceasingly; unremittingly.* 2. *all during; all over; all through; everyplace; everywhere; throughout.*

(up) to the hilt ▪ A moribund metaphor. *altogether; completely; entirely; fully; perfectly; quite; roundly; thoroughly; totally; unreservedly; utterly; wholly.*

to the letter ∎ A moribund metaphor. *accurately; correctly; exactly; faultlessly; flawlessly; ideally; just right; perfectly; precisely; rightly; strictly; to perfection; unerringly.*

(dressed) (up) to the nines ∎ A moribund metaphor. *elaborately; elegantly; extravagantly; fashionably; flamboyantly; flashily; gaudily; lavishly; ostentatiously; profusely; richly; showily; smartly; stylishly.* • The house was decorated to the nines. REPLACE WITH *lavishly.*

> Happily enough, it did not rain next day, and after morning school everybody dressed up to the nines.—Evelyn Waugh, *Decline and Fall*

to the point of (that; where) ∎ A wretched redundancy. *so; so far (that); so much (that); so that; to; to when; to where.* • It's gotten *to the point that* I even flirt with operators. REPLACE WITH *so that.* • But it has now evolved *to the point where* they do it all the time. REPLACE WITH *to where.*

to the teeth ∎ A moribund metaphor. *altogether; completely; entirely; fully; perfectly; quite; roundly; thoroughly; totally; unreservedly; utterly; wholly.*

to the tune of ∎ A wretched redundancy. • It cost him *to the tune of* $4,500 to buy his new computer system. DELETE *to the tune of.*

to the victor belong the spoils ∎ A popular prescription.

to thine own self be true ∎ A popular prescription.

touch and go ∎ A moribund metaphor. *dangerous; precarious; risky; uncertain.*

touch base with ∎ A moribund metaphor.

(as) tough as leather ∎ An insipid simile. 1. *athletic; beefy; brawny; burly; energetic; firm; fit; hale; hardy; hearty; healthful; healthy; husky; leathery; manly; mesomorphic; mighty; muscular; powerful; puissant; robust; rugged; sinewy; solid; sound; stalwart; stout; strapping; strong; sturdy; tough; vigorous; virile; well-built.* 2. *constant; dependable; determined; faithful; fast; firm; fixed; inexorable; inflexible; loyal; obdurate; resolute; resolved; rigid; solid; stable; staunch; steadfast; steady; stern; strong; tenacious; unflinching; unwavering; unyielding.*

(as) tough as nails ∎ An insipid simile. 1. *athletic; beefy; brawny; burly; energetic; firm; fit; hale; hardy; healthful; healthy; hearty; leathery; manly; mesomorphic; mighty; muscular; powerful; puissant; robust; rugged; sinewy; solid; sound; stalwart; stout; strapping; strong; sturdy; tough; vigorous; virile; well-built.* 2. *constant; dependable; determined; faithful; fast; firm; fixed; inexorable; inflexible; loyal; obdurate; resolute; resolved; rigid; solid;*

stable; staunch; steadfast; steady; stern; strong; tenacious; unflinching; unwavering; unyielding.

tough sledding ∎ A moribund metaphor. *arduous; backbreaking; burdensome; difficult; exhausting; fatiguing; hard; herculean; laborious; not easy; onerous; severe; strenuous; toilful; toilsome; tough; troublesome; trying; wearisome.*

(it's) tough to teach an old dog new tricks ∎ A moribund metaphor.

towering inferno ∎ An infantile phrase. *blaze; conflagration; fire; holocaust; inferno.*

(proven) track record ∎ A moribund metaphor.

tread water ∎ A moribund metaphor. • He is now *treading water*, deciding what to do next.

treat (us) like royalty ∎ An insipid simile.

très ∎ A foreign phrase. *very.* • She is *très* happy now that she is working. REPLACE WITH *very.* • Two New Yorkers we recently sent out on a discount shopping spree were *très* impressed with the hippness quotient. REPLACE WITH *very.*

trials and tribulations ∎ An inescapable pair. *adversity; affliction; calamity; catastrophe; difficulty; distress; hardship; misadventure; misfortune; ordeal; trial; tribulation; trouble; woe.* • It also presents a first-hand account of the *trials and tribulations* of living in a lesbian family. REPLACE WITH *ordeal.*

tried and true ∎ An inescapable pair. 1. *constant; dependable; faithful; firm; loyal; reliable; solid; staunch; steadfast; strong; true; trustworthy; trusty.* 2. *authentic; authenticated; established; reliable; substantiated; sound; verified; well-founded; well-grounded.*

trim (her) sails ∎ A moribund metaphor.

trip the light fantastic ∎ A moribund metaphor. *dance.*

triumphant return ∎ An inescapable pair.

trouble in paradise ∎ A moribund metaphor.

true blue ∎ A moribund metaphor. *constant; dependable; faithful; firm; loyal; reliable; solid; staunch; steadfast; strong; true; trustworthy; trusty.*

true facts ∎ A wretched redundancy. *facts; truth.* • Sometimes I wish the papers would print the *true facts*. REPLACE WITH *facts* or *truth.*

true love ∎ A suspect superlative.

(the course of) true love never runs smooth ∎ A popular prescription.

truthfully honest ∎ A wretched redundancy. *honest; truthful.* • To be *truthfully honest*, I do want to be her friend. REPLACE WITH *truthful.*

truth is stranger than fiction ▮ A popular prescription.

truth, justice, and the American way ▮ An infantile phrase.

try it, you'll like it ▮ An infantile phrase.

try, try again ▮ A popular prescription.

turn a blind eye to (toward) ▮ A moribund metaphor. *brush aside; avoid; discount; disregard; dodge; duck; ignore; look away from; neglect; omit; overlook; pass over; shrink from; shun; shy away from; turn away from; withdraw from.* • And Chile, at least, is learning the risks of *turning a blind eye to* the past. REPLACE WITH *ignoring.* • Yet some of Bolt's advertisers, while lured by the site's demographics, may be *turning a blind eye to* content they normally find questionable in other media. REPLACE WITH *overlooking.* • The donors have *turned a blind eye toward* allegations of corruption. REPLACE WITH *disregarded.*

> The scholarly badger, who hated contradiction and despised the Socratic method, would cast a blind eye to the twitching braid until her pupil's gasps became too insistent to ignore.—George Hagen, *The Laments*

turnabout is fair play ▮ A popular prescription.

turn a (the) corner ▮ A moribund metaphor. 1. *advance; awaken; better; expand; flourish; gain; gain strength; grow; heal; improve; increase; pick up; progress; prosper; rally; recover; recuperate; refresh; renew; revive; rouse; strengthen; thrive.* 2. *adjust; alter; change; modify; transform.* • Our No. 1 goal is to reestablish reliability and customer satisfaction, and we think we have started to *turn the corner.* REPLACE WITH *improve.*

> Two weeks was only one day more than thirteen days, but I felt we'd turned a corner that shouldn't have been turned, and I couldn't get myself out of bed.—Ann Packer, *The Dive From Clausen's Pier*

turn a deaf ear to ▮ A moribund metaphor. *brush aside; avoid; discount; disregard; dodge; duck; ignore; neglect; omit; pass over; recoil from; shrink from; shun; shy away from; turn away from; withdraw from.* • Wilson should *turn a deaf ear to* HMO lobbyists and sign it. REPLACE WITH *disregard.* • Congress has *turned a deaf ear to* the public and taken the next step to unplug PBS and NPR. REPLACE WITH *ignored.*

turn a negative into a positive ▮ A torpid term. • The revolution in traditional family ties has *turned a negative into a positive* for most singles today. SEE ALSO **negative; positive.**

turn (their) back on ▮ A moribund metaphor.

abandon; abdicate; avoid; brush aside; deny; desert; disavow; discount; disinherit; disown; disregard; dodge; drop; duck; forgo; forsake; give up; ignore; leave; neglect; omit; pass over; quit; recoil from; reject; relinquish; renounce; shrink from; shun; shy away from; snub; surrender; turn away from; withdraw from; yield. • It will be unfortunate, indeed, if the countries of Western Europe *turn their backs on* their Eastern neighbors. REPLACE WITH *disregard.*

turn back the clock (of time) ▮ A moribund metaphor.

turn (your) dreams into reality ▮ A popular prescription.

turn inside out ▮ A moribund metaphor. *agitate; confuse; disorder; disorganize; disquiet; disrupt; disturb; fluster; jar; jolt; jumble; mess up; mix up; muddle; perturb; rattle; ruffle; shake up; stir up; trouble; unnerve; unsettle; upset.*

turn into (to) stone ▮ A moribund metaphor. *calcify; fossilize; harden; petrify; solidify.*

turn like the weather ▮ An insipid simile. *capricious; changeable; erratic; fickle; fitful; flighty; fluctuating; haphazard; inconsistent; inconstant; intermittent; irregular; mercurial; occasional; random; sometime; spasmodic; sporadic; unpredictable; unsettled; unstable; unsteady; vacillating; volatile; wavering; wayward.*

(another) turn of the screw ▮ A moribund metaphor.

turn over a new leaf ▮ A moribund metaphor. *alter; begin again; begin anew; change; convert; improve; metamorphose; modify; reform; remake; remodel; rethink; transform.*

turn sour ▮ A moribund metaphor. • Banks caught in the euphoria of a construction boom have watched the economy *turn sour.*

turn (my) stomach ▮ A moribund metaphor. *appall; disgust; horrify; nauseate; offend; outrage; repel; repulse; revolt; shock; sicken.*

turn tail ▮ A moribund metaphor. *abscond; clear out; decamp; depart; desert; disappear; escape; exit; flee; fly; go; go away; leave; move on; part; pull out; quit; retire; retreat; run away; take flight; take off; vacate; vanish; withdraw*

turn the other cheek ▮ A moribund metaphor.

turn the page ▮ A moribund metaphor. 1. *alter; begin again; begin anew; change; convert; improve; metamorphose; modify; reform; remake; remodel; rethink; transform.* 2. *discount; dismiss; disregard; forget about; ignore; overlook; set aside; shelve.* 3. *go on; move on; proceed.*

turn the tables (on) ▮ A moribund metaphor.

turn the tide ▮ A moribund metaphor. *alter; change; rearrange; reverse; switch; transpose.*

turn up like as bad penny ▮ A moribund metaphor.

> He should have figured the faux Nancy Drew would be here, seeing as she kept turning up like the proverbial bad penny.—Judi McCoy, *Hounding the Pavement*

turn up (her) nose ▮ A moribund metaphor. *contemn; deride; despise; detest; disdain; jeer at; laugh at; mock; ridicule; scoff at; scorn; shun; slight; sneer; snub; spurn.*

turn up the heat ▮ A moribund metaphor. *coerce; command; compel; constrain; demand; enforce; force; goad; impel; importune; incite; induce; insist; instigate; make; oblige; press; pressure; prod; push; spur; urge.*

(sit and) twiddle (our) thumbs ▮ A moribund metaphor. *be idle; be inactive; be lazy; be unemployed; be unoccupied; dally; dawdle; loaf; loiter; loll; lounge; relax; repose; rest.*

twilight zone ▮ A moribund metaphor.

twist (his) arm ▮ A moribund metaphor. *bulldoze; bully; coerce; compel; constrain; demand; drive; enforce; enjoin; exhort; goad; force; impel; incite; insist; intimidate; make; necessitate; obligate; oblige; order; press; pressure; prod; require; threaten; tyrannize; urge.*

twist (wrap) (him) around (her) little finger ▮ A moribund metaphor. *administer; boss; command; control; dictate; direct; dominate; domineer; govern; in charge; in control; in command; manage; manipulate; master; misuse; order; overpower; oversee; predominate; prevail; reign over; rule; superintend; tyrannize; use.*

twist of fate ▮ A moribund metaphor.

twists and turns (of fate) ▮ A moribund metaphor.

twist slowly in the wind ▮ A moribund metaphor. *afflict; agonize; crucify; excruciate; harrow; martyr; persecute; rack; torment; torture.*

two heads are better than one ▮ A popular prescription.

(like) two peas in a pod ▮ An insipid simile. *akin; alike; correspondent; corresponding; equal; equivalent; identical; indistinguishable; kindred; like; matching; one; same; selfsame; similar; twin.*

> I winced every time I heard someone refer to another girl or boy my age to be so much like his or her father or mother that they were like two peas in a pod.—V. C. Andrews, *Secrets in the Shadows*

two's company, three's a crowd ▮ A popular prescription.

two-way street ▮ A moribund metaphor.

two wrongs don't make a right ▮ A popular prescription.

Uu

(as) ugly as a toad ∎ An insipid
simile. *deformed; disfigured; disgusting;
displeasing; distorted; freakish; frightful;
ghastly; gorgonian; grisly; grotesque;
gruesome; hideous; homely; horrendous;
horrible; horrid; monstrous; offensive;
plain; repellent; repulsive; revolting; ugly;
unsightly.*

(as) ugly as sin ∎ An insipid simile.
*deformed; disfigured; disgusting;
displeasing; distorted; freakish; frightful;
ghastly; gorgonian; grisly; grotesque;
gruesome; hideous; homely; horrendous;
horrible; horrid; monstrous; offensive;
plain; repellent; repulsive; revolting; ugly;
unsightly.*

ugly duckling ∎ A moribund metaphor.
*deformed; disfigured; disgusting;
displeasing; distorted; freakish; frightful;
ghastly; gorgonian; grisly; grotesque;
gruesome; hideous; homely; horrendous;
horrible; horrid; monstrous; offensive;
plain; repellent; repulsive; revolting; ugly;
unsightly.*

unbeknownst ∎ A withered word.
unbeknown; unknown. • *Unbeknownst* to
his girlfriend, he made a videotape of them
having sex. REPLACE WITH *Unknown.*

unbelievable ∎ An overworked word. 1. *beyond
belief; beyond comprehension; doubtful;
dubious; implausible; imponderable;
improbable; incomprehensible; inconceivable;
inexplicable; questionable; unfathomable;
unimaginable; unthinkable.* 2. *astonishing;
astounding; breathtaking; extraordinary;
fabulous; fantastic; marvelous; miraculous;
overwhelming; prodigious; sensational;
spectacular; wonderful; wondrous.*

uncharted territory (waters) ∎ A moribund
metaphor.

under a cloud ∎ A moribund metaphor.
*discredited; disfavored; disgraced;
dishonored; distrusted; in disfavor; in
disgrace; in disrepute; in ignominy; in
shame; suspect; under suspicion.* • He
became the only vice president to leave
under a cloud. REPLACE WITH *in disgrace.*
• He left the police department *under a
cloud of suspicion.* REPLACE WITH *under
suspicion.*

under (my) belt ∎ A moribund metaphor.
*background; education; experience;
grooming; grounding; instruction; learning;
knowledge; maturity; practice; preparation;
qualifications; schooling; seasoning; skill;
teaching; training.*

More precise words also might be used,
and when a more precise word can be
used, it should be used.

> Both took the bar exam three times; Wally
> had four divorces under his belt; Oscar could
> only dream.—John Grisham, *The Litigators*

(come) under fire ∎ A moribund metaphor.
*be admonished; be assailed; be attacked;
be castigated; be censured; be chastised;
be chided; be condemned; be criticized; be
denounced; be rebuked; be reprimanded; be
reproached; be reproved; be scolded; be set on;
be upbraided.*

(keep) under lock and key ∎ A moribund
metaphor. 1. *confined; imprisoned; in jail;
locked up.* 2. *guarded; protected; safe; secure;
sheltered; shielded.*

under (his) own steam ∎ A moribund
metaphor.

understaffed and overworked ∎ An
inescapable pair.

under the gun ∎ A moribund metaphor. *be at
risk; be at stake; be endangered; be imperiled;
be in danger; be in jeopardy; be jeopardized;
be menaced; be threatened.* • The American
way of life, long taken for granted, was
under the gun. REPLACE WITH *being
threatened.*

under the same roof ∎ A moribund
metaphor. *be as one; be indissoluble; be
indivisible; be inseparable; be together.* • The
who's who of world power, gathered *under
the same roof* in a public place, poses an
unparalleled security headache for Italian
authorities. REPLACE WITH *together.*
• While he understands those living in
the house could live anywhere in the
community, he sees a danger in putting
them all together *under the same roof.*
DELETE *under the same roof.*

> I hold it singular, as I look back, that I should
> never have doubted for a moment that the
> sacred relics were there; never have failed to
> feel a certain joy at being under the same
> roof with them.—Henry James, *The Aspern
> Papers*

under the sun ∎ A moribund metaphor. *in
existence; known.*

under the table ∎ A moribund metaphor.
*clandestinely; confidentially; covertly;
furtively; mysteriously; in private; in secret;
privately; quietly; secludedly; secretly; slyly;*

stealthily; surreptitiously; undercover.

under the weather ▮ A moribund metaphor.
1. *afflicted; ailing; debilitated; diseased;
enervated; feeble; frail; ill; indisposed;
infirm; not (feeling) well; sick; sickly;
suffering; unhealthy; unsound; unwell;
valetudinarian.* 2. *besotted; crapulous;
drunk; inebriated; intoxicated; sodden;
stupefied; tipsy.* • It doesn't matter if some
days I'm feeling a little low or *under the
weather.* REPLACE WITH *unwell.*

under the wire ▮ A moribund metaphor.

under (his) thumb ▮ A moribund metaphor.
*dependent; subject; subordinate; subservient;
under.*

> A part of her wanted to say "Fuck you" to
> both of them and let Kevin see how happy he
> was in the arms of that sleazy whore. If that
> was what he wanted, fine. Let her destroy
> him. Let him see what life would be like under
> her thumb.—Brian Freeman, *Immoral*

under (his) wing ▮ A moribund metaphor.

(keep) under wraps ▮ A moribund
metaphor. *camouflage; clandestine; cloak;
conceal; cover; covert; disguise; enshroud;
harbor; hide; out of sight; secret; mask;
screen; shroud; suppress; surreptitious; veil;
withhold.* • Radcliffe tried, and failed, to
keep its list *under wraps.* REPLACE WITH
hidden. • Negotiations have been kept
largely *under wraps.* REPLACE WITH
secret.

uneasy calm ▮ An inescapable pair. • By
midafternoon, an *uneasy calm* returned to
much of the capital.

**uneasy lies the head that wears a
crown** ▮ A popular prescription.

united we stand (divided we fall) ▮ A
popular prescription.

unite in holy wedlock (marriage) ▮ A
wretched redundancy. *marry; wed.*

unless and (or) until ▮ A wretched
redundancy. *unless; until.* • I am opposed
to the imposition of any new taxes *unless
and until* major cuts in spending have been
implemented. REPLACE WITH *unless* or
until.

unmitigated gall ▮ An inescapable pair.

untenable position ▮ An inescapable pair.

until and (or) unless ▮ A wretched
redundancy. *unless; until.* • *Until and unless*
these two conditions are met, the second
rule does not fire. REPLACE WITH *Unless*
or *Until.*

until such time as ▮ A wretched redundancy.
until. • Lessee shall not be liable for
any rent *until such time as* Lessor can
deliver possession. REPLACE WITH *until.*
• The FBI would cooperate but play a
subordinate role *until such time as* it

became evident that the explosion was
caused by a criminal act. REPLACE WITH
until.

up a blind alley ▮ A moribund metaphor. 1. *at
risk; endangered; hard-pressed; imperiled; in
a bind; in a dilemma; in a fix; in a jam; in
a predicament; in a quandary; in danger; in
difficulty; in jeopardy; in peril; in trouble;
jeopardized.* 2. *caught; cornered; enmeshed;
ensnared; entangled; entrapped; netted;
snared; trapped.*

up a creek ▮ A moribund metaphor. *at risk;
endangered; hard-pressed; imperiled; in a
bind; in a dilemma; in a fix; in a jam; in a
predicament; in a quandary; in danger; in
difficulty; in jeopardy; in peril; in trouble;
jeopardized.*

up against the wall ▮ A moribund
metaphor. 1. *at risk; desperate; endangered;
frantic; hard-pressed; imperiled; in a
bind; in a dilemma; in a fix; in a jam; in a
predicament; in a quandary; in danger; in
difficulty; in jeopardy; in peril; in trouble;
jeopardized.* 2. *caught; cornered; enmeshed;
ensnared; entangled; entrapped; netted;
snared; trapped.*

(right) up (her) alley ▮ A moribund metaphor.

up and running ▮ A moribund metaphor.
1. *at work; functioning; going; in action;
in operation; operational; operating;
performing; producing; running; working.*
2. *able-bodied; active; fit; healthy; robust;
strong; vigorous; well.* • We intend to have
a smoothly functioning, well-integrated
unit *up and running* when we start in
February. REPLACE WITH *in operation.*
• This country needs massive amounts of
aid to get these people *up and running.*
REPLACE WITH *well.*

> Everyone, even Liam, offered their expertise
> to get her up and running.—Rebecca Bloom,
> *Tangled Up in Daydreams*

(dance) up a storm ▮ A moribund metaphor.
1. *ceaselessly; constantly; continually;
endlessly; extensively; incessantly;
interminably; perpetually; persistently;
unendingly.* 2. *greedily; insatiably;
rapaciously; ravenously; voraciously; wildly.*
• Though I ate *up a storm,* I was petite and
underweight. REPLACE WITH *rapaciously.*

up a tree ▮ A moribund metaphor. 1. *at risk;
endangered; hard-pressed; imperiled; in a
bind; in a fix; in a jam; in a predicament; in
danger; in difficulty; in jeopardy; in peril;
in trouble; jeopardized.* 2. *caught; cornered;
enmeshed; ensnared; entangled; entrapped;
netted; snared; trapped.*

up close and personal ▮ An infantile
phrase. *close; intimate; personal.*

up in arms ▮ A moribund metaphor. 1.
*agitated; alarmed; angry; annoyed; aroused;
choleric; enraged; fierce; fuming; furious;
incensed; indignant; inflamed; infuriated;*

irate; irked; irritable; mad; maddened; raging; resentful; splenetic; vexatious. 2. *factious; insubordinate; insurgent; mutinous; rebellious; seditious.* • The nurses were *up in arms* because of their work conditions. REPLACE WITH *incensed.*

up in the air ∎ A moribund metaphor. *confused; dubious; indecisive; in doubt; irresolute; open; questionable; tentative; uncertain; unconcluded; undecided; undetermined; unknown; unresolved; unsettled; unsure.* • The issue is still very much *up in the air* despite a series of rulings in the 1980s. REPLACE WITH *unsettled.*

> Or depending on his work schedule, which was now up in the air, he could urinate on them at whatever time he got up.—James Whorton, *Approximately Heaven*

ups and downs ∎ A moribund metaphor. *alterations; changes; erraticism; fluctuations; fortuitousness; inconstancies; shifts; uncertainties; vacillations; variations; vicissitudes.* • A community that can meet many of its needs by using locally available natural, human, and financial resources will be less affected by the *ups and downs* of the national and global economies. REPLACE WITH *vicissitudes.*

upset the apple cart ∎ A moribund metaphor. *confuse; damage; disorder; disrupt; disturb; jumble; mess up; mix up; muddle; ruin; scramble; spoil; upset.*

up the ante ∎ A moribund metaphor.

up the creek (without a paddle) ∎ A moribund metaphor. 1. *at risk; endangered; hard-pressed; imperiled; in a bind; in a dilemma; in a fix; in a jam; in a predicament; in a quandary; in danger; in difficulty; in jeopardy; in peril; in trouble; jeopardized.* 2. *caught; cornered; enmeshed; ensnared; entangled; entrapped; netted; snared; trapped.*

up the food chain ∎ A moribund metaphor. *to the bosses; to your superiors.* • Associates should consider asking one another to review drafts before sending them *up the food chain.* REPLACE WITH *to their bosses.*

up the river ∎ A moribund metaphor. *in (to) prison.*

up till (until) ∎ A wretched redundancy. *till (until).* • *Up until* the day he left, they hoped that he would play a major role in the new company as a key senior executive. REPLACE WITH *Until.*

> I'd given him the pipe for Father' Day. Up until then he had never even smoked.—Sue Monk Kidd, *The Mermaid Chair*

up till (until) this point (time) ∎ A wretched redundancy. *until now.* • *Up until*

this point we have been working in the dark. REPLACE WITH *Until now.*

(step) up to bat ∎ A moribund metaphor. 1. *aim for; attempt; endeavor; engage; participate; pursue; seek; strive for; try.* 2. *advance; appear; approach; come forth; come forward; emerge; rise; show; surface; transpire.* 3. *act; perform; speak; talk.* 4. *be accountable; be answerable; be responsible.* • In this regard, one campus organization has *stepped up to bat.* REPLACE WITH *emerged.* • First *up to bat* is Philip Cercone, director of McGill-Queen's University Press. REPLACE WITH *to speak.*

> So now Lora comes up to bat and tells a story that is basically the same as mine but utterly different...—David Margolis, *The Stepman*

up to (my) ears ∎ A moribund metaphor. 1. *bury; deluge; flood; glut; immerse; infest; inundate; overburden; overload; overpower; overrun; overwhelm; sate; swamp.* 2. *altogether; completely; entirely; fully; perfectly; quite; roundly; thoroughly; totally; unreservedly; utterly; wholly.*

up to (my) eyeballs (eyebrows; eyes) ∎ A moribund metaphor. 1. *bury; deluge; glut; immerse; infest; inundate; overburden; overload; overpower; overrun; overwhelm; sate; swamp.* 2. *altogether; completely; entirely; fully; perfectly; quite; roundly; thoroughly; totally; unreservedly; utterly; wholly.* • The campaigns' organizations are all *up to their eyeballs* with delegate-counting. REPLACE WITH *overrun.* • We are in this now, *up to our eyebrows* and for the long haul. REPLACE WITH *fully.*

up to par ∎ A moribund metaphor. 1. *average; common; commonplace; customary; everyday; mediocre; middling; normal; ordinary; quotidian; regular; routine; standard; typical; uneventful; unexceptional; unremarkable; usual.* 2. *acceptable; adequate; fine; good; good enough; healthy; passable; satisfactory; sufficient; suitable; tolerable; well.*

up to scratch ∎ A moribund metaphor. *acceptable; adequate; fine; good; good enough; healthy; passable; satisfactory; sufficient; suitable; tolerable; well.*

up to snuff ∎ A moribund metaphor. *acceptable; adequate; fine; good; good enough; healthy; passable; satisfactory; sufficient; suitable; tolerable; well.*

up to speed ∎ A moribund metaphor. *acceptable; adequate; fine; good; good enough; healthy; passable; satisfactory; sufficient; suitable; tolerable; well.*

use and abuse ∎ An inescapable pair. • We all agree that we have been racially *used and abused.* • Lil Franklin said her son had been *used and abused* by two fundamentalist ministers.

utilize ∎ A torpid term. *apply; employ; make use of; use.* • I *utilize* my bike for nearly everything. REPLACE WITH *use.* • These are all expository techniques that you will be *utilizing* once you have mastered the basics of writing. REPLACE WITH *using.* SEE ALSO **finalize**.

Vv

valuable asset ∎ An inescapable pair. This phrase is, like many inescapable pairs, also redundant, for an *asset* is *valuable*.

variations on a theme ∎ A torpid term.

> Once she allowed herself to think that, then there was no stopping a flood of other suspicions—primarily variations on the theme of the power and ubiquity of Ray's "friends."—Jane Smiley, *Duplicate Keys*

variety is the spice of life ∎ A popular prescription.

various and sundry ∎ An inescapable pair. *assorted; diverse; sundry; varied; various; varying.* • I tried *various and sundry* ways to get her to see me. REPLACE WITH *various*. SEE ALSO **all and sundry**.

vehemently oppose ∎ An inescapable pair. • MCA *vehemently opposed* Sony's Betamax and the VCR invasion.

verboten ∎ A foreign phrase. *banned; disallowed; enjoined; forbidden; prohibited; proscribed.* • But once everything was set up, my analog modem worked on a previously *verboten* digital phone. REPLACE WITH *disallowed*.

verily ∎ A withered word. *actually; indeed; in fact; in faith; in reality; in truth; truly.*

very ∎ An overworked word. The word *very* is often a needless intensive, but preceding words like *excellent, major,* and *delightful,* it is ludicrous. • I think that's a *very* excellent thought. DELETE *very*. • It's a *very* major plus for our state and our region. DELETE *very*. • You seem *very* delightful. DELETE *very*. • She's a biochemist and *very* brilliant. DELETE *very*. • If the test cells were to be shut down, it would be *very* detrimental to the operation. DELETE *very*. • Moreover, the wind at the peak can be *very* deadly. DELETE *very*. SEE ALSO **really**.

viable alternative ∎ An inescapable pair.

vicious circle ∎ An inescapable pair.

vicious rumor ∎ An inescapable pair.

vim and vigor ∎ An inescapable pair. *animation; ardor; dash; dynamism; élan; energy; fervor; force; intensity; liveliness; passion; potency; power; spirit; stamina; strength; verve; vigor; vitality; vivacity; zeal.*

virtue is its own reward ∎ A popular prescription.

vis-à-vis ∎ A foreign phrase.

viselike grip ∎ A moribund metaphor.

visible (invisible) to the eye ∎ A wretched redundancy. *visible (invisible).* SEE ALSO **audible (inaudible) to the ear**.

vive la différence ∎ A foreign phrase.

voice (crying) in the wilderness ∎ A moribund metaphor.

vote with (their) feet ∎ A moribund metaphor. • People are *voting with their feet,* and politicians know this.

Ww

wages of sin ∎ A moribund metaphor.

(just have to) wait and see (what happens) ∎ A torpid term. *I don't know; (it's) not (yet) known; (that's) uncertain; (that's) unclear; (it's) unknown.* SEE ALSO **(it) remains to be seen; your guess is as good as mine.**

wait for the ax to fall ∎ A moribund metaphor.

wait for the other shoe to drop ∎ A moribund metaphor.

waiting for Godot ∎ An infantile phrase.

waiting in the wings ∎ A moribund metaphor.

wake the dead ∎ A moribund metaphor. *blaring; boisterous; booming; deafening; earsplitting; fulminating; loud; noisy; obstreperous; piercing; plangent; resounding; roaring; shrill; stentorian; strident; thundering; thunderous; tumultuous; vociferous.*

wake up and smell the coffee ∎ A moribund metaphor. *be alert; be attentive; be awake; be aware; be cognizant; be conscious; be mindful; be perceptive; be sentient; be wakeful.*

wake-up call ∎ A moribund metaphor. *admonition; caution; warning.* • The priest sexual scandal is a *wake-up call* for the church.

walk a fine line ∎ A moribund metaphor.

walk a tightrope ∎ A moribund metaphor. *chance; dare; endanger; gamble; hazard; imperil; jeopardize; make bold; peril; risk; venture.*

walk away from ∎ A moribund metaphor. *abandon; abdicate; avoid; brush aside; deny; desert; disavow; discount; disinherit; disown; disregard; dodge; drop; duck; forgo; forsake; give up; ignore; leave; neglect; omit; pass over; quit; recoil from; reject; relinquish; renounce; shrink from; shun; shy away from; snub; spurn; surrender; turn away from; withdraw from; yield.* • The state cannot *walk away from* that obligation. REPLACE WITH *disregard.*

walk on air ∎ A moribund metaphor. *blissful; blithe; buoyant; cheerful; delighted; ecstatic; elated; enraptured; euphoric; exalted; excited; exhilarated; exultant; gay; glad; gleeful; good-humored; happy; intoxicated; jolly; jovial; joyful; joyous; jubilant; merry; mirthful; overjoyed; pleased; rapturous; thrilled.*

walk on eggs (eggshells) ∎ A moribund metaphor. *be careful; be cautious; be circumspect; be delicate; be guarded; be sensitive; be vigilant; be wary; be watchful.* • For years, Robinson *walked on eggshells* as the first black baseball player in the major leagues.

> Walking on eggshells, trying not to put a foot wrong, takes a lot out of you. Someone else was walking delicately, too.—Marian Babson, *Only the Cat Knows*

(all) walks of life ∎ A moribund metaphor.

walk softly and carry a big stick ∎ A popular prescription.

walk (me) through ∎ A moribund metaphor. *clarify; clear up; describe; disentangle; elucidate; enlighten; explain; explicate; illume; illuminate; interpret; make clear; make plain; reveal; simplify.* • Can you *walk me through* the process of how you wrote it? USE *explain.* • Middle-school students will be told the details of the drill in advance, and their teachers will *walk them through* the steps on the day of the event. USE *describe.*

wall of silence ∎ A moribund metaphor.

(the) walls have ears ∎ A moribund metaphor.

want to bet? ∎ An infantile phrase.

war clouds ∎ A moribund metaphor.

war is hell ∎ A quack equation.

(as) warm as toast ∎ An insipid simile. *heated; lukewarm; mild; temperate; tepid; toasty; warm; warmish.*

warm the cockles of (my) heart ∎ A moribund metaphor.

warn in advance ∎ A wretched redundancy. *warn.* • Management should be *warned in advance* that fines are no longer the way to satisfy the system for a careless disaster. DELETE *in advance.* SEE ALSO **advance warning; forewarn.**

war of words ∎ A moribund metaphor. *altercation; argument; bickering; conflict; contention; controversy; disagreement; disputation; dispute; feud; polemics; quarrel; row; spat; squabble; strife; wrangle.* • Yesterday's *war of words* seemed like a replay of the bitter 1988 campaign. REPLACE WITH *squabble.*

wash (their) dirty linen in public

wash (their) dirty linen in public ▪ A moribund metaphor.

(all) washed up ▪ A moribund metaphor. *beaten; condemned; conquered; cowed; cursed; damned; defunct; doomed; fated; finished; gone; lost; ruined; vanquished.*

wash (her) hands of (it) ▪ A moribund metaphor. *abandon; abdicate; avoid; brush aside; deny; desert; disavow; discount; disinherit; disown; disregard; dodge; drop; duck; forgo; forsake; give up; ignore; leave; neglect; omit; pass over; quit; recoil from; reject; relinquish; renounce; shrink from; shun; shy away from; snub; surrender; turn away from; withdraw from; yield.*

> The gambler apparently had washed his hands of me, but he didn't seem to hold any stubbornness against me.—Dashiell Hammett, *Red Harvest*

waste not, want not ▪ A popular prescription.

(like) watching grass grow ▪ An insipid simile. 1. *banal; barren; bland; boring; deadly; dreary; dry; dull; everyday; flat; humdrum; inanimate; insipid; jejune; lifeless; lusterless; mediocre; monotonous; prosaic; routine; spiritless; stale; tedious; tiresome; unexciting; uninteresting; vapid; wearisome.* 2. *dawdling; hesitant; laggardly; lagging; leisurely; slothful; slow; slow-paced; sluggardly; sluggish; snaillike; tortoiselike; unhurried.*

> He'd chosen the field of surgery because of the sheer challenge of it; obstetrics, in comparison, had seemed kind of like watching grass grow.—Linda Howard, *Cry No More*

watch (him) like a hawk ▪ An insipid simile. *be alert; be attentive; be awake; be aware; be eagle-eyed; be heedful; be informed; be keen; be observant; be vigilant; be wakeful; be watchful.*

water over the dam ▪ A moribund metaphor. 1. *completed; concluded; done; ended; finished; over; passed; through.* 2. *history; the past; yesterday.*

water (runs) under the bridge ▪ A moribund metaphor. 1. *completed; concluded; done; ended; finished; over; passed; through.* 2. *history; the past; yesterday.*

> A lot of water runs under the bridge, a lot of it dirty.—Thomas Savage, *The Sheep Queen*

(like) waving a red flag (rag) in front of a bull ▪ An insipid simile.

wax and wane ▪ An inescapable pair.

way ▪ An infantile phrase. • I'm *way* better than this. USE *much.* • The Internet is potentially *way* more powerful than television ever dreamed of being. USE *far.* • In some places, it is *way* below zero.

USE *far.* • *Way* too frequently, the family goes on a trip. USE *Far.* • It's *way* too soon to say they are going to begin an investigation. USE *much.* • Cooper Street is *way, way* in debt, and the sale only begins to dig us out of the hole. USE *deeply.*

Way in the sense of *much* or *far*, is informal, even ugly. It's unacceptable to use this sense of *way* in your writing, and it's unbecoming in your speaking.

ways and means ▪ An inescapable pair. *approaches; means; mechanisms; methods; techniques; ways.*

(as) weak as a baby ▪ An insipid simile. *dainty; debilitated; delicate; enervated; feeble; fragile; frail; infirm; nonmuscular; puny; sickly; unhealthy; unwell; valetudinarian; weak; weakly.*

(as) weak as a kitten ▪ An insipid simile. *dainty; debilitated; delicate; enervated; feeble; fragile; frail; infirm; nonmuscular; puny; sickly; unhealthy; unwell; valetudinarian; weak; weakly.*

> The diagnosis was in on love, the diagnosis was coming in; and love was as weak as a kitten, and pitifully confused, and not nearly strong enough to be brave or even understand.—Martin Amis, *London Fields*

weak in the knees ▪ A moribund metaphor. *dizzy; faint; giddy; lightheaded; weak.*

wears (her) heart on (her) sleeve ▪ A moribund metaphor. *demonstrative; emotional; emotive; sensitive; sentimental.*

wear the pants ▪ A moribund metaphor. *administer; boss; command; control; dictate; direct; dominate; govern; in charge; in command; in control; manage; manipulate; master; order; overpower; oversee; predominate; prevail; reign over; rule; superintend.*

weather the storm (of) ▪ A moribund metaphor. • A tremendous thank you goes out to each of you who has helped our family *weather this storm.* SEE ALSO **reach epidemic proportions**.

weighs a ton ▪ An insipid simile. *bulky; heavy; hefty; weighty.*

weight in proportion (proportionate) to height ▪ A torpid term. Men should eschew women (and women, men) whom they've not yet met and who describe their physiques as *weight in proportion (proportionate) to height.*

Let us men prefer an *athletic; brawny; firm; fit; medium-build; mesomorphic; muscular; robust; sinewy; toned; well-built* woman or a *bony; ectomorphic; lanky; lean; petite; rail-thin; scraggy; scrawny; skeletal; skinny; slender; slight; slim; small; spare; spindly; svelte; sylphid; thin; tiny; trim; wispy* woman or a *big-boned, big-breasted, big-bellied, or big-bottomed; bulbous; bulky; busty; buxom; chubby; chunky; corpulent;*

curvaceous; curvy; dumpy; endomorphic; enormous; fat; flabby; fleshy; full-figured; globular; heavy; heavyset; hefty; huge; large; obese; plump; portly; pudgy; rotund; round; squat; steatopygic; stocky; stout; voluptuous; zaftig woman—if not for her *womanliness* then at least for her *words*.

weird ∎ An overworked word. *aberrant; abnormal; anomalistic; anomalous; atypical; bizarre; curious; deviant; different; distinct; distinctive; eccentric; exceptional; extraordinary; fantastic; foreign; grotesque; idiosyncratic; independent; individual; individualistic; irregular; novel; odd; offbeat; original; peculiar; puzzling; quaint; queer; rare; remarkable; separate; singular; strange; uncommon; unconventional; unexampled; unique; unnatural; unorthodox; unparalleled; unprecedented; unusual.* SEE ALSO **strange**.

(all) well and good ∎ A wretched redundancy. *adequate; all right; excellent; fine; good; O.K.; satisfactory; well.* • That's *all well and good* for the hobbyist running a bulletin board or the IT worker who does side programming jobs in his off-hours at home. REPLACE WITH *good*. • Well, this is *all well and good,* but who's going to pay for it—not my insurance company! REPLACE WITH *fine*. • This is *all well and good*, but what do experts say? REPLACE WITH *good*. • That's *all well and good, but what about my son?* REPLACE WITH *fine*. SEE ALSO **fine and dandy; still and all**.

well-nigh ∎ A withered word. *almost; nearly.*

wet behind the ears ∎ A moribund metaphor. *artless; awkward; callow; green; guileless; immature; inexperienced; inexpert; ingenuous; innocent; naive; raw; simple; undeveloped; unfledged; unskilled; unskillful; unsophisticated; untaught; untrained; unworldly.*

wet (my) whistle ∎ A moribund metaphor. *drink; guzzle; imbibe; quaff.*

we've all got to go sometime ∎ A popular prescription.

we've got to stop meeting like this ∎ An infantile phrase.

what a difference a day makes ∎ A torpid term.

what are you going to do ∎ A plebeian sentiment. This is still another expression of resignation. Though phrased as a question, it is rarely spoken interrogatively, so resigned, so hopeless are those who use it. SEE ALSO **such is life; that's how (the way) it goes; that's how (the way) the ball bounces; that's how (the way) the cookie crumbles; that's life; that's life in the big city; that's show biz; what can you do.**

what can I say? ∎ An infantile phrase.

what can I tell you? ∎ An infantile phrase.

what can you do ∎ A plebeian sentiment.

SEE ALSO **such is life; that's how (the way) it goes; that's how (the way) the ball bounces; that's how (the way) the cookie crumbles; that's life; that's life in the big city; that's show biz; what are you going to do.**

what (he) doesn't know won't hurt (him) ∎ A popular prescription.

whatever ∎ An infantile phrase. As a one-word response to another's comment or question, *whatever* is as dismissive as it is ill-mannered. SEE ALSO **excuse me.**

whatever happens happens ∎ An infantile phrase. SEE ALSO **it just happened; what(ever) must (will) be, must (will) be.**

what goes around, comes around ∎ A popular prescription. This is the secular equivalent of "as you sow, so shall you reap." As such, it is nonetheless a moralistic prescription—intoned by those who think in circles—that too easily explains the way of the world.

what goes up must come down ∎ A popular prescription.

what happened (is) ∎ An ineffectual phrase. • *What happened was* I woke up one morning and just decided to leave. DELETE *What happened was.* • *What happened was* we applied for welfare. DELETE *What happened was.* • *What happened was* when I said that to him he got upset and left in a huff. DELETE *What happened was.* • *What has happened is,* my identity has gotten lost in this ordeal. DELETE *What has happened is.* SEE ALSO **what is.**

what ... is ∎ An ineffectual phrase. • *What you want is* someone who will stand by his work once it is completed. DELETE *What is.* • *What we are finding is* that they want to measure up to our standards of integrity. DELETE *What is.* • *What this course is about is* empowerment. DELETE *What is.* • *What we have is* a program that asks some important questions. DELETE *What is.* SEE ALSO **what happened (is).**

what is the world coming to? ∎ A plebeian sentiment.

what's done is done ∎ A quack equation. • *What's done is done,* but rethinking the choice now will help you make a better choice next time.

what's good for (the goose) is good for (the gander) ∎ A popular prescription.

what (which) side (her) bread is buttered on ∎ A moribund metaphor.

Can't help but wonder if it would have stayed a secret if it had been anyone else. People here know which side their bread's buttered on.—Simon Beckett, *Written in Bone*

what will they think of next? ∎ A plebeian sentiment.

what you don't know can't (won't) hurt you ▌ A popular prescription.

what you see is not always what you get ▌ A quack equation.

what you see is what you get ▌ A quack equation.

wheel and deal ▌ An inescapable pair. *bargain; contrive; deal; do business; machinate; negotiate; plan; plot; scheme.*

when and if ▌ A wretched redundancy. *if; when.* • People are asking *when and if* there will be a democratic government. REPLACE WITH *if* or *when.* SEE ALSO **if and when; if, as, and when; when and whether; when, as, and if; whether and when**.

when and whether ▌ A wretched redundancy. *when; whether.* • She will decide *when and whether* and under what circumstances she'll become a mother. REPLACE WITH *when* or *whether.* SEE ALSO **if and when; if, as, and when; when and if; when, as, and if; when and whether; whether and when**.

when, as, and if ▌ A wretched redundancy. *if; when.* SEE ALSO **if and when; if, as, and when; when and if; when and whether; whether and when**.

whence ▌ A withered word. 1. *from where.* 2. *from what source.* 3. *from which.*

when (you) come right down to it ▌ A wretched redundancy. *all in all; all told; altogether; eventually; finally; in all; in the end; on the whole; overall; ultimately.*

when hell freezes over ▌ A moribund metaphor. *never; no; not at all; not ever; not in any way; not in the least.*

when in Rome (do as the Romans do) ▌ A popular prescription. *abide by; accede; accommodate; accord; acquiesce; adapt; adhere to; agree; behave; comply; concur; conform; correspond; follow; harmonize; heed; mind; obey; observe; submit; yield.*

when it comes to ▌ A wretched redundancy. *about; as for; as to; concerning; for; in; of; on; over; regarding; respecting; to; toward; when; with.* • I feel I'm more experienced *when it comes to* looking for a job. REPLACE WITH *in.* • I'm an expert *when it comes to* marriage. REPLACE WITH *about.* • *When it comes to* middle-age dating, there are four stages. REPLACE WITH *As for.* • She is not reasonable *when it comes to* me. REPLACE WITH *with.*

when it rains, it pours ▌ A moribund metaphor.

when push comes to shove ▌ A moribund metaphor. • *When push comes to shove,* liberalism collapses, society polarizes itself, and the gloves are removed.

when the cat's away, the mice will play ▌ A moribund metaphor.

when the going gets tough, the tough get going ▌ A popular prescription.

where angels fear to tread ▌ A moribund metaphor.

whereat ▌ A withered word. *at which point.*

wherefore ▌ A withered word. 1. *why.* 2. *for which.* 3. *therefore.*

wherein ▌ A withered word. *how; in what way.*

where … is concerned ▌ A wretched redundancy. *about; as for; as to; concerning; for; in; of; on; over; regarding; respecting; to; toward; with.* • Our gangs are just getting off the ground *where* violence *is concerned.* REPLACE WITH *concerning.* • Obviously, time doesn't heal all wounds, especially *where* the Red Sox *are concerned.* REPLACE WITH *regarding.* SEE ALSO **as far as … (goes; is concerned)**.

whereon ▌ A withered word. *on what; on which.*

where's the beef? ▌ An infantile phrase.

where there's a will, there's a way ▌ A popular prescription.

where there's smoke there's fire ▌ A popular prescription.

where the rubber hits the road ▌ A moribund metaphor. • That, for Christians, is *where the rubber hits the road*—where we intersect with people who are poor or marginalized.

wherethrough ▌ A withered word. *through which.*

whereto ▌ A withered word. *to what; to which.*

whereunto ▌ A withered word. *to what; to which.*

wherewith ▌ A withered word. *with what; with which.*

whet (my) appetite ▌ A moribund metaphor.

whether and when ▌ A wretched redundancy. *when; whether.* • Lee will be the one to determine *whether and when* he isn't up to the job. REPLACE WITH *when* or *whether.* SEE ALSO **if and when; if, as, and when; when and if; when and whether; when, as, and if**.

which way the wind blows (is blowing) ▌ A moribund metaphor.

while at the same time ▌ A TOP-TWENTY DIMWITTICISM. A wretched redundancy. *at the same time; while.* • It provides us with an opportunity to honor his memory *while at the same time* assisting future students. REPLACE WITH *at the same time* or *while.* SEE ALSO **simultaneously at the same time; while simultaneously**.

> Once in the elevator, it was important to stand in silence beside the bags, to erase oneself behind the dignity of the uniform, while at the same time not seeming cold or indifferent and indeed remaining alert to any sign of helplessness in the traveler.—Steven Millhauser, *Martin Dressler*

while simultaneously ∎ A wretched redundancy. *simultaneously*; *while*. • So you can work on applications *while simultaneously* watching TV in a resizable window. DELETE *simultaneously*. SEE ALSO **simultaneously at the same time**; **while at the same time**.

whilst ∎ A withered word. *while*. • *Whilst* it delivers the required protection, most users will probably feel strangely unsatisfied after some hard use. REPLACE WITH *While*. • Some imply a functional relationship between variables *whilst* others are of a more exploratory nature. REPLACE WITH *while*.

whip into a frenzy ∎ A moribund metaphor. *acerbate*; *anger*; *annoy*; *bother*; *bristle*; *chafe*; *enrage*; *incense*; *inflame*; *infuriate*; *irk*; *irritate*; *madden*; *miff*; *provoke*; *rile*; *roil*; *vex*.

whip into shape ∎ A moribund metaphor.

whistle in the dark ∎ A moribund metaphor.

whistling Dixie ∎ A moribund metaphor.

(as) white as a ghost ∎ An insipid simile. 1. *anemic*; *ashen*; *blanched*; *bloodless*; *cadaverous*; *colorless*; *deathlike*; *doughy*; *haggard*; *lusterless*; *pale*; *pallid*; *pasty*; *peaked*; *sallow*; *sickly*; *wan*; *whitish*. 2. *achromatic*; *alabaster-white*; *albescent*; *bleached*; *chalky*; *colorless*; *ivory*; *milk-white*; *milky*; *niveous*; *pearly*; *pearly-white*; *snow-white*; *snowy*; *uncolored*; *whitish*.

> He tells me that the Dictator was receiving all this in silence, but that he was as white as a ghost.—Thornton Wilder, *The Ides of March*

(as) white as a sheet ∎ An insipid simile. 1. *anemic*; *ashen*; *blanched*; *bloodless*; *cadaverous*; *colorless*; *deathlike*; *doughy*; *haggard*; *lusterless*; *pale*; *pallid*; *pasty*; *peaked*; *sallow*; *sickly*; *wan*; *whitish*. 2. *achromatic*; *alabaster-white*; *albescent*; *bleached*; *chalky*; *colorless*; *ivory*; *milk-white*; *milky*; *niveous*; *pearly*; *pearly-white*; *snow-white*; *snowy*; *uncolored*; *whitish*.

(as) white as snow ∎ An insipid simile. 1. *achromatic*; *alabaster-white*; *albescent*; *bleached*; *chalky*; *colorless*; *ivory*; *milk-white*; *milky*; *niveous*; *pearly*; *pearly-white*; *snow-white*; *snowy*; *uncolored*; *whitish*. 2. *anemic*; *ashen*; *blanched*; *bloodless*; *cadaverous*; *colorless*; *deathlike*; *doughy*; *haggard*; *lusterless*; *pale*; *pallid*; *pasty*; *peaked*; *sallow*; *sickly*; *wan*; *whitish*.

(like) white on rice ∎ An insipid simile. 1. *congenital*; *fundamental*; *genetic*; *hereditary*;

inborn; *inbred*; *ingrained*; *inherent*; *inherited*; *innate*; *intrinsic*; *native*; *natural*. 2. *all over*; *everywhere*; *omnipresent*; *ubiquitous*.

whither ∎ A withered word. 1. *where*. 2. *wherever*.

(my) whole, entire (life) ∎ An infantile phrase. • People like you laughed at me *my whole, entire life*. • With this on, you will attract more women than you have in *your whole, entire lives*.

who let the cat out of the bag? ∎ A moribund metaphor.

whoop it up ∎ A moribund metaphor. 1. *be merry*; *carouse*; *carry on*; *celebrate*; *debauch*; *disport*; *frolic*; *party*; *play*; *revel*; *riot*; *roister*; *rollick*; *romp*; *skylark*. 2. *bay*; *bawl*; *bellow*; *blare*; *caterwaul*; *cheer*; *clamor*; *cry*; *holler*; *hoot*; *howl*; *roar*; *screak*; *scream*; *screech*; *shout*; *shriek*; *shrill*; *squawk*; *squeal*; *vociferate*; *wail*; *whoop*; *yell*; *yelp*; *yowl*.

who's minding the store? ∎ A moribund metaphor.

who would have (ever) thought ∎ A plebeian sentiment.

(the) why and (the) wherefore ∎ A wretched redundancy. *aim*; *cause*; *goal*; *motive*; *purpose*; *reason*.

why didn't (I) think of that? ∎ A plebeian sentiment.

why me? ∎ A plebeian sentiment.

wide of the mark ∎ A moribund metaphor. *erroneous*; *false*; *incorrect*; *inexact*; *mistaken*; *untrue*; *wrong*.

wild and crazy ∎ An inescapable pair.

> However wild and crazy they may be, they stand by their friends.—Matthew Reilly, *Scarecrow*

wild and woolly ∎ An inescapable pair.

wild blue yonder ∎ A moribund metaphor. *air*; *atmosphere*; *biosphere*; *empyrean*; *ether*; *firmament*; *heaven*; *heavens*; *outer space*; *sky*; *space*; *stratosphere*.

wild goose chase ∎ A moribund metaphor.

> Copulatory leads to copulation, the union of the sexes in the art of generation and I don't know what that means and I'm too weary going from one word to another in this heavy dictionary which leads me on a wild goose chase from this word to that word and all because the people who wrote the dictionary don't want the likes of me to know anything.—Frank McCourt, *Angela's Ashes*

wild horses couldn't (keep me away) ∎ A moribund metaphor.

wild horses couldn't drag it from (me) ∎ A moribund metaphor.

window dressing ∎ A moribund metaphor.

window of opportunity ∎ A moribund metaphor. *chance; occasion; opening; opportunity; possibility; prospect.* Only able writers know that *window of opportunity* is unable to influence or engage us. *Window of opportunity* is wording that lulls and then deadens.

• I think we have a terrific *window of opportunity* to make progress this year. REPLACE WITH *chance.* • There may be a *window of opportunity* between 12 and 1 for us to talk. REPLACE WITH *time.* • One redesign of an ASIC can cause the system vendor to completely miss the *window of opportunity* for a particular product. REPLACE WITH *opportunity.* • On the conflict in Darfur, the High Commissioner said he saw a *window of opportunity* to reach a political settlement for the strife-torn region. REPLACE WITH *chance.* SEE ALSO **a barrage of**.

> The phrase 'window of opportunity' had gone on for ever, syllables clambering over each other to give the pain more time to do its thing.—Glen Duncan, *Death of an Ordinary Man*

window on the (world) ∎ A moribund metaphor.

winds of change ∎ A moribund metaphor.

wine and dine ∎ An inescapable pair.

win hands down ∎ A moribund metaphor. *beat; conquer; crush; defeat; outclass; outdo; overcome; overpower; overwhelm; prevail; quell; rout; succeed; triumph; trounce; vanquish; win.*

win, lose, or draw ∎ A moribund metaphor. *regardless.*

win (his) spurs ∎ A moribund metaphor.

wipe off the map ∎ A moribund metaphor. *annihilate; assassinate; butcher; demolish; destroy; devastate; eradicate; exterminate; kill; massacre; murder; obliterate; pulverize; rack; ravage; raze; ruin; shatter; slaughter; slay; smash; undo; wrack; wreck.*

wipe the slate clean ∎ A moribund metaphor. *begin anew; start afresh; start over.*

-wise ∎ A grammatical gimmick. • I've been very successful *businesswise*. REPLACE WITH *in business*. • *Burialwise*, I don't feel they're responsible enough to take care of *my wishes*. REPLACE WITH *my burial wishes*. • I do have a photo of a model *who resembles me bodywise*. REPLACE WITH *whose body resembles my own*. • And *academicwise*, he's made the honor role every year. REPLACE WITH *academically*. • She is attractive and much smaller *sizewise* than me. DELETE *sizewise*. • I'll let you know *what I get from them informationwise*. REPLACE WITH *what*

information I get from them. • By spending our development time, future ads will be very *reasonable pricewise*. REPLACE WITH *reasonably priced*.

> The cream of the East and Middle West, engineering-wise and managerwise, was met in the amphitheater of the Meadows.—Kurt Vonnegut, Jr., *Player Piano*

(as) wise as Solomon ∎ An insipid simile. *astute; bright; brilliant; clever; discerning; enlightened; insightful; intelligent; judicious; keen; knowledgeable; learned; logical; luminous; penetrating; perceptive; perspicacious; rational; reasonable; sagacious; sage; sapient; sensible; sharp; shrewd; smart; sound; understanding; wise.*

wit and wisdom ∎ An inescapable pair.

with a big (capital) (A) ∎ An infantile phrase. • It's crisp, *with a capital C*. DELETE *with a capital C*. • He loves conversation—*with a big C*. DELETE *with a big C*. • These establishments offer *dining with a capital D*. REPLACE WITH *elegant dining.*

> So he knew a little bit about Beauty too. Beauty with a capital B: not just a pretty face or a picturesque landscape, ...—Robert Hellenga, *Philosophy Made Simple*

(go over) with a fine-toothed comb ∎ A moribund metaphor. *analyze; canvass; comb; examine; explore; filter; forage; hunt; inspect; investigate; look for; probe; quest; ransack; rummage; scour; scrutinize; search; seek; sieve; sift; winnow.*

with a heavy hand ∎ A moribund metaphor. *coercively; draconianly; harshly; oppressively; severely.*

with all (my) heart ∎ A moribund metaphor. *earnestly; fervently; genuinely; heartily; honestly; sincerely; unreservedly; wholeheartedly.*

with an open hand ∎ A moribund metaphor. *altruistically; beneficently; bountifully; charitably; generously; liberally; munificently; unselfishly; unstintingly.*

with a vengeance ∎ A moribund metaphor. *actively; aggressively; dynamically; emphatically; energetically; fast; furiously; fervently; fiercely; forcefully; frantically; frenziedly; furiously; hard; intensely; intently; mightily; passionately; powerfully; robustly; savagely; spiritedly; strenuously; strongly; vehemently; viciously; vigorously; violently; wildly; with vigor.*

with a wink and a nod ∎ A moribund metaphor. *clandestinely; confidentially; covertly; furtively; in private; in secret; mysteriously; privately; quietly; secludedly; secretly; slyly; stealthily; surreptitiously; undercover.* • Boston's most infamous criminal partnership began *with a wink* *and a nod.* REPLACE WITH *furtively.*

with bated breath ▪ A moribund metaphor. *agitatedly; anxiously; apprehensively; excitedly; fearfully; nervously; suspensefully; timidly; timorously; tremulously; worriedly.*

with bells on ▪ A moribund metaphor. *animatedly; eagerly; ebulliently; effervescently; effusively; enthusiastically; excitedly; lively; spiritedly; sprightly; vivaciously.*

with (their) eyes wide open ▪ A moribund metaphor. *by design; consciously; deliberately; intentionally; knowingly; on purpose; purposely; willfully; with intent.* • They did this *with their eyes wide open.* REPLACE WITH *deliberately.*

with flying colors ▪ A moribund metaphor. *beautifully; brilliantly; dazzlingly; excellently; grandly; impressively; magnificently; marvelously; outstandingly; splendidly; sublimely; successfully; superbly; triumphally; triumphantly; victoriously; wonderfully.*

with (her) heart in (her) mouth ▪ A moribund metaphor. *anxiously; apprehensively; fearfully; pavidly; timidly; timorously; tremblingly; tremulously.*

within a hair's breadth of ▪ A moribund metaphor. *(very) close (to); (very) near (to).* • Some visionaries are *within a hair's breadth of* achieving unattended computer center operation. REPLACE WITH *close to.*

(beaten) within an inch of (his) life ▪ A moribund metaphor. *brutally; cruelly; ferociously; fiercely; harshly; mercilessly; ruthlessly; severely; viciously; violently.*

> Alderman Schlumbohm, heckled to within an inch of his life, followed to the council door by three hundred of his fellow-citizens, was there left with the admonition that they would be waiting for him when he should make his exit.—Theodore Dreiser, *The Titan*

within a whisker of ▪ A moribund metaphor. *(very) close (to); (very) near (to).*

(handle; treat) with kid gloves ▪ A moribund metaphor. *carefully; cautiously; delicately; gently; gingerly; mildly; sensitively; tactfully; with care.*

with machinelike precision ▪ An insipid simile. *accurately; easily; exactly; excellently; faultlessly; flawlessly; flowingly; impeccably; indefectibly; methodically; perfectly; precisely; regularly; smoothly; systematically; well.*

with might and main ▪ A moribund metaphor. *actively; aggressively; dynamically; emphatically; energetically; ferociously; fervently; fiercely; forcefully; frantically; frenziedly; furiously; hard; intensely; intently; mightily; passionately; powerfully; robustly; savagely; spiritedly; strenuously; strongly; vehemently; viciously; vigorously;*

violently; wildly; with vigor.

with (her) nose in the air ▪ A moribund metaphor. *arrogant; cavalier; condescending; contemptuous; despotic; dictatorial; disdainful; dogmatic; domineering; haughty; imperious; insolent; lofty; overbearing; overweening; patronizing; pompous; pretentious; scornful; self-important; supercilious; superior; vainglorious.*

(welcome) with open arms ▪ A moribund metaphor. *affectionately; cheerfully; eagerly; enthusiastically; gladly; happily; joyously; readily; unreservedly; warmly.* • We have welcomed them *with open arms.* REPLACE WITH *cheerfully.* • I hope I am welcomed back *with open arms.* REPLACE WITH *unreservedly.*

(went off) without a hitch ▪ A moribund metaphor. *accurately; easily; exactly; excellently; faultlessly; flawlessly; flowingly; impeccably; indefectibly; methodically; perfectly; precisely; regularly; smoothly; systematically; well.*

without cost or obligation ▪ A wretched redundancy. *free.*

without further ado ▪ An infantile phrase. *at once; directly; forthwith; immediately; instantly; promptly; right away; straightaway; summarily; unfalteringly; unhesitatingly; without delay.*
  Of course, any speaker who drones *without further ado* at the end of his prefatory remarks probably ought never to have been introduced.

without missing a beat ▪ A moribund metaphor. *accurately; easily; exactly; excellently; faultlessly; flawlessly; flowingly; impeccably; indefectibly; methodically; perfectly; precisely; regularly; smoothly; systematically; well.*

without rhyme or reason ▪ A moribund metaphor. *decerebrate; foolish; idiotic; illogical; incomprehensible; meaningless; nonsensical; senseless; stupid; unintelligent; unintelligible.*

with (my) tail between (my) legs ▪ A moribund metaphor. *abjectly; ashamedly; humbly; ignobly; ignominiously; ingloriously; in humility; in shame; meekly; shamefully; submissively.* • But she was not happy at the school and left before graduation *with her tail between her legs.* REPLACE WITH *ingloriously.*

> Anne came home with her tail between her legs and slumped into her father's smoking chair.—Elle Eggels, *The House of the Seven Sisters*

with the exception of ▪ A wretched redundancy. *apart from; aside from; barring; besides; but for; except; except for; excepting; excluding; other than; outside of.* • We found that our first **50** patients were wide awake and alert the next day *with the* *exception of* one patient. REPLACE WITH *except for.*

woefully inadequate ▌ An inescapable pair. Little is *inadequate* that isn't *woefully* so.

wolf in sheep's clothing ▌ A moribund metaphor. *apostate; charlatan; deceiver; dissembler; fake; fraud; hypocrite; impostor; knave; mountebank; pharisee; phony; pretender; quack; rascal; recreant; renegade; scoundrel; swindler; tergiversator; traitor.*

(he) won't bite ▌ A moribund metaphor.

won't budge (an inch) ▌ A moribund metaphor. *be adamant; be close-minded; be contumacious; be firm; be immovable; be immutable; be inflexible; be intransigent; be invariable; be obdurate; be obstinate; be resolute; be resolved; be rigid; be steadfast; be stubborn; be tenacious; be unalterable; be unbending; be unchangeable; be unchanging; be uncompromising; be unmovable; be unwavering; be unyielding.* • I heard owner Jerry Jones on 105.3 The Fan yesterday still bristling and decreeing that Jumbo Jerry *won't budge an inch.* REPLACE WITH *is resolute.*

> I speak warily, slowly. Hardness comes over her swiftlike and then, like a limpet, she won't budge an inch.—D. C. Reid, *The Knife Behind the Gills*

won the battle but lost the war ▌ A moribund metaphor.

won't take no for an answer ▌ An infantile phrase. *insist.*

words cannot describe (express) ▌ A plebeian sentiment. • *Words cannot express* the terrible emptiness we feel or how much we miss her. SEE ALSO **there are no words to describe (express).**

work (my) butt (tail) off ▌ A moribund metaphor. *drudge; grind; grub; labor; moil; slave; strain; strive; struggle; sweat; toil; travail; work hard.*

work (his) fingers to the bone ▌ A moribund metaphor. *drudge; grind; grub; labor; moil; slave; strain; strive; struggle; sweat; toil; travail; work hard.*

working stiff ▌ A moribund metaphor. *aide; apparatchik; assistant; cog; dependent; drudge; flunky; helper; hireling; inferior; junior; minion; secondary; servant; slave; subaltern; subordinate; underling; vassal.*

work like a dog ▌ An insipid simile. *drudge; grind; grub; labor; moil; slave; strain; strive; struggle; sweat; toil; travail; work hard.*

worlds apart ▌ A moribund metaphor. *different; discordant; discrepant; dissimilar; dissonant; divergent; incommensurable; incommensurate; incomparable; incompatible; incongruent; incongruous; inconsistent; inconsonant; inharmonious; unlike.*

worn threadbare ▌ A moribund metaphor. 1. *banal; bromidic; common; commonplace; hackneyed; overused; overworked; pedestrian; platitudinous; prosaic; stale; trite.* 2. *damaged; decayed; decrepit; deteriorated; dilapidated; ragged; shabby; shopworn; tattered; worn.*

worried to death ▌ A moribund metaphor. *agitated; anxious; apprehensive; distraught; distressed; fearful; nervous; panicky; stressed; stressful; tense; tormented; troubled; uneasy; worried.* SEE ALSO **to death.**

(he) worships the ground (I) walk on ▌ A moribund metaphor. *adore; cherish; esteem; eulogize; exalt; extol; glorify; honor; idealize; idolize; laud; love; panegyrize; prize; revere; treasure; venerate; worship.*

worst-case scenario ▌ An overworked word. • The *worst-case scenario* would be for Question 3 to pass and for Question 5 to fail. • The indictment of a top executive on child-porn charges represents a *worst-case scenario* for any company and its IT managers. • He could ultimately be a progressive's *worst-case scenario.*

> Sometimes the worst-case scenario comes true. But, of course, it wasn't the worst-case scenario at all: she could have died; she could have been paralyzed from the neck down rather than the waist; she could have been disfigured as well.—Daniel Stolar, *The Middle of the Night*

(every parent's) worst nightmare ▌ A moribund metaphor. • It's *every mother's worst nightmare.* • This defendant is *every person's worst nightmare.* • Being a stepparent is *my worst nightmare.* • Perhaps the cliché is true about its being a woman's greatest fantasy and *a man's worst nightmare.* SEE ALSO **it was a nightmare.**

> Mariah awakens to her worst nightmare: Ian Fletcher has disappeared with Faith.—Jodi Picoult, *Keeping Faith*

worth (her) salt ▌ A moribund metaphor. *advantageous; beneficial; cost-effective; effective; effectual; efficacious; gainful; lucrative; productive; profitable; serviceable; useful; valuable; worthwhile.*

worth (its) weight in gold ▌ A moribund metaphor. 1. *costly; dear; expensive; inestimable; invaluable; precious; priceless; prized; valuable.* 2. *advantageous; beneficial; effective; effectual; efficacious; essential; helpful; indispensable; profitable; serviceable; useful; valuable; vital; worthwhile.*

> A loyal one was worth his weight in gold; a disloyal or lazy one should be dismissed at once. Never keep a bad servant.—Karleen Koen, *Through a Glass Darkly*

would appear (hope; imagine; seem; submit; suggest; suspect; think) ❚ A wretched redundancy. *appear (hope; imagine; seem; submit; suggest; suspect; think)*. • I *would think* so. DELETE *would*. • I *would hope* a decision would be reached before the term of office expires. DELETE *would*. • It *would appear* that the state wants to jeopardize the project. REPLACE WITH *appears*.

Not only is the *would* in *would appear (hope; imagine; seem; submit; suggest; suspect; think)* superfluous, it calls into question the accuracy and knowledge of whoever uses the phrase. Only the intellectually timorous, the dimwitted, need to so qualify their words.

wouldn't be caught (seen) dead ❚ A torpid term. 1. *abhor; abominate; detest; hate; loathe.* 2. *averse; disinclined; loath; opposed; reluctant; unwilling.*

> Jason wouldn't take her on dates, wouldn't be caught dead holding hands with her in public or stepping onto a dance floor.—Tom Perrotta, *Little Children*

wouldn't hurt a flee (fly) ❚ A moribund metaphor. 1. *affable; agreeable; amiable; amicable; compassionate; friendly; gentle; good-hearted; good-natured; humane; kind; kind-hearted; personable; pleasant; tender; tolerant.* 2. *dovish; irenic; nonviolent; pacific; pacifist; pacifistic; peaceable; peaceful; peace-loving; unbelligerent; uncontentious.*

(I) wouldn't touch it with a ten-foot pole ❚ A moribund metaphor.

wrap (get) (his) arms (head; mind) around ❚ A moribund metaphor. 1. *accept; advocate; back; champion; embrace; support; welcome.* 2. *appreciate; apprehend; comprehend; grasp; understand.* • People are really struggling to *get their arms around* this bill. REPLACE WITH *support*. • It's a selective organization, inherently biased and fallible, but likewise incapable of *wrapping its arms around* every problem and every controversy. REPLACE WITH *embracing*. • It's hard for people to *get their arms around* this. REPLACE WITH *understand*.

> He's never once tried to wrap his head around what time is doing to us, to our family.—Richard Powers, *The Time of Our Singing*

wrapped up in (herself) ❚ A moribund metaphor. *egocentric; egoistic; egotistic; egotistical; narcissistic; self-absorbed; selfish; solipsistic.*

wreak havoc ❚ An inescapable pair. *demolish; destroy; devastate; injure; obliterate; rack; ravage; ruin; shatter; smash; undo; wrack; wreck.* • A handful of companies is *wreaking havoc on* the rest of the industry. REPLACE WITH *ravaging*.

wreathed in smiles ❚ A moribund metaphor. *beaming; glowing; smiling.*

(it's) written all over (you) ❚ A moribund metaphor.

wrong end of the stick ❚ A moribund metaphor.

(what's) wrong is wrong ❚ A quack equation.

(he) wrote the book (on) ❚ A moribund metaphor.

Xx

x marks the spot ∎ A moribund metaphor.

Yy

year in (and) year out ∎ A moribund metaphor. *always; ceaselessly; constantly; continually; continuously; endlessly; eternally; everlastingly; evermore; forever; forevermore; immortally; indefinitely; interminably; permanently; perpetually; persistently; unceasingly; unremittingly.*

(62) years young ∎ An infantile phrase. • I'm 43 *years young.* DELETE *years young.*

yell and scream ∎ An inescapable pair. *bay; bawl; bellow; blare; caterwaul; clamor; cry; holler; hoot; howl; roar; screak; scream; screech; shout; shriek; shrill; squawk; squeal; vociferate; wail; whoop; yell; yelp; yowl.* • Two months later, he'd lost all his hair, and his wife started *yelling and screaming* about my not making him continue. REPLACE WITH *scream* or *yell.* SEE ALSO **yell and scream.**

yell (her) head off ∎ A moribund metaphor. *bay; bawl; bellow; blare; caterwaul; clamor; cry; holler; hoot; howl; roar; screak; scream; screech; shout; shriek; shrill; squawk; squeal; vociferate; wail; whoop; yell; yelp; yowl.*

yes, Virginia, (there is) ∎ An infantile phrase.

you are what you eat ∎ A popular prescription.

you can catch more flies with honey than with vinegar ∎ A popular prescription.

you can fool some of the people some of the time, but you can't fool all of the people all of the time ∎ A popular prescription.

you can lead a horse to water, but you can't make (him) drink ∎ A popular prescription.

you can make a difference ∎ A popular prescription.

you can say that again ∎ An infantile phrase.

you can't be all things to all people ∎ A popular prescription.

you can't buy love ∎ A popular prescription.

you can't change the world in a day ∎ A popular prescription.

you can't fight city hall ∎ A popular prescription.

you can't fit a square peg in a round hole ∎ A popular prescription.

you can't get blood from (out of) a stone ∎ A popular prescription.

you can't get there from here ∎ An infantile phrase.

you can't go home again ∎ A popular prescription.

you can't have everything ∎ A popular prescription.

you can't have it both ways ∎ A popular prescription.

you can't have something for nothing ∎ A popular prescription.

you can't have your cake and eat it too ∎ A popular prescription.

you can't judge a book by its cover ∎ A popular prescription.

you can't live on love alone ∎ A popular prescription.

you can't live with (them) and you can't live without (them) ∎ A popular prescription.

you can't lose what you never had ∎ A popular prescription.

you can't make a silk purse out of a sow's ear ∎ A popular prescription.

you (just) can't make this stuff up ∎ An infantile phrase.

you can't please everyone ∎ A popular prescription.

you can't put new wine in old bottles ∎ A popular prescription.

you can't serve God and mammon ∎ A popular prescription.

you can't take it with you ∎ A popular prescription.

you can't teach an old dog new tricks ∎ A popular prescription.

you can't win them all ∎ A popular prescription.

(so quiet) you could hear a pin drop ∎ A moribund metaphor. 1. *dumb; hushed; motionless; mum; mute; noiseless; quiet; reticent; silent; soundless; speechless; stationary; still; stock-still; subdued; taciturn; unmoving; voiceless; wordless.* 2. *becalmed; calm; halcyon; irenic; pacific; peaceable; peaceful; placid; quiescent; reposeful; serene; tranquil.*

you don't miss what you never had ❚ A popular prescription.

you do the best you can ❚ A suspect superlative. Dwelling on our failures is no better than dismissing them, but *you do the best you can,* still another expression of resignation, may too easily excuse us for our missteps and mistakes, our failures and inadequacies. Here, *the best* is surely suspect.

you (have to) do what you have to (do) ❚ A popular prescription.

you get what you pay for ❚ A popular prescription.

you had to be there ❚ A grammatical gimmick. This is merely an admission of having badly told a tale.

you have everything to gain and nothing to lose ❚ A popular prescription.

you have nothing to lose ❚ A popular prescription.

you have to give to get ❚ A popular prescription.

you have (got) to start somewhere ❚ A popular prescription.

you have to understand (that) ❚ An ineffectual phrase. • First of all, *you have to understand that* many black men are in prison. DELETE *you have to understand that.* SEE ALSO **it is important to understand (that)**.

(do) you know? ❚ An ineffectual phrase. • I felt like I was enlightened, *you know?* DELETE *you know?* • You never know what's going to happen, *you know?* DELETE *you know?* • The translation sounded too straightforward, *you know?* DELETE *you know?* • To an extent, I think everybody is racist. *You know?* DELETE *You know?* SEE ALSO **(you) hear what I'm saying? (you) know what I mean? (you) know what I'm saying? (you) know what I'm telling you?**.

you learn something new every day ❚ A plebeian sentiment. It's the event of having learned something—something taught, not thought—that gives rise to the remark.

you made your bed, now lay in it ❚ A popular prescription.

you name it ❚ A grammatical gimmick. *and others; and so forth; and so on; and the like; etc.* • Today, in our state, those who do the public's work—teachers, cops, public-health nurses, social workers, highway builders, prison guards, *you name it*—are held up to ridicule.

you never know ❚ A plebeian sentiment.

you never know till you try ❚ A popular prescription.

young and foolish ❚ An inescapable pair.

you owe it to yourself ❚ A popular prescription. • Believe me, *you owe it to yourself* to take advantage of this exciting opportunity.

you're (only) as old as you feel ❚ A popular prescription.

you're either part of the solution or part of the problem ❚ A popular prescription.

you're either with (me) or against (me) ❚ A popular prescription.

you're kidding ❚ An infantile phrase. This expression is among the most banal we utter. We say it uncontrollably—less in stupefaction than in stupidity—and without a moment's reflection.

The more commonplace the words you use, the more commonplace the person you are. SEE ALSO **really? you've got to be kidding**.

you're not alone ❚ A plebeian sentiment. • Feeling depressed, lonely, restless, bored, upset? *You're not alone.*

you're not the only one ❚ An infantile phrase. *as I do; I do too; neither do I; no more do I; nor do I; so do I.*

you're only young once ❚ A popular prescription.

your guess is as good as mine ❚ An infantile phrase. *I don't know; (it's) not (yet) known; (that's) uncertain; (that's) unclear; (it's) unknown.* SEE ALSO **(it) remains to be seen; (just have to) wait and see**.

yours truly ❚ An infantile phrase. *I; me.* • And you can bet that *yours truly* will do something crazy. REPLACE WITH *I.* • Reading it over, I notice that there is an error, but it was committed by *yours truly.* REPLACE WITH *me.*

you scratch my back, I'll scratch yours ❚ A popular prescription. • It's an approach that resonates equally with businessmen steeped in the win-win jargon of negotiations and politicians deep in the pragmatic *you-scratch-my-back-I'll-scratch-yours* conversations that make Washington run.

you think too much ❚ A plebeian sentiment. *You think too much* is, of course, commentary that only those who rarely think could ever offer. These are the people who cower from consciousness, who fear feelings and discourage thinking. SEE ALSO **I (just) don't think about it**.

you've come a long way (baby) ❚ An infantile phrase.

you've got to be kidding ❚ An infantile phrase. SEE ALSO **really? you're kidding**.

you win a few (some), you lose a few (some) ❚ A popular prescription.

Zz

zigs and zags ∎ An inescapable pair.

> To love the way someone's mind zigs and zags; to know that, as frustrated as you may get during the telling, every story is worth listening to; that after every movie you see together he will point out something you've missed . . . that is rare indeed.—Rachel Toor, *The Pig and I*

(a) zillion(s) (of) ∎ An infantile phrase. Doubly infantile are the phrases *ba-zillion* and *ga-zillion*. • I'll bet their mothers spent *a zillion* hours trying to get their sons to clean up after themselves. REPLACE WITH *countless*. • I made *a zillion* mistakes. REPLACE WITH *innumerable*. • There may be grating aspects to 20- and 30-somethings earning *kazillion*-dollar bonuses, but at least wealth gives them the self-confidence to ask for a date. REPLACE WITH *million*.

Appendix

Top-Twenty Dimwitticisms

In 2006 and 2007, Factiva, a Dow Jones Company, provided *The Vocabula Review* with monthly graphs showing the top-twenty dimwitticsms used in U.S., U.K., Canadian, Australian, and Indian newspapers and magazines. I had supplied Factiva with a list of 200 dimwitticisms, and they searched for the terms among thousands of publications. On the next few pages are the graphs for April 2007.

U.S. Press

Analysis conducted by Factiva showed that of two hundred dimwitticisms used by the U.S. press during April 2007, the most common was *ongoing*.

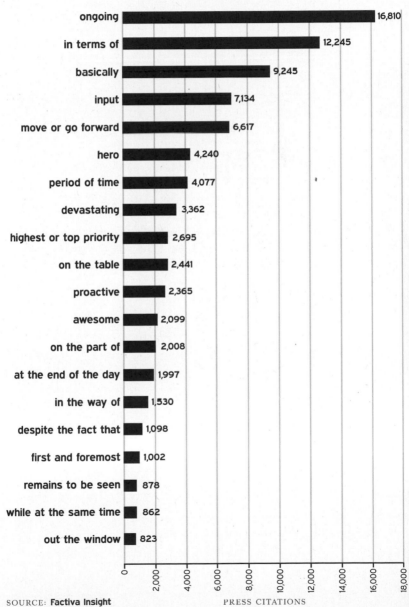

ARTICLE MENTIONS: 83,708

ongoing	16,810
in terms of	12,245
basically	9,245
input	7,134
move or go forward	6,617
hero	4,240
period of time	4,077
devastating	3,362
highest or top priority	2,695
on the table	2,441
proactive	2,365
awesome	2,099
on the part of	2,008
at the end of the day	1,997
in the way of	1,530
despite the fact that	1,098
first and foremost	1,002
remains to be seen	878
while at the same time	862
out the window	823

PRESS CITATIONS

SOURCE: **Factiva Insight**

PERIOD: **April 2007**

U.K. Press

Analysis conducted by Factiva showed that of two hundred dimwitticisms used by the U.K. press during April 2007, the most common was *in terms of.*

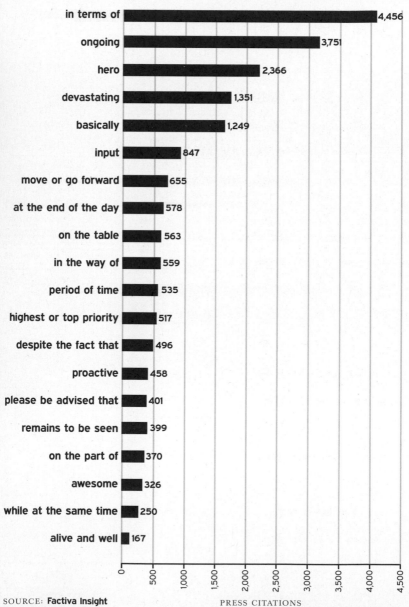

ARTICLE MENTIONS: 20,294

in terms of	4,456
ongoing	3,751
hero	2,366
devastating	1,351
basically	1,249
input	847
move or go forward	655
at the end of the day	578
on the table	563
in the way of	559
period of time	535
highest or top priority	517
despite the fact that	496
proactive	458
please be advised that	401
remains to be seen	399
on the part of	370
awesome	326
while at the same time	250
alive and well	167

PRESS CITATIONS

SOURCE: **Factiva Insight**

PERIOD: **April 2007**

Canadian Press

Analysis conducted by Factiva showed that of two hundred dimwitticisms used by the Canadian press during April 2007, the most common was *ongoing*.

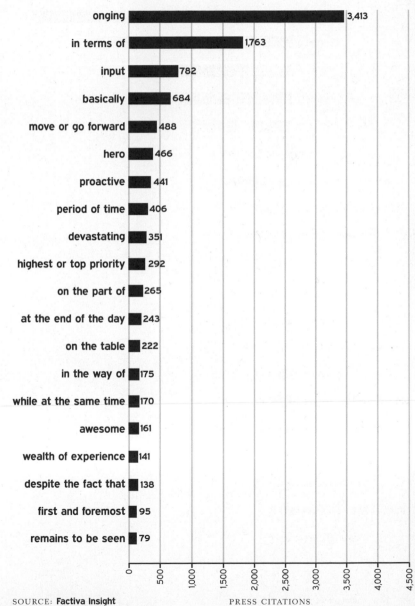

ARTICLE MENTIONS: 10,765

Term	Citations
onging	3,413
in terms of	1,763
input	782
basically	684
move or go forward	488
hero	466
proactive	441
period of time	406
devastating	351
highest or top priority	292
on the part of	265
at the end of the day	243
on the table	222
in the way of	175
while at the same time	170
awesome	161
wealth of experience	141
despite the fact that	138
first and foremost	95
remains to be seen	79

PRESS CITATIONS

SOURCE: **Factiva Insight**

PERIOD: **April 2007**

Australian Press

Analysis conducted by Factiva showed that of two hundred dimwitticisms used by the Australian press during April 2007, the most common was *in terms of.*

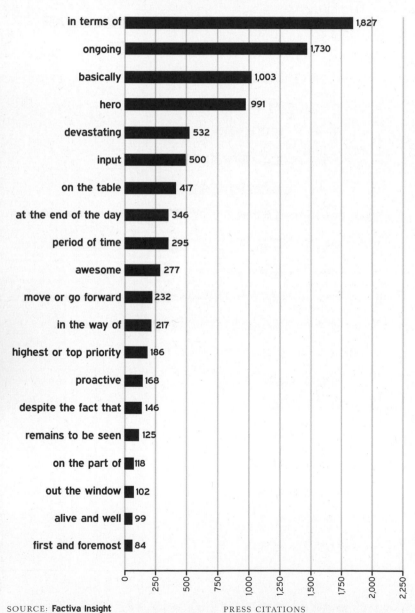

ARTICLE MENTIONS: 9,395

in terms of	1,827
ongoing	1,730
basically	1,003
hero	991
devastating	532
input	500
on the table	417
at the end of the day	346
period of time	295
awesome	277
move or go forward	232
in the way of	217
highest or top priority	186
proactive	168
despite the fact that	146
remains to be seen	125
on the part of	118
out the window	102
alive and well	99
first and foremost	84

PRESS CITATIONS

SOURCE: **Factiva Insight**

PERIOD: **April 2007**

Indian Press

Analysis conducted by Factiva showed that of two hundred dimwitticisms used by the Indian press during April 2007, the most common was *in terms of.*

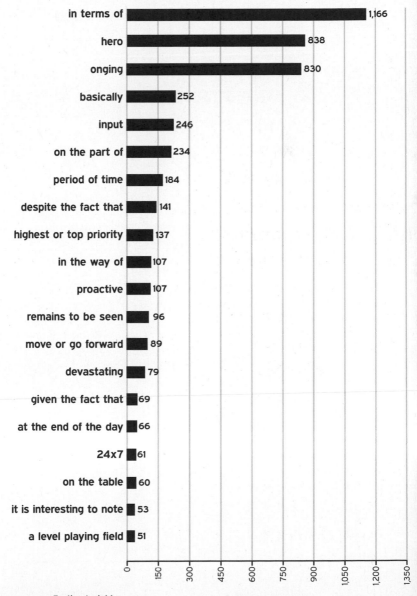

ARTICLE MENTIONS: 4,866

Phrase	Citations
in terms of	1,166
hero	838
onging	830
basically	252
input	246
on the part of	234
period of time	184
despite the fact that	141
highest or top priority	137
in the way of	107
proactive	107
remains to be seen	96
move or go forward	89
devastating	79
given the fact that	69
at the end of the day	66
24x7	61
on the table	60
it is interesting to note	53
a level playing field	51

PRESS CITATIONS

SOURCE: **Factiva Insight**

PERIOD: **April 2007**

235